A Clashing of the Soul

A Clashing

of the Soul

John Hope

and the Dilemma of

African American Leadership

and Black Higher Education

in the Early Twentieth Century

Leroy Davis

THE UNIVERSITY OF GEORGIA PRESS

ATHENS AND LONDON

© 1998 by the University of Georgia Press
Athens, Georgia 30602
All rights reserved
Designed by Erin Kirk New
Set in 10 on 13 Janson by G & S Typesetters, Inc.
Printed and bound by Braun-Brumfield, Inc.
The paper in this book meets the guidelines for permanence
and durability of the Committee on Production Guidelines
for Book Longevity of the Council on Library Resources.

Printed in the United States of America
02   01   00   99   98   c   5   4   3   2   1

Library of Congress Cataloging in Publication Data

Davis, Leroy.
    A clashing of the soul : John Hope and the dilemma of
African American leadership and Black higher education
in the early twentieth century / Leroy Davis.
        p.   cm.
    Includes bibliographical references (p.   ) and index.
    ISBN 0-8203-1987-2 (alk. paper)
    1. Hope, John, 1868–1936.   2. Afro-American college
presidents—Biography.   3. Afro-Americans—Education
(Higher)—History—20th century.   4. Afro-American
leadership—History—20th century.   I. Title.
LA2317.H72D38   1998
378'.0092—dc21
[B]   97-42440

British Library Cataloging in Publication Data available

To my mother, Frances Harris Major,
and the numerous African American institutions,
black leaders, and community activists
who carried the torch forward when few others would.

Contents

Foreword

His was a name I heard almost daily for the first decade and a half of my life. It was not merely because I bore the name, but also because Dr. John Hope was invoked regularly by my mother and my father, who had both been in Dr. Hope's classes at Roger Williams University in Nashville, Tennessee. And my parents, even as young college students, thought that he, coming out of Rhode Island's Brown University, might have had a special message from the original Roger Williams for those who sought wisdom and enlightenment from his legitimate surrogate. When my mother left Roger Williams University to teach in west Tennessee near her home, my father literally followed Dr. Hope when he went to teach at Atlanta Baptist College, an early incarnation of Morehouse College.

I knew of most of the major principles in their lives for which my parents gave credit to Dr. Hope: absolute racial equality without delay; staunch support for his close friend W. E. B. Du Bois; the highest and most rigorous standards for our schools and colleges, if their graduates were to compete successfully in the larger world; and impeccable public and private morality, if blacks were to eradicate unjust accusations of laxity and licentiousness. There were other principles—some large, some small—that also became a part of the honorable precepts of living my parents recited almost daily and attributed to Dr. Hope. Thus, not only was his name a household word, but the principles by which we lived were his, at least in part.

In 1934, when I found myself as a nineteen-year-old senior at Fisk University among those in Atlanta for the Fisk-Morehouse football game, it dawned on me that I was in Dr. John Hope's city. By this time he was the president of Atlanta University, but that made no difference to a self-confident youngster who wanted to meet this person who had become a veritable icon in the Franklin household. It never occurred to me that he might not be in his office on a Saturday morning or that he might be busy with long-arranged appointments. I *had* to see him, so I went to his office and asked if I could see him. His secretary asked if I had an appointment. When I replied in the negative, she asked for my name. When I gave it, her eyes brightened. She told me he was in a conference, but she would inform him that I wished to see him. In a very few minutes the door of the inner office opened and out walked John Hope, teacher and mentor of Mollie Parker Franklin and Buck Colbert Franklin, president of Atlanta University, and role model for his namesake. Without exaggeration I can say that this was not only an unforgettable moment, but one of the most exciting of my entire life. He did not have much time, but his generosity made it seem like an eternity, especially since I was so excited that I was almost speechless.

Placing his hands on each of my shoulders he said quietly, but firmly, "So this is John Hope Franklin." He asked about my parents and my progress in college, and wanted to know what I planned after college. I said quite confidently, but with no reason to be confident, that I would be going to Harvard to do graduate work in history. He apologized for having to return to the meeting over which he was presiding and disappeared behind the inner door as quietly as he had appeared a few minutes earlier. Only later did I fully appreciate his graciousness in coming out of a meeting to greet a youngster known to him only by name. Much later, I would learn how flattering it is to have someone named for oneself. Under such circumstances, one is prepared to find reasons to make any and all arrangements to meet one's namesake.

It would also be years before I would fully appreciate Dr. Hope's great contributions to civil rights and education. I was filled with pride—as though I had something to do with it—when Dr. Du Bois told me, in the late 1950s, how Dr. Hope supported him in his early struggles to secure full equality for African Americans. Not until I read Dr. Hope's letters and occasional pieces did I fully understand the depth of his commitment to the struggle to bring America's practices in line with its preachments. Only when I read the history of Morehouse College by E. A. Jones, the history of Spelman College by Florence Read, and the history of Atlanta University by Clarence A. Bacote did I appreciate the educational leadership of Dr. Hope. My parents described him to me, but I did not fully comprehend until I read this work by Leroy Davis.

Dr. Hope seemed never to tire in his lifelong struggle to improve and extend educational opportunities to African Americans. He seemed to see better opportunities at Atlanta Baptist College than he had seen at Roger Williams University. Indeed, he seemed almost prescient; the fortunes of Roger Williams declined while those of Atlanta Baptist College rose as it became Morehouse College. His vision of an educational intellectual capital in Atlanta, where there was a cluster of colleges, gradually took shape, and he inevitably became the central figure in the planning of what became the Atlanta University System in 1929.

Despite the fact that Ridgely Torrence published a biography of John Hope some fifty years ago, Hope remained, as Leroy Davis remarks here, the least known major figure in the annals of African American history between Booker T. Washington and Martin Luther King Jr. Perhaps that is because he was also one of the least understood figures during that period. Dr. Hope consistently fought on the civil rights front as well as on the educational front. There were times when the two great passions of his life seemed to be at odds with each other, but he regarded both as indispensable for the future of his people. Davis sees this problem quite clearly, and he treats the dual objectives in Hope's life as the central feature of this work. Surely, this biography by Davis will place Dr. Hope in the prominent spot he deserves in African American history. It will also provide a much needed understanding of the manner in which this great leader appreciated and worked for the attainment of the twin goals of educational and political equality.

JOHN HOPE FRANKLIN

Preface

       The historian's craft is illuminating. In the process of what we do, we often learn that our work includes an element of autobiography, revealing perspectives and experiences that help us sustain interest in our subjects over a long period. Within that autobiographical context there are often answers to questions we never knew we had, questions hidden deep in our subconscious minds.

    I am fascinated by those questions and answers. Eight years ago, when I completed the dissertation phase of this project, I acknowledged my gratitude to the late Elliott Rudwick for suggesting a biography of John Hope as a doctoral dissertation. However, I now realize that the genesis of my interest in African American leadership, black education, and black institutions dates back to my teen years in the black working-class community of Smoketown in Louisville, Kentucky. Specifically, my interest was sparked by an incident that took place back in 1963. No, it was not the March on Washington. At only fifteen, and just beginning high school at still all-black Central High, I was much more interested in girls, having a few dollars in my pockets, and wearing nice rags on my back (that's fancy clothes for those of you who do not speak "ebonics") than in political activism. Yet, as the son and grandson of black domestics who instilled an unconscious pride in black institutions (especially the church), transmitted the values of our community, and inspired in me a respect for black leaders, I was sensitive enough to the politics of my racial identity to recognize a subtle insult when I heard one.

    Though it occurred more than thirty years ago, I remember the incident vividly. It was a crisp fall Saturday afternoon, and I was working my part-time job at a white barbershop cleaning up and shining shoes. These were the days before McDonald's, Burger King, and Wendy's. The only fast food joint I remember was White Castle, and they hired few African Americans. My white employer (who I later learned was Jewish) was kind enough. He knew I played high school football and trusted me to come in after practice at night during the week to clean up the place. I worked all day on Saturdays, shining numerous pairs of shoes and boots and keeping the floor clean of shaven hair. My employer was the master barber.

One of his customers that day was a huge, bearded man clad in a black motorcycle jacket and big black boots. His words to me: "Boy, I need a shine. If you do a good job, I will give you a buck; if you give me a damn good shine, I will give you two bucks." Though a little intimidated, I was elated at the prospect of getting for one shine what I normally received for two or three. I had just started to shine the man's boots at the foot of the barber chair when, with his gaze fixed on me, the man suddenly bellowed out: "That Martin Luther King is some colored boy, ain't he?" I pretended not to hear him, never looking up, snapping the shine rag across his boots to make it pop and increasing the saliva to enhance the shine on the boot toe. He repeated the sentence, this time adding: "I'm talking to you, boy." Until this day I do not know why, but I heard myself saying that King was a "good Negro leader." The emphasis, I remember, was on the term "Negro."

The chattering in the shop ceased, and everyone turned eyes and ears on the strange threesome: the customer, the barber/owner of the shop—and me. "What did you say, boy?" the patron asked, leaning forward toward me. Slightly above a whisper, my voice cracking, I repeated my response with the same emphasis. I glanced at the owner of the shop, who had turned red with rage. With comb in one hand and scissors in the other, he leaned halfway way down to me at the foot of the barber chair and said with a sly grin on his face: "That's not what he asked. He said that King is some 'colored boy,' ain't he?" The gesture and the look on his face were more revealing than what he said. I knew, and he knew, that my job was on the line. How I responded in the next few seconds would determine whether or not I would go home with a job. It was his way of exerting his influence, of showing the collective power of whites over blacks in the workplace and everywhere else. I needed my job—wanted my job—and responded with what was pretty much, as I interpreted it, an accommodationist answer. I simply said in a half-muffled tone, looking downward, "Yes." Both the customer and the barber smiled with an air of victory and accomplishment. The barber then raised up and continued to cut the patron's hair, and the customer started another conversation with others in the shop. I remember thinking, even then, that they believed an uppity "young nigger" had been put in his place and everything was back to normal.

I left the shop a little early that day, upset, beaten down, and a little ashamed that I had not stood my ground and insisted on referring to King as a "Negro man" instead of a "colored boy." On the way home, I sought answers on the streets from people I respected. These were not traditional African American leaders, yet they must be acknowledged here as a major impetus for this work. My conversations with them were not even contextualized by the incident; I managed to sneak it in as we spoke of other things. There was slightly older Clint Lovely—we called him "Fudd" because he resembled a popular cartoon character. I also ran into "Blue" (I never knew him by any other name), who was also older but was known for listening to us "young bloods." If I remember correctly, a few short years later Blue was killed trying to rob a white neighborhood grocery store.

A little closer to Grace Presbyterian Church and Recreation Center, a white church and settlement house located in the middle of Shepherd's Square (the Smoketown housing project where I hung out), I ran into the notorious "Cokey." Though only a few years older than I, Cokey was what rap artists today would call an original "gansta," the familiar "bad nigger" known in working-class African American communities across the country. Only about five feet five inches tall, bronze Cokey weighed no more than about 130 pounds. He was always super sharp, known for his highly starched and perfectly creased jeans and very stylish shirts. He also wore a "bebop" cap, or sometimes a derby or a wide-brimmed hat, usually cocked "ace-deuce" to the side. Though I never saw it, Cokey allegedly carried an automatic weapon in a violin case when he was going to "take care of business" (I remember seeing the violin case but never really wanted to see the contents). I do know Cokey was often armed, and in those days, carrying any kind of pistol was a big deal. When I got around to mentioning the incident, Cokey acknowledged his respect for King and other African American leaders in his own way, suggesting responses ranging from "taking the man out" to burning down the barber shop. I don't know if he was bluffing or not, but I decided to move on. After I got out of the United States Air Force in 1970, or perhaps shortly before, Cokey was shot and killed by his abused wife as he tried to break down her front door. Depending on the situation or the people involved, Cokey could move from "Dr. Jekyll" to "Mr. Hyde" with ease.

When I finally got to Grace, as we called the church and community center, I ran into Frederick Stoner. Freddie was the director of the recreation component of the church and settlement house. But to me and all the other kids from the housing project and surrounding communities, he was much more. In addition to teaching and organizing competitive sports like training for boxing (which we all did, including, at an earlier time, Cassius Clay, later known as Muhammad Ali), basketball, and even roller skating, Freddie was our adviser, confidante, and grown-up friend. In between other subjects, I told him about the incident. Also joining that conversation were my former little league football coaches (I played for the Grace Bears), Camp and Merrell. I honestly don't remember what they had to say about the incident, just that they took the time to listen with a sympathetic ear.

I then strolled over to the church I attended, black Bates Memorial Baptist Church, which was located in the middle of the housing project. Though the white minister and members tried desperately to lure us, few African Americans in Smoketown attended the predominantly white Grace Presbyterian Church for religious services. When I stopped at Bates to get some cold water from the water fountain, I encountered the church custodian (a porter by profession), Mr. John White, and his wife, Miss Leora. Mr. Moore, a postal employee, local black leader, and important official for the "colored" branch of the YMCA on Chestnut Street, was also present, along with his schoolteacher wife. All of them were members of Bates Memorial, and I told them the story as well.

I don't remember if I mentioned it to people like Efufee (pronounced *e-FEW-fee*) Carney, a cousin of track and Olympic star Wilma Rudolph (and almost as fast), or "Bubble" Nelson, David Earl Lewis, Lawrence Williams, Irvin Dickerson, Ronald Golden, or Willie Leonard, just a few of the guys I ran with in those days. Today our group would be called a gang. There was also a female counterpart group that included Quimiller (pronounced *Q-miller*) Scruggs, Beverly Taylor, Patricia Leach, Ann Ferguson, Janice Winburn, and Ruth Edwards. But *gang* is really too strong a word. We had few fights with rivals, and there was practically no crime except for an occasional unlawful entry into two local factories—one made ice cream, the other pies. Most of the time we just hung out together. We played on the same teams, sometimes shared a little cheap wine, and at night harmonized under the lamppost adjacent to the front steps of the Grace recreation center.

My intellectual interest in that "black world" of my youth actually began after my discharge from the United States Air Force in March 1970, when I was twenty-three years old. The incident at the barbershop had by then receded to a corner of my unconscious, and I no longer wondered why that "redneck's" disparagement of King had struck such a nerve in me. Like many others in those days, I returned home as one of the militants and revolutionaries my friends and family had been hearing about, complete with a wardrobe of African garb (most of it made by Asian tailors). In the military I had finished the conventional Black Power reading list: *The Autobiography of Malcolm X*, *Native Son*, Chancellor Williams's *Destruction of Black Civilization*, all of Frantz Fanon's works, and a few other books.

I had always liked to read, and my family always encouraged the practice. They never knew that way back in junior high school I would hide my books under the steps of the segregated East End Public Library (after I did my homework) while I went across the street to play basketball at Grace. I now realize that I hid the books for two reasons: I did not want to lose them, and I wasn't quite sure what my macho buddies would think about me bringing library books like *Buffalo Bill Cody* to the gym.

My old running buddies did not know what to think of the "new" Leroy Davis. On one level, they believed I was still "regular" (acceptable). Like everybody else, I usually showed up at local nightspots such as the J & H, the Top Hat, and the Circle Bar wearing platform shoes, wide-brimmed hats, bloused silk shirts, and sleeveless three-quarter-vest suits with bell-bottoms. I still loved the music—blues, jazz, soul, whatever—and I could still dance. And I was still comfortable in the guarded backrooms where heavy gambling took place before and after the "nightspots" closed.

But on occasion I would bounce into a club wearing my traditional African garb. Instead of talking about the "ladies" (a few of my friends were pimping, and a few others were big-time drug dealers), I would talk about the need for all of us to learn African American history, take control of our neighborhoods, and create independent black schools. I talked about the danger of "the pig," and I even indirectly mentioned the option of "offing the pushers" (eliminating the drug dealers). I was able to get away with this because I was from the neighborhood (today that wouldn't matter; I would be killed). On occasion, some of the pushers would respond, reminding me of the lack of opportunities available for black folk, the difficulty of getting a decent job after doing time in prison, and the general reality—the need to create an underground economy out of what was, instead of what could be. These guys were not Marxists or socialists, and they had no ax to grind with capitalism. They accepted the tenets of materialistic society and simply wanted more access to what America valued most.

I owe a lot to those guys and to that period (I don't want to mention names even now). They taught me a lot about class differences in the African American community. My experiences in the military broadened my horizons in ways I never dreamed possible. My tours overseas gave me a perspective on America that is impossible to get anywhere within the country. Yet, my time in the military also allowed me to escape some of the experiences that led a few of my friends down the road to petty (and not so petty) crime. One of my good friends went into the military too, but instead of becoming involved in what we then called the "black liberation movement," he was devastated by drugs. He overcame his drug problems, only to become one of the biggest and most respected drug dealers in Louisville.

I took a different path. I decided to use the GI Bill to go to college. I didn't know what college was really about, but I liked to read, and in my view that was (and still is) the most important tool anyone could bring to the academy.

Like many other veterans, I was at first drawn to business courses. But I knew even then that my true love was history, not so much for its intellectual rewards as for its importance in African Americans' struggle for liberation. I attended college full time during the day and worked the midnight shift at the local General Electric plant. I was active in the Black Worker's Coalition at the plant and also served as the president of the college's Black Student Union. On Saturdays, I tramped through the housing project with flyers trying to drum up support for a Saturday school for kids at Grace where I taught African American history (my reading of history never ceased). I attempted to do the same thing at my own church (which I attended a lot less frequently), but the minister did not want "that mess" going on in his church. All of this was in addition to trying to settle down and adjust to my first marriage.

During those years my circle of associates expanded to include African Americans from all over the city. Though not exclusively, most of my new acquaintances were from the black middle and upper middle classes. Some were professional leaders of the organizations—and coalitions—that I interacted with as president of Jefferson Community College's Black Student Union. Others were black professionals who held both conventional occupations and leadership positions in black organizations. My interaction with whites was still mainly limited to my instructors and fellow classmates at the college and my employers and fellow workers at General Electric and, after leaving that job, the Louisville Gas and Electric Company.

I tried to maintain my association with my old friends in Smoketown, but that became increasingly difficult. Many of them had moved to the more affluent west end of the city, my family and I had moved out of the area as well, and I was incredibly busy besides. As time went on, many of those involved in major illegal activities shied away from me and others not involved in their "professions." Yet, when we did happen to meet in various places, we always talked about the old days. Louisville was rapidly changing. Old Walnut Street, the central business district of "black Louisville," was no more (even the street's name had been changed, to Muhammad Ali Boulevard). Urban renewal took its toll on Smoketown as well, and the area lost much of its past vibrancy.

I left Louisville in 1974 to finish my education at Howard University in Washington, D.C. Before leaving, however, I visited the first friend from the old neighborhood who had ever allowed me to discuss my ideas about race, leadership, and class on an intellectual plane. He came scrambling back to my mind time after time as I conducted the research for this biography. We called him "Soc," short for "Socrates." I had known him for years, but we became close only after I returned from the military. Soc was a small black man. He probably weighed 110 pounds or less and stood only a little over five feet. He was from a large family that struggled much more than mine to survive. Although he had a brilliant mind, Soc dropped out of high school; by the time I returned from the air force he had become a professional thief. One never knew from month to month, or year to year, whether Soc was "in" (prison) or "out."

Soc and I often sat for hours—sometimes on the steps of the Grace recreation center late at night, sometimes in local bars over a drink—talking about race issues, books we had read, and possible solutions to social problems. We had read the same things; the only difference was that his reading had been done in prison, mine in the military. Both of us had spent enough time on the same streets to unconsciously incorporate an animated urban demeanor in our mannerisms that was visible in our oratorical style and expression. People in the nightspots and on the streets—at times including the hookers and their pimps—would pause to listen to our debates. Soc was the first intellectual giant I ever knew, a natural philosopher who needed only one small break.

Though I tried hard—desperately hard—I couldn't get Soc to shake his life of crime. Eventually, in his own way, he asked me to stop begging him to change. I realize now that it was embarrassing for him to have to continuously reject my overtures. He finally said to me when I decided to leave Louisville: "Look, man, I'm trying to understand your need to move on, to go to Howard, and all that s——, so you have to understand. Like you, I am what I am, I've got to continue what I know best, and that's just how it is, dig it?" I didn't "dig it," but I did accept it, and I never mentioned his lifestyle again. Whenever I visited Louisville from Washington, I always asked whether Soc was "in" or "out." The answer to the question was as unpredictable as my trips back home.

My acknowledgments must inevitably include people such as Soc and others I encountered and interacted with in my years growing up in Louisville, including the participants in the barbershop incident. But I also feel a deep sense of gratitude to a more conventional group that directly or indirectly contributed to the completion of this work. After all, although the groundwork was laid elsewhere, I actually came to intellectual maturity at Howard University. With the assistance of committed and dedicated professors such as Arnold Taylor, Olive Taylor, Joseph Harris, Adell Patton, Rev. Carl Hayden, and Charles Johnson, I began to think deeply about gender, class, and race relations both along and across race lines. I was also fortunate to have dynamic classmates who are now highly respected professional historians. They include Maceo Dailey, Sharon Harley, Rosaland Terborg-Penn, and Gerald Gill. It was at

Howard that I began to appreciate the importance of African American educational institutions and decided to become a professional historian.

I have already acknowledged my gratitude to the late Professor Elliott Rudwick for suggesting the specific topic for my research. But others at Kent State were also helpful. They included the venerable August Meier, from whom I learned much about writing and the discipline required to remain in the archives for long periods. Though Professor Meier and I often disagreed, I respected his opinion, and I hope he respected mine. I also owe a debt of gratitude to Professor John Hubbell, who allowed me to impose on his valuable time as director of the Kent State University Press by taking over the project as a dissertation after Rudwick's untimely death. He never ceased to provide invaluable advice and encouragement as I worked on the book. This work was also enhanced by the valuable comments of friends like Vincent Fort, Donal Lindsey, Gary Clark, Barbara Bowman, Ernie Dover, Charlyn Harper-Brown, Rodney Lester, and Joe Windham.

Above all at Kent State University, I owe a special debt to the living "godfather" of the scholar-activist tradition (I prefer that term to the more contemporary "public intellectual"), the former chairman of the Pan-African Studies Department, Edward Crosby, and his wife, Shirley, who together still represent the "first black family" of Kent, Ohio. In addition to asking important intellectual questions about black leadership and institutions, Crosby insisted that I resume my own community activism. In addition to teaching in the Pan-African Studies Department under his guidance, I was "volunteered" to take charge of programs that served the greater Kent African American community. Because of Crosby, my trips back to Louisville became more frequent, and I consciously sought out old friends and acquaintances to ensure that I maintained perspective—something easy to lose in the world of academia. It is because of Crosby that I continue to try to integrate academics and community activism.

This book was further aided by my first full-time teaching job at Spelman College in Atlanta. I went from there to Morehouse College, continually deepening my intellectual interest in black education and black leadership and, with the assistance of my Morehouse colleague Jackie Rouse, enhancing my sensitivity and appreciation of gender-centered issues. I owe a special thanks to my friend Alton Hornsby, chairman of the Morehouse History Department, a meticulous historian who kindly and graciously made the Hope Papers available to me even before he had completed the arduous task of editing them.

I also received several grants that allowed me to conduct research in more places across the country than I care to remember. A Rockefeller Foundation grant allowed me to conduct research at the Rockefeller Archives Center in Tarrytown, New York. A United Negro College Fund Development Grant allowed me to finish my dissertation and continue the research for this biography. I also received a generous grant from the University Research Council of my present employer, Emory University. That grant's support allowed me to conduct invaluable research in Washington, D.C.; Valley Forge, Pennsylvania; Providence, Rhode Island; Princeton, New Jersey; and New York City.

Good librarians are a special breed. My model was Miss McCoy, the librarian at the East End Public Library where I used to hide my books. She was always gracious, providing me with attention and information even when I did not ask for it. While I was reading one book or looking for sources for a report, she was constantly bringing me new material to add to what I already had. In those early days at Booker T. Washington Elementary School and Jackson Jr. High School, Miss McCoy probably saw something in me that I did not see in myself. The librarians I met while researching this biography duplicated the character and commitment to service of Miss McCoy. The staffs of special collections at the Atlanta University Library, the Moorland-Spingarn Research Center at Howard University, the Schomburg Research Center in New York City, and the Manuscript Division of the Library of Congress and National Archives were extremely helpful. So were the staffs of the Rockefeller Center in Tarrytown, the Brown University Library Special Collections and archives, Worcester Academy in Massachusetts, the Special Collections at Princeton University, the Georgia State Archives, and the American Baptist Historical Society in Valley Forge. And of course I cannot omit the staff of Emory University Library. I owe all of them an intellectual debt I will never be able to repay.

The students in my graduate seminars and my colleagues at Emory University also helped in the completion of this book. Special thanks are due to Winston Grady-Willis, Bobby Donaldson, and especially Bill Carrigan, who found an important missing piece to the John Hope family. I can never thank my colleagues Jim Roark and Mary Odem enough. Both read every paragraph of every draft and provided invaluable insights that undoubtedly made this a better book. I owe a very special thanks to Professor Willard Gatewood, who also took time to carefully read each draft. I admittedly borrowed heavily from his conceptual framework on black elites. I also owe a debt of gratitude to those who allowed me to interview them for this work. I especially want to recognize the information provided by the Hope family: my subject's son and daughter-in-law, Dr. and Mrs. John Hope II, and their son, Professor Richard Hope, a sociologist by training and the current director of the Woodrow Wilson Foundation at Princeton.

I cannot end this without also acknowledging my debt of gratitude to Atlanta deejays Nadeem Suliman Ali, Steve Bowser, and especially Abdul, whose program of "straight-ahead" jazz from 12:00 to 5:00 A.M. on WCLK kept my thoughts percolating as I wrote through the wee hours of the morning. And to the fine staff at the University of Georgia Press, from Karen Orchard, the director, to Malcolm Call, Kelly Caudle, and Jennifer Rogers. I certainly could not have done without my very able and competent copy editor, Melinda Conner.

Finally, I have to thank and pay tribute to my family. First my mother, Mrs. Frances Major, who always, ever since I can remember, made it clear that I could accomplish anything in spite of the obstacles. I also thank my offspring, who were children when this project began. My daughter, Kamaria Ife, who became computer literate typing an early version of the manuscript, is now the proud mother of twins and won't let me forget that I am a grandfather. She has no conscious memory of life without John Hope. The same is true for my sons, Jumaane Haki and Rahsaan Jamil. At the time of this writing, they are eighteen and twenty-one years old, respectively. I know they tire of me using Hope's life as a model for their own commitment to family, community, and belief in social responsibility. All three of them have been my inspiration and are in part what this book is all about. Their mother—and my first wife—also deserves thanks. While I hesitated more than twenty-five years ago, she insisted that college was not beyond my capabilities, and that majoring in history instead of business was not an unforgivable sin.

I am most indebted to my wife, Ann. Ever since our marriage in 1993 she has been forced to share me with John Hope. Not only has Ann failed to complain, she has been my most avid supporter and cheerleader, and at the same time a consistent and constructive critic. Though at first timid about commenting on drafts of the manuscript, she eventually became very bold and asked valuable questions that led to important rewrites. We spent so many hours discussing Hope's life that she probably knows him as well as I do. Because of Ann I have tried hard to include aspects of Hope's life I might otherwise have omitted. She convinced me that readers would be interested in how people of Hope's generation interacted with their spouses, socialized their children, and spent their leisure time.

I, of course, accept all responsibility for any errors. My Smoketown friend Soc would get a kick out of me admitting that.

Introduction

Perhaps too frequently, it takes death to make the living pause to appreciate an important figure. On 22 February 1936, a dark cloud hovered over the campus of Atlanta University. Rain began to fall around 3:30 P.M. on the hundreds gathered there for a solemn occurrence. John Hope, one of the premier African American leaders of his time, was being laid to rest. Students, faculty, and staff, college and university presidents, and a host of relatives and friends had come to pay their last respects. The simple ceremony was exactly what Hope wanted. Only two years earlier he had written that "people should get on with their work and not spend too much time with the dead." Nevertheless, by the time the service ended, tears of emotion mixed freely with the rain that poured from above.

This book encompasses the life of John Hope, an important black educator and race leader of the early twentieth century. Throughout his life Hope was relentless in his support of public education, adequate housing, health care, job opportunities, and recreational facilities for African Americans in Atlanta and the nation. As an advocate of full black equality, he also embraced civil rights organizations such as the W. E. B. Du Bois–led Niagara Movement, the NAACP, and the southern-based Commission on Interracial Cooperation. No less renowned as an educator, Hope eventually became the first black president of two important colleges. In 1906 he ascended to the presidency of Morehouse College, an all-male liberal arts school in Atlanta. In 1929 he was selected to be the president of Atlanta University (now Clark-Atlanta University), which under his leadership became the first college to provide exclusively graduate education for African American students.

"Who was John Hope?" people ask today. "Do you mean John Hope Franklin, the distinguished historian?" It may surprise some to learn that Franklin's parents named their son after the educator and race leader, John Hope. Although Hope was well known early in this century, he is largely forgotten today. He could very well be the least known major figure in the annals of African American history between Booker T. Washington and Martin Luther King Jr. Yet John Hope meant as much to the development of black higher education as Washington meant to the development of black industrial education.

The title of this book, *A Clashing of the Soul: John Hope and the Dilemma of African American Leadership and Black Higher Education in the Early Twentieth Century*, derives in part from Gunnar Myrdal's monumental classic study of the "Negro problem" in the United States. Myrdal's meticulous research and penetrating analysis revealed what he called an "American dilemma," a predicament created by two patterns of contradictory behavior. On the one hand, Myrdal found that white Americans clung to the moral principles of the American creed, which included racial tolerance, fundamental equality, and access to equal opportunity. On the other hand, however, their interactions with African Americans revealed desires, traditions, and special interests that often contradicted that creed. As a race, African Americans were generally believed to be biologically inferior, thus justifying their treatment as second-class citizens without the fundamental rights given to all Americans. Ironically, racial bigotry was also "American," and its roots were just as deep in the country's historical traditions.[1]

White America's dilemma had serious repercussions in the African American community. One result was the legalization of segregation at the beginning of the twentieth century and the "black" world it created. Within this setting, African Americans developed their own values, dynamics, tactics, and objectives, which were deeply rooted in their collective experiences. Yet in spite of their isolation, and perhaps because of it, African Americans were often plagued with dilemmas as paradoxical and contradictory as those in white society.[2]

A study of Hope's life in the first three decades of the twentieth century illuminates many of the complex issues that vexed African American leaders in segregated America and created what Mordecai Johnson, Howard University's first African American president, called a "clashing of the soul." John Hope grappled with two dilemmas practically all of his adult life. First, there was the inner turmoil that resulted from attempting to balance John Hope the college president and John Hope the race leader. Hope often gave up his best faculty members and administrators to race advancement organizations such as the NAACP and the Urban League and to service organizations such as the Colored Men's Department of the YMCA and the National Council of Churches. He frequently contemplated leaving Morehouse and becoming a professional race leader himself.

John Hope also epitomized radical black leadership in the South during the age of Booker T. Washington.[3] He made a conscious choice to join the ranks of black radicals such as W. E. B. Du Bois, William Monroe Trotter, J. Max Barber, and Ida Wells-Barnett who insisted on full black equality without compromise. With that decision, Hope turned his back on the conservative philosophy of Booker T. Washington, thereby alienating powerful white philanthropists and arousing the suspicion and hostility of prominent Atlanta whites.

Hope's image as a militant race leader, especially within the African American community, created tensions that eventually resulted in his second major dilemma. Increasingly in the 1920s, influential blacks and whites tended to evaluate Hope's leadership differently. The potential for race warfare after the "Red Summer" of 1919 led white leaders to turn to Hope and other established black leaders of his generation for advice and assistance. Many of those same white leaders reevaluated their commitment to black higher education and decided the time had come for increased financial support. Morehouse College, with its African American president and successful record of educating black males, benefited enormously from this new direction. Yet it was not Hope the militant who attracted these prominent and influential whites, but Hope the conservative educational statesman, who was willing to compromise and adjust to the realities of the segregated South.

Some African American leaders rejected Hope's leadership style. Leaders of the New Negro Movement such as Mordecai Johnson, Walter White, James Weldon Johnson, and even Hope's good friend Du Bois often disagreed with Hope's increasingly moderate stances. Many African American students of the 1920s went further and labeled Hope a conservative—even an accommodationist—badly out of step with the times. Hope struggled to resolve his dilemmas until he died in 1936.

Readers looking for a detailed history of Hope's administration at Morehouse or Atlanta University will be disappointed; the subject receives only brief attention here. Other important areas of Hope's rich life also receive little attention. My purpose throughout is to focus on what I see as the central and most instructive dynamic of his life: his dual roles as black college president and race leader. Most African American leaders of Hope's era were not confronted with this dilemma. Professional race leaders, though they were few, usually held paid positions in protest, nationalist, or other types of race improvement organizations. Most African American leaders, however, worked in conventional occupations. Their leadership roles owed much to their positions and standing within the black community, and sometimes within the white community as well. As a class they were usually professionals in segregated black America, in occupations ranging from ministers and educators to journalists and businesspeople. The tensions Hope experienced as a black college president and race leader were unique. More than anything else, they resulted from his interaction with and dependence on influential whites.

Booker T. Washington, the most famous African American college president in the late nineteenth and early twentieth centuries, seems not to have grappled with Hope's dilemma. He did not confront an image problem in the African American community (or the white community) that seemed to change drastically late in his life. In addition, Washington's relationship with prominent whites was cordial from the very beginning. Most whites supported both the style and direction of Washington's leadership and his philosophy on African American education. If Washington agonized over his role as a black leader and college president or experienced tensions resulting from that duality, the story has not yet been told.[4]

A biography of John Hope can add much to our knowledge and understanding of the world of African Americans at the beginning of the twentieth century. Although Hope's problems were rooted in systemic discrimination, they also reflected issues, desires, and expectations that emanated from the African American community itself. Instead of an external view of segregated black life, this work looks at that community from the inside out. Like Louis Harlan in *Booker T. Washington*, I look at the peculiar nuances that went into the making of a black leader who was also a black college president. However, in contrast to what Harlan has argued regarding Washington, I believe it was not power that motivated Hope (though he clearly was not without power) but a sense of obligation and commitment to perform two difficult tasks equally well: developing black higher education and resolving other "race problems" as he interpreted them.

This biography of John Hope also contributes to our understanding of color, class, and caste within the African American community, especially the group Willard Gatewood identified as "aristocrats of color."[5] Born of a biracial union in Augusta, Georgia, shortly after the Civil War, Hope belonged to a small black upper-class elite whose history predated the coming of freedom. Though technically a mulatto, John Hope looked like a white man with no visible traces of African blood.

Considering the perilous status of African Americans during his lifetime, why, given the opportunity, did Hope not pass for white? That question was often raised by some whites while Hope still lived, especially while he was in prep school and college. It continued to be raised after his death, and is even raised in some circles today. The question itself is a sign of unfamiliarity with black experience. It both devalues African American community and ignores the trauma associated with severing relationships with family, friends, and institutions. Perhaps the question should be just the opposite, even for those African Americans with complexions as fair as John Hope's: Why would African Americans born and socialized in the African American community, in spite of the social milieu, give up their racial identities?

W. E. B. Du Bois, whom Hope counted as one of his best friends, agreed about the importance of a distinct African American identity even while acknowledging that some African Americans chose to cross the "color line." About John Hope, Du Bois wrote that "he was at once white and glad to be black." Annoyed at repeated requests for an explanation of why Hope did not "pass," the noted race leader, sociologist, and historian finally elaborated on the question years after Hope's death: "There was nothing extraordinary in Hope's being a Negro. He did not consciously choose to be a Negro. He was a Negro. Because being a Negro, or a German, or a Chinese is primarily a matter of friends, surroundings, habits of life; and not merely a question of appearance or biology." Du Bois correctly believed Hope's identity was deeply rooted in his experiences as a child growing up in Augusta:

> For a boy raised to regard himself as colored; to have colored relatives, friends, and neighbors; always to have been taught to look upon "whites" as mainly belonging to an alien, antagonistic body of human beings, for such a boy to desert his folk even in spirit and loyalty, much less in physical withdrawal, would have been more unnatural than to remain true to this race despite appearance. To white people, naturally a course of action, thus natural and expected, seemed inexplicable, if not Quixotic. We, within the Veil, see analogous phenomena in reverse; obviously negroid folk who by action and choice are white.[6]

Du Bois's views applied to many African American leaders whose physical features gave no hint of their racial identity. Hope's own wife, Lugenia Burns Hope, along with Mary Church Terrell and Adella Hunt Logan quickly come to mind among the women, and Walter White, William Jefferson White, and Mordecai Johnson come to mind among the men. African American leaders in the black community, often called "race" men and women in the late nineteenth and early twentieth centuries, were usually selected because of their fierce race loyalty and deep sense of social responsibility. Race was deeply embedded in their identities, and as Du Bois pointed out, "firmly established in their childhoods." I believe Du Bois's analysis is correct, and for that reason I do not spend time trying to explain Hope's decision to remain a part of the African American community. I do, however, try to explain how Hope reacted when two members of his own family decided to pass.

Hope's racial identity was irrevocably linked to his dilemmas as a black college educator and national race leader. His tensions obviously emanated from a societal structure that separated African Americans from the rest of society and, in practice, saddled that separation with a badge of inferiority. Within their separate black world, African Americans insisted on a pragmatic, not idealistic, leadership. In the South, where there was no chance for integration, African American leaders had little choice but to fight for progress and advancement within the segregated setting. That reality also proved to be a major factor in John Hope's "clashing of the soul," as he tried desperately to balance his roles as a southern black college president and militant race leader in the first three decades of the twentieth century.

1

"Oh Mary Don't You Weep"

John Hope was born on 2 June 1868, yet his story does not begin on that date. Like most Africans who would become "African Americans," an important part of his history—the story of his mother's people—lies hidden, perhaps forever lost, in the oral traditions and literature of the nations along Africa's coasts. Fortunately for historians, remnants of Hope's family history have been preserved. Though nothing of his background in Africa survives, there is a New World record that extends back three generations.

Hope's roots in this country began early in the nineteenth century in Hancock County, Georgia, approximately 30 miles west of Augusta. The county is located on the Fall Line where the Piedmont joins the Coastal Plain. Travelers to the area at the close of the eighteenth century saw tremendous potential there for moderately sized family farms. In addition to the fine hardwoods and pines for timber, the rich red soil seemed ideal for growing several cash crops. Early in the nineteenth century, this vision proved to be both right and wrong. Hancock County, as part of Augusta's hinterlands, did become an agricultural paradise. Yet it was not small farmers who reaped the economic rewards, but plantation owners who used enslaved African labor.[1]

Mary, John Hope's maternal great-grandmother, was just one of numerous slaves scattered among several Hancock County plantations in 1820. No information survives of her origins, and the little that is known about her comes from family traditions and the estate records of her owner, Hugh Taylor. In 1820, sixteen-year-old Mary was looked on as a beautiful young woman by many people in the slave quarters and in the master's household. Such attention might have been flattering in another time and place, but for enslaved African American women in the antebellum South, it was more often a curse. While serving in her master's household, Mary was raped by a visiting planter. Late in 1820, according to the family's oral history, she gave birth to a mulatto daughter and was "nominally married" to an unidentified man in the slave quarters. That daughter would become John Hope's maternal grandmother.[2]

Mary named her daughter Lethe (pronounced *leeth*), or "Lethi." Years later Lethe took the name Lethea. Little is known about Lethe. Her first five years were probably spent with her mother. She resurfaced in 1825, when the Marquis de Lafayette, a Revolutionary War hero, visited the county seat in Sparta. As he traveled by stagecoach over the rugged, virtually impassable roads from Augusta, Lafayette was given a tremendous welcome by prominent citizens of Hancock County. Mary's owner, Hugh Taylor, helped to organize the festivities and attended the welcoming celebration at the Eagle Tavern with his family. Taylor's ten-year-old daughter, Mary Elizabeth, also cheered the war hero, along with a "petite, mulatto slave-child" companion called Lethe.[3]

The death of a slave master aroused mixed emotions and much uncertainty among the slaves. In 1826, just one year after the visit of Lafayette, Hugh Taylor died. Taylor's will divided his estate among his heirs, with the largest portion held in trust for Mary Elizabeth. Her share included twenty-one slaves, Mary and Lethe among them. Although the slave Harry was allowed to choose his own master, who "would pay Harry the sum of two dollars annually to his own use," Mary and Lethe, like most of the Taylor slaves, received no special treatment.[4]

Lethe and her mother probably remained together until 1830. After that, Lethe began to spend more and more time with her owner, Mary Elizabeth Taylor. Taylor initially attended school in one of the many private academies in Hancock County, then finished her education in New York after her father's death. She traveled extensively in the Carolinas, Louisiana, Virginia, and New York. Estate records show that she owned nineteen slaves in 1830. Mary and seventeen others were hired out; Lethi was retained for Mary Elizabeth's own use.[5]

In 1833, Mary Taylor married Edward Bustin, a prominent businessman from Augusta. That same year Lethe and her mother were hired out to a local planter and his mistress. It was probably the last time they spent together. In 1834, Mary was sold to one of Mary Elizabeth's brothers, and Lethe accompanied the Bustins to Augusta, where she remained one of the many slaves in the Bustin household.[6]

Augusta is located on a rich and fertile plain at a bend on the Savannah River. The first city map, drawn in 1780, showed six streets running east to west, parallel to the river: Bay, Reynolds, Broad, Ellis, Greene, and Telfair. Seven other streets ran north and south: Houston, located on the east at the lower end of the city, was followed by Lincoln, Elbert, Center, Washington, McIntosh, and Jackson. Ten years later, the small southern town had only about 1,100 residents.[7]

Urban slavery in Augusta was far different from plantation slavery in rural Hancock County. When the city was founded in 1735, the role of slavery in the town's political economy was not yet clear. Augusta's size and population exploded in the nineteenth century, when it became an important commercial center. In 1841, the first city directory reported that approximately 6,300 people resided in Augusta, practically half of them enslaved African Americans. By 1860 the population had swelled to approximately 12,500, with the African American population remaining around 50 percent of the total. Though small by most states' standards, Augusta was the second largest city in Georgia. Cotton dominated its commerce, which accounted in part for the large number of slaves, but the economy was by no means one-dimensional. Several banks, textile industries, and other economic ventures contributed to Augusta's prosperity, as did the railroad and steamboat, important modes of transportation.[8]

Augusta's most knowledgeable historian correctly noted that the city's traditions were rooted in a unique blend of New England commercialism with a distinct Virginia ethos. The commercialism emanated from the city's close historical relationship with Charleston, South Carolina, which emphasized a cosmopolitanism associated more with cities in the Northeast than in the South. That strain was balanced by the Virginia-influenced "Code of the Old South," which Augusta adopted as a standard of behavior. This code was based on a belief, to use Edward Cashin's words, "that all men were created equal, but then they rose more or less high to the station for which nature fashioned them." According to the code, white men's opportunities were unlimited, but blacks' opportunities were limited by their biological and genetic inferiority. In addition, the Virginia influence held that "making money was un-southern." Augusta's political elite was often criticized for running a "Yankee town." In their defense, however, Augusta's leaders thought of themselves as "urban Virginians, as merchants, but planters, too." This blend of Virginia socio-political culture and Charleston commercialism shaped Augusta's worldview.[9]

Neither enslaved nor free African Americans were unaffected by Augusta's dual personality. Throughout the antebellum period the city tried to define the correct place for the enslaved. According to the Virginia tradition, that place was on the plantation. The Charleston influence, however, wanted slaves wherever it was cost-effective to use them. City officials argued vociferously about whether slaves should be employed in factories and on steamers, and whether they should be allowed to keep public stables and shops without white supervision. There were also arguments about African Americans selling items on the streets, in direct violation of city ordinances. That these ordinances were seldom enforced was pointed out by one writer who complained, "Every-day I see women, girls, and boys of color selling in the public streets, cakes, biscuits, custard, pickles, pies, etc., and they carry spirituous liquors to sell to the wagoners on the camp grounds." [10]

Enslaved and free blacks alike benefited from Augusta's indecision. Urban slaves frequently lived among free persons of color and enjoyed more freedom than plantation slaves. They often hired themselves out for wages, freely attended black churches, and wandered in the night without supervision. With approximately 3,700 slaves in the city in 1860, Augusta officials were frequently frustrated in their attempts to identify who was free and who was not. [11]

The census of 1860 records only 386 free persons of color in Augusta. Though few in number, free blacks had always been permanent fixtures in the city. They worked as draymen, blacksmiths, barbers, hired laborers, and in other professions—including one piano tuner. A few free persons of color managed to do fairly well in the marketplace. They also established churches, secretly educated their children, and at times helped fugitive slaves to escape. [12]

Social relations between Augusta's whites and free blacks were governed by the city's unique character. Early in the nineteenth century, free persons of color were officially required to register with the city. They also had to have white guardians who would agree to take full responsibility for their welfare and behavior. Relationships between guardians and their black charges varied, but there was little social interaction across racial lines; Augusta's free blacks attended their institutions, and whites attended theirs. Most interaction between guardians and their charges took place in the workplace or when the latter needed a pass. Free blacks usually remained independent as long as they acknowledged and accepted their place in the society.

Nevertheless, it should not be surprising that many free persons of color were mulattoes who maintained more than cordial relations with their white benefactors. Georgia law prohibited interracial marriages, and more informal relationships were officially forbidden as well. In 1852 the legislature increased the penalties for white men living with African American women. The *Augusta Chronicle* reported that a white man and a "woman of color, of any shade or complexion whatever, free or slave," who lived together in "a state of adultery or fornication" could be fined and imprisoned for three months. The issue divided Augustans, for many prominent male citizens lived with African American women. No one dared to officially sanction the "degrading practice," but some Augusta leaders believed the stronger penalties against interracial cohabitation were futile. Social interactions between free persons of color and prominent whites in Augusta play a crucial role in the John Hope story. [13]

The Bustins resided in the First Ward of Augusta on Broad Street at Elbert, not far from the Bustin and Walker grocery store, one of the family's many businesses. Augusta must have seemed strange to fourteen-year-old Lethe when she arrived in 1834, for it was very different from rural Hancock County. In many ways, unfortunately, it was the same. What happened to Lethe in 1836 was painfully similar to what had happened to her mother only sixteen years earlier: at the age of sixteen, Lethe was also raped by a Hancock County slave owner. It is unclear whether the attack took place in Sparta, where the Bustins spent considerable time, or in Augusta. In 1837, Lethe gave birth to a mulatto son whom she named Benjamin. The same slave owner, said to have been a Virginian by the name of Butt, fathered all of Lethe's children. She would have six more.[14]

Relationships between masters and slaves were often as complex as the institution that spawned them; Lethe's relationships with Mary Elizabeth and Butt were probably not unusual. Ridgely Torrence, John Hope's first biographer, acknowledged that Butt's initial sexual encounter with Lethe was rape, but he strongly believed their alliance after that was based on mutual consent, and over time went beyond even cordiality. Their sexual encounters continued until Butt's death. In addition, Torrence was convinced that Lethe and Mary Elizabeth Bustin were never simply master and slave. He believed they were friends as well, and that Lethe accompanied her mistress as a companion rather than a servant. Like the indomitable, high-spirited slave in Alex Haley's novel *Queen*, Lethe rarely noticed the invisible chains that bound her—or so Torrence thought.[15]

Torrence's conclusions stemmed from several different sources. First, the fact that Butt and Lethe's relationship continued for several years somehow softened the impact of what Torrence called "the morganatic nature" of their connection. In addition, Butt's family—then and much later—acknowledged the illicit affair to Lethe and her descendants, which also seemed in Torrence's mind to mollify the rape of the sixteen-year-old slave. With regard to Mary Elizabeth Bustin, Torrence believed Lethe's wide-ranging experiences with her documented their mutual affection. Lethe certainly traveled with Mary Bustin on many of her journeys before her marriage, including perhaps one or more trips to New York. Mary Elizabeth also secretly taught Lethe to read and write, in spite of laws prohibiting that practice.[16]

But while it seems fair to say that Mary Elizabeth Bustin provided Lethe with experiences denied to most other slaves, to suggest that her relationships with Bustin and Butt transcended the boundaries of master and slave seems to go too far. Instead of traveling with her master, for example, Lethe might have preferred to remain with her mother and others in the African American slave community. Strong bonds existed between enslaved African American women in the quarters, especially among mothers and their adolescent daughters. There is no record of Mary's response to their forced separation or to Lethe's rape. Yet we do know from other accounts of enslaved African American women that these experiences were too common and were always traumatic.[17]

There is no question that Mary Bustin herself sold Lethe's mother, but her complicity in Lethe's rape is more difficult to discern. Quite possibly it was Edward Bustin who permitted the sexual assault on Lethe, without his wife's knowledge. Though in very different circumstances, black women and white women were often caught in a web of despair within plantation households controlled by slave owners.[18] On the other hand, the Bustins did not live on a plantation; they lived in the city, and there was much more interaction between master and slaves living in urban households. Furthermore, estate records show that Mary Bustin continued to manage her slaves after her marriage and kept them separate from those belonging to her husband. Torrence suggested that Mary Bustin and Lethe were extremely close. If this were true, it seems unlikely Bustin's husband could have permitted the rape of his wife's "best friend" without her consent. Even if she was unaware of the initial encounter, Mary Bustin certainly did not remain ignorant of Lethe's continuing sexual encounters with Mr. Butt, which produced children almost yearly.[19] We do not know whether Mary Elizabeth knew of or consented to Lethe's rape; nor do we know whether she attempted at any time to halt the sexual abuse. It may be that Lethe was not really that special to Mary Bustin. She may have been just another female slave whose personal well-being was of only peripheral concern to her master.

Lethe herself may have left indirect clues that reveal her thoughts about her own situation and that of her mother, Mary. In 1860 Lethe appeared for the first time in the federal census as a free person of color. She chose to retain her mother's surname, Taylor, and gave it to all of her children instead of naming them Bustin, after her own mistress, or Butt, after their father. This may have been a deliberate choice. In his study of the African American family, Herbert Gutman determined that slaves used names to make statements about their identity and to reject their enslaved condition. Perhaps in selecting "Taylor" after becoming free, John Hope's grandmother revealed that her relationship with Bustin and Butt was that of master and slave, no more and no less.[20]

By 1860 John Hope's grandmother, now known as Lethea Taylor, resided in the Fourth Ward of Augusta and headed an extended family that included nine people. The exact date of her manumission is unknown. It probably occurred sometime after 1850, as her name does not appear in the census of that year. Yet she is also absent from the slave schedules, and there are no clues to her status in tax digests or other local records. Family members believed she was freed sometime early in the 1850s, and that Mr. Butt, the father of her children, became her guardian. When he died, her guardianship passed to Isaac Tuttle, a business associate of Butt's who lived in Augusta.[21]

Like many African American women in the antebellum South, John Hope's grandmother dreamed of making her seven children's lives better than her own. Unlike most of those women, however, Lethea's wide-ranging experiences had equipped her with resources that helped her to realize that dream. The census indicates she worked as a seamstress. Family members added the information that Lethea Taylor also secretly taught her children and other free persons of color to read and write.

Though not as common as free black academies in Charleston, schools run by free persons of color did exist in Augusta. Ex-slave Eugene Wesley Smith remembered that "going to school wasn't allowed, but still some people would slip their children to school. There was an old Methodist preacher, a Negro named Ned Purdee, he had a school for boys and girls going on in his back yard. They caught him and put him in jail. He was put in stocks and got so many lashes every day for a month. They put his feet and hands in the holes, and he was supposed to be whipped across his back." [22] Another free black Augustan secretly operated a school for thirty students in a black-owned building. After the Civil War, when it was safe to talk about it, the teacher explained that the "children entered it by different doors, the girls with their books strapped under their skirts, the boys with theirs concealed under their coats." Secret passages provided quick exits when whites were in the area.[23]

Eventually the state of Georgia clamped down on all efforts to educate African Americans, slaves and free blacks alike, making the practice extremely dangerous. In 1852, Lethea arranged (probably with Butt's help) for two of her children to attend school in Charleston. Though Lethea Taylor's status in 1852 is unclear, contemporaries later remembered that "there would have been nothing at all unusual about the Butt father sending his daughters to school even if they were slaves so long as he was rich enough and prominent enough to protect them." They also remembered that two white lawyers operated a school "for the colored children of wealthy white men." [24]

Lethea Taylor's children attended a school run by a black woman—who, ironically, was also a slave owner. Though records do not identify the school or the woman, she was probably someone Lethea had met earlier while traveling with her mistress. Quite possibly the woman was Frances Pickney Bonneau Holloway, member of a Charleston family with a long tradition of free black educators and slave owners.[25]

The two children educated in Charleston were Lethea Taylor's two oldest daughters. Mary Frances, named after Lethea's mother, Mary, was born in 1839. Anna, often called "Nannie," was born in 1841. In 1854, when she returned home from school at the age of fifteen, Mary Frances was a beautiful "slender girl with a proud bearing, a dark olive complexion, finely spaced eyes, and broad forehead." Six years later, Lethea's eldest daughter had given birth to two children; in time she would become John Hope's mother.[26]

Few job opportunities were available to free women of color in 1854 outside the realm of domestic service. In spite of her education, charm, and sophistication, a year passed before Mary Frances (often called "Fanny") took a job. Perhaps others were offered in the meantime, but Lethea tended to be very protective of her oldest daughter in Augusta. Though the children's father had died, Lethea managed to keep the household together with the money she earned as a mantua maker (seamstress) and the economic help of her grown children. In 1855, though with some hesitation, Lethea allowed Mary Frances to work outside the home.

Early that same year, Isaac Tuttle, a prominent businessman and philanthropist, died, leaving his stepson, Dr. George M. Newton, a large inheritance. That inheritance included a substantial sum of money in addition to several slaves, which the stepson added to his own fifteen. George Newton also inherited the guardianship of several free blacks, including Lethea Taylor and her family. Newton approached Taylor and asked her to help him find someone to manage his crowded household. Late in 1855 Mary Frances Taylor became George Newton's housekeeper.

Born in 1810, Newton was an Augusta native with medical degrees from Pennsylvania and Europe who returned home to become a prominent physician and businessman. He played a major role in establishing the Medical College of Georgia early in the 1830s. For a short time he was the dean of the school's faculty, but he served most of the time as a professor of anatomy. City directories and tax digests show that Newton also served on the boards of several banks and owned considerable real estate.[27]

Newton's home was on Greene Street, an avenue described by one visitor as "lined with fine mansions; tall, spreading trees not only grace[d] the sidewalks, but a double row, with grassy spaces between, [ran] down the centre of the ample roadway." Newton's house was an "intellectual and social center, fortified by a large library in many languages and a cellar of such sumptuous character that the remnant of its rare imported vintages sold after his death for $6,000." It was this household that Mary Frances was expected to manage just one year after she finished school. Like her grandmother and mother before her, Mary Frances had reached the age of sixteen. Newton was then forty-five years old and no doubt one of the most eligible bachelors in Augusta.[28]

Later that year, when Mary Frances moved into the Greene Street home with Newton, it was apparent she was pregnant with their first child. On

28 February 1857, Mary Frances gave birth to Madison J. Newton, who would become John Hope's half-brother. Above the protests of his students and colleagues at the medical college, Newton immediately handed in his resignation.[29]

Little is known of the Newton family the first year after Madison's birth. A family friend interviewed years later speculated that Newton took Mary Frances to South Carolina and secretly married her. There is no conclusive evidence for that, although Mary Frances appears in the Augusta directory for 1859 as "Mrs. George Newton" at the Greene Street address.[30] The Newton union, however, was not to be a long one. In 1858, Newton had a bad accident that left him very ill. Early in 1859 he died of tetanus. The Newton household was shattered. Mary Frances, with a child barely a year old and pregnant with another, was suddenly without any means of support. Eventually she moved back home with her mother.

What Lethea Taylor thought of her daughter's plight in 1860 is unknown. Perhaps she recalled her mother's history, and her own, and wished she had not violated a cardinal rule. Lethea, of all people, was aware of the risks for African American women working in the homes of white males, particularly unmarried ones. Possibly that explains why, initially, Mary Frances arrived early in the morning at the Greene Street residence, managed to go undetected by Newton, and left before he returned home from the medical college. Once Mary Frances had attracted Newton's attention, however, there was little Lethea Taylor could do to alter events, despite her free status. It is impossible to say with certainty that Mary Frances was forced into a sexual relationship with Newton, although she was only sixteen and he was thirty years her senior. Ridgely Torrence, for example, was convinced she loved George Newton and that their relationship was based on mutual admiration.[31]

There were also rumors around town that the wealthy Newton had included Fanny in his will. The rumors were false. Newton's will was hastily written on 2 January 1859, shortly after he was diagnosed with tetanus. He left more than $12,000 to white members of his family; the rest of the estate went to a local orphanage founded in 1852. There was nothing in the will for Mary Frances, Madison, or the unborn child. That is not to say conclusively that Newton did not care for his black family. In 1859, white members of prominent families would certainly have contested wills that included large bequests to blacks, slave or free. That fact notwithstanding, there is still no evidence that Newton intended in any way to provide for his black family after his death.[32]

In 1912, John Hope wrote a letter to his wife vividly describing a four-hour visit during his first trip to Europe. In a valley beneath an imposing hill stood a row of blue-roofed houses in close proximity to a large river. Hope gazed momentarily at one of the houses, then walked across an old bridge and stopped at a spot where a school once housed students studying Greek and Latin. Torrential rain poured down on John Hope and his guides during most of that visit. Yet that did not dampen his excitement as he laughed at the children in wooden shoes scattering for shelter. Hope was in Langholm, Scotland. His father, James Hope, had been born there in 1805.[33]

In 1817, James Hope, the eldest of five children, arrived in New York City with his father, Matthew. The elder Hope had come to America to make a new start after the failure of his cotton mill in Langholm. Years after James Hope's death, family members remembered that the thing that most impressed him when he arrived in the United States was his first view of African Americans: "dark-skinned boys, agile and strong, rhythmically unloading huge bales of cotton from the ships that plied coast-wise from Savannah to the port of New York." There were also "brown girls moving like queens as they balanced bundles or brimming pitchers on their erect heads," and "small dark children at their dancing play."[34] Although Matthew Hope died in 1827, James and his brothers had developed a flourishing grocery business by 1831. But James's real ambition was to follow in his father's footsteps and establish a cotton factory. Thus, in 1831, James Hope left New York and moved south to Augusta to make his dream a reality.[35]

Ten years later James Hope had become a successful businessman and prominent Augusta citizen. The 1841 city directory lists him as a director of the Augusta Insurance and Banking Company. He boarded with another Scotsman, J. Kerrs, the man who had ignited Hope's interest in moving to Augusta and became his business partner when he arrived. In 1842, James was part of a delegation that invited Henry Clay to Augusta, and he became a familiar face at the meetings of the Augusta City Council. Hope later served as the secretary and general manager of the Augusta Manufacturing Company, and in 1847 helped organize a steamboat company and other enterprises. The census of 1860 and city tax digests show that Hope was a wealthy man on the eve of the Civil War.[36]

Part of James Hope's wealth was derived from shrewd investments in real estate. His business partner in these transactions was Dr. George Newton, the father of Mary Frances Taylor's two children. The two men met early in the 1840s and became good friends. Hope, five years older than Newton and like him unmarried, spent many hours at the Greene Street home and was attracted to the young, vibrant, and very efficient Mary Frances Taylor. Ironically, James Hope became the father of John Hope by a twist of fate.

Early in June 1859, six months after George Newton's death, James Hope bought an expensive piece of property on Ellis Street between Kollock and Marbury, approximately one mile from the bustling Savannah River business district, that became the home of Mary Frances Taylor. Hope left Augusta and returned to New York early in 1860, but returned late in December. Early in 1861, James Hope moved into the Ellis Street house with Taylor and her children. James Hope was then fifty-six years old; Mary Frances Taylor had not yet turned twenty-two.[37]

Details regarding the events surrounding the early relationship between Taylor and Hope are sketchy. According to one story, Hope promised George Newton he would use Newton's half of their joint investments to take care of Taylor and her children. The house was purchased with these funds and simply fulfilled the promise made to his good friend on his deathbed. Distraught over Newton's death, Taylor turned to Hope for advice and assistance with matters relating to the estate and the care of her children. However, so the story goes, it was not long before their platonic relationship turned into something stronger. Personal responsibility replaced obligation, gratitude turned to love, and Mary Frances Taylor and James Hope decided to live together as husband and wife.[38]

Local records challenge some aspects of this account. Tax digests and Richmond County land records show only four joint ventures that involved James Hope and George M. Newton. All were real estate transactions completed long before Newton's accident. Three properties they purchased jointly in 1853 were sold early in 1858, and the only other property they owned jointly was purchased and resold in 1853. There simply were no joint ventures of record between the two men when George Newton died, and thus no funds available from that source to maintain Newton's African American family.[39]

Nor did Hope, one of Newton's three executors, oversee any money Mary Frances inherited from Newton's estate, because she was not mentioned in the will. James Hope may have been genuinely concerned with Fanny's welfare, but his concern was not predicated on matters dealing with George Newton's estate. There were rumors that James Hope had always been romantically attracted to Mary Frances Taylor, and that the purchase of the Ellis Street home was simply the first move in Hope's plan to replace George Newton as head of the Taylor family. Though his intent cannot be determined, there is no doubt James Hope paid close to $2,000 for that property in 1861.[40]

Members of the Hope household on Ellis Street in the early 1860s, though crowded, were cautiously optimistic about the future. In addition to James Hope and Mary Frances Taylor, the household included James and Anna Taylor, Fanny's brother and sister; Fanny's two children by George Newton, Madison J. Newton and baby daughter Georgia Frances Newton (called Sissie); and several of Newton's slaves and James Hope's slaves. In 1862, Mary Frances gave birth to the first John Hope, who did not live to see his fourth birthday.[41]

Although James Hope was semiretired, his stocks continued to yield high profits and his real estate investments remained sound. The Hopes were certainly not plagued with money problems in the early 1860s, but there was tension—tension generated by the uncertainties of war. In October 1859, news of the events at Harper's Ferry reached Augusta by telegraph. John Brown's failed crusade against slavery heightened the city's awareness of its own vulnerability. Practically half the inhabitants of Augusta were slaves, and there was also an arsenal in Augusta. Paranoia blanketed the city, enabling the city council to intensify its restrictions on free blacks as well as those enslaved. New ordinances passed in December prohibited "balls, dancing parties, fairs, singing meetings, or meetings for any other purpose of negroes, except sitting up with the dead and funerals." Even those functions were allowed only with written permission from a white person and the city council. Curfews were reset for 11:00 P.M. in the summer and 10:00 P.M. in the winter. City officials hoped to limit masters' practice of hiring out their slaves by charging $100 per slave instead of $10. Organizations like the Agricultural and Police Society and the Savannah River Anti-Slave Traffick Association, formed earlier to control slaves in and around the city, strengthened their patrols.[42]

Other ordinances passed early in 1860 specifically targeted free persons of color. In January the Augusta City Council decided to levy a tax of $20 on every free black living in the city. The state of Georgia went even further and authorized the sale of free blacks into slavery. Augusta's free black community did not remain silent. Several delegations presented the city council with petitions protesting the new laws. During the first six months of 1860 the *Chronicle* was full of news items that highlighted the dissatisfaction of Augusta's small free black population. There is no evidence that any free blacks were forced to give up their freedom as a result of the laws.[43]

Controlling the behavior of enslaved and free African Americans was not the only thought on the minds of Augusta's leaders. There was a real possibility that Georgia would secede from the Union. The strain of waiting was finally ended on 19 January 1861 when piercing clangs resonating from "Big Steve," a four-ton bell located high above Greene and Jackson Streets, alerted Augusta that Georgia had seceded from the Union. That night, fireworks illuminated Broad Street and people danced frantically in the streets.[44]

James Hope may or may not have taken part in the celebration, for many of Augusta's residents were not secessionists. Yet Hope's loyalty to Augusta was unquestionable. In time he volunteered his services and took an oath of allegiance to the Confederacy. He was already in his middle fifties then, past military age, still broad shouldered but now completely gray. State records show that he served in the Silver-Grays, an infantry company organized in Augusta for local defense that guarded river bridges, powder works, and Union prisoners during the war.[45]

Meanwhile, back in the house on Ellis Street, Mary Frances gave birth to the second Hope child. Jane Hope was born in 1863, the year of the Emancipation Proclamation. An editorial in the *Augusta Chronicle* probably expressed the sentiment of many white Augustans when it stated that the Emancipation Proclamation "changes nothing except behind Union lines. There it brings poverty to the master and misery to the slave."[46] No celebrations were recorded among slaves or free persons in the Hope household, yet they could not have been oblivious to the dramatic changes occurring all around them.

By 1864 the Confederate cause was in jeopardy. Augusta braced for an attack from General William Tecumseh Sherman's forces marching out of Atlanta. The attack never came; Sherman chose to take Savannah instead. Yet Augusta suffered from the war nevertheless; there were shortages of every kind, including the need for more labor. Some of the city's leaders strongly encouraged impressment of slaves, but enslaved and free African Americans had become very unpredictable. When a series of fires mysteriously swept the city, a *Chronicle* editorial thinly disguised its belief that slaves had set the torch. Free blacks boldly ignored city ordinances, riding vehicles of various kinds all over the streets, buying liquor at will, and continuing to schedule balls and parties without "proper supervision." Black refugees poured into the city late in 1864, and the *Chronicle* reported the story of a beggar who, on asking for money, was handed a Confederate dollar bill and handed it back. The end was obviously near.[47]

On 3 May 1865, Union forces marched into Augusta and occupied the city. A former slave later recalled the scene: "Yas'm I seen 'em comin' down de street. Every one had er canteen on he side, a blanket on his shoulder, caps cocked on one side de haid. De cavalry had boots on and spurros on de boots. First de sot de niggers free on Dead River, den dey come on here to sot us free. Dey march straight up Broad Street to de Planter's Hotel, den day camped on de river." Two or three months after the arrival of the first Union troops, the Thirty-third Regiment of U.S. Colored Infantry arrived. Unable to hide his pride, a former slave of William Eve sang along with others:

> Don't you see the lightning?
> Don't you hear the thunder?
> It isn't the lightning, it isn't the thunder,
> But its the buttons on the Negro Uniforms.[48]

Augusta quickly became caught up in a whirlwind of revolutionary change. Just three weeks after Robert E. Lee surrendered, General Davis Tillson established headquarters for the Freedmen's Bureau in the city. Former slaves continued to pour into Augusta, but the old Democratic leadership could no longer do anything about it. Though the city had not been devastated by the war, there was nevertheless a great deal of political and economic rebuilding ahead.

How the Hope household responded to this scenario is difficult to determine. Their private thoughts were not recorded, and interviews conducted later did not pose the question. The enslaved members of the household were at one end of the spectrum, and of course the war set them free. James Hope, at the other end, owned those slaves and had put on a uniform in support of the Confederacy. Somewhere in the middle stood several people of color whose freedom had come long before the Civil War began. Were their loyalties with the slaves—and the Union—or were they more inclined to support the Confederacy? Many of Augusta's free blacks did openly support the Unionist position, particularly in the war's waning years. Free blacks residing in homes of white men were understandably silent. Perhaps they harbored mixed loyalties that reflected their distinct class position in the society. They existed in a twilight zone, floating somewhere between slavery and complete freedom. Living as they did on the margins of a society designed for free whites and enslaved blacks, free persons of color in families headed by white men were in an even more peculiar position.

All southern families experienced changes after the Civil War, changes not always related to the defeat of the Confederacy. In 1865, tragedy unrelated to the events occurring in Augusta and elsewhere in the South struck the Hope family when Mary Frances and James's first child, little Johnny, died of diphtheria. Shortly thereafter, James Hope left Augusta and went north to check on his business interests. Unexpectedly, he decided the time had come to move his family away from the devastated South. In the meantime, Mary Frances gave birth to James Hope's third child, "dark-eyed, olive-cheeked" Alethea, named after Mary Frances's mother. The thought of moving to the North did not please Mary Frances, perhaps because she would not be able to bring the Newton children, yet sometime late in 1866, James Hope, Mary Frances Taylor, and their two daughters left Augusta for New York.[49]

Hope owned a store in what is now Harlem on 125th Street. At that time, before the great migration of blacks to the North, Harlem was still a small, isolated village of white residents. At the spot where the Harlem meets the East River, Hope bought a house and land with room for a garden, orchard, and meadow. Two things about the James Hope family remain mysteries. First, did James Hope ever marry Mary Frances Taylor? Years later, Lugenia Burns

Hope, John Hope's wife, stated that "there was a rumor among Augusta people that there was a marriage license hanging on the wall of the Hope household." Yet there is neither recorded evidence nor family corroboration that a marriage ever took place.[50] If not, why? No New York law prevented interracial marriages. And that question leads to another. Did Mary Frances live in New York as a woman of color, or did she pass for white? With her dark olive complexion and fine chiseled features, twenty-seven-year-old Mary Frances and her children could easily have lived in New York with no questions asked about their racial origins.

In any case, the family's time in New York was very short. Mary Frances found it difficult to adjust to the hustle and bustle of New York City. She missed her extended family in Augusta and wanted to go home. In New York, a daughter remembered years later, Fanny met the venerable Frederick Douglass, who tried to persuade her to change her mind and stay in the North. Douglass lived in Rochester then, and they were probably introduced on one of his frequent trips to New York City. James Hope, along with his sister and brothers, who visited often, agreed with Douglass that it would be dangerous raising her children in a "reconstructing" South. Undaunted, Fanny's love of family seems to have overruled her fear of any dangers that might await her in Augusta. Years later, John Hope said that "loyalty to her dependent brothers and sisters and to her mother made her return home, and he [James], who had in mind to remain in New York in business with his brothers, returned to Augusta to be with her."[51]

The Hopes arrived back in Augusta sometime in 1867. Shortly thereafter, the highly venerated Lethea Taylor turned forty-seven. She was still a small, slender, and very pretty woman who was usually immaculately dressed in a dress of bombazine over a spreading hoopskirt. She had successfully raised seven children and was taking care of several grandchildren (including the Newtons during Mary Frances's stay in New York). Though she continued her sewing at home, Lethea had not been well for more than a year. Sometime after the Hopes arrived back in Augusta, she took a turn for the worse. In later years Lethea Taylor's granddaughter Jane remembered someone rushing into the Hope home on Ellis Street and whispering something to her mother, and the two storming out of the house and disappearing up the street. Though they were unaware of it, Jane scurried along behind them, puzzled by the cries of sorrow coming from inside her grandmother's house a few blocks away. Young Jane Hope soon learned that her grandmother, Lethea Taylor, had just died.[52]

Lethea was buried in Cedar Grove Cemetery, established in 1825, the same year the five-year-old slave child Lethe had cheered Lafayette in Sparta. Built for Augusta's people of color, Cedar Grove Cemetery was located next to the better kept, and fenced, Magnolia Cemetery for whites. Mary Frances was present at her mother's funeral, of course, but James Hope probably did not accompany her. Perhaps as Mary Frances stood mourning at her mother's graveside she took some time for deep reflection.

Family and friends believed Fanny was thrilled to be back in Augusta but also recognized that something was troubling her. Life in the South was fraught with uncertainties, and there were no assurances that sixty-two-year-old James Hope could protect his family. Jane, her oldest daughter, was only four years old, and baby Alethea was barely one. The future was even less certain for the Newton children—the independent Madison, then ten, and his shy sister, Sissie, two years younger. Like her mother and grandmother before her, Mary Frances Butts was worried about her children's future.

After the Civil War, Mary Frances and all of Lethea's children took the name of their father, Mr. Butt, adding an *s* to the name to make it their own.[53] Lethea, of course, never did. Perhaps that represented a generational change in attitude among formerly free persons of color that was symbolic of the new freedom. At any rate, it does help to gauge the changes that had occurred in the lives of three generations of African American women by 1867. John Hope's great-grandmother, Mary, his grandmother, Lethea, and his mother, Mary Frances, had survived in a society where they were victims of race, sex, and class-based oppression. Two of them had most likely been raped as sixteen-year-olds by men old enough to be their fathers. Even Hope's relationships with George Newton and James Hope were centralized by her political and socioeconomic place in the antebellum South. Yet, like many other African American women, both slave and free, the women in John Hope's family had visions of a brighter future for their children. In some respects, though not without personal sacrifice, that goal was already being realized.

2 Identity

"My mother told me that while she was heavy with child, my father told her that this child would be a comfort," John Hope wrote years later. "I understand that they kept deferring a name for me until my aunt and the nurse and my little sisters began to call me 'John.' Thus, I suppose, I can have my dead brother's name without feeling under the curse of destiny through the impiety of naming a child after a dead brother."[1]

The perceptive historian Rayford Logan once wrote: "The time and place of an individual's birth quite often affects the rest of his or her life."[2] John Hope, Mary Frances Butts's sixth child, was born on 2 June 1868. A year earlier, Congress had wrestled the reins of Reconstruction away from President Andrew Johnson, and Georgia, like the other southern states, was furious. City newspapers in Augusta, a hotbed of Republicanism, were filled with local and statewide political news. On 21 April 1868 the *Augusta Chronicle* criticized African Americans for voting for Georgia's new constitution: "April 20th will be remembered as a day of 'most stupendous farce.' Negroes were driven like dumb . . . cattle to the polls and intimidated to vote for the Constitution and Bullock."

Only months after Hope's birth, the Georgia legislature expelled its African American members on the grounds that the constitution did not permit them to hold office. Official figures showed that blacks slightly outnumbered whites in Augusta, a fact that contributed to tensions that were already high as the November presidential election approached. Earlier, the *Chronicle* had reported that the "Klan has been organized in this place. . . . Success say we to the Ku Klux Klan."[3]

Both the ballot and the bullet were used on election day in Augusta. At one voting station an argument broke out between two men, one black and one white; both drew pistols and fired, prompting others with pistols to do the same. When the smoke cleared, one black man was dead, shot in the back; two other blacks were wounded, as was one white. A full-scale riot was averted only by the timely arrival of troops from the federal arsenal. There were a few other cases of scattered violence that day, but African Americans, despite the intimidation, turned out in large numbers at the polls.[4]

John Hope was too young to remember that turmoil, but the early days of Reconstruction helped to shape the Augusta he experienced as a child. Hope's earliest memories were of what the family called the "homestead" at 1108 Ellis Street. Just inside the entrance was a hall that led all the way through the center of the house "to the dear old back room," a gathering place for the entire family. Adjacent to the back room was a comfortable parlor that led into Madison's book-filled room. James and Fanny occupied a spacious room to the right of the hallway, and young John's room was next to that of his parents. The dining room was next to John's, followed by several other bedrooms. Family members remembered a house filled with exquisite furniture that included many antiques and fine upholstery. Gas brightened the Hopes' home when most other Augustans were still using coal oil.

When young John Hope ventured out into the backyard, he was greeted by a mulberry tree whose roots rose two or three feet above the ground and extended fifteen or twenty feet in every direction. Neighbors complained that the tree rotted the fence, but James Hope said he would rather build new fences than cut down the tree. Beneath the huge tree, which was not far from a rusty water pump, stood a giant swing where John and his siblings played.[5]

The house seemed like a fairy-tale castle to the young John Hope. No fewer than fifteen people lived there. In addition to his parents, the 1870 census listed John and his three sisters, Jane, Alethea, and three-month-old Grace; the Newton children, Madison and Georgia Frances, who were then away at school; and four of Mary Frances's siblings: Anna, Jane, and Katherine, all seamstresses, and James, a barber, as residents. Three servants lived in the household, too: Cato and Julia Habersham and seven-year-old Martha Willis. James Hope was listed as white, the three servants were in the black column, and the rest of the residents were listed as mulattoes.[6]

When John Hope turned five, his father was already sixty-eight, old enough to be his grandfather. James Hope did not live to see his son's ninth birthday, and John Hope cherished the few memories he could muster of the short time he and his father shared. Strange as it may seem, one of his most vivid surviving memories came from a dream he recorded during an illness in 1933. Hope dreamt about small things, like the beauty of his father's grate fires, which burnt brightly during the winter. He also remembered his father's reserve, his aristocratic bearing, the deep and abiding respect he silently commanded from adults and children alike. "For we venerated him but did not exactly fear him,"

Hope continued. "I used to sit with him and walk with him even when neither of us was saying anything to each other."[7]

Hope's most extensive memories of his father were recorded in 1934 when he began writing his autobiography (which was never finished). He defended his parents' union, insisting it was built on nothing less than deep mutual affection. "I speak reverently of my mother and father as wife and husband," he wrote, "although the laws of Georgia would not recognize such a thing." James and Mary Frances did not try to hide their relationship. As early as 1861 they were often seen sitting on the front porch holding hands. It was John Hope's belief that his father had fiercely defended his relationship with his mother and had demanded that others show her the same respect they would show to a white woman. Although white women did not visit the Hopes, many distinguished Augustans did, and they usually dined with the entire family present. Of course, these memories were the musings of an adult son defending his parents' controversial union many years later. Some of the incidents he "recalled" actually occurred before his birth or when he was only two or three years old.[8]

In many respects Hope's childhood adventures were no different from those of other children growing up in Augusta. "Big Nan" (his aunt Anna Butts) closely supervised all of the children in their early years, but John managed to venture out on his own to explore the neighborhood and its surroundings. His older sister Alethea, who was a bit of a tomboy, was his earliest pal. Together they flew kites, walked on stilts, and climbed fences and trees. Sometimes they would sneak away to play in the big ditch that ran down the side of Greene Street, two blocks away around the corner. Though great fun, it was an activity certain to earn a switching from Big Nan or their mother if they were caught.

Other activities were closer to home and less risky. The 1877 city directory indicates that G. H. Kernaghan's Planters Livery and Sale Stables were located about a block from the Hope house. Barefoot and clad in "knee-breeches," young John would meander over to the shop to work the bellows and watch the iron heat up. He was fascinated with the stables and yearned to learn the art of driving a buggy.[9] It was probably in this same stable that Hope met and befriended Smart, an elderly ex-slave who kept his pipe and matches in his tangled white hair and made his living as a hostler. The young boy and the old man spent many pleasant hours together. When Smart took a job as a coachman, John often accompanied him, riding "shotgun" on the box. The two continued to be friends until Smart's death, years later.[10]

Young John Hope's most exciting explorations took him on journeys designed to end at the Savannah River. Usually accompanied by his older sisters

Alethea and Jane, Hope preferred to take the long way: up Ellis about three quarters of a mile to Center (Fifth) Street, then left and down into the old Lower Market in the middle of Broad Street. Everything was sold in the market, from fresh vegetables and fruits to caged chickens, farm animals, and pets. Drivers of donkey carts packed with items from the countryside competed with African American women hawking their wares from large baskets on their heads. The market doubled as an information center for Augustans and Savannah River area farmers: "The latest news was spread, political issues debated, gentlemen's agreements made, gossip swapped, and advice, sought or unwanted, given." Mesmerized by the sights and sounds of the busy market, the young Hopes sometimes never made it to the river at all.[11]

John Hope probably knew the market by its more common name: the Augusta Slave Market. Although Augustans spoke of it only in hushed whispers, it was a well-known fact that African American slaves had been bought and sold before the Civil War in that very place. "They made a scaffold whenever they was goin' to sell anybody, and would put the person up on this so everybody could see him good," a freedwoman later recalled. "Then they would sell him to the highest bidder. Everybody wanted women who would have children fast."[12]

Before the Civil War, slave auctions were held at least once a month in the Lower Market. Potential buyers and curious onlookers packed the grounds to watch the spectacle. In 1878, ten years after John Hope's birth, a cyclone destroyed all but one pillar of the Lower Market. A mysterious handprint remained visible on that lone structure as late as 1938. Young John, along with many other Augustans, believed the print belonged to a slave who had returned to haunt the spot where he had been sold.[13]

The sights and sounds of the half-mile journey to the river evoked much excitement from the three young explorers. Once they reached Broad Street, looking east, they could take in the entire three-block Augusta business section. Most of the banks, hotels, and office buildings they saw were either brick or wood, usually two or three stories high, with iron-railed balconies on the second story. Trees edged both sides of the street, and there were several watering troughs directly down the middle. Moving on to Reynolds Street the children passed along "Cotton Row," the center of the cotton business, where in early fall hundreds of wagons clamored over cobblestone streets waiting to unload their precious "white gold." It was said that one could walk a mile on the cotton bales without once touching the street.[14]

Beyond the hustle and bustle that was Reynolds Street lay the banks of the Savannah River. The river's personality was as unpredictable as the town that sprang from it. The Savannah could be as peaceful as a "noble limpid stream," noted its poet, Eugene Murphey, yet also had "her times of rage in which she scourges us and . . . slays." Floods, common occurrences before the levees were built, did not frighten the young Hopes. They often trailed floodwaters to the river's edge and were disappointed when they realized the water would not reach their house. Years later, Hope remembered taking trips across small streams, and once, no doubt without his parents' knowledge, crossing the Savannah River itself in a bateau (a light, flat-bottomed boat).[15]

John Hope's childhood was not all fun and games and adventure, however. African Americans in Augusta and throughout the South viewed education as an important symbol of freedom. Many African Americans took the initiative and began to educate themselves secretly even before the Civil War. They accelerated the process once freedom came, predating educational efforts by northern missionary organizations, the Freedman's Bureau, and, eventually, reluctant state and city officials.[16]

In his early years, John may have received private instruction from an African American woman from Charleston. Hope's sister Jane later recalled that she attended Mrs. Holloway's private school and was relatively sure John had attended it, too.[17] Young John's public education took place in a rickety old wooden school down by the river on Reynolds Street, about three blocks from his house. Each of the four rooms in the airy building packed in forty students, with each allowed half a desk. In the 1870s the Fourth Ward Colored School included eight years of instruction divided into three levels. Three years of instruction in the primary or elementary school were followed by two years in the intermediate school and then three years in the grammar school. The standard curriculum included reading, spelling, and arithmetic, with writing and geography added the third year. Composition, penmanship, and history were added the fourth year, and the final years included declamation and recitation, and science.[18]

Only two of Hope's teachers are known; both were African American women educated at Atlanta University. Lucy Laney, the better known of the two, was born in Macon, Georgia, in 1854 and was one of four students to graduate in Atlanta University's first class in 1873. She was brought to Augusta through the efforts of one of the city's prominent black leaders. Laney taught young John in the primary grades. She eventually left Augusta for a time, and then returned in 1886 to establish the renowned Haines Institute, which she ran for the rest of her life.[19]

Georgia Swift was born in Athens, Georgia, in 1854. Like Laney, she was recruited to teach in Augusta's black public schools after she graduated from Atlanta University. Her teaching career began in another ward in Augusta, but she was eventually transferred to the Fourth Ward, where she said the "rusti-crats" lived, a term that poked fun at the old aristocratic families of color whose members had been free before the Civil War and had almost no distinguishable African characteristics. Georgia Swift became the principal of the school and remained there until she married and moved away from Augusta.[20]

Lucy Laney believed strongly that students should receive training in the classics. In addition to the standard curriculum, the stocky, dark-skinned Laney, usually plainly dressed and with close-cropped hair, made sure her students were familiar with both Greek and Latin. Georgia Swift was John Hope's favorite teacher. Several speeches he made as an adult sang her praises. "Miss Georgia," Hope remembered, "had a peculiar facility for making pupils efficient in arithmetic and instilling the principles of a true gentleman." Besides the standard curriculum, Swift tried to instill the Protestant Ethic in her students, encouraging hard work and thrift, Victorian manners and ideals, and preaching the importance of democracy. She was fiercely opposed to drinking, and she campaigned for the Women's Christian Temperance Union in every county in Georgia after she left the school system.

It was a credit to the established black leadership in Augusta that these two dynamic African American women were successfully recruited. Education officials were usually suspicious of Atlanta University graduates and others who had received degrees from the private black "colleges." Many of these graduates had been taught by northern white missionary teachers, whose ideology of "evangelical abolitionism" sent shivers down the spines of local school board officials.[21] When the state of Georgia finally decided to support African American education with public money in the early 1870s, it was in part to rid the state of the New England missionary influence.

Young John Hope was oblivious to the politics of his early education. He plowed through Sterling's Readers, practiced his penmanship, suffered through part 1 of Derry's *History of the United States*, and agonized over long division and fractions. On occasion he followed an older boy through the back fence behind the schoolhouse and crept down to the river. Unlike clever Alethea and his bright younger brother, Thomas, John Hope was a "plodder," his sister recalled. He eventually got the job done, but it took him longer and he studied harder to achieve the desired results. His father often assisted young John with his homework, sometimes spending hours going over his arithmetic. His half-siblings, Madison and Sissie, were away at Atlanta University in the early 1870s but kept him on his academic toes when they were home.

The good times were not to last. In 1874, the family experienced a crisis from which it never fully recovered. James Hope suffered a stroke that left him impaired but not disabled. He continued to oversee his business interests, and young John was often seen gently leading him downtown to his office. Although his recovery was miraculous for a sixty-nine-year-old man, James Hope must have recognized that his end was near. In 1867 he had deeded the Ellis

Street residence to Mary Frances Butts, a practice forbidden before freedom. After his stroke, the deed was officially recorded in the county courthouse. Surprisingly, James Hope did not make out a will at that time. He lived only two years more.[22]

Aside from a small circle of close friends, the "prim and reserved" Hopes generally kept to themselves in the years after James Hope's stroke. Yet neighbors knew the elder Hope's health was deteriorating. Friends later recalled that shortly after the stroke, visitors arrived in a rented buggy from Kernaghan's, perhaps driven by John's friend Smart. Jane and Thomas Hope, had arrived from New York to check on their elder brother's health.

John Hope remembered that he tagged along when "Uncle Thomas and Aunt Jane took the two youngest girls, Grace and Anna, on a buggy ride sporting new clothes purchased in New York." Anna, a golden-haired baby with no visible traces of African blood, had been born in 1873. Eventually James's sister admitted that she wanted to adopt Anna and raise her as a white child. "It was a critical time," Hope later wrote. "My mother then had seven living children, it was not certain that my father would live, it was very certain that Anna would have exceptional opportunities; so that the decision of my mother, especially at this time of pressure, must have been difficult." Despite the difficulty, however, Mary Frances politely but firmly said no.[23]

During the summer of 1876 James Hope's health continued to deteriorate. He was seventy-one years old, and it was clear that this time he would not bounce back. Late in October, while John Hope lay awake in the next room, his father died: "Finally, my mother came in and lay in the bed with me. She just put her arms around me, kissed me, and wept, saying, 'You have no father now.'" James Hope did not live to see the birth of his second son and sixth living child, Thomas Hope, who was named after James Hope's wealthy brother in New York.

Eventually, Thomas and Jane Hope returned to Augusta to take James home to be buried in the family plot in New York. No one, including Mary Frances, wanted him buried in Augusta. "I see that now very clearly," Hope wrote years later; "the thought of my father being in a white cemetery." John Hope was only eight years old when his father died. Although it was not immediately apparent, his life had changed forever.[24]

The death of James Hope in 1876 removed any protection that may have shielded his family. While Reconstruction rushed to an anticlimactic conclusion nationally, the process of "redemption" had long been under way locally. Of course, 1876 was an election year, and election years in the South were always tense. During the summer, violence exploded in a city called Hamburg on the South Carolina side of the Savannah River.

Hamburg could have easily been the setting for D. W. Griffith's controversial movie, *Birth of a Nation*. A Georgia publication in 1938 described Hamburg during Reconstruction as the "Negro town of Hamburg, with its colored mayor, town marshal, and justice of the peace. . . . Wagon loads of cotton en route to Augusta were seized by Negro leaders for mythical taxes, and upon sale, the money went into Negro pockets."[25] Tensions between white Augustans and black Hamburg existed as early as 1871. In March of that year the *Augusta Chronicle* asked in its pages, "Shall we have war with Hamburg? since the Africanization of Hamburg good feeling has disappeared." About two weeks later William Markwalter went to Hamburg to practice shooting his pistol and was arrested by two African American constables for violating a Hamburg city ordinance. Shots were exchanged, and Markwalter fell, wounded in the leg.[26]

On a hot July fourth in 1876, the spark ignited five years earlier erupted into a full flame. Two white Augustans in Hamburg were required to wait a few moments while a drilling militia unit crossed the road. Insulted, the whites unsuccessfully demanded that the black militia be disarmed. The next day, an ex-Confederate general and Klan member returned with a mob of angry Augustans determined to take matters into their own hands. The Hamburg troops barricaded themselves in an armory on the edge of town and exchanged fire with the mob for two hours. Eventually a cannon was brought up and fired point-blank into the small building.

Two separate groups of militiamen fled the burning building, but only one group escaped. The other group decided to surrender, unknowingly sealing their fate. Several of them were taken to a cornfield near the river, released, and then ordered to run. As soon as they took off, the men were shot. Later that evening, Klansmen led the white mob on a rampage, killing more black Hamburg residents and destroying their property. An embarrassed *Augusta Chronicle* reported the grim scene: "A final picture shows a deserted town; old Negro women hurrying across the bridge with all their worldly possessions in pillowslips. Augusta Negroes remained throughout the episode quietly in their homes, and took no part in the trouble across the river, After the carnage, Hamburg ceased to exist."[27]

Hope's memories of that Fourth of July weekend confirm the *Chronicle*'s report. Most of Augusta's citizens were unaware of the events in Hamburg, but word of impending trouble crept through the African American community. The same "quiet before the storm" existed a month later when Augusta experienced its first lynching. A group of men broke into the Augusta jail and took out and shot Robert Williams, who was accused of raping a white woman. Hope did not recall this incident, but the events in Hamburg haunted him the rest of his days. When other tragedies struck African Americans, Hope would always say: "And remember, I heard the guns of the Hamburg Massacre."[28]

James Hope probably understood there was little he could do to protect his family from the increasingly hostile and racist environment. Yet their financial security was within his grasp. James Hope's estate was valued early in 1877 at $56,000. In his hastily drawn will, Hope left $30,000 in trust to Mary Frances Butts and her children. The rest of the estate he left to his family in New York.[29] He named three close business associates in Augusta to be his executors and trustees, but only one, it seems, bothered to qualify through the courts. Five years later there had been no accounting of the estate except for the sale of old wines valued at a little over $1,000. The Augusta Hopes had received nothing.

It appears that James's brother Thomas Hope brought suit against Phillip, the executor, in 1891, claiming he was incompetent. Perhaps the suit was filed on behalf of the Hope family, but no evidence supports that claim. More likely, the New York Hopes wanted their $25,000. Nothing came of the suit, however. Although records show that no one received any proceeds from the estate even into the twentieth century, John Hope later recalled that his mother did receive a small income for the rest of her life. That income more than likely came from several rental properties owned by James Hope that passed to Mary Frances on his death.[30]

It is difficult to understand why James Hope did not entrust his estate to Thomas and name him the sole executor. Thomas Hope had a vested interest in his brother's estate and certainly would have benefited by its proper execution. Most of Hope's investments were in railroad and other stocks; less than 5 percent of the estate was invested in local real estate. Thomas Hope, a self-made millionaire in his own right, could have managed those investments from New York. Butts or Hope family members could have managed James's few local properties in Augusta, as they did later. Why James Hope entrusted his family's financial future to outsiders, even "close" business associates, remains a mystery.[31]

Though they were far from destitute, the loss of their father's inheritance was a severe blow to the Hope family's financial situation. Fortunately, Mary Frances owned the house, so they all had a place to live, but with no revenue from the estate, the oldest children—Madison, Georgia Frances, and Jane— were forced to withdraw from Atlanta University. Private school for young John Hope was out of the question. According to the 1877 city directory, thirty-eight-year-old Mary Frances decided to take in sewing and Madison tried his hand at barbering and a number of other odd jobs. The Hopes may have been helped by Mary Frances's brothers, who lived nearby. Benjamin, a painter, and Joseph, a harness maker, were in their late thirties. James Butts, who had just turned thirty, also lived in the vicinity and was a frequent visitor to the Hope household.

For the first time in their lives, Mary Frances Butts and her children became simply another black family trying to survive in a hostile environment. They were still part of the elite black upper class. But it was no longer their wealth and white head of household that placed them there, but their status, ancestry, and heritage as free persons of color before the Civil War.[32]

John Hope was certainly cognizant of his family's straitened circumstances. He saw other family members make financial sacrifices and believed the time had come to do his share. He needed to find work. "Negro children become rather mature in practical affairs before their childhood has passed," Hope remarked years later in a speech. "I myself ceased to be a child at eleven years of age." The end of his childhood was still a couple of years away when John Hope, against his mother's wishes, took his first job in June 1878. He had just turned ten.[33]

Hope worked that summer at the law firm of Capers and Habersham, located a couple of blocks away on Johnson Street near the cotton district. His job included keeping the offices clean and running errands. He was promised four dollars a month but usually received about half that amount. Nevertheless, he managed to save enough to buy a pair of brass-tipped brogans. There were other jobs as well. Later he took on a paper route for the *Augusta Chronicle*. It was on this paper route a year later that Hope first saw African American men and boys setting type, at the office of the *Georgia Baptist*.[34]

John Hope's life after his father's death was not all work. As he got older, Hope ventured much farther away from home. Male companions had replaced his erudite sisters. The "Bridge Row Gang," prostitutes on Center Street between the Lower Market and the river, were a sign of Augusta's unsavory side unseen on his earlier journeys with Jane and Alethea. Perhaps continuing east beyond Center Street for the first time, Hope and his buddies passed the Richmond County Jail at Elbert and Watkins. The youngsters were probably unaware that before the Civil War, slaves were sent there with notes to be punished. Instead of being incarcerated, they were secured in X-shaped wooden stocks and whipped according to the instructions provided in the notes. More familiar, but farther away at the south end of the city, stood the Terri, an oasis of freedom for ex-slaves seeking a new beginning in Augusta. Later in his life Hope remembered these "human wrecks of swift emancipation. People left too old and helpless or too ignorant, though young, to discharge a freedman's obligation to society. . . . They were poor, but they were individual people."[35]

"Terri" (or "Terry") was short for "Negro Territory," the name given to the area in Augusta where the first freedmen settled immediately after the war. Gwinnett Street (renamed Laney-Walker), its main thoroughfare, later became a dynamic, thriving black commercial district with hotels, insurance companies, churches, schools, and movie theaters. In Hope's youth, however, there were only unpaved streets that bore instructive names like Thank God

Alley, Electric Light Alley, Walker Baptist Alley, and Slopjar Alley. He remembered it as a den of iniquity infested with gambling, prostitution, and other criminal activities.

The houses in the Terri were generally one-room unpainted shacks occupied by one to three families. Their exteriors were decorated with "lard cans brightly painted," which lined "porches fitted with ferns, palms, geraniums and verbena." Backyards were usually "cluttered with outhouses, chicken coops, and wood piles." There is no evidence that Hope spent much time in the Terri, and he had not yet come to grips with the class differences that separated his upper-class world from that one.

In spite of the intraracial differences separating residents of the Fourth Ward, where Hope lived, from the Terri's inhabitants, both groups of African Americans shared a common cultural worldview: the church was the religious and social center of their lives.[36] James Hope had belonged to the white Saint Paul Episcopal Church on Reynolds Street. The rest of the family attended Springfield Baptist Church less than a mile away. Black Springfield Baptist had a rich history. Its roots were in colonial South Carolina, in a place called Silver Bluff. Founded sometime between 1773 and 1775, Silver Bluff Baptist Church is often credited with being the first organized black church in America. After the American Revolution, some of its members crossed the river into Georgia and established a church in the small village of Springfield around 1787 or 1793. The village became part of Augusta in 1798. What was later described as a "cluster of houses and a house of worship for colored people at the intersection of Broad and Marbury streets" became Augusta's first free black community.[37]

Springfield "African" Church, as it was called during much of the nineteenth century, became a religious and social icon in the lives of enslaved and free black Augustans. Until 1840 it was the only black church in Augusta. That year, Independent Baptist Church, soon called Thankful, grew out of Springfield to accommodate slaves who lived in the southeast part of the city. Springfield Baptist gave birth to several other churches as well. Very little is known of its political activities before the Civil War, but given its members' precarious position in society, discretion was probably the rule. The veil of secrecy was lifted after Emancipation, however, and Springfield became a powerful instrument in the crusade for black equality. Within its sanctuary African Americans held mass meetings, debated strategies designed to improve their lives, and created important organizations such as the Georgia Equal Rights and Education Association, which was formed in 1866.

But Springfield was more than a hotbed of political activity. Several programs were developed there to aid black Augusta residents. A YMCA was organized shortly after the Civil War, and Hope remembered church-sponsored bazaars, festivals, and Sunday school picnics across the river in Hamburg. Children gleefully played "clap in and clap out," and more timidly played the kissing game, "turn the bottle." Already a center of religious instruction, the Sunday school became a conventional school for the first time in 1867 and was called Augusta Institute. It later moved to Atlanta and became Morehouse College.[38]

Without doubt Springfield Baptist was the most prominent black church in Augusta, and its members represented some of the oldest black families in the city. Many were mulattoes who lived in the same area as the Hopes. Harpers, Ladevezes, Barefields, Smythes, and Fosters dotted Springfield's membership rolls and at one time or another claimed the Hopes as close friends. The Whites—William Jefferson and Josephine—were perhaps closer than the others. The two families had known each other at least since 1856, when Mary Frances stood up with Josephine at her wedding. The Whites at first lived farther east, over by the cemeteries, but eventually moved to Campbell (Ninth Street) only a block from the Hopes. When William Jefferson White withdrew from Springfield and formed Harmony Baptist Church in 1868, Josephine continued to attend Springfield, often walking up Ellis Street and stopping to see Fanny Butts on her way to church.[39]

Many of the White and Hope children were the same ages. Anna White was born the same year as Madison Newton, and Isaiah White was Georgia Frances's age. Two daughters who died young were born the same years as Jane and Alethea, and Mary and William White Jr. arrived the same years as Grace and Anna. In addition, Claudia White was born the same year as the baby, Thomas, and Lucian Hayden White, a boyhood playmate of John Hope, was also born in 1868.[40]

It was not the White children's closeness in ages that most impressed John Hope, however, but their dynamic and sometimes controversial father. William Jefferson White, allegedly the son of a white father and a woman of African and Indian blood, epitomized black leadership in Augusta, if not in the state of Georgia. Legend has it that he was a free man of color who made his living as a carpenter. White joined Springfield Baptist in 1855, the year before he and Josephine Thomas were "married" and began living in her master's household. Little is known of his prewar political activities, but it was widely believed that he secretly taught many of Augusta's African American children reading and arithmetic.[41]

White exploded onto Augusta's political scene during Reconstruction. He helped organize the Georgia Equal Rights and Education Association at Springfield Baptist Church in 1866 and served as one of its officers. Aspiring white politicians in need of support from the increasing black electorate sought White's endorsement. In exchange for his support, White wanted pol-

iticians to place increased economic opportunities, funding for black education, and overall improvements in the quality of black life on their agendas. In
this he sometimes opposed the more conservative black leaders in Augusta,
who preferred to avoid confrontations over potentially explosive racial concerns. White was probably Augusta's most consistent and outspoken advocate
of African American equality.[42]

White was best known for his steadfast commitment to black education, a
commitment that earned him the title "Father of Negro Education in Georgia." Shortly after the Civil War, White traveled as an agent of the Freedmen's
Bureau, helping to establish black schools throughout the state. He also operated a Sabbath school at Springfield Baptist Church, an important precursor of
the missionary schools that would soon come to the area.[43] White pushed city
officials to establish a high school for African Americans in the early 1870s.
Repeatedly appearing before the school board, he promised buildings from the
Freedmen's Bureau, offered space at his own Harmony Baptist Church, and
went out and recruited first-rate instructors. It was he who recruited Lucy Laney and Georgia Swift, and he later recruited Richard R. Wright, Atlanta University's first valedictorian, to run one of Georgia's first black high schools.[44]

As important as White's efforts to support black education were, however,
it was his passionate and dedicated commitment to black leadership—evident
in his fervent pitches for race loyalty, his solid belief in the efficacy of black
self-help, and his support of black institutions and businesses—that impressed
the young John Hope. White's racial pride may also have been puzzling. He
looked like a white man, and there were rumors that his African blood was
negligible, if it existed at all. Yet he insisted on his "colored" identity and spent
most of his life as a race leader. Years later, Hope wrote on the occasion of
White's death that "earning a living was never his chief aim and function. He
was a leader of great ability, unusual outlook, and sustaining philosophy."[45]

William J. White was a role model for John Hope early in his life. In 1880,
White became the editor and proprietor of the *Georgia Baptist*, the official paper of the black Missionary Convention of Georgia. He combined the newspaper office with a printshop and used only African American employees.[46]
When Hope was growing up, the shop was located on Ellis Street below Macintosh, only four blocks from his home. "How thrilling it all was to me as a
boy," he later remembered, "to look for the first time into that printing office
of the *Georgia Baptist* in the little brick building on Ellis Street!" Hope had seen
white men setting type, but a printshop operated by black people was something new. "William J. White showed me for the first time in my life," he
continued, "that Negroes could operate and own a newspaper."[47] For Hope,
the brick building on Ellis Street represented a marriage of philosophy and
practice. And it awakened a racial pride that he carried into adulthood. In

addition to adopting White's ideological principles, he would also support African American attempts at economic self-help.

John Hope's adolescent years passed quickly. He completed the eighth grade in 1881 but passed up high school, thinking his formal education was finished. Booker T. Washington founded Tuskegee Institute that year, but that was probably out of Hope's reach. Augusta Institute had moved to Atlanta two years earlier, so there was no chance that he might go there. In 1880, Ware High School for African Americans began full operation. Though it was near his home, Hope passed up that opportunity as well. The school's first principal, Richard Wright, remembered later that Hope's relatives attended, but not Hope. Nor did he attend Paine Institute, which had opened in 1882. He passed up all these educational opportunities and stepped instead into the working world.[48]

John Hope acquired his first full-time job at Lexius Henson's Exchange Saloon and Restaurant. The city directory of 1872 shows that Henson and his brother, Charles, operated a small restaurant at Ellis and Macintosh close to the Hope residence. By the late 1870s Lexius Henson had become the proprietor of one of the most elegant restaurants in Augusta. The ads for his whites-only establishment boasted of "fine wines and liquors, all the delicacies of the season served in the best style and at all hours." The *Augusta Chronicle* compared it with the best restaurants in New York, Savannah, and Charleston. A separate women's section was adorned with a fine Brussels carpet, lace curtains at the windows, and tables laid with snowy linen and gleaming silver.[49]

Henson himself was a controversial character. In 1875, a group of black Augustans tested the recently passed Civil Rights Act by entering a number of whites-only establishments. Though Henson was a black entrepreneur, his place was first on their list. Blocking their entrance, Henson reminded them that "this is a white man's bar, and you ought not to try to injure my business in that way." Although he was apparently very well respected by Augusta's white community, Henson was not popular among blacks. It was said that he was denied membership at the elitist Union Baptist Church because he sold intoxicating liquor (and perhaps also because of his exclusionary policies), and that in response he erected a Presbyterian church and invited only his friends to attend.[50]

By the time Hope began working at Henson's Restaurant in 1881, the business had moved to a three-story building on Broad Street at Seventh. If thirteen-year-old John Hope had qualms about working in the all-white restaurant and bar, no one knew it. In later years he referred to Henson only once (and then not by name, but as "that God-less man") in a brief sentence in his autobiographical sketch. Yet contemporaries remembered that the two got along fine. Employed first as a wine steward, Hope in time kept Henson's books and eventually helped to manage the restaurant. He learned valuable lessons from this African American entrepreneur that served him well first as a college student and later as a black college president.[51]

In addition to sharpening his managerial skills, Hope also interacted with an elite group of Augusta's whites at Henson's Restaurant. Many were ex-planters—unrepentant and still blaming the Yankees for the destruction of their world. Hope was still a rather young boy; he was charming, reserved, efficient, but remarkably shy. It is likely that Henson's customers felt at ease being served by the nonthreatening, extremely fair-complexioned mulatto boy, whose history they probably knew well. Hope and Levi White, a boy-hood friend who believed he had been cheated out of his white father's inheri-tance, often escorted prominent white patrons home, sometimes struggling as they attempted to keep the inebriated bodies (some of them women) upright between them.[52]

Hope's experiences at the Beech Island Farmer's Club in South Carolina were less embarrassing, perhaps, but just as insightful. The club was established in 1846 by James Hammond, a prominent slave owner and former governor of South Carolina. It grew out of the Agricultural and Police Society, which had been formed to keep slaves away from Augusta and Hamburg, South Carolina. Hammond's grandson, Judge Henry Hammond, often held private meetings with the aristocratic elite of Augusta and neighboring South Carolina that were catered by Henson. Hope at first served as the wine steward for these monthly meetings, but in time he managed the entire operation.[53]

Hope performed his duties well and became very popular with the white southerners who patronized the Beech Island Farmer's Club. Accustomed to quality service, they appreciated Hope's knowledge of wines, business acumen, and conciliatory demeanor. Judge Henry Hammond's uncle, Major Joseph B. Cumming, late of the Confederate Army, took special notice of John Hope. Cumming, Speaker of the Georgia House of Representatives after Augusta's "redemption" and a leader in the New South, was one of the few white Au-gustans blacks counted on in times of trouble. Soon, Cumming would loom large in Hope's decision to continue his education.[54]

Hope's social life gradually changed over the five years he spent at Henson's Restaurant. Church remained at the center of his activities, but there were other enterprises as well. Excursions up the canal to the locks replaced the chil-dren's games of his youth. With his brother Madison, Hope attended concerts featuring the black Madame Selika and lectures delivered by Frederick Doug-lass and Frances Ellen Watkins Harper at the old downtown Market Hall. He watched plays from the segregated balconies of the old Girardey Opera House only a few blocks away from his home on Ellis Street. With his sister Jane,

Hope was active in the black Sumner Literary Society and Lending Library, which was formed after the Civil War. The society was a major gathering place for Augusta's black elite, at times hosting noted lecturers such as Dr. J. T. Robert, a northern-educated southerner who returned to the South to become the Augusta Institute's first president.[55]

Young John also found himself drawn to Paine Institute's rented rooms on Broad Street. The major attractions there were Sarah (Coot) Curry and Georgia Foster, particularly the former. Contemporaries remembered that Hope's shy, reserved, and formal ways in the middle 1880s tended not to attract many young women. However, John and his good friend John Barefield scurried up to Broad Street every evening to "carry home" Sarah Curry and Georgia Foster. Foster was the attractive daughter of a prominent white man and an African American woman. Ironically, Sarah Curry's identity remains a mystery. None of Hope's formal correspondence mentions her by name, although a letter written years later to his wife suggests the relationship may have been serious: "I was so . . . attached to a girl that she and I would have been married before I was twenty-one if I had not left Augusta to attend the Academy [Worcester] just after I became eighteen years of age."[56]

John Hope never elaborated on his decision not to attend high school in Augusta. Though the family's finances had deteriorated, the Hopes were by no means destitute, and there is no evidence that his mother tried to influence him one way or the other. It may simply have been a preference for work rather than a rejection of high school. High schools, public and private, were relatively rare in the 1880s, and most young men in the South did not attend. Even those lucky enough to finish grammar school usually started to work afterward; high school attendance was very much the exception for both races.[57]

As late as 1885, a year before Hope left Augusta, he had no plans to continue his education. Most of his friends and co-workers spent their leisure time patronizing public dance halls or "house parties" where the "smoke was thick and the drinking heavy." They often played the lottery or enjoyed card games and the comical free theater at Augusta's city court. In general, however, those friends and co-workers belonged to a different class. Though he was not officially in school, Hope continued to read, to attend lectures and plays, and to associate with others continuing their education.[58]

Much of Hope's intellectual interest can be attributed to the influence of his brother Madison Newton, who had an impressive home library and was rarely seen on the streets of Augusta without a book under his arm. Contemporaries remembered that his dates usually consisted of taking women to lectures or reading to them on their front porches. Newton never returned to school after he left Atlanta University. He took a job as a letter carrier in the local postal system and wound up working there for the rest of his life. With

Newton as his role model, John may have intended to follow the same life-style—reading during his leisure time while continuing to work at Henson's Restaurant.[59]

John Hope's years at Henson's Restaurant paralleled a steady period of growth in black Augusta. Census records show that a little more than ten thousand African Americans, representing roughly 46 percent of the population, were scattered through the four wards of the city by the middle 1880s. More than ten churches served the city's black residents, along with numerous lodges, benevolent societies, and black military organizations. Two newspapers and at least one volunteer fire department also occupied the African American land-scape. African American leadership in the 1880s reflected the growing diversity of the black population. The new leaders came out of an expanding black middle class drawn mainly from the old mulatto families who were free before the Civil War and ex-slaves who rose to prominence after freedom.[60]

Augusta's African American leaders sponsored an array of public activities, including mass meetings and parades and celebrations for Emancipation Day, the Fourth of July, and the passage of the Thirteenth, Fourteenth, and Fifteenth Amendments to the Constitution. John Hope especially enjoyed the Emancipation Day speeches. The speakers often included educators such as Lucy Laney and Richard R. Wright; Judson Lyons, a brilliant lawyer and later a prominent politician in Washington; and Hope's cousin Robert Bradford Williams, one of the first African Americans from Augusta to attend Yale. Williams later enjoyed an illustrious political career in Europe. Young John Hope was also impressed by John Wesley Gilbert, who had attended Brown University, studied in Europe, and returned to Augusta as the first black teacher at Paine Institute (later Paine College). Hope loved listening to the oratory of prominent minister Dr. Charles T. Walker, a former slave who became one of the nation's great preachers.[61]

African American leaders in Augusta whose success predated the Civil War were not as visible on the leadership platforms of the 1880s, but they remained powerful forces in the community and were still members of the postwar black elite. In addition to the venerable William J. White, these men included Robert A. Harper and Charles Ladeveze, whose names appeared on "free black" registration lists as early as 1858. That year Harper was a thirty-five-year-old piano tuner, and Ladeveze, the descendent of refugees from the Haitian Revolution of the early nineteenth century, was a twenty-nine-year-old cabinet-maker. Harper studied music in Boston but returned to Augusta before the Civil War and reportedly secretly aided slaves along the Underground Rail-road. Family members later revealed that he had also circulated copies of *Uncle Tom's Cabin*. Charles and his sister, Laura, operated one of the most popular art stores in Augusta. Laura married Robert Harper, and Charles's son, John Ladeveze, became a vice president of the Workingman's Loan and Building Association, the first black bank in Georgia.[62]

Long before race ideology placed African American leaders squarely behind either W. E. B. Du Bois or Booker T. Washington, Augusta's black leaders differed over strategy, even while trying to maintain a united front. The need for education was never a debatable issue, and all defended the race against charges of inferiority, yet leaders of the older generation tended to be more conservative and were often willing to make controversial compromises with Augusta's local white elite. When city officials encouraged black Augustans to shun the Freedman's Bureau and schools taught by northern missionaries, Robert Harper advised blacks to "cast their lot with Augusta whites." Even the ratification of the Fifteenth Amendment was initially met with mixed emotions among black Augustans. When more than four thousand blacks paraded to City Hall to celebrate the amendment's passage, one carried a banner that read "Georgia, Our Native State, with all thy faults we love thee still." Then, according to the *Chronicle*, "the crowd marched over to the residence of the mayor, J. V. H. Allen, and gave him three cheers."[63]

Conservatism and factional squabbles were not limited to the African American leaders who had been free before the Civil War. William J. White and Richard R. Wright, for example, were frequently at odds in the 1880s. Wright refused to attend White's "colored conventions," telling the *Augusta Chronicle* that they "simply raised the racial issue, and our people cannot afford that." In time, Wright's influence in Republican party politics matched White's, and the two sometimes wrangled violently in the 1880s. There were also disputes between William J. White and prominent minister Charles T. Walker. Both Wright and Walker later became valuable allies of Booker T. Washington.[64]

Hope never commented on the disputes between African American leaders in Augusta, but he was surely familiar with them, for they were frequently played out in the pages of the *Georgia Baptist*, and at times even in the *Augusta Chronicle*. Moreover, many of the city's most prominent black leaders were closely associated with Hope and his family in the 1880s. Lucy Laney had taught him in primary school, and the White and Hope families were close friends. The Hopes were also close to the Ladevezes and Harpers, who lived nearby. Eventually, two of Hope's sisters married Ladevezes (who were related to the Harpers), and another married Judson Lyons. Bradford Williams was his cousin, and Hope later regarded John Wesley Gilbert as among the greatest teachers he had ever known.[65]

In June 1885, John Hope turned seventeen. Before reaching his next birthday he made two decisions that drastically changed his life. John was heavily influenced by the evangelical teachings of Big Nan, the aunt who had instilled in the Hope children a strict code of behavior. "I was taught at home not to lie and steal. As a very little child I shuddered at the thought of Hell . . . if I should die unregenerate," he once said. Yet in spite of his aunt's tireless efforts, Hope did not join a church in those early days. Not until years later did he explain why: "I began to reckon how long I should live, and then to console myself that for me Hell was still a comfortable distance away." [66]

When Hope was eleven years old, his family left Springfield Baptist Church to join another Baptist congregation. According to one source (whose views are echoed by many black and white Augustans today), Springfield split along color lines in 1879, and "the yellow people, the mulattoes, started the Union Church." The official church records tell a different story. When the congregation was unable to agree on the next minister, between sixty and eighty members left in 1879 and formed Union Baptist Church. Hope family members, including Uncle James Butts and Aunt Nannie, played significant roles in creating the new church, as did John Ladeveze. Union Baptist's congregation soon became one of the most prosperous in Augusta. [67]

The change in churches did not significantly affect John Hope's religious views until 1885, when a charismatic and well-traveled Charlestonian replaced Union Baptist Church's ailing minister. Born in 1854, Rev. John Dart was the son of an ex-slave and a prominent mulatto woman. The younger Dart attended Charleston's Avery Institute after the Civil War, graduated from Atlanta University in 1879, then went on to Newton Theological Seminary in Newton, Massachusetts, where he received his degree in 1882. Dart received valuable preaching experience at the Newton Center in Massachusetts, then taught for two years in Washington, D.C., and pastored a church in Providence, Rhode Island. He was called to Union Baptist Church in 1885. [68]

John Hope and his mother were caught up in the new minister's first annual revival early in February 1886. Both were captivated by the thirty-year-old Dart's fiery sermons and mesmerizing presence as he strutted up and down the church aisle, his hands on his hips. Dart convinced Hope that "religion was a good thing for this world" and that the Christian life was "simple and rational." Hope was won over. Church records show that Hope and thirty-one other converts, including Mary Frances Butts, were baptized in March 1886. [69]

John Hope took his religious conversion seriously. Always thoughtful—"meditative" is how he described himself in later years—Hope pondered long over his decision to become a Christian. He believed that going before the entire church, confessing his sins, and promising to lead the life of a Christian was more than part of a ritual, more than simply preparation for baptism in the cold waters of the Savannah River. When Hope rose from those waters he believed he had been spiritually transformed, and he committed himself to

lead a life that would be markedly different than before. He had already taken
"the pledge" never to drink. He did not smoke or play cards. Even dancing
was off-limits in the Hope household, where the evangelical Aunt Nannie was
the spiritual leader. Then and in the years that followed, Hope thought seriously of entering the ministry, and though he did not, a sharp religious edge
remained an important part of his personality.

Although he remained in August only five months, Rev. John Dart was an
important actor in Hope's spiritual transformation. No other person matched
Dart's influence on John Hope in 1886. By the time Dart departed, John
Hope's life course had been altered immeasurably. Even before Hope joined
the church, Dart nudged him to continue his education. Years later, Dart's
grown children recalled that their father "was always after young people." He
would often say, "Boy, make something of yourself. Read. Get Books. Start to
think." Predictably, Dart suggested that Hope attend a northern school. Hope
later remembered that Dart's suggestion "got working in my mind almost like
a command."[70]

At first, Dart's words fell on deaf ears. Hope had put in five years at Henson's
Restaurant and could see no logical reason to leave his comfortable position
there. He consulted other Augustans, black and white, whom he believed understood the situation of a seventeen-year-old "southern boy" better than the
more cosmopolitan Dart. Robert Bradford Williams and John Wesley Gilbert
thought school "up North" was a good idea; both were already matriculating
in northern schools and had made only minor adjustments. Friendly white
educators thought it was a marvelous idea, too. Dr. George Walker, who had
become Paine College's second president, offered to assist with John's academic preparation. A friendly white lawyer suggested that Hope study law,
and Major Joseph B. Cumming not only endorsed the idea but also gave him
advice on his reading and loaned him books, including his own son's volumes
of *Plutarch*, and even donated a five dollar bill to help him get started.[71]

Once his mind was made up, Hope was no less serious about his schooling
than he was about religion. Money was certainly a legitimate obstacle. Education at prestigious Atlanta University was expensive, but it paled in comparison to the costs of attending school in New England. Dart knew about
Worcester Academy in Massachusetts, and also knew that its principal was
particularly interested in attracting African American students. No scholarships were guaranteed, and competition for them was stiff; yet determined
students often received some financial assistance. Students were expected to
reach Worcester on their own, however. Family and friends helped, but it was
his brother Madison's donation of $100 that John remembered years later.
"Through his generosity . . . I was lifted out of an environment that would

probably have held me down for the rest of my life." It was a major sacrifice for Madison. His annual salary at the time was only $500.[72]

By May 1886 John Hope had made up his mind. He would attend Worcester Academy. Although he continued to work at Henson's, he was preoccupied with his academic preparation, which Rev. Dart had already initiated. Dr. Walker probably helped with that preparation, and over the summer both Robert Bradford Williams and John Wesley Gilbert may have pitched in too. Hope's correspondence does not mention that Dart left Augusta shortly before Hope turned eighteen early in June. Hope undoubtedly missed his mentor, but he probably understood the reason for Dart's departure. "Union Baptist Church wanted him to stay," Dart's family later explained, "but he was dissatisfied with the people at Union, dissatisfied with the South. He was too far ahead of his time." Dart returned to Charleston and eventually started the Charleston Normal and Industrial School, serving as its principal until his death in 1915.[73]

John Hope did not record his thoughts as he drifted off to sleep that last night before leaving Augusta. Leaving home and family for the first time was undoubtedly traumatic, and though Hope had worked for five years, he was still only eighteen years old. He had never been out of the South, and almost certainly he was a little fearful. Perhaps Hope's father comforted him in his dreams. Because of him, John Hope was born into a family where the color line was blurred, if not ignored. James Hope's wealth exposed his son to a world virtually unknown to most black Augustans. That early family background would prove helpful when John Hope began to interact with privileged New Englanders.

Other prominent whites may also have crowded into those dreams. Cumming, Walker, Roberts, and others may have slowly passed by, smiling and waving their farewells. A good friend would later write that "it was possible for a Negro in the Augusta of John Hope's boyhood to aspire to the heights and to receive encouragement from white people in so doing."[74] Hope's Augusta experiences had taught him that the welfare of African Americans was irrevocably linked with cooperation between black leaders and the white elite. Several years passed before this notion emerged into the forefront of his thinking, but the seeds of interracial cooperation were firmly planted in his mind in the town of his birth.

Yet Hope's Augusta was more black than white. His dreams could not have omitted the fiery militancy of William J. White, the conservatism of Robert Harper, the charismatic and cosmopolitan John Dart, or the resourceful and indomitable Lucy Laney. Augusta was no oasis of freedom, and African American leaders fought hard against the evils of discrimination. Some, like Hope himself, could easily have left Augusta and lived out their lives as whites. Yet most did not. In spite of their physical appearance, they chose to be African Americans. John Hope would follow the same path.

Big Nan may have paid him a visit that night too. Her comfort was perhaps most reassuring. She was his earliest religious teacher, and she set the standard for his behavior and prepared him for his spiritual rebirth. John Hope's religious fervor would deepen in New England, but its seeds were sown in Augusta. Perhaps John Hope awoke the next morning with a smile on his face. It was time to leave Augusta for Massachusetts and Worcester Academy. He was better prepared than he realized.

3

Worcester and Brown

John Hope arrived by train in Worcester, Massachusetts, early in September 1886, a week before the beginning of the fall term. His first impressions of this quaint New England town have not survived, but comparisons with his beloved Augusta were probably inevitable. Like Augusta, Worcester's origins predated the American Revolution. Founded in 1674, the city lies inland in a narrow, winding valley nearly surrounded by hills. There is no Savannah River there, of course, but Lake Quinsigamond and several smaller brooks skirt the city's eastern side, providing it with important natural resources. Agriculture, the first mainstay of the economy, had gradually given way to manufacturing by the beginning of the nineteenth century. Workers turned out everything from firearms, wire, and textiles to coaches, leather goods, and clocks. Sparked by the demands of the Industrial Revolution, inventions like the loom, sewing machine, and cotton gin were created within twenty miles of Worcester. The railroads were soon transporting the city's industrial goods fifty miles in either direction to Providence and Boston, and Worcester became a busy center of New England travel.[1]

John Hope was impressed with the city's setting. Before he left Augusta for Worcester, Hope's contacts with the outside world had been limited to an occasional short trip to Atlanta and work in neighboring South Carolina. The North was still a "promised land" where freedom resided beneath the protection of the shining North Star. It was also the headquarters of the Underground Railroad and the home of the venerable Frederick Douglass, Harriet Tubman, Ida B. Wells, and other African American leaders whom John idolized. He was not yet familiar with the harsh realities of black life in the North, and for the time being Worcester seemed like a fantasy come true. John Hope had finally reached the pot of gold at the end of the rainbow.[2]

Worcester's political history in the mid-nineteenth century supported John's vision of a northern paradise. Before the Civil War the town had been a hotbed of abolitionism and a prominent stop on the Underground Railroad. In 1848, Worcester politicians had denounced the Mexican War as an "arrogant proslavery war of conquest." They also rejected the nomination of presidential Whig party candidate Zachary Taylor and urged the state to "go for free soil and free men . . . free land, and a free world." The Fugitive Slave Law of 1850 found little support in Worcester, and some citizens took it on themselves to defy the law openly. Worcester also contributed nearly four thousand men to the Union Army during the Civil War. In short, Worcester in the nineteenth century exemplified everything John Hope felt a northern city should be, and more.[3]

In spite of its abolitionist past, however, few African Americans actually called Worcester home. In 1860 there were only 769 blacks in the entire county, compared with 158,881 whites. When black migrants moved up from the South in large numbers after the Civil War, they bypassed Worcester and settled instead in the more cosmopolitan cities of Providence and Boston. In 1870 the population of Worcester consisted of 513 blacks and 41,105 whites; in 1880 there were 763 blacks and 58,291 whites; and by the turn of the century only a few more than 1,100 African Americans called Worcester home.[4]

In addition to the absence of a noticeable black presence in Worcester, the social atmosphere contrasted sharply with Augusta's. Worcester had long boasted of a tradition that encouraged strict morality, rigid discipline, and puritanical values. There were no brothels in Worcester, nor were streetwalkers visible anywhere in the city. Saloons in Worcester bore little resemblance to Henson's Restaurant in Augusta. The few saloons that did exist closed promptly at eleven; no separate rooms served women; and no saloons were open on holidays. An academy classmate of John's later insisted that bartenders were so solicitous of minors in Worcester that even some "men in their twenties carried their Poll Tax receipts in their pockets." Sunday closing laws were strictly enforced, of course, and Sabbath observance prohibited everything from baseball games to spending a quiet day fishing on the lake.[5]

John was also impressed with the beauty of Worcester Academy's ten-acre campus. The school sat atop a steep hill that provided a breathtaking view of the city and countryside below. Distinguished-looking elms and oaks dotted the campus landscape, and in the crisp early fall, gold and red leaves floated gently in the breeze. Worcester Academy opened in 1834, the brainchild of deeply religious New Englanders committed to the spiritual and academic development of young men. Although interdenominational in its origins, the school had come under the influence of Northern Baptists by the 1850s. An early copy of the *Academy*, the school magazine, boasted that Worcester was a "thoroughly Christian school, founded and built upon Christian principles." The faculty included only Christian men who valued "character above scholarship" and were expected to find "constant opportunities to . . . suggest the true aim of life, and direct the pupil's attention to the gracious person and holy life of our Saviour."[6]

The school's religious activities matched the advertisements in its catalogues. Revivals were frequent, and faculty members regularly knelt in prayer at students' bedsides at night, hoping to save them from eternal hellfire and damnation. Each morning began with a church service, and students attended two religious exercises on Sunday. Parents were allowed (with the approval of the principal) to select the church their sons attended, but the weekly prayer meetings and religious instruction were not optional. Predictably, many of Worcester Academy's students became ministers.[7]

For many years after it opened, Worcester Academy paid much more attention to religion than to academics. Like other academies in the nineteenth century, its curriculum inclined toward Greek and Latin studies, and classes were usually small. Teachers fiercely dedicated to the school's mission combined inspirational instruction with rigid discipline. While a science option was available, most students chose the "college preparatory track," which in principle prepared them for admission to New England's best colleges. In the decade following the Civil War, however, most Worcester students did not go on to college, and some even failed to finish at the academy. Worcester struggled to keep its doors open during those years with no more than fifty students registered in any one quarter. Administrators and faculty complained privately about the students' intellectual character and "lack of higher mental ability and power of application." They later admitted that "scholarship was low and marks signified little" in those days.[8]

By focusing on academics, administrators and faculty managed to turn the program around, and by the time John arrived in 1886 the school's academic program had improved dramatically. The change began early in the decade with the introduction of biweekly examinations. At first, students struggled, literally, to "make the grade," but soon the averages rose significantly in both tracks of study.

In 1886 the college's academic reputation was at an all-time high, enrollment was up, and some students actually had to be turned away. That same year the academy's literature boasted that graduates with certificates from the principal had been admitted without examination to New England universities such as Brown, Dartmouth, and Amherst. Worcester Academy had at last joined Holy Cross, Clark University, and several other local schools with superior academic reputations. Together these schools formed an emerging intellectual center whose fame was increasing throughout the Northeast.[9]

There were only two main buildings on campus when John arrived at Worcester. Davis Hall, the larger of the two, sat slightly back from the main street on the right. But it was the grand house immediately to the right of the campus entrance that John first noticed. Painted bright yellow with a white wraparound porch, the building was the home of the school's principal, the venerable Daniel Webster (D. W.) Abercrombie. Neither Hope nor Abercrombie realized that the histories of their families had intersected years ago in antebellum Sparta, Georgia.

Abercrombie was a grandson of General Anderson Abercrombie, a native of Sparta and a business partner of Hugh Taylor, onetime owner of John Hope's great-grandmother and grandmother. D. W. Abercrombie was born in Alabama to a southern planter and northern mother. After his father died during the Civil War, Abercrombie's mother moved the family to the North. He eventually received a law degree from Harvard, but instead of practicing law, he decided to teach.[10]

John Hope had fond recollections of his first meeting with Dr. Abercrombie. It did not, however, seem very promising at the start. Though eighteen years of age, John Hope was still shy. Meeting new people was never easy for him, yet he wanted desperately to make a good first impression. Although Hope had been born into an interracial family, his schooling and social life in Augusta had all taken place behind a racial veil. The white world was largely unknown to him. Worcester Academy was virgin territory, and John's five-minute wait to see the principal probably seemed like hours. Glancing around the office, Hope looked unsuccessfully for something familiar. Portraits of all sizes and shapes returned his curious gaze. In a few short months he would know they were the founders and recite the academy's history with pride. But that familiarity was in the future. The silence was suddenly interrupted when sharp-eyed, black-haired Abercrombie walked into the room.[11]

"What a difference two or three steps in a room can make in the life of a boy," Hope recalled of the moment more than twenty years later. At the principal's aggressive approach, hand extended, John breathed a sigh of relief. Hope later learned that the perceptive thirty-three-year-old Abercrombie made a habit of treating shy and inexperienced freshmen like familiar, seasoned seniors. Abercrombie seemed not to notice that a young man so clearly white in his appearance was the school's only black freshman that academic year. That was fortunate, for the sensitive Hope might have misinterpreted a sudden frown, curious look, or embarrassing question.[12]

Hope's first conversation with Abercrombie eventually turned to money. Fees at Worcester Academy were $62.50 per term, or approximately $200.00 for the academic year. Confident he could handle the initial costs, Hope pressed Abercrombie for some commitment regarding his future financial support. He cautiously inquired first about jobs, then about scholarships and other ways he might earn his tuition. Abercrombie was noncommittal. Scholarships were available, but they were highly competitive; worthy students could find jobs, but those also depended on merit and exemplary behavior. Nothing was guaranteed. Outwardly, Hope appeared pleased to learn of the opportunities. Privately, he questioned his ability to compete. Those private thoughts, of course, were only revealed to Abercrombie years later.

A lull in the conversation was interrupted by a loud knock at the door. Abercrombie's wife desperately needed some absorbent cotton from the city down below. With no hesitation Abercrombie gave the job to the surprised young freshman, who scampered off to run the errand. The true meaning of that event dawned on Hope only many years later. *Absorbent* was a new word added to his vocabulary, but far more important, the small task placed him squarely in the realm of the familiar and gave him a much-needed boost in self-confidence. Hope also interpreted the errand as a genuine gesture of Abercrombie's faith, his confidence in John's ability to get through the academy. For the time being, Hope was satisfied in this new world, secure and at ease. It was time to meet the student body.[13]

John's first impressions of student life at Worcester Academy were either not recorded or were written in letters that no longer exist. Nevertheless, photographs taken during his freshman year hint at the racial and gender composition of the student body. There is no record of any African American woman ever being admitted to the academy, but a few white female students were still there when Hope arrived. Their numbers declined quickly, however, and by 1890 women were no longer admitted. On the other hand, male students of different racial and ethnic groups were visible everywhere on campus. African Americans, Europeans, Jews, and a few Asians shared the space with white Americans from all over the country. The founders' vision of what today would be called a "racially diverse" student body had begun to take shape.[14]

Diversity at Worcester Academy was not limited to race, however. Though perhaps more subtle, other differences in the composition of the student body were also apparent. Hope's contemporaries remembered that "juvenile delinquents, misfits and thwarted theologians" often found their way to Worcester Academy. There were also sons of prominent families who chose Worcester's rugged and sometimes spartan existence over the more genteel academic environments of Groton, Exeter, or Andover. Students from working-class families were usually older and were expected to work their way through school with employment on campus. Some were day students who commuted from the surrounding communities. Other students, like Hope, had experienced the "real world of work" and decided to return to school to continue their education.[15]

Thus, it was class more than racial distinctions that stood out in the students' living conditions. All the students on campus lived in Davis Hall. Most of them were in second-floor rooms in the two wings off the recitation rooms. John Hope and other students with limited financial resources occupied rooms above the third-floor chapel, under the roof.

Hope's roommate the first two years was John Harvey Wigginton, a fellow African American who went on to attend Yale, graduated from the law school, and became a successful lawyer. John Holmes, the only other African American on campus during Hope's tenure, was a popular athlete—a varsity football and baseball player—who later became a physician in Kentucky. None of Hope's surviving correspondence mentions his black classmates. Perhaps they were not very close, or they may simply have failed to keep in touch after graduation.[16]

Other Worcester students, however, remained Hope's friends many years after graduation. Some were among the original thirty-nine freshmen who arrived with Hope in 1886, including Harold Hazeltine, who later attended Brown with Hope and ultimately became a distinguished professor at Cambridge University in England. Albert Bailey was an even closer friend whom Hope met in his sophomore year. After graduating from the academy in 1890, Bailey attended Harvard and became first a prominent academician and later a businessman in Worcester. He did not see Hope again until the 1920s, when both men booked passage on the same European steamer returning to the United States. Bailey's memories had not faded over the years. He recalled even then that Hope read vociferously at the academy: "He could always be found in the newspaper room, digesting the most significant social and political news of the day." Perhaps because of his age, Hope seemed more serious, more focused on his studies than most of the students. He had an engaging personality that was often described as gracious and mild mannered. Although always soft-spoken and reserved, Hope was gifted with a delightful sense of humor. He "never antagonized," Bailey remembered, "never took up cudgels."[17]

Other Worcester Academy classmates remembered a less genteel John Hope. Robert Drawbridge worked his way through prep school and college, played football at both Worcester and Brown, and later became a prominent Congregationalist minister. Erastus Starr and John Swain were sons of prominent New England families. Swain eventually became an important journalist and, at Hope's request, wrote a few articles at the turn of the century for the Atlanta-based *Voice of the Negro*.[18] Starr became a prosperous engineer. In addition to echoing some of Bailey's sentiments, these men remembered Hope's enthusiasm for sports at Worcester Academy and later at Brown. Though never an outstanding athlete, Hope enjoyed sports and did make the second team in football and baseball. And, according to a classmate, he was a "fair boxer with the gloves on." He could even be a little mischievous. He admitted to Draw-bridge years later, in 1912, that he "raised the dickens" sometimes and gave the dormitory monitors some trouble.[19]

The school records for Hope's Worcester years are spotty at best, yet it is certain he chose the college preparatory course. Unlike some students, who dreaded plowing through Collar and Daniell's *Latin Book for Beginners* and Tetlow's *Latin Lessons*, Hope devoured them with an intellectual appetite that knew no boundaries. He loved to read the classics—Homer, Herodotus, and Ovid—and he also admired Shakespeare, Eliot, Hawthorne, and Thoreau. Besides these favorites he relished history, English grammar, and reading; he tolerated math and science.

Hope's academy grades are not available, but students' and teachers' com-ments about his performance reveal a certain continuity with his academic ex-perience in Augusta. In spite of his high motivation and intellectual curiosity, Hope's academic performance that first year was only average. He continued to be a plodder, and test results seldom revealed the depth of his prepara-tion. "He studied twice as long and hard as other Academy students," said one classmate, but his marks were not appreciably higher than theirs. Math and science were particularly troublesome. His close friend Erastus Starr had to help him with algebra and geometry.[20] In his defense, this was Hope's first year back in school after a five-year interruption, and he was in a superior preparatory school in a world far from any he had ever known. In view of these considerations, it is perhaps commendable that he performed as well as he did his first year.

Hope's first year in Worcester passed quickly. Before long the academic year was over and he found himself aboard a train headed south. Physically John had not changed much; he remained about five feet seven inches tall and still weighed about 135 pounds. Inside, however, his worldview had begun to ex-pand, even though he barely realized it at the time. In Augusta, Hope had no white friends his own age. Most of the whites he knew were older adults, men he had met through work or former acquaintances of his father. His "friends" in Augusta—his peers at work and play—were African Americans like him who shared the collective experience of their racial group.

In Worcester, Hope's circle of friends had widened to include young men whose regional, class, and racial backgrounds were far different from his own. He had been taught by Abercrombie that "a man's race made no difference . . . that character was everything." Hope's experiences at the academy seemed to confirm the school's democratic creed. Though clearly aware of his racial iden-tity, Hope's closest friends at Worcester were white, and there seemed to be no racial barriers that separated them on campus or off. Erastus Starr and John Swain, for example, invited Hope to spend vacations and holidays with their families. In addition to expanding his circle of friends, Hope became more disciplined at Worcester, more confident of himself and his abilities. Over time he also became more self-reliant and, according to his sister Jane, less tolerant of discrimination at home.[21]

John Hope returned to his old job at Henson's Restaurant to work away the summer of 1887. It was a familiar routine, a job he performed effortlessly and with precision. His experiences that summer at Henson's probably made him realize how much he had changed in the intervening year. Friends later remembered that he kept to himself, socialized little, and daydreamed a lot. "John did his work well," a co-worker remembered, yet "his mind was somewhere else."[22] The truth was that John had outgrown Henson's. For him it was now a dead-end street. He missed the academic challenges of the academy, the camaraderie of his classmates, and the freedom of New England.

Nevertheless, Hope was practical enough to recognize that Henson's provided a job, and he desperately needed the income. He needed money to return to the academy, and he dared not appeal to his family, which was already operating on a shoestring budget based mainly on Madison's wages as a postal employee. Hope soon realized that even if he saved every dime he made at Henson's that summer, he still would not be able to pay his Worcester Academy fees in the fall. He asked for a raise, but Henson refused. Hope was thus placed in a difficult position. If he left the restaurant and no other job materialized, he would face an even greater deficit at the end of the summer. In the end, the inadequate salary notwithstanding, John Hope stayed at Henson's.[23]

At least one major event that summer temporarily diverted Hope from his financial problems. His sister Alethea, then twenty-two, was married on 5 July 1886. The ceremony took place in the Hope home on Ellis Street instead of at Union Baptist Church. Alethea, like the rest of the Hope family, could easily have passed for white. Contemporaries described her as a beautiful woman with an olive complexion. She looked, someone recalled, "almost a little Jewish." Alethea married Charles Ladeveze, prominent member of an old and aristocratic black family whose complexion matched her own. The couple remained in Augusta for a time but moved to Providence, Rhode Island, early in the twentieth century.[24]

Shortly after his sister's wedding, Hope developed a new relationship that helped him resolve his financial dilemma. Alethea was married by the new minister of Union Baptist Church, Rev. John W. Dunjee, who liked to tell the story of his escape from slavery. Like Henry "Box Car" Brown, who told a similar tale, Dunjee spent part of his freedom trek concealed in a box. Dunjee liked to boast that his tale had been included in the popular collection of stories of the Underground Railroad published by William Still.[25]

When John Hope told Dunjee about his financial situation, Dunjee offered to contact an acquaintance in Ohio who often helped young men trying to obtain an education. Edward Burr Solomon, a businessman and philanthropist in Dayton, offered to lend Hope some money, but only if he promised to become a minister. The ministry was certainly on John's mind, but he had made no final decision and refused to accept any money on that basis. Solomon admired young John's honesty and determination, gave him the money without stipulation, and helped him periodically throughout his years at the academy. Hope never forgot Solomon's generosity and in 1901 named his firstborn son after him.[26]

The John Hope who returned to Worcester Academy in 1887 was no longer the shy, inexperienced lad who had timidly climbed the steep hill a year earlier. He received only a partial scholarship that year, but Abercrombie kept his word and provided him with employment on campus to help him make ends meet. John worked two jobs his second year at the academy: washing dishes and waiting on tables in the dining hall, and keeping the campus stoves loaded with firewood. His vast experience at Henson's paid off. He was soon elevated to the headwaiter position in the dining hall and supervised several full-time employees. A classmate remembered that in his senior year Hope supervised the entire dining hall staff. He also gained a favorable reputation in the hotels and restaurants of Worcester, and instead of returning to Augusta, John spent his last two summers in Worcester working at local restaurants.[27]

John's busy work schedule did not adversely affect his academic performance, and he even found the time for extracurricular academic activities. Taking Abercrombie's advice, he joined Lego, the school's debating society, and in time became its president. At the end of his junior year Hope participated in the highly touted Dexter Prize speaking contest and won second place. He also showed promise as a writer. In his junior year Hope was invited to join the staff of the *Academy*, the school's monthly magazine, and he became its editor in 1890.

There was a rigid code of behavior at Worcester Academy. Smoking and card playing were grounds for immediate expulsion. A student did not have to be caught smoking cigarettes or playing cards; simple possession of either constituted grounds for dismissal. Cursing and attendance at dances and other variety shows also incurred stiff penalties. Young men could always find ways to get into trouble. John Swain, one of Hope's best friends, remembered that "the town had just one variety show . . . where terrible things took place; Lottie Collins sang 'Ta-ra-ra-BOOM-de-ay!' A troupe of French poodles jumped through hoops, and girls actually wore tights before the lecherous eyes of men." Swain later admitted that he kept his trunk fully packed because when a student was "fired," he was not even allowed time to gather up his things before leaving.[28]

There is no evidence that Hope found the inflexible rules at Worcester burdensome. His free time was limited, and his mind had already been set against most of those "vices" during his years in Augusta. In a few years, in fact, Hope would support the very same rules at Morehouse College. He nevertheless participated in the few sanctioned social activities at Worcester Academy. In addition to sports, he belonged to the Worcester chapter of the YMCA, taking a special interest in the religious activities. He also enjoyed an occasional visit to Boston. He usually traveled there by train, which took about an hour, and met his good friend John Swain. Although he made numerous trips to Boston, none was as exciting as the first, which he described in an essay written during his first year at the academy. He was particularly impressed with Bunker Hill and its breathtaking view of the city. Over the years, Boston remained one of his favorite cities.[29]

In 1890, as John's time at Worcester Academy came to an end, he looked back on an exhilarating four years. His easy acceptance by his classmates, the school's religious orientation and emphasis on classical culture, and his virtual adoption by Dr. Abercrombie were all John had hoped for and more. Perhaps he marveled at how easily he had made the transition from the red clay of Georgia to the rolling hills of New England. As Commencement Day approached, John seemed to have his future well in hand. He had decided to continue his education, and Brown University was his choice.

Hope first learned about Brown from the charismatic John Dart, his mentor in Augusta. Dart had once pastored a church in Providence and knew that Brown accepted African American students. And it was Dart who told John he should "aim high."[30] Although the idea of attending Brown had been planted in Augusta, it grew to fruition in Worcester, Massachusetts, under the skillful guidance of D. W. Abercrombie. The headmaster and John Hope became increasingly fond of each other over the four years John spent at Worcester. He spent considerable time at the Abercrombie residence and became the childhood idol of Abercrombie's teenaged daughter. Few of John's important decisions were made without Abercrombie's wise counsel. Thus, when Abercrombie strongly encouraged him to seek admission to Brown, Hope did not hesitate.

Hope never knew that Abercrombie worked hard behind the scenes to find financial aid for him. His grades were good, but the competition for aid at Brown was keen. Because of the school's denominational affiliation (it too had strong Baptist connections), Abercrombie managed to get philanthropic Baptists to pay for Hope's tuition and housing his first year at the college.[31]

Hope was far less sanguine about his professional destiny than he was about his choice of a college. Hope's friend W. E. B. Du Bois once wrote of his disdain for "any human being of the mature age of 22 who did not have his life all planned before him."[32] He would have been disappointed with the indecisive John Hope in those days, for at the "mature age" of twenty-two, Hope had still not decided on a career. For a fleeting moment he considered studying the law; he also thought briefly of studying medicine. Most seriously, however, John wanted to become a minister. His religious zeal had only increased at the academy, and one of Brown's attractions for him was its strong religious foundation.

Yet Hope hesitated; he had not been able to resolve certain religious issues, though he dared not mention it to even his most intimate associates. It was only years later that he revealed his dilemma in a speech: "I got to thinking about evolution and the Immaculate Conception . . . between 1886 and 1890, when young students hardly dared tell their teachers that they were thinking about those things." There were things in the spiritual realm that John had difficulty accepting: the ideas of a virgin birth and a universe created by God tested the limits of his faith. He was probably not the first student in the 1890s unable to resolve the conflict between science and religion, but until he did, he dared not commit himself to the ministry. Thus John went to Brown still undecided about a career, yet unwilling to discuss his problems with anyone who could help.[33]

But that tendency to keep his difficulties to himself was characteristic of John Hope. He worked out his problems alone during hours of intense introspection, and he was always his own best critic. Even his most deeply held convictions did not escape his blend of idealism and pragmatism. His way of solving his most troublesome problems was an important part of his personality, but it frequently created unnecessary difficulties for him. His inability to share his burdens often led him to draw faulty conclusions, manifested at times in what appeared to be low self-esteem, even low self-worth. He sometimes appeared to lack confidence, was often too modest about his accomplishments, and tended to magnify his failures. Of his religious dilemma he admitted in retrospect that "it seems a tragedy that I could not have gone to a pastor or a teacher and talk out my spiritual difficulties." Yet John was almost sixty-seven when he made that speech. It never did become easy for him to talk over his difficulties with others.[34]

John Hope's class was the first to graduate in Walker Hall, a new two-and-a-half-story building of Romanesque Revival design. On Commencement

Day John was a handsome lad of twenty-two with light brown hair and a matching handlebar mustache that had just begun to curl. Without doubt he felt a surge of pride as he marched into the edifice and prepared to read the class history. His selection as reader was a tribute to his outstanding speaking and writing abilities. Yet his joy may have been tempered with sadness. Not one member of his family attended the commencement exercises, although he knew he had their support. Graduation from Worcester meant that John Hope had cleared an important hurdle in a place and society far away from the Augusta of his childhood.

On 17 September 1890 John Hope enrolled at Brown University. Widely acclaimed as the seventh oldest college in America, Brown first opened its doors in 1764 as Rhode Island College in Warren, Rhode Island. The school moved to Providence in 1770 and was renamed Brown University in 1804. By 1890 it was well on the way to becoming one of the most prestigious colleges in the nation.[35]

Hope's first week at Brown was a stern reminder that he was no longer a seasoned veteran senior, as he had been at Worcester, but an inexperienced first-semester freshman. But he was not alone; seven other Worcester Academy graduates entered Brown that fall. All eight of the young men were deeply religious and were looking toward the ministry as a possible career.[36]

Some of the Worcester graduates, like his friend Harold Hazeltine, lived in luxurious University Hall, a four-story building with a central pedimented pavilion and a roof topped by a deck and a cupola. The first building erected on the Brown University campus, University Hall had undergone extensive renovations during the summer of 1890 and was now used as a dormitory. Poor students like John Hope, however, lived in far less commodious quarters. He shared a small room, number 45, on the top floor of a building constructed in 1822 that was ironically called "Hope College." When John moved in, the north wall was cracked, the timbers were rotting, and the interior was worn and dingy. Although renovations had been promised and were always hoped for, students knew it was the dormitory to avoid.[37]

The semester began early on Wednesday morning when the bell atop University Hall summoned students to the opening ceremonies. Widely covered in the local papers, the affair took place in the second-floor chapel of Manning Hall, an impressive building erected in 1835 that resembled a Doric temple. Students packed the chapel, with the few remaining seats taken up by friends and former graduates. Women crowded into the gallery; for them this was an especially memorable occasion. Their presence in the freshman class of 1890 represented the first victory in their long and arduous struggle for admission to Brown.[38]

Flanked by the faculty on the platform, President Elisha Benjamin Andrews rose to welcome more than one hundred new freshmen. After reminding the new students that they were privileged indeed to be at Brown, Andrews delivered an address entitled "The Idea of a Collegiate Education." The theme resonated well with John and others in attendance, and affirmed the president's reputation as a dynamic and energetic speaker.[39]

It was President Andrews who laid the groundwork for Brown University's emergence as a modern university. Described as a "powerful personality, strong of body, intellect, and will, racy in speech, of large outlook, and great of heart," Andrews took over the presidency of Brown University in 1889. His appointment followed an already distinguished career as a soldier, politician, college educator, and lawyer. Andrews served in the Civil War but was discharged in 1864 after losing an eye at the Battle of Petersburg. He entered Brown University in 1866 and graduated in 1870. After a successful career as a university professor, Andrews began a distinguished, though short, career as president of Brown University.[40]

Throughout John Hope's life, he tended to attract the attention of liberal white men with power. It had been the case in Augusta and Worcester, and it continued to be the case in Providence. Hope first met Andrews when he enrolled in the university president's "Moral and Intellectual Philosophy" class. Hope was mesmerized by Andrews's electrifying lectures and sound philosophy on life. Andrews challenged students to expand their horizons and inspired them to excel beyond their wildest expectations. His students were also imbued with a deep sense of school loyalty. Prompted in part by Andrews, John abandoned the classics and decided to major in philosophy instead.[41]

Hope's academic record at Brown improved significantly over his performance at Worcester. He did well in the liberal arts curriculum, which completely replaced the mandatory mechanics program in his sophomore year. He took courses in Greek, Latin, French, philosophy, geometry, trigonometry and algebra, chemistry, botany, physics, literature, history, political economy, fine art, geology, and physical education. Brown had not yet adopted an alphabetical grading system and used a numerical evaluation for each class, with 10 the highest grade. Hope's average his first year was 8.097. It would be his lowest. Although his sophomore year was the most difficult by his own account, it also represented his best average of the four-year period: 8.733. When he graduated, his cumulative average was 8.473; his lowest grades were in introductory physics classes. His best grade, a perfect 10, was in advanced philosophy. A few years later Hope would draw on Brown's curricula to support his belief in the efficacy and superiority of a liberal arts education.[42]

Hope's grades are even more remarkable in view of the amount of time he had to work to support himself. He later wrote that both his "prep school and college were unceasing burdens with reference to money." While his financial situation had been precarious at Worcester Academy, it by no means matched his financial struggles at Brown. The subject clearly dominates his Brown correspondence.[43] The higher fees and limited one-year scholarship made financial survival much more difficult for him. Though his grades were good, they were not excellent, and additional scholarship money did not materialize. John rarely revealed his financial problems to his family in Augusta and did not embarrass them by asking for money they could not supply.

There *were* family members with the financial resources to help John at Brown. The Hopes of New York, John's paternal uncle Thomas and aunt Jane, were financially secure. Thomas Hope had amassed a fortune in the merchandising business. After the death of James Hope, the white New York Hopes showed no interest in continuing the relationship with their black relatives in Augusta. The Georgia Hopes were not surprised. Many of them believed that Jane Hope never forgave Mary Frances for not allowing her to adopt Anna back in 1874 and welcomed the opportunity to sever the relationship after her brother's death. Still others believed the New York Hopes had never accepted their brother's black family and did not expect the relationship to continue after James Hope died. There is no conclusive evidence to confirm or deny either story. It is likely that both racism and Jane Hope's failure to adopt Anna played roles in severing the bonds between the black Hopes and the white Hopes.[44]

Ironically, the New York Hopes resurfaced in 1890, shortly before John graduated from Worcester Academy, although not to reestablish old family ties. The New York Hopes reentered John's consciousness when he read about them in the pages of the *New York Times*. Thomas Hope, over eighty and unmarried, died in March and left most of his $600,000 fortune to build a hospital for the poor in Langholm, Scotland, the place of his birth. Thomas Hope's survivors, according to the *Times*, were his sister, Jane, and family members of a "deceased brother." That brother, however, was not James, John Hope's father, but Anthony S. Hope. The *Times* did not mention the Hope family in Augusta at all.[45]

Thomas Hope's will generated a good deal of controversy. A white cousin whom John never met contested it, questioning the large donation slated for the hospital in Langholm. Ironically, this cousin was also named John, and he was only two years younger than John Hope of Augusta. The will also included a provision not found initially in the list of people receiving money from the estate. To John Hope's delight, his brother Thomas, named after the deceased Thomas Hope, was to receive $3,000 for his education, a sum that would allow him to attend both Worcester Academy and a college of his choice. John, whose financial needs were more immediate, received nothing from his rich uncle's estate.[46]

John Hope did what he had always done when he needed money. Though no more financial aid was available on the university campus, he found part-time work with the caterers and local restaurants of Providence. Most of those businesses hired on a first come, first served basis, making it necessary for Hope to scurry down the steep hill each afternoon to claim his place in line. Most of his earnings went to pay his tuition; there was very little left over for food. Lack of food became a constant concern: "I hope my boys will never have to go through what I went through in college," Hope said to his wife a few years later. On another occasion he wrote to one of his sons, then in graduate school: "A man who has never gone hungry because of lack of funds has missed an experience not easily forgotten. I suppose my egregious appetite and liking for food is due to the fact that for a good part of four years I was not able to buy enough to eat."[47]

Hope was sternly reminded of his own meager existence in his sophomore year when tragedy struck and claimed his roommate, Frank Levi Trimble of Winchester, Tennessee. Trimble, a handsome, powerfully built black man, was already a junior when Hope arrived at Brown. Trimble's father was a Baptist minister and leader among his people who had passed his commitment on to his son. To his white friends on campus, Trimble appeared quiet and reserved: "He was always very courteous, and had a pleasant smile," one student remembered. Hope, however, remembered Trimble's "burning desire to serve his race." Unlike the indecisive Hope, Trimble's direction was clear: he had come to Brown University "with the avowed purpose of being a teacher among his people."[48]

His outstanding performances on the track team and in the classroom had made Trimble a well-known and popular student on the Brown campus. He was "a good scholar in the languages, did particularly well in Latin," and was a gifted orator. As a tribute to his academic success, Trimble was awarded the coveted Phi Beta Kappa key his junior year.[49] Yet Trimble, like Hope, seldom discussed his hardships, and his years at Brown had also been characterized by a continuous struggle to survive without the financial help of family or friends. As Trimble entered his senior year with the class of 1892, it appeared on the surface that his battle had been won. Unfortunately, things were not as they seemed. For three years Trimble denied himself adequate clothing and food in order to pay his tuition and housing fees. He had also managed to save $429 to do graduate work at Harvard University. Not even his own roommate, John Hope, realized the extent of his suffering.

Early in the fall of 1891 Trimble collapsed on campus. No immediate diagnosis was forthcoming, but there were rumors, later confirmed, that it was tuberculosis. Winter had come early to Providence that year, and it proved to be an especially harsh one. Trimble's diet often consisted of only syrup and bread, which even Hope recognized was insufficient. In a somber letter written in 1930, Hope told the story to his son John: "I shall never forget what he said to me one day as he looked out from the covers rather wild-eyed, and spoke in that husky voice of a man with both lungs almost gone. 'If I ever get well again, I shall eat more meat.'" Frank Levi Trimble did not get well again. He dropped out of school that fall and died early in 1892, only a few months before graduation. John remembered Trimble in his class oration in 1894. He also remembered a Worcester Academy classmate, Edward Makepeace, who died at Brown in November 1890.[50]

References to his economic circumstances dominate Hope's Brown correspondence, but his campus activities and social life receive scant attention. He was especially active in campus activities, which makes the void even more puzzling. For example, in his freshman year, Hope worked as the Brown correspondent for several newspapers, and he joined the staff of the *Brown Daily Herald* on its debut in 1891. In his sophomore year John was president of the Worcester Academy Club and served as the class treasurer. Sports continued to be a major attraction. Though he played only sandlot football, he was a competitive boxer: "Remember how you plugged me in the eye? It aches yet," wrote a former classmate more than twenty years later. In Hope's senior year he became an editor of the *Brown Daily Herald* and was also chosen to deliver the class oration.[51]

John Hope's social status at Brown is more difficult to discern. Evidence of social interaction, even with his close Worcester friends, is conspicuously absent from the oral and written testimony of his Brown years. Gone, for example, were the weekend visits with classmates' families, the occasional outings in Boston with friends, and the camaraderie that came from his leadership of the debate team. An earlier biographer wrote that Hope's colleagues at Brown "were no doubt cautiously aware that from a University it is but a step to the world outside." That reality was probably far more obvious to the introspective and mature John Hope.[52]

Greek fraternities increased in number during Hope's tenure at Brown and were immensely popular centers of social activity. They became even more popular after the erection of the Psi Upsilon chapter house on Thayer Street.[53] Like most college fraternities in John Hope's day, however, those at Brown did not admit persons of color. A classmate later remembered that "because of the segregation of the college fraternities, I didn't have a chance to know Hope well." Though the whites-only rule was often unwritten, it was common knowledge at the university.[54]

Hope's insistence on maintaining his African American identity was no secret either. In 1893 he revealed to a black friend at Brown that one fraternity
did consider admitting him. Although a Worcester classmate promoted his
admission, nothing ever materialized from the discussions and no invitation
was ever extended.[55] The reason why is not difficult to discern. John could not
have entered the fraternity as a white man because he was unwilling to "pass."
That would have left the fraternity with only one option—to admit him as an
African American. But such a decision would have opened the doors to other
persons of color, a price the fraternity obviously was not willing to pay.

Hope's experience with the fraternity perhaps hints at his social status during his years at Brown. His refusal to deny his racial identity precluded his
participation in most campus social activities. There is no evidence of blatant
or overt acts of discrimination, but Hope would never have put himself in a
position where such acts could occur. That Hope was consciously concerned
with a racist atmosphere at Brown is even harder to document. Many years
later he provided a clue to his social status at Brown when he wrote that it was
at Worcester Academy, not Brown, that he experienced a truly democratic atmosphere. And it was only in a speech given in 1928 that he revealed that he
had "gone through the entire range of embarrassment from fear of lynching . . . to the finest, most subtle condescension that one person could feel
from another." That "subtle condescension" may have been a thinly disguised
description of his social experiences at Brown University.[56]

For whatever reasons, it was not the Brown University campus that was
Hope's social center in those years but the African American community in
Providence. Unlike Worcester, Providence had a substantial African American community with a distinguished history that dated back to the American
Revolution. The gradual abolition of slavery began in Rhode Island in 1784.
By the early years of the nineteenth century, most of the African Americans
in Providence were free, except for "a few," wrote William Brown in his autobiography, "who declared their masters had been eating their flesh and now
they were going to stick to them and suck their bones."[57] Blacks nevertheless
continued to be victims of racial violence and discrimination. In 1822, Rhode
Island passed a stringent disfranchisement law that stripped African American
property owners of all political rights. Two years later, whites destroyed the
Providence black community of "Hard Scrabble," and in 1831 a race riot destroyed the black sections in "Snow Town" and on Olney Lane.[58]

African Americans fought back by establishing their own organizations to
address their needs. There were earlier attempts late in the eighteenth century, but the most successful organization, the African Union Meeting House
near Brown University, was established in 1819 with the help of white friends.
The meeting house of the "Afro-Yankees," as one historian has called them,

operated out of what C. Eric Lincoln and Lawrence Mamiya, in *The Black Church in the African American Experience*, called a "black sacred cosmos," an African American religious worldview that owed much to the African heritage. As a holistic enterprise, the organization placed a special emphasis on providing black education; it emphasized temperance, housed several black militia companies, and included the Prince Hall Masonic Lodge and several relief societies. Over time the African Union Meeting House of Providence evolved into the city's first African American church.[59]

By the middle of the nineteenth century the interdenominational African Union Meeting House Church could no longer meet the religious needs of black Providence. New black churches sprang up representing every conceivable denomination. The most popular were the African Methodist Episcopal (AME) Church, the AME Zion Church, the Episcopal Christ Church, and the Second Free Will Baptist Church. The old African Union Meeting House became the Meeting Street Baptist Church.

Most of Providence's African American leadership came from these churches, sometimes with their ministers in the vanguard. Alexander Crummell, pastor of the small Episcopal Christ Church, was an outstanding African American leader both before and after he left Providence. The history of black Providence confirms the view of Lincoln and Mamiya that the "black Church has no challenger as the cultural womb of the black community."[60]

The church was still the center of African American life in Providence when John Hope arrived in 1890. Brown, like Worcester Academy, expected its students to select a church at the beginning of their freshman year. In Worcester, Hope had chosen to attend D. W. Abercrombie's white church; in Providence, he selected the black Pond Street Baptist Church on the west side of the city. Why John chose Pond Street Baptist remains a mystery. There were two black Baptist churches on the east side not far from the Brown University campus. Most likely, Frank Trimble attended Pond Street and pushed his freshman roommate in that direction.

Whether a link already existed between black Providence and African American students attending Brown is unknown, but Hope had no problem gaining acceptance among Providence's African American elite. His experiences at Springfield and Union Baptist churches in Augusta had been ample training. Given Hope's rigorous academic schedule and constant search for work, it is remarkable that he spent so much time in black Providence. Less than a month into his first semester, he served on a local committee that arranged for the Honorable John Mercer Langston of Virginia to visit.

Born before the Civil War, Langston, like Hope, was the son of a black mother and white father who acknowledged his African American son. Unlike

Hope, however, Langston did not have his father's name. By 1890 Langston had already enjoyed an illustrious career as distinguished diplomat, college president, educator, and lawyer. In 1888, Langston ran for Congress as a representative from the Fourth Congressional District of Virginia and won. However, he was not seated until September 1890, after an election committee finally decided the seat was rightfully his. In celebration of that victory, the state Republican party invited Langston to visit Providence. Local African American leaders quickly moved to see that the distinguished congressman, second in popularity only to Frederick Douglass, was received by a larger audience.[61]

John later recalled that the event was a festive occasion. It began with a parade at Langston's hotel, complete with flying banners and bands playing, and ended at a local auditorium where Langston was scheduled to speak. John was quite visible in the procession, perched high in a carriage between Langston and the chairman of the Republican Central Committee. He remembered Langston's keynote address as "the boldest and most impassioned utterance I ever heard from him. It stamped him as a Negro, an American citizen, and a scholar." The evening ended with a formal banquet for the congressman that Hope attended as one of the platform guests.[62]

The next day the charismatic Langston spoke at Brown University. Though chapel services were held daily at Brown, this was the first time an African American had graced the pulpit. John Hope could hardly contain himself: "There where Wayland and Lincoln and Robinson had sat, educators whose impress on the country's culture cannot perish with the years, sat Hon. John M. Langston, a fit representative of my people." Historian August Meier may well have been correct in asserting that Langston "was the epitome of [ideological] inconsistency," but to the young John Hope he was the epitome of loyal race leadership.[63]

Hope's interaction with Providence's African American community deepened during his years at Brown University. He met several people his own age and formed friendships that continued long after his graduation. Mary E. Jackson and Roberta Dunbar, who would one day become charter members of the Providence NAACP, were early associates who belonged to the Pond Street Baptist Church. The two women joined Hope in organizing a small African American literary club called the Enquirers. At weekly meetings held in the home of one of its fifteen members, the Enquirers devoured the works of Shakespeare, Wordsworth, Poe, and Byron. They also enjoyed reading the writings of African American Phillis Wheatley. In addition the group shared in the biographical experiences of Frederick Douglass and Toussaint-Louverture. The feisty Miss Emily Tolliver, who lived to be almost a hundred, remembered "a party when they all came in costume, representing books, and the game was to guess what the other members represented."[64]

Roberta Dunbar later admitted that even though the "race question" was not the subject of much discussion in those days, the Enquirers spent considerable time talking about racial issues. There is no record of specific topics, but clues scribbled across class notes and scraps of paper seem to reflect Hope's thoughts on an array of African American concerns (for example, "The oppression of the Negro is for the time being causing him conservatism—notice his views on expansion and other manifesting new movements"). At the bottom of the same page Hope scribbled in quotes, as if remembering some kind of sign, "'No dogs nor Niggers Allowed in this park.'" On a scrap of paper he doodled: "The reason why many know so little about [African Americans] is because they think they know so much."[65]

There were plenty of racial issues in Providence for the Enquirers to discuss. After the Civil War, Rhode Island's African American population increased sharply as immigrants moved up from the South and settled in Providence or Newport. Neither city turned out to be the paradise many had expected. Until Rhode Island passed its first civil rights law in 1885, laws denied blacks access to public accommodations and transportation and prohibited their service on juries. Also in the 1880s, interracial marriages were banned. In the 1890s, most African Americans in Providence worked in menial occupations, black juvenile crime was on the rise, and health conditions were appalling.[66]

The Enquirers filled an important void in Hope's life. Predominantly white Brown University had little to offer to a developing African American leader. No university forums provided thorough discussions of racial problems and issues that could match those he found with the Enquirers. Nor could Brown keep Hope abreast of the cultural mores and class values that were so much a part of upwardly mobile "aristocrats of color." The club was more than an organization represented by rings with an engraved question mark symbolizing its members' intellectual curiosity. It was also a center of social activity. The Enquirers sponsored parties, teas, receptions, and balls—outlets that simply did not exist for African Americans at Brown University.[67]

John Hope's interactions in Providence were not all with the city's black elite. His continuing need to work gave him an opportunity to associate with the black working class as well. In spite of his aristocratic origins and white complexion, Hope was popular with his much darker fellow workers at the restaurants and catering places that frequently employed him. Hope could have made more money if he had not rejected all opportunities to pass for white. His insistence on working only with African Americans often puzzled his fellow workers, but Hope said he did it "to show his standing with his people."[68]

"His people" apparently appreciated the gesture. One of John's white class-mates at Brown decided to throw a graduation party his senior year at a popu-lar hall in Providence, and his family contracted with a local caterer to use a crew of black waiters that included John Hope. But John had also been invited to attend the party. The financially strapped Hope's first inclination was to work the affair, but the headwaiter and other African Americans on the crew insisted he attend as a guest instead. Hope revealed the story many years later to Florence M. Read, the president of Spelman College, who recorded it: "The waiters seemed to be rather pleased to see him there—proud of it. If he had ever high-hatted them, they would have acted quite differently." [69]

Apparently Hope was well liked by many in the Providence African Ameri-can community. Students at Ivy League Brown often appeared snobbish, aloof, and condescending toward the local inhabitants, but John Hope knew how to make his working-class friends feel comfortable without appearing patroniz-ing. Part of that ability has to be credited to his personality. But just as impor-tant was the fact that the relatively small black community in Providence was, by and large, made up of working-class people. Unlike Nashville and Atlanta, as Hope would soon discover, Providence did not have a large enough black population to support an elitist class-based existence. In black Providence, es-pecially in view of Hope's financial situation, he had to cross intraracial class lines. [70]

As John Hope entered his junior year at Brown in the fall of 1892, his financial worries had become almost unbearable. The work he found in Providence and the little assistance he received from the university's Aid Fund "for deserving young men of limited means" just did not pay the bills. Hope worked his first two summers in Rhode Island at the famous Watch Hill resort, a small, pic-turesque seaside vacation community. But there was no work available there during the summer of 1892. With his college debts continuing to mount, he went back to Augusta to work for the first time since arriving at Brown.

Although there is no record of it, John probably worked at Henson's Res-taurant. Whether or not he did, however, he returned to Providence in the fall still unable to pay his bills. President Andrews, the man responsible for the little money Hope received from the Aid Fund, used his influence and power to go one step further. Though it was against the rules, Andrews allowed John to register in the fall with a deficit. "I can't keep from telling you how thankful I feel to Mr. Andrews for his kindness to you," Hope's mother wrote in Oc-tober, shortly after John's return. "If I had the least thought that you were so uncertain about getting back in school when you left home, I would have been very unhappy." [71]

John was also thankful and relieved, but this was only a temporary reprieve, not a permanent solution. If he did not find a job that would allow him to pay back his debts, he would have to leave school. To make matters worse, the country slipped into a financial panic in 1893, and the downturn in the economy further restricted job opportunities.

Just when Hope had almost given up, word came of a position in Chicago. Though it was a few months late, America had decided to celebrate the four hundredth anniversary of Columbus's arrival in 1492. The event was staged in Chicago and was called the World's Columbian Exposition. Here was an opportunity to pay his debts and finish his education at Brown. John did not hesitate. As soon as final examinations ended, he was on a train headed for the Windy City.[72]

John Hope later remembered in a speech: "When I was in college in my junior year I got what the boys call 'in the hole,' and went out to Chicago and worked for about six months, and paid my debts."[73] As usual, he did not tell all; it was not quite that simple. The promised job did not materialize, and at first Hope had no luck finding anything else. The Panic of 1893 had become a depression, the worst the country had experienced up to that point. Cities and rural areas alike were affected, and jobs of any kind were scarce.

Yet the persistent Hope did not give up. He was finally sent to see someone who knew Chicago's restaurant scene and had enjoyed some success in placing young waiters. John's first job lasted only a few days before all the waiters, including John, the crew's only black man, were laid off. Undaunted, he again contacted the man who had referred him and learned that his complexion was working against him. Mistaken for white, John had been sent out on his first job as an easy way to let him down. Jobs for white waiters were scarce. However, jobs for colored men were not.

The next time, Hope was sent to the Lexington Hotel in Chicago, where he remained the rest of the summer. His complexion continued to be a source of some embarrassment to him. The headwaiter, whose name was Johnson, exploited every opportunity to poke fun at Hope's pale skin. During roll call on one occasion he pretended not to know Hope and called out: "Who is this man John Hope?" Other black waiters, unaware of Johnson's facetious game, quickly identified Hope to show Johnson that he had not missed roll call. With a sly, mocking grin, Johnson bellowed out: "Oh, that half-white man there." Hope would later acknowledge that he "supposed he came as near to hating Johnson while he worked for him as he ever had any man."

Throughout his trials, Hope remained resolute in his claim to his African American identity. As it had been in Providence, his decision was at times an economic disadvantage. The Metropole Hotel, for example, which preferred to hire white crews, paid $60 a month; the black crews at the Lexington made only $50, later reduced to $40. His darker companions in Chicago were as puzzled as his fellow workers in Providence: "What's the difference?" a young man asked on one occasion. "I have a friend down there [at the Metropole]; he plays around with us at night but in the daytime he is a white man and gets paid like the others." But that was not John Hope's way. He resented the attention his complexion engendered but seemed to relish every opportunity to reinforce his African American identity.[74]

John's work in Chicago caused him to miss a few weeks of the fall term. Although it was his senior year, Hope simply could not pass up the opportunity to make enough money to pay off his college debts. Yet it was more than just money keeping John in Chicago. Lugenia D. Burns, a lovely twenty-two-year-old African American woman, had swept Hope off his feet. The two met at the Columbian Dancing Party, a social function sponsored by the city's black elite. The party was a gala event with everyone dancing to the pulsating beats of the Second Regiment Band. Between the graceful waltzes, quick-paced quadrilles, and vivacious Bohemian polkas, John tried to become more than just one more suitor competing for Lugenia's attention. Jacqueline Rouse, who wrote a fine biography of Lugenia Hope, claimed Lugenia did not find John especially attractive; in fact, she was a little offended by "the steady gaze from his blue eyes."[75] The two did get together, and they dated frequently the rest of the summer. They went to the Columbian Exposition, although it is not clear whether or not they attended the controversial Colored People's Day events organized by Frederick Douglass.[76]

There were other dates, too—picnics, boat rides, and an occasional trip for an ice-cream soda. John had not had much experience with women, but he sensed something unusual about Lugenia. She was a fiercely independent woman whose desire to address the problems of her people matched Hope's own. Lugenia, however, had more experience and tended to dominate their conversations. Though she was born in St. Louis, the youngest of seven children, Lugenia had spent most of her life in Chicago and was now her mother's primary source of support. She worked for eight years in a printing company and as a seamstress. Later she was appointed the first African American secretary to the Board of Directors of Kings Daughters, a social service organization deeply respected in the community. Her experiences in the real world made Hope's struggles at Brown seem mundane. Perhaps that is why he left the relationship in Chicago open-ended. He may have believed that the worldly Lugenia was out of his league. Yet shortly after returning to Providence, he sent her a letter timidly asking her to help out a friend on his way to Chicago. The friend never arrived, but John's letters kept coming.[77]

Hope's senior year at Brown was as busy as the previous three, yet he performed both his academic duties and his work responsibilities with a happier disposition. He had paid off his debts to the university, although doing so left him with less than two dollars to his name. The funds he earned in Providence all went for tuition, and there was no money left to buy clothes. John's poverty must have been evident. A professor gave him a pair of secondhand trousers he had brought from Germany. "Can you imagine wearing a pair of these odd-looking breeches with an American-made coat?" he asked an amused audience many years later. Hope, however, went right through the year, "broke all the time, working when I could get work, and putting a hitch in my breeches when I couldn't get work and when invited out to a nice dinner I ate heartily but tried to act as if I had them every day." [78]

Two African American freshmen enrolled at Brown during Hope's senior year. One of them was his new roommate, Edward Delano Stewart of Mystic, Connecticut. Hope was closer, however, to Ted Owens, who adopted Hope as his mentor. Owens, who had prepared for Brown at Howard University, rarely made a move without Hope's advice—he asked his opinion on everything from housing in Providence to which instructors he should avoid on campus. The two men formed a relationship that lasted for the next thirty years. [79]

Hope's senior year passed quickly; soon he was preparing for graduation. His final examinations had given him little trouble, allowing him to concentrate on the Class Day activities scheduled for 15 June. He had been chosen as the class orator. Hope was not the first African American awarded that distinction at Brown, but few remembered Inman Edward Page of Washington, D.C., the first of his race to receive that honor. Page is usually credited with being one of the first two African Americans to matriculate at Brown. The other was another Washingtonian, George Washington Milford. Both graduated in 1877. [80]

Others were excited about John's oration in Sayles Hall even if he seemed unusually calm. Immediately preceding his address, the orchestra played "Old Brown," an appropriate tune to introduce Hope's oration, which was simply entitled "Brown University." John prefaced his remarks with moving tributes to Trimble, Makepeace, and Professor of Latin Language and Literature John Larkin Lincoln, a favorite teacher who also died during Hope's tenure at Brown. He then turned to his primary theme, the concept of the university as developed by a "superior Western Civilization." The oration was both an uncritical history of the West and a sermon of praise—equally uncritical—to Brown University itself: "Let us observe . . . that to have been at Brown University is to have drunk in the unpretentious, unobtrusive, yet all pervading idea of liberty and brotherhood, and to have acquired a breadth of culture which means the erasure of all lines, be they of race, or sect, or class, and recognize no claim other than that which highest manhood makes." [81]

The address epitomized the best that a late-nineteenth century Western-centered curriculum offered in 1894. Nevertheless, those in attendance may have been expecting something else, perhaps some acknowledgment, however subtle, that African Americans were living in a society that had not yet lived up to its democratic creed. In his graduation address four years earlier at Harvard, W. E. B. Du Bois ended with a dramatic line that paid tribute to Africans in the diaspora of North America: "You owe a debt to humanity for this Ethiopia of the Outstretched Arm." Yet John Hope's speech was conspicuous for its absence of any references to "his people" in America or anywhere else. [82]

This is not to suggest that an audience in 1894 would have accepted an oration whose thematic focus was the centrality of the African American experience. But there was excitement about a "Negro" delivering Brown's oration, and expectations were high. People were curious about what he would say as well as his ability to say it. After it was over, Ted Owens heard a woman outside the chapel remark: "I heard that a Negro was going to deliver the oration so I came to hear him; and after all, he was only a white boy." Her disappointment may have revealed more than a simple mistaken identity. It may have reflected her assessment of the oration itself. [83]

The Class Day exercises continued over the weekend in an unceasing round of festivities and entertainment, "a brilliant spectacle of everything calculated to dazzle," one newspaper described it. Later that afternoon there was the traditional tree planting, and late that evening the Promenade Concert. Seniors at Brown lived for the gaiety of the promenade, an outdoor concert that took place on the front campus. Young men and women dressed in evening attire heightened by "dazzling incandescent colors of fraternity insignia" formed a maze of colors in and about the campus, "constantly moving to the orchestral tunes of the Reeves American Band." Most of the participants ended up at the dance in the gymnasium hall or at one of the numerous "college spreads" hosted by Theta Delta Chi, Alpha Delta Phi, Delta Upsilon, or one of the other fraternities. [84]

Predictably, Hope's correspondence mentions none of these activities. Perhaps it was too painful for him. His heart was in Chicago with Lugenia, and the lovesick Hope found it difficult to go stag to celebrations meant for couples. Further, the social milieu at Brown had not changed. In spite of his praise of the university in his oration, neither racial nor gender discrimination had disappeared from Brown's social environs in 1894, and Hope's participation in the social activities of Class Day might not have been welcomed.

Certainly there were other things he deemed more important than parties.

John Hope was twenty-six years old and about to graduate from college, but he still remained unsure of what he wanted to do as a profession. Should he become a minister? His religious convictions had deepened during his years at Brown, but there is no evidence that he had been able to resolve the conflict between science and religion that had bothered him at the end of his Worcester Academy days. Teaching had become increasingly attractive to him. President Andrews certainly encouraged him to take that direction, and had done so from the beginning of his freshman year.[85] It was not Andrews who first opened Hope's eyes to the joys of teaching, however, but an experience in the Providence African American community.

Hope seems never to have mentioned to anyone at Brown that it was John Mercer Langston who led him to view teaching as a serious career option. It happened during Langston's visit during John's freshman year, when Hope and several people met with the congressman in his hotel room. Suddenly Langston recognized a former student and began to reminiscence about being an old teacher who loved teaching and was at home in the schoolroom. Langston's emotional response startled John. "The way in which he made the remark, the beam on the countenance of the young man as they looked into each other's face, gave me a new insight into this man of whom I knew up to that time especially as a political figure."

Hope probably did not recognize in 1890 that teachers rarely see the fruits of their labors. More often than not, students go on to the next stage in their lives while teachers remain behind to educate a new group. Hope recognized something majestic in the reunion between Langston and his former student, but only years later was he able to articulate exactly what he felt: "There they stood, student and teacher, eyeing each other as visions of past association came into their minds, the master who had started the questing fire in this young man, the young man who remembered with gratitude the new, strange fire and felt a new glow with his old teacher."[86]

By the time Hope entered his senior year, teaching overshadowed the ministry as an immediate career choice. Yet he delayed making the final decision. The issue was more complex than it appeared on the surface. Hope's white complexion provided him with more options than he actually wanted. He had never wavered on his racial identity and had consistently chosen to cast his lot with other African Americans who shared his collective experiences. It was a decision rife with danger. African American life in the 1890s, especially in the South, was disgracefully cheap.

His white teachers at Brown forced Hope to consider another option. It was well known that he intended to return to the South. The afternoon before commencement, John was summoned by a faculty advisory committee to present his plans. No record of the conversation exists, but Hope later shared his

WORCESTER AND BROWN 65

memory of the deliberations with his friend Ted Owens. The chairman of the committee was the stern Professor John H. Appleton, whose icy glare through horn-rimmed spectacles was as foreboding as it had been in chemistry class, where Hope had not done well. Appleton wore an unusually long handlebar mustache with an equally thick full beard that together revealed little of his mouth. According to Owens, when Appleton spoke, he emitted a muffled sound that seemed to be coming from someone else.[87]

It was Appleton's job to find out if Hope did indeed plan to return to the South, and if so, to persuade him to forsake his African American identity and live in New England as a white man. Allegedly, a position had already been secured for him at the *Providence Journal*, the city's leading newspaper. Appleton acknowledged that he knew Hope was anxious to work among his own people, but he dismissed the idea as "very foolish. Because if you do, it will be measured merely by a Negro yardstick."[88] John had heard all that before. His white friends at Brown had likewise tried to persuade him to choose their world with its unlimited opportunities, and he was well aware of the segregated and inferior world that increasingly engulfed African Americans. Still he remained undaunted, although he promised the committee he would think about it.

Hope, of course, had decided to return to the South, even though his friends thought his decision "not only quixotic but foolish." They could not understand a voluntary return to such an oppressive existence. In their minds, any rational person would seize the opportunity to escape, to pass for white. What his friends failed to realize is that John Hope was socialized by his formative years in Augusta long before he arrived in New England, although his roommate Frank Trimble may have reinforced that early socialization. And peculiar as it must have seemed to them, most African Americans were not willing to give up their black identity and escape at all costs.

More than anything else, it was the centrality of Hope's socialization as an African American that contributed to his dilemma over choosing a career. Within black America, professionals were expected to assume some responsibility for the improvement of their race, and that realization had to be factored into any career choice. That expectation further complicated Hope's options. It was more than a simple choice between occupations, and "to pass or not to pass" was not even a serious consideration. What was most difficult for John Hope was deciding on a profession that best suited his personality and was also commensurate with his obligation to assume some responsibility as an African American leader.

John Hope marched into the historic First Baptist Meeting House as part of the 126th Brown University Commencement exercise at 9:00 A.M. on

Wednesday, 20 June 1894. It was the largest class ever to graduate. John perhaps smiled as his friend Harold Dexter Hazeltine, a classmate since Worcester days, read his oration called the "Destiny of Africa." Hazeltine's call for a more enlightened policy toward Africa offered a welcome respite from the brutality carried out in the name of Manifest Destiny and the "white man's burden," the rationales that dominated most official Western thinking on Africa in the late nineteenth century. John Hope would maintain a strong interest in African affairs for the remainder of his life.[89]

Yet his smile at commencement may also have been in response to thoughts of the promising future that lay just ahead. He had accepted a teaching position at Roger Williams University, a struggling liberal arts institution for African Americans in Nashville, Tennessee. His colleagues and friends at Brown probably shook their heads in disagreement, if not disgust, but they wished him well anyway. It was not yet a permanent career decision, for he had not closed the door on the ministry. John Hope was returning to the South, and there, among "his people," he would make the final decision.

4

The Return South: Nashville

John Hope's return to the South began with a detour to Richfield Springs, New York, where he spent the summer working as a waiter in a fashionable restaurant. The bills for his final year at Brown had not yet been paid, and he refused to arrive at his first job penniless. At Richfield Springs, Hope met another African American waiter who was also working to pay for his college expenses. William Taylor Burwell Williams was a brilliant undergraduate at Harvard University whose quest for a first-class education equaled Hope's.

Born in Virginia, W. T. B. Williams was a year younger than John Hope. He attended the public schools in Clarke County and then taught there when he was only seventeen. He next enrolled in Hampton Institute's normal course and taught in the elementary department after graduation. Before arriving at Harvard in 1893, Williams spent four years at Phillips Academy, a prestigious preparatory school in Andover, Massachusetts. After graduating from Harvard, Williams went on to an illustrious career in education and government service. The two young men formed a close friendship that summer that lasted for many, many years.[1]

John could always count on Williams to say the right things: "You are right in believing that there are in you the instincts of a gentleman," Williams wrote to Hope in response to one of John's recurring moments of self-doubt. "They are no latent propensities either, believe me, my boy. They are the things that have won you friends and admirers everywhere. To uproot them, if it were possible, would be to destroy John Hope as we know him." Williams was free with advice on affairs of the heart as well as the mind.[2]

John Hope finally arrived in Nashville in September 1894. On one level the change of location was refreshing, for it ushered in a new phase in Hope's widening range of experiences. His teaching contract perhaps said it best. Roger Williams University Teacher's Certificate no. 17714 stated that John's eight-month appointment was to commence on the first of October 1894 at a salary of $500. Like the other ten faculty members, including the president, Hope was required to raise $1,000 from outside sources and pay it into the treasury of the American Baptist Home Mission Society (ABHMS) no later than April 15, 1895. Faculty who failed to raise all the money were docked the equivalent amount from their salaries.[3] It is difficult to believe that the stiff ABHMS rule was enforced, but even if the entire salary was paid, it was a paltry sum. John was satisfied nevertheless. The country was still in the midst of a depression, and he had never earned more. With his return to the South, Hope looked forward to a promising career and a more prosperous economic future.

On another level, John's return was a mixed blessing for him. All was not well in the South at the turn of the century. As early as 1871, when John was still a child, southern Democrats had mounted a vigorous campaign to "redeem" the South in the name of white supremacy, "redemption" being a veiled code for "black disfranchisement." The Compromise of 1877 left the door open for widespread racial violence and intimidation. Poll taxes and literacy clauses were introduced in the 1880s, further restricting blacks' already meager political power. By the 1890s, black disfranchisement legislation had cropped up in state legislatures throughout the South. It was merely a matter of time before African Americans' participation in the political process came virtually to a halt.[4]

In the view of historian Rayford Logan, the Compromise of 1877 ushered in the "let alone" policy of President Rutherford B. Hayes and initiated a downward spiral that reached dead center during the Cleveland administrations in the 1890s. Democrat Grover Cleveland, elected for his second term as president in 1892, was not unlike most of his predecessors who occupied the presidency after the Compromise. He too believed African Americans were better off in a "reconstructed South." In any case, Cleveland had his hands full trying to deal with a devastating depression, mediating the debate over the silver or gold standard, and placating an incipient radical agrarian reform movement whose economic concerns would soon garner enough strength to become a potent political force. In 1894, however, Cleveland found the time to sign several bills that erased many of the remaining vestiges of Reconstruction legislation from federal statutes. He had already opposed a federal elections law, he approved the virtual disfranchisement of African Americans in Mississippi, and he stood silently by as Ben "Pitchfork" Tillman vociferously demanded that similar measures be taken in South Carolina.[5]

Segregation steadily increased throughout the South in those years, economic opportunity was often determined by skin color, and the image of African Americans as inferior beings biologically incapable of high achievement appeared practically everywhere. The 1890s also saw an unprecedented number of lynchings, most of them in the South. John Hope was particularly aware of these developments in Georgia, especially in his hometown, Augusta. Although there were not many lynchings in Augusta in the 1890s, economic opportunities for blacks were decreasing, and black political appointments were increasingly challenged. Reminiscing about politics in Augusta during his boyhood, Hope wrote around the turn of the century that "then the opposition was to Republicans, today it is to Negroes. It is not a party line, but a race line."

Black leaders in Augusta, including one of Hope's brothers-in-law, loudly protested racist reporting in white newspapers and the use of scientific racism to justify African American disfranchisement. The aging black activist William J. White joined in the protest through the pages of his newspaper, the *Georgia Baptist*. He sharply criticized the usually friendly *Augusta Chronicle* for encouraging its readers to draw the color line in employment practices. In 1893, Aunt Nannie also noticed the downward trend in economic opportunities: "There is nothing that a colored man can get to do [in Augusta]," she wrote to her nephew John. "He has either to sit on a carriage box or wait on some white man's table or dig in the ground." Eventually the unfriendly racial atmosphere drove two of Hope's sisters and their families permanently out of the South.[6]

John's return to the South placed him once again in a world that was more black than white. The history of Roger Williams University, which began as the Nashville Institute in 1867, set the stage for his reentry into the heart of black America. The school owed its beginnings to the confusion during the years immediately following the Civil War in the South when newly freed men and women were passionately interested in acquiring an education. They would gather around anyone, black or white, who was willing to teach them the mysteries of reading, writing, and arithmetic. Daniel W. Phillips, a northern Baptist minister who had been educated at Brown University and Newton Theological Seminary, was the minister of a Baptist church in Nashville. He also taught a class for African American ministers in his home. The class quickly outgrew the residence and the church, forcing Phillips to seek larger facilities. Although other African American churches immediately answered the call, they soon realized that the demand for black education far outstripped any church's capacity to provide space. African Americans in Nashville convinced Phillips that a permanent building was absolutely essential.[7]

Phillips was also a member of the American Baptist Home Mission Society, one of the numerous missionary organizations that ventured south after the war to minister to the needs of the freedmen. With funds raised during trips to the North, he eventually purchased a building in Nashville and moved his school to a site near Fort Gilliam, northwest of downtown. In August 1867, the Nashville Institute opened with two teachers. By the middle 1870s the school had once again outgrown its space. Phillips at first eyed a spot at Fort Gilliam perched high above the school's present location, but that site had already been secured for Fisk Free Colored School (later renamed Fisk University), sponsored by the ABHMS's arch competitor, the American Missionary Association (AMA).[8]

In the 1880s a new site was found on thirty acres of land about two miles south of Nashville on a gentle slope facing the city. In 1883 the school was incorporated as Roger Williams University. The "university" part of the name was ambitious, more a reflection of where the school wanted to go than how far it had actually come. Yet the new name was not totally farfetched. Roger Williams University had granted its first A.B. degree in 1877. It became the first ABHMS school to offer college work and continued to lead all of the missionary organization's schools in the size of its college student body until it closed its doors in 1905.[9]

When Hope arrived at Roger Williams in 1894, the school was still recovering from a scandal that had begun in 1887 and was not settled until several years later. Student activists had charged several administrators, including the incumbent president, William H. Stifler, with a number of offenses. The treasurer and superintendent of industrial work was accused of everything from unscrupulous financial dealings to serving "nauseous food and accusing students of theft." He was also charged with propositioning a white female instructor and a black female student. For these insults, student leaders wrote in a local newspaper, "the boys would have used a rope, but for good old Dr. Phillips."[10] The signature of F. L. Trimble appeared on many of the students' petitions—most likely it was the same Frank Levi Trimble who roomed with Hope later at Brown until his death in 1892.

President Stifler refused to meet with the students and denied their request to meet with the school's board of trustees. The local African American community sided with the students, as, eventually, did most of the faculty and the local board of trustees. The ABHMS would not relinquish control over the school, but did dismiss the president and the treasurer. The society also wanted to expel the major student leaders of the rebellion. The controversy brought out into the open an issue that had been brewing for years: Who was really in control of ABHMS-sponsored institutions? In addition to concerns over the extent of African American control, regional factors were involved as well: North versus South, and local versus national control of what was perceived as a community institution. Records show that the student leaders of the protest did graduate, but the situation was not completely resolved until 1890.[11]

President Stifler's replacement died of a heart attack only months after taking office. His supporters blamed the death on stress produced by the contro-versy. Alfred Owen, the president when Hope arrived, had been appointed to the post in 1887. Presidents of ABHMS schools personally interviewed and briefed each new faculty member about their schools' academic and religious culture. We do not know whether Hope's briefing included information on the recent scandal.

If John Hope knew of the scandal at Roger Williams when he arrived in 1894, he kept it to himself. Many of those around him knew, of course, and sto-ries continued to circulate around the campus. The math professor, John W. Johnson, knew almost everything there was to know about the scandal. He had been one of the original student leaders of the rebellion, although he was later denounced as a traitor when he refused to sign a telegram from the students giving ABHMS headquarters an ultimatum.[12] Born of free parents before the Civil War, the tall, handsome, light-skinned Johnson had also struggled to get an education. Hope met him at breakfast on his first morning on campus, and the two became close friends. In later years Johnson would become Roger Williams's first African American president.[13]

In spite of all the turmoil, Hope was genuinely happy at Roger Williams University. Its strong religious character and dedication to Christian prin-ciples made him feel very much at home. Many of the practices at Roger Williams were no different from those at Worcester Academy and Brown. He did not mind that all the faculty and administrators were staunch Baptists who were expected to concern themselves as much with the students' souls as with their ability to read, write, and do arithmetic. Each day began with chapel services, and boarding students ended their evenings with prayer in their dor-mitories. Daily Bible classes were a mandatory part of the school's curriculum, and students were required to attend church all day on Sundays. To ensure there was no mistake about the school's mission, administrators maintained records on students who continued to be "sinners," and ABHMS headquarters expected periodic progress reports on student conversions to Christianity. It was standard procedure at missionary schools, and Hope was very comfortable with it.[14]

For the first time, though, John Hope was on the other side of the podium. At Worcester and Brown he had been the recipient of religious and academic instruction and had looked to the faculty for guidance. At Roger Williams he was expected to be the mentor, to disseminate valuable knowledge to students as enthusiastic about learning as he had been only a short time before. It was not always an easy task. During Hope's four years at Roger Williams the an-nual student enrollment hovered around 175, and a mere ten faculty members tried to offer the same range of courses as would be found at the elite northern universities. Everything was taught—from Latin, Greek, history, and science to modern languages, business, and law. Hope taught science, which was not his favorite subject. More than once, J. W. Johnson had to come to his rescue.

On one occasion, however, Hope managed to rescue himself. One of his students, Arthur M. Townsend, who became the valedictorian of his class (and later the president of Roger Williams), remembered Hope conducting an experiment during that first year that went haywire. There was a sudden explosion. Instead of a protective Hope following his hurrying students to safety in the yard outside, however, the science professor led the charge. Two years later, Hope helped raise money to build a science lab. It was his first attempt at fund-raising, but he knew from personal experience how much the lab was needed.[15]

No faculty member had the luxury of teaching only in the area specified in his contract. In addition to science (which he would have gladly given up), Hope jumped at the opportunity to teach Greek and Latin. Students remembered that his knowledge of the classics was second only to that of Dr. Owen, the president of the college. The extra classes were a mixed blessing. Hope welcomed the extra pay he received for teaching additional classes, yet he often wound up with six or seven classes, and preparing for them left little time for the other responsibilities expected of ABHMS teachers.[16]

Nevertheless, Hope did more than just teach. The mission society officials demanded that faculty and administrators take their religious mission as seriously as they did academics. Hope attended all school-sponsored religious gatherings and frequently led the services himself. The pious Hope maintained an open-door policy when it came to students but extended himself even more to those who had not yet accepted Christianity. In 1896 Hope revealed to his future wife, Lugenia Burns, that students sought him out for religious counseling, which often took place in the privacy of his room on Sundays following one of the three services. Some of these sessions often went on for more than an hour of intense testimony, confession, and reading selected passages from the Bible. "I got down on my knees and prayed for him," Hope wrote about a student who visited him on a typical Sunday evening. John's religious resolve was often tested: "In such moments I feel my spiritual weakness, and long for more grace from God." Actually his religious base was solid, and his interactions with students on spiritual matters matched his academic zeal in the classroom.[17]

Unlike Worcester and Brown, Roger Williams University had women students. Teaching women was a new experience for John Hope. They were considerably younger than the male students, averaging only seventeen years to the males' twenty-five. School administrators and community leaders were especially sensitive to the presence of women after the allegations that sparked the student revolt of 1886, and took measures to ensure that rectitude prevailed. Students were forbidden to smoke, play cards, dance, and utter profanities, of course, in line with the rigid New England Victorian code of conduct espoused by all ABHMS schools. Roger Williams, however, added some rules that applied only to women. Most referred to types of clothing. For instance, no jewelry was allowed, nor were silk, satin, velvet, or "fancy trimmed dresses" or hats, even for church or commencement. Women were forbidden to leave the campus except under emergency circumstances, and males and females were not permitted to visit each other's dormitories under any circumstances. In fact, male and female students interacted very little beyond the watchful eyes of the seasoned and vigilant dean of women and other female chaperons who monitored campus behavior.[18]

Along with the other faculty members, Hope shared the responsibility of ensuring that the rules governing interactions between male and female students were strictly enforced. On one occasion during his first year, a male and female student dared to walk across the campus grounds in broad daylight holding hands. The incident had the whole campus buzzing, and no one was surprised when both students were expelled. A faculty member remembered that Hope thought it was the right decision. Later, as the president of Morehouse College, Hope continued to believe that the ideal college educated male and female students separately. Rigid codes of conduct existed at both black and white schools in the 1890s, of course, but African American schools tended to retain their puritanical rules long after these had been abandoned by their white counterparts.[19]

Students did not take up all of Hope's time at Roger Williams University. He took brisk three-mile walks to keep himself fit. Sometimes the walks took him across Hillsboro Road, through the Vanderbilt campus, and all the way into urban Nashville. Yet the university's country setting suited John perfectly. The teachers lived a relatively spartan existence in their quarters in Hayward Hall, a large and spacious building constructed in part by students in 1886. In those days, there was no indoor plumbing, gas, or electricity anywhere on campus, even in the president's quarters. Now and then, John left his upstairs room to spend an evening playing sports—sometimes tennis but more often football. "Football is no game for a coward. I am no player, but do not fear to play and I do play," Hope insisted in a letter to Lugenia. Apparently, his enthusiasm for the sport had not waned in the years since he was first introduced to it at Worcester Academy.

Football was still quite new in the 1890s. No equipment protected players in those days, and at only five feet seven inches and 135 pounds, Hope was by no means a big man. The sport nevertheless had a strange allure for him. It was more than an athletic contest between two robust teams, each trying to score more touchdowns than the other. Hope developed a race-based philosophy that rationalized the game as sound training for black leaders destined to confront a hostile, racist environment. In his view, the game instilled discipline and determination: "I try to put games into prominence among our people," Hope wrote in a revealing letter to Lugenia. "Sports teach them how to contest without losing self-respect. It is a means of acquiring bravery and gentility." Hope believed that the heightened adrenaline levels that accompanied the game's physical requirements and maddening pace contributed to a highly charged emotionalism that sharpened the senses: "The man who can't get his blood up, can't yell his throat hoarse on an occasion, who can't throw his arm around the man who makes a good play and almost . . . curse a man who makes a bad one, is a cold, bloodless sort of an individual. Such a man cannot easily resent an insult. The same instincts that make a man love dangerous sports make him dare to do noble deeds."

In his second year at Roger Williams, Hope volunteered to coach the school's first football team, and he would support the sport later in Atlanta when Morehouse developed a championship team. There is no reason to believe that he was not sincere when he wrote: "I know of no game that can do so much for developing sportsmanship among my people as football, and it is with some such notion that I am giving it my time and interest."[20]

In addition to physical activity, Hope read voraciously in his leisure time and tried his hand at writing poetry. He spent some of his spare time in the Nashville African American community. Roger Williams was only two miles from Nashville, a large city by southern standards and full of African Americans who had migrated there soon after the Civil War. Their situation was an all-too-familiar refrain. By the 1890s, most of them were tucked away in unsanitary slums with few municipal services and rampant disease. Nashville had its own "Hell's Half Acre" and "Black Bottom," names commonly given to black slums in urbanizing black America all over the country.

Nor did the rising tide of racism that swept across America in the 1890s bypass Nashville. By 1894, the state had passed a poll tax, Democrats had adopted the all-white primary, and other electoral hurdles were in place that practically eliminated the black vote. Segregation's sprawling tentacles separated everything from seating at the racetrack to burial in the cemeteries. Most African American males in Nashville worked in unskilled jobs, and close to half of all black women worked outside the home, most in domestic occupations.[21]

In 1892, two years before Hope arrived, an estimated ten thousand men, women, and children witnessed a particularly brutal lynching that took place in broad daylight. An African American man accused of rape was forcibly removed from the city jail, lassoed with a rope, and then thrown over the Cumberland River bridge with the noose still drawn tight around his neck. Some members of the mob amused themselves by snapping the rope up and down,

then riddling the dead body with bullets. One year earlier there had been several unprovoked attacks by whites on black bystanders. One man claimed he
had simply awakened from a drunken stupor "to the sight of a Negro boy leaning against a pole and had plunged a knife into his heart." After two more
blacks were murdered, a local newspaper warned that "human life—even
though it be that of a Negro—is not of so little value that our whole people
will not be shocked and astounded at seeing it snuffed out." Obviously the
"human life of a Negro" was as cheap in Nashville in the 1890s as it was elsewhere in the South.[22]

The black Nashville that Hope knew best contrasted sharply with the squa-
lor of the slums, whose residents were the ones most likely to be victims of
racist whites. Hope usually socialized with Nashville's African American elite,
aristocrats of color with class origins similar to his own. Many were mulattoes
and almost white in appearance, and most had achieved some notoriety as a
result of wealth, occupation, or education and could point to family members
free before the Civil War.[23]

The Napiers—James Carroll and Nettie Langston—were the first family of
upper-class black Nashville. Napier was one of four children born near Nashville of free black parents in 1845. He was educated at a private school for
African American youth in Nashville and later attended Wilberforce University and Oberlin College in Ohio. In 1868 his association with the Republican
party in Nashville landed him a job at the State Department in Washington,
D.C. There Napier caught the attention of Hope's hero, John Mercer Langston, who encouraged him to get a law degree from Howard University. In
1872 Napier returned home to Nashville and set up a law practice, at the same
time dabbling in real estate and increasing his influence in the state Republican
party. Napier's career really took off in 1878 when he married Nettie Langston, John Mercer Langston's daughter. In addition to building a successful
law practice, Napier held several government appointments under four presidents, served seven years on the Nashville City Council, and was a successful
businessman and banker.[24]

Nettie Langston Napier was born Nettie DeElla Langston in Oberlin,
Ohio, in 1861. Before marrying Napier in 1878, she attended Howard University for one year and then transferred to Oberlin College to complete her
studies in music at the Oberlin Conservatory. It was Nettie Napier, a charming hostess with an outgoing personality and pleasant sense of humor, who was
mentioned most frequently in Hope's correspondence. She alone seemed able
to penetrate Hope's icy exterior and keep him consciously aware of his aloof
demeanor. "She takes very little stock in my association with you [Lugenia
Burns] or anyone else I suppose," Hope wrote affectionately about Nettie
Napier. "She gives me credit for a coldness that does not admit of such things

as affection." Even Hope's "cold, dead, old handshake" did not escape the attention of the observant and humorous Nettie. Unable to master the "pump-
handle shake," John confessed that he tended to "press the hand like the
French" instead.[25] As the first lady of Nashville's black elite, Nettie Langston
Napier was often singled out in local newspapers as "a leader in the colored
social circles of Nashville" and the "model woman."[26]

The site of John's first meeting with the Napiers remains a mystery, but it
was probably at the unnamed social club Hope frequently mentioned in his
letters to Lugenia. Within a year of his arrival in Nashville Hope had become
a frequent visitor in the Napier household, the undisputed center of Nashville's African American upper class. Newspaper coverage of the Napiers and
other Nashville aristocrats of color was not always favorable. The "bright colored" Napiers on occasion found themselves answering charges of separating
themselves from other African Americans and drawing a color line within their
own racial group. The Napiers' wedding was a case in point. Napier married
Nettie Langston in 1878. The ceremony took place in Washington, D.C., in
the predominantly white Congregational church where the Langston family
worshipped. One Ohio newspaper reported that five hundred invitations went
out—with half going to whites, "and no person of *dark* [emphasis in original]
color being included." James Napier vehemently protested the account but
added that while "true in respect to his marriage in Washington," it was "false
in every other particular." In other words, he practiced no color discrimination after he returned to Nashville.[27]

Some African Americans in Nashville frowned on the black upper class for
their elitist lifestyle and color-conscious social functions. Years later, when the
light-skinned Arthur Langston (Nettie's brother) married the equally "bright"
Ida Napier (James's sister) at the family home, one newspaper reported it "took
but a glance to discover that those present represented the intelligentsia of
their race." There was also criticism of the city's "Blue Vein Society"—African Americans with complexions so light that their blue veins were easily visible. Local folklore among Nashville's black community long had it, incorrectly, that Fisk University, which educated many elite family members, had
been founded to educate the black children of white fathers. It was also a
common belief that Howard Chapel, an American Missionary Association–
supported Congregational church attended primarily by the city's black elite,
"opened its membership only to those who were light."[28]

One can only speculate on Hope's perceptions of the black upper class and
whether he felt a part of it during his years in Nashville. His correspondence
provides a few clues. References to a black elite appear only in his letters to
Lugenia, often concealed in descriptive subordinate phrases, and even then
reveal only his perceptions of black "society" (Hope's generation's term for

the African American upper class) in Washington, D.C., not in Nashville. By the 1890s the African American elite in Washington, which Willard Gatewood referred to as the "Capital of the Colored Aristocracy," was often characterized by its lavish and exclusive social functions, color prejudice, ambivalence toward the masses, and relative economic security. Increasingly in the 1890s, celebrations like Emancipation Day, an event Hope had enjoyed since his boyhood in Augusta, were shunned by Washington's "black 400." One African American newspaper editor wrote that "if any of the leading colored citizens of Washington . . . looked at the Emancipation procession . . . at all, it was just as the leading white citizens looked at it."[29]

Without doubt Hope did not look favorably on the African American upper class, especially in Washington. The group's elitism and lavish displays of wealth and refinement offended him. "I do not care to go into society and should much rather be away from here," he wrote to Lugenia while on a visit to Washington. When by necessity Hope was forced to stay in the city, he made a special effort to stay with friends who in his words were "not 'society' people."[30]

If John never commented specifically on color prejudice among the black elite, he was nevertheless well aware that a person with an almost white complexion and Caucasian features was more likely to be accepted into their ranks than someone without them, regardless of other qualifications. In cities like Washington, even though it did not guarantee his acceptance, his complexion caused African Americans (and perhaps some whites) to rush him off to meet other aristocrats of color, believing that he must identify with them and desire to move in their circles. Without mentioning color, John wrote to Lugenia from Washington that he did not like "being paraded," even though his temperament would not permit him to refuse a direct invitation. He usually avoided being placed in that position by keeping a social distance between himself and the African American elite. "I can tell you much about Washington society," he again revealed to Lugenia, "for, while I have not been in it, I have known of it for years through good sources for reliable information."[31]

John's views on Washington society seem to contradict his social behavior in Nashville. He often attended the teas, balls, literary society meetings, and especially the plays frequented by Nashville's upper-class elite. It was not unusual for him to attend respectable events like the "grand musical and literary entertainment" sponsored by the YMCA at Spruce Street Baptist Church. He would not, however, be found at Nashville's Oddfellows Hall, or any local club, listening to "Mr. Dock Lines" provide music for the "Barnyard Dance." He was equally opposed to what he called "that infernal rag-time music," whose cadence he thought "peculiarly the property of our people." "I have seen it now in secular pleasure and heightened religious expression," he wrote to

Lugenia, and it is "a part of the Negro emotional Nature to use that time and movement." John believed that the popular ragtime made "men and women, boys and girls forget their surroundings" and put them "in direct line by a very short route from the dance floor to the deepest hell." [32]

But it was not only his perceptions of what constituted proper music and entertainment that placed Hope among the elite. He socialized with the Napiers, and on at least two occasions dated Ida Napier before her marriage to Arthur Langston. John was also no stranger to Howard Chapel. Although it was not restricted to a light-skinned elite, as many thought, Howard Chapel was an upper-class church very similar to his own Union Baptist Church in Augusta, whose members were also very "bright." Hope was a good friend of Jesse Moorland, the chapel's light-skinned minister (and also of free black ancestry), in Nashville, and the two would become even closer a few years later. [33]

There were other obvious similarities between John Hope's preferences and those of Nashville's upper-class elite. He not only possessed the free ancestry and education, he was also pursuing an "acceptable" occupation and measured the existence of culture by a European yardstick. Nevertheless, Hope did not see himself as a black aristocrat. In his mind, the point of separation between the upper class and himself was rooted in the economic opportunities free blacks passed on to their offspring born after freedom. Nettie Langston and James Carroll Napier, for example, had inherited the opportunities that paved the way for each to obtain a high-quality education and set them on the road to material prosperity.

John Hope believed that he had not been that lucky. Although he too was born with a "silver spoon in his mouth," that spoon was yanked away after his father's death. From that point on, his life, and that of his family, while still privileged in many respects, was fraught with hardship and struggle. Financial hardship terminated the education of his oldest brother and sister and forced another sister to postpone the completion of hers. John himself struggled for eight years to get a first-class education at Worcester Academy and Brown, more often than not working to pay his own way. In Augusta and Providence, his fellow workers were primarily from the working class, even though some of them, especially in Augusta, were as white as he. John's interpretation of his own life thus set him outside the experience of the African American elite. Their snobbishness and elitism annoyed him, and he disapproved of their ostentatious lifestyle.

Further, John Hope's financial situation was still a source of much worry. He was in his late twenties and had finally finished school, but he was still struggling to make ends meet. He wanted to marry a woman who expected financial security. Hope may have envied the economic security of the African

American elite, and perhaps his perceptions of them stemmed from his dissatisfaction with his own situation.

John identified much more closely with the new middle class that was rising in power and influence within black America. Its members in many ways represented the black side of the Horatio Alger story. Many, like John, were still in the process of raising themselves up by their own bootstraps. That group included friends like Ted Owens, W. T. B. Williams, and his colleague J. W. Johnson, as well as people in Augusta like Madison Newton, his brother-in-law Judson Lyons, and educators such as Georgia Swift, Lucy Laney, and Richard R. Wright. And John would probably have agreed that success through struggle marked not only his own life but also the life of another up-and-coming African American leader named Booker T. Washington.[34]

The cluster of African American schools in Nashville gave birth to the city's burgeoning black middle class. Crowned by students as the "colored Athens of the South," Nashville boasted of Roger Williams and Fisk Universities, Central Tennessee College (later Walden University), Meharry Medical College (which broke away from Central Tennessee), and later Tennessee Agricultural and Industrial State Normal School (which became Tennessee State University). These schools produced doctors, lawyers, businessmen, educators, ministers, and other professionals. The new southern African American middle class was in many ways similar to the upper-class elite. Certainly many graduates of Fisk and Roger Williams were light skinned, and almost all of them enjoyed the same social activities as the elite. Black middle-class graduates of the city's colleges were also critical of the behavior and social activities of the black rank and file, and believed their only salvation lay in education and the adoption of a "high" European culture.[35]

The fine line that distinguished the black upper class from the black middle class may have been, as Hope believed, inherited opportunity versus self-made opportunity. Surely there was overlap between the two classes in Nashville's black "world-within-a-world." Historian Faye Robbins recognized the existence of an upper-class elite in Nashville, yet believed that the line separating the middle class from the upper class in the 1890s "cannot be drawn with the evenness of a board sawed in two pieces, but is more like the jagged edge of one broken across the knee." On reflection, John Hope probably would have agreed.[36]

John's first year in Nashville passed quickly. At the end of the spring term in 1895 he turned in his grades and took a train directly to Chicago. The pretext for his trip was the University of Chicago's popular and affordable program in religious studies, where Hope took two classes in theology. He had not yet completely given up on the ministry, though his interest was fading, but there was a stronger pull. Lugenia Burns lived in Chicago, and while he was staying in the dormitory at the university he was close to his "Genie." John's friend Ted Owens, who was still an undergraduate at Brown, was not fooled by John's interest in studying theology. On hearing of John's plans, he quickly concluded: "What John's studying is that girl." [37]

Even before he reached Nashville John knew that he wanted to marry Lugenia Burns; his interest in her had not waned one iota. That first year in Nashville, John kept Lugenia's postman busy delivering bulky letters daily. Sometimes a twenty-page letter would have a ten-page postscript. In passionate and poetic words he tried to convey the depth of his love for her. Letters that began with casual news of family members, his work at Roger Williams, or how he spent his leisure time somehow wound up as testaments to his love and pleas for an early marriage.

He was not yet secure in his relationship with Lugenia, for there were still many unanswered questions. Love was a new emotion to the rather icy John Hope, and the ups and downs of the long-distance relationship sent him clamoring for advice. How should he approach Lugenia, and what should he expect of her? Was it really fair to ask a woman raised in the relative comfort of the North to wed a man who had committed himself to a life in the turbulent South? Uncharacteristically, John sought answers from everybody he respected. In addition to his family, especially Aunt Nannie, John consulted his friends W. T. B. Williams at Harvard and Ted Owens at Brown. With Owens he was a bit more cautious; he and Hope had pledged not to consider marriage for another ten years.

He received varying answers. Owens and Williams thought John was being too hard on himself, "accentuating the negative and undermining the positive," as Owens described it. Williams tried to convince Hope that he was "not the meanest creature God ever made, God has richly endowed you and has made you for far better purposes than self-introspection." Aunt Nannie advised him to think about his strengths, his commitment to family, and his strong moral character. The relationship was still new in 1894, and all of his confidants advised him to spend more time with Lugenia before coming to a permanent decision. John planned to do just that in Chicago. [38]

All in all, it was an enjoyable summer. His classes at the University of Chicago went remarkably well, and John even contemplated working on a graduate degree. The time spent with Lugenia deepened their relationship, although John brooded over the fact that no formal engagement materialized. Twenty-four-year-old Lugenia was no passive player in this game of love. She remained cautious, hesitant, and noncommittal, even while she enjoyed Hope's passionate letters and displays of affection. Lugenia was always direct and could never be accused of hiding anything from her "Jack," including her reservations about becoming his wife. It was no secret that she had other suitors. She questioned John's ability to support her and did not relish the thought of life in the South. Notwithstanding her own male suitors, Lugenia was not enthusiastic about Hope dating other women, and he knew the Burns family was lukewarm to him at best.[39]

With his mind still on Lugenia, John headed south to Augusta to spend some time with his family before the beginning of the new academic year. Though his visits had become rare, Hope wrote home almost daily while he was at Roger Williams. The Ellis Street homestead was still the clan's center, but there had been changes since Hope left Augusta nine years earlier. John's favorite aunt, Nannie, then forty-eight, still resided in the household along with his mother, Mary Frances Butts. His youngest sisters, Grace, twenty-four, and Anna, twenty-two, were still unmarried and also lived at home. Grace and Anna taught school in the city's Fourth Ward. John's older brother, Madison (also called Buddie), thirty-six, the only male in the household, continued to work at the city post office. Thomas Hope, John's eighteen-year-old younger brother, was away at Worcester Academy. Georgia Frances (Sissie), Jane, and Alethea, Hope's older sisters, had all married and maintained households of their own in Augusta.

Grace and Anna were happy enough, and it was to them that John revealed things about himself that he would tell only a close brother or sister. Grace learned, for example, that John was attracted to northern women, particularly (though this was probably unknown to Lugenia) New Englanders. He also enjoyed cooking, particularly fish and other meats, but continued to stay away from alcohol and tobacco.[40]

Other family members did not seem happy, and John worried about them. Fifty-five-year-old Mary Frances ventured out of the house a bit more now than she had in the years immediately following James Hope's death, though she continued to wear only drab, dark clothing. Cakewalks sponsored by the church still excited her, and she enjoyed picnics in the park with her grandchildren. Nevertheless, Hope was convinced that his mother was lonely. Many of her friends, including some of the older Barefields, Harpers, and Ladevezes, had died or moved away. John often remarked that his mother was only in her mid-thirties when his father died, yet there was never another man in her life. He blamed himself for her loneliness and felt guilty about leaving home.

Mary Frances did little to assuage that guilt. She made sure that her son never forgot the words James Hope whispered to her the day John was born: "This child will be a comfort to you and will never leave your side." The words haunted John whenever he returned from a visit or read one of her letters. No matter how cheerful his mother tried to be, Hope always sensed a melancholy tone that left him feeling depressed and guilty.[41]

Hope worried about other family members as well. Buddie was thirty-six and still single, and he wanted desperately to leave the South. He had tried unsuccessfully to open a restaurant, and his other business ventures in partnership with his uncles never quite got off the ground. Buddie continued to keep an eye open for opportunities outside the region, but jobs were scarce and he was reluctant to leave the security of his postal job in Augusta. John probably had mixed emotions about Buddie leaving. He was the main support of their mother in Augusta and managed several rental properties that had been part of James Hope's estate. At bottom, John simply felt that there needed to be a man in the house. Nevertheless, he did everything he could to keep his older brother aware of job opportunities outside Augusta.[42]

Hope's older sisters were married to prominent black Augustans. Thirty-one-year-old Jane was married to Judson Lyons, an attorney, important figure in Republican party politics, and influential race leader who would one day become the register of the United States Treasury.[43] Though the Lyonses were happy enough in their situation, thirty-four-year-old Sissie and twenty-eight-year-old Alethea and their families were not. Sissie and Alethea had married the Ladeveze brothers, John and Charles, proud sons of black Augustans whose free ancestry dated back to the early nineteenth century. During Hope's childhood in Augusta, the Ladevezes had been prominent entrepreneurs and race leaders who enjoyed considerable respect from the city's black and white communities. All that changed in the hostile racial environment of the 1890s. Whites no longer recognized class distinctions within the African American community. As the nineteenth century wound down, families like the Ladevezes, Whites, Barefields, and Buttses watched helplessly as their hard-won gains seemed to evaporate before their eyes. Both of the Hope-Ladeveze families were strongly considering turning their backs on the South and abandoning their racial identity.

Thomas Hope, the youngest and, many believed, the brightest of the Hope clan, had finished school in Augusta and was matriculating at Worcester Academy—following in the footsteps of his older brother John. The money inherited from his rich uncle's estate had ensured Thomas's education and brilliant future—or so everyone thought. The handsome Thomas, however, had gone to Worcester only because he was expected to, not because of any compelling desire to broaden his horizons. Thomas often wrote to John that he would rather be making money. Had there been a good job for him in Augusta, he would have remained there in spite of John's insistence that he continue his education. Thomas kept John constantly on pins and needles, for the younger

Hope was impulsive and changed his mind often. John wanted to believe that Thomas would become more stable, mature, and organized as he aged, but deep down, he knew that was unlikely.[44]

Hope did not spend all his time in Augusta with his family. He also visited friends and discussed the race-related issues of the day. Race leaders in Georgia were very concerned about whites' attempts to eliminate the black vote. The newspapers were full of South Carolina's disfranchisement deliberations, and many Augusta leaders wondered how closely Georgia's legislature was following the debates. Segregation was steadily increasing, jobs were scarce in Augusta, and Georgia had the dubious honor of leading the nation in lynchings. Hope could provide comparable details from Tennessee. That state had practically disfranchised its black citizens on the state level, segregation was virtually a reality in most of the state, and "lily whiteism" was eating away at local political opportunities in Nashville. And Tennessee had its own share of grotesque lynchings.

Black intellectuals' discussions of lynching in the 1890s at times took a curious twist. Though all condemned lynching as savage and barbaric behavior, individuals differed regarding whether most victims of "Judge Lynch" were the "respectable Negro," as Ida Wells-Barnett claimed in the *Indianapolis Freeman,* or the "common Negro," as Emmett J. Scott of Texas believed.[45]

Hope and his friends in Augusta were not concerned solely with domestic issues that summer of 1895. The violent struggle going on in Cuba was also a hot topic among African American intellectuals. John staunchly supported the Cubans, viewing their conflict with Spain as a Cuban war of liberation. He would be no less supportive when the United States entered the conflict three years later. But most of Hope's interest in foreign affairs focused on Africa. Like many members of his social class in black America in the 1890s, he rejected an exodus to Africa as a solution to America's race problem but was less opposed to the selected emigration of those who wanted to go. Hope continued to condemn encroaching European colonialism and believed that missionary activity in Africa served the religious needs of both Africans abroad and African Americans in the United States.[46]

Eighteen ninety-five was a significant year in the history of African Americans. Two related events of that year were known to practically every black man and woman in America, even if the connection between them was not immediately apparent. John Hope and the rest of black America probably paused for a moment of reflection when in February they learned that Frederick Douglass had died suddenly in his Anacostia home in Washington, D.C. His death left a leadership void within the African American community that many felt would not be easily filled. Only seven months later, a young educator by the name of Booker T. Washington delivered a ten-minute speech in Atlanta,

Georgia, that had enormous repercussions. Sooner than anyone expected, the shoes of Frederick Douglass had been filled. John Hope witnessed that historic moment in Atlanta and would help to determine its meaning in America for many years to come.

Hope decided that the Atlanta Cotton States and International Exposition, which was to open on 18 September, was worth a layover on his way back to Nashville, but he certainly did not expect to witness a historic event there. Hope was, of course, familiar with Booker T. Washington and his increasingly popular industrial school in Tuskegee, Alabama. Washington's popularity followed the establishment of the Slater Fund in 1881, which directed its money to support black industrial education. Hope was also aware that Washington had become the most prolific spokesman for black industrial education since the death of Hampton Institute's Samuel J. Armstrong.

Hope was curious about Booker T. Washington and wanted to know what his rising prominence might mean for black colleges. His own Roger Williams University offered courses in industrial education, but as was the case at most African American colleges, the subject was relegated to a subordinate role.[47] That fact notwithstanding, Hope still wanted to hear what Washington would say as the black leader chosen to represent the race at the opening of the Atlanta Exposition.

The Atlanta Cotton States and International Exposition was conceived by New South leaders determined to heal old wounds between the states and cast Atlanta and the rest of the South in a new light. Business leaders hoped to bring about an economic reconciliation that would pave the way for increased trade, larger markets, and bigger profits. The show was not designed to attract the attention of northern business interests alone, however. Though this exposition was much smaller than the Chicago World's Fair of 1893, its organizers planned to showcase the New South's economic potential to countries all over the world. It would take place in Atlanta's own backyard, in redesigned Piedmont Park with its celebrated new lake.

Separate black and white crews worked around the clock to ensure that the exposition opened on time. The *Augusta Chronicle* reported that the avenues were covered "with crushed limestone . . . whose blue paving . . . approximates the color of the blue sky [which] harmonizes well with the green of the plaza and the terraces." The *Atlanta Constitution* promised that the exposition would "shape the future history of the south." "The cotton exposition of 1881 was only a bud," boasted the *Constitution*'s editors; "this is the full blown rose."[48]

African Americans were expected to play an important part in the grand event. As close to one-third of the South's population, blacks were essential to the region's economic livelihood, even though their treatment in the political and social orders remained a disgrace. For the exposition, image was everything, and New South leaders in Atlanta knew they needed to paint an image of African American life that was acceptable to the rest of the nation.

The *Atlanta Constitution* periodically highlighted black Atlanta's support. A little more than a week before the exposition opened, a large article appeared with a big, bold caption: "What the Negro Is Doing. Matters Concerning the Progress and Development of the Colored Race." Black Atlanta leaders had actually approached white leaders about opening a black exhibit in the exposition. African American women worked hard to promote the exposition by sponsoring concerts, dinners, and other social events to raise money for the "Negro Building." Atlanta's black businesses and organizations were as anxious to attract new consumers and show off their wares as the owners of Rich's Department Store and the Coca-Cola Company were. The *Constitution* reported that "Butler, Slater and Company, pioneer colored druggists of Georgia, had completed their booth," and African American–owned hotels like the European House on Auburn Avenue and the Howell on West Mitchell Street advertised their availability for black visitors. African American organizations such as the three-year-old Southern Empire State Medical Association of Georgia, "composed entirely of the colored regular physicians of the state," were careful to schedule their professional meetings in Atlanta during the exposition, and the most distinguished visitors received a special invitation from the black-owned Pierian Club. The *Constitution* boasted that "the colored people are greatly interested in the progress of Atlanta and the success of the exposition." Atlanta's New South leaders believed they had successfully brought it all together; the exposition was Atlanta's "great enterprise, the climax of her endeavors—the crowning glory of her career."[49]

John Hope arrived by train in time for the grand opening. The eighteenth of September was a hot and humid day in Atlanta, with the temperature climbing to a sweltering eighty-eight degrees. Nevertheless, the streets were full of people. Before the day ended, five thousand would marvel at the many sites and flinch at the sudden bursts of cannon fire that punctuated the day. John had been at the Columbian Exposition in Chicago and may not have been impressed with the parade that began at the intersection of Broad and Marietta Streets late in the afternoon and ended three hours later at the foot of Fourteenth Street at the main entrance to Piedmont Park—then slightly outside the city limits. The parade featured mounted police and military bands from all over the region, trailed by Atlanta's Second Battalion of Colored Infantry and the black Lincoln Guard of Macon. The first carriages to appear carried the exposition's dignitaries and their families: *Atlanta Constitution* editor Clark Howell, C. A. Collier, the president of the exposition, and other prominent white officials. The carriages of the distinguished African American guests brought up the rear. A nervous Booker T. Washington rode with Negro Building organizer Garland Penn and Bishop Wesley Gaines of the AME church. Following them were other prominent African Americans including Rev. Henry Hugh Proctor, the pastor of Atlanta's First Congregational Church, who would one day become one of John Hope's good friends.[50]

Hope was seated inside the auditorium at least an hour before the ceremonies began. Eventually the platform guests walked across the stage, and a spontaneous burst of enthusiastic cheering went up from the crowd. It was followed just as suddenly by almost dead silence: Booker T. Washington had appeared among the distinguished guests on the platform. John may not have heard, as the *Indianapolis Freeman* later reported, that "one after another asked angrily, 'What's that nigger doing on the stage,'" for as soon as Washington became visible to those seated in the black section, wild cheers drowned out everything else.[51]

Washington's speech followed the address of Mrs. Joseph Thompson, head of the Women's Department of the Cotton Exposition and coordinator of the Women's Building, who sat down to vigorous applause. Washington rose and edged toward the center of the platform beneath the arch, in full view of the audience of more than three thousand. He had recently shaved off his mustache and looked younger than his thirty-nine years. When he finally began to speak, John listened intently. Though Hope was certainly familiar with Washington's speeches, there is no evidence that he had ever heard him speak in person. Thunderous applause shook the building at the speech's conclusion.

Constitution editor Clark Howell stepped boldly forward and stated: "That man's speech is the beginning of a moral revolution in America." The *Augusta Chronicle*'s response was more pointed. While praising the speech, the *Chronicle*'s editors took the opportunity to lambast African Americans for attempting to call themselves something other than "colored" or "Negro." The paper urged them to follow Washington's example:

> There is no nonsense or affectation about Booker Washington. You see nowhere in any of his speeches anything about Afro-Americans. His race is the negro race and he does not stultify himself or make himself and his people ridiculous by tacking on any such hyphenated nonsense to designate them. In the very opening sentence of his speech he properly referred to his people as negroes, and frankly gave tribute to the white men of the South as the negro's best friend.[52]

When he arrived back in Nashville, John Hope said nothing about the exposition. Students, faculty, and even President Owen and Lugenia Burns learned nothing of Hope's impressions of Washington or the speech he delivered at the Atlanta exposition.[53] Early in the spring semester, Hope finally broke his silence in a speech before a Nashville "colored debating society." He minced no words, going directly to the part of Washington's speech that had caused considerable discontent among some African American leaders: "If we are not striving for equality, in heaven's name for what are we living? I regard it as cowardly and dishonest for any of our colored men to tell white people or colored people that we are not struggling for equality. If money, education, and honesty will not bring to me as much privilege, as much equality as they bring to any American citizen, then they are to me a curse, and not a blessing."

Hope's words were direct, penetrating, and full of fire. There could be no mistaking his position: "Now, catch your breath, for I am going to use an adjective: I am going to say we demand social equality. If equality, political, economic, and social, is the book of other men in this great country of ours, of ours, then equality, political, economic, and social, is what we demand." Hope knew that any suggestion that blacks and whites were social equals touched a sensitive nerve in most white Americans. Yet he did not let up. "Why build a wall to keep me out?" he asked white America rhetorically. "I am no wild beast, nor am I an unclean thing."

Hope held no illusions about the need for protest and the importance of struggle. He knew that African American rights would not come on a silver platter. "Rise Brothers! Come let us possess this land." "Never say, 'Let well enough alone,'" he advised his audience. "Cease to console yourselves with adages that numb the moral sense." Reminiscent of the philosophical underpinnings he associated with football, Hope further advised his audience to "be discontented. Be dissatisfied. 'Sweat and grunt' under present conditions." Like Washington, he used an analogy that included the sea. But it was not a calm and docile sea that called to blacks and whites, "cast down your buckets where you are," but a raging sea of black protest moving endlessly against the tide of inequality: "Be as restless as the tempestuous billows on the boundless sea," he said, climaxing his address. "Let your discontent break mountain-high against the wall of prejudice, and swamp it to the very foundation. Then we shall not have to plead for justice nor on bended knee crave mercy; for we shall be men. Then and not until then will liberty in its highest sense be the boast of our Republic."[54]

Hope was not the first African American to publicly criticize Washington's speech. Critiques had already appeared in the *Washington Bee, Atlanta Advocate, Cleveland Gazette,* and a few other African American newspapers. The *Christian Recorder* published a critical editorial asking "Is Booker T. Washington's Idea Correct?" on 28 November 1895; and the *Voice of Missions* published an equally critical letter a month later that argued that Booker T. Washington was no Frederick Douglass: "To compare Mr. Booker T. Washington with Frederick Douglass," the angry writer from Washington, D.C., clamored, "is as unseemly as comparing a pygmy to a giant."[55]

None of these critiques, however, pierced the heart and soul of Washington's speech on an intellectual plane equal to that of Hope's speech in January. W. E. B. Du Bois wrote his famous critique of Booker T. Washington in *Souls of Black Folk* seven years later. But even he lagged behind Hope in recognizing the danger of Washington's views. "Let me heartily congratulate you upon your phenomenal success at Atlanta," Du Bois telegraphed Washington shortly after the speech; "it was a word fitly spoken." Du Bois then followed up his endorsement with a letter to the *New York Age* that stated, "Here might be the basis of a real settlement between whites and blacks in the South, if the South opened to the Negroes the doors of economic opportunity and the Negroes co-operated with the white South in political sympathy." Neither Hope nor Du Bois was a prominent figure in black or white America in 1896, and their political views scarcely ever appeared in print. But Du Bois would later emerge in the vanguard of African American opposition to Booker T. Washington; ironically, Hope would be known only as one of Du Bois's disciples.[56]

Hope said nothing about education in his Nashville speech, but neither had Washington in Atlanta. The Tuskegee principal's preference for industrial education was already well known, however, and his elevation to a position of leadership was bound to bring his educational philosophy to center stage. The *Christian Recorder* seemed cognizant of the consequences in its November editorial: "Mr. Washington's position, whatever he may mean, is interpreted as against the higher education of colored people. His position is that a colored boy should not be educated in the same way as a white boy. He evidently is not in favor of the higher education. In his mind Oberlin, Lincoln University, Wilberforce, Fisk, Atlanta University and the like are mistakes." The *Washington Bee* attacked Washington's views on education in its critique of the Atlanta speech in October 1895, and the letter from the Washingtonian printed in the *Voice of Missions* did likewise. "General Armstrong introduced him [Washington] to the public, and others made his path easy," wrote Smith of the *Cleveland Gazette*, still comparing Washington with Douglass. "He was lifted up and continued to sail on the reputations of General Armstrong and Hampton, for Tuskegee is known everywhere as 'the child of Hampton'—part of Hampton."[57]

The writer's association of Washington and Tuskegee with Armstrong and Hampton is instructive. It is James Anderson's view that the educational philosophy pioneered by Samuel Armstrong at Hampton Institute linked industrial education with a subordinate role that Armstrong believed African Americans were destined to play in the southern economy. Like many southern leaders at the end of Reconstruction, Armstrong was in favor of black disfranchisement. He believed in social inequality and expected African Americans to occupy the lower stratum of the South's occupational ladder. Yet Anderson makes a convincing case that Armstrong differed from other southern leaders with regard to the importance of universal schooling. While white southern leaders in general believed that education would ruin blacks, "Armstrong held a deep faith in the powerful capacity of moral and industrial education to socialize blacks to understand and accept their disfranchisement and to make them more productive laborers."[58]

Armstrong's thinking, according to Anderson, was firmly rooted in the educational philosophy that governed Hampton Institute, where training leaders for the South's black educational system was considered a much more important goal than teaching agricultural skills. In exchange for universal schooling, Hampton's brand of industrial education became part of a continuing New South ideology that sacrificed African American social and political interests to the need for black workers in an economy based on agriculture. This "Hampton model" of black industrial education was on a collision course with institutions of black higher learning whose philosophy was just the opposite.[59]

Missionary organizations like the ABHMS and the AMA, sponsors of Roger Williams University and Fisk University, respectively, were concerned about Washington's increasing popularity. So were many African American leaders and some black teachers. Only weeks before Washington spoke in Atlanta, ABHMS and AMA leaders got together at the annual meeting of the American Social Science Association to discuss the growing tendency to support only industrial education for blacks.

Critiques of the trend appeared in the pages of the ABHMS journal, the *Home Mission Monthly*, and the *New York Independent* (whose associate editor was an influential member of the AMA) late in September and continued from that point on. Writers argued that the "Negro industrial education concept was based upon the denial of the humanity of a whole race" and was calculated to make the "Negro absolutely content with his lot as a servant." On the other hand, higher education, according to missionary organization writers, rested on a belief in "the thorough humanity of the black man, with divine endowment of all the facilities of the white man; capable of culture, capable of high attainments under proper conditions and with sufficient time; a being not predestined to be simply a hewer of wood and drawer of water for the white race." Henry L. Morehouse, the executive director of the ABHMS, believed African Americans would "progress largely through the wise leadership of a gifted intelligentsia," and he gave top priority to educating the "talented tenth." He was not alone. The editor of the *Home Mission Monthly* also believed that African American progress would come through the leadership of "noble and powerful minds raised up from their own ranks."[60]

Hope was certainly aware of the controversy brewing over industrial education versus higher education in 1896, and he recognized, in Anderson's words, that "Washington and Tuskegee were Armstrong and Hampton in blackface." Hope was also an avid reader of both the *Home Mission Monthly* and the *Independent*, and knew their arguments well. As a product of Worcester and Brown, he had long cast his lot with the proponents of higher liberal arts education and was comfortable with their ideology. Though he did not mention education in his first speech in 1896, it was not long before he raised his voice in defense of black higher education.

He revealed his views in another speech that took place in Nashville late in the spring semester of 1896. It was probably given either in one of the weekly chapel talks with students at Roger Williams or on a public platform elsewhere in Nashville to an African American audience. The speech was entitled "The Need of a Liberal Education for Us, and That, Too, in the South." Like other proponents of college education for African Americans in this period, Hope used the terms *higher education* and *liberal* or *liberal arts education* interchangeably. Although this speech lacked the passion of his speech on full black equality, Hope made sure his listeners carried away with them the meaning of a liberal arts education, how it differed from the Hampton model of industrial education (even though the latter was not mentioned), the role of higher education in the African American struggle for complete freedom, and higher education's place in the development of African American leadership.[61]

As Hope gave more talks and public speeches, he began to develop a distinct style of speaking. He avoided clichés and jokes and went directly to the heart of what he had to say. In his speech on education, he began with his own definition of liberal arts education, which was not "mere attainment" or "merely packing the mind with information. Training. Whatever else it may be, it must first be that," he said. "It is training the mind in the various realms of knowledge," based "*first* [on] well-grounded *principles*" (emphasis in original). Probably with his own academic experiences in mind, Hope lectured his audience about the advantages of a liberal arts education in helping students make intelligent decisions about their careers: "A man has to wander in the paradise of knowledge picking of this and that fruit, getting a taste of this, that and the other, until he finds that which is best to his liking, that which . . . is the most life-giving. If he had not eaten from many [fruits], he would not have been able to make comparisons."

Hope's view of the role of a liberal arts education in African American progress was unmistakable in the speech, as was education's place in the training of African American leaders. Like Henry L. Morehouse and other proponents of black college education, John Hope also believed in training a black intelligentsia. In the same speech, which was given several years before Du Bois popularized the concept of a "talented tenth," Hope said:

Now we consider it right and proper that a certain percent of our people should have such training as will put them on a level with all other races in their quest for higher knowledge in letters and science. The progress, dignity, and respectability of our people depend on this. Mere honesty, mere wealth will not give us rank among the other peoples of the civilized world; and, what is more, we ourselves will never be possessed of conscious self-respect, until we can point to men in our own ranks who are easily the equal of any race.

Hope concluded his speech by recognizing the need for a broad-based curriculum and support for southern black higher education, and calling for college-level work in African American institutions. "We are not all going to be members of the broad-clothed professions," he said. "Some of us must develop the material resources and look after the commerce, both of which a university training fits us to do." Hope believed both that the development of black businesses would play a key role in the "essential progress of the race" and that black colleges would play a major role in that development. They needed only "the proper facilities and adequate appliances" from the friends of black higher education to succeed.

Hope also recognized that little actual college work went on even in the institutions that called themselves colleges: "Too much quarter is given, and the result is too much loafing in our schools." But he also reminded his audience that black college students were enthusiastic and had potential. They "responded cheerfully when given additional work," he said. "If we do not move rapidly, it is largely because we are [only] permitted to move slowly." Finally, Hope expressed his belief that African Americans were destined to remain in the South, and it was therefore essential that high-quality collegiate education be sustained and nurtured in the region where most African Americans lived.[62]

John Hope's speeches on the need for black higher education and full equality helped to launch him as an important African American leader. It was only a beginning, of course, and as yet very few people outside black Nashville and the academic community at Roger Williams University knew of this twenty-eight-year-old college professor. There is no doubt that Booker T. Washington was the most recognized African American leader in black and white America in 1896. Hope himself would say that "beside Booker T. Washington I am a pygmy."

Ironically, it was also in 1896 that the United States Supreme Court upheld racial segregation in its decision in *Plessy v. Ferguson*. That decision accelerated legal discrimination against African Americans and isolated them more than at any other time in their history. But there was ample room for African American protest in the black world-within-a-world, and for the emergence of a dynamic oppositional leadership. John Hope, with his speeches on full African American equality and the importance of black higher education, consciously stepped forward to challenge Washington's most celebrated positions. If that move did not make Hope the first black intellectual to publicly oppose Washington, it certainly made him one of the earliest and most consistent critics of the Tuskegeean's most prized philosophies.

Owen James, the new president of Roger Williams University, was quick to identify Hope as a rising star who might represent and forward the interests of all the ABHMS schools. Hope had all the right credentials. He was an articulate and intelligent black southerner thoroughly committed to the society's mission. Though not a mission school graduate, he was a deeply religious man who had received his liberal education at two of the finest Baptist-affiliated schools in the Northeast. Both Worcester and Brown had connections to the American Baptist Home Mission Society. John already knew Thomas J. Morgan, Henry L. Morehouse, and Malcolm MacVicar, powerful figures in the ABHMS administration. Morgan was the executive secretary of the ABHMS and the editor of the society's influential journal, the *Home Mission Monthly*. Henry L. Morehouse was the executive secretary of the American Baptist Education Society. MacVicar, the superintendent of the Home Mission Society's Education Department, would one day become the president of another ABHMS school, Virginia Union University. During a visit to Nashville, MacVicar advised Hope to take summer courses at the University of Chicago toward a Ph.D. in the classics, and told him the mission society would pay the bill. Hope wrote to Lugenia that it was preparation for the time "when he hopes to land me at a larger school than Roger Williams at a larger salary." There were other plans on the horizon as well, but neither John nor ABHMS officials knew in 1896 just what role Hope would eventually play in marketing the "mission school idea."[63]

In his private life, however, John had definite plans. He would go back to Chicago in the summer of 1896 and convince Lugenia Burns that she should become his wife. And so he did. By the end of the summer Lugenia had finally consented to marry him, but John had to agree to keep their engagement secret. There were still a few problems to overcome, and Lugenia did not yet want to confront her family. There was also a big question to be answered: Where would they live? John had earlier mentioned that he was interested in returning to Georgia, and that casual reference did not escape Lugenia. Both she and her mother already resented the idea that the marriage would take the couple as far south as Nashville. Lugenia bristled at the idea of living in Georgia, and Hope, for the time being, let the matter drop.

In addition, Lugenia remained unconvinced that John had given up other women. Neither wanted to presume too much, and their exchanges are often comical. In one letter Lugenia told Hope, *"you have really never loved before,"* then added a timid *"—have you?"* John replied, "I wish you had not put in that 'have you?' If you had just told me that I had not, I should have allowed myself to believe that you knew more about me than I did myself." It seemed not to matter that John was as open about his occasional dates in Nashville as Lugenia was about her "prosperous gentlemen friends" in Chicago.

Perhaps he was too open. Unlike Lugenia, he often revealed exactly whom he dated, where they had gone, speculated on what kind of wives his dates would make, and explained why they did not appeal to him. On one occasion John mentioned that one of his former dates had married, even though it was a "marriage of convenience not love." Lugenia wrote back asking more questions about his female acquaintances and advising him to watch his affections toward the married woman. In thanking Lugenia for her advice Hope admitted: "I checked myself several times in my attentions to her . . . for I never tried to take advantage of him even when the way was open, and I could have made honorable approaches to the woman who is now his wife." Instead of seeing the larger picture—Lugenia's implicit objection to his courtships in Nashville—John simply took her specific advice at face value. "If he accused me," Hope wrote about the potential jealous husband, "I should feel called upon to defend my honor." It was not Hope's honor that most concerned Lugenia, however, but his continued relationships with other women.[64]

There were other obstacles to the marriage as well. When Lugenia feared that John's family would interfere in their lives, Hope promised her that in their household she would be queen and he would be king. The main obstacle in Lugenia's mind, however, continued to be economic. Her mother, Louisa Burns, was getting older, was often sick, and was permanently deaf, and Lugenia was her primary source of support. It was difficult for Lugenia to place her personal happiness before the welfare of her mother. For that reason she encouraged John to reconsider what she believed would be a more profitable career in journalism. John wrote: "You ask me about having a Negro corner in some reputable publication. That is possible, I suppose; but even if I had a 'pull,' I could not work it at such long range." In spite of continued offers from Providence, he had lost all interest in working for a white newspaper. John had already accepted his role as a "race man," and he believed that white newspaper editors did not allow black writers to express themselves freely: "White people sometimes let Negroes write for their periodicals, but they usually say what kind of an article they want," he told Lugenia. "The Negro cannot always express his views." Privately, John Hope had already decided to remain in education.[65]

Early in 1897 it seemed that all the problems had finally been resolved. John and Lugenia openly professed their love for each other to both families and set a date for their wedding, 29 December 1897. John should have been happy, but he still felt an undercurrent of despair. His letters to Lugenia suggest he worried that he could not erase his solemn "poker face" or shed what appeared to be a cold and indifferent demeanor. The John Hope known to students and acquaintances was not at all like the John Hope his letters revealed. The latter bubbled with enthusiasm as he unlocked the recesses of his mind and heart. Conversation and other face-to-face interactions were always more difficult for him than writing. To Hope's surprise, even Lugenia believed he needed to be more "kind and gentle, and above all *affectionate*" (underlined in original). John himself admitted: "My self-consciousness and accompanying effort at appearing dignified keep me in such bounds as to cause many to regard me as an iceberg." [66]

Yet Hope's gloom only months before his marriage was not solely the result of his inability to combat his stern personality. Roger Williams University was increasingly feeling the economic crunch brought on by philanthropists' preference for black industrial education. The missionary societies did what they could to supplement the shrinking funds, and African American religious groups helped out with contributions, but only sporadically. Industrial philanthropists had always been slow to support black liberal arts schools, but after the ascendancy of Booker T. Washington their money flowed almost exclusively into institutions that supported the Hampton-Tuskegee idea.

Roger Williams University had been plagued with problems from its very beginning. There had been seven presidents since the school was incorporated in 1881 as a degree-granting university, including two in the four years Hope had taught there. Student enrollment continued to increase, but faculty salaries did not, nor did the number of faculty positions. Teachers taught ever more classes and counseled an ever increasing number of students. Hope's workday usually started at five in the morning and seldom concluded before six in the evening. In the spring of 1897, Hope revealed to Lugenia that the thirteen-hour workday left him tired most of the time and he wished he could move to a larger school. [67]

There were problems back home in Augusta as well. John's oldest half-sister, Georgia Frances, along with her husband and two children, had decided to leave the South. The specific reason for their decision, if there was one, remains a mystery. [68] Sissie's husband, John Ladeveze, as mentioned earlier, was an important race leader and businessman in Augusta who had on occasion loaned Hope small sums to help him through college. Ladeveze had also unsuccessfully urged Judson Lyons, another of Hope's brothers-in-law, not to resign as postmaster of Augusta, a position to which he had been appointed by

President McKinley.[69] Whatever his reasons, John Ladeveze decided to leave Augusta and take his family to Pasadena, California. The actual move did not take place until early in October 1897, yet the anticipation of it had weighed heavily on Hope's mind since it became clear early in the spring that the Ladevezes had decided to leave.[70]

Hope also continued to worry about the direction in which Booker T. Washington was leading the race. The danger of Washington's philosophy to higher education, and to the race in general, hit close to home around the end of the spring semester in 1897. On the first of May, the Tennessee Centennial Exposition opened in Nashville. Determined to outdo Atlanta, Nashville's separate Negro Building stretched 250 feet along the east bank of what is now Lake Watauga and was financed in part with $12,000 provided by Tennessee's New South leaders. In all, eight special days were set aside to honor African Americans, starting off with Negro Day. Newspapers reported that one of the most popular attractions was the replica of a plantation "befo de wah," complete with "genuine plantation darkies . . . pickaninnies with their wooly and white-headed grandmas, young bucks and thick lipped African maidens" who were "happy as a big sunflower." With "broad-mouthed grins" they invited others to "dance the old-time breakdowns" and watch their demonstrations of "crap games, camp meeting scenes, and cake walks." Indeed, Tennessee's racist depictions had accomplished the planners' mission: they had outdone Atlanta.[71]

But there was more. The black industrial education theme was much more prominent in the Nashville exposition than it had been in Atlanta. It was vividly displayed throughout the Negro Building in numerous exhibits. Industrial education was the slogan of the day, and it was linked inextricably with African American progress. "An exposition determines their industrial status," noted a pleased white observer. "This done, we shall be able, with each succeeding exposition, to measure their strides and determine their progress." The conservative William H. Councill, an African American educator from Alabama, was even more direct: "The Negro needs a higher industrial education," he said at the official opening of the building on Negro Day. "Congressional enactments can not make us a race. The race must make itself."

Booker T. Washington spoke from the steps of the Negro Building in Nashville and again resounded the theme of racial harmony through economic progress—albeit at the expense of full rights for blacks. While education received virtually no mention in his speech in Atlanta, its importance was made clear in his Nashville oration: "Slavery was an industrial school that trained more men than in the whole city of Nashville today," he said. There is no direct evidence placing Hope at the Tennessee Exposition, yet he probably attended. He was certainly aware of the event's marketing of racial harmony through economic progress and its linking of both directly to industrial education.[72]

It was difficult after 1895 for two race leaders to occupy the same space without discussing the pros and cons of Washington's philosophy. A few weeks after the opening of the Tennessee Centennial Exposition, the black National Baptist Convention held its meeting in Nashville. John was delighted when his brother Madison took the opportunity to come up for a visit. No doubt they discussed their sister's plan to go to California, but it seems that ample time was also spent discussing Booker T. Washington's leadership. Hope and his brother were joined by William E. Holmes, another Augustan who taught in Atlanta, and Richard R. Wright, the first principal of Augusta's Ware High School. Since 1889 Wright had been the president of the State Industrial College for Colored Youth near Savannah (now Savannah State College). The four men spent hours on the back porch of Hope's residence discussing Washington's philosophy. After Wright left around midnight, the discussions often continued inside until the early morning hours.

Hope described the discussions in a letter to Lugenia written in June 1897. The same ten-page letter shows that his objections to Booker T. Washington were more ideological than personal. Washington's jokes to white audiences about African Americans made him uneasy: "Any man who talks to southern white people as he does about the Negro cannot receive my commendation." Yet it was clear that John respected Washington as a race leader, calling him "unquestionably the greatest Negro we have had since Douglass." Hope apparently believed, as he wrote to Lugenia, that "we can recognize greatness even when we do not agree with it." Like most of the race leaders who opposed Washington, Hope did not disagree with all of his objectives even though he questioned many of his tactics. Hope also supported African American self-help and economic development, and believed there was a place for industrial education, but he was unwilling to sacrifice full political equality and black higher education in the process. In a rare display of anger (to say nothing of informality), Hope continued in the same June 1897 letter to Lugenia: "I should not mind meeting him [Booker Washington] some day and bitching with him for he is certainly not doing our ultimate cause *all* good and *no* harm" (emphasis in original).[73]

Hope's letters confused Lugenia, who failed to distinguish between his feelings for Washington's philosophy and for Washington the man. Earlier that month, Lugenia Burns had written to Hope asking him indirectly what he thought about her participation in an upcoming event that included Booker T. Washington. Booker T. Washington was scheduled to speak in Chicago later that summer, and Lugenia was expected to work on the local arrangements committee and to serve as one of the hostesses. She wanted to know what Hope thought about her in that role. The naive Hope failed to recognize (or simply chose to ignore) that Lugenia in her own way was asking for advice.

Lugenia by no means approved of Booker T. Washington and had not wanted to take part. Yet she interpreted Hope's response to mean that she had his approval and that he would appreciate an invitation to the reception himself. His words probably resonated in her ears: "We can recognize greatness even if we do not agree with it." The independent Lugenia, however, chose not to violate her own ideological principles, even if they were in conflict with those of her future husband. She refused to take any official role in the festivities, although she still planned to get John an invitation to the reception, which meant she would go as his escort. It seemed to Lugenia that this was what Hope wanted.[74]

Hope's response to this arrangement is significant, for it places him consciously and squarely in opposition to the philosophy of Booker T. Washington before the beginning of the twentieth century. It also shows his desire to prevent even the perception of his being a Washington supporter. John apologized to Lugenia for his inconsistency and for asking her to do something she "thought was wrong in principle." He reiterated that no one knew who he was, and that Washington was a giant in comparison, although as an educator, he wrote, "I am in Washington's class." He did not want those in attendance at the affair to "put me down as being present because I advocated the same notions as to Negro education that B.T.W. does." It is not known if that reply satisfied Lugenia, but it left no doubt about his opposition to Booker T. Washington's educational philosophy and his sensitivity to any social interaction that could be misinterpreted.[75]

Later in June 1897, Hope went to the University of Chicago and enrolled in courses toward his Ph.D. in the classics. Already tired and somewhat nervous, his stress level rose even higher that summer. He was unhappy with his academic performance. Compared with these Ph.D. courses, his previous classes in theology had been easy. John had hoped to see a good deal of Lugenia, but he often had to cancel their dates to study for exams. When they did meet, John was visibly despondent, often brooding over his meager income (his expected annual salary at Roger Williams was $650) and fearing that Lugenia would not be happy once they were married. Yet he managed to get through the summer. He finished his schoolwork, took care of some last-minute details associated with the wedding, and was back in Nashville by the middle of September.[76]

John Hope rode an emotional roller coaster the last two months before he and Lugenia were married. His correspondence is dominated by personal concerns. There is no mention of his academic activities—or any reference to Roger Williams at all except for an occasional reminder that he was over-worked. His letters to Lugenia were constant, sometimes three a day and fre-quently totaling as many as thirty to forty pages. A telegram that arrived early in October added to his anxiety. His sister and her family were on their way to California and planned to spend a night with John in Nashville. Outwardly Hope appeared happy, "endeavoring (rather successfully) to be light-hearted so as to make them cheerful," he wrote to Lugenia. Privately, however, he was devastated at the thought of them moving so far away. It was not a good time for him, but he broke down only when writing to his mother after the Ladev-ezes departed.[77]

It seems that Sissie and her family had decided not only to leave the South but to abandon their racial identity as well. Perhaps the decision to pass had already been made and was conveyed to John, which would explain why their leaving filled him with so much grief. He had written to Lugenia that he was confused by their decision but "half believed it was for the better," but he did not fill in the details. None of his letters mentions why the Ladevezes left or what they planned to do.

Passing was an extremely private matter fraught with danger and uncer-tainty. Many families chose to deal with the practice by simply not mention-ing—even to other family members—that it had occurred. The practice was not uncommon in Augusta, and there were rumors that others in the Hope family, especially one or two of John's uncles and aunts, had also "passed to the other side." Those who passed permanently left family members feeling am-bivalent, yet very seldom were they betrayed. It would be twenty-eight years before Hope saw his sister again, and the meeting then would be strained.[78]

John chose to believe that Sissie's husband, John Ladeveze, was the architect of their move to the far West. "It certainly was not Sissie's idea," he wrote to Lugenia. Yet that was not a critical assessment, for John envied his sister's seventeen-year marriage and looked on that relationship as a model for him-self and Lugenia. "Nothing but love could make Sissie leave her house and go away to that great distance from her kin. She loves her husband and trusts him, she loves her children and makes every sacrifice for them," he wrote. In spite of the many unknowns that awaited the Ladevezes in California, Hope took comfort in his sister and her husband's long-standing union.[79]

To moderate the stress engendered by the working conditions at Roger Williams, his sister's move to California, and his upcoming wedding, John made his three-mile walks more regular. He needed the stamina, for Louisa Burns continued to plant seeds of doubt in her daughter's mind. Though she was aware of the engagement, Mrs. Burns had not yet given the union her blessing. Lugenia had mentioned that Hope wanted to leave Nashville and

would consider moving farther south. The idea made Lugenia's mother furious, but her anger did not cloud her thinking. In return for her consent, she
asked John to promise not to take her daughter farther south than Nashville.
John refused and promised only to do his best to make Lugenia "a proper
husband." Shortly thereafter, Lugenia brought up the idea of going to Africa
and becoming a missionary. Hope had heard it before. Lugenia had asked him
a year earlier what he would say if she decided to "give up everything and go
to Africa." Hope had said that he would not oppose it then and timidly replied
that he would not oppose it now. "Now," however, was only weeks before the
wedding. Hope braced for the worst and was relieved when it did not come.[80]

His relief was short-lived. Everything was set on campus for the newlyweds.
With the help of President James, John had secured two well-lighted rooms
with a front view of the campus. Lugenia would have an outlet to the women's
side of the house without having to come into the men's hall at all, and John
had purchased a stove and storm windows to help keep out the draft. The new
apartment was much cozier than his present room and would provide them
greater privacy and, as John preferred, "less contact with the administration of
affairs." He had also proudly informed Lugenia of his purchase of a thousand-
dollar life insurance policy that would provide her with some security if anything happened to him.

Approximately two weeks before the wedding, Lugenia dropped another
bombshell. She had been offered a position in Chicago at a salary that would
allow her to care for her mother, earn her own living, and, as Hope put it, "be
her own boss." Hope was not to fear, she said. She had already refused the
position, and thus "turned her back on mother and everything" for him.[81]

John's three-mile walks suddenly increased to four. He felt enormous guilt.
Lugenia's concern for her mother's welfare was genuine, and Hope was very
sensitive to that concern. Leaving Chicago would be a painful sacrifice for
Lugenia. Hope recognized that his meager salary would not provide financial
security for him and Lugenia, let alone for her mother. He decided to put it
all on the line and allow Lugenia to bow out gracefully. "I do not want you to
deceive yourself," he wrote. "In refusing this new offer I want you to see the
dark side too." There was no question about their love for each other, but,
Hope wrote, "I am not the only one . . . who is depending on you for happiness." He did not want to compete with her mother and plainly stated, "I am
not worth it in the first place, and in the second place I am not selfish enough
to win happiness at the expense of your mother's happiness. Do what you are
sure is best." [82]

In the end, Lugenia decided not to postpone the wedding. Few letters from
Lugenia are included in the extant Hope correspondence for these years, but
those few clearly show that their love was mutual in spite of Lugenia's misgiv-

ings. Two days before Christmas, and only six days before their wedding, Lugenia confirmed her commitment to John in a letter as poetic and passionate as anything John had ever written to her.[83] As planned, the couple was married on Wednesday, 29 December 1897. The ceremony took place at Lugenia's church in Chicago, Grace Presbyterian, a church of the African American elite established by black Presbyterians from Tennessee and Kentucky. Lugenia's family was present, but none of Hope's family had been able to come. However, his good friend W. T. B. Williams stood proudly with him at the altar. It was a quiet wedding conducted without much fanfare, and was over almost as soon as it began. Late that evening Hope and his new bride took a carriage to the train station, where they boarded a train for Nashville.[84]

John's friend and colleague J. W. Johnson made sure there was a welcoming committee at Roger Williams University. Probably sleepy-eyed and exhausted from the long train ride from Chicago (it was already after one o'clock in the morning), the last thing the newlyweds expected was a surprise party. When the Hopes reached their building, students with kerosene lamps were there to greet them, lining both sides of the staircase and leading them into the reception area. There the party began with light refreshments and speeches of welcome. The new Lugenia Burns Hope later remembered that John was his "normal shy and cold self, but his bride was neither." The party was enjoyed by all.[85]

The Hopes eventually settled in for what they thought would be the quiet, ordered, and serene life of a college professor and his wife. It was not to be. In 1898, midway into the spring semester, Hope received word that a teaching position was available at Atlanta Baptist College (ABC). The thought of returning to Georgia had never been far from his mind. Although he probably did not tell Lugenia, in December 1894 he received a letter from his friend William E. Holmes, the only black faculty member at Atlanta Baptist, that confirms Hope's interest in returning to Georgia: "It was absolutely impossible to see Dr. MacVicar. He was much too hurried, but I hope to see him, Dr. Morehouse, or Gen'l Morgan at our board meeting at Spelman in February, when I shall advise you as to the result of my efforts."[86]

Hope's desire to leave Roger Williams for Georgia had not wavered since he had written to Lugenia in 1896 that Atlanta "has fewer objectionable features than Nashville. There are more northern people in Atlanta, [it] is larger, has more business, and the colored people have a much better commercial and political standing than they do here." Though neither Lugenia nor her mother was enthusiastic about the move, Lugenia did recognize that Atlanta held more opportunities for African Americans.[87]

Hope refused to become too excited when Atlanta Baptist College's president, Dr. George Sale, wrote to offer the job. The $650 salary only matched what he was making at Roger Williams. He discussed the proposal with his family in Augusta and with W. T. B. Williams. Williams agreed with Hope's elder brother, Buddie, that "Atlanta was the place." Next, Hope contacted Dr. MacVicar, superintendent of education for the ABHMS, in New York. Mac-Vicar assured John that he was free to make a choice and seemed to push him toward Atlanta. Meanwhile, in Atlanta, the president of ABC was getting nervous. It was May, and he had heard nothing from Hope. He raised the salary offer to $700 and offered to add another $100 if Hope would take on the job of bookkeeper. "The plan would have this advantage," President Sale wrote to John about the additional job, "it would give you insight into the workings of the H[ome] M[ission] School on the business side, which knowledge might be of great use to you in the future." [88]

Despite Hope's reservations, the lure of a return home to Georgia was too great. Atlanta was a bustling metropolis with a large African American community and, perhaps even more important, a burgeoning black middle class. It was not too far from Augusta, which would make the care of his mother and visits with the rest of his family much easier. Certainly ABC's reputation was growing, and there appeared to be room there for his own intellectual growth. As an added incentive, he would be teaching his beloved classics. Thus he informed the New York office and President James at Roger Williams that he had decided to leave Nashville. [89]

Since leaving Augusta in 1886, Hope's life seemed to unfold in four-year intervals. Though not without hardship, his four years at Worcester Academy built successfully on a foundation already established in Augusta. His years at Brown University in Providence built on his experiences at Worcester and gradually reintroduced John Hope to an African American world that did not exist in Worcester, Massachusetts. His eight years in New England unquestionably broadened his horizons, added to his moral convictions, and kept alive the flame that seemed to guide his destiny. John needed all of these experiences to survive his return to the South and to offset the blatant racism, bigotry, and violence that beset his people in the 1890s.

The last four years in Nashville, though a short time in the scheme of things, had been a trial by fire. On one level it was a love story between a man and a woman with a happy ending. Yet even that bliss took place behind an ever-thickening racial veil that limited choices, defined realities, selected leaders, and forged personalities. Like most other African Americans, Hope did not allow the exigencies of the racial milieu to drown him in a sea of despair, though on occasion he came dangerously close to the edge. He managed to survive and emerged with his feet firmly planted in reality. The experiences in Nashville would be adequate training for the years ahead—back to the Deep South and the red clay of Georgia.

5

The Return South: Atlanta

John and Lugenia Hope arrived in Atlanta late in September, shortly before the beginning of the fall semester. The Atlanta that became Hope's home in 1898 looked radically different from the glamorous New South city visited by thousands during the Cotton States Exposition of 1895. Atlanta Baptist College sat high on what a contemporary called a "bare red hill" on fourteen acres of land about a mile west of the heart of Atlanta. The front of the campus offered a good view of the city, and the rear view consisted of rolling country that on clear days revealed Mount Kennesaw (now Kennesaw Mountain) twenty miles away. The bloody battle for Atlanta during the Civil War had left scars on the college's campus. Muddy trenches, deeply eroded pits, and gun emplacements were constant reminders of the Confederate soldiers' unsuccessful attempt to head off Sherman's deadly advance.[1]

The college's first permanent Atlanta location, built in 1879, was at Elliott and West Hunter Streets, sandwiched between a lumber mill and the Southern Railway railyard in an industrial area that in a few years would become part of the Atlanta Terminal Station. Students had to strain to hear their teachers, who were often drowned out by the noise of the locomotive whistles and lumberyard machinery. When class ended and students ventured outside, they were often greeted by a haze of literally breathtaking soot and grime that on occasion even drifted into the classrooms. One ABC president wrote that "in those days, lung power was a prime qualification in the teacher."[2]

The new school was a four-story red brick building with a white marble face that glittered in the sunlight. Built just eight years before John and Lugenia arrived, Graves Hall was named after the president who preceded George Sale. Unfortunately, the building was already bursting at the seams. Practically every inch of its space was used to full capacity. Students lived in the basement, where they also ate their meals, washed their own dishes in the kitchen, and did their laundry before retiring to their rooms. The upper stories in Graves Hall included a small chapel, a one-room library, eight classrooms, the president's quarters, and rooms for six teachers.

All the rooms for teachers were filled when the Hopes first arrived, and they spent their first month in Atlanta as the guests of President George Sale and his wife, Clara Goble. Decent housing was expensive and scarce in Atlanta, and the Hopes probably preferred to live on campus in the unfamiliar city. The Hopes could not complain about the Sales' hospitality; they were welcomed with open arms. Canadian-born George Sale was a forty-one-year-old Baptist minister, eleven years Hope's senior, who had long been associated with the ABHMS. He and his wife came to Atlanta from Toronto in 1890 when President Graves decided to relinquish the presidency (although he remained as a teacher). A reserved and devout man, Sale was also an experienced fund-raiser and an able administrator. Although he got along well with the students, he was uncomfortable interacting with them. A former student remembered that President Sale "had a stilted manner and seemingly cold disposition that kept students at a distance."[3] President Sale depended on William E. Holmes, the school's only African American full-time faculty member before Hope arrived in 1898, to compensate for his shortcomings in this area.

Atlanta Baptist College owed its origins to three men: William J. White; Richard C. Coulter, an escaped slave; and Edmund Turney, a devout white Baptist minister from the North. When Coulter met Turney in Washington, D.C., in 1864, the latter had just founded the National Theological Institute (later called the National Theological Institute and University). The institute, designed to educate freedmen for the Baptist ministry, represented the first step in Turney's grandiose plan to establish a national Baptist university in Washington, D.C. Meanwhile, he planned to establish "minister's institutes" throughout the South (actually branches of the D.C.-based Theological Institute) to meet the educational needs of the African American ministers he hoped to produce. Turney's school was chartered in May 1866, and it rivaled and at times duplicated the work of the ABHMS before the two organizations merged in 1869.[4]

Inspired and energized by Turney's vision, Coulter returned to Augusta determined to establish a branch of the Theological Institute there. Turney was unable to assist Coulter directly, but he did provide him with a letter authorizing Coulter to use his name. In Augusta, Coulter turned to the venerable William J. White, who turned Coulter and Turney's dream into a reality. In 1867, White established the Augusta Institute in Springfield Baptist Church. When the Theological Institute merged with the ABHMS, the Augusta school came under the control of the Home Mission Society. During the Augusta

Institute's early years, the ABHMS had few resources and could offer little support to the new school. Hope probably did not know that his mother had sent furniture and food to the needy students when the school first opened. In fact, it was only through the efforts of Augusta's African American community that the school survived its earliest years.[5]

Augusta Institute's future began to look brighter when the ABHMS appointed Dr. Joseph T. Robert, a southerner, to run it in 1870. The sixty-four-year-old Brown University graduate soon developed the institute into a first-rate school for the training of African American men interested in becoming ministers. The school already had prominent graduates, some of them relatives of John Hope. In addition to William J. White, who had completed the institute's course himself, there was Hope's cousin James Wesley Gilbert and his brothers-in-law John Ladeveze and Judson Lyons. In 1879 the Augusta Institute moved to Atlanta, changed its name to Atlanta Baptist Seminary, and began to hold classes in the basement of Friendship Baptist Church, the first African American Baptist church in Atlanta. The school then offered a theology program that trained ministers, and the equivalent of a grammar through high school curriculum with an individual college course offered only periodically.[6]

In 1897, the year before Hope arrived, the school became Atlanta Baptist College. Until that time all of the school's graduates had come from its elementary, high school, and theology departments, even though a "college course" had been listed in the catalogue since the early 1890s. The name change, however, represented more than a vision of what ABC hoped to become. In 1897 Atlanta Baptist awarded diplomas to its first three college graduates, Henry A. Bleach, John W. Hubert, and Major W. (M. W.) Reddick, who went on to become prominent educators, race leaders, and ministers. They joined a growing list of outstanding graduates that included Lyons, who entered politics; Baptist ministers E. K. Love, C. T. Walker, and Edward R. Carter; and William E. Holmes, who became a respected educator.[7]

These men were not strangers to John Hope. Lyons was his brother-in-law, of course, and Holmes had played a prominent role in bringing him to Atlanta Baptist College. E. K. Love was the minister of the largest black Baptist church in Savannah, a fine writer, and a vocal leader of the African American separatist movement in Georgia. Dynamic C. T. Walker was the minister of the prominent Tabernacle Baptist Church in Augusta, where he was known for his fiery orations, and was also prominent in state and national African American Baptist organizations. Edward R. Carter, who succeeded Frank Quarles as minister at Friendship Baptist Church, was also influential in state and national black Baptist organizations and was well known as a scholar, a writer, and a prominent African American Baptist ambassador of goodwill.

These men were among the most respected and powerful race and religious leaders in Georgia.[8]

Hope met the other six ABC faculty members and teaching assistants before the semester began. He probably did not know that his $800 a year salary made him one of the highest paid members of the faculty. In addition to Holmes and President Sale, the faculty included Carrie E. Bemus, Waldo Truesdell, teaching assistant John Hubert (one of ABC's first college graduates), and matron Mary Hyde. Bemus, a northern white woman educated in Pennsylvania and Boston, arrived at Atlanta Baptist in 1892 with considerable teaching experience. She taught English and was the principal of the English Preparatory Department, where Hope would teach the classics. Truesdell, another white northerner, came to ABC in 1897 and taught science. He had just graduated from Harvard and, like Hope, had attended Worcester Academy. The two men first met at Worcester when Hope delivered a speech there during his time at Brown. Hope and Truesdell became good friends at ABC but differed philosophically over the leadership of Booker T. Washington. The faculty was a diverse group, but all welcomed Hope as an equal member of their small family.[9]

September passed quickly, and Hope began a tenure at Atlanta Baptist College that would last for more than thirty years. A student later remembered that Hope "beamed with confidence" as he faced his first class in October 1898. Hope exuded self-confidence for a number of reasons. First, and perhaps most important, he was happily married. The "poker face" that camouflaged his uncertainty over his relationship with Lugenia in Nashville was no longer needed. In addition, unlike his first appointment teaching science at Roger Williams, Hope had been hired at ABC to teach the classics, his area of expertise.[10]

For the moment Hope had definitely decided to remain in academia, turning his back on what might have been a promising journalism career. Still passionately interested in religion and the ministry, Hope continued to take summer classes at the University of Chicago. He no doubt recognized, as a former student would later remark, that "it was the preachers in those early days who were most respected at the Seminary [Atlanta Baptist]." All the ABHMS schools operated within a religious culture, and doors of opportunity opened to educated ministers. Virtually all ABHMS school presidents were ministers, as were some of the faculty members. His career decided, happy in his personal life, and secure in his ability to teach the subject matter, John Hope seemed more content in 1898 than he had ever been before.[11]

Hope quickly recognized that the one hundred or so students enrolled at Atlanta Baptist College in 1898 were a diverse lot. But it was a diversity based not on race, gender, or even class as much as on age. During ABC's early years, many of its students were adults. This age diversity reflected the tremendous importance African Americans placed on education in the post–Civil War era. It was not uncommon to find twenty-five- and even thirty-year-old men in ABC's grammar and high school departments (which enrolled most of the students). By the time Hope arrived, younger students had become more common, but they often found themselves sitting side-by-side in classrooms with students old enough to be their fathers. Perhaps to avoid confusion, and certainly as a badge of respect, all ABC students were called "men" and were usually addressed as "Mister" whether they were in the grammar school or the college department, a tradition that persists to this day. The title was designed to instill pride in students, acquaint them with the institution's traditions, and make them aware of the high achievement expected of ABC graduates.[12]

If there was a great difference in the ages of students in 1898, their regional and class makeup was far more homogeneous. Although a few students from bordering states were sprinkled in, most were "Georgia boys straight from the farm," one student recalled, whose circumstances reminded Hope of his own financial struggles in New England. Most students arrived with few essentials, sometimes only with the clothes on their backs. Their parents or the students themselves had already made remarkable sacrifices just to get to ABC. Most could not afford even the $30 annual tuition and expected to work to pay their way through school.

The "dignity of work" philosophy popularized by Booker T. Washington was not new among African Americans. Administrators at ABC had always believed that work was dignified, and they hired no outside workers for jobs students could perform. The eight cents an hour wage earned by student employees went directly to pay their bills. Thus, for both social and economic reasons, students did all the housework in Graves Hall, including the washing and ironing. They also helped prepare meals in the dining room, and passersby saw students everywhere on the campus trimming walks and flower beds, making drives and terraces, and repairing fences and outbuildings. One student of that time, James Nabrit Sr., later recalled that "many looked down at the preachers on the hill." Yet Atlanta Baptist's students were a proud group who valued their emerging institution and believed it was as fine an example of black self-help as the better-known Tuskegee Institute or any of the other Atlanta institutions.[13]

By the time John Hope arrived, Atlanta Baptist College placed more emphasis on its academic program than its department of theology. Yet the school's image as a strict Bible seminary was slow to die. Some students were shocked at the rigid discipline, puritanical values, and religious indoctrination that all students received regardless of their age or program. As at Roger Williams, no card playing, smoking, dancing, or other activity deemed immoral by administrators was allowed. Sam Nabrit, a second-generation ABC student and later a faculty member, recalled that students attended two religious services a day during the week, and three on Sundays. Many ABC graduates went on to study theology at Virginia Union University (called the Richmond Theological Seminary until 1899) and other seminaries, including the University of Chicago's Divinity School. In part because of its strict rules of conduct and heavy emphasis on religion, it would be many years before ABC would shed its image of a strictly denominational institution designed to train "preachers and teachers."[14]

Before John Hope arrived, William Holmes had been the only black faculty member in Atlanta Baptist's thirty-one-year history. He began as a teaching assistant under President Robert and received full faculty status in the 1880s. By 1898, the Augusta-born Holmes, a dark man of medium height, had been with the school for twenty-five years. Although much revered by students as the "intellectual father of us all," their contact with Holmes had significantly diminished in the late 1890s; his administrative responsibilities simply prohibited it. In addition to teaching several classes in English and history—and occasionally theology—Holmes was secretary of the faculty, college librarian, and from time to time the school's bookkeeper. He also usually worked summers for the ABHMS and participated in several black state and national Baptist organizations. In spite of his busy schedule, Holmes continued to counsel students on everything from academics to religion, and was continuously held up as a fine example of the kind of Christian man the Home Mission Society produced at Atlanta Baptist College. Yet there was simply not enough of him to go around. The students were delighted to learn in 1898 that President Sale had hired a second African American faculty member—a "colored man from Brown" who had taught at prestigious Roger Williams University—to relieve Holmes of some of his responsibilities.[15]

Though happy with his arrival, it seems that the students warmed rather slowly to John Hope. Certainly he faced the same problem that plagued all faculty members at ABC: It was not easy to instruct students with such varying degrees of maturity. A student assistant believed that the problem was "Hope's lack of theological credentials in a religious school where ministers were everything." Students no doubt were put off by Hope's stern disposition and formal manner. The students at Roger Williams had reacted to him the same way at first, and Hope's personality had not changed in the intervening years. Some students were startled by Hope's white features and aristocratic bearing—characteristics many of them associated with the more elitist Atlanta

University. They appreciated Hope's knowledge of Greek and Latin but privately criticized him for being too demanding. "Professor Hope expected too much of us too soon," one student recalled.[16]

There were important differences between the students Hope had taught at Roger Williams and those he encountered at Atlanta Baptist College. His students at Roger Williams had been mainly in the college department, or at least in college preparatory classes. Atlanta Baptist's college department had only nine students. Hope's students that first year also included the twenty-five in the high school (which included a small number of students preparing for college) and sixty-six in the primary and secondary grades. It took him awhile to make the necessary adjustments.[17]

Though formal in manner, Hope had a dry sense of humor, which he used sometimes to put students at ease and sometimes to drive home a particular point. He had an uncanny ability to lift the subject matter out of its historical period and place it in a practical, contemporary context that commanded the students' attention. Passages from classical literature, for example, were often used first to emphasize values Hope deemed relevant to the lives of students, and then to emphasize practical points that represented the interests of the college. Though at times baffled by his technique, students nevertheless retained the passages and were able to recall them and their meaning even after leaving school.

Charles Hubert, an Atlanta Baptist graduate hired many years later by President Hope to teach at a salary larger than his own, recalled an amusing episode that both showed Hope's superior teaching skills and revealed students' inability to figure him out. The subject was the Gallic Wars, Hubert remembered, "where Aedui had promised Caesar supplies of grain but failed to produce it, though they kept declaring it was being collected. . . . Hope walked over to the window then turned and reminded his Latin class that 'you boys mustn't say that your money is coming until it is really on the way.' The boys had not been paying their bills," Hubert concluded, yet Hope delivered the statement without cracking a smile, and the students did not know "whether to chuckle or ask for his forgiveness."[18]

By the end of the first semester, Hope's interactions with students outside the classroom had broken down the barriers between them and eventually led to his becoming one of the most popular teachers on campus. With Holmes increasingly absent, students bypassed President Sale and went to the soft-spoken Hope for counseling. "He could be stern as Caesar and tender as a mother," one student recalled. Students sought his advice on everything from finances to health and family. Those assigned to other advisers frequently sought Hope's opinion first. One student remarked that "if a boy needed a dose of medicine, castor oil, or a reprimand, he [Hope] gave it to him. He had no hours."[19]

Hope's support of student athletics, so much a part of his life at Roger Williams, continued at Atlanta Baptist College, further endearing him to his students. At thirty, Hope no longer played football, but he introduced the game to delighted ABC students shortly after his arrival. Benjamin Brawley, an early student and later a scholar, faculty member, and administrator, remembered that in the school's earliest days, formal exercise was the only physical activity sanctioned by ABC administrators. Many of the New England missionary teachers frowned on competitive sports and paid little attention to them. Nevertheless, the students were proud of their baseball team and took their sports seriously. Hope spent much of his spare time on campus helping out with the baseball team. He coached intramural football in 1899, and by 1900 had helped to organize the school's first competitive team. A note in the student magazine, the *Athenaeum*, aptly sums up the students' growing affection for Hope: "We are well pleased with our new professor, John Hope, A.B. He has made himself quite popular already with students. He's alright for he takes an active interest in our athletics."[20]

Hope now played tennis instead of football to keep fit, and continued to take long walks. His journeys often led him down the red clay roads leading to nearby Atlanta University (AU), whose very appearance perhaps evoked mixed emotions. He had looked with awe at the ivy-covered buildings of coed Atlanta University when he was only four years old. Georgia Frances and Madison Newton had attended the university in the early 1870s, and young John and his father had come to visit them. Those were happy times in Augusta. The Hope family was content then and looked forward to a promising future. But Atlanta University also reminded Hope of the unhappy time in 1876 when the reduced income that followed the death of his father had forced Sissie and Buddie to leave the prestigious school.[21]

In many ways Atlanta University was a lot like Nashville's Fisk. It also owed its origins to northern Congregationalist missionaries, who established the school shortly after the Civil War and left it economically on its own in the 1880s. And in spite of the pretentious "university" surname, it too was primarily a normal school with a well-established college department, but with most of its students enrolled in the lower grades. By the turn of the century, AU was less dogmatic in its religious zeal than the other five colleges for African Americans in Atlanta, although chapel attendance was still mandatory and most of the puritanical rules and strict discipline practiced at the other schools were maintained. AU's highly visible bright-complexioned students led many African Americans to believe that the school, like Fisk, had been founded by white fathers interested in educating their colored children. Hope's early family history tended to give the story credibility. Hope never publicly commented on the widely held belief, and there is no evidence that the American Missionary Association founded AU or Fisk with any such intention. What is certain is that in Atlanta and Nashville—cities that could (and did) claim to house the largest conglomerate of black colleges in the world—Fisk and Atlanta Universities stood head and shoulders above the other schools in academics, administrative organization, and reputation.[22]

Two of Hope's most enduring friendships were formed with AU faculty members. George A. Towns, a black southerner born in Albany, Georgia, in 1870, first arrived at Atlanta University in 1885 for his last year of grammar school. He remained there off and on for the next nine years, graduated in 1894, and taught physics in the science department until 1898. Towns went on to Harvard and received another bachelor's degree in 1900, then returned to Atlanta to teach at AU, where he was often seen in later years riding his bicycle rather than using the city's segregated transit system. A staunch proponent of full equality, Towns remained an Atlanta icon for the next sixty years.[23]

Hope and Towns first met in Chicago during the 1893 World's Fair. As youngsters, both men had been taught by early graduates of Atlanta University, who instilled in them rigid ideological principles rooted in New England cultural influences. That New England culture, reinforced and strengthened by their northern academic experiences, remained a permanent part of their personalities that fueled their passionate insistence on full equality, their demand for African American higher education, and their opposition to the philosophy of Booker T. Washington.

Hope met and befriended another AU faculty member who came to epitomize the best of the African American scholar-activist tradition. W. E. B. Du Bois had arrived at the university in 1897. He lived with his wife, Nina, and their year-old son, Burghardt, in faculty rooms in AU's South Hall. In his prizewinning biography of the intellectual giant, David L. Lewis pointed out that Du Bois considered Hope "his most intimate male friend" and always dealt with him as an equal.[24]

Born just four months apart in 1868 into very different situations, the early backgrounds of the two men were in some respects similar. Both were members of the first black generation after the Civil War whose family heritage included a privileged free status unknown to most others of their racial group. Yet Hope's Deep South origins contrasted sharply with Du Bois's early life in Great Barrington, Massachusetts, a town that counted few African Americans among its residents. Although race was a factor in his western Massachusetts home, as a teenager Du Bois (whose interactions with recently arrived immi-

grants were not always cordial) seemed convinced that class was a larger barrier to privilege in America than skin color. Hope, on the other hand, in spite
of the peculiarities of his blended family, recognized as a teenager that race
was a pervasive fact of life in Augusta.[25]

Ironically, the two men gained valuable insights when they traveled in opposite directions to continue their education. Their new academic environments expanded and altered their worldviews. Du Bois went south to Nashville to attend Fisk University in 1885, and one year later Hope traveled north
to Worcester Academy. At Fisk, the reality of race in America hit Du Bois like
a thunderbolt and led to his spiritual transformation and inevitable emergence
as a "race man." Du Bois's world became increasingly black as he immersed
himself in the intraracial reality of a southern African American elite who by
a variety of means made their way to the prestigious Fisk University. Hope,
on the other hand, "whitened" his worldview at Worcester Academy. He
easily blended in with both the working class and an elite group of young
white men who tended to accept him as an equal in spite of his racial identity.
Just as important, in New England Hope became even more familiar with the
high ideals and Western-based culture of his teachers. Like Du Bois at Fisk,
Hope absorbed that culture because of his personal belief in its intellectual
superiority and its efficacy in the struggle for African American advancement.
Although John Hope's experiences "behind the veil" in Augusta had planted
the seed of his racial destiny, his commitment to race work and leadership had
begun to bloom by the time he was ready to leave Brown.[26]

There was at least one major difference between the two men, however.
Hope was attracted to the New England culture's emphasis on fervent religi-
osity, missionary zeal, and evangelicalism. In addition to his personal belief in
its epistemology, Hope also viewed religion as a useful tool in the fight against
prejudice. It produced what he and many of his contemporaries called "Christian character," a sort of invisible armor that helped to insulate African Americans from insults and allowed them to maintain their dignity. Hope wrote
years later that the "mere reading of the scriptures and the hearing of singing,
even though they [students] may not participate in the singing, has a cultural
effect and more frequently than not, a very lasting spiritual influence in the
fight against prejudice."[27]

For the more scholarly Du Bois, religion remained a gray area. Hope left
Brown University, a school that still boasted of its Baptist origins, to work at
Roger Williams University, a school even more deeply entrenched in religious culture. Du Bois went on to the more secular Harvard, eventually doing
graduate work there and in Germany. Lewis wrote that when Du Bois took his
first teaching job, at Wilberforce University in Ohio, a black institution that
was also intensely religious, he "found the pastoral campus parochial . . .

primitive and hysterically religious"; people "flaunted their religion at every opportunity." By the time he reached Atlanta, Du Bois was convinced that reasoned study and analysis, not religion, would break down the walls of discrimination.[28]

The two men's views of the role of religion represented slight differences in their strategic approaches, not an unbridgeable philosophical void. Both believed passionately in the same objectives: full African American equality and training for African Americans in higher education. They also agreed fundamentally on the methods by which equality would be obtained. Along with religion, Hope also believed in the importance of scientific study, and both men promoted Western culture as a fundamental basis of good character. In addition, both men agreed that every attempt to heighten the wall of racial discrimination should be met with an army of resistance just as determined to tear it down. Their differences in religious outlook notwithstanding, in 1898 Du Bois and Hope held mutual beliefs that formed the basis for a deep and enduring friendship.

Du Bois was Hope's closest friend in those early Atlanta years, but he forged other friendships as well. His friends included men (and they were all men) like William Pledger, Henry Lincoln Johnson, William Crogman, J. R. Porter, Dr. William Penn, and Rev. H. H. Proctor. Pledger and Johnson were law partners in Atlanta and prominent figures in the state Republican party. Pledger, born the slave of a plantation owner around 1851, cultivated the right political contacts during Reconstruction and became one of the most powerful men in the Georgia Republican party until early in the twentieth century. Both he and Johnson were political mavericks who rejected cooperation or fusion with the state Populist party, opting instead for a closer association with paternalistic white Democrats. However, they were best known among African Americans in the late nineteenth century as race men, civil rights activists who spoke out about injustice and were committed to full equality. Pledger especially was appalled at Georgia's dismal record in protecting African Americans against lynching. Privately, both men straddled the tactical fence, often personally benefiting from a friendly relationship with Booker T. Washington while simultaneously acting in ways that violated key elements of the Tuskegeean's program.[29]

William Crogman, the oldest of the group, was born in the West Indies in 1841 and orphaned at the age of twelve. Educated in Massachusetts and later at Atlanta University, he was a respected professor of Greek and Latin at Clark University (later Clark College and now Clark Atlanta University), a Methodist "college" for African Americans then located in south Atlanta close to the present location of the federal prison.[30] In 1903 Crogman began a seven-year stint as Clark's first African American president, perhaps the first black ever to serve as president at any of the southern black schools supported by northern missionary societies. The small, bronze-colored Crogman (who with his spectacles looked a lot like Gandhi), who was in his sixties, shared Hope's love of the classics and commitment to liberal arts education. He was also a race man committed to full equality and protest who especially deplored segregation. He liked to boast that he chose to walk the three or four miles to town and back from the college, regardless of the weather, rather than suffer the humiliation of riding on Atlanta's segregated streetcars.[31]

Porter, Penn, and Proctor were closer to Hope's age. The Savannah-born Porter was a dentist who arrived in Atlanta in 1893 and set up a private practice, leaving behind a successful business career in banking and real estate in Birmingham. Penn was a prominent physician and surgeon, chubby but handsome, who came to Atlanta fresh out of Yale Medical School in 1897. Penn, whose brother, I. Garland Penn, had been in charge of the Negro Building during the Atlanta exposition, had a thriving medical practice and served as "physician-in-residence" at three of the six black Atlanta schools. Both Penn and Porter were emerging as race leaders in the early twentieth century, and both insisted on full equality, racial self-help, and solidarity.

Proctor attended Fisk (Du Bois was a classmate) and then Yale University. After graduation he became the first African American minister of the First Congregational Church of Atlanta. As a result of Atlanta's changing demographics, the congregation of the mainly upper-class church had become increasingly black, although the class composition of its approximately one hundred members remained the same. In time, Proctor's "institutional church" became a hallmark of social responsibility. Proctor had played a prominent role in the Atlanta exposition and missed few opportunities to protest against racial injustice. As is true of most African American leaders of his time, his actions defy strict ideological categorization. He got along well with both Washington and Du Bois, and claimed both men as two of his dearest friends. He saw himself as primarily an interracial leader—an intermediary—and later called his autobiographical sketches *Between Black and White*.[32]

In his later years Hope would remember these men as important contributors to black community life in Atlanta. They helped to perpetuate a tradition of African American activism that earned Atlanta a reputation as a hotbed of African American political protest. By its example, black Atlanta helped define the very meaning of African American leadership—race men and women—committed to a society free of racial prejudice, poverty, and injustice, and consciously aware of a distinct African American ethos born of their hyphenated group experience in America. Cut from a variety of cloth, these leaders brought to Atlanta a wide range of experiences and backgrounds.

They were by no means a perfect group. They chose different tactical approaches, and personal ambitions and opportunities at times compromised their idealistic objectives, yet these men managed to pass on their spirit of service to a younger generation that would carry the leadership torch forward. Hope recognized as much in 1928 when he wrote to Du Bois that "much that is being done today, I think, grew rather directly out of the work that colored men did in Atlanta as far back as twenty-five, nearly thirty years ago. It really is history, Du Bois."[33]

During his first semester at ABC, Hope confined his activity to the campus—teaching his classes, counseling students, and generally learning his academic responsibilities. After visiting both families—in Chicago and Augusta—during the Christmas vacation, Hope returned to school in 1899 with a bad case of the flu. Winter had come early that year, and the temperature had plummeted to an unheard-of nine degrees below zero.

The spring thaw brought more than relief from frigid temperatures, however; it also brought racial violence. Georgia mobs murdered twenty-seven African Americans in 1899, an all-time high, earning the state the dubious honor of being responsible for murdering 31 percent of all the African Americans illegally executed in the nation.[34]

Palmetto, Georgia, then a small railroad town about twenty-five miles southwest of Atlanta (now south Fulton County), figured prominently in two of the lynchings, which received national attention and forced Hope to recognize how fragile black existence was in his home state. On 16 March 1899, seven black men were accused of arson in Palmetto, arrested, and placed in an iron-barred room in a warehouse until they could be taken to the county jail the next day. Late that night, meeting no resistance from the six armed guards, a masked mob of fifteen broke into the room and shot all the men at point-blank range, then reloaded and fired a second volley into their prostrate bodies, killing five of them. Miraculously, two were only wounded.[35]

The *Georgia Baptist* of Augusta reported the crime seven days later and correctly predicted that in spite of a bounty offered by the state, "we have not the slightest idea that the governor will ever be called upon for the rewards offered [$500 for the arrest and conviction of the first man and $100 for every subsequent one] and we do not believe he expects ever to see these men brought to justice." The *Georgia Baptist* called the lynching "the most horrible crime of the age." In a very short time, however, William J. White, the editor, would realize that he had been sadly mistaken.[36]

The Sam Hose (or Holt) lynching near Newnan, Georgia, about ten miles south of Palmetto, was one of the most publicized in United States history. It occurred on 25 April, approximately a month after the *Georgia Baptist* reported the lynching of the "Palmetto Five." Sam Hose, a black farmer in Palmetto, had hurled an ax in self-defense and killed his white employer, a man named Cransford. By the time news of the incident reached the state capital, a few details had been added. According to the story told in Atlanta, Hose had not only brutally murdered the farmer, he had also snatched the farmer's child from its mother and thrown it across the room, and had repeatedly raped the farmer's wife in the same room where her husband was dying. Eventually the 140-pound, five-foot-eight-inch Hose, depicted in newspapers as a "burly black brute," was captured, tortured, mutilated, and burned to death in a carnival atmosphere in Coweta County. Two thousand men, women, and children witnessed the execution, with that many more arriving too late from Atlanta to get in on "the main event." They were not too late, however, to purchase Hose's scorched body parts, charred bones, and other bloodcurdling relics that were sold as souvenirs.[37]

Like other African Americans in Atlanta and across the country, Hope was outraged by the lynchings in Georgia, which a black newspaper editor called the "string em up state." As the offspring of an interracial relationship, he may have been particularly angered by the local newspapers' emphasis on the alleged rape of the dead farmer's wife. Many, if not most, southern whites chose to believe that only rape could explain sexual encounters between black men and white women. For several years, Atlanta newspapers had been justifying lynching as a legitimate punishment and a potent deterrent of the "constant" rape of white women by black men. In 1897, a woman writer warned in the *Atlanta Journal* that "if it takes lynching to protect women's dearest possession from drunken, ravening human beasts, then I say lynch a thousand a week if it becomes necessary." An *Atlanta Constitution* journalist encouraged the paper's readers to "let the good work go on. Lynch em! Hang em! Shoot em! Burn em!"[38]

The Hose lynching forced Du Bois to recognize that "one could not be a calm, cool, and detached scientist while Negroes were lynched, murdered and starved." It was necessary at times to leave the ivory tower of academia for the more dangerous arena of social activism.[39] Hope did not record his feelings about the lynchings that occurred during his first year in Atlanta, but Lugenia said later that he was outraged. When his students bombarded him with questions, Hope condemned Atlanta and the state of Georgia for their silence in the face of the lynchings. He surely also discussed the murders with Du Bois and others within his circle of friends.[40]

Hope may well have been part of a delegation from Friendship Baptist Church that protested the Palmetto lynchings to Governor Candler. Led by William E. Holmes, the delegation presented resolutions that condemned the Palmetto tragedies as a "menace to popular government, an abridgement of civil liberty and a crime against humanity." Five years later, in 1904, Hope and

Du Bois led their own delegation to see the governor about an especially horrible lynching in Statesboro, and eight others that took place in Georgia that year. However, Atlanta's African American leadership, including John Hope, remained silent during and after the Sam Hose lynching, causing the governor to blast the "better class" of African Americans for not condemning and turning Hose over to the authorities.

The governor's views were given wide coverage in the pages of the *Atlanta Constitution* and the *Atlanta Journal*. He claimed that members of the African American middle class and their leaders were "blinded by race prejudice, and can see but one side of the question." "I want to protect them in every legal right and against mob violence," he continued, "but they must show a willingness to at least aid in protecting the community against the lawless element of their own race. To secure protection against lawless whites, they must show a disposition to protect the white people against lawless blacks."[41]

Governor Candler misread the meaning of the silence within Atlanta's African American community. Perhaps it did not occur to him that African American leaders—and certainly those in Atlanta—did not know Sam Hose's whereabouts, or that many may have doubted his guilt. After the lynching, there was even more reason for all classes within black Atlanta to remain silent. Antiblack feelings were running high. The climate was not conducive to any kind of protest against the lynching (especially one led by blacks) or lingering questions about Hose's guilt or innocence. Even whites who questioned the official story of the incident were liable to suffer the wrath of the hysterical city. On the Monday that the *Constitution* reported Hose's ghoulish execution, it also reported the arrest of a white man on the charge of "criticizing Mrs. Cransford." The man, a railroad watchman and Atlanta resident, had been heard suggesting that Cransford's wife had "aided and abetted the negro in the commission of the crime," and that "he didn't believe Holt was as guilty as he was represented to be." The *Constitution* reported that police were aware of the tensions in the city and decided that it was best to "arrest the old man and keep him safe in jail for his own good." Yet the paper identified him by name and printed his exact address. Perhaps the only thing that saved him from bodily harm was his denial that he had said anything derogatory about "Mrs. Cransford," and the paper's report that he confessed, "If I could have gone to Newnan I would have helped the people burn the negro at the stake."[42]

If it was dangerous for a white citizen to question the events surrounding the Hose incident, certainly African Americans, including John Hope, had good reason to remain silent. But there were other reasons for Hope's silence as well. The ABHMS schools operated in an environment that was increasingly hostile to African American higher education. Though this would change, in 1899 the Home Mission Society measured its faculty members by a yardstick that rarely extended beyond the boundaries of its institutions. Teaching, counseling, and other interactions with students on campus were the activities that counted. Of course ABHMS officials endorsed the right of African Americans to enjoy the privileges of a participatory democracy, and there was no shortage of rhetoric about community service. Such service, however, was best restricted to politically safe activities like defending African American higher education and raising funds to support the mission schools. Before Hope arrived, with the occasional exception of Holmes, ABHMS faculty rarely participated in "radical" activities like public protests, writing articles, or making speeches against discrimination or lynching.

The scholar-activist tradition emerged slowly at Atlanta Baptist College and tended to coincide with the arrival of new African American faculty members. In 1899 there were only two regular black faculty members at ABC. Hope was new there and was just beginning his career, and he was not yet in a position to become an activist. In fact, it was only after Hope became the school's president in the first decade of the twentieth century that community activism among faculty and administrators became an important part of the Atlanta Baptist College (and later Morehouse) tradition.[43]

John Hope seems to have controlled his outrage early in 1899 as one racial incident followed another. He probably joined Du Bois in lamenting the Palmetto and Hose lynchings, the bloody riot in Wilmington, North Carolina, in 1898, the mob murder of a black postmaster, and other racial incidents Du Bois wrote about later that year in the *New York Independent*. John Hope understood restraint. A veteran faculty member of ABHMS schools, he was well acquainted with the society's unwritten policy on African American activism. One's outrage over racial problems was expressed privately, among friends and immediate family.

Although such occasions were rare, the usually mild John Hope could and did erupt in emotional outbursts when confronted with injustice to blacks in the South. Lugenia Hope later remembered that in those early days in Atlanta "John used to set the table on fire. I used to say to him, 'Jack, don't be so savage at the table.'" By June he had decided to test the Home Mission Society's policy by writing a restrained letter to T. J. Morgan, the organization's corresponding secretary: "Might speaking out cause any embarrassment to the American Home Baptist Missionary Society?" he prodded Morgan gently. As Hope probably expected, Morgan wrote back a conciliatory but paternalistic letter that more or less confirmed the society's position. Patience, Morgan wrote, was still the most effective tool in bringing about racial change in the South.[44]

Hope may have vented his frustrations over Georgia's increasingly notorious race relations record in a way that was not immediately apparent. Early in May 1899, Du Bois wrote to Hope asking him to present a paper at a planned conference on African American business, to be "pitched on a little higher plane than most of the tradesmen will reach."[45] The occasion was the Fourth Atlanta University Conference on Negro Problems, an annual conference whose proceedings became a part of the invaluable Atlanta University Studies series. The conferences received a much-needed boost when Du Bois arrived in Atlanta to take control of the series in 1897. His four-pronged attack included a nationalistic, yet intellectual and philosophical foundation for the development of African American business and a nationwide scientific study of black enterprise. There were also two symposiums: one provided an opportunity for potential entrepreneurs to interact with established veterans, the other was a "mother's meeting" allegedly called to address the business concerns of women. The conferences ended with resolutions drawn from the research on black businesses that illuminated both strengths and weaknesses. Though not without problems, the AU conferences (like the Farmers Conferences at Tuskegee) were laudable early attempts at meshing the needs of the community with the resources of the academy.[46]

John Hope's role in the conference on African American business was pivotal. His paper, designed to define the key issues in the intellectual rationale, was the most scholarly of all the presentations. He was perhaps a little nervous about it, having been in Atlanta for only a short time. Outside the classroom and his small circle of friends, he was not yet a recognizable figure in the city's activist and scholarly communities. It was probably his first exposure to a diverse interracial and somewhat national audience in Atlanta. The AU Conferences on Negro Problems already had a reputation in the black world, and there were high expectations for those presenting papers in the general sessions.

The conference began at eight o'clock in the evening on 30 May at Ware Memorial Chapel. Hope sat patiently on the guest platform as Atlanta University's president, Horace Bumstead, opened the conference and introduced Governor Allen D. Candler. Candler's presence may have been a bit disturbing. The Hose lynching was still fresh in most minds, and Candler had not been kind to this mainly black middle-class group in the pages of the *Atlanta Constitution*. His unprepared and hurried opening address revealed no new thinking in the New South of the late 1890s. It was over almost as soon as it began, and Hope was the next to speak. After being introduced by Du Bois, Hope walked to the podium to read his paper.[47]

He began with a strong opening statement: "The Negro status has changed considerably since the Civil War, but he is today to a great extent what he has always been in this country—the laborer, the day hand, the man who works for wages." In the conference proceedings the paper was called "The Meaning of Business." The original title of the speech, however, was more nationalistic: "The Business Man's Contribution to the Development of Our Race." The paper echoed the central theme of the conference. African Americans needed both "capital to dictate terms" and more producers, not just consumers. On the surface, the paper is no more than a call for African American self-help in an age of business enterprise rooted in the economically conservative and imperialist orthodoxy of the day.

Yet, a closer reading of the speech and the subsequent paper reveals an angry tone. Whites appeared only as vague figures used variously as positive and negative models for black behavior. In the speech, most whites were presented as representatives of the capitalist class, whose understanding of business and its place in world affairs was worthy of emulation. But the "so-called Anglo-Saxons" had less admirable traits as well: "They are a conquering people who turn their conquests into their pockets. Now our end as a race most likely will not be of the same nature as that of the Anglo-Saxon," Hope predicted. In Hope's view, African Americans had "emotional and spiritual elements that presage gifts . . . more ennobling and enduring than factories, railroads and banks."

Hope's belief in innate characteristics peculiar to the two races was a view shared by many blacks and whites in the late nineteenth and early twentieth centuries. Yet he did not attempt to bring black and white Americans together through the speech; nor did he speak of mutual economic interests. The speech was directed exclusively at African Americans and seemed to ignore the few whites in the audience and on the platform. It may have seemed curious to those in the audience seeing Hope for the first time—a man who appeared Anglo-Saxon himself—to hear him speak so passionately about "service in the elevation of my people."

Although no reaction to Hope's speech has survived, its tone reveals an anger absent from any other address he ever made before an integrated audience. This speech is far different from those he would soon deliver in the North. Perhaps it was Hope's way of expressing his anger over the recent lynchings. It was a safe forum. The governor of the state was seated on the platform (if he had not already left), and Hope had the ability to disguise what may have been his protest in a speech on an acceptable subject.[48]

Three or four months passed before black Atlanta got another glimpse of ABC's new African American professor. The American Baptist Home Mission Society had other plans for John Hope that were less confrontational and more in line with the society's view of community activism. The liberal arts colleges supported by the ABHMS were increasingly threatened by the growing support for Booker T. Washington's philosophy of education. After the publication of Washington's *Up from Slavery* in 1900, support for African American industrial education became even more widespread. Many private philanthropists thought the "Tuskegee idea" made good practical sense and chose to direct their contributions toward vocational schools, thus further reducing the already limited economic pool for financing black higher education. It did not help that some African Americans increasingly agreed with the gospel of vocational education and were joined by a number of whites, even a few influential members of the ABHMS.[49]

The ABHMS had no choice but to mount an aggressive offense against the assault on African American higher education. At the end of John Hope's first semester at Atlanta Baptist College, the Home Mission Society made good on its earlier promise to give Hope a larger role in the business side of the organization, which had been plagued by financial crises for most of the past decade. Hope took a summer position with the ABHMS that called for him to travel to specified northern cities and speak on the need for liberal arts colleges in the South. It was a strategy designed to raise money for both Atlanta Baptist College and Spelman Seminary (now Spelman College) and regain valuable philosophical support eroded by Booker T. Washington's emphasis on vocational education. Lugenia did not accompany him. Since she had to vacate Graves Hall, she went to Salt Springs (now called Lithia Springs), a picturesque resort developed as Georgia's first chautauqua by New South advocate Henry Grady.[50]

Hope spent that first summer speaking in the Midwest. From his base of operations in Detroit he traveled to other urban centers like Toledo, Dayton, Cincinnati, and Louisville, usually by boat or train. It was an arduous schedule that at times included smaller and more rural areas. Late in July, for example, he arrived in Detroit one morning, spoke to a group in Toledo that evening, and then traveled all night and part of the next day to speak to another group in southern Ohio. Nearly three hundred miles of travel on a hot summer day was not uncommon, he wrote to Lugenia, sometimes with nothing "to go on but one doughnut, one cup of coffee and the August number of McClure's Magazine."[51]

Though the regimen was difficult, Hope's instructions were relatively simple. It was his responsibility to convince Baptists to donate money to southern schools for blacks, particularly to Atlanta Baptist College. Church groups were his primary targets, but Hope also spoke at secular functions such as women's club meetings and fraternal societies. His message rarely changed: African Americans needed higher education. The future of the race depended on it, and the missionary schools, struggling desperately to remain afloat, needed financial support. His white audiences were often receptive enough, but the "northern colored folks," Hope wrote to Lugenia, "need to be worked up to a missionary spirit." [52]

Hope enjoyed that first summer of speaking and traveling. His letters to Lugenia reveal a relaxed and reflective man who was enjoying the "rolling hills and meadows" of Portsmouth, Ohio, and South Bend, Indiana, and the "quiet still waters" of Lake Erie. These letters also provide rare glimpses of Hope's likes and dislikes, visions of the future, deepening concern at deteriorating race relations, and constant self-evaluation. Impressed with the serene country atmosphere of southern Ohio, for example, Hope wrote to Lugenia of his wish to buy a farm where they could live out their lives "away from uncertainties." He imagined Lugenia "cooking, canning, milking and churning" in a "blue gingham frock," and himself doing chores in "a big straw hat and washable trousers with patches in the knees and seat." At the time Lugenia did not think much of the idea, but a few years later the Hopes did purchase a farm in Powder Springs, Georgia. Hope's letters (luckily for the historian) continued to reveal much more than he ever would in face-to-face interactions. [53]

Hope also enjoyed meeting African Americans in northern urban areas like Detroit. They seemed to like him and often commented favorably on his speeches. Though Hope continued to be dissatisfied with their financial contributions, he looked forward to attending their social events, including a celebration in Toronto of Canadian blacks commemorating the emancipation from English slavery. Nevertheless, Hope's puritanical beliefs prevented his enjoyment of all their recreational activities. On one occasion, three hundred northern African Americans shared a boat with Hope, laughing, singing, and dancing to ragtime music for five delightful hours. Hope wrote to Lugenia that they were "as fine-looking, neatly dressed set of colored people" as he had ever seen. Yet they were noisy and indiscreet, with "sweet looking young girls allowing fellows to en-arm them, throwing themselves into all sorts of indiscretions for a day's fun." In the view of the rigid John Hope, that was not proper behavior. Yet, except for telling Lugenia, Hope kept his views of African American social behavior to himself. It enabled him to maintain valuable contacts in the North that would become very useful to him in a few short years. [54]

Hope enjoyed the racial tranquility of the American North and the "equal Northern *law*," as opposed to "unequal southern *law*." His spirits soared as he crossed the Mason-Dixon line, perhaps recalling cherished memories of the peaceful years spent in New England. Yet even in the North there were reminders that African Americans and whites were not equal citizens in the late 1890s. Although he was never personally mistreated by any of his white hosts (who, he said, only "professed to be Christians"), racism on a more subtle plane did sometimes raise its ugly head.

Sly gestures or off-the-cuff remarks sent Hope scurrying for a pen to vent his frustrations in private letters to Lugenia. In Kentucky, for example, Hope "had his feelings touched" many times as he suffered silently through conversations offensive to his people. He revealed to Lugenia, as he would many times throughout his life, that he would not mind being "darker for then I should have some relief from those things I suffer through being taken for a white man." Yet the instances of prejudice only reinforced his racial identity: "From the bottom of my heart, as long as the Negro is a sufferer, and as long as the white man makes him suffer," he confessed to Lugenia, "I prefer to be with the oppressed, feel with the oppressed, and, if need be suffer with the oppressed, rather than be as . . . mean and uncharitable with white men, rather than have a share with oppressors."[55]

Hope refused to allow his frustration over white racism to interfere with his work for the Home Mission Society. He never shared his views with ABHMS officials, or with any whites for that matter. As far as they knew, Hope was content, and his work was exemplary. Though admittedly anxious when the tour first began, Hope became more relaxed, composed, and deliberate as he repeated the philosophy of the ABHMS in speech after speech. He was a perfect spokesman: young, debonair, handsome, articulate, educated in New England, and loyal to the ABHMS. Even though industrial education continued to command the attention of philanthropists, Hope's work impressed Henry Morehouse, T. J. Morgan, and Malcolm MacVicar, the most powerful men in the ABHMS, who increasingly viewed Hope as a rising star in the Home Mission Society.

Hope did not spend all his time polishing his image as an African American leader, teaching classes at Atlanta Baptist College, and delivering speeches for the ABHMS. Lugenia was an important part of his life. The couple eventually moved to their own rooms on the second floor of Graves Hall, which Benjamin Brawley described as "the center" of the college's life.

Shortly after they arrived at Atlanta Baptist, Lugenia had been both frightened and attracted by the disturbing sounds she heard one night coming from a nearby neighborhood. The next morning she said to John, "I wonder what was happening over there last night." As Lugenia later told the story, John was busy shaving at the time. He paused, perhaps razor in hand, and replied: "That's for you to find out." Lugenia never said whether or not she responded to John's reply, but she did find out.[56]

The sounds she heard that night could have been anything from echoes of a vociferous argument to desperate screams for help to gunshots. Atlanta's west side had been a neglected part of the city for years. The area around Atlanta Baptist and Spelman Seminary was rife with gambling, prostitution, murders, and robberies, and was a general haven for Atlanta's criminals. City officials used it as a dump for rubbish; the area streets were full of holes, mud, and debris; and residents had no city services like water mains, sewage, or lighting. Only Chestnut Street (now James P. Brawley Drive), where a few members of the black middle class were beginning to settle, buffered the colleges from dangerous crime-infested areas like West Fair Street Bottom, Battle Alley, and the notorious community high up on a hill later called Beaver Slide.[57]

Lugenia Hope rolled up her sleeves and commenced doing social work in the slum areas around ABC and elsewhere in black Atlanta. Eventually she founded the Neighborhood Union, an organization of African American women that became one of the earliest and most successful efforts in progressive reform in the country.[58]

In spite of their busy schedules, John and Lugenia shared more of each other's lives in the years before he became the president of Atlanta Baptist College than they did after his appointment. Each understood the other's commitments, and they tried to be mutually supportive. Du Bois and Hope were close, but Lugenia was John Hope's best friend. She alone shared his most personal thoughts, cheered his triumphs, and consoled his failures. When possible, the couple spent a week or two together at Lithia Springs before he began his summer work for the ABHMS. If not Lithia Springs, the two stole away to a remote hideaway they had discovered in Marietta, Georgia, near Kennesaw Mountain. The letters Hope wrote to Lugenia while traveling for the ABHMS reveal much about his love for her. By midsummer, signs of Hope's yearning for his wife usually cropped up in his letters between descriptions of his activities. Readers can almost see his eyes twinkle and feel his spirits rise when he acknowledges receiving one of Lugenia's letters.[59]

Out-of-state trips together were rare for John and Lugenia Hope, but there were a few. In the spring of 1900 they managed to attend a convention in Detroit together and visited Niagara Falls for the first time. Perhaps they treated it as the honeymoon they had never had. Their driver and guide on the Canadian side of the falls was an old former slave who impressed them with his vast knowledge of the black presence in Canada. "Together we trod the whole journey from slavery into freedom," Hope remembered in a speech a year later, "the old ex-slave and the two Negro children of a new order of things." It was an experience Lugenia and John remembered with affection.[60]

For most of 1900 Lugenia was pregnant with the couple's first child. There is no record of complications, but the Hopes may have been anxious nonetheless. A year earlier, shortly before the start of the AU Conference on Negro Problems, Burghardt Du Bois, the only son of Nina and W. E. B. Du Bois, died of diphtheria at the age of two. In his "Passing of the First Born" in the

Souls of Black Folk, Du Bois hinted at the scarcity of medical services available to African Americans in Atlanta. There were only two or three black physicians in the city, and they lived across town in south Atlanta in what was then called Brownsville. There was no telephone in the Du Bois family's South Hall faculty apartment, and appealing to white doctors was out of the question. By the time a physician was contacted, it was too late. Du Bois's biographer wrote that the couple was devastated and Nina Du Bois never really recovered from the tragedy.[61]

As their close friends, John and Lugenia Hope must have shared the couple's pain. Perhaps John was a member of the funeral procession of horse-drawn carriages that moved slowly (probably up West Mitchell Street) toward the train station to send Burghardt's body to its final resting place in Great Barrington, Massachusetts. Along the way, impatient whites called them "niggers," deeply affecting the Du Boises and the funeral party. Burghardt's death probably reinforced Hope's determination to see that Lugenia received the best care available in Atlanta. The person who delivered the Hopes' first child remains a mystery, but John Hope may have had his friend Dr. William Penn, a black surgeon and Yale graduate, standing by in case he was needed.[62]

Edward Swain Hope was born healthy on 28 August 1901. Though probably relieved for the moment, Hope continued to be vigilant. Du Bois's son was two when he died, and Hope was well aware of the stories handed down in his own family of his namesake, the first John Hope, who died of the same disease at three years of age. The names given to his firstborn son represented crucial episodes in Hope's life. "Edward" was the first name of Edward Burr Solomon, the Ohio philanthropist who had loaned John money to continue his studies at Worcester Academy. "Swain" was the last name of John Swain, a fellow student at Worcester and the son of a prominent Boston family whom Hope visited often while he was a student in New England. Swain and Hope had continued their friendship, and Swain always donated money to ABC when Hope made his summer trips north to raise funds. In addition to showing gratitude, naming his son Edward Swain Hope was perhaps John's way of immortalizing those early experiences and emphasizing the importance he placed on education.[63]

After Edward's birth, the Hopes moved out of their second-floor rooms in Graves Hall to larger rooms downstairs. Surely Lugenia would have preferred a larger residence, perhaps even a house, but Hope was adamantly determined not to accumulate a large debt. Money was scarce in those years, even though John received a small income from his share of properties owned by the family in Augusta. Neither John's mother nor Lugenia's was in the best of health, and at times the parental households in Augusta and Chicago needed financial assistance.

In addition, Hope had already begun a practice that would continue to wreak havoc on his finances for the remainder of his life: he donated more money than he could actually afford to African American organizations, institutions, and charities that he believed were worthy of his support. Those contributions included monthly sums to ABC and regular donations to organizations like the Foreign Mission Board of the National Baptist Convention, the Butler Street YMCA, the black National Baptist Young People's Union,[64] and the American Baptist Home Mission Society. It was also difficult for Hope to turn down requests for donations for new African American libraries, parks, kindergartens, and other facilities. He strongly believed in the work of the organizations he supported, and—as he echoed over and over in his speeches, talks, and papers—in the importance of African American self-help. Yet his financial records show that in the eight years before he became president of Atlanta Baptist College in 1906, he borrowed money twice against the life insurance policy he had taken out when he and Lugenia first married. The borrowing continued into his presidency, which suggests that the Hopes lived above their means.[65]

In spite of the money shortage, the birth of Edward brought great joy to John and Lugenia Hope and their families, particularly to Hope's mother, whose life otherwise seemed characterized by despair. Hope believed that Mary Frances Butts had never completely recovered from his father's death in 1876. She had worn only black in all the years since, and although she was not yet forty when James Hope died, she never had another close relationship with a man. She chose instead to live her life alone, saving her affection for her children and grandchildren.[66]

Trips to Augusta were frequent when Hope first returned to Georgia in 1898. Over the years, however, as Hope became increasingly busy, letters replaced visits to the Augusta homestead. Those letters show that Hope's mother had not been well for years. Her close friends were dying, and her letters seem to indicate that a part of her died with each. One of her good friends had been gravely ill and died early in 1900, and it upset her to know that the woman's adult sons, who were generally known to be passing for white, failed to visit their mother before she died. They also failed to return for her funeral. The woman was deeply pained by the absence of her sons and communicated her sorrow to Mary Frances. Fearing that she, too, might die alone, Fanny wrote to John and saddled him with the responsibility of ensuring that all her children were present when she died and would remain in Augusta for her funeral.[67]

Late in the spring of 1903, Mary Frances's health declined abruptly. Only a few months earlier she had lost her best friend, Josephine White, the wife of William J. White. The Augusta Hopes believed that Mary Frances never recovered from Mrs. White's death, and that event plus her insistence on traveling to visit her children may have precipitated her own death. Ever since 1898, after President McKinley appointed Judson Lyons register of the United States Treasury, Mary Frances Butts had made frequent visits to Washington, D.C., to see her daughter Jane and the rest of the Lyons family.

When she planned another visit in early April 1903, her family warned against it because of her failing health. Nevertheless, Mary Frances was determined to visit her youngest son, Thomas, who also lived in Washington, and then to travel to Atlanta to see her youngest grandson, "dear little Edward." It was as if she had a premonition of the inevitable. On her return from Washington, Fanny wrote to John Hope: "There is to be an excursion to Atlanta Friday week, and I thought I would come up. I think the change might do me good. I am sorry that you will not be there when I come." John Hope labeled this letter "The last letter my mother wrote me." It was dated 30 April 1903.

While she was in Atlanta, Fanny took a sudden turn for the worse and Lugenia had her escorted back to Augusta. John, who had already begun his summer traveling for the ABHMS, was finally located in Boston and arrived in Augusta sometime late in May. Mary Frances Butts died of apoplexy on the third of June, just two weeks before her sixty-fourth birthday. John Hope turned thirty-five the day before she died.[68]

The funeral took place at Augusta's Union Baptist Church. There is no record of Hope's thoughts as he listened to the minister eulogize his mother. They had always been close, and she, along with other family members, had figured heavily in his decision to return to Georgia. It is not abnormal for adult children to wish they had spent more time with their parents. John Hope, who had always felt guilty about leaving his mother seventeen years earlier, believed she understood the reason for his infrequent visits when he was in New England and Nashville. But saying that he was simply too busy to visit from nearby Atlanta, Hope wrote to Lugenia later that summer, was no excuse and "asked too much of my poor mother."[69]

Yet, Hope knew that he needed to put his own grief aside and remain strong; other family members needed his support. First there was his older brother, Madison, who had continued to work at the city post office all those years and to manage several family-owned properties. He was still unmarried—and unhappy—and still wanted to move north, but that opportunity never came. He was buried two decades later in segregated Cedar Grove cemetery beside Mary Frances.

There was also his younger brother, Thomas, whose erratic behavior frustrated Hope and confirmed his belief in his brother's immaturity. Eventually Tom graduated from Brown University and—with the help of his brother-in-law Judson Lyons—secured a job in the District of Columbia public school system. However, he was constantly in trouble in Washington, sometimes disappearing for weeks, with no family member (or school official) having the slightest clue to his whereabouts.[70]

One of John's sisters and her family were conspicuously absent from the funeral, leaving Fanny's wish to have all of her children present at her death unfulfilled. Georgia Frances did not come home to bury her mother. California was a long way from Georgia, of course, and the distance alone may have explained her absence. Hope's correspondence provides no direct explanation; however, an apologetic letter from Georgia Frances to Aunt Nannie written later that year provides a few clues. "No one knows but the Lord what I suffer," Georgia Frances wrote. "I often think if it wasn't for my two little children I would rather go and rest from the curses and trials of this world." The references to suicide are not just implied. "Since I begun this letter," she continued, "I heard the sad news of a woman living near committing suicide. I suppose the result of some serious trouble." The letter hints at some undisclosed disfavor toward her husband that deepened after her mother's death. Whatever the problem, Georgia Frances loathed being caught in the middle. She was especially concerned about the feelings of Madison. "I love my brother as I do myself and I hope some day to see him and explain things in full."[71]

California census records confirm that by the second decade of the twentieth century, Georgia Frances and her family had crossed the color line and were living as whites in Los Angeles. "Permanent passing" continued to be an undertaking fraught with uncertainties, one of those being the possibility of discovery. Hope believed, as did his mother, that it was fear of discovery that kept the sons of Fanny's deceased friend away from her bedside and funeral back in 1900. Though it pained families to "lose" loved ones, most often those who made the decision to pass were not betrayed. African Americans generally understood why that choice was made and the humiliation that came with exposure. There was no doubt in Hope's mind that Sissie's decision to pass permanently as white explained her absence from her mother's funeral. Publicly he said nothing; privately, however, he never forgave her. Ironically, his anger had less to do with her decision to pass than with her failure to fulfill her mother's last wish.[72]

When Mary Frances Butts died in 1903, Hope had just completed his fifth year at Atlanta Baptist College and was about to begin his tenth year in the service of the ABHMS. He was comfortably settled in Atlanta and had begun to establish himself as an African American leader and educator. Hope was popular with the ABHMS officials in New York who looked after the interests of the society's African American schools. They were especially impressed with Hope's skills as a fund-raiser and equally moved by his persuasive speaking abilities and his dedication to the ABHMS philosophy.

Hope no longer took classes in theology at the University of Chicago, but he retained an academic and personal interest in religion—an important point not lost on officials within the ABHMS educational hierarchy. In retrospect, it seems clear that by 1903 John Hope was destined to play a larger role in advancing the educational interests of the ABHMS. The form that service would take was not yet certain. In fact, it remained to be seen just what role the politics of African American higher education would play in determining whether Hope would make his contribution in Atlanta or another institution administered by the American Baptist Home Mission Society.

6

The Making of a "Militant"
African American President
in a Southern City

Hope began the fall semester of 1906 as Atlanta Baptist College's first African American president—in fact, the first of his race ever appointed president of any ABHMS school in the organization's seventy-four-year history. The Home Mission Society's revolutionary decision came only after a protracted struggle between liberal whites in the ABHMS and increasingly nationalistic African Americans in Georgia, who had very different perceptions of John Hope.

Within the black world Hope was viewed as a militant, a fierce advocate of black community interests who participated in bold and sometimes dangerous confrontations with powerful local and state officials. Nor did he shy away from lending his expertise as a skilled administrator, organizer, and educator to radical organizations pursuing "militant objectives" that included an insistence on equality and the right of African Americans to share equally in America's participatory democracy.

A different John Hope appealed to the liberal white leaders of the American Baptist Home Mission Society. Their John Hope was much more restrained, a devout Christian, an excellent teacher, and a skilled administrator. Above all else, their John Hope was fiercely loyal to the ABHMS and aggressively attacked the organization's critics while ignoring its shortcomings. The ABHMS recognized Hope's radical image among African Americans, and eventually publicly applauded his principled stance on full equality. Privately, however, ABHMS leaders recognized that Hope's militancy was always tempered with a moderation that met the needs of their organization. When it came to ABHMS control of African American higher education, for example, Hope was a staunch conservative, an accommodationist who defended the ABHMS even in the face of opposition from some of the most powerful African American leaders in the state. On the other hand, in the debate over the efficacy of a liberal arts education versus vocational education for African Americans, the

ABHMS appreciated Hope's militancy and vehement defense of black college education, even though his stance was in opposition to powerful Booker T. Washington and most philanthropists.

On the surface, it seemed that the two groups' perceptions of John Hope were too disparate to result in any meaningful black-white cooperation. However, Hope satisfied important mutual interests shared by African Americans in Georgia and the predominantly white Home Mission Society. Hope was not necessarily a perfect candidate, and elements in both groups had reservations about him. Yet by 1906, the ABHMS believed John Hope to be the best candidate available and moved quickly to capitalize on a golden opportunity.

Few periods in the life of John Hope are more crucial or complex than the eight years preceding his selection as president of Atlanta Baptist College. Those years saw issues of race, leadership, ideology, and religion divide African American Georgians. The mainly white, northern-based Home Mission Society found itself unable to operate within an environment characterized by a divided African American Baptist constituency. The drama was further complicated by a social environment that was increasingly hostile to African American advancement generally, and to black higher education in particular.

Ironically, Hope's ascendancy to the presidency was set in motion by the resignation of Atlanta Baptist's first African American faculty member, William E. Holmes, who fell victim to the continuing conflicts between African American Baptists and the ABHMS. Since the 1880s, African Americans had waged an unending struggle for more influence in the ABHMS mission schools and in Baptist literature.[1] By the late 1890s, African American Baptists in Georgia and throughout the nation seemed hopelessly divided into factions they called "separatists" and "cooperationists." Separatists (who at times also called themselves "anticooperationists" or "progressives") believed that the interests of black Baptists were best served without any support from or official ties with the ABHMS or its affiliate, the American Baptist Publication Society (ABPS). Cooperationists (sometimes called "antiseparatists" or "conservatives") chose to accommodate to the ABHMS, continue the cooperative relationship, and gain more influence within their organizational structures whenever opportunities arose. Along with other, local concerns, these issues deeply divided African American Baptists in Georgia and contributed to the split into two separate black state conventions in 1893, a split that destroyed long-standing friendships among black Georgians.[2]

The same summer that Booker T. Washington delivered his famous speech at the Atlanta Cotton States Exposition in 1895, three factions of African American Baptists came together at Friendship Baptist Church and formed the first national organization to address African American Baptist concerns. The meeting resulted in what the late historian James Washington called "the Other 1895 Atlanta Compromise," which brought into existence the National Baptist Convention (NBC).[3] The compromise resolved some national differences, and the NBC included both cooperationists and separatists among its members. In spite of this show of unity, however, tensions continued between black cooperationists and separatists.

In Georgia, where African American Baptists were particularly concerned with the issue of black influence in ABHMS schools, the tensions only deepened. In an effort to moderate that tension and reunite the factions at least in their support of the mission schools, the ABHMS in 1897 encouraged black Baptists in Georgia (and in other states as well) to form the Negro Education Society. The result was yet another organization drawn from the ranks of the two state black Baptist conventions, the Missionary Baptist Convention of Georgia (MBC) and the General State Missionary Baptist and Education Convention of Georgia (GSMC). The Negro Education Society was designed to give African Americans more influence in directing the affairs of Atlanta Baptist College and Spelman Seminary by increasing the number of African Americans on their boards of trustees.[4]

Two years later, however, in 1899, African Americans still found themselves on the periphery of power in the Home Mission Society matrix. Policy, as always, emanated not from black or white local trustees but directly from ABHMS headquarters in New York. William E. Holmes submitted his resignation and left Atlanta Baptist College late in September 1899 to become the president of recently created Central City College in Macon, Georgia. Earlier in September the *Georgia Baptist* had reported that Holmes had been "tendered the presidency and a man sent to Atlanta to urge his acceptance." Most black Baptists in the state did not believe that Holmes would really resign from ABC after spending more than twenty-five years there. Separatists believed that the popular Holmes would attract students away from ABC to the new school in middle Georgia. When the events leading to Holmes's resignation were eventually made public in the pages of the *Georgia Baptist*, the antagonism between cooperationists, separatists, and the ABHMS deepened.[5]

President Sale saw Central City College as a threat to the interests of the Home Mission Society. Though Holmes had promised to honor the contract he had signed with Sale earlier in June and remain at Atlanta Baptist College, Sale demanded that Holmes take a public stand against the establishment of Central City College. "The spirit in which the movement to establish that college was born, and its attitude toward the work of the Home Mission Society are such that a man cannot be wholly in sympathy with both," Sale wrote, "thus I ask of you an unequivocal statement of your position." Holmes refused and cut his ties with ABC. Initially, he refused to discuss the conflict publicly.[6]

In the meantime, ABHMS officials T. J. Morgan and Malcolm MacVicar commented on the dispute with tactless outbursts that fanned the flames. MacVicar repeated a statement he had made many times before, that "it would be one hundred years before the colored people would have men prepared to be presidents to preside over colleges." Morgan wrote directly to Holmes on receiving a copy of his resignation: "It would require your people two centuries to build up such institutions [Atlanta Baptist College and Spelman Seminary] as we have built up in the city of Atlanta." And he did not stop there. The establishment of Central City College, Morgan wrote, was "foolish, well nigh criminal, and doomed to ignominious failure." It was only after receiving Morgan's letter that Holmes took all the correspondence associated with the dispute to the *Georgia Baptist* for publication.[7]

What John Hope knew about the rumblings at ABC is difficult to determine. None of his surviving letters includes anything about internal politics at the school or makes any reference to Holmes other than casually mentioning his departure. President Sale had presented Hope to the General State Missionary Convention at its annual meeting in Atlanta shortly after his arrival in 1898. Eventually Hope joined the GSMC, which seemed only slightly more receptive to the ABHMS than the other state black convention, the Missionary Baptist Convention of Georgia. John Hope had been back in Georgia for only a year and was probably not yet embroiled in any of the state's black religious or academic controversies. And although Holmes had been instrumental in Hope's appointment at ABC, there is no evidence that the two men were especially close.

Atlanta Baptist College students, however, were well aware of the dispute. In intraracial politics, ABC students tended to be conservative. They usually followed the lead of the president and were unlikely to be critical of any administrative decision. Only a small blurb about Holmes's exit appeared in the October issue of the student magazine. The passion of one year earlier—when the students had acknowledged Holmes as the "intellectual father of us all"—was conspicuously absent. In 1899, the heading was simply "Holmes Gone to Macon." Though the students "reserved a tender place" for him in their hearts, they added this instructive postscript: "We confidently assert that no student, during all of the years of his connection with the College, has come under his influence."[8]

Holmes was a renowned black leader, educator, and Baptist statesman who commanded respect from such esteemed peers as William J. White, E. R. Carter, C. T. Walker, E. K. Love, and, before his death, the founder of Friendship Baptist Church, Frank Quarles. Younger men such as Hope,

Towns, Penn, and Proctor looked on Holmes as a model of African American leadership and held him in the highest regard. Holmes was more knowledgeable about African American Baptists in Georgia and the machinations of the ABHMS than anyone else in the state.[9]

Yet there was also a sinister side to William E. Holmes. He was ambitious and may have been an opportunist. In the late 1880s he secretly informed the ABHMS on the activities of prominent black Baptists in Georgia. He was most critical of William J. White, who was then associated with the separatist faction, and E. K. Love, the separatist leader. In 1887, before the black Baptists split in Georgia, Holmes learned that leading members of the Missionary Baptist Convention had devised a plot to wrestle control of both ABC and Spelman Seminary away from the ABHMS if their demands were not met. Furthermore, MBC leaders also threatened to establish a rival institution that would be staffed and supported by black Baptists. Holmes, a former corresponding secretary of the Missionary Baptist Convention, informed the Home Missionary Society's H. L. Morehouse of the plot, closing his letter with the following critique of black Baptist leadership: "Colored pastors are not above their people; having little or no sense of honor, they regard with indifference the failure to fulfill a promise, or to meet an obligation. This is true of them both individually and collectively, for the [Missionary Baptist] Convention as a whole is as slow to make good a promise as is any member of it."[10]

This complex scenario took a turn toward the bizarre in the early 1890s. E. K. Love and another black Baptist separatist leader, J. C. Bryan, called for more representation on ABC's and Spelman's boards of trustees. They also wanted African American presidents at the head of each school and an African American majority on both faculties. Meanwhile, William J. White had changed his mind and was calling for greater cooperation between the ABHMS and the mission schools, and he led that faction of the Missionary Baptist Convention of Georgia by the spring of 1892.[11]

Sometime in the 1890s, perhaps after the split in 1893, the most bizarre about-face of all took place among African American Baptists in Georgia. William E. Holmes became a staunch separatist and aligned himself with E. K. Love. Given his role and association with Atlanta Baptist and the ABHMS, the change is baffling, and the records reveal few clues that explain his drastic change in position. There is, however, at least one plausible explanation. It seems likely that Holmes expected at some time to become ABC's president. But when ABC looked for a new president in 1890, it was not Holmes who was offered the position, after practically twenty years of service, but the Canadian George Sale. Perhaps it was his realization at that point that his chances of becoming president of ABC were growing dim that caused Holmes to reexamine his position on cooperation. By 1899, Holmes may have been pushed by the ABHMS—and pulled by African American separatists—to believe that it was not at ABC that he would fulfill his presidential ambitions but at Macon's Central City College.

John Hope was probably unaware of the profound changes taking place among Georgia's black Baptists in the early 1890s and of the politics surrounding the split. In those years he was still struggling to finish his education and focusing his attention on his future bride, Lugenia Burns. Nevertheless, Georgia's African American Baptist history is important to the story of John Hope because it provides clues to what was expected of loyal ABHMS mission school teachers. With Holmes's resignation in 1899, Hope became the only permanent African American faculty member at Atlanta Baptist College. To what extent he would follow in his predecessor's footsteps, private and public, remained to be seen.

In fact, Hope's response to the events in 1899 was probably no different from that of most other African American Baptists in Georgia. Most of Georgia's African American leaders were cooperationists and hated to see Holmes sever his relationship with ABC. Georgia separatists, however, saw it as a window of opportunity to erect a college of their own—one with not only African American faculty and students, but a black president as well. The idea of establishing an African American Baptist college in Georgia was not new. African American Baptists had placed a priority on creating a black Baptist college in Georgia since their missionary association was founded in 1870. Cooperationists believed that wish had been fulfilled in Atlanta Baptist College and Spelman Seminary. Separatists believed ABHMS officials would never share power in the mission schools, and they thus had no choice but to establish one of their own. In 1901 the issue of shared governance would explode once again. At that time Hope was undoubtedly in the cooperationist camp. It is highly likely that he was a conservative on this issue in 1899 as well.[12]

Another of the realities shaping the lives of African American leaders tended to unite instead of divide them. Even though the bickering over Holmes's resignation did not die down until late December, black leaders could ill afford to spend time divided in Georgia's hostile racial climate. The lynchings, which had continued unabated since Sam Hose's execution early in the spring, demanded a united front. Black leaders, religious and secular, were also united in their opposition to increasing segregation, exclusion of blacks from public facilities, and attempts at legalized disfranchisement.

John Hope had just returned from a successful summer working for the ABHMS in 1899. His future looked promising, and he was probably less angry than he had been when he left the state a few months before. Once back in Georgia, however, Hope recognized that nothing had changed. If he pondered the Home Mission Society's unofficial opposition to faculty activism, it was not for long. His second year in Atlanta commenced with a series of protests that continued unabated until he became president of Atlanta Baptist College seven years later. His activities added luster to his stature as a new and emerging African American leader, deepened his commitment to Atlanta's radical tradition, and increased his popularity in the community as a militant defender of equal rights.

It was in opposition to disfranchisement that Hope made his first appearance as an activist against inequality late in 1899. By that time, in spite of African American protests, poll taxes and the adoption of county primaries (which became a state white primary in 1900) had already begun to shrink the black electorate in Georgia. Thomas Hardwick, a Washington County legislator who still bristled over the recent Populist uprising, believed further measures restricting the black vote were necessary. The Hardwick Bill called for measures already used in other southern states, like literacy tests and the grandfather clause, to remove the few remaining African American voters in Georgia and ensure that there was no black political participation at all.[13]

Throughout the fall, Hope joined Du Bois, Crogman, Proctor, Pledger, and other African American leaders in Atlanta in developing a strategy to combat Hardwick's proposal. Booker T. Washington also opposed the bill and often went to Atlanta to map out his strategy. Though probably not at the same time, their strategy meetings were often held at the parsonage of Henry Proctor, the minister of the First Congregational Church and a good friend of Hope, Du Bois, and Washington. Washington revealed his views publicly in a conciliatory interview in the *Atlanta Constitution* in November. Hope, Du Bois, and twenty-one other African American leaders in Atlanta signed an equally deferential petition expressing their opposition to the bill which they presented to the state legislature. Du Bois followed that up with an article criticizing Hardwick in the pages of the *New York Independent* a few weeks later.[14]

Ironically, the Du Bois–Hope and Washington positions expressed the same concerns. On the surface, what seemed to bother them most was the Hardwick Bill's failure to recognize class differences among African Americans, not the bill's threat to eliminate all black voting. "So far as the Hardwick Bill proposes to restrict the right of suffrage to all who, irrespective of race and color, are intelligent enough to vote properly," the petition read, "we heartily endorse it." The petition, however, was more than an elitist document designed to protect the political interests of the black middle class. It also condemned those features of Hardwick's legislation, like the grandfather clause, that were overtly racist and would affect all African Americans regardless of class. Even their endorsement of suffrage restrictions based on education has perhaps been misunderstood. It was not an endorsement without qualification. An education-based restriction would be satisfactory only if there were free schools for all children. The inclusion of this prerequisite, obviously aimed at expanding black educational opportunities, showed their concern for the African American rank and file and their adherence to the principle of equal opportunity.[15]

Nothing, however, stemmed the tide then moving in the direction of African American disfranchisement in Georgia, even though African Americans helped to defeat the Hardwick Bill in 1899, and again in 1901. By 1905 a discouraged John Hope would write about politics in Georgia: "There was a time when we knew conditions in our state and town, but so little influence does a Colored man have in politics now that I do not even know the name of the alderman in my ward, although I am a registered voter, have paid my poll tax and voted for President Roosevelt."[16]

Predictably, Hope focused his efforts on African American education. His emergence as a leader owed much to his attempts to expand educational opportunities for African Americans in Atlanta. In the 1880s black leaders had successfully pushed the school board and city council to staff black public schools with African American teachers.[17] By the late 1890s, however, some of the African American teachers were ill trained, and practically all were overworked and grossly underpaid. Although conditions in urban areas were not as bad as in the countryside, double sessions were still the rule instead of the exception in Atlanta, and African American children attended school in buildings that were dangerously substandard. In addition, there were no black high schools in Atlanta, and students who wanted to continue beyond the eighth grade could not do so at public expense. The Georgia legislature later eliminated the eighth grade and threatened to drop the seventh as well. From the system's inception, noted one historian of the period, "education for black Atlantans was inferior in every respect to that of whites."[18]

In the early 1900s, Hope joined other leaders in petitioning the state legislature, school board, and city council for better accommodations for black students. He wrote and spoke about the intolerable conditions and participated in conferences in support of efforts to maintain and increase revenue to Atlanta's black public schools. Opportunities for change were limited to Atlanta's segregated environment, of course. At the onset of America's "apartheid," as urban historian Howard Rabinowitz has clearly shown, exclusion— not integration—was the alternative to segregation. It was a reality well understood by Hope and other African American leaders protesting inequalities in education and other areas of African American life. That same reality influenced and helped to shape black objectives and methods of protest in the late nineteenth and early twentieth centuries.[19]

The increasing segregation did create problems for African American leaders. Their constituencies expected leadership on two fronts that probably now seem inconsistent and contradictory. In Atlanta, with its tradition of black radicalism, African American leaders were expected to wage aggressive campaigns against lynching, disfranchisement, and perhaps even selected separate accommodations, especially in public facilities like transportation.[20] Black leaders like Hope found it easy to engage in such activities without violating their ideological commitment to an open democratic society. Yet Atlanta's black radical tradition also called for efforts to create and improve facilities *within* the separate black community. African Americans in Atlanta expected such efforts from their leaders even if these violated philosophical principles about the importance of an open society. At times, leaders were frustrated by having to straddle the ideological fence between the principle of integration and the reality of segregation. Certainly this became more and more a problem for Hope as the years went by. Yet for those who valued their status as leaders within the African American community, such stances were necessary and their only claim to legitimacy.

African Americans in the South developed an affection for their own institutions that would only deepen over the years, and African American leaders could ill afford to ignore that. Most important, perhaps, were the black public and private schools. But African American leaders were also expected to acknowledge and respect other institutions in the segregated black world as well—churches, businesses, fraternal orders, organizations, and in time the black Greek societies that emerged on black college campuses.

The importance of African American institutions, and their relationship to the larger African American community, was not lost on John Hope. Belonging to and supporting African American institutions was no more unnatural for blacks than it was for their white counterparts who supported and belonged to their own separate institutions. These separate "race" institutions became integral components of African American communities throughout the South and were supported and loved by the black rank and file. Hope belonged, for example, to the oldest African American Baptist church in Atlanta, Friendship Baptist Church, which was then located on the northwest corner of Mitchell and Haynes Streets. He would eventually become a member of the Odd Fellows and the black Greek fraternity Alpha Phi Alpha, and was already a member of the National Baptist Convention and the General State Baptist Convention of Georgia. As the years passed, Hope became more entrenched in the internal affairs of the African American world, unconsciously building the support he would need when George Sale decided to give up the presidency of Atlanta Baptist College in 1906.

Thus, Hope continued to function as a scholar-activist trying to improve conditions within segregated black America while at the same time protesting the very existence of his racial group's second-class status. Few petitions to city and state officials were submitted without his signature, and rarely was he absent from public protests against injustice. Hope read widely, digesting current events both at home and abroad. He became a popular speaker known for the breadth of his knowledge, his uncanny ability to recall facts instantly, and his mounting confrontations with the status quo. Talks to local churches, public schools, and black community organizations filled his schedule.

It was not long before the other African American "colleges" on the south side of town—Morris Brown (the only truly African American–run and –controlled college in Atlanta), Clark University, Spelman Seminary, Gammon Theological Seminary (now the Interdenominational Theological Center), and, of course, Atlanta University—took note of Hope's rising star among Georgia's African American leaders.[21] His speeches at these colleges both broadened Hope's leadership base and helped him to sharpen and refine his views and positions on contemporary issues. The addresses were always carefully prepared and showed an awareness of the school's (and the denomination's) specific mission and a sensitivity to popular student positions.

In 1900, for example, Hope spoke to students at Morris Brown College, an African Methodist Episcopal school most closely associated with the controversial Bishop Henry McNeil Turner, who was the chancellor of the college between 1896 and 1908. Though better known for his support of the back-to-Africa movement of the late nineteenth century, Turner helped to establish Atlanta's African American protest tradition after the Civil War with his calls for better public education facilities, his insistence on the franchise, and his fierce opposition to lynching. John Hope and other African American leaders in Georgia held Turner in the highest esteem, both for his contribution to the development of African American leadership and for his long-standing reputation as "the acknowledged spiritual leader of the Negroes in Georgia."[22]

Morris Brown was a hotbed of support for African emigrationism, particularly during the volatile 1890s. The issue was discussed almost daily in African American newspapers across the country, and few were unaffected by Turner's pleas for continental African and African American interaction on some level. Lugenia's fleeting interest in African missionary work before her marriage, for example, probably owed much to Turner's influence in Chicago during the Columbian Exposition. A group of African American women from Atlanta petitioned the legislature as late as 1903 to take their families and themselves to Africa, and even Hope and Du Bois, perhaps in an angry moment, briefly flirted with separation. Along with a few other friends, the two men considered moving to the Georgia Sea Islands and starting an African American colony they hoped would extend "clear to the bottom of Brazil, including the

West Indies," ensuring their isolation from whites. The idea never got off the ground, however, and remained only a romantic fantasy.[23]

Like many of his contemporaries, including Washington and Du Bois, Hope did not generally support African emigration. His view of Africa at the beginning of the twentieth century did not differ substantially from that of other Americans, black or white. Seen through a parochial American lens, his Africa was a country (not a continent) "dark and mysterious" and in dire need of "God and western civilization."[24] Yet Africa intrigued him. He recognized the link between continental Africans and black Americans, and he believed African Americans had a vital role to play in Africa's development. Perhaps predictably, that role was couched in a Western-based paternalism that was a part of conventional African American thought at that time. "It is our simple duty to these people [the Africans] and the world to protect them," he told Morris Brown students in his speech, "protect them by our teaching and our life." Intraracial class factors also played a role in Hope's vision. "African Negroes need the American Negroes not of the vicious, ignorant, or thriftless classes, but the noble, the intelligent, the busy, self-respecting . . . Negro. Not the Negro who can't succeed at home but the Negro who can succeed anywhere because within him are the qualities that make success."[25]

Overall, Hope's speech at Morris Brown was militant in tone. It was not the divisive intraracial concern over emigration that stood out, but the more unifying emphasis on opposition to European colonialism. Hope stated that "English capital, English pluck, English brains and English desires to possess the world are surely going to run a railroad clear through that [African] continent from North to South, and its branches will pierce the most remote jungles." He was as critical of British militarism as he had been years ago at Brown and in his speech at the Fourth AU Conference on Negro Business the year before. His anticolonialism covered not only European adventurism in Africa but earlier conquests of indigenous peoples in the Americas as well. "I am not sure that a mistake was not made," he said, "when the Aztecs' remarkable civilization was crushed by one full blow from Spanish greed. Nor do I see how God's Kingdom on Earth can be hastened by the extermination of millions of African Negroes before the iron heel of Anglo-Saxon civilization." Hope's attitude toward Europe, and especially England, would change in time, but his anti-imperialist views, especially his defense of African rights, were stated eloquently among African Americans at Morris Brown in 1900.[26]

At the same time Hope was making his mark as a leader among African Americans, ABHMS officials continued to recognize his importance in furthering the work of their organization. That Hope was being recruited by another ABHMS school reveals how valuable he had become. By the fall of 1901 Hope had spent three successful summers working for the ABHMS and had established an exemplary record as a loyal Atlanta Baptist College faculty member. After Holmes resigned in 1899, Hope was the only African American on the faculty, although recent graduates of the college continued to serve as teaching assistants.

Shortly before the beginning of the fall semester, Hope received notice that a teaching position in theology would be opening up at Virginia Union University in Richmond. Virginia Union was an ABHMS school created when Wayland Seminary in Washington, D.C., merged with Richmond Theological Institute. In 1899, Malcolm MacVicar had resigned as the corresponding secretary of the ABHMS to organize the new school. He also served as its first president. Benjamin E. Mays, a highly revered former president of Morehouse College, was probably correct when he said years later that Virginia Union was the society's favorite in those days.[27]

Home Mission Society officials strongly encouraged Hope to consider the faculty position at Virginia Union University. However, George Sale was just as determined to keep him in Atlanta. Angered at the overtures toward his only black faculty member, Sale fired off a letter to ABHMS headquarters in November expressing his opposition. "Professor Hope is the one man upon whose judgement and counsel I rely on in matters of general policy and management," he wrote to ABHMS corresponding secretary T. J. Morgan. Not only could Sale ill afford to lose John Hope for those reasons, he was also particularly valuable, Sale wrote, "in continuing the growing harmony in the state between the college and the Negro Baptists." "You can easily see how trouble would arise if we are compelled to replace Professor Hope with a white man, as I fear we should have to do."[28]

The letter provides insights into Hope's value to the ABHMS early in the century. Sale and other members of the society recognized his growing stature as a leader and had already begun to place him alongside some of the most dynamic African American leaders of the state, and to a lesser extent the nation. The letter also illuminates the importance ABHMS officials attached to the relationship between African American leaders and the black community. Of course, many of Atlanta's black leaders were faculty members or administrators at the city's six African American institutions. While some of the other colleges could boast of two or more such leaders, however, President Sale had only Hope. Sale did not hesitate to make that point clear in his letter to Morgan. Hope, he said, was the only man at ABC who could measure up "with such men as Du Bois [AU], Turner [Morris Brown], Crogman [Clark] and Towns [AU]." It was a fact not lost on ABHMS headquarters.[29]

Although Sale deplored the thought of losing his only African American faculty member, he nevertheless left the final decision up to Hope. MacVicar and Morgan met with Hope in Atlanta early in December. Though he showed no enthusiasm for leaving Atlanta Baptist, Hope agreed to consider their proposal. He discussed the matter with Lugenia, then sought advice from his brother Madison and his sister Grace in Augusta. He probably discussed it with friends such as Du Bois and Towns as well. In the meantime, Hope's unenthusiastic response led Morgan to send a letter to Sale withdrawing the offer. "In view of your strong protest and especially in view of Professor Hope's evident reluctance to make the change," Morgan wrote, "I shall give the matter no further consideration." [30]

Hope received a copy of the letter and did not appreciate the manner in which the offer had been withdrawn. "When you give me a choice between actions, I seriously consider which is for the best; and perhaps you will some day agree that my seeming reluctance was only the proper care that any safe man would exercise," Hope wrote in a rare candid reply. Morgan conceded the point and responded with a conciliatory and apologetic letter that he hoped would clear up the misunderstanding. [31]

The verbal sparring between Hope, Sale, and Morgan reflected more than a president's interest in retaining a valued faculty member or Hope's slow and deliberate way of reaching important decisions. The sudden interest in recruiting Hope at Virginia Union University took place amid renewed tensions between the ABHMS and African American separatists. In 1899 Virginia's African American Baptists had divided along separatist and cooperationist lines when the ABHMS appointed Malcolm MacVicar, a white man, president of the school. As in Georgia, African American Baptists in Virginia had also split and formed two different state religious conventions. In the fall of 1901, Virginia Union anticipated losing an African American theology professor, and ABHMS officials desperately wanted Hope to replace him. Sale had written an official of the ABHMS shortly before Hope was approached about the vacancy that "if there is to be trouble on that ground, I feel that the University at Richmond should meet it and not transfer the difficulty to us and so endanger a rupture where a spirit of harmony and peace is growing." Hope most likely knew about the political situation at Virginia Union and did not want to be embroiled in what was obviously a potentially explosive situation. [32]

Meanwhile, back in Georgia, there had been several meetings in Atlanta between ABHMS officials and representatives of black and white religious conventions by 1901. [33] These meetings had done little, however, to bring separatists back into the cooperationist fold. The separatist leaders were well respected among antiseparatist black Georgia Baptists, and it pained both groups to air their differences in public. Hope and other cooperationists had stood shoulder to shoulder with separatists, for example, on issues involving the value of African American college education and improving community facilities. They were usually also in agreement on the need for full equality.[34] Yet the division among African American Baptists over the Home Mission Society's policies just would not go away. An ABHMS annual report issued earlier in 1901 indicated that trouble was brewing once more among black Baptists in Georgia, but things seemed to have settled down by the end of the year.[35]

Later in December, however, after talking to Morgan and MacVicar about the Virginia Union position, Hope delivered a blistering speech at Clark College that showed the issue was still very much alive. Hope's speech left no doubt that he was squarely in the ABHMS ideological camp in 1901. It also showed that, among different groups within the African American world at the turn of the century, labels like conservative and progressive, radical and liberal, often referred to issues not generally recognized among whites. To distinguish their position from African American separatists, for example, Hope and other cooperationists called themselves conservatives. Hope stated in his Clark College speech that "the radicals think that the only safe solution . . . is total separatism, and the conservatives believe in union of interests, and in cooperation." Separatists, he believed, were taking the issue of group solidarity and racial pride too far, and he warned that "Negro business, Negro church, Negro school and Negro country—for the Negro by the Negro and nobody but the Negro" was self-destructive and represented "wasteful crudeness." In Hope's view, the separatist philosophy only strengthened arguments for blacks' biological inferiority and inability to compete in the larger society. "The success that may come from total separation will bring with it that fatal idea that . . . we cannot succeed in any other way," he said. "Along with the bigotry and conceit of isolation will come an unwillingness to risk coping with the other race; and this will be an acknowledgement of inferiority."[36]

The conservative position, however, sacrificed nationalist ideals and considerations that were important to many African Americans. In addition to the pride they took in their own institutions, African Americans recognized that the racist environment denied them opportunities in the larger society and forced them to confront their inferior legal status on a daily basis. Hope conceded these points but still believed the conservative position was more realistic. Most important, the conservative position provided opportunities for competition: "With the two [black and white] men working together, mutual respect will surely be enhanced as each sees the other succeed." Ironically, when it came to the cooperation-separation dispute, Hope tended to subordinate collective African American advancement to a belief in the primacy of individualism. "Let me say this: If your ideal is the highest *individual* development for the greatest number of individuals, you ought to choose the conservative position. And after all, if the essence of life be character, what other view can be taken except that which admits of highest individual growth."[37]

Hope's rationale for promoting the cooperationist position in black education does not lend itself to simplistic analysis. On one level, his position made perfect economic sense. As a realist fully in tune with the numerous obstacles confronting black education, Hope understood that African Americans did not yet have the economic resources, administrative skills, or political clout to assume full responsibility for their own educational development. He would give many more speeches with essentially the same message.

Hope's ideological position on black education also reflected his personal interests. He taught at an ABHMS school and was a relatively young teacher looking out for a promising academic career. By May 1902 he had so impressed ABHMS officials that they paid him an additional salary "to visit churches and associations in Georgia in the interests of cooperation and education." Though no doubt committed to the cooperationist position, Hope was also not one to pass up an opportunity to advance his career.[38]

Yet Hope's rationale for supporting the conservative position was in many ways contradictory. Not only was it at odds with his earlier speeches in Atlanta—the speech on Negro business he delivered in 1899, for instance—it also contradicted his behavior in promoting race-specific organizations and institutions in black Atlanta. Leaders like Hope who had a "professional foot" in the white world were often troubled by intraracial issues with nationalist sensibilities. Practically all race men and women of the early twentieth century had some nationalist sensibilities, but that does not mean that they were all interested in going back to Africa or even that they had a conscious understanding of their African origins. A definition of African American nationalism in the early twentieth century that is limited to a conscious recognition of an African heritage or a desire for expatriation is simply too narrow. Mechal Sobel correctly stated in her instructive book on the "Afro-Baptist faith" that "every culture has a worldview that it uses to order and evaluate its own experiences." In the African American worldview, nationalist tendencies were rooted in blacks' collective historical experience as African Americans. That experience united them and was manifested in their support and pride in the creation and preservation of their own institutions.[39]

African American leaders who questioned the value of black control of community institutions were especially vulnerable to criticism from both groups. Hope and other cooperationists recognized that black separatists voiced valid concerns. All black Baptists recognized, for example, that the mission schools were owned by and would remain under the control of the ABHMS. Equally significant was the realization that ABHMS mission schools trained primarily

African American students. As black Baptist leaders gained in knowledge and skills, they became less willing to leave the education of their own college elite solely in the hands of a white organization. Separatists therefore chose to publicly condemn what one historian labeled the Home Mission Society's "cultural imperialism and tokenism" and decided to try alternative ways of influencing their racial group's educational future. Cooperationists certainly recognized the problem, but they disagreed with the separatists' solution.[40]

Cooperationists also understood that African American Baptist leaders had long been concerned about the way the ABHMS handled the funds it received in the name of southern education and evangelization. Melvin Washington has convincingly shown in his fine work on African American Baptists that "nothing gave greater impetus to the separatist tendency . . . than their belief that they had the right and responsibility to share in the administration of all Baptist funds collected in the name of aiding the freedmen." Although cooperationists still hoped to reach an agreement with the ABHMS, by the early 1900s separatists had virtually given up on the possibility of ABHMS officials ever sharing any financial accountability with African American Baptist leaders.[41]

The cooperationists were aware that the Home Mission Society's intransigence had helped to push the separatists to their extreme position, leading them to encourage students to withdraw from better equipped ABHMS-owned African American schools and transfer to less well equipped but black-controlled Baptist educational institutions. That stance was intended in part to preserve black dignity, respect, and pride, nationalist sensibilities shared by most African American leaders at the beginning of the twentieth century. Though Hope chastised African Americans for their support of "Negro" businesses, churches, and schools, he himself belonged to many of those institutions, and he personally supported black enterprises then and later.[42]

Despite sharing certain nationalist sensibilities with the separatists, Hope was nevertheless unwilling to give up what he called the "best college educational opportunities available to Negroes in the South." In the early 1900s, Hope probably knew more about black higher education in Georgia than anyone else. After Holmes resigned in 1899, no one was more knowledgeable about the intricacies of the ABHMS organization and the administrative complexities associated with running mission colleges in a hostile southern environment. That special insight no doubt contributed to Hope's belief that the separatists' brand of nationalism simply went too far. As cultural artist and historian Bernice Reagon once explained, nationalism can be a double-edged sword. It is a crucial tool in drawing attention to group interests. At some point, however, it becomes reactionary, stifling progress and survival "in the world with many peoples."

Though others disagreed with him, Hope saw separatist nationalism (like the nationalism of the African emigrationists in another context) as reactionary and therefore incapable of moving his race forward. It was actually an impediment in African Americans' quest for the best college education then available. In his view, the cooperation of whites was still necessary to maintain "Negro institutions" such as Atlanta Baptist College and Spelman Seminary.[43]

Hope's position on cooperation resonated well in the ABHMS and increased his value as an important voice within the organization. At the same time, however, he continued his local activities in Atlanta's African American community. Since not all African Americans were Baptists, it was relatively easy for Hope to maintain his positive image as a militant African American leader in spite of his conservative stance on the Baptist mission schools.

In the spring of 1902 Hope became deeply involved in a protest designed to provide black Atlantans with library facilities. His activities helped to magnify his image as a militant African American leader sensitive to black needs across class and denominational lines. The library protest was typical of the protests conducted by African Americans leaders in Atlanta during the late nineteenth and early twentieth centuries, and it illustrates how potentially dangerous such public protests were. In 1899 the president of the all-white Young Men's Library Association secured conditional aid from philanthropist Andrew Carnegie to build a public library in Atlanta. In March 1902 the library opened at Forsyth and Carnegie Place on a site furnished by the Library Association. The city promised the new library an annual maintenance appropriation of $5,000 from city taxes.[44]

African American leaders in Atlanta had long hoped for library facilities to serve "the general public" (i.e., blacks as well as whites) and the needs of the city's black colleges. Back in the 1870s a local African American minister had helped organize the Abyssinian Library (actually a reading room), which opened in March 1880. Two years later, the organization boasted two thousand volumes and more than two hundred members. In July 1882, however, a fire destroyed the building, and in spite of their efforts African Americans in Atlanta simply could not raise the capital necessary to rebuild the library facility. When the Carnegie Library opened, the African American community had been without any library facilities for more than twenty years.[45]

Ever vigilant, Hope, Du Bois, and other African American leaders had heard that blacks would not be admitted to the free "public" library. The news was probably not unexpected, yet these men, led by Du Bois, "thought it well to ask why." The opening ceremony began promptly at three o'clock on the third of March. The exercise was full of pomp and circumstance, with city leaders, library trustees, and a host of invited guests congratulating each other over their "marvelous accomplishment."

Hope left no record of what he and others in the delegation of eight thought as they walked downtown and climbed the hill to the new marble structure. They, of course, had not been invited, and their appearance drew cold stares and expressions of wonder, Du Bois later wrote, as to "what business we had there." According to Du Bois, after some waiting, the trustees received them courteously and gave them seats.[46]

Du Bois began the protest with the deference and delicacy necessary in all confrontations with white officials: "Gentlemen, we are a committee come to ask that you do justice to the black people of Atlanta by giving them the same free library privileges that you propose giving the whites." While Du Bois continued his carefully prepared remarks, Hope and other members of the black delegation sat silently by, keenly aware of the hostility that emanated from the library trustees. Du Bois went on to question the use of public monies in any facility that excluded a segment of the tax-paying public. Hope later remembered that the chairman of the trustees became most uncomfortable when Du Bois lectured the committee on the "spirit of this great gift to the city," which was not "caste or exclusion, but rather the catholic spirit which recognizes no artificial differences of rank or birth or race, but seeks to give all men equal opportunity to make the most of themselves." Du Bois finished his bold statement and sat down.

There was a deafening silence. It lasted only for a moment, but it probably seemed an eternity to Hope and the other African American delegates. The members of the library committee stared at the eight black spokespersons (neither Du Bois's correspondence nor Hope's reveals the identities of the others), perhaps probing for some sign of weakness, discomfort, or strain. Hope, ever sensitive to his white complexion, may have thought he was being singled out for special scrutiny. At last the chairman of the committee spoke: "Do you not think that allowing whites and negroes to use this library would be fatal to its usefulness? . . . Can negroes be admitted to the use of public libraries in the South?" The delegation remained silent.

Before the committee delivered the obvious answer to the black delegation's request, one of the delegation chimed in with a reminder that "we did not ask to use this library, we did not ask equal privileges, we only wanted some privileges somewhere." The library chairman then made several things clear: "Negroes would not be permitted to use the Carnegie Library in Atlanta; . . . some library facilities would be provided for them in the future; the City Council would be asked to appropriate a sum proportionate to the amount of taxes paid by negroes in the city; . . . an effort would be made, and had been made, to induce Northern philanthropists to aid such a library."[47]

The unsuccessful fight to establish a public library for African Americans in Atlanta was perhaps one of the bitterest disappointments of Hope's early activist career. Within a few years, however, a separate library was built for Atlanta's African American community. In 1903 Carnegie donated $25,000 for a library to be built on the campus of Atlanta University. It opened its doors in 1906 to AU faculty and students as well as the general public. No public library for African Americans was built in Atlanta until the Auburn Avenue Branch Carnegie Library opened in 1921. John Hope played a vital role in that campaign. Annie L. McPheeters, an icon among black librarians in Atlanta, noted that it became the "community's cultural and intellectual center and contributed much to the total cultural and social development of this population from 1921 to its untimely closing in 1959."[48]

Hope's importance as a spokesman for the American Baptist Home Mission Society was raised another notch in 1902 when industrial education received an added boost. John D. Rockefeller founded the General Education Board (GEB) that year and endowed it with $1 million to aid southern education. The GEB consisted of a small but powerful group of businessmen that controlled several other philanthropic agencies and, in Louis Harlan's words, assumed "virtual monopolistic control of educational philanthropy for the South and the Negro." The board paid little attention to the black mission colleges, even though most of their students were enrolled in the grammar and high school departments. The southern states did little to promote African American public education at the beginning of the twentieth century, and for that reason the GEB did, on occasion, provide small amounts of money to specific projects at the mission schools.[49]

Booker T. Washington's industrial education philosophy continued to dominate thinking on African American education and to command the attention of philanthropists. The values Washington encouraged—thrift, respect for work, and the dignity of labor—were the values America's most prominent businessmen respected. The Hampton model of industrial education provided them with a convenient rationale for the role they saw African Americans fulfilling in the southern political economy.[50]

With the creation of the GEB and its growing monopoly over funding for southern African American education, the ABHMS wasted no time in providing John Hope with additional platforms to challenge Washington's assumptions. In a speech delivered in Detroit around the turn of the century, Hope declared that "liberal education for Negroes is a boogie to frighten people, especially those philanthropists who give much and study very little the objects of their beneficence, while industrial education has come to be a shibboleth." True to the mission school ideology, Hope acknowledged the importance of black industrial education but rejected the assumption that it was the only way African Americans could appreciate labor. Citing his own experience during his college years "working in high places and in menial employment," Hope said, "I give you my word, the Negro does not despise labor, and he who says the Negro needs industrial training to keep him from despising toil had better find a more plausible reason." Just as significant, Hope rejected the assumption that African Americans were less frugal than their white counterparts. "Do your white artisans in the north who earn from two to ten dollars a day know the value of a dollar and save it?" he asked rhetorically. "If you think so, watch their condition ten days after they have gone on strike." [51]

But Hope did more than simply challenge the popular assumptions that supported black industrial education. He also offered his own blueprint for the skills African Americans needed in a changing industrial economy and chastised white Americans for shutting blacks out of the new and most advanced trades. It was plain that in addition to a South without job discrimination, Hope's schematic envisioned the needs of an expanding separate black world.

Hope believed that African Americans needed professional training in administrative skills so that black businesses could survive. Along with "trained preachers and teachers," Hope stated, the African American community needed "business education for lawyers, physicians, dentists and storekeepers." He was just as insistent that "Negro workers ought to have access to apprenticeships in the rubber, paint and chemical industries," areas then closed to African American workers. "From newsboy to engineer," Hope informed the audience, "as white people have the capital you can see that in the long run white labor is given not only a chance but a preference. All the skill in the world would not stop such competition." There was room for both industrial training and higher education, and Hope did not understand why "big-minded men" should be so intent on ensuring that the "industrial feature is the only good feature in Negro education." [52]

Hope's message on the attributes of a liberal arts education increasingly found its way into speeches he made at Atlanta's other African American colleges. He delivered the same message to black women's groups, public school students, and general African American audiences. In addition to challenging Washington's assumptions about the primacy of industrial education, Hope, like Du Bois and others, linked his defense of higher education to the training of African American leaders—to manhood—and full equality for the race. "There must still be a deliberate effort on the part of schools to bring Negroes to see everything," Hope stated in another speech, "to comprehend all, to be dismayed by nothing, but to continue the chartered course to democracy, to brotherhood through intelligent leaders who rate their personal success and happiness by the enlarged welfare of those among whom they work and strive and live." [53]

Hope rarely if ever mentioned—or criticized—Washington by name in his speeches, but he did not extend the same courtesy to Andrew Carnegie, the steel magnate and philanthropist who joined other powerful businessmen in supporting the industrial school idea. Carnegie admired Booker T. Washington and provided Tuskegee Institute with its first significant endowment in 1903. [54] One of the most articulate of the industrialist philanthropists, Carnegie linked African American industrial education to the South's need for black labor. "The Hampton Institute shows the only useful solution," he said in a speech reprinted in Hampton's *Southern Workman*. "The Negro is 'placable and lovable.' These men give us eleven million bales of cotton a year and this I contend helps to make the United States the most powerful nation in the world." Carnegie—like Washington and his mentor, Samuel Armstrong— linked his vision of black education to his perception of blacks' economic possibilities and to what he saw as the inefficacy of black participation in politics: "My knowledge . . . leads me to the opinion that no political measures can ever save or benefit the Negro." [55]

Hope had little respect for Andrew Carnegie or his views on African American economics and politics. He was particularly upset with the piece that appeared in the *Southern Workman*, and made it the subject of an Emancipation Day address in 1902 (a few months before the library protest). Hope began the speech by reading portions of Carnegie's article aloud, then stopped to elaborate on the philanthropist's description of African Americans as "placable and lovable," and the black worker as "a good-natured obedient fellow that does what you tell him and is satisfied with what . 1 give him." "If his estimate [Carnegie's assertion that African Americans produced eleven million bales of cotton a year] be correct," Hope continued,

> that makes more than a bale of cotton for every Negro man, woman and baby. No such productivity is accorded any other laborer in this country, and we ought to enjoy the fruits of our labor. But see what this philanthropic Northern gentleman with his pocket full of libraries says: "These men give *us* eleven million bales. Who are these *us*? Is it fair to have us Negroes heap up riches for others without securing in wages, in civil and political rights the same blessings that other laborers less productive than Negroes get in this country?

Hope's disparaging attacks on Carnegie's views would come back to haunt him a few years later, after he became the president of Atlanta Baptist College. The ABHMS no doubt appreciated Hope's unwavering stance on the value of a liberal arts education, but had the speech been delivered to a white group on Hope's summer speaking circuit, even the ABHMS might have been a little uneasy. It was an Emancipation Day speech, however, probably delivered at either Friendship or Wheat Street Baptist Church to an all–African American audience. The speech probably went over well there in "radical black Atlanta," further polishing Hope's image as a militant African American leader.[56]

By the early 1900s Hope had met some of the most militant African American leaders in the nation. Some of them belonged to the elite Washington-based American Negro Academy, founded by the prominent race leader Alexander Crummell. In 1899, during his second year as president of the organization, Du Bois asked his friend John Hope to attend the academy's annual meeting in March. A year later, in 1900, Hope was invited to join. The academy's membership then included prominent African American radicals and some of the intellectual giants of the era. In addition to Du Bois, there were the Grimké brothers, Francis and Archibald; educator Kelly Miller; Bishop Alexander Walters of the AME church; and another recent inductee, Charles C. Bentley of Chicago, a prominent dentist who would become a good friend of Hope's and would help organize the first meeting of the Niagara Movement in 1905.

Ironically, the idea for the academy originated with Georgians William H. Crogman and Richard R. Wright, both friends of Hope's and members of the organization when Hope joined it. According to Alfred Moss, Crogman and Wright wrote to Crummell with the idea "of bringing together a group of black scholars and thinkers to establish a national society whose main work would be to formulate strategies for solving the problems of their people and to respond to the attacks of white intellectuals." When the organization held its first meeting in 1897, Booker T. Washington signed the roll as one of the thirty-six charter members. One year later, Washington was no longer a member. By then it was clear that the academy's insistence on full equality and its strong endorsement of African American higher education placed it within the realm of militant African American organizations.[57]

In 1905, Hope delivered an important paper on African American disfranchisement to the academy that demonstrated his continuing contribution to Atlanta's militant scholar-activist tradition. The address, eventually published as one of the academy's Occasional Papers, was called "The Negro Suffrage in the States Whose Constitutions Have Not Been Specifically Revised." Though not as comprehensive as the title suggests, as a scholarly work the paper shows a keen awareness of history and politics, citing in detail the peculiar economic and political factors that helped to explain Georgia's first and second bouts with Reconstruction. Unlike some other states, where black disfranchisement had already been legislated by the end of the Reconstruction period, Hope wrote that in Georgia, "the best things have happened or rather the worst things have not happened for Colored people." Nevertheless,

Hope made few distinctions between states that disfranchised blacks outright and those like Georgia that did it "stealthily or by indirection." "The purpose of all is the same," snapped a militant John Hope: "a hatred for Colored people and a determination to have white supremacy at any cost of life and honor."[58]

Just as important on the activist side of the equation, a careful reading of the paper reveals Hope's continuing efforts to protest racial injustice in Atlanta and improve the conditions of the black rank and file. In his rationale for the ballot, Hope indirectly mentioned his attempts to improve education, the confrontation at the Carnegie Library, protests against the Jim Crow streetcar, and attempts at reforming the penal system. After that presentation, the academy membership must surely have thought that Georgia's John Hope epitomized the scholar-activist tradition.[59]

In 1903, two years before Hope delivered his paper to the academy in Washington, he met the leaders of Boston's African American radicals for the first time. The group was led by the editor of the *Boston Guardian*, William Monroe Trotter, and his coeditor, George Forbes. The Harvard-educated Trotter was the embodiment of the anti-Washington forces whose vitriolic assaults on the Tuskegeean in the *Guardian* would later embarrass both Hope and Du Bois. Trotter came from a wealthy African American family with a tradition of taking uncompromising stands against all forms of discrimination. While Hope was in Boston speaking in the interest of the ABHMS, he, Trotter, and others spent time discussing the race problem, with all venting their frustrations with Booker Washington's leadership. However, the more reserved Hope later admitted in a letter to his wife that he was uneasy with Trotter's boldness, total lack of discretion, and emotional outbursts during the discussion. Nevertheless, at the close of their talk Trotter and Hope viewed one another with mutual admiration. Later that summer Hope wrote to Lugenia that the Boston group's dedication to race issues was "a real heart matter with them." With special reference to Trotter, and seeming surprised, Hope wrote: "He is absolutely immersed in the subject of *Equal Rights* for Negroes." Two months after Hope left Boston, Trotter took part in the infamous Boston "riot," which began as a peaceful protest against Washington and his policies. Hope was lucky he had already left the city.[60]

In 1905, around the time Hope delivered his address to the Negro Academy, Theodore Roosevelt was being inaugurated for the second time as president of the United States, elected this time in his own right. Like other African Americans, Hope had been slightly encouraged by Roosevelt's promise of a "square deal" and by the friendship he extended to blacks on the campaign trail before the November election. African Americans had not forgotten their shock and anger over Roosevelt's negative portrayal of black troops' performance during the Spanish American War, but he won many of them over when he dined with Booker Washington at the White House in 1901, after only one month in office. Also during his first administration, with Booker T. Washington's approval, Roosevelt continued to appoint loyal African American Republicans to federal positions, and to stand behind them. Though the practice delighted African Americans, it outraged southern Democrats.[61]

In spite of the cautious optimism engendered by Roosevelt's election, life for most African Americans continued on a downward spiral, and, in the view of Hope and other leaders like him, Washington's philosophy of conciliation and accommodation did nothing to arrest the deterioration. America's militant black leaders felt they could not wait for President Roosevelt to do something; change needed to come from within—beginning with a reevaluation and new directions from African American leaders themselves. To accomplish that goal, early in June 1905, Hope joined some sixty other members of the "talented tenth" nationwide in signing the initial call to establish the Niagara Movement. The thirty who eventually showed up at the secret meeting in Buffalo, New York, in mid-July left no doubt of their intentions.[62]

Historians often emphasize the anti-Washington bias reflected in the Niagara Movement's principles and objectives. While it is correct that the impetus for the organization developed out of a concern for what its organizers saw as the failure of Washington's policies, during its short life the movement did, in fact, address issues that no African American leader, certainly in the South, could afford to ignore. Niagarites insisted on full "manhood suffrage" and encouraged African Americans "to vote intelligently and effectively." They also advocated civil rights, demanded social equality, and re-emphasized the need for both college and vocational education. And because Booker T. Washington used his power to control certain African American newspapers, they also insisted on "freedom of speech and criticism" and "an unfettered and unsubsidized press."[63]

However, the movement's objectives also included fostering belief in the dignity of labor and aiding the development of more African American businesses and business cooperation. In many ways the declarations reflected the reality of an increasingly separate African American existence. While continuing to fight for full participation in the larger society, the Niagarites accepted, as a practical matter, the need to improve conditions and services within the expanding black world. Thus, in addition to the emphasis on business, Niagarites recognized the need for employment in traditional areas as well as in new fields then opening up. Facing a choice between separate education and no education at all, Niagarites did not waste time insisting on access to educational facilities provided for white children. They supported the right of African Americans to attend college (which, of course, in the South meant the traditional black colleges), but also called for improved state assistance to the existing separate public grammar and secondary schools, new facilities, and expanded educational opportunities for African Americans. Finally, the Niagarite declarations called for more health care facilities within black America and asked that "tracts and information in regard to the laws of health" be distributed. While acknowledging the need to curb violence directed at African Americans "by all civilized authorities," movement members were just as committed to stemming crime within the African American community by establishing more YMCAs and other social service outlets designed to achieve that objective.

That the Niagara Movement could embrace these issues, which transcended the ideological positions of accommodation and protest often assumed to dominate black thought in the age of Booker T. Washington, is in itself important. However, the issues become even more significant in view of the fact that Hope, Washington, and other African American leaders in the South spent much of their time addressing concerns essential to an expanding separate existence.[64]

His summer commitments to the ABHMS prevented John Hope from attending the first meeting of the Niagara Movement, but he was nevertheless enthusiastic about the militant organization and was delighted to receive Du Bois's letter late in July informing him that the Niagara Movement was growing. Sometime between the July meeting and Hope's return to Atlanta in the fall, he and Du Bois probably decided what role Hope would play in the organization's work. Both men recognized Hope's popularity among African American leaders in Georgia and his increasingly evident administrative skills. One year earlier Hope had been described in a popular journal as "a strong young man of the race" who was "fast becoming one of the prominent colored men of the country."[65]

During the Niagara Movement's first year, Hope was assigned the title "state secretary for organization" in Georgia. No description of his responsibilities exists, but the position probably entailed attempting to organize and set an agenda for a local branch in Georgia. Only a year earlier, twenty-seven-year-old J. Max Barber, a Virginia Union University graduate, had established the radical African American monthly *Voice of the Negro* in Atlanta. Barber frequently opened the magazine's pages to radical leaders like Hope and Du Bois, and for a while it ranked among the best sources for Niagara Movement news. Within the southern states the Niagara Movement remained small, however, and neither Hope nor Du Bois was able to make Georgia an exception.[66]

Inspired in part by the militancy of the Niagara Movement, early in February 1906 William J. White issued a call for a convention in Macon, Georgia, to be organized along the same lines as the Niagara Movement. Two hundred delegates representing the eleven congressional districts in the state attended the Georgia Equal Rights Convention. In addition to White, signers of the call included recognized leaders like Hope, Du Bois, Bishop Henry McNeil Turner, Judson Lyons, J. Max Barber, A. D. Williams (grandfather of Martin Luther King Jr.), and a number of others. Among its other demands, the convention called for eliminating lynching and Jim Crow cars on railroads, and for allowing African Americans to become members of the Georgia militia (National Guard) and to serve on juries. The Macon convention also demanded better educational facilities and called for an end to both excessive judicial punishment and blatant attempts to disfranchise Georgia's blacks.[67]

The Georgia Equal Rights Convention was a much larger assembly than the founding meeting of the Niagara Movement, and Hope played an important role on its organizing committee. It was a difficult task, not simply because of the logistics involved, but also because of the wide-ranging ideological points of view held by the participants. Though dominated by militants, the convention also included Baptist separatists and cooperationists, emigrationists, and pro-Washington and anti-Washington forces (including Washington's spies). Macon itself was a separatist stronghold, and the meeting was addressed by Central City College's William E. Holmes, who had resigned from Atlanta Baptist College in 1899.[68]

Hope's work behind the scenes leading to the final public resolutions was characteristic of the quiet yet effective leadership style that would become his trademark. The stars of the show were the leaders of the two most divisive and controversial ideological camps in Georgia. W. E. B. Du Bois, by then the recognized leader of the anti-Washington forces, delivered the keynote speech. William J. White, the editor of the pro-conservative *Georgia Baptist*, delivered the presidential address.[69] Hope was inconspicuous in the deliberations; he maintained a low profile and delivered no speeches before the delegates. His presence, nevertheless, was not lost on J. Max Barber, who praised him in the pages of the *Voice* as "another one of the guiding factors in the convention." Though Hope's voice was seldom heard on the floor in debate, Barber wrote, he "worked like a beaver in the committee rooms."[70]

Whether it was planned or not, Hope avoided the criticism leveled against both the Georgia Equal Rights Convention and the Niagara Movement in the pages of the pro-Washington *Atlanta Independent*, then in its third year of publication. The *Independent*'s colorful editor, the outspoken Benjamin Davis, wasted no time in lambasting what he believed were the negative aspects of the convention's resolutions and its most noticeable supporters. He reserved most of his criticism for Du Bois, who in Davis's view had controlled the conference. William J. White's presidential address, Davis concluded, "was the hand of Dr. White, but the voice of Professor Web. [*sic*] Dubois." Du Bois had already come in for criticism in the pages of the *Independent* for being the leader of the "headless" movement, which opposed the doctrines of Booker T. Washington.

Davis, an influential member of the Republican party's state committee, took special aim at the convention's resolution on disfranchisement and its opposition to segregated transportation. He no doubt knew of the radical leaders' widely held view that it was not separation that offended them "half as much as the unjust discriminations imposed as soon as the law becomes operative." The grossly unequal facilities were the most offensive, prompting the *Voice of the Negro* to report in 1904 that "only then" does the "principle of it [separation] grind and sting." Davis nevertheless concluded in the *Independent* that the "Du Bois conference at Macon was opposed to the white primary and separate cars. The conference then must favor social equality and Negro participation in Democratic politics." [71]

Though Hope perhaps flinched at the derogatory arrows Davis launched at his friend, he was probably relieved that his own name had not been mentioned. Benjamin Davis did not hesitate to show his disdain for the light-skinned aristocracy, or to hide his ideological disagreement with policies or issues. In addition to educators like Du Bois, ministers like Proctor and politicians like Henry Rucker were his frequent targets. Willard Gatewood was correct when he wrote that Benjamin Davis was "always a maverick . . . often detecting 'colorphobia' . . . where it did not exist and occasionally where it probably did." [72]

While Hope was busy participating in the Niagara Movement and the Georgia Equal Rights Convention, a major shakeup took place in the administrative hierarchy of the Home Mission Society organization. MacVicar and Morgan had died, and Henry L. Morehouse, whose service to the organization already exceeded twenty years, was once again the corresponding secretary of the organization. One vacancy, however, remained. The ABHMS needed a new superintendent of education, and it wanted George Sale to take that position. When he accepted, the presidency of Atlanta Baptist College became vacant. His record in the service of the ABHMS made Hope a serious contender for the job. The stage was thus set in 1906 for another explosive dispute between Georgia's separatists and cooperationists and the American Baptist Home Mission Society. [73]

It is not known just how much had been leaked about Sale's proposed retirement from Atlanta Baptist. Hope and Sale were close, and Sale undoubtedly informed Hope of the society's deliberations. Perhaps that information affected Hope's behavior in the months before the ABHMS made a decision.

Hope no doubt recognized that he could ill afford negative publicity in the precarious atmosphere of divided black Georgia.

In Atlanta, there may have been some inkling of the impending change at ABC as early as January, if not sooner. Late that month Benjamin Davis stated a position in the *Atlanta Independent* that echoed the sentiments of many black separatists, and perhaps shows that rumors were already in the air. African American presidents were more useful at black institutions, Davis said, because "the white college president cannot because of his race, instinct and training, inspire the Negro youth."[74]

It appears likely that George Sale, in conjunction with the ABHMS, had been grooming John Hope to take over the presidency of Atlanta Baptist College for some time. Since 1903, in addition to teaching his classes, Hope had served as principal of the preparatory department of the college, which former student Mordecai Johnson later called "the tail end of the whole educational process."[75] Hope also sometimes served as the school's chief administrator when Sale's travels took him out of the city for long periods. As early as 1904, the *Voice of the Negro* began referring to Hope as "Vice President" of Atlanta Baptist College.

Hope realized that the ABHMS was genuinely interested in increasing African American representation on the ABC faculty. Though African American assistant teachers were common, Hope was for years the only black full-time faculty member. By 1906 there were three more African Americans on the faculty, two of them graduates of ABC, but that was still a far cry from appointing a black president. Finally, it was obviously to Hope's advantage that he attended Brown University at the same time that John D. Rockefeller Jr. was there as an underclassman. They were not friends at Brown, nor is there any evidence that they were even acquaintances, yet the powerful family that controlled the General Education Board was no doubt aware that Hope was a "Brown man," and that fact may also have been factored into the decision-making process.

Hope could only wait while the Home Mission Society deliberated. Correspondence written later between Hope and H. L. Morehouse reveals some of the questions that Hope pondered in the months before the decision was made: What would be expected of the first African American president? How much freedom would he have to make curriculum changes, add new faculty, or simply restructure the institution to reflect his short and long-term objectives?[76] Hope probably shared his thoughts with Lugenia, and perhaps even with Du Bois, other friends in Atlanta, and his family in Augusta. There is no record of the ABHMS deliberations, so it is difficult to determine if other candidates were seriously considered for the position. The school term ended early in May, and still there was no word. According to the ABHMS minutes, a decision was finally reached a few days after ABC's spring term ended.

On 7 May 1906, officials at the American Baptist Home Mission Society voted to appoint John Hope acting president of Atlanta Baptist College. His yearly salary of $1,500 matched George Sale's and was comparable to the salaries of other ABHMS school presidents. Hope's "acting" status, however, was a different matter altogether. It no doubt reflected an attempt to maintain some control over the revolutionary decision the ABHMS had just made. In spite of Hope's proven abilities, the Home Mission Society was still not totally convinced that he—or any African American—could run one of their schools effectively. Thus they decided to make his position temporary, retaining the power to make it permanent one year later or to appoint someone else (probably a white man) instead. With that in mind, the ABHMS did two things. First, it was decided that Superintendent of Education Sale would work out of Atlanta that first year instead of moving to New York. A clause was included in Hope's contract that allowed Sale to remain in the president's quarters while President Hope and his family remained in their Graves Hall apartment. The society's intention was obvious: Sale could watch out for the interests of the organization and ensure that Hope made no irreversible mistakes.[77]

Second, in addition to arranging for Sale to monitor Hope's administration, the ABHMS decided not to publicize Hope's appointment. There were no press releases or notices to philanthropic agencies or black religious organizations. The only mention in the official ABHMS publication, the *Home Mission Monthly*, appeared in the August issue tucked away in a corner under the caption "Home Mission Appointments." It simply listed "'Rev' John Hope, acting President," followed by other faculty appointments.[78]

The ABHMS knew that word of Hope's appointment would spread quickly without any effort on the society's part to publicize it. That was both good and bad. On the one hand, for financial reasons, the ABHMS probably wanted the news to get out. On the other hand, the organization recognized that once Hope's appointment became public knowledge, African American Baptists would immediately intensify their efforts to get black presidents at other ABHMS schools. Limiting publicity about the appointment and bestowing on Hope the title "acting president" thus bought the ABHMS time—time both to evaluate Hope's performance after a year and, if he was successful, time to prepare for the demands to appoint African American presidents at other ABHMS schools that would surely come.

In many ways, Hope's appointment to the presidency owed much to the severe economic problems the ABHMS had faced since the depression of the early 1890s. Donations had fallen off drastically, and Washington's industrial education philosophy siphoned off much of the money that was available for African American education. By the early 1900s, the ABHMS desperately needed more financial support from Georgia's African American Baptists. Even though black Baptists nationwide accounted for a quarter to a third of the support for all ABHMS schools, their contributions in Georgia were meager. Georgia's African American Baptists tended to give their money to private African American Baptist academies located in their respective regions of the state—Walker Baptist Institute in Augusta, Jeruel Academy in Athens, and Americus Institute in Americus, for example. Contributing to ABHMS mission schools was simply not a priority, even for those who professed to be cooperationists.[79]

Annual reports and minutes from the late 1890s and early 1900s show that ABHMS officials knew exactly why the shortfall occurred. The little support provided by the cooperationists did not go very far, and the separatists contributed nothing at all. They, of course, were unhappy at the lack of black influence at ABC and Spelman; some actually dismissed the former as a "white" school. Unless this problem was somehow resolved, the ABHMS could not expect donations from Georgia's African American Baptists to increase.[80]

Whether planned or coincidental, the decision to appoint Hope president of ABC was a stroke of genius on the part of the society. The timing was perfect. At an earlier time and place, an African American president would have been out of the question at Atlanta Baptist College. For years the ABHMS had tried to reunite the two state Baptist conventions, thinking that the split itself was the reason the society had been unable to generate significant contributions to its mission schools. But they failed to realize that there were other issues dividing African American Georgia Baptists that were no less important than the question of mission school influence. The split was also the result of strong egos and personality conflicts, and questions over leadership, the importance of missionaries, and the role of women within the state convention.[81] Further, ABHMS officials ignored the fact that cooperationists and separatists were found in both state organizations. Even the creation of the Negro Education Society in 1897, with members from both conventions, failed to significantly increase African American contributions to the ABHMS, or to reunite the two conventions.

African American Baptists in Georgia wanted a signal that the ABHMS was willing to give them a greater voice in directing the policies of the ABHMS schools. The appointment of John Hope—popular teacher, skilled administrator, and highly respected African American leader—to the presidency of Atlanta Baptist College was just the sign many Baptists needed.

Hope's contemporaries were convinced that the ABHMS had no choice but to appoint Hope president of ABC if it wanted to avoid creating even deeper divisions among African American Baptists in the state. James Nabrit Sr., an early ABC graduate and the pastor of Atlanta's Mount Olive Baptist Church, stated years later in an interview that "John Hope was appointed president of Atlanta Baptist College by the New York Office to alleviate the tension . . . it was a fight between those groups that wanted to cooperate with the northern baptists and those that didn't, because they wanted to run things themselves." Lugenia Burns Hope echoed those sentiments, as did Benjamin Mays. Edward Jones stated in his 1967 history of Morehouse that John Hope "was so highly regarded by the Trustees and his colleagues, and his qualities of leadership were so evident to all . . . that no other possible successor was considered." Home Mission Society records confirm Jones's contention.[82]

Hope's selection took most of the steam out of the separatists' argument because it gave them what they had been demanding all along. African American Baptists in Georgia continued to have their differences and did not reunite their conventions until 1915. Yet Hope's appointment did end most of the tensions between the separatists and the cooperationists. The two groups were able to unite in support of Spelman Seminary and Atlanta Baptist College, and to form a united front against external forces that questioned the validity of any black college education at all.[83]

Several important factors had brought John Hope to this point in history. His importance to the ABHMS and his stature as a leader among black Georgians in both the secular and religious communities was a significant factor in his appointment as president of ABC. In addition to helping settle the cooperationist-separatist dispute, Hope's appointment satisfied the needs of the ABHMS in a number of critical ways that were in some cases equally important to different groups of black Atlantans. He was an avid fund-raiser and administrator who in the last eight years had gained the financial trust and confidence of ABHMS officials. He expressed a passionate commitment to the efficacy of black higher education while remaining pragmatic enough to see the advantages of continued cooperation. Equally significant, John Hope was a "Georgia Baptist"—not a minister, but a deeply religious man who many believed was as comfortable in the pulpit as he was behind the lecture rostrum. He was also a familiar face at the black National Baptist Convention and was active in religious activities statewide.

Of equal importance to black Georgians and ABHMS officials alike was the fact that Hope was a native southerner—a Georgian by birth. More important, he was from Augusta, the "black Baptist citadel" that had been home to the state's first African American Baptist convention and was the first home (as Augusta Institute) of Atlanta Baptist College. Hope and his family personally knew prominent African American leaders such as George Dwelle of

Springfield Baptist Church (who at one point led the General State Convention, of which Hope was a member) and the venerable William J. White, who had been Hope's idol since childhood. In a society in which the rank and file of both races were still suspicious of Yankees, Hope could also lay claim to a personality that was perceived as uniquely southern. He was slow and deliberate in his speech, conciliatory in tone, and mild in temperament. There was a trust in him, a willingness to negotiate and, perhaps, if necessary, compromise with well-meaning whites. Whether Hope's personality was a direct result of his southern upbringing may be debatable. Among black southerners and the whites with whom he interacted in the ABHMS, however, Hope's demeanor stood in sharp contrast to the "arrogance" of northern black leaders like W. E. B. Du Bois and the fiery "never-say-compromise" William Monroe Trotter. In a few short years, because of his leadership of Atlanta Baptist College and the role he would play as the dean of African American higher education, Hope would be affectionately called "the Booker T. Washington among Baptists." Ironically, even in 1906, Hope was not unlike a stripped-down Washington—redressed in mind and spirit, then fitted in a tailored suit of southern militancy.[84]

That militant element in Hope's personality was the one thing that troubled the ABHMS. Though the society's officers appreciated and expected his unwavering stance on African American college education, Hope at times exhibited a free spirit. He clearly had a mind of his own, and he participated in activities and made speeches that made ABHMS officials uneasy.

There was no activist tradition among ABHMS presidents. They did not participate in confrontational protests against black disfranchisement and lynching, for example, or belong to militant organizations like the Niagara Movement and the Macon Equal Rights Convention. Nor were they apt to petition for black library facilities or parks and recreational areas, or to confront city officials about better public school facilities and better pay for teachers in those segregated schools. Hope, of course, had assumed his role as an African American leader long before he was offered the opportunity to become ABC's first black president. The roots of his commitment to a black leadership tradition ran deep, and there was no sign that he was about to abandon it.

It was a risk the ABHMS was willing to take. Quite frankly, there was no other choice. John Hope was selected, it seems, not only because of his popularity as a leader among black Baptists in Georgia, but also because, as Sale knew even in 1901, only Hope at ABC measured up to the other national and nonsectarian African American leaders such as W. E. B. Du Bois. Though the ABHMS remained silent, the militant but nondenominational *Voice of the Negro* did not hesitate to proudly display Hope's picture on the front page of its July issue. It was not Hope's conservatism that impressed the editors of the journal, but his militancy. With perhaps some exaggeration, the accompanying article observed: "In all things affecting the life and progress of the race in the United States in particular and in the world in general, Mr. Hope usually shows what side of the fence he is on. Nobody has ever called him a straddler." [85]

Officials of the Home Mission Society probably did not appreciate this publicity, but they recognized that there was a new dawn on the horizon, and that their continued interests were inextricably linked with the reality of an increasingly separate black world whose people demanded accountability from their leaders. ABHMS officials would soon learn that those leaders who happened to be presidents of mission colleges would not be exempted.

7

The Hope Presidency:
The Crucial First Year

On 1 June 1906, the eve of his thirty-eighth birthday, John Hope officially became Atlanta Baptist College's first African American president. When he took office Hope realized southern African American college presidents were expected to follow the conservative path established by Booker T. Washington. But he had other intentions. A few years later he wrote to W. E. B. Du Bois that he had made a conscious decision at the beginning of his presidency to continue his participation in all the causes and organizations that had characterized his racial leadership before his appointment. In the early years of his presidency, Hope saw no reason to curtail his race work activities or to moderate his criticism of discriminatory practices in the South and of northern philanthropists. He was not yet fully cognizant of the demands placed on presidents of African American colleges operating within the political economy of the South. That knowledge would come, but only gradually.[1]

John Hope's militant intentions were announced dramatically during his first summer as president of ABC with his participation in the second meeting of the radical Niagara Movement. The meeting took place at Harpers Ferry at historic Storer College, a mission school established by the American Missionary Association after the Civil War. For four days, the one hundred participants—mostly blacks with a sprinkling of a few northern whites—rededicated themselves to the principles of full equality. A highlight of the conference for John Hope occurred one day at dawn when he joined others in a barefoot pilgrimage to the restored site of John Brown's famous 1859 raid on the federal arsenal.

The second meeting of the Niagara Movement was not completely harmonious. Although they participated in other activities, no women—of either race—were actual members of the Niagara Movement. The issue was debated and resolved in the women's favor for the next meeting in 1907.[2] But no amount of controversy could stem Hope's enthusiasm. He had missed the first meeting in 1905, and as state secretary in Georgia he had not succeeded in arousing much interest in the movement at home. The 1906 meeting thus presented Hope with an opportunity to place his special stamp on the proceedings.

As chairman of the Education Committee, Hope prepared the report and led the session that reflected the organization's steps to improve African American education. The recommendations were predictable: prepare a pamphlet on conditions in southern black schools to be sent to legislators and the public, increase efforts to secure the cooperation of African American editors and ministers, and sponsor educational forums. The issues and solutions were already reflected in the organization's declarations and were included in Du Bois's compelling "Address to the Country," which was delivered by Lafayette Hershaw of Washington on the last night of the conference.[3]

Hope took away fond memories of the 1906 summit at Harpers Ferry. A photograph taken during the meeting captures the seriousness of the affair. Posed in front of one of the Storer College dormitories, Hope stands on the second row slightly left of center, with bushy auburn hair and a thick mustache that curls slightly at the ends. Seated on the front row, hats gripped firmly in hand, are a relaxed, photogenic W. E. B. Du Bois and an intense William Monroe Trotter, along with Hershaw and Clement Morgan of Boston. Like the other participants, Hope is immaculately dressed in a suit, starched collar, and bow tie. Present at the meeting were some of the most radical African American leaders of the day. What Hope chose to remember a few years later, however, had less to do with names than it did with occupations. He took great pleasure in being the only president of "our colleges" present at the meeting.[4]

Back in Atlanta by early September, Hope made last-minute preparations for the first year of his administration, which was slated to begin on the third of October. The transition from Hope's dual roles as race leader and faculty member to race leader and college administrator was more difficult than he had anticipated. The presidency required focus, detailed organization, and meticulous planning; yet the other side of the equation would not be denied. Hope's administrative duties were often interrupted by race issues that commanded the attention of African American leaders nationwide.

There was concern, for example, for the African American soldiers charged with shooting up the small town of Brownsville, Texas, shortly before the Niagarites met at Harpers Ferry. When none of the soldiers admitted to any wrongdoing, the military said there was a "conspiracy of silence." A military tribunal found virtually all of the First Battalion of the Twenty-fifth Infantry Regiment (Colored) guilty and recommended dishonorable discharges for all without any possibility of reenlistment. Among the 170 men in the crack regiment were recipients of the Medal of Honor, Spanish American War veterans who had been cited for their bravery, one man with more than twenty-seven years of military service, and several men with more than ten. President Roosevelt, fully aware of the approaching congressional elections, promised an investigation.[5]

John Hope did not know early in September that political considerations would play a major role in Roosevelt's handling of the Brownsville affair. He was aware, however, of the role politics was already playing in contributing to the tense, volatile atmosphere in Atlanta. For close to eighteen months the city had been embroiled in a fierce, race-baiting gubernatorial campaign that was based in part on the strange bedfellows of southern politics and white fears of miscegenation. Daily newspapers, led by the sensational *Atlanta News*, fanned the flames of racism with bold and potentially explosive headlines: "Half Clad Negro Tries to Break into House," "Negro Grabs Girl as She Steps Out on Back Porch"; and "Woman Brutally Attacked by a Black Fiend." Sometimes the papers included bizarre, sexually suggestive news from other states. On 14 September, for example, the *Atlanta Journal* printed a story from Columbus, Ohio, under an outlandish caption: "Horror of a Dream Kills This Woman: Dreamed That She Was Carried from Her Bed by a Negro and Assaulted and, Waking, She Died of Fright." A photograph of the woman (who actually died of a heart attack and had not been well for some time) appeared in the paper beside a cartoon depicting her being awakened by a knife-wielding black caricature complete with bulging eyes and thick, protruding lips. The Associated Press articles intensified racial tensions in Atlanta. Many of the lurid reports were later found to be wholly without foundation. Nevertheless, the newspapers made little attempt to distinguish facts from figments of what appeared to be deranged imaginations.[6]

Bombarded for months with daily reports of black crime, African American leaders in Atlanta were in a precarious situation. On the one hand, they wanted desperately to believe the reports were false; on the other hand, they wanted to distance themselves from the "criminal element of the race" usually associated with lawlessness. Middle-class blacks detested the dives, saloons, and houses of prostitution as much as the whites who believed such places were the breeding ground of African American rapists.

Late in August 1906, Booker T. Washington expressed his concerns about African American crime in a keynote address to the National Negro Business League meeting in Atlanta. African American leaders needed to take the responsibility to ensure that the "criminal negro is gotten rid of whenever possible," he said, identifying that element as "the loafers, the drunkards and gamblers, men for the main part without permanent employment . . . who glide from one community to another without interest in any one spot." "We cannot be too frank or too strong," Washington continued, "in discussing the harm that the committing of crime is doing to our race."[7]

Black Atlantans also condemned the African American "criminal element" in print, buying into the notion of a black crime wave. Hope's good friend Henry Proctor, pastor of the black First Congregational Church and a man highly respected by white city officials, echoed the sentiment. Excerpts from one of his sermons chastising African Americans who patronized the dives and saloons found its way into the *Constitution*. Proctor's view of the black criminal class was similar to Washington's. It consisted, Proctor said, of the "weaker elements of the race," recent migrants from the countryside who "in their ignorance . . . are entrapped before they know it, and join the criminal element." Antioch, an AME church in suburban Decatur, also bought into the idea of a black crime wave. Early in September, sparked in part by a stirring sermon by their minister, J. G. Robinson, church members drew up a set of resolutions that was also printed in the *Atlanta Constitution* under the caption "Negroes Condemn Crimes." The resolutions pleaded for "White Citizens of DeKalb and Fulton Counties" to distinguish between the "criminal element" of the race and "law-abiding citizens." They vehemently condemned the "outrages" against white women and resolved unequivocally "that under no circumstances would we shield, or sympathize with the perpetrators of these hellish deeds." The church group also resolved "to call upon members of our race in order that our hands may be clean and we be seen in the right light, that we do not give shelter nor bread to suspicious characters; and further, that we notify officers of the law of the whereabouts of any suspicious characters seen by us at any time or place."[8]

If some black Atlantans were concerned about an African American crime wave, many white Atlantans were on the verge of complete hysteria. Political candidates Hoke Smith and, to a lesser extent, Clark Howell had done their jobs well. Their message—that the security of whites could be assured only by tight control over blacks—found an especially willing audience among recent white immigrants to the city. It did not matter that the slogan was designed primarily as a political strategy aimed at black disfranchisement. After Hoke Smith won the primary in August, with white emotions at peak levels, newspapers continued to fuel the popular belief that tight control over the entire African American community was the best way to protect white women from "black brutes."[9]

By the middle of September the race-baiting campaign and inflammatory news reporting, combined with Thomas Dixon's controversial play *The Clansman*, which had filled Atlanta theaters to overflowing a few months earlier, had built anti–African American sentiment to an uncontrollable frenzy. The alleged "flood" of black criminal behavior called for drastic solutions. Fulton and Dekalb Counties joined the city of Atlanta in beefing up their police forces, and prominent citizens recommended that a "protective league similar to the Ku Klux Klan" be formed. Citizens' groups held meetings at which they passed resolutions on the "criminal tendencies of the negro," and Sheriff Nelms of Fulton County stated publicly that the "outrages upon white women must stop, if every negro in many miles of Atlanta have to be killed." John Hope, who prided himself on reading all the Atlanta papers daily, recognized that the city was a powder keg waiting to explode.[10]

That explosion came on a warm Saturday night on 22 September 1906. The Hopes had already settled down in their tiny Graves Hall apartment. Mrs. Hope was in her bedroom, John was in the study, and little Edward was probably fast asleep. A series of piercing sirens that could only mean trouble startled Hope, who rushed outside into the dark, tranquil campus searching for someone who knew what was happening. Though he encountered many people, no calming explanation was forthcoming. Eventually a far-off roar broke the silence. Though frightening, it had a familiar ring. Thirty years earlier, in 1876, John Hope had heard that sound as a child. Then, it had signaled the beginning of the violent end of the African American community of Hamburg, South Carolina.

Walter White, member of a prominent black family in Atlanta and a future leader of the NAACP, also heard the roar. Although he was only thirteen at the time, Walter remembered it clearly in later years. The sound, he said, "the like of which I had never heard before . . . sent a sensation of mingled fear and excitement coursing through my body." The eerie sound of the mob, the shrieks of the victims, the clanging of bells, and the shrill of whistles announced that the city was in chaos. One of the worst race riots in American history had begun.[11]

Hope found out the next day that the trouble started when newsboys from competing papers appeared in Decatur Street hawking their "extras" between five and nine o'clock on Saturday evening. The newspapers carried word of new assaults against white women, a subject already being vigorously discussed among black and white men on different street corners. Rumors of a "Negro uprising" spread among the whites. Eyewitnesses reported white men "mounted on soapboxes holding copies of the extras high." The men admonished the gathering crowds for not protecting the "sanctity of white womanhood in the past" while challenging them "to do something now." Whipped into a wild frenzy, the white men dispersed in all directions looking for blacks on whom to vent their anger. The first clashes occurred in the upper Decatur Street area, with both sides using clubs, iron pipes, brickbats, and whatever else came to hand. Soon, however, African Americans realized that they were grossly outnumbered by the mob, which had grown to more than ten thousand, and that armed resistance out in the open was fruitless.[12]

The mob concentrated on unsuspecting African Americans caught in the downtown area. It was the weekend, and Lugenia Hope's rough notes of the events indicate that many of them were out doing their marketing. The victims were maimed, mutilated, and killed in the most grotesque fashion. Men and women passengers were attacked on streetcars, and cabbies were dragged from their wagons, never to pick up another fare. African American businesses, especially those that catered to an exclusive white clientele, felt the full wrath of the mob. White rioters demolished plate-glass windows in restaurants and barbershops to get to their black victims, shattering at the same time Booker Washington's promise and belief that dutiful, apolitical black entrepreneurs had nothing to fear in the reconstructed "New South."

Young Walter White and his father, who had just punched out from his job at the post office, nearly came face to face with the mob as they drove down Marietta Street toward the heart of the business district at Five Points, the most direct route to their Houston Street home. They were almost run down by a fast-moving funeral wagon driven by a heroic and frantic white man. Three African Americans were crouched in the rear, holding on literally "for dear life." Walter White never forgot the taut expression on the driver's face as he "alternately . . . lashed the horses and, without looking backward, swung the whip in savage swoops in the faces of members of the mob as they lunged at the carriage determined to seize the three Negroes."

Changing routes quickly, young Walter and his father, protected only by their white complexions and features, added their own heroics on that first night of rioting. On Pryor Street the two spotted a stout African American woman whom they recognized as a cook at a downtown hotel. She ran toward them as fast as she could, but the mob was gaining ground, and only a few yards separated her from a nasty death. Young Walter remembered that his father, not by any means a large man, handed him the reins and then hoisted the woman into the cart. "I did not need to be told," he also recalled years later, "to lash the mare to the fastest speed she could muster." Most African Americans caught downtown that Saturday night were not that lucky. The carnage ended only when fierce thunderstorms blanketed the city around three o'clock in the morning. Walter remembered the grim scene on Sunday morning: "Like skulls on a cannibal's hut the hats and caps of the victims of the mob . . . had been hung on the iron hooks of the telephone poles. None could tell whether each represented a dead Negro. But we knew that some of those who had worn the hats would never again wear any."[13]

Meanwhile, back in west Atlanta on the Atlanta Baptist College campus, Hope and the other residents (minus most of the students and faculty, who had not yet arrived for the fall term) braced for an attack they thought would surely come. Hope and a few other men began patrolling the campus early on Sunday morning. Lugenia later said that a man on furlough from the army brought Hope a gun and cartridge belt.

W. E. B. Du Bois was on his way back to Atlanta where he would guard his family with "shotgun in hand." The director of the physical plant at Atlanta University claimed to have prepared a box to hide the Du Bois family if necessary. Mrs. Du Bois knew about it, he reportedly said, but he was not sure whether or not Du Bois ever did.

Soon the militia arrived on campus, reluctantly deployed by the governor shortly after midnight on Sunday the twenty-third. Stretched thin throughout the city and suffering from lack of sleep, the young white men were not in a good mood. Hope recognized as much and tried to break the ice. C. H. Wardlaw, an ABC faculty member, recalled seeing Hope walk briskly toward a soldier, who nervously cried out: "Stop. What do you want? Put up your hands!" The soldier raised his firearm and pointed it directly at the new president of Atlanta Baptist College. Hope slowed his pace considerably, put up his hands, and began to smile, then invited the man into the house for a cup of coffee. Disarmed by Hope's cordiality, and perhaps unsure of Hope's racial identity, the soldier lowered his weapon and accepted the invitation.[14]

Not all of the militia on the campus were that friendly. According to Lugenia (who referred to the soldiers as "gangsters camped at our gates") and another campus resident, some of the soldiers were recognized as participants in the violence of the night before. Although the soldiers may not have been actual participants, the *New York Times* did report that the mobs "paid little attention to soldiers because they felt strong bonds of common emotion and sympathy with the troops and did not expect forceful military action."[15] Hope and other ABC residents continued to patrol the campus for the next three days. In spite of continuing rumors that rioters planned to invade the campuses and other African American communities on the west side, that part of town remained relatively untouched by the four days of violence in Atlanta.

Brownsville, a well-kept black middle-class area in south Atlanta, was not so lucky. By Monday, 24 September, the African American residents had armed themselves. Some reports claimed that guns had been shipped in from as far away as Chicago hidden in coffins. When they arrived in Atlanta, the guns were distributed in soiled laundry bags. In Brownsville, near Clark University and Gammon Theological Seminary, guns and ammunition were furnished by storekeeper, postmaster, and Atlanta University graduate J. L. Price.[16] As his good friend John Hope had done on the west side, J. W. E. Bowen, the president of Gammon Theological Seminary, opened the school's buildings to local residents, mainly women and children seeking refuge from the rioters.

Most of the men vowed to stay and defend their homes if rioters invaded their community. On Monday night their worst fears materialized.

Bowen had requested protection for the African American colleges. Instead, Fulton County officers, joined by other white men with guns, marched into the community and began arresting the residents for possessing weapons. When a group of African Americans was sighted on a narrow, dark street, part of the unidentifiable "police force" moved in their direction and began to shoot. Their barrage was answered by the crackle of small arms and rifle fire, which "rained down bullets" on the white group, killing a county officer. The skirmish quickly escalated into a full-blown, and highly publicized, battle. Before it ended with the retreat of the county forces, several black and white men lay wounded or dead in the street.

At daybreak a few hours later, hundreds of soldiers and policemen returned to Brownsville, allegedly to arrest the men responsible for the death of the fallen officer. They also expected to finish disarming the residents. Before the day ended, four more African American men had been placed on the casualty list. Journalist Ray Stannard Baker heard later that police officers and white citizens entered the home of a wounded man shot the night before, "opened his shirt, placed their revolvers at his breast, and in cold blood shot him through the body several times in the presence of his relatives." [17]

That same Tuesday, close to three hundred African American men were arrested, including several Clark University students who had just returned for the start of the fall semester. More than seventy of them were charged with the death of the county officer, although most were released later. Three other men charged the night before were held. Sheriff Nelms (the same man who a few weeks earlier had said that African American men within miles of Atlanta would have to be killed to prevent "outrages" against white women) reportedly resisted attempts to lynch the accused men, but all three were fatally shot on the way to the jailhouse, one of them dying later at Grady Hospital. [18]

John Hope largely escaped the direct effects of the rioting in Atlanta, but that was not the case for several of his close friends. According to some reports, President Bowen was accused of starting the riot in Brownsville. He was beaten over the head by one of the police with a rifle butt even before any charges were levied against him. William F. Penn, a prominent physician, also came close to losing his life during the Brownsville phase of the riot. Penn reported in an interracial meeting held on Tuesday, 25 September, that ten white men (some of whom Penn knew and had treated professionally) had invaded his home looking for weapons, and his young daughter had gone from one to the other begging them not to shoot her father. Though he was not harmed, Penn and his family were threatened and forced to leave their home. [19]

Bishop Henry McNeil Turner and James G. Robinson (pastor of the De-catur AME church whose resolutions were printed in the *Atlanta Constitution*) were met by a "hail of bullets" as they stepped outside Turner's house on their way to that same Tuesday meeting. Robinson was armed, and he "ran to the Tabernacle and . . . prepared to die with [Turner]." The two men hid under the church, where they protected two African American children who were also fleeing from the rioters. Miraculously, all escaped injury.[20]

J. Max Barber and the aged William J. White, also close associates of John Hope, were forced to leave town as a result of the Atlanta riots. Barber was outraged by a letter to the *New York World* written by John Temple Graves that, in Barber's words, "placed all the blame for the riots on the black man's back." Barber eventually wrote an anonymous letter explaining that it was not a "carnival of rapes" that had caused the riots but sensationalist reporting by Atlanta's white newspapers. City authorities traced the letter to Barber and offered him a choice between three distasteful options: deny authorship and retract the contents of the letter, leave town, or serve a sentence on the chain gang. Barber chose to leave town and resettled in Chicago. His view of the events was later confirmed by the mayor's own investigative committee. The *Voice* resumed publication for a short time, but eventually one of the most influential radical magazines of the era ceased to exist.[21]

William J. White, editor of the esteemed Augusta-based *Georgia Baptist*, a trustee of Atlanta Baptist College and Spelman Seminary and Hope's idol since boyhood, was also victimized by the riots. After he wrote editorials in his newspaper that condemned the rioters and their backers, hostile whites threatened to burn down his printing office and home and kill him if he did not leave the city. George Sale, the superintendent of education for the American Baptist Home Mission Society (and Hope's predecessor at ABC), accompanied White on a visit to the mayor of Augusta to complain about the threats. Though the mayor promised all the protection "in his power," he "feared that he might not be able to control the situation." The mayor strongly encouraged White to leave "for the good order of the city." Within hours of the meeting, William J. White temporarily left Augusta.[22]

Hope's thoughts about the victimization of his friends during the riot have not survived; nor do we know what he thought about the controversies that emerged in the riot's aftermath. Few African Americans, for example, agreed with the official reports, which seemed to undercount casualties on both sides; and African Americans leaders were divided over the role of the black under-class in precipitating the disturbance. President William Crogman of Clark University, for instance, told Mary White Ovington (then a correspondent for the *New York Evening Post*) that it was the "lawless element"—those African Americans often condemned by the middle class—who fought back, "and it is to these people that we owe our lives." Black leaders also had differing opinions of the hundreds of African Americans who left Atlanta after the riots.[23]

Several of Hope's close friends attended the interracial meetings that followed the riot. White city leaders apologized for the widespread devastation, set up funds to assist victims, promised progressive reforms, and established separate racial committees to ensure that Atlanta would never again experience that level of racial violence. Hope was not among the conservative men invited to attend the initial meeting on Sunday, 23 September, the second day of the riot; nor does it appear that he attended the larger meeting held two days later on Tuesday that included more than a thousand white citizens. Perhaps he attended other meetings in subsequent months; but even if he did, there is no evidence that he played a significant role in any of their deliberations. He remained uncharacteristically quiescent, as if the riot had occurred a thousand miles away instead of in his own backyard.[24]

It may be that Hope simply wasn't invited to the meetings. Like Du Bois, Hope had fashioned himself a radical in a city where white leaders, if they talked with African American leaders at all, chose those whom they believed were conservative members of the "substantial and property-holding class." Successful businessmen usually headed the list, but boosters (or exemplars) of the city's New South image and well-established and respected African American ministers were also included. More often than not, white city leaders in Atlanta acknowledged African American leaders who were friendly, or at least not openly hostile, to the philosophy of Booker T. Washington. Thus, in the wake of the Atlanta riot, city leaders chose businessman Alonzo Herndon, druggist Dr. H. H. Slater, black patriarch Bishop Turner, and Rev. Henry Proctor (all men who had agreed that African Americans themselves were partially responsible for the riot) as the "leading conservative Negroes" to help stop the riots and ensure some form of peaceful coexistence between the races.

Later, black journalist Benjamin Davis, Presidents Bowen of Gammon and Crogman of Clark, and others were added to the list of conservative African American leaders acknowledged by the city's white leadership. Although no ideological blanket could cover them all, Atlanta's "progressive" white leadership perceived these men as acceptable spokesmen for the African American community in 1906. Barber, Du Bois, Hope, and others like them were just too radical to be useful.[25]

In sum, Hope was probably either not chosen to participate in the deliberations after the riot or refused to take part in them. John Hope did not trust most southern white men in 1906. In his view, only northern white liberals had demonstrated a sincere and genuine interest in the welfare of African Americans in the South. In 1906, Atlanta whites who favored African American higher education and endorsed full black equality were rare. Hope seemed convinced that the organizers of the interracial meetings with selected African American leaders—businessmen, members of the city council and school board, and representatives from the mayor's office and police department—were more concerned with Atlanta's image than with genuine progressive change.

Like J. Max Barber, Hope rejected the official explanations of the riots dispatched to the world and was not convinced that the apologies were sincere. In a letter written to his friend W. T. B. Williams early in October, Hope wrote that "Atlanta is badly disfigured and full of apologies, but explanations do not explain, if you will pardon the paradox." Hope's view of southern leaders eventually changed, and one day he would count them among his most valuable allies. That reevaluation took place years later, however, and was far from his mind in 1906.[26]

Yet, Hope's silence after the Atlanta riot went beyond his response (or lack of response) as a militant African American leader. He was about to begin his administration as ABC's first African American president. The explosion in Atlanta literally days before that historic undertaking may have affected him in two contradictory ways. John Hope the African American college president was preoccupied with worries over how the riot would affect his ability to run Atlanta Baptist College. How would the turmoil affect parents' legitimate concerns for their sons' safety? Would faculty—old and new—have second thoughts about teaching in Atlanta? How would the riot affect northern philanthropists, who already favored African American industrial education? Would the turmoil affect ongoing attempts to get charitable foundations to pay more attention to African American higher education? And finally, how would Atlanta's white leaders respond to ABC and the other private schools in the aftermath of the riot? Would the riot engender a more positive attitude toward African American higher education, or would it be a death blow to institutions already operating precariously in a hostile racial and academic environment? There was no way to foresee the future—and no precedents—because no college president of any Atlanta school had ever experienced events such as those the city saw during those four September days in 1906. Only time would bring answers. John Hope could do nothing but hold his breath and hope for the best, and perhaps at the same time prepare for the worst.[27]

Despite the uncertainty, there was a side of John Hope that remained unduly optimistic. In Atlanta, he kept his positive outlook to himself, but it comes through in a private letter to his friend W. T. B. Williams. "You know Williams," Hope wrote in a letter a few weeks after the riot, "when everybody else has the blues, I get merry." The tone is apologetic, as if Hope wanted Williams to explain the source of this optimism at a time when the future seemed so bleak. The feeling was more than a quirk in Hope's personality.

Though reluctant to admit it, Hope refused to drown himself in a sea of despair and pessimism at the very time he had been given his greatest opportunity. The riot notwithstanding, a part of John Hope remained enthusiastic about the future, even cheerful, as he looked forward to a brighter day.[28]

Classes began at Atlanta Baptist College about a week after the riot. Everything was prepared and in place. Hope had listened carefully to friends who held administrative positions and heeded their counsel. Shortly before the September riot, Robert Moton, commandant of students at Hampton in 1906 and a future president of Tuskegee, had visited Hope to offer his assistance. Moton was another of the people Hope had met at the 1893 Chicago World's Fair who in time became prominent African American leaders. The two would remain lifelong friends.

Hope probably benefited from the experience of other African American presidents in Atlanta as well, including J. W. E. Bowen, an attendee at the first Niagara Movement meeting who had become Gammon's first African American president in the spring of 1906. Hope's friend William Crogman had been serving as the first black president of Clark since 1903. At one time, both Bowen and Crogman had been closely identified with Atlanta's black radical tradition; after their presidential appointments, however, both succumbed to the powerful influence of Booker T. Washington. Bowen in particular owed his appointment to the Tuskegean. His first Niagara Movement meeting was also his last, as his ideological stance thereafter moved gradually to the right. In time, Hope too would have to come to grips with Washington's powerful influence.[29]

Hope soon realized that presidents of missionary colleges in the early twentieth century carried an enormous responsibility. Hope personally interviewed and hired every faculty and staff member at ABC and was held responsible for their behavior (and that of students) on and off campus. He taught two scheduled classes. In addition, when faculty members were unable to teach, the president stepped in and taught their classes, no matter the subject or discipline. Furthermore, as president of Atlanta Baptist College, Hope was also the official treasurer and chief fund-raiser. Though he was allowed to approach African Americans everywhere in the United States for donations, ABHMS policy restricted his fund-raising among whites to specific northern locales. Atlanta Baptist had a local board of trustees, but power remained in the hands of the New York–based Home Mission Society, which refused to share administrative responsibilities locally. In one way that was to Hope's advantage. His allegiance was to the ABHMS. It was to the parent organization that Hope looked for guidance, administrative help when necessary, and, above all, money. Though black and white local trustees were always cordial with ABHMS presidents, they were powerless when it came to direct control of the president or of any of the administrative apparatus at Atlanta Baptist College, and they knew it.[30]

The faculty at ABC had changed considerably since Hope arrived in 1898. The school's first African American president was greeted in 1906 by a virtually all-black faculty. Among its members was tall, dark, and athletic Samuel Howard Archer, who had come to ABC a year before Hope became president. A graduate of Colgate University, Archer taught mathematics and coached all the team sports. Like Hope, he had also been a faculty member at Roger Williams University. There was also the scholarly Benjamin Griffith Brawley, fair of complexion, slender, with impeccable manners and fastidious tastes. A 1901 graduate of Atlanta Baptist College, Brawley began his teaching career that year as an assistant teacher. He had since received another B.A. degree from the University of Chicago, and would receive a master's degree in English from Harvard in 1908. Brawley taught English at ABC and in 1917 wrote the school's first history. Later, he and Archer served as deans of the college, and Archer would eventually follow Hope as ABC's second African American president. Edward Jones, the author of the definitive history of Morehouse College, said that Brawley and Archer left their "mark on the College by infusing into its traditions and personality, something of themselves."[31]

Brown University graduate John B. Watson, another outstanding African American faculty member, had already been on board for two years when Hope took over the presidency in 1906. A close friend of Hope's, Watson taught science and math and later distinguished himself as an administrator for the Colored Department of the YMCA. In time he would become the president of two other African American colleges.

Rounding out the faculty at ABC were several ABC and Spelman Seminary graduates who were employed as assistant teachers. Hope strongly believed that the future of ABC and other private African American schools would depend ultimately on its own students. For that reason, he offered outstanding graduates the opportunity to teach in the lower grades, thereby furthering their commitment and loyalty to ABC and promoting their development as excellent teachers. Often, such graduates continued their education in northern universities with ABC's help, but they were expected to return to ABC as full faculty members. In part, that tradition reflected the lack of opportunities for African Americans to teach in major white colleges and universities elsewhere in the nation. However, the policy also clearly benefited ABC, and certainly it became an important factor in helping to shape the "Morehouse mystique."[32]

The students were the heartbeat of the college. "We have fifty boarding students and a good number of day pupils," Hope wrote to a friend in a tone that was cautiously optimistic. Students were slow to return during the first semester following the riots; by the beginning of the second semester, however, the trickle had become a flood. The dormitories filled quickly, and, to no one's satisfaction, students were forced to live off-campus.

Not unlike the student body before Hope's presidency, most ABC students were from poor, uneducated families in rural Georgia who sacrificed much to send their sons to school. A few, however, were following in the footsteps of earlier graduates. Familiar names like Nabrit, Hubert, Walker, and Reddick represented a second generation of Atlanta Baptist College men. Though rare, a few students came from as far away as Pennsylvania, Florida, Texas, Alabama, and Tennessee.

From Tennessee, for example, came the brilliant and athletic Mordecai W. Johnson. As the captain and quarterback of ABC's outstanding football team, he threw numerous touchdown passes to his equally brilliant and athletic right halfback, John W. Davis. The men were roommates who received their B.A. degrees during Hope's first ten years at ABC and returned to teach there after graduation. Years later, Johnson became the first African American president of Howard University, and Davis became the president of black West Virginia State College.[33]

Hope soon recognized that his previous tenure as a teacher at ABC was both an asset and a liability. On the one hand, currently enrolled students were delighted with his appointment and made a special effort to ensure they did nothing to reflect negatively on his administration. President Sale first announced Hope's appointment as acting president in a chapel service at the end of the 1905–6 academic year. Mordecai Johnson, then in the academy (ABC's high school department), remembered that students quietly got together and agreed "there must be no untoward act of ours that will put a strain on him." The word was passed along to new students entering that fall semester.[34]

Yet Hope's appointment also raised unrealistic expectations among both ABC students and their parents. More than a white president, a black president of an African American institution was expected to somehow miraculously ease the economic burden of education. Congratulatory letters poured into his office during the summer, but so did endless requests for financial aid.

A widow from Johnsonville, Tennessee, whose "desire was great toward trying to get my son in a school I have heard so much about," promised to get the young man there if Hope would assure him a "state scholarship." A student from Barnesville, Georgia, whose "farm was very poor this year" wanted to come a month early to work on his board before school opened. Currently enrolled students needed more time to finish paying their bills. A father pleaded with Hope to let his son "go out in the city and get him a job . . . to finish paying for his schooling because I haven't any money to send him." A sickly mother behind in paying her son's bills wrote to Hope that her husband and two children at home were sick. "I haven't been able to get out anywhere to attend to any business," she wrote. Yet the determined mother told Hope, "Don't be uneasy, I will send every cent of it." On occasion, the letters informed Hope that students would not return. A lad from Dothaw, Alabama, for example, was sorry not to return, but "my father is going into a new business, and he will need me." It appears that Hope took time to answer every one of the many letters, even though in most instances he could not grant the requests.[35]

Nevertheless, Hope developed close and enduring relationships with the parents of ABC students. They expected him to act as a surrogate parent, and Hope usually did not disappoint them. A mother from Darien, Georgia, could not believe her son had already outgrown his "nice school suit." "I want you to be kind enough to see after DeWitt's clothes for us . . . some things strong and good and plenty large enough," she wrote to Hope. A father concerned about his son's safety asked Hope "to hurry him in his studies . . . and please don't let him go out in the city too often. Let him go out when you think it is necessary for him to go." Parents' questions and concerns never ceased: "Is he a good boy in school? Does he give you any trouble? I have tried the best that I could to give him a good training at home." In the early years of his administration, Hope tried hard to see to it that parents were well informed of their sons' needs and progress at Atlanta Baptist College.[36]

Hope insisted on maintaining the strict New England code of conduct already in existence at ABC. Victorian in his own ideals, he often went beyond parents' expectations. Students were suspended or expelled for cursing, smoking, misbehaving in class, playing cards, and comparable infractions. Mordecai Johnson, for example, a mischievous student in his early days at ABC, wrote to Hope from his home in Memphis in 1907: "I intend to make up for all that I have failed to do in the past years both in scholarship and deportment." Nevertheless, two years later Johnson was suspended for a semester for allowing card playing in his room. He again wrote to Hope, this time from his job in Chicago: "Although a strayed sheep, I am still interested in the fold and other members of the flock, and I sincerely hope that all the others may remain in the shelter of the fold and be spotless in the eyes of the shepherd."[37]

There were stringent penalties for "fraternizing" with women, including those at Spelman Seminary. Holding hands while walking across campus was strictly forbidden. Such "high crimes" could result in a scolding on the spot, and, for second offenses, even expulsion. Hope was reluctant to accept students who had been expelled from other schools for "ungentlemanly-like" behavior. The father of a Knoxville College student suspended for "kissing a girl behind a car" wanted to enroll his son at all-male ABC because the boy spent "too much time with girls when the opportunity permits." Hope denied the student admission because he was a "bad influence that could not be tolerated."[38]

Parents often unsuccessfully pleaded with Hope to give their sons second chances. The son of a prominent Baptist family in Augusta was suspended the semester he was supposed to graduate. The family was sorry their son had been "naughty," but pleaded with Hope and the faculty "to forgive him, and let him pull through and finish with honors." The student had to wait another semester for that. A family from Birmingham, Alabama, wrote a long letter to Hope in 1907 pleading that two students who had spent a night and part of a day away from school without permission not be expelled. Though they acknowledged the gravity of the offense and Hope's insistence on strict discipline, they wondered, "Is it not possible to do this without resorting to the extreme penalty, expulsion?" Privately, some students called Hope a benevolent despot. "I don't mean he was a tyrant," a former student said; " . . . he handled things in a nice way, but he meant what he said or else." To that generation of Morehouse men, "or else" meant suspension or expulsion.[39]

John Hope's firm control over his students did not immediately translate into ABHMS confidence in his ability to run the institution. There were obvious reminders that the ABHMS was not yet sure of him, such as his "acting" status and Sale's continued occupation of the president's quarters while Hope and his family remained in their tiny Graves Hall apartment. As early as May 1906, ABHMS corresponding secretary H. L. Morehouse, had written a letter to Hope that left no doubt about the society's expectations: "With such suggestions and advice as President Sale may give you . . . I am sure you are thoroughly familiar with the spirit and the methods of his administration, and will endeavor to conduct the institution on essentially the same basis as that which had it so successful in the past."

Though Hope respected the former president, he had no intention of operating Atlanta Baptist College as if he were a clone of George Sale. He had already begun to think of expansion: more faculty, a revised and more focused curriculum, a larger college department, and, foremost on his list, a new dormitory so that all ABC students could live on campus. Hope replied to Morehouse in a restrained letter that he would "endeavor to conduct the institution on essentially the same basis" as it had been run before, but warned him not to "construe that expression to mean that I am expected to follow the methods of others."[40]

Improvements took money. Hope had established a good relationship with Wallace Buttrick, the executive director of the General Education Board, but their cordiality had produced no new funds for Atlanta Baptist. Buttrick was fifty-three years old when Hope became president of ABC. He was a former postal clerk, railroad brakeman, and Baptist minister from New York who claimed some theological training and admitted that he knew little about African Americans before being chosen to lead the GEB in 1902. Buttrick cheerfully described himself as "bald, bespectacled, inclined to corpulence and equatorially large." He was a good listener, thoughtful, at times appearing conciliatory and in agreement with his adversaries. In spite of his excellent diplomatic skills, however, Buttrick was a company man. Although in time he came to question his own beliefs in African American inferiority, he never failed to follow the directives of the Rockefeller-controlled GEB. Therefore, the GEB under the direction of Wallace Buttrick continued to limit its financial gifts to African American schools whose mission focused primarily on industrial, rather than college, education.[41]

Early in the century, all of the Atlanta colleges, even prestigious Atlanta University, scrambled to expand their industrial programs to take advantage of GEB money. In 1904 George Sale tried to convince the GEB that Atlanta Baptist had moved toward industrial education, but the board was not fooled.[42] W. T. B. Williams, one of Hope's best friends, was working for the Slater and Jeanes Funds—both controlled by the GEB—at the time, and he also tried, unsuccessfully, to persuade the GEB to pay some attention to struggling black colleges.[43]

In 1907 President John Hope revealed his plans for Atlanta Baptist College to the General Education Board. The immediate need was still a new dormitory, but he also mentioned future plans that included expanding the college department and eventually eliminating the preparatory (elementary and secondary) departments altogether. Hope soon learned to keep some plans to himself. Predictably, the GEB was not impressed. The board continued to believe in the Hampton-Tuskegee model of black industrial education, and backed that belief with hefty appropriations to those institutions.[44]

Undaunted, Hope tried another approach. He appealed directly to Andrew Carnegie for money "to build a good manual training shop in which to conduct an industrial night school for most backward and undeveloped boys of the city." Carnegie had visited Atlanta, however, and had come away convinced that already "more was being done for the Negro than the White man in the state of Georgia." The existence of five black colleges in Atlanta did not help Hope's case. Late in 1906 Hope wrote to Booker T. Washington that only he could change Carnegie's mind. Washington responded that it was not that easy: "In regard to Mr. Carnegie, I would say that he is a very curious proposition. He gets ideas into his head in his own way, and when they once get there, it is very hard to get them out." Carnegie never responded to Hope's request, but he did pass the letter along to the GEB.[45]

Hope worked hard among African Americans, especially Baptists, to get a

financial commitment that he could take to the GEB to show that blacks supported the institution. In December 1907, he wrote to the GEB's executive
secretary: "Don't you believe, Doctor, that your Board would give us at least
10,000 on condition that we raise 15,000 more, provided at least $5000 came
from colored people? If you have any idea that there is one chance in ten of
the Board granting this slight request, please let me know and I shall make a
formal request to the Board." Again there was no positive response, and again
Hope appealed to African American friends who were squarely in the industrial education camp. Robert Moton wrote to Buttrick on Hope's behalf and
asked him to appeal directly to Rockefeller and Carnegie, and W. T. B. Williams wrote a passionate report and letter to Buttrick that explained why he
felt Atlanta Baptist College should be singled out for special attention in Atlanta. Though the board was impressed with Williams's report, neither Williams nor Moton could coax the GEB into giving ABC an appropriation.[46]

At the end of his first academic year, Hope had been no more successful at
getting money from the GEB than his predecessor, George Sale. Nevertheless, it had been a good year, and everyone seemed pleased with Hope's administration, including the ABHMS. In spite of the Atlanta riot, enrollment
at the college had skyrocketed, and faculty, staff, and students seemed to appreciate the school's first African American president. And although he had
been unsuccessful at getting money, Hope got along well with the GEB officials. His reserve, mild manner, and acute diplomatic instincts were valuable
assets. He pleaded his case for financial assistance aggressively, but he never
crossed the socially forbidden line that separated powerful and influential
white philanthropists from their dependent African American cohorts. His letters show that he sometimes came dangerously close to the edge, but he always
withdrew before permanent damage was done to the fragile relationship.

Hope had been even more successful at gaining the confidence of ABHMS
officials. The minutes of the society's June board meeting recorded that Hope
had "administered the affairs of the college with such marked efficiency that he
was unanimously appointed president," thus terminating his "acting" status
and making his appointment permanent. Only then was there widespread
publicity about Hope's selection.[47]

Congratulations poured in from everywhere. Below Hope's photograph in
the December issue of the *Home Mission Monthly* was a two-page article written by George Sale, now the superintendent of education for the ABHMS,
praising Hope as a "man of modest and retiring disposition, who has come
into prominence by his ability and force of character rather than by any effort
of his own."[48] Sale had always maintained the utmost confidence in Hope's
abilities, and he played a major role in pushing the ABHMS to make Hope's
appointment permanent. As early as March 1907, he wrote to Henry More-

house that "there is an opportunity in this college of doing a splendid thing for the Negro race by demonstrating that an institution with a Negro President and a faculty almost wholly Negro can be most efficiently conducted." By June of that year it had been arranged for Hope to receive an honorary master's degree from his alma mater, Brown University. The *Providence Journal* noted how unusual it was for Brown to bestow an honorary degree on an alumnus a mere thirteen years after graduation. In presenting the award, Brown University president William H. P. Faunce said it was given because Hope "as teacher and leader of his people . . . with patience, sanity and zeal" was helping in the "slow solution of one of the great problems of our time." The *Boston Transcript* added in an editorial, perhaps with some exaggeration, that Hope "had made a name for himself hardly less than second to that of Booker Washington as an educator and worker for the uplift of his own people in the South."[49]

Hope's permanent appointment to the presidency was more than a reward for his performance at the college or the ease with which he followed southern etiquette with white philanthropists, and it was more than a statement of abstract confidence on the part of the ABHMS. Hope was also being recognized for his work within the African American community and for the new developments and directions he sponsored. The division between the two worlds separated by race that began late in the nineteenth century further widened early in the twentieth. The decision rendered in *Plessy* v. *Ferguson* in 1896 and the violence in Atlanta—and elsewhere in the South—tended to widen the racial gulf and to elicit more social and legal rationalizations for segregation. After the Atlanta riots, African Americans themselves seemed more bent than ever on going it alone—on creating their own institutions and solving what they defined as their own social problems. Special efforts were made to expand black social services through institutions such as the African American YMCA. Hope's friend H. H. Proctor, through his idea of the "institutional church," intensified efforts to aid black juvenile delinquents and newly arrived immigrants from the countryside. Attempts were also made to expand recreational facilities and to create more programs, like the one run by Lugenia Hope, to develop opportunities and support for working girls and women.[50]

The postriot environment no doubt contributed to an increased nationalist spirit in black Atlanta that emphasized racial self-help and solidarity, and eventually developed into an expansion of black Atlanta. New businesses and churches were created, and there were even unsuccessful calls for African American policemen to patrol increasingly all-black neighborhoods. After the riot, African Americans were forced to abandon the central part of the city, and most of the new development took place east of the old downtown area along a corridor that would come to be known as "sweet Auburn Avenue."[51]

This separate existence was not solely of their own making. African Americans who remained in the South needed to feel safe and secure in a region where a hostile white majority seemed bent on their destruction. And in spite of the inequalities between the two worlds, many believed that peaceful coexistence was possible only within the separate world being forced upon them. There had always been a love affair between African Americans and their own institutions, but in the early twentieth century that affection intensified and gradually became an integral component of a distinct and dynamic culture and worldview.[52]

African American leaders in the early twentieth century did not see this development as an "accommodation to the system." Within their separate world, many of them continued to fight for equality. In fact, many of the protests that took place in the South, especially those in Atlanta that included known "radicals" like Hope and Du Bois, centered on equality *within* the segregated setting.[53] Historians need to factor in both intraracial and interracial realities when they reexamine African American leadership in this period— and move beyond simply labeling activities and ideologies as "accommodation" or "protest." Such a reevaluation may (or may not) retain Booker Washington among the conservatives, in that he rarely spoke out publicly even about inequalities within the segregated system. On the other hand, many of Washington's supporters (especially in Atlanta) did speak out against unequal facilities within that separate framework, yet some historians have insisted on placing them alongside Washington on the conservative bench as well. Ironically, such "conservative protests" about inequalities within the black world have been used to label men such as Hope and Du Bois radicals.[54]

Perhaps there is something to a prominent Atlanta African American physician's quip late in the nineteenth century that blacks "objected to discrimination, not separation." A prominent graduate of Atlanta University even believed the "entire issue of race would disappear if government would provide rigid enforcement of the law" and "assure fair and just dealings between the races." African Americans realized that racism and whites' belief in blacks' inferiority were at least partly responsible for their separate existence, yet many were not yet convinced in the early twentieth century that American democracy could not include two societies that were "separate but truly equal." That understanding would eventually come, but structural changes in the southern political economy had to occur before an effective fight could be launched against the system of segregation itself.[55]

Meanwhile, after the riots of 1906, African Americans in Georgia increas-

ingly believed they were on their own. John Hope benefited from this increased nationalist sentiment as a closer relationship developed between ABC
and the 200,000-plus African American Baptists in Georgia. Baptists' financial
support of mission schools in Georgia had always been meager, lagging far
behind their support of other ABHMS institutions. Georgia's African American Baptists had always claimed that their poor showing was a response to the
Home Mission Society's reluctance to appoint black administrators. Though
Hope's temporary appointment in 1906 raised expectations among some
ABHMS officials (and Wallace Buttrick of the GEB), there was not yet proof
it would result in significant changes in black Baptist contributions. The stage
was therefore set to evaluate Hope's economic importance as ABC's first African American president.

The society's seventy-fifth anniversary celebration provided the perfect opportunity. Early in January 1907, the Home Mission Society widely circulated
a special appeal to "Negro Baptists" to help offset a $100,000 deficit. The
glossy circular, with its boldface heading tucked neatly between photographs of
Presidents Abraham Lincoln and George Washington, attracted a lot of attention. It called for a mass rally to take place shortly after Lincoln's Birthday.
Corresponding Secretary H. L. Morehouse wanted to raise at least $10,000
and hoped African Americans would contribute substantially to that amount.
Anticipating all of the possible negative responses, the circular reminded African Americans of the Home Mission Society's role in creating a number of
the existing institutions, its aid to those created by black initiative, and its help
in providing "a large number of professors of their own race."[56]

Perhaps still uneasy about publicizing Hope's appointment, the ABHMS
did not mention in the circular that one of its most important schools was
headed by an African American president. Nevertheless, Hope worked long
hours to see that African American Baptists in Georgia contributed their share
of the $10,000. He probably understood that this small fund-raising campaign
was an opportunity to show his ability to raise money from African Americans
in Georgia, a task no prior president of ABC had been able to accomplish with
much success. There is no doubt that ABHMS officials were also waiting to
see what effect Hope's racial identity would have on black Baptists' support
for ABHMS schools in Georgia. For more than a month, Hope and his teachers spoke each morning in chapel on some phase of what Hope called the
"Home Mission Work." By April, only one of the scores of ABHMS schools
across the South (the now defunct Alabama Baptist Colored University) had
raised more money than Atlanta Baptist College. Home Mission Society officials were both surprised and ecstatic at Hope's success, especially so soon
after the Atlanta riot. It was one month later that the board decided to make
John Hope the school's fourth permanent president. Of course, it was white

officials of the Home Mission Society who made the final decision, but Hope's relationship with the African American community coupled with his ability as a fund-raiser and the rapidly changing social milieu had figured prominently in the decision.[57]

Practically all the congratulatory notes Hope received on his appointment in 1907 made reference not only to his competency as an administrator but to his role as a race leader as well. In reality, Hope's activities as president of ABC completely overshadowed his role as an African American leader during that first year. There is no evidence of his involvement in the events that followed the Atlanta riots, and he did not respond publicly to the unsettling news about the African American soldiers involved in the Brownsville affair that surfaced shortly thereafter in November. President Roosevelt continued his retreat from black interests and upheld the dishonorable discharges of practically all the men of the popular First Battalion of the Twenty-fifth Infantry Regiment.

In all likelihood, Hope was too busy establishing his authority over Atlanta Baptist College and trying to raise desperately needed funds for the struggling liberal arts institution to respond to these issues. Nevertheless, what Hope called "the race question" was never far from his mind. He was an avid reader and rarely missed any news that affected African Americans. He was most likely troubled by his inability to find time for activities not directly related to his work at Atlanta Baptist College.

Yet he was also a realist. He knew that his future at Atlanta Baptist would at least in part be determined by the impression he made on ABHMS officials his first year as president. The 1906–7 academic year was perhaps the most crucial year of his early presidency. He knew there would be time to regain his reputation as an active African American leader after he had surmounted that hurdle. His stature as the permanent president of Atlanta Baptist College would in fact increase his influence when his outside leadership activities finally resumed.

8 Continuity and Change after a Decade of Service

Between 1906 and 1916, John Hope emerged as an educational statesman and African American leader of national stature. That prominence did not come without a price. The decade produced significant changes in Hope's thinking as well as new alliances and directions that would move him several notches from the left of the black ideological spectrum toward its center. Deep inside, Hope would question his convictions and be plagued by an inner turmoil that at times caused him to question his desire to continue in his profession. By the end of the decade, John Hope was in some respects a different man from the one who had taken up the reins of Atlanta Baptist College in 1906.

Although the activist side of John Hope remained dormant for most of his first year as president of ABC, a glimpse of the militant race leader appeared briefly in the summer of 1907. In between recruiting faculty, helping students find summer jobs, and the always exhausting task of fund-raising, Hope remained an active member of the radical Niagara Movement and managed to find time to attend the third annual meeting in Boston. Partly because the group was officially accepting female members for the first time, the eight hundred people who met at Parker Memorial Hall constituted the largest gathering thus far. In addition to issues reminiscent of those taken up at the two earlier meetings, resolutions were adopted at this meeting condemning the violence in Atlanta, Georgia's continuing attempts at disfranchisement, and the Interstate Commerce Commission's upholding of what Niagarites called "social slavery and the vicious and nasty Jim Crow car." Nor did the Niagarites fail to condemn President Theodore Roosevelt for riding "roughshod over the helpless black [Twenty-fifth Infantry] regiment whose bravery made him famous." Finally, they urged African American voters in the North to use their ballots "to defeat Theodore Roosevelt, William Taft, or any man named by the present dictatorship." In both temperament and ideology, the Niagara Movement remained the most militant voice of the African American community.[1]

Hope fully supported the movement's official resolutions but, as he had at the earlier conventions, continued to append his special concern about public and private African American education in the South. Hope's correspondence does not hint at his position on the internal bickering that was an undercurrent at the Boston meeting. Differences between Niagarites William Monroe Trotter and Clement Garnett Morgan eventually led to an even more damaging feud between W. E. B. Du Bois and Trotter. The latter rift never mended, and historian David Lewis is correct in asserting that the meeting that August was "the beginning of the end of Niagara." Hope was a member of the Niagara Movement's Executive Committee, where the differences between the feuding leaders were most apparent. Although obviously aware of the factional infighting, Hope seemed not to take sides but rather to try to unite the opposing factions by reminding them that African Americans needed the movement.[2]

While the Niagara Movement continued to hobble along on the national level, Hope resumed his activism in Atlanta, revitalizing his role as a local African American leader. As always, however, it was not only his demands for full equality that endeared him to the African American community, but also his work on behalf of the increasingly segregated world dependent on its own leaders and institutions. John Hope was particularly proud of black Atlanta's involvement in the Young Men's Christian Association (YMCA), an organization that first earned his respect and admiration at Worcester and Brown.

The YMCA came to the United States from Europe in 1852 as an organization dedicated to serving the spiritual and educational needs of young men and boys. The association did not seriously consider the plight of the African American male until 1875. The eventual result was the creation of what African Americans called the "Colored Men's Department," a separate component of the YMCA designed to provide an umbrella for all affairs related to African American YMCA work.[3]

The Colored Department took off in the 1890s when it divided its work into two major fields headed by two tireless workers totally dedicated to the organization's mission. One of them, W. A. Hunton, the first African American international secretary, took charge of the branches that were just beginning to appear on African American campuses. The other, Jesse E. Moorland, an old friend of Hope's, took charge of the city branches. Hope had first met Moorland in 1894 when he pastored a Congregational church in Nashville. But it was the older, Canadian-born Hunton who most impressed Hope with his relentless energy, his dedication to the YMCA cause, and his wise counsel on how to increase African Americans' loyalty to and affection for their institutions. In a letter to Hunton's wife (also a tireless worker in the interest of the black YMCA) written years later on the occasion of her husband's death, Hope recalled Hunton's simple yet profound advice when he first became president of ABC: "Make the boys love the college." Hope cherished the words, he wrote, "as much as any one thing that was ever said to me."[4]

As they did with so many other American institutions, African Americans transformed the Colored Department of the YMCA into a vehicle for racial uplift. If whites regarded the YMCA "as an organization that safeguarded the morals of young uprooted men in the city by surrounding them with a proper and wholesome environment," African Americans regarded it as one designed to help blacks and instill race-based community responsibility. It was also a training ground for black leaders, who were expected to be role models within the African American community. Moreover, the city branches paid special attention to education and a religion-based morality designed to develop character.[5]

John Hope became an avid supporter of the black YMCA branches on the ABC campus and in the city almost as soon as he arrived in Atlanta. By 1900 he had been the faculty adviser to the Y Club at ABC and had delivered numerous speeches to the organization. One of the most memorable, entitled "Ambassadors for Christ," moved the students to show their appreciation by mentioning it in the student publication, the *Athenaeum*. Hope was no less active in the black Atlanta branch, which then operated out of an old house on Wheat Street (later renamed Auburn Avenue). Hunton described the Atlanta branch as a "veritable bee-hive of activity that enrolled adults, young men and boys in their educational programs, and offered them alternatives to the saloons, gambling houses, and dives with wholesome recreational activities." The Wheat Street facility also provided limited shelter and a bathhouse for recent arrivals from the countryside looking for opportunities in the city. John Hope was most involved in the organization's educational programs. He regularly taught in the night school, lecturing on everything from politics to religion; he especially enjoyed teaching adults to read and write. When the Colored Department's annual convention met in Atlanta in 1903, Hunton and Moorland asked Hope to deliver one of the major addresses.[6]

In spite of the other demands on his time, Hope gradually resumed his active role in the Atlanta YMCA after he became the president of ABC. Early in 1908 he was appointed to the Management Committee, which was responsible for the overall direction of the local organization. Eventually Hunton and Moorland brought Hope to the attention of prominent whites on the International YMCA Committee in the organization's New York headquarters. Willis D. Weatherford, a Vanderbilt-trained southern liberal, was an international student secretary who was especially interested in the work of the African American branches. Shocked by the "lawless barbarism" of the Atlanta riot, Weatherford took a keen interest in the race problem and in 1907 established a summer training school for YMCA secretaries at Blue Ridge, North Carolina, that included a course in race relations. The course, however, excluded African Americans. Nevertheless, the favorable response of those who took the course led Weatherford to call together a group of blacks and whites in Atlanta to discuss a book he planned to write to use at the Blue Ridge facility. The meeting took place in April 1908 and included, among others, Hope, Hunton, and Moorland. Though not completely comfortable with the book, all three men supported it and the all-white Blue Ridge facility. Two years later, in 1910, Weatherford published *Negro Life in the South*, which was marketed as a major text on race relations and used widely throughout the region.[7]

Hope's apparent capitulation to the racialized policies of the YMCA International Committee cannot be ignored; after all, Hope prided himself on his militant image, which was based in part on a principled rejection of segregation. The YMCA was certainly not without African American critics. For example, Calvin Chase, editor of the *Washington Bee*, insisted that Christians should not "worship separate and apart from each other. If they believe in a God they ought to know there is but one heaven and one hell." Du Bois was also critical: "It is an unchristian and unjust and dangerous procedure which segregates colored people in the Y.M.C.A." African American leaders in such Niagara Movement strongholds as Boston, Detroit, Chicago, and Cleveland also resented the YMCA's Jim Crow policies, even though some of them later accepted segregated facilities in their own northern cities. Like most African American leaders in the South (including Booker T. Washington), John Hope recognized the contradictions but never wavered in his support for the YMCA. At the same time, however, like other Niagarites (although less vociferously), he criticized the YMCA's policy of segregation. For John Hope personally, the opportunity to develop "Christian character," the promise of religious training and wholesome recreation for what he perceived as underprivileged African American males, even within a segregated setting, appealed too much to his Victorian and paternalistic sensibilities to be denied.[8]

Hope and other southern race leaders—conservatives *and* militants—often shared views that set them apart from their northern counterparts. For example, race leaders in the South were forced to come to grips with the realities of de jure segregation. More than two-thirds of all African Americans still lived in the South, and southern leaders (and perhaps many of those in the North as well) recognized that blacks simply had too many needs to reject separate development out of hand. The alternative to segregation was usually exclusion, not integration, and leaders in the early twentieth century believed it was unrealistic to waste valuable energy on the unlikely prospect of achieving immediate integration.

In his role as an African American leader in the South, Hope endorsed other separate organizations that were frowned on by some of his northern counterparts. He staunchly supported the black branch of the Atlanta Anti-Tuberculosis Association and became its chairman in 1915. He was also prominent in the National Association of Teachers in Colored Schools (NATCS), an organization started in 1904 that was designed to improve the quality of African American education and address the problems of African American teachers. By 1909 Hope had become very active in the NATCS, and eventually he served a term as its president.

A few years into his ABC presidency, Hope realized that he was taking on too many outside responsibilities. He wrote to a friend that "the Y.M.C.A. in the city and other uplift movements keep me working all the time." Yet he refused to slow down, trying to devote as much attention to his role as a community activist and race leader as he did to his job as president of Atlanta Baptist College.[9]

The tensions between the two roles increased over the decade as new organizations competed for Hope's attention. As the Niagara Movement continued to die a slow death, a new interracial organization called the National Negro Committee arose to take its place. Hope was present at the second meeting of the organization, when it became the National Association for the Advancement of Colored People (NAACP), and he may have been at the founding meeting in 1909. Though Hope remained silent at the early meetings of the NAACP, he prided himself on being, as he wrote to Du Bois later, "the only president, colored or white, of our colleges that took part in the deliberations." His association with the radical NAACP kept alive his image as a militant race leader committed to full equality and tended to balance out his activity in southern-based segregated activities.[10]

The NAACP's biracial composition troubled some of the old Niagarites. Trotter and Ida Wells-Barnett, for example, were skeptical of the organization's structure, paternalism, predominantly white leadership, and refusal to publicly condemn the policies and leadership of Booker T. Washington. Like Du Bois, however, Hope was enthusiastic about the NAACP's potential and comfortable with its racial composition. Progressives like William English Walling, Lillian Wald, Oswald Garrison Villard, Mary White Ovington, and John Milholland—all northern white liberals—were the kind of white people Hope trusted. In Hope's view, their temperaments, and perhaps even more their geographic location, freed them of the infectious racism that plagued their counterparts in the South. They reminded him of old associates like Abercrombie at Worcester, Andrews at Brown, Sale in Atlanta, and Henry L. Morehouse of the American Baptist Home Mission Society. An interracial organization dedicated to full equality for African Americans was a radical new departure, and Hope was eager to help the NAACP achieve its goals.[11]

But Hope had little time to spend with any outside organization in 1909 or 1910. The requirements of the presidency pulled and tugged at him and demanded his full attention. Atlanta Baptist's financial coffers were drastically low, but a new dormitory was essential and the school needed a chapel. The college's entertainment and recreation events were being conducted in local African American churches when they should be housed on campus. Friends like Robert Moton and W. T. B. Williams, as well as ABHMS officials Morehouse and Sale, had done virtually everything they could to influence white philanthropists, but the response was always the same: Philanthropists preferred to support African American industrial education; denominational schools should look for "independent sources"; there were simply too many black schools in Atlanta—Atlanta University, ABC, Spelman, Clark, and Morris Brown—and these duplicated programs and resisted all pleas for cooperation or consolidation.[12]

Hope usually remained calm in his deliberations with the GEB and other philanthropic agencies, holding his anger until he could release it to their agent, his good friend W. T. B. Williams. When advised by foundation officials to find independent sources, Hope quipped to Williams in an angry moment in 1908: "Where are they? I will take the train tomorrow at my own expense, if you just telegraph me one man to talk to." To Williams, Hope admitted there were indeed four colleges in Atlanta (he did not count Morris Brown or Gammon as colleges), but there were only six bona fide colleges for African Americans in the entire state (including Paine in Augusta and Central City in Macon along with Atlanta's four). In regard to Atlanta Baptist, Atlanta University, Clark, and Spelman, Hope argued: "Here, then, are four colleges representing over a million colored people within the state of Georgia, to say nothing of the work we have to do for other adjacent states." In Hope's view, consolidation was impractical: "Sacrificing all denominational sentiment to say nothing of other traditions that are dear and sacred" would result in a "cut and dried education program." Yet he also knew that if the schools rejected consolidation out of hand, the funding organizations would expect the schools to help themselves or get help from their own denominational societies.[13]

Hope rejected that idea as well, believing it contradictory to the expressed policies of the GEB, which claimed to base its awards on the work of the educational institution, not its sponsor. "Suppose denominational schools are doing just as good work as undenominational ones, ought the fact of denomination be a barrier with a board that professes to take no account of denomi-

nation whatever, but looks only to the merit of the institution?" Hope asked
Williams. "There is only one argument, and that is the fact that four schools
are assembled here in Atlanta. When you look that argument squarely in the
face you will see that it is by no means a strong one."

Hope tried to assure Williams that the criticism was not meant for him
personally, for Williams was among his dearest friends, yet the end of the
letter clearly shows his dejection: "Now, I have told you all I know and all I
feel; and when you and others with your critical eye, with your professional
impartiality, examine this letter it will amount simply to this, 'Well that same
old request, we had it before; we cannot handle it, the work is duplicated.' Into
the waste basket. I call it hard, downright hard." [14]

In the fall of 1909 Hope tried once again to solicit financial aid from an
independent source. He appealed once more to the philanthropist Andrew
Carnegie, who had turned down or ignored his request two years earlier. This
time, Hope asked for a new building estimated to cost $40,000, on the condi-
tion that ABC raise half the money. Early in November, Carnegie asked his
agent, James Bertram, to get more information on Hope and ABC. Perhaps
the aging Carnegie had forgotten—or had never known—that Hope had
sharply criticized his "selected philanthropy" and "his pocket full of libraries"
back in the early 1900s. Certainly nothing suggests that the steel magnate
had changed his mind about the importance of African American college
education. [15]

At least in part, Carnegie's reconsideration of Hope's request was prompted
by a favorable recommendation from Booker T. Washington, whose record
for assisting African American college presidents in Atlanta was good. A few
years earlier the powerful Washington had assisted William Crogman of Clark
University and J. W. E. Bowen of Gammon Theological Seminary. Privately,
John Hope had asked for, or at least accepted, the Tuskegeean's endorsement
on his behalf. Later Hope felt some guilt about Washington's role and wrote to
Du Bois that "a good friend of the college" had approached Washington
without his knowledge, implying that only then had he taken advantage of a
golden opportunity. [16] That "friend" could have been his college roommate
Ted Owens, who taught at Tuskegee, or possibly Moton or even Williams,
who had taken an extensive trip with Washington earlier that year. On the
other hand, Hope may have approached Washington himself. The two men
maintained a professional cordiality that provided some basis for a tenuous
friendship even though they were at separate ends of the ideological spectrum
on the issues of black college education and full racial equality. On at least one
occasion Washington had used an Atlanta associate to gather confidential information about John Hope and a number of other Atlanta black leaders who
had aroused his suspicions. [17]

Though letters between Hope and Washington are few, those that exist show that the two men and their families visited on occasion and enjoyed the arch rivalry between their football teams. There were ABC graduates on Tuskegee's faculty, and one or two of the vocational teachers at ABC were graduates of Tuskegee. Almost none of the surviving correspondence between Hope and Washington discusses their ideological differences, but when the matter came up, neither man tried very hard to persuade the other to accept his point of view.[18]

Washington decided to do what he could to assist Hope, and approached Bertram, Carnegie's "right-hand man." Bertram advised Washington to write directly to Carnegie and give his opinion of Atlanta Baptist College. In a letter dated 13 November, Washington wrote to Carnegie that ABC was one of the "oldest and best established colleges for our people in the South." It was doing "real college work and sending out men of the highest type of usefulness," he said, and "President Hope is a man of the highest and cleanest character." He also told Carnegie to disregard the school's religious affiliation, "as it does not mean much in this case." Two days later, on 15 November, Washington attempted unsuccessfully to follow up his letter with a visit. He did see Bertram, however, who convinced him that the prospects were good. The next day Washington penned an optimistic letter to Hope: "Mr. Bertram seems deeply interested, and that is always a favorable sign. My own belief is that the effort is going to succeed, though you may have to wait a little while for a decision."[19]

Louis Harlan has written that "Washington and Carnegie belonged to a mutual admiration society that knew no restraint."[20] Perhaps that is why Carnegie decided to give ABC half of the $20,000 in matching funds that Hope had asked for late in 1909. Carnegie's gift, given with the blessing of Booker T. Washington, certainly sparked the school's growth in the early years of Hope's presidency. An early Hope biographer wrote that as "if by magic, things began to happen . . . the General Education Board made a gift; the society in New York voted a large sum, and the future of a new building, Sale Hall . . . was assured." The Home Mission Society added $35,000 to Carnegie's $10,000, and the GEB donated another $5,000, although the latter depended on Georgia's African American Baptists contributing an additional $5,000, a sum they had never before managed to raise. They were given until the end of December 1911 to raise the money, and they were successful.[21]

On one level, this episode shows the powerful influence of Booker T. Washington. But it also demonstrates blacks' support of ABC, black Baptists' appreciation of the college's first African American president, and the continuing importance of African American self-help when it came to supporting their own institutions. Two years earlier, in 1907, W. T. B. Williams had written a twelve-page letter to Wallace Buttrick emphasizing the need for support for African American colleges and explaining why he felt Atlanta Baptist College deserved special consideration. It was "the only college of importance for the Negro Baptists of Georgia and Florida," he said, and it attracted students and support from western South Carolina, eastern Alabama, and Tennessee as well. Williams believed African American Baptists outnumbered all other denominations (there were close to 300,000 Baptist church members), and "these Baptists are proud of the school, and . . . keenly appreciative of a colored man as its president." Most of the African American Baptist organizations in Georgia had sent resolutions to the ABHMS "expressing their appreciation of the appointment of Prof. John Hope as president and pledging him their support," Williams told Buttrick. This idea of African American self-reliance, as we have seen, was not lost on philanthropic agencies or missionary boards. In addition to being influenced by Washington, arguably the most powerful black man in America at that time, philanthropists and the ABHMS took the opportunity to test African Americans' support of their own institutions.[22]

Perhaps most significant, the episode reveals the growing awareness of the importance of African American college education in an increasingly segregated world. This is not to suggest that the GEB or any other charitable foundation had decided that black college education was as important as industrial education; for the next ten years, foundations continued to treat black liberal arts institutions as stepchildren.[23] Nevertheless, the issue of college education had at least been placed on the table, and the increasing segregation gave it an urgency that was not easily ignored. Among other things, African Americans needed their own college-trained leaders, teachers, businessmen, and physicians in this expanding black world. The passionate tone of Williams's letter to Buttrick left no doubt about his belief in the importance of college-educated African Americans to serve black America:

> The increasing intelligence and prosperity of the colored people together with the more rigidly enforced separation of the races increase the demands for greater numbers of professional men among the colored people. . . . The farther the colored people are removed and kept from the more cultivated white people the greater becomes their need for having considerable numbers of educated cultivated people of their own race among them. Otherwise there must come a general retrogression from lack of ideals and competent leadership.[24]

Both Buttrick and the General Education Board were impressed with Williams's reasoning, particularly in the aftermath of the riot in Atlanta. Buttrick was so impressed that he wrote to the president of the GEB that the "report is so valuable that in my judgment all the members of the Board ought to read it just as it stands." In addition to the $5,000 the GEB promised for ABC's new building, the board also voted to give the school a small annual appropriation of $5,000 for operating expenses. Ironically, the emergence of what was expected to be a permanent and separate black existence helped crack open the door that eventually led to philanthropists' acceptance of the importance of black higher education.[25]

Late in 1909, however, John Hope was wondering what his militant friends would think when they found out that he had been assisted by Booker T. Washington and Andrew Carnegie. His militant image was at stake. Would they wonder that a member of the Niagara Movement, follower of Du Bois, and supporter of the infant but seemingly radical National Negro Committee had sought assistance from men whose ideas were so radically different from his own? Even the conservative National Baptist Convention, whose meetings Hope always attended, knew and respected him as a militant race leader unwilling to compromise his principles and fully committed to black college education. What did his acceptance of Washington's endorsement mean? Would ABC's curriculum move from its present emphasis on liberal arts subjects to focus on industrial education? Would Hope himself change his principles? Would he remain firm in his commitment to full equality, both social and political, or would he join other African American presidents of black colleges in Atlanta like Crogman and Bowen, who tended at the very least to straddle the ideological fence once they were ensnared in Washington's powerful web?

For days, his dual roles as militant African American leader and black college president created an almost unbearable inner turmoil for the sensitive John Hope. He decided not to wait for the news to come out, but rather to test the water early by informing his closest Atlanta friends of the Carnegie gift before it became public knowledge. He braced himself for their reactions. He assured them he had not compromised his own principles or changed the direction of Atlanta Baptist College in exchange for Washington's influence. Practically all voiced their approval, recognizing Hope's precarious position as president of an African American college no one wanted to see fail, although some questioned the wisdom of owing a favor to Booker T. Washington. In a social gathering at the home of George Towns early in January, Hope's friends could not resist teasing him for "selling out" to the Washington camp. He had "often taken and given 'roasts,'" Hope wrote to his friend Du Bois afterward, and he was glad that this one "was so light for me—not a scorching, just a comfortable warm brown."[26]

Privately, however, Hope took the criticism to heart. In many ways he believed he had become a victim of his own success. He had received the gift in part because of his popularity in the African American community, yet part of that community—the group that shared most of his ideological principles—

seemed to question his judgment. It bothered him more than he wished to admit. Du Bois had been one of the ringleaders at the roast, and Hope was unable to detect what his friend actually believed.

Later that month, while visiting Providence, Rhode Island, Hope's uncertainty prompted a nineteen-page letter to Du Bois. He needed to reassure his friend, and perhaps himself as well, that he had done the right thing. To show he was yet committed to his original principles, Hope reminded Du Bois that he had been the only African American president present at the Harpers Ferry meeting of the Niagara Movement and at the founding meeting of the NAACP. Unlike Du Bois, who was now a professional race leader, Hope did not have the luxury of making decisions based on principles alone. That simply was not possible for an African American college president. "The opposing views of other men do not so much concern you in your thinking because you have hardly needed them in your equation. . . . I am a plodder. My even petty thinking calls for great travail of mind and spirit. . . . I carry along . . . all opposing views with which I am acquainted."

Hope returned to the point he had tried to get across at the roast: the mission and direction of ABC had not been compromised by his acceptance of the Carnegie money, nor had he changed his personal stance on civil rights. Hope rejected the presumption of guilt by association, although years earlier he had embraced that principle himself with regard to Booker T. Washington.[27] "But Du Bois," Hope quizzed his friend, "may there not be a tyranny of views? Have we not required such severe alignments that it has been sometimes as much a lack of courage as a mark of courage to stand either with Du Bois or Washington to the absolute exclusion of one or the other in any sort of intercourse?" Hope feared losing Du Bois's friendship, but he stood his ground: "I am glad that as a man interested in education I can associate properly with another man who is interested in education yet from a different angle as Washington is." Du Bois, of course, did not dissolve the friendship. He remained one of Hope's closest friends for the rest of his life. But he did warn Hope that he was treading on dangerous ground: "You have done what you have to do under the circumstances. I only trust that the pound of flesh demanded in return will not be vital."[28]

There is no evidence that Washington ever exacted his "pound of flesh" from John Hope. In fact, Hope continued to guide Atlanta Baptist College in the same ideological direction as always, at times offending the Tuskegeean's most cherished sensibilities. When the National Negro Conference became the NAACP at Charity Hall in New York on 12 May 1910, Hope was there. Only a few months later, Washington's already precarious relationship with the NAACP reached rock bottom. Criticized widely for deemphasizing America's racial problems on a European tour, Washington, through Robert

Moton, sought Hope's, Villard's, and Du Bois's help in reducing public criticism of his policies and bringing about some kind of reconciliation between the Tuskegeean and Du Bois.[29]

Moton got nowhere with the three men. Du Bois, who had circulated an appeal condemning Washington's European lectures on the plight of blacks in America, refused to retract anything he had written. He even tried to recruit Moton into the NAACP. Villard, a founding member of the NAACP, also endorsed Du Bois's "Appeal" (although he had not signed it) and asked Washington, through Moton, to join their ranks. It was Hope, however, whom Washington perhaps most hoped to influence. Only a year earlier Washington had given Carnegie his endorsement on Hope's behalf, and he had noted that Hope had not signed Du Bois's "Appeal to the People of Great Britain and Europe." Enclosing a copy of the letter he had sent to Villard, Moton wrote to Hope asking for his assistance. Though more conciliatory in tone than the responses of Villard and Du Bois, Hope sent back the same message. He too refused to speak out publicly against the NAACP and rejected Moton's presumption that the organization was anti-Washington.[30]

Hope did offer a suggestion for bringing Du Bois and Washington together. "If some of us could have these two gentlemen meet and then leave them to talk out their ideas for five or six hours in the freest possible way," Hope wrote, "they would know each other better and probably all of us would be better off." The suggestion was a classic John Hope solution for reducing friction, but it was not what Moton or Washington wanted to hear.

Early in December, Moton wrote to Washington, enclosing all three men's responses and adding this postscript: "I must confess that I doubt whether we can do anything with these people." Washington obviously agreed. Perhaps with Hope in mind, four days later Washington wrote to Emmett Scott, his secretary, that "as usual our friends are silent." John Hope and Booker T. Washington continued to be on cordial terms until the latter's death in 1915, but Washington now knew he could not count on Hope's unwavering support in a crisis.[31]

A few months before Washington tested Hope's loyalty, Du Bois left Atlanta for New York to become the director of research and publications for the NAACP. Hope was saddened by his friend's departure, but the two men remained close and became strong allies in the work of the organization. Over the years Hope provided Du Bois with important information from the South that Du Bois used as propaganda in the *Crisis*. Because of his vulnerability as the president of ABC, Hope's own views rarely appeared in print, but he privately passed information to Du Bois on subjects ranging from discrimination in education to injustices in the judicial system and lynching to the names of possible recruits for the NAACP. In later years, Hope and Du Bois frequently disagreed. Yet Du Bois always valued Hope's perspective and vast knowledge of both intraracial and interracial relations in the South.[32]

Most of Hope's work for the NAACP was conducted out in the open, however, not in secret. During the first ten years of his presidency he attended all the annual meetings and shared his expertise on educational issues involving the race, just as he had done for the Niagara Movement. He also shared his thoughts on other concerns. At the NAACP's fifth annual conference in 1913, for example, Hope read a paper called "The Struggle for Land and Property," which showed that he still supported the idea, popular among many African American leaders, that race-based economic development was necessary.[33]

Hope used his contacts to see that the NAACP's message reached organizations like the National Baptist Convention. In time, NAACP officials also counted on Hope to help raise money. And, of course, he provided a forum for the work of the NAACP at Atlanta Baptist College. Joel Spingarn, a prominent member of the NAACP and later the chairman of its board of directors, visited Atlanta in 1912 and delivered a lecture on the organization's principles. As a guest of the ABC president, Spingarn spent considerable time with Hope, and the two became close friends.[34]

Before long, Hope's name was familiar in NAACP circles across the country. He was a prominent member of the organization's Advisory Committee and of the distinguished Spingarn Medal Committee as well. African American community groups regularly invited him to speak on NAACP principles and to help launch new branches or increase participation in already established chapters. Hope spoke often in local churches and town halls in Providence, Rhode Island, for example, usually as a guest of his good friends William Freeman and Mary E. Jackson, former members of the Enquirers, the literary club Hope had helped organize back in his student days at Brown. Freeman and especially Jackson—who worked by her own admission "like a galley slave" for the organization—were responsible for the Providence branch of the NAACP being one of the most active in the nation.[35]

Though Hope also spoke at local venues in Atlanta, the NAACP was much slower to catch on in the South. Atlanta Baptist College students took part in NAACP activities as early as 1912, yet Hope was surprised that they did not form an official student chapter until one was organized in 1925 by faculty member E. Franklin Frazier, who was destined to become a prominent African American sociologist. When Atlanta formed a permanent branch of the NAACP in 1917, Hope's name was at the top of the membership list.[36]

Hope became increasingly restless at Atlanta Baptist College, particularly after the NAACP was founded. His responsibilities (and headaches) continued to pile up, even though his teaching and administrative responsibilities were substantially reduced in 1912 when he created the position of dean. Thereafter, the everyday running of the college was left largely in the hands of Benjamin Brawley, closely assisted by his fellow faculty member Samuel Archer.[37] The administrative reorganization gave Hope more time to raise much-needed funds. He was never happy or comfortable with that responsibility, however, even though he did it exceedingly well.

Hope's dislike of fund-raising was only part of the problem. It was the part of him that yearned to be a professional race leader that was restless. In his view, William Howard Taft's election as president in 1908 neither promised nor delivered improved conditions for African Americans, nor did Woodrow Wilson's election in 1912. It seemed to Hope that in their respective ways, organizations like the NAACP, the Colored Department of the YMCA, and the Urban League (in which he was also active and served on the advisory board) were on the battlefront, and those working to improve African American higher education lurked somewhere in the rear. Though he rarely showed it, Hope was torn between remaining in education and seeking a professional position in a race advancement organization. He increasingly recognized that the professional happiness and freedom he longed for would be difficult, if not impossible, to find within the confines of academia. As an African American college president, his freedom was restricted by the fragility of his position in the South. His work with the NAACP and other organizations had taught him that hard lesson by the time he reached the middle of his first decade at Atlanta Baptist College.

What troubled Hope most was his self-imposed silence. It compromised his principles and made him uncomfortable. Though he shared these thoughts with few people on paper, a glimpse of his inner turmoil is revealed in a long letter to his old schoolmaster, D. W. Abercrombie of Worcester Academy. To the man who seems in many ways to have been his surrogate father, Hope wrote that in order for him to carry on his work in Atlanta, he needed "courage and silence." "Silence is almost absolute," Hope wrote, "for I will not *speak* a lie. How much I lie by remaining silent only God knows." Hope did not explain these curious generalizations, but it seems clear that some things associated with his role as a college president made him uncomfortable.[38]

As always, Hope was unusually hard on himself and allowed negative thoughts to consume him. In fact, Hope's record during his first decade as president of Morehouse College (Atlanta Baptist College had been renamed in 1913 in honor of ABHMS official Henry L. Morehouse) was exceptional. He had survived in Atlanta when the first African American presidents of two other institutions had failed. In 1910, both Crogman of Clark and Bowen of Gammon Theological Seminary had been asked to step down, and Methodist officials were "looking to replace them with white men."[39] Student enrollment at Morehouse more than doubled during that first decade, the academy had expanded, and the college department was three times as large as before. Atlanta Baptist was becoming a college in fact as well as in name. Hope had also significantly increased the size of the physical plant. Sale Hall had been built with the Carnegie money, and a campaign for an additional building, Robert Hall, was under way. During that first decade John Hope had put Morehouse on the road to what Edward Jones called the "period of self-assurance and early prestige."[40]

Hope's contribution to the growth of Morehouse College involved more than increasing the student enrollment, physical plant, and number of buildings. In Hope's day, the school's academic credibility—indeed, its overall reputation—depended largely on the quality of its teaching, which was usually determined by the success and character of the school's graduates. The faculty understood that above all else they were hired to teach, and with most course loads including four to six classes daily, opportunities for research were scarce anyway. Within the first ten years of his administration, Hope developed an uncanny ability to attract faculty fiercely dedicated to the school's mission, and they in turn recruited other outstanding teachers and students. Virtually all the faculty members Hope recruited were African American men who were not only competent in their respective disciplines but were also squeaky clean in character, making them excellent role models for Morehouse students.[41]

The Morehouse College that emerged under John Hope's guidance represented both continuity of the history of the small, black all-male school that had begun in Augusta back in 1879 and change. From its early New England influence, Morehouse inherited what would today be called its "Eurocentric curriculum" (classes based completely on the Western tradition), its strong emphasis on religion, and its insistence on building strong character. John Hope ensured that these traditions continued, but he also introduced new measures that became vital components of the Morehouse tradition. Relationships between faculty and students were closer than at any other time in the school's history. In spite of Hope's reserve, timidity, and what an official of the GEB would later call "lack of aggressiveness," he worked hard to keep students in school, at times even borrowing money from friends to help students meet their financial obligations. He also worked tirelessly to find summer jobs for his students. Through Hope's efforts, Morehouse students worked on tobacco farms in Connecticut, in restaurants in Chicago, and in insurance companies in Durham and Atlanta. His relationship with his students did not end at graduation. He continued to advise them on everything from jobs to social relations—although in the case of the latter the advice was not always well received. A graduate of the school who was teaching in Missouri was interested in a young lady whose father preferred that he "never more pen a line to his home." As a last resort, the girl's father contacted Hope, who wrote to the man that he "ought to do the square thing. That girl is young, her father is opposed to you corresponding with her, [and you] ought not to do so." If he did not desist, Hope warned the young man, he would embarrass his friends and "injure the good name of the college."[42]

Most significant, Hope imbued Morehouse College with a spirit of race leadership—of commitment, obligation, and personal responsibility. Whatever their chosen professions, Morehouse students were expected to be "race men" who by their actions, demeanor, and character epitomized black America's finest. In many ways, Hope tried to live his own public life in a way that exemplified this model. He commanded the highest respect from students and faculty alike, who often marveled at his dedication to the college and to race advancement organizations locally and nationally. No previous president of ABC had ever been as socially active; of course, all the previous presidents had been white. Thus, during his first decade of service, Hope added both a race-based spirit of social responsibility and a closer faculty-student relationship to the school's already well established liberal arts tradition.

Hope was responsible for hiring men such as Kemper Harreld, the fine musicologist from Chicago; Matthew Bullock, a graduate of Harvard; and former students John W. Davis, Mordecai Johnson, and Zachary Hubert to teach at Morehouse. Many of these men went on to become African American college presidents, important and influential race leaders in African American churches, civic leaders, and leaders in organizations like the YMCA, the NAACP, and the Urban League. A former student remembered that "it was the end product of the Morehouse College experience" that "contributed to the school's outstanding reputation in the Negro community." That "end product" also led to increasing recognition by influential whites. Nevertheless, John Hope could not see the forest for the trees. He seems to have convinced himself that the clash between Hope the race leader and Hope the African American college president nullified his successes and left only failure as his legacy.[43]

It is impossible to say whether or not Lugenia Hope knew of the stresses and strains affecting her husband. Hope often kept things to himself. Furthermore, Lugenia Hope was a race leader and community activist in her own right and was often just as busy as her husband. In 1907 she taught millinery at Spelman College. Her social reform work in Atlanta had not abated since her arrival and actually accelerated after the riot of 1906. In July 1908 her social work led to the creation of the Neighborhood Union. With Lugenia Hope as president, the Neighborhood Union created an elaborate network of African American women that increased communication between neighbors and addressed everything from the lack of recreational facilities and decent housing for blacks to providing forums to "impart a sense of cultural heritage." Members of the union appeared before the board of education and the city council with petitions protesting the inadequate school facilities. By 1935, when Lugenia retired, still holding high their motto, "Thy Neighbor as Thy Self." As Jacqueline Rouse, Lugenia Hope's biographer, has written, the efforts of this group of educated middle-class black women "had run the gamut from services and programs to issues and protests." [44]

During most of the Neighborhood Union's crucial first year, Lugenia was pregnant with her second son. John Hope II, affectionately called "John Jr.," was born on Christmas Day 1909. In 1912 John Hope particularly remembered John Jr.'s triumphant emergence from the "terrible twos" and the twelfth birthday of their oldest son, Edward, who took great pride in sleeping by himself in a double bed in his own room. The Hopes took Edward out of the Roach Street public school after the fifth grade and enrolled him in the Morehouse Academy. "Negro children in Atlanta have no opportunity for industrial education in the public schools," Hope once wrote. Edward had shown an interest in engineering at the age of five, and Hope did all he could to encourage his son in that direction. During the summers, Edward worked with the supervisor of the school's physical plant. It was an invaluable experience that paid off later when he attended the Massachusetts Institute of Technology. The family had finally moved into the president's quarters in 1907, providing more room for John II to play and for Edward to tinker. [45]

Around 1912, D. W. Abercrombie began to hint that he wanted Hope to send Edward to Worcester Academy. Four years later Abercrombie's hints turned to pleas, but Hope continued to stall until his former schoolmaster dropped the idea. It is difficult to say with certainty why John and Lugenia refused Abercrombie's requests. Rumors of racial discrimination had surfaced at Worcester Academy around 1911, but even without them, John and Lugenia Hope were probably hesitant to send their son so far away. In addition, an African American president of a black college that included an academy could hardly send his son to a white school in New England without raising eyebrows among his black constituency. "There are some reasons why I might be misunderstood by my constituency if I were to send him," Hope wrote to Abercrombie. Furthermore, by the beginning of the second decade of the twentieth century Hope had good reason to believe that the academy at Morehouse offered his son academic preparation equal to that offered by Worcester Academy; there was simply no reason to send Edward to New England. But Hope would never have said that to his former schoolmaster. [46]

Most of the time, the running of the household, including disciplining the boys, was left to Lugenia, but neither parent spared the rod when punishment was deemed necessary. When his sons were grown, Hope did not look favorably on that form of punishment and wished he had chosen other means instead. Yet John Hope's relations with his sons were always excellent. Edward was eight years older than his brother, and the two did not always share the same memories. John II's lingering images of the household included memories of his father stretched out on the couch, half asleep (though the elder Hope rarely admitted it) or listening intently to a boxing match on the radio. Edward's memories were more often of a crowded household with visitors from practically everywhere.[47]

Of the two boys, Edward had the most exciting experiences. He spent one summer working on a yacht based at Hampton that traveled up and down the east coast, and another summer in Chicago working as a bus mechanic. On occasion John Hope secretly paid Edward's salary in these jobs to ensure that his son received good job experience. Though Edward seemed closer to his mother, both parents were very protective of their two sons, oftentimes playfully accusing one another of being overly protective and refusing to allow the boys to grow up. In fact, both parents wanted to keep the boys children as long as they could. Once, for example, Hope urged Lugenia not to encourage Edward to work one summer because "Negro boys grow up too soon already" and should be allowed "to enjoy their childhood as long as they can." On another occasion, Lugenia wrote to Hope scolding him for allowing Edward to put on long pants. "I could not keep back the tears," Lugenia jested, and "I could not help blaming you." Back then, long trousers symbolized maturity and opened the door for relationships with girls and women. In 1915 she wrote to Hope, "I want him a boy awhile longer." Edward was then fifteen years old.[48]

John Hope looked to his family as a source of joy in what was otherwise a stressful existence. In addition to spending quiet time with his family at home, Hope found relief from his strenuous schedule by spending one or two of the summer months in Europe. Hope was forty-four years old when he first crossed the Atlantic Ocean in 1912 at the invitation of an English minister he had met the year before in Atlanta. The man had promised to create opportunities for Hope to lecture that would more than pay for his expenses. Furthermore, he wrote to Hope as an added incentive, "the freedom from all racial feeling will put new life into you."[49]

Hope believed some "new life" was very much needed; his only regret was that Lugenia could not accompany him. Both could not afford to make the trip, and Lugenia was busy with the Neighborhood Union. The union had been incorporated in 1911, and the summer months, with programs and projects in abundance, were a particularly busy time. Thus, John Hope traveled to Europe in 1912 alone. In England he met up with his friend E. R. Carter, who had also been invited to lecture.[50]

Hope's letters to his family from that first summer abroad are revealing. He had not lost the journalist's ability to describe in vivid detail what he saw and experienced. He also continued to be far more open in letters than he ever was in face-to-face conversation. His hopes and desires for his children, expressions of love for Lugenia, concerns for fellow African Americans, and mundane instructions to Morehouse staff come brilliantly alive in his written words. He wrote two ten-page letters—one to Lugenia and another to Edward—his second day aboard the ship. To his wife he wrote about the people, claiming he talked little but observed much about the mannerisms and personalities of the other passengers and what he believed to be "the complete absence of a color line."[51]

He was particularly attracted to an unidentified African missionary and clergyman he met the first day out. Long interested in educational and religious exchanges between Africa and black America, Hope made sure the minister knew that Africans were welcome at African American schools in the South, and that he wanted African students to consider Morehouse. He promised to accept a student from the man's country and communicated his long-held belief, also written to Lugenia in a letter, that "Africans and other foreigners should be treated in American schools, not as freaks or paupers but just like other people."[52]

In fact, it was under Hope's leadership at Morehouse that students from Africa and the Caribbean first matriculated at that institution. Among Baptist institutions in black America at that time, Richmond's Virginia Union was widely known as the leader in recruiting African students. They were usually educated and trained in the ministry, and then sent home as missionaries. In 1898, Hope had met and been impressed by one of Virginia Union's star pupils, John Chilembwe from Nyasaland (now Malawi), who finished school and returned home an ordained minister sometime around the turn of the century. Chilembwe became a staunch anticolonialist and in 1915 led an unsuccessful but highly publicized freedom struggle.[53]

Hope made sure that his letters to almost twelve-year-old Edward were always written on official ship's stationery. Those letters were both vivid descriptions of the vessel's mechanical and technological characteristics and subtle reminders and encouragement of his son's wish to become an engineer. Edward's jobs during his summer vacations "for a dollar a week in the grime and grease" were good training for a variety of engineering options that might someday include, Hope wrote, "taking your old white-haired daddy in your own ship." Or, Hope continued, "maybe it won't be a ship but a train or an airship. Maybe it will be a machine shop. Maybe it will be a mine that you will be bossing. We don't know just what, but we know that you will finally get your pay, and it will not be the dollar a day or the $100 a week but Edward Swain Hope, Engineer."[54]

Hope arrived in Europe early in July. His itinerary included visits to England, France, Italy, and finally Scotland. Not knowing what to expect, Hope was relieved when he was graciously welcomed by his English hosts and escorted to their home in Leeds, which became his base of operations. His letters to Lugenia and Edward help the historian to reconstruct what impressed Hope most that summer. Hope took in a bit of history first, visiting the ruins of Kirkstall Abbey, which was settled by monks in A.D. 1152. Less than a week later, on 20 July, he was in London. He stayed at the Charterhouse Hotel and visited the British Museum, where, he wrote to Lugenia, he went straight "for the room that I have wanted to see ever since I studied Greek Art and Architecture under old man Pollard [at Brown] in 1893–4." Hope spent the next day in Cambridge with Harold Hazeltine, an old classmate from Worcester and Brown who was then teaching at Cambridge University. Back in London, there were constant invitations from his new acquaintances, including the fifty-year-old daughter of Ira Aldridge, "perhaps the greatest Negro tragedian our race has produced." The daughter lived with her mother ("a white Germany lady") and her sister in a "section of London that has been dear to artists and authors for nearly . . . a century."[55]

Trained in the classics at both Worcester and Brown, Hope was elated to set foot on the same ground trod by his heroes and heroines. "I went to church this morning back in a court several gates removed from the street. It was the place where Thackeray went to school and went to church as a boy." In Italy he wrote to Lugenia: "I am in Rome! I got here at sunset, winding up the ride by passing along the ancient walls of Rome and landing my foot on Roman soil." He also saw Saint Peter's Cathedral and the famous statue of Moses by Michelangelo. In Scotland he visited Dumfries: "Robert Burns came here for Ayr; lived here; wrote here; drank a great deal of liquor here; died and was buried here. I love Burns," he wrote to Lugenia. "It gives a fellow a funny feeling to see for the first time something that he has all his life long wanted to see."[56]

Scotland, the birthplace of his father, held a special attraction for Hope. On learning from his sister Grace that Langholm was his father's hometown, Hope went there shortly before he left Europe.[57] The visit evoked emotion-filled memories of the happy moments he shared with his father as a boy, and sad memories of his father's early demise and the events that followed. In his last letter to his wife before returning to the United States, Hope recounted the painful story—perhaps long repressed—of the squandering of his father's estate and his having to go to work at a young age "not for the fun of it but for a downright living." John Hope seemed to hold his father responsible for his own premature death, for consigning the family's economic future to less than trustworthy executors, and for resigning his mother to a life of sorrow and unhappiness.[58]

Hope's dual roles as race leader and college president required him to be sensitive to popular views and expectations within the African American world. In 1912 that sensitivity may have caused him to be far less comfortable with his biracial origins than he would be twenty years later when he began to put autobiographical notes on paper. For example, it was probably at least partly his understanding of popular opinion that convinced Hope not to send Edward to Worcester Academy. Like other racial groups, African Americans at all levels of society harbored prejudices that were reflected in negative assumptions about other African Americans. Skin color was a major source of intraracial prejudice. Scholars have long recognized that within black America, one could be "too black" or "too white." African American leaders could not ignore these prejudices, whether or not they agreed with them. Certainly as it pertained to skin color, African American leaders had to be cognizant of the existence of such a prejudice and understand the many ways it could be expressed. They also had to conduct themselves publicly in ways that were not offensive.[59]

Hope knew very well that his light skin invited suspicion among some African Americans. That was especially true in Atlanta, where black journalist, Washington supporter, and "mulatto-baiter" Ben Davis was constantly poised to attack the city's light-skinned elite. Booker T. Washington was also a mulatto, an African American leader, and a college president, of course, but Hope had the extra burden of a white skin and European features. Quite simply, he looked white, and he may have felt more compelled to downplay or ignore the white side of his racial identity (except, perhaps, to close family members) than even slightly darker colleagues.[60]

John Hope recognized in 1912 that to extol the white side of his biracial origins would have been no more "politically correct," to use today's jargon, than sending his son to a northern white academy. When he wrote to Lugenia in July about his plan to visit his father's home, he asked her not to tell anyone because "such things are so misunderstood by our people."[61] In this he was reacting to sensibilities within the African American community. As a race leader and African American college president whose complexion was fair enough to allow him to pass for white, Hope may have had no other choice.

It was perhaps for the same reasons that Hope shielded his sons from details about the white side of their racial identity. Hope told only Lugenia about his trip to his father's birthplace. In interviews years later, neither John nor

Edward could recall discussions about any white members of the family, even though as children they visited one aunt who passed for white in Providence.[62] Perhaps all this was a calculated move on Hope's part to deal with yet another complexity associated with his roles as race leader and college president. Nevertheless, it could also have been simply a stall for time—time he needed to work out his own feelings about his father and the European side of his identity.

His mixed emotions about his trip to Langholm aside, John Hope began a love affair with Europe that summer that lasted the rest of his life. Gone forever were the anti-European tones that characterized some of his earlier orations. From that point on, he spoke of Europeans, and the British in particular, with warmth and affection. In large part the change came about as a result of the warm hospitality and friendliness, without regard to race, exhibited by his hosts. Hope later wrote to his host family that he loved them, their country, and all of their friends. Like the stately Frederick Douglass, the indomitable Ida Wells-Barnett, and other African American leaders, Hope found in Europe a temporary reprieve from the pressures of an overt and obsessive racism that appeared even more foreboding when the United States was viewed through a foreign lens. Refreshed and energized, he was ready to return to America.[63]

John Hope's views of some American whites were also changing. Even before his trip to Europe he had written to an associate that southern "white people . . . are trying to become more honest, fairer, and more Christian." After he returned to Atlanta, his belief in the emergence of a new southern white man grew stronger. In the fall of 1913 he expressed this sentiment to his friend Joel Spingarn of the NAACP. He was seeing "a certain progressive element of the South," he wrote, that seemed more friendly and anxious to "cooperate with the Negro in his religious, education, and even financial enterprises."[64] Though they were scarce before the First World War, there were a few southern liberals Hope felt he could trust. For example, Hope knew and respected John E. White, pastor of Atlanta's First Baptist Church and a member of Morehouse College's local board of trustees. Though no correspondence between the two men exists, White on occasion spoke at chapel services at Morehouse College. For his time he was an outspoken liberal southerner who wrote often about "Anglo-Saxon obligation and opportunity" in the South to improve race relations. Hope also knew W. D. Weatherford of Nashville. He had consulted with Hope on his first book, and Hope respected his efforts to encourage southern college students and faculty to study the race question.[65]

In 1913, when Hope expressed his changing attitude to Spingarn, he probably had in mind the second annual meeting of the Southern Sociological Congress, which had recently met in Atlanta. Along with other white southern leaders, Weatherford had organized the congress to address an array of social issues, including race relations. Although initially no invitations were extended to African Americans to join the organization, more than ninety of them showed up at the Atlanta sessions without objections from the white membership. The African Americans in attendance undoubtedly saw the gathering as a step in the right direction; one said it demonstrated "the possibility of young white men of the new order sympathizing in and appreciating the hopes and aspirations of the Negro today." Hope probably would have agreed, and he may have been one of the African Americans attendees.[66]

Hope was well aware, however, that this emerging group of southern liberals did not challenge the idea of white supremacy. In Atlanta, the support that existed for African American institutions—churches, schools, and even businesses—was often geared toward avoiding racial friction (certainly after the riots of 1906) and preserving the city's New South image. Even southern liberals insisted on segregation and refused to support any form of political or social equality. Nevertheless, Hope was willing to give them the benefit of the doubt: "We shall have to let white opinion drift a little bit until it finds itself more thoroughly committed in spirit to human rights as these rights relate to the Negro along with other people," he wrote to Spingarn. In Hope's view, southern liberals needed encouragement, not criticism. Perhaps they were more honest than many believed, had "good intentions," and only needed time to develop "in the line of real brotherhood and human rights."[67]

Yet as soon as he had written those words to Spingarn he wanted to retract them. They frightened him. Were they really his? He tried to explain, not only to Spingarn but to himself as well, perhaps: "I say we may have to do this, yet I feel the downright fear of doing it. It seems to me that there must be on our part some proper direction of this new and better thought and feeling of the moral South towards the Negro." Though unsure how to channel this "enlightened southern thought," its very existence raised his spirits, made him more "cheerful and courageous." Yet Hope continued to question his own optimism. In closing, he wrote to Spingarn: "Whether this on my part is due to better health, advancing years or a real improvement in the situation, I do not know. It may not be any of these three things but just a dogged determination on my part not to have the blues."[68]

On 2 June 1916, John Hope celebrated his forty-eighth birthday. Due in part to his daily two-mile walks, his weight remained constant at around 135–40 pounds in spite of his love for good food. His face, however, had grown fuller, and his auburn hair was succumbing to an onslaught of gray. There had been

occasional illnesses. Simple exhaustion often led to colds that kept him bedrid-
den for two or three days. Though he often cautioned others to take better
care of themselves, when it came to his own health Hope rarely took his own
advice or anyone else's. "There is no need of having two fools in the world if
you can get one of them to be sensible," he wrote to W. T. B. Williams about
his health. "I advise you to be sensible as there is no hope for me." [69]

None of Hope's illnesses during the first decade of his presidency was life-
threatening. Unfortunately, such was not the case for many of his friends and
associates. Death claimed George Sale, his predecessor at Morehouse College,
in 1911. Two years later, in 1913, the eminent race leader William J. White
died. Hope had no memory of a world without William Jefferson White, who
had been a boyhood idol and a close family friend. White was the founder of
the infant—Augusta Institute—that grew into Morehouse College, a member
of Morehouse and Spelman's local boards of trustees, and an avid supporter
of John Hope's presidency. Ironically, the year White died was the year the
school's name was changed from Atlanta Baptist College to Morehouse College to honor Henry L. Morehouse of the ABHMS. William J. White, whose
life epitomized the best of the Morehouse tradition, died too late for his name
to be seriously considered for the school he helped found and nurture through
its most difficult years. [70]

Before the decade ended, there were additional illnesses and deaths among
family and friends. In 1912, Lugenia Hope had surgery. In fact, according to
her biographer, Jacqueline Rouse, she seemed to be constantly in poor health.
In 1916 Lugenia's mother, Louisa Burns, became very ill, and Lugenia spent
several months in Chicago until her mother died early that spring. Also in
1916, Hope's good friend W. E. B. Du Bois underwent two complicated surgical procedures that left him with only one kidney. Though the operations
were successful, Hope was still concerned about Du Bois's health in January 1917. [71]

But perhaps the most significant death of the decade—for John Hope and
for all African American leaders—occurred on 14 November 1915 when
Booker T. Washington, aged fifty-nine, died at his Tuskegee home in Alabama. Neither friend nor foe could deny Washington's impact on African
American life in America. Even Du Bois, among other less flattering thoughts,
managed to admit in the *Crisis* that Washington's death marked "an epoch in
the history of America," and that he was the "greatest Negro leader since
Frederick Douglass." [72] John Hope had just left Providence for New York
when he received word of Washington's death. He wired Morehouse College,
instructing the faculty to get together with Lugenia and "send an appropriate
floral piece in the name of Morehouse College." He also advised Lugenia to
go on to Tuskegee without him. He had already secured Pullman accommo-

dations to Tuskegee and expected to pass through Atlanta early Wednesday morning. Meanwhile, Washington's secretary, Emmett Scott, sent Hope a letter at Morehouse asking him to serve as an honorary pallbearer. Hope met the other participants at The Oaks, Washington's home, early on Wednesday, 17 November, and they proceeded to the chapel where the funeral took place.[73]

Hope's opinion of Washington had evolved over the years. In spite of deep ideological disagreements, he had moved from disdain toward Washington to respect—perhaps even admiration. His own entrance into the fragile world of African American presidents and race leaders contributed to his understanding of Washington's behavior. In addition, Hope could not forget that at a critical juncture in Morehouse College's history, Washington had intervened with Andrew Carnegie to help move Hope's school forward. Had he not done so, Atlanta Baptist might have remained just another of the numerous black religious academies or prep schools scattered throughout Georgia.[74] John Hope believed Washington's interest in helping ABC was genuine despite his occasional, but highly publicized, vilification of black higher education.

By his example Washington had schooled Hope on the political economy of African American education and had made him cognizant of the perilous plight of African American leaders who were also black college presidents. Unlike other race leaders without comparable responsibilities, presidents were far less free to publicly say and do as they wished. Hope learned, for example, that targeting influential philanthropists for public criticism was very risky business for African American college presidents dependent on external funds. He also learned to moderate his criticism of the South. By the end of the decade Hope had begun to seek out southern allies, even if that meant accepting a relationship based on something less than a mutual goal of full racial equality. Hope would have eventually learned these lessons without Washington's guidance. However, the men also became friends over the years, and though their discussions at Tuskegee and in Atlanta were not recorded, it is likely that Hope learned a great deal from the man Louis Harlan called the "Wizard of Tuskegee."

Hope recognized that he and Washington were similar in many ways—more ways than he probably cared to admit. Both were African American presidents who doubled as race leaders. Both men dearly loved the South and were not enthusiastic about the northern migration of blacks. Just as significant, both men defended the existence of separate African American institutions and worked enthusiastically for their creation and preservation. Many northern African American leaders also supported separate black institutions, but Washington and Hope seemed to have a special energy, a passionate commitment to African American community building born of the stark realities of black life in the South.

Nevertheless, John Hope was an anomaly in the South. His public views on the importance of higher education and social and political equality placed him squarely among the northern black radicals. Booker Washington's supporters recognized that Hope was a moderate among the Tuskegeean's detractors and often tried to use him to close the ideological gap between Washington and Du Bois. On the other hand, most African American radicals (including Du Bois) tended to overlook Hope's acceptance of southern realities, choosing instead to see in him those qualities that made him one of them. Hope actually operated somewhere in the middle: militant enough to maintain his association with the Du Bois faction, yet moderate enough to earn the respect of Washington's supporters and keep open the lines of communication. By the time Washington died, Hope had grown weary of the factional bickering among the different leadership camps, and as the funeral ended, he hoped that reconciliation was not far away.[75]

Others were also tired of the ideological bickering. Two days after Washington's funeral, Hope went to New York to attend an interracial conference sponsored by the General Education Board. Along with influential members of the GEB and other foundation representatives, an elite group of black and white educators had been assembled to discuss the future of African American education. The meeting included four presidents of what the GEB considered the leading industrial and liberal arts African American institutions of the time. Two of the four presidents—Hope and his good friend Robert Moton, who replaced Washington at Tuskegee—were also African American leaders highly respected by the General Education Board. The other two white presidents were H. B. Frissell of Hampton and Fayette A. McKenzie of Fisk University. Other important participants included W. T. B. Williams; Thomas Jesse Jones, a white former Hampton faculty member who was then conducting a survey of black education for the federal Bureau of Education; GEB executive director Wallace Buttrick; GEB board member Abraham Flexner; and James Dillard, then president of the Jeanes Foundation.[76]

Although he admitted that he was not against black vocational education, Hope held fast to his belief in the need for high-quality black liberal arts institutions and adequate funds to secure and maintain quality instruction. He also adamantly opposed the idea of black colleges merging or consolidating, even though that might prevent some duplication of efforts. Flexner favored letting the weaker colleges "sweat," neither suppressing nor consolidating them, in the hope that they would eventually disappear. When Flexner asked whether that would "in the long run . . . stigmatize the inferior institutions [so] that they would give up, the way the poor medical schools are giving up," Hope knew he was talking about the black colleges in Atlanta.[77]

Hope had earlier written to an ABHMS official that he thought it interesting that "years after the criticism was made on the over-massing of Negro educational institutions in Atlanta, white people are beginning to do the same thing." He was referring to the Georgia School of Technology (now Georgia Tech University) and Agnes Scott, a school for "young ladies." He also mentioned "the great Presbyterian University" (Oglethorpe University) and the "great Methodist University" (now Emory University) as schools duplicating resources, and cautioned against ignoring the importance of religious tradition in the development of schools throughout the North and South, whether black or white.[78]

Hope defended Atlanta's black denominational schools by appealing to something the GEB understood very well: "If we should do away with these denominational schools that are run very largely by the Northern societies and are giving the best sort of education that is being given, what would happen? The Negroes would say, 'We are going to educate our children in our own schools,' and they would start up another college and we would be worse off than we are now." Hope further warned the conference participants that eliminating any of the schools would "seriously hamper Negro attempts at self-help." He saw Morris Brown College, the African Methodist Episcopal school in Atlanta, as a prime example. "Morris Brown College has a great big Negro constituency back of it, and with all of its faults, is an example of Negro self-help, which you have got to reckon with." He used Morehouse and Spelman to further emphasize his point: "But what is happening? Here come along 300,000 Negro Baptists who say, 'We will do more for education this year than we have ever done.' You have to think a long while before you get rid of those schools, because if you did, you would be getting rid of a certain amount of incentive of Negroes to pay for their own education." GEB officials were well aware that black denominationalism was a real obstacle to cooperation and consolidation, and they certainly did not want to discourage African American attempts at self-help.[79]

The GEB conference was significant for several reasons. Historian James Anderson wrote that it "pointed to the pressing need for industrial philanthropists to become involved in the development of black colleges and professional schools if they were to be successful in redirecting the scope and function of black higher education." Though this may be true, the GEB was motivated by another interest as well. After W. T. B. Williams's report was submitted in 1907, the GEB had come to realize that African Americans needed their own institutions—including colleges—to train leaders and pro-fessionals for their self-sufficient and (the GEB anticipated) permanently separate existence. By 1915, the GEB's support of a separate black society had begun to include at least thinking about supporting selected black colleges.[80]

The conference also signaled a change in the ideological debate about Af-rican American education. African American educators had grown weary of the debate over education and now believed there was room in black Amer-ica for both industrial and liberal arts educations. In spite of the ideological sparring between Hope, GEB officials, and Frissell of Hampton, the African American participants were generally united. Hope, Moton, and Williams had attended Washington's funeral just a few days before the New York con-ference. The three were good friends who no doubt discussed what to expect at the conference, and perhaps decided to present a united front.[81]

The conference also shows the extent to which Hope's stature as an African American educator and black college president had grown over the decade. His selection as one of only two African American presidents invited to attend the Negro Education Conference—representing a "leading Negro liberal-arts institution in the South"—was a sign of his growing importance to pow-erful and influential whites. The black education pendulum was beginning to move in the opposite direction, and as Washington had done for industrial education, Hope would help guide black higher education in the direction he wanted it to go.

Hope felt good about the conference and the role he had played in the de-liberations. Admittedly with some conceit, he wrote shortly afterward to a friend in Providence, "I think I had a chance to say some things that might not have been said by others there."[82] Privately, a part of him still yearned for a professional position as an activist and race leader. His activism in Georgia never came to a complete standstill. He continued to be influential in advanc-ing black public education, and he put his influence and financial support sol-idly behind organizations such as the African American YMCA, NAACP, Ur-ban League, and others.

Violence directed against African Americans continued to disturb him most. He was particularly moved by the lynching of an African American family—including two young girls—in Monticello, Georgia, early in 1915. Shocked at the state's continuing racial violence, Hope formed a committee and led a delegation to see the governor, begging him, unsuccessfully, to do something to stop the lynching.[83] Periodic activism, however, was unsatisfac-tory. A part of Hope still wanted relief from the fund-raising, the compro-mises, and the role playing that ordered the life of a black college president.

Hope's opportunity to serve as a professional race leader came much sooner than expected. In January 1916, Du Bois wrote to Hope that May Childs

Nerney, the executive secretary of the NAACP, had resigned. In fact, Hope was already aware of her resignation and had sent a warm letter asking her to reconsider a week before he received Du Bois's letter. The editor of the *Crisis*, however, was providing more than just information. Perhaps with the thought of increasing his own power within the NAACP in mind, Du Bois wanted Hope to take over as executive secretary. He had already discussed the possibility with NAACP board chairman (and Hope's good friend) Joel Spingarn, who had voiced his approval.[84]

John Hope now faced a dilemma. The position offered an opportunity to fulfill both his personal and professional desires. He could become a professional African American race leader doing the activist work he claimed to love. Personally, this was an opportunity to take his family and move north—to New York, a city full of the culture he sorely missed in Atlanta. New York was also the workplace of important northern white liberals like Spingarn, Villard, and Ovington. Even more significant, he would be able to spend more time with his best friend, Du Bois, and a number of other African American acquaintances who lived in the city. In a nutshell, New York City offered more freedom for Hope and his family than he could ever expect in Atlanta, or anywhere else in the South.

Yet Hope hesitated. Certainly there were aspects of his job at the helm of Morehouse College that he did not like. But in spite of its shortcomings, Hope loved the South. Perhaps even more significant, he loved Morehouse College. The bond that linked him with the progress and interests of his faculty and students could not easily be severed. Especially with the optimism engendered by the Negro Education Conference, it would be difficult to abandon his responsibilities as an African American educator at precisely the time that his dreams—his vision for his school and for African American higher education in general—seemed on the verge of being realized. Hope wrote to Du Bois early in February that he had decided to remain at Morehouse College.[85]

Hope continued to serve on the NAACP's advisory board and on the prestigious award committee for the Spingarn Medal. The committee, which also included Villard, James Dillard, Bishop John Hurst of the AME church, and former president William Howard Taft, was established in 1915 by Joel Spingarn to award a gold medal "for the highest and noblest achievement of an American Negro." Hope also played a role in the first Amenia Conference, organized by Spingarn and Du Bois and held at Spingarn's Troutbeck, New York, estate during the summer of 1916 to reconcile African American leaders separated by the leadership and ideologies of Washington and Du Bois.[86]

Hope used his influence with Du Bois to ensure that the conference included leaders from a broad ideological spectrum. Always the peacemaker, Hope wrote to Du Bois early in July that Robert Moton was enthusiastic about the conference and wanted to be present. Du Bois wrote two letters to Moton. The first was the "Open Letter to Robert Russa Moton" that appeared in the July *Crisis* before Hope sent his letter to Du Bois. The public letter was a barely disguised warning to Moton to curtail his conservative stances on African American issues. Du Bois's second, private letter to Moton, probably written at Hope's request, was more conciliatory. Hope also urged Du Bois to intervene with Spingarn to invite W. T. B. Williams. "I am sure that Dr. Spingarn would know little or nothing about Williams unless he was told because his work does not bring him a great deal of prominence, but it does bring him a great deal of authority and information."[87] At the Amenia Conference, Hope bunked in tent number 10, the sole "Niagara Man," as delineated by Spingarn, among "Washington Men" like Moton (who did not attend), James Napier, and "undifferentiated" W. T. B. Williams. Hope and Williams led the first session, "Industry and Education."

In many ways the first Amenia Conference (the second was held in 1933) was similar to the Negro Education Conference of 1915. Both conferences sought to reduce the factional fighting among African American leaders following the death of Booker T. Washington and to outline an agenda for continued black progress. All the black participants in both conferences agreed on the need for both industrial and college education for blacks. The participants at the Amenia Conference, whose agenda was larger, in principle also recognized the importance of the NAACP and full political freedom for African Americans. They also acknowledged the unique circumstances of southern African American leaders and vowed to refrain from public denunciations of opposing points of view. Many of the resolutions would not withstand the test of time, but Hope nevertheless believed they were a step in the right direction.[88]

John Hope was as impressed in 1916 with the first Amenia Conference as he had been with the Negro Education Conference held the previous year. Not long afterward, he received a letter from Joel Spingarn. The NAACP had decided to create a new position in the organization, modeled in part on the bureaucracy of the Urban League and suggested by May Childs Nerney before she resigned as secretary. Although a white man, Roy Nash, had filled Nerney's position, the board had decided to split up the work of the NAACP Secretariat by employing a field organizer. The idea was to divide the major work of the organization between two people—one black and one white—and thus attract African American support for the organization. Hope was offered the position of "field organizer." Though some members of the NAACP questioned the effectiveness of an academic in such a raw position, Hope did have the support of his friend Spingarn, and most likely of Du Bois as well. As before, Hope gave the proposition serious thought. In many ways

214 A CLASHING OF THE SOUL

he was suited for the job. He was very well known and respected in African American communities across the country; he had already established a reputation as an avid supporter of the NAACP; and he was moderate enough, perhaps, to penetrate even the most resistant conservative strongholds. The position was also yet another opportunity to fulfill his desire to serve as a professional activist and race leader.

In October 1916, Hope sent his final answer to Spingarn: "It is one of the most attractive offers that can come to a colored man at this time and I wish I could take it." Once again, Hope decided to remain at Morehouse College. He committed his support to Mary E. Jackson, a good friend and one of his key contacts in Rhode Island, who had shown an interest in applying for the position.[89] Jackson was a race woman in her own right, one who tackled issues of gender and racial discrimination head-on. She offered her vast experience in the National Association of Colored Women, the Alpha Suffrage Club, and the Labor Department of Rhode Island.[90] On 24 October, just three days after he penned his letter to Spingarn refusing the national organizer position himself, Hope wrote Mary White Ovington a sparkling recommendation on Jackson's behalf.

In spite of her many qualifications, Jackson's gender was obviously an obstacle. Seven days later, on 31 October, Ovington sent Hope an appreciative but unenthusiastic acknowledgment of the recommendation. Though she acknowledged Jackson's qualifications, Ovington wanted to know: "Is there any man whom you believe we might possibly get who could hold down the job?" Hope recognized that the NAACP had not yet begun to address its own gender biases when it came to African American women. He later wrote to an NAACP official congratulating the organization on securing James Weldon Johnson's services as field organizer and also mentioning an earlier conversation regarding "whether the organization wanted a man or a woman." Without further comment or explanation, he simply added that he did not believe the organization could have found a better "man than Mr. Johnson."[91]

Nevertheless, Hope's commitment to Mary Jackson by itself fails to explain his decision to reject the newly created NAACP position. It seems that Hope had reached what he thought was a permanent decision. His primary professional obligation would remain focused on black higher education. The presidency of Morehouse College allowed him enough flexibility and time to continue his work with race organizations without totally abandoning his responsibilities as an educator. His work with the Colored Department of the YMCA, the Urban League, and the National Association of Teachers in Colored Schools might not have been possible had he become the national field organizer for the NAACP. He might also have been forced to give up his work as honorary president of the Association for the Study of Negro Life and History (organized by Carter Woodson in 1915) and his membership on other boards, committees, and organizations that were very important to him.

Hope was not unaware of his growing influence in the development of African American higher education. He seemed to enjoy the prestige and clout—perhaps even influence and power—that were beginning to come his way in both the black and white worlds. His presence at the Negro Education Conference and first Amenia Conference and the efforts to recruit him for two important NAACP positions testified to his rising status. Though reluctant to admit it, Hope enjoyed his dual roles and was not about to give up either. The true test of his commitment and ability to perform both jobs with equal vigor was not far away. America was about to enter the First World War. In the war era Hope would face challenges far greater than any he faced in his first decade of service as president of Morehouse College.

9

The War Years: 1917–1919

John Hope once gave a speech in which he explained why European alignments along nationalist lines were becoming increasingly dangerous: "France is as offensively French as her delicate position will permit. Austria is tottering because it is heterogeneous," and "Germany has been welded into a mighty empire along narrow race lines." England has never been more "lordly Anglo-Saxon," and "Slavonic Russia" is "wedging its way through hitherto impregnable positions," causing the "yellow races" to come "together like frightened sheep." Hope did not speak these prophetic words on the brink of America's official entry into the First World War, or in 1914 when the war first engulfed Europe. The speech was delivered thirteen years earlier—in 1901—at an unknown observance called Negro Day at Clark University in Atlanta.[1]

From 1917 to 1919 John Hope operated in an environment increasingly dominated by the realities of world war and rising African American expectations. He believed war to be an "abomination." "To talk about righteous wars," he wrote to an English friend in 1916, was "many parts humbug." While sensitive to the plight of the German people, whom he believed to be victims of the German government's policies, Hope never wavered in his support for the Allied powers and his country's official posture.[2]

Along with other African American leaders, Hope expected the war to bring true democracy to his people. With that idea in mind, he became for the first time in his life a professional race leader working among African American troops in France. His work brought Hope national recognition as an African American leader. As the war continued, his patriotism collided with his commitment to his people, placing him at times in awkward, even compromising positions. By 1919, increased racial violence, widespread discrimination in the military, and negative reports about the behavior and performance of African American soldiers had shattered Hope's dream of a racially enlightened America. Ironically, at the end of the war years, at almost the height of his own popularity, Hope privately believed his country had reached the nadir— the height of resistance to blacks' attempts to achieve equality. His faith in America's ability to extend democracy to its darker citizens would be shaken as never before.

Woodrow Wilson was reelected president in November 1916 after a tough fight with the Republican party's candidate, Charles Evans Hughes. Wilson's campaign slogan, "He kept us out of war," lost its validity in the early months of 1917 as the United States inched toward official entry into World War I. For John Hope, however, the threat of war took a backseat to more immediate concerns at the beginning of 1917. The tone of his correspondence is often melancholy, as though the burdens of the world rested on his shoulders. Problems seemed to multiply daily, but solutions seemed as scarce as snow in a Georgia summer. Hope was weary of the endless battles to bring financial security to Morehouse, improve relations between the races, and bring some semblance of equality to black life within a segregated setting.

There was also guilt about his family. He wanted to spend more time with sixteen-year-old Edward and eight-year-old John II. Hope was convinced that he and Lugenia Hope neglected their boys. And though he tried to disguise it, he was not completely comfortable with his wife's work outside the home. He understood her leadership of the Neighborhood Union intellectually, but found it difficult to cope emotionally. His letters to her were often reminders of her "primary responsibilities as a mother" and the "boys' need for nurturing and care." Yet, deep down, he understood; there were just not enough hours in the day for either of them to accomplish their goals as race leaders while conforming to conventional wisdom about raising two children. He had convinced himself that it was all his fault. In a particularly solemn letter written to a friend in the middle of January, Hope wrote, "I think my family is neglected most of all the organizations with which I am connected."[3]

Hope's gloom early in 1917 also stemmed from his concern for W. E. B. Du Bois, who had not yet recovered from his two major surgeries—the first to remove kidney stones, the second removing the entire left kidney. Hope remained in constant contact with both Du Bois and his wife, Nina, throughout the ordeal. Hope understood the *Crisis* editor better than most of his contemporaries and was among the few who had penetrated Du Bois's complex exterior and seen the sensitivity and compassion that lay beneath. "He does what so many people do," Hope wrote to another friend in March, "show[s] his worst side to company." Hope's personal interactions with Du Bois had convinced him that "at heart he is one of the sweetest fellows that I know and one of the most easily imposed upon." But Du Bois kept that part of himself hidden from the public. "What people see is his mask," Hope wrote. "It will never be otherwise."[4]

While he continued to monitor Du Bois's progress, John Hope's January was filled with activities. Morehouse College was planning a gigantic celebration of its fiftieth anniversary late in February—an event that kept Hope in the South. But the extended time in the region pulled Hope in other directions. On 15–17 January he attended the Twenty-sixth Annual Tuskegee Farmers Conference, which this time focused on the widely discussed theme of African American migration to the North. Back in Atlanta by the twentieth, he took part in a concerted effort to build a new black YMCA building and to get the city to provide land and maintenance for an African American library. On 31 January 1917, Hope and other local leaders organized the Atlanta branch of the NAACP at the offices of the Standard Life Insurance Company on Auburn Avenue. They had tried to organize an Atlanta branch a year earlier, but without success. Black Atlantans in the early twentieth century tended to rally around issues that directly affected their interests within the African American community rather than supporting the dim prospect of any kind of integration.

It was the very real threat of decreased public education opportunities that finally galvanized black support of an Atlanta branch of the NAACP.[5] The number of African American public schools came nowhere close to meeting the demand for them, and those in existence were deplorable. African American youth had no real opportunities for vocational training, there were no black public senior high schools, school buildings were substandard, and students were forced to accept the inconvenience of double sessions. City administrators usually ignored the protests and cut financial corners in black schools whenever they wanted to improve the quality of the city's white schools.

In 1913 Lugenia Hope's Neighborhood Union conducted a six-month survey of the black schools in Atlanta and presented the findings to the *Atlanta Constitution*, the mayor, and members of the school board and city council. In 1915 city officials eliminated the eighth grade in Atlanta's black and white schools to save money. There were rumors early in 1917 that in order to provide more money for the city's white public senior high schools, Atlanta officials planned to eliminate the black seventh grade as well. The African American community decided it was time to take a stand.[6]

Reluctantly, John Hope interrupted the planning of Morehouse's fiftieth anniversary to address the public school issue. He became a key figure on an emergency committee whose task it was to decide how the protest against the city's plans should be conducted. There were calls for drastic measures like boycotting the schools, refusing to pay taxes, and organizing a mass protest against the seventh grade closing. Late in February, however, Hope helped persuade the group to present a more conservative petition to the school board which he helped to draft. If that approach proved unsuccessful, they would then move on to one of the more radical alternatives.[7]

On 22 February, just three days before Morehouse's fiftieth anniversary celebration, Hope went to his office as usual. Sometime that morning he received a call from Walter White, the secretary of the Atlanta branch of the NAACP, who had just learned that the board of education planned to meet at three o'clock that afternoon to decide the fate of the black seventh grade. Hope quickly left the office to meet with the emergency committee, which also included Benjamin Davis of the *Atlanta Independent*, physician William F. Penn, and Harry H. Pace of the Standard Life Insurance Company (Walter White was not on the delegation). They were joined by members of the Allied Ministers' Union, an organization comprising the city's leading Baptist and AME ministers that included W. S. Cannon, a Morehouse graduate, chairman of the alumni association, and prominent member of the powerful General Missionary Baptist Convention; and A. D. Williams (grandfather of Martin Luther King Jr.), a member of the Missionary Baptist Convention and the pastor of Ebenezer Baptist Church.

Penn and Cannon addressed the school board while Hope and the others stood quietly at their sides. They reminded the board of its charge to all of Atlanta's children, stressing the board members' double responsibilities as citizens and public servants: "You are servant of all of the people—the white and black in common, and the services that you render each must be equal in adequacy and efficiency. If you discriminate in favor of either, you are recreant to the trust imposed." The men also reminded the board that Atlanta's African Americans paid taxes and were entitled to their constitutional right of petition. "We do not ask that the white boys and girls be denied any facility that they now enjoy," they said, "but if you can increase the facility for their education and enlightenment, we sanction it, and ask that you discharge your public function honestly and conscientiously to the black boys and girls by providing them with the same adequate, ample and efficient facilities in the grades, in industries, in preparation for a high school and [to build] a high school." The board's response was more favorable than the delegation expected. Board president R. J. Guinn and board member (and future mayor) James L. Key pledged their best efforts to "be fair and provide the most liberal advantages and opportunities for the education of all the children, without regard to race or color." In the end, the seventh grade was not eliminated, although the other problems within Atlanta's segregated school system continued.[8]

With that issue at least temporarily resolved, Hope turned his attention back to Morehouse's fiftieth anniversary. The three-day celebration included conferences on moral and religious training and African American education, and the list of invited speakers charted Hope's meteoric rise as an educational statesman and black leader. They also represented significant epochs in his personal history, from his early days in New England to his presidency in Atlanta, and his many friends and associates across the "color line." William Faunce of Brown University delivered the anniversary sermon; D. W. Abercrombie, Hope's principal at Worcester Academy, also spoke, as did the leading white officials of the ABHMS and William Buttrick of the GEB.

African American leaders were also well represented. Most were longstanding friends whom Hope had known most of his adult life and who had stood shoulder to shoulder with him in the development of Morehouse College and in protests against inequality. They included W. T. B. Williams, Robert Moton, and a still recovering W. E. B. Du Bois. The program also included an up-and-coming generation of African American leaders, many of them Morehouse men. Mordecai Johnson, who had left the ABC faculty to become an international secretary with the Colored Department of the YMCA, was there, as was M. W. Reddick, the principal of Americus Institute, a black academy in Georgia, and president of the state Baptist organization. Local leaders included Morehouse men A. D. Williams, P. James Bryant of Wheat Street Baptist Church, and W. S. Cannon. It was truly a Morehouse celebration, and according to the *Atlanta Independent*, "just about every prominent black Baptist minister claimed the school as his Alma Mater." Perhaps that was why few women were on the official program, though many attended all three days of the festivities.[9]

Hope was particularly pleased at the presence of Du Bois. The letters the two men exchanged discussing Du Bois's attendance at the celebration reveal how they tended to let down their guards with one another. They joked, ribbed, and teased each other in ways that would have surprised most people who knew them. Hope wanted Du Bois there even if he was too weak to speak because "your mere presence would make me very happy and would add to our conference." He promised to pay all Du Bois's expenses and provide a quiet room "where you could smoke to your heart's content without embarrassing anybody who does not like to smoke." He even promised to allow Du Bois to drink something "stronger than tea or coffee," although he would have to bring it with him because "Georgia is now bone dry, at least to the innocent." (Hope still did not drink or smoke.) Du Bois accepted the invitation but jokingly wrote back that after all his "flirting with the gay and festive surgeon it will cost you every damned cent of my expenses. So figure it out carefully and see if its really worthwhile." [10]

Du Bois's address, the finale of the program on Tuesday, took place shortly before the Morehouse Glee Club concert began. It was entitled the "Negro Press as an Educative Influence," and according to the *Atlanta Independent* "was awaited with eagerness by the audience." Du Bois's address was short and sweet compared with the much longer speech of Robert Moton that preceded it. With perhaps a disguised warning to the more conservative Moton, in "brilliant language" Du Bois said the *Crisis* and other black publications should tell the truth about race relations. "Lying is inadequate as a possible solution of the race problem," he said, and "more and more we must be honest with ourselves and not dwarf our souls by pretending that is the truth which is not." In Du Bois's view, World War I was a startling example of the "havoc wrought by men who were not honest with each other in diplomacy." The black press had a role to play in the "shaping of opinion in the new Europe and must lead as a constructive force." At the end of the short address, Hope led the audience in giving his best friend a standing ovation. [11]

John Hope had already electrified the predominantly black middle-class audience two days earlier with his formal presidential address. Entitled "Fifty Years of Negro Education and the Outlook," the speech was both the longest and the most eloquent Hope had ever given. In it, he interwove the threads of black and white influences in the historical development of education at Morehouse and in the history of African Americans in general. He paid homage to the New England schoolteachers who journeyed into the dangerous South to "administer to the educational needs of the freedmen," and also to the missionary organizations, foundations, and individual philanthropists that were "the financial backbone" of many of the South's educational institutions. Hope did not imply, however, that the northern groups and individuals had arrived to find a docile group of newly freed blacks with no clue to the meaning of freedom or the value of education. They had found a population of African American men and women whose "yearning and striving had already existed during two centuries of slavery, so that laws had to protect masters in their effort to hold their slaves by perpetuating ignorance." [12]

Hope's presidential address showed that he was still the same leader he had always been: a man working to improve relations between the races while acknowledging and supporting nationalist sentiment and black realities within the segregated black world. But there were other yardsticks beyond education for measuring African American progress. In the last fifty years there had been tremendous developments in the African American community—in businesses, churches, organizations such as the Neighborhood Union, and other self-help enterprises. "More and more," Hope told his audience, "the college must lead in vital matters respecting the race." To that end it needed to be more independent, free to make decisions without strings attached. Hope warned against too much dependence on white philanthropy: the "Negro race must not always have to go outside of itself for support"; and "the merit of a college, like that of a man, depends not only on what it does, but what it is."[13]

This section of Hope's discourse may have produced both frowns and smiles on many white faces in the audience, but it produced no mixed emotions among the many African American Baptists present, who remained uncomfortable with the amount of control wielded by the missionary societies and philanthropic agencies over African American educational institutions. Yet Hope managed to strike a balance. Resonating loudest was the theme that both blacks and whites had been essential to African American progress since the Civil War and would continue to be essential for years to come.

The speech epitomizes Hope's inseparable roles as an African American educator dependent on broad-based support and a leader committed to progressive change in both the African American world and the larger society. It shows his skill in balancing black and white support in those roles, even while he aroused suspicion about his objectives. In March he wrote to a newspaper editor that he was surprised when "colored and white men stood up and applauded his address." It was one of the few times he felt truly appreciated.[14]

As 1917 continued, World War I gradually came to dominate Hope's thoughts. He followed the news of the war religiously but revealed his deepest thoughts only in letters to close friends and associates. In 1914 he had doubted that America would actually fight, but that view changed as the war dragged on. In February 1917 he revealed to a missionary associate in China that the United States was "restless and anxious." With German submarines roaming the seas and destroying commerce, the United States might find itself in the war at any time. The war had already wreaked havoc on a French family Hope had visited in 1912. Their son had been killed early in 1917, and Hope had sadly reported the news in chapel at Morehouse. In his condolence letter to the family written late in March, Hope admitted that their son's death had "brought the war closer to me than anything that had occurred up to that time."[15]

Black Americans were already experiencing the side effects of the war in Europe. Immigration from Europe had slowed, and the demand for labor in the North far exceeded the supply. African Americans were encouraged to fill the void. The lure of economic opportunity in the North coincided with deteriorating economic and social conditions in the South. The boll weevil destroyed the cotton crop, drastically reducing income from farming. Except for the most menial occupations, economic opportunities were scarce even in urban Atlanta, and the city's record in providing political and social opportunities for African Americans remained as dismal as ever.

Georgia continued to lead the nation in lynching. Sparked in part by the lynching of Jewish entrepreneur Leo Frank, the Klan was revived on Thanksgiving night 1915 on Stone Mountain, a high peak not far from Atlanta. The December premiere in Atlanta of the film *Birth of a Nation*, which was based on Thomas Dixon's racist book, *The Clansman*, gave the Klan an added boost. The Klan's membership would eventually include prominent officials of the Atlanta Police Department, the Georgia speaker of the house, and a future congressman. In spite of efforts by New South leaders to discourage black migration, close to fifty thousand black Georgians packed up their things during the war years and headed for the "promised land." [16]

Neither John Hope nor other African American leaders could ignore such an exodus. Hope had known for about a year that African Americans were working in northern jobs usually reserved for whites. While traveling in New England in 1916, he wrote to an English friend that he had never before seen "black men working on the New York, New Haven, and Hartford railroad as section men with pick and shovel." Hope had mixed feelings about the migration. It troubled him that it was a movement of the rank and file that seemed "unled and unguided." Deep down, he believed that African Americans should and would remain in the South, and he warned against the exodus as a solution to the problems of racial inequality. He also warned those Americans quick to label adverse race relations as strictly a southern problem that the North was by no means a racial paradise. [17]

Nevertheless, for both ideological and pragmatic reasons, Hope did not openly discourage black migration out of Georgia and did not hesitate to lay the blame for it at the feet of southern white leaders. Though recognizing that natural disasters were beyond their control, Hope criticized southern leaders for ignoring lynching, failing to encourage improvements in black public facilities, and pretending that political and economic inequities based on race did not exist. For that reason Hope supported the part of the resolution engineered through the January Tuskegee Farmers Conference by Robert Moton that insisted that only better treatment would halt the black exodus from the South. [18] He vehemently disagreed, however, with the parts of the resolution that urged African Americans to remain in the South "no matter what" and claimed that "future economic opportunities would be even greater than in the North." He also remained unconvinced that southern white leaders were doing all they could to improve conditions, as the resolution implied, and were thus deserving of African American support. He later wrote to a friend in

South Carolina that the state had no real "scientific conception of the economic and moral loss it will stand in the departure of Negroes." The "better class of whites" were generally indifferent, he thought, and poor whites were "downright happy as they believe they will have a better chance with us out of the way."[19]

Hope realized that the war was creating economic opportunities for African Americans, and he exploited those opportunities to help Morehouse students. It was already an established tradition among southern black male students (including Hope and many of his close friends when they were students) to seek summer employment in the North. Most of the jobs for blacks were in plush restaurants or other service-oriented industries in the large northern cities and coastal resorts. Through his contacts among blacks and whites in the North, Hope found jobs for students in the tobacco and railroad industry in Connecticut, the meat-packing industry in Chicago, and in other industries in Massachusetts, Ohio, and Pennsylvania. Although newspaper editor Benjamin Davis publicly criticized black college presidents "who were no more than northern agents," Hope did not hesitate to help his students capitalize on the labor shortages created by the First World War.[20]

As the United States moved closer to an official declaration of war, Hope's thoughts switched to the question of black participation. There had been widespread rumors that the Germans were seeking secret alliances with African Americans in the South, and the government was concerned. On 25 March, however, the black First Separate Battalion, District of Columbia National Guard unit, was ordered to protect the entrances to the Capitol. This decision convinced African American leaders that the Wilson government trusted African American troops and believed blacks were loyal. Hope was delighted. Certain that positive changes were just over the horizon, he was already thinking about who among African Americans should take the lead in the coming new world order. Perhaps bubbling with excitement, Hope wrote to a friend that "young people of our race must decide quickly what part the Negro is to play in the new world civilization which is to follow this great war."[21]

By early May his optimism had begun to fade. When the groundswell of patriotism that followed the declaration of war prompted African Americans to converge on the recruitment centers in April, many of them were discouraged from enlisting, and some were actually turned away. The War Department quickly established quotas for African American enlistees, and just as quickly sent word throughout the country that slots in the "colored organizations" had been filled. "If the country needs me, I shall respond readily," Hope then wrote to another friend with an obvious loss of enthusiasm, "but I very much fear . . . it is not going to call on colored people to do much fighting." The passage of the Selective Service Act on 18 May, providing for the enlistment of all Americans, raised Hope's spirits a notch, but they plummeted again when he realized that the principles of segregation had been written into the legislation. Hope continued to alternate between optimism and despair with each new development related to the role of African Americans in the country's participation in the First World War.[22]

John Hope was no stranger to segregation, of course, and had often supported it at home even when it violated his principles. Endorsing it as a national policy was a different matter. At the beginning of the year, acting on his own, Joel Spingarn had introduced a proposal to establish a separate facility for the training of African American officers. Impressed with a similar whites-only facility in Plattsburg, New York, Spingarn correctly believed that African Americans would have no commissioned officers unless they had a training facility of their own. The declaration of war in April and the passage of the Selective Service Act in May gave the proposal an urgency that could not be ignored. African American leaders such as the much-heralded military hero Colonel Charles Young; NAACP member William Pickens, then dean of Morgan College for Negroes in Baltimore (now Morgan State University); Jesse Moorland of the YMCA; and George Cook, secretary of Howard University, supported the measure from the very beginning and worked hard to publicize the opportunity for potential candidates. A number of other African American leaders, however, were reluctant to support a government-sponsored segregated military facility.

In May, the NAACP board finally caught up with the black rank and file's overwhelming support for the camp. The organization officially decided to support the facility if there was no chance of African Americans training with whites. John Hope was present at the sixth annual conference of the NAACP held in May 1917 when a resolution supporting the camp was presented. In spite of its acceptance of segregation, Hope enthusiastically endorsed the resolution, as he had from the beginning.[23] He had written to Spingarn late in January that he thought it a good idea, and early in April he informed George Cook of Howard that he could not "pressure the boys [Morehouse students] into joining, but personally, I am heartily in favor of the Training Camp and wish that hundreds of our young men would enter." If he didn't pressure them, he did strongly encourage Morehouse students to sign up for the camp. Perhaps for John Hope, a *southern* African American leader, the decision was not the "perpetual dilemma" (to use David Lewis's words) that it was for W. E. B. Du Bois, who also endorsed the facility.[24]

Like Du Bois, Hope was committed to improving relations between the races and helping to engender structural changes in American society that would eliminate racial injustice. But he was also an intraracial leader keenly sensitive to the needs of blacks within the African American world. Southern leaders like Hope, who out of necessity vigorously supported the black YMCA, churches, businesses, schools, and other black enterprises in the South, seemed to understand that sometimes the principle of integration had to be weighed against the real threat of exclusion. Like it or not, the gray area in between was often the acceptance of a segregated enterprise. It was a lesson African American leaders outside the South were only just beginning to learn.

Hope's concerns about African American soldiers increased rapidly after the passage of the Selective Service Act and the opening of the black officer training camp in Des Moines, Iowa. The War Department soon realized that many of the black and white men already in the military—and those expected to be drafted—had almost no education; many were unable to sign their own names. It was an embarrassment to the United States government, for it was an indication that the men were ill prepared to accept the responsibilities of citizenship. In conjunction with the War Department, the War Council Advisory Board developed far-reaching educational programs designed to aid the war effort and turn draftees into citizen-soldiers. The board consisted of prominent philanthropists like George Peabody; liberals Oswald Garrison Villard, Walter Lippmann, and future Supreme Court justice Felix Frankfurter; and Commissioner of Education P. P. Claxton. All the troops were slated to receive the same education, but it would take place within their segregated units. John Hope, Robert Moton, Emmett Scott, Bishop George W. Clinton of the AME Zion church, and a few other black leaders were called on for advice in the creation of this monumental education project. Hope particularly welcomed the opportunity to serve the educational needs of black soldiers.[25]

Most of the War Department's policies did not meet with Hope's approval, however, especially those surrounding the officer training camp in Des Moines and the activation of the all-black Ninety-second Division. To Hope's dismay, and that of many black college students, the twenty-five-year minimum age requirement automatically disqualified many students and recent graduates interested in joining the camp. In addition, nearly a third of the slots were reserved for African American soldiers already in the four regular army units. Few denied that members of the existing black units deserved a chance to become officers, for they had paid their dues in bloody combat on the western plains, in Mexico, in the Philippines, and elsewhere. But many black leaders were concerned over what seemed to be the War Department's deliberate plan to commission a significant number of poorly educated black soldiers who were accustomed to taking orders from white superior officers.

In addition, only white officers would receive commissions above the rank of captain. Privately, the War Department stepped up its efforts to staff existing and future new black units with white officers. The man appointed to command the black Ninety-second Division, for example, was the well-meaning and competent, but soon to be controversial, Major General Charles C. Ballou. General Ballou would draw the jeers of Hope and other African American leaders a year later when he confined his men to their post because a black sergeant had insisted on being admitted to a movie theater in a Kansas town. To justify his decision, Ballou issued the infamous "Bulletin 35," which publicly proclaimed that although the theater manager was "legally wrong," the "GREATER wrong" was the sergeant's for provoking "race animosity." [26]

Hope was especially vigilant over policies that involved the Ninety-second Division. Though committed to its activation, the government had no intention of training the black division in one camp, choosing instead to scatter the men in seven locations throughout the Midwest and Northeast. White attitudes in the South contributed to that decision. Southern politicians, including those in Georgia, had already begun to voice their opposition to African American soldiers, even native southerners, training in the region. Though they did not always admit their concerns publicly, many African American leaders were disturbed by the department's policies early in the mobilization. Hope privately wrote to his friend W. T. B. Williams to "expect trouble" if the War Department did not give black soldiers a "square deal." [27]

The trouble came much sooner than Hope expected. On 23 August 1917, one hundred or so black soldiers of the Twenty-fourth Infantry descended on Houston, Texas. Frustrated by events that ranged from unanswered complaints of police brutality to racial insults and Jim Crow accommodations, the soldiers struck at the first police station in their path. In less than two hours the troops killed or wounded close to thirty civilians, including five policemen. Nineteen black soldiers were tried and hanged; several more received life sentences. [28]

Racial violence was occurring in many places. More than three thousand witnesses applauded the burning of a "live Negro" in Mississippi. On 5 July, a former ABC student living in Chicago wrote to Hope describing a small racial skirmish there. Just before that, blacks and whites had clashed in a violent race riot in East St. Louis. At least forty African Americans were brutally killed, some of them in the most grotesque manner. The East St. Louis riot had the dubious honor of eclipsing Atlanta as the worst race riot in American history. Hope's pessimism reached new depths. He wrote many friends of his complete disgust with the rioting in East St. Louis and Houston, echoing the concerns of his former student in Chicago that the "country seemed to be moving toward an internal rebellion." [29]

Deteriorating race relations did not occupy all of Hope's thoughts as the country mobilized for war. His nephew James Ladeveze—the son of his forty-nine-year-old sister Alethea—was eligible for the draft. James's low registration number led his uncle (mistakenly) to believe he would probably not be called. Alethea and Charles Ladeveze, however, were not comforted; they wanted Hope to see about getting James into an officer training camp. Hope was unable to help. On Sunday, 8 December 1917, James Ladeveze left to join the navy. Alethea was devastated. Hope wrote to his sister Anna that "it was a rather sad time, Leith really needed me and I was glad that I could be there to comfort her."[30]

John Hope's relationship with Alethea provides some insight into the range of interactions that existed within early twentieth-century mulatto families with members who had chosen to pass for white. Back in the early 1890s, Charles Ladeveze had packed up his family and his art store and moved from Augusta to Savannah. By 1895 he was thinking about moving north, and through Alethea sought Hope's advice about cities along the northeastern corridor where the family might settle. Census records show that in Savannah the Ladeveze family, including the three children—Victor, Medora, and James— were still acknowledging their racial identities. Alethea correctly listed her father in the census as a Scotsman and her mother as a mulatto from Georgia.[31]

When the Ladevezes left Georgia, they left their African American racial identity behind. The family settled in Providence, Rhode Island, sometime after 1905. No correspondence between the Hopes in Georgia and the Ladevezes in Providence prior to 1917 exists, and the details of their lives in the interim are somewhat sketchy. Like Sissie and her family in California, the Providence Ladevezes apparently abandoned their racial identity, although they did not cut all ties with their relatives, as the California Ladevezes did. The 1920 census lists Alethea and her family as white. She still listed her father correctly as a white man from Scotland, but instead of listing her mother as a mulatto from Georgia, she put her down as a white woman from New York.[32]

Even after crossing the color line the Providence Ladevezes maintained their relationship with the rest of the Hope family in Georgia. Hope's sisters Grace and Anna, and his half-brother, Madison, all visited the Ladeveze house at 193 Reynolds Street in Providence. John Hope apparently accepted his sister's decision to pass, and he continued to associate with the Ladevezes at least until 1920. Hope's response to his sister's request about getting James into the officer training camp is a perfect example of one of the problems involved in passing. Hope did not refuse to help his nephew. He could not help him, he explained, because James was living as a white man "and I have no influence in any of the white camps." James had earlier written a warm letter to his uncle John describing his draft status, a recent visit by "Uncle Buddie" (Madison Newton) from Augusta, and the activities of his brother, Victor, who was still "doing his bit on the farm at Kingston" (Rhode Island). Hope was just as cordial to James: "If we could just sit down and have a conversation with Lloyd George, Premier Ribot, and Emperor William," Hope joked in a letter to his nephew, "perhaps we might get things straight in a few days. I think, however, if they let me put across one of my lobster salads I might settle them whether I settled the War or not." The letter's tone is warm and familiar, as if Hope were writing to one of his own sons. John, Lugenia, and their youngest son, John Hope II, visited Alethea and her family in August 1917. Alethea later wrote to tell the Hopes how much they enjoyed the visit, and particularly seven-year-old John II, who seemed to have had a wonderful time. Hope's relationship with the Providence Ladevezes shows that passing for white did not necessarily involve the termination of all relationships with family members on the opposite side of the color line.[33]

Nevertheless, Hope may have been somewhat ambivalent about the matter, for he was forced to play an active role in keeping the family's identity secret. During the war years, Hope usually stayed with the Ladevezes when he visited Providence, and often had his mail delivered there. Hope also had good friends in Providence—the Tolliver sisters, Mary E. Jackson, and William H. P. Freeman—all prominent race leaders he had known since his days at Brown. There is no concrete evidence that any of them ever knew about his sister; if they did, they kept the secret well.[34] It is certainly not mentioned in his correspondence with any of his closest friends, or even with members of his own family. Since Hope was so well known, his friends may simply have assumed that he was staying with a white family when he came to Providence, an error Hope did nothing to correct.

If his sister's racial identity did not cause John Hope much concern, the wartime racial violence and discrimination did. Hope's ideas of what to do about it were in a constant state of flux. Several of his letters to friends and associates written in the fall of 1917 offer bits and pieces of what seems to be a coherent philosophy and plan for using the war as a vehicle for African American advancement.

Hope strongly believed racist whites were aware that the war was providing new opportunities for blacks but, as he wrote to a friend in Massachusetts, they were "determined to keep colored people in their place." He also seemed convinced that the war in Europe had focused the world's attention on race relations in America. "We must now very speedily become free," he wrote to Du Bois in support of the New York Silent Parade (which protested the carnage in East St. Louis), "or saddle slavery upon ourselves for the next one hundred years." In Hope's view, black progress rested on the ability of African Americans to continuously demonstrate their patriotism through their unqualified support of the war. That support included everything from concerted and well-publicized purchases of liberty bonds to enthusiasm for "our boys" in uniform. African American leaders, he believed, had a special responsibility to take the lead in demonstrating blacks' support by accepting every opportunity presented to them to aid the war effort. He also saddled black leaders with the responsibility of first ensuring that influential whites kept black patriotism uppermost in their minds and then pushing those whites cautiously toward the idea of full black equality.[35]

But what of African American protest, resistance, and agitation? Hope's plan addressed that component as well: "We must continue to show dissatisfaction with our plight in America," he wrote to a former Worcester classmate, while at the same time continuing "our patriotic support" to show that "colored people deserve a square deal." Though admittedly difficult, Hope believed the dual approaches were absolutely essential, and he expected African American leaders to lead in both directions.

Hope's plan to dismantle discrimination in America thus involved specific tasks for blacks and progressive whites. African American expressions of patriotism—and dissatisfaction with the status quo—would increase whites' sensitivity. Nudged by world opinion, that sensitivity would help facilitate a significant change of conscience and would bring African Americans under the umbrella of American democracy. Hope obviously had not yet lost his faith in his country's ability to change. His correspondence from late 1917 shows that he had less faith in the ability of African Americans to keep the protest tradition alive than he had in progressive white America's ability to do its part.[36]

Meanwhile, Hope deepened his commitment to war work, in what seemed to be the implementation of his own strategy as well as a true reflection of his patriotic support. Very few opportunities went unnoticed. When the educational unit of the Food Administration sought African Americans' help in easing war-generated shortages, Hope immediately volunteered his assistance. Once officially on board, he lectured groups of African Americans on the need for conserving resources and actively recruited other blacks to join the lecture circuit as well. He also played a major role in the founding of the Atlanta-based Colored American Society for the Relief of Orphaned Children and Widows, an organization established to assist families of African soldiers (particularly Senegalese fighting in France) killed in combat during the war. As the organization's vice president, Hope raised funds, provided information, contacted influential people in other states about the organization's work, and encouraged Morehouse College and other black schools to establish chapters.[37]

Also in line with his strategy, Hope took advantage of every opportunity to protest discrimination in Atlanta. Late in September, he was again part of a committee that petitioned the city council to eliminate double sessions in Atlanta's black public schools. The council had promised to eliminate the practice in the white schools, but ignored the problem in the black schools. After a two-hour session during which the delegation tried to convince Atlanta officials of the need for improved African American schools, one council member said that he was opposed "to giving one nickel more for the education of the Negro children as they were already getting more than they deserved." Whites' attitudes had obviously hardened since blacks had successfully protested the elimination of the black seventh grade. Hope was outraged and wrote to a former student that "Georgia on the Negro School question is probably the coldest state in the South."[38]

Of all his war work, John Hope enjoyed his interactions with African American soldiers the most. By the end of 1917 the men at the Des Moines officer training camp had received their commissions, the Ninety-second Division had been activated, and the first round of inductees had been drafted. Hope had visited the Des Moines camp several times to see former students and other friends who had been doctors, lawyers, teachers, and ministers before signing up for the officer training camp. He visited their stateside training stations in Camp Meade in Maryland, Camp Dix in New Jersey, and Camp Upton in New York. He also made frequent trips to Camp Gordon near Atlanta to see the nine thousand black troops training there.

At first, his romps on military bases seemed to feed a personal pride in being in the company of African American soldiers. Hope had admired "his people in uniform" since his days at Brown when he fraternized with black Civil War veterans. The visits, however, soon came to seem like work and demanded more and more of his time. Especially at Camp Gordon, Hope conducted prayer services, held educational forums, and helped secure sports equipment to provide "wholesome opportunities for recreation."[39]

In time, Hope began to encourage African American soldiers to talk about daily life in the military camps. Complaints emerged of discrimination in recreational facilities, health care, and living conditions, and segregated or nonexistent facilities in nearby towns. African American officers echoed the complaints recorded by government officials of white enlisted men refusing to salute them, and of white troops of every rank calling them "nigger," "coon," and "darkey." In October, Emmett Scott (Booker T. Washington's former secretary) was appointed to the position of special assistant to Secretary of War Newton Baker with the job of overseeing matters pertaining to African American troops. In conjunction with Raymond B. Fosdick, chairman of the Commission on Training Camp Activities (commonly referred to as the Fosdick Commission), Scott surveyed conditions in training camps throughout the country. Though the Fosdick Commission found many instances of discrimination, the War Department refused to make changes.[40]

Hope did not immediately reveal the complaints he was hearing from black troops to military or civilian authorities, or even to close friends. His reasons for that are not clear, and his silence seems to contradict his wartime philosophy. Of course, he was not working in an official capacity—although he wanted to—and perhaps he believed that any negative comments would jeopardize any chance he had to do so. Perhaps more important, he may have felt it dangerous to point out any disunity within the military, since he believed, correctly, that the War Department was still uneasy about both the events in Houston and German propaganda. Although he continued his unofficial investigations, Hope remained silent about what he learned for almost two years.[41]

While happy in his role as an African American leader, Hope was increasingly reminded that he was also a professional educator, and the president of a black college experiencing its own wartime problems. When Hope was on the road, as he frequently was, Deans Archer and Brawley took care of day-to-day matters at the college. The war wreaked havoc on the school's operations. Essentials for the physical plant and general academic supplies were scarce. Many of the students were drafted, and those who were not drafted enlisted. The increasing number of faculty vacancies was even more disturbing. Younger faculty were as likely to be drafted as students. "They were always up in the air," Hope wrote later in disgust, "as to whether they would have to go at once to Camp." Each semester it became increasingly difficult to secure faculty replacements before the term began.[42]

Many of Morehouse College's wartime problems were beyond Hope's control. Yet, as usual, he tended to blame himself. He was a workaholic, a perfectionist who believed everything he did had to be done exceptionally well. Though often critical of others for the same behavior, Hope did not allow himself to slow down. Then almost fifty years old, he continued to operate as if he had two full-time jobs and was able to do both equally well. He put just as much energy into his race work as into his career as a college president. He seems never to have consciously recognized that his commitment to these dual responsibilities represented a dilemma, what a former student would later call a "clashing of the soul." Both responsibilities were demanding, required enormous energy, and produced almost unbearable stress. Like many other "race men and women" of that time, John Hope seemed willing to pay the price.

Once again he considered leaving Morehouse College. He had been at the school for nineteen years, and in the service of the American Baptist Home Mission Society for twenty-three. He wrote to Lugenia that "the strain on me is too severe." Perhaps it was time to move on, for "quite frankly," he wrote, "I am insufferably weary of it all." Hope later retreated from that drastic conclusion and decided he simply needed a rest—a year away from Morehouse. If the ABHMS and GEB "should not think well of giving it to me," he wrote to his wife, "this is a very good time to know it because now I can get something else . . . if they do not regard me of sufficient value to let me rest for a year."[43]

There had been hints earlier, but Hope finally admitted to Lugenia what was really on his mind: He wanted to work professionally with African American soldiers, perhaps go to France and work with the Ninety-second Division. In many ways this was a compromise. If granted the opportunity, he could take a leave of absence and become a professional race leader without feeling guilty for neglecting his work at Morehouse. Privately, he allowed it to leak to close friends and family that he might be ready to move on, and a year in France would help him reach a final decision.

To some extent Hope's desire to work professionally with black soldiers was sparked by his envy of those who were already working in an official capacity, and he did not have to look far to find them. His own wife had been working with African American soldiers in New York at Camp Upton since late in December. Lugenia's work was a constant reminder of what Hope thought he ultimately wanted to do and be. Though her absences from home did not always set well with him, he admired her work as a professional race leader and respected her leadership of the Neighborhood Union. In addition, she made time to work with the "colored committee" of the Red Cross and eventually with the Colored Women's War Work Council (part of the Atlanta War Work Council). In 1917 she had earned special accolades for her work during a horrendous spring fire in Atlanta. She was honored at a special session of the National Negro Business League meeting in Chattanooga, Tennessee, for her social work and the national attention she had brought to the work of "colored women." When it was clear that African American troops would be stationed in Camp Upton, Lugenia Hope was called on to help organize an African American hostess house and train women for work in other hostess houses to be established across the country.[44] Lugenia's work no doubt contributed to Hope's own personal desire to serve. He probably reasoned that if Lugenia could be spared from the Neighborhood Union to work in New York, he could temporarily leave the running of Morehouse to Archer and Brawley to serve in France.

There were other friends doing admirable work as well. The Federal Council of Churches operated the Committee on the Welfare of Negro Troops, which investigated discrimination complaints against service agencies at home and abroad. The two field secretaries of that committee were personal friends of his, and Robert Moton was also a member. Major W. Reddick was the assistant state director of the National War Savings Committee for Georgia, and Joel Spingarn of the NAACP was actively serving in the military. Hope was envious when he learned in February that the president of the Georgia School of Technology was going to Europe. "Perhaps I could not speak entertainingly so as to be attractive to soldiers," he wrote to Lugenia, "but there might be something that I could do for them, either with them or near them."[45]

The segregated YMCA, with its shrewd leader, Jesse Moorland, offered Hope the best opportunity to serve black soldiers in an official capacity. The National War Work Council of the YMCA worked closely with the United States government and was chiefly responsible for providing American soldiers with education, recreation, and religious and other services both at home and abroad. As the head of the popular Colored Men's Department, Moorland oversaw all YMCA activities directly related to African American soldiers. Moorland's work with the YMCA had always represented a double-edged sword to John Hope. On the one hand, Moorland was partly responsible for Hope's sustained interest and dedication to black YMCA work. On the other hand, Moorland's aggressive recruiting of black secretaries forced Hope to make difficult choices between his responsibilities as an African American leader and his role as a black college president. Moorland was always in need of YMCA secretaries, and the Morehouse College faculty was a reservoir of talent. Hope faced a dilemma: give up the faculty and have the college suffer, or retain them and deny their services to a race institution he deemed enormously important. Hope usually acquiesced and allowed Moorland to directly contact his most outstanding faculty members. By the time Moorland retired in 1923, he had recruited scores of Morehouse men, three of whom later became presidents of major African American colleges.[46]

Hope was not surprised when Moorland wrote late in October 1917 to offer him a secretarial position in France working with African American soldiers. Hope's work at Morehouse prevented a serious consideration of the offer at that time, but he hoped to get an opportunity to serve later. On the night of 22 January 1918, he confided to a friend that he would "love to have a hand in demobilizing the Negro soldiers," for it would be "such a great opportunity for helping not only the Negro soldiers but our country and our civilization." The next morning Hope penned a letter to Wallace Buttrick of the GEB, expressing the same desire but couching it in a context he may have believed would be more palatable to northern white philanthropists. His presence in France for the demobilization would ensure that Morehouse College "was doing its part making Negroes more useful—no longer a nation's problems, but a nation's asset." At that time, however, no approach worked; Buttrick and the GEB remained indifferent to Hope's wishes.[47]

Perhaps that is why Hope temporarily suspended his interest in going to France and placed more emphasis on working professionally in the United States. Yet he continued to be weary of his work at Morehouse and to press for a year's leave of absence. He also increased his unofficial work with African

American soldiers and uncovered numerous incidents of discrimination. Letters from former students serving in France added to the complaints he received locally. In Atlanta, the white members of the War Work Committee practically ignored the black members, causing Hope to concede that black Atlantans, men and women, would have to do war work "by ourselves without any leaning whatever on white people." Furthermore, he wrote to Lugenia from Atlanta, "there is absolute unanimity among us that we shall not stand for any further jim-crowing."[48]

Hope also continued to protest injustice to African Americans in general. In 1918, white Georgians lynched nineteen African Americans, more than double the number lynched the year before. In March, John Hope joined with more than 110 Georgia black leaders in signing his name to a strongly worded protest to the secretary of labor:

> During the past three decades nearly three thousand American colored men, women and children have suffered butchery and death in almost every conceivable form at the hands of the lynchers of America. . . . We regard lynching as worse than Prussianism, which we are at war to destroy. It decreases faith in the boasted justice of our so-called democratic institutions. We are the one group of American people, than whom there is none more loyal, which is marked out for discrimination, humiliation and abuse. . . . When we reflect upon these brutalities and indignities we remember they are due to the fact that in almost every southern state we have systematically, by law or chicanery, been deprived of the right of that very manhood suffrage which genuine democracy would guarantee to every citizen in the republic. . . . We shall exert our righteous efforts until not only every black man but every eligible black woman shall be wielding the ballot proudly in defense of our liberties and our homes. We are loyal and will remain so, but we are not blind. We cannot help seeing that white soldiers who massacred our black brothers and sisters in East St. Louis have gone scot free. We cannot help seeing that our black brothers who massacred white citizens in Houston have paid the most ignominious penalty that can come in this country to a man in uniform. Do not these undemocratic conditions, these brutalities and savageries provoke the Rulers of the nation to speak out of their long sphinxlike silence and utter a voice of hope, a word of promise for the black man? . . . May not your silence be construed as tacit approval or active tolerance of these things. The effect on the morale of black men in the trenches, when they reflect that they are fighting on foreign fields in behalf of their nation for those very rights and privileges which they themselves are denied at home, might be discouraging. We appeal to you in the name of democracy! We appeal to you in the name of our American citizenship! We appeal to you in the name of God, and *We would be heard!*[49]

Despite the government's stranglehold on free speech during the First World War, Hope's personal attitude was beginning to match the tone of this long petition. He seemed increasingly less patient with flagrant violations of black civil rights in the spring of 1918 and more militant and confrontational. He could not publicly criticize any activities directly related to the prosecution of the war, of course, which explains at least in part why he remained quiet about the complaints from black soldiers. However, his discontent came out in his interactions with the ABHMS and GEB. He dropped his conciliatory tone and made it clear that he needed a rest and intended to pursue work in some professional capacity with African American soldiers. The Morehouse College Board of Trustees apparently realized that Hope meant business. Late in March the board approved his request for a six-month leave, and in private conversations some GEB officials offered to help him get to France. Lugenia Hope had influence with members of the Fosdick Commission and had already begun to inquire about a position for her husband. Hope discouraged her efforts, however, both because it would involve war work only in the United States, and also because he did not want it to appear that she had been promoting his interests. "If I should go into any sort of War Work," he wrote to Lugenia, "I would want to go in the very first place because somebody else thought that I was needed."[50]

In fact, Hope had already turned to his friend Jesse Moorland, who was doing all he could to turn the YMCA into an organization more friendly toward African American soldiers at camps across the country and overseas. "With Moorland," Hope wrote to his wife, "we might be able to break down some of this devilish prejudice and give Jesus Christ an opportunity to operate among these needy soldiers white as well as black." On 27 April, Moorland wired Hope: "My plans for you approved yesterday as per our conversation Wednesday. Can shorten regular time of service but this must be confidential for the present. . . . Hope you can arrange to go soon." The shortened time of service was a reference to Hope's leave of absence being granted for six months instead of a year. By early May it was common knowledge that Hope was going to France. The public announcement came two weeks later.[51]

Exactly what Hope was expected to do in Europe remained vague. His appointment coincided with an expanded role for the YMCA beginning in March 1918. Impressed with the success of its stateside educational work, the War Department approved two educational plans for American troops in France. One involved educational work that would aid the war effort, the other a program that would be initiated during demobilization to prepare the men to reenter civilian life. The *Crisis* reported that Hope was to go as "sort of a general inspector of colored Y.M.C.A. work in France." Another source indicated that his job was simply "educational—visiting and lecturing."[52]

Even Hope was unsure. He hoped to visit all the African American troops at "the front," investigate their complaints, and report these to the proper authorities. He also wanted complete access to all educational material provided to African American soldiers and to help the black YMCA secretaries accomplish their goals. Word was already reaching the United States of white opposition to black educational work, of personnel shortages, and of a lack of facilities and equipment. Of course, whatever work he performed would have to be cleared with military officials overseas. Just what restrictions would be imposed on Hope's broad-based agenda remained to be seen. He was happy, however, that he would be working exclusively for the YMCA at an annual salary of $2,500 plus expenses—$1,000 more than he made at Morehouse.[53]

Hope rushed to get things in order and prepare for his scheduled departure in July. Family matters topped his list of priorities. It had been touch and go with eight-year-old John II, who suffered most of late April and May with stomach cramps, a cold, "billious fever," and a "liver badly out of fix." A very disturbed Lugenia Hope demanded assurances from her husband and sister-in-law Jane Hope, who took care of the Hope household while she and John were away, that it was not typhoid fever. Without waiting to hear from them, she shortened her stay in New York and returned home to be with her son. Even before her arrival in late May, however, John II was on his way to a full recovery.[54]

Seventeen-year-old Edward, then a rising senior in the Morehouse Academy, had, according to his father, "the automobile repairing 'Bee in his bonnet.'" He was also adventurous and full of dreams of far-off places away from parental control. In spite of limited opportunities in segregated America, Edward believed he had found a way to explore America. He would become a porter in the Pullman Car Service—at least for the summer, just to get the experience. When Edward told his father of his summer plans, the elder Hope was outraged. "It was just a thought," Edward wrote to his father. To ensure that it remained only a thought, Hope arranged for Edward to spend the summer in Chicago under the watchful eye of an officer of the black Wabash YMCA. Unable to secure a job in the automobile industry, Edward landed a position learning to repair bus engines, at times working seven days a week, usually twelve hours a day. Hope believed the long hours accounted for his son's run-down appearance when he saw him just before leaving for Europe. Edward never mentioned working on a Pullman car again.[55]

A crisis at Morehouse came close to derailing Hope's plans to go abroad. Hope announced his trip at the end of the 1918 spring semester and appointed Samuel Archer to the position of acting president, with Benjamin Brawley as his assistant. Both men had vast experience conducting the college's business. They were older and not likely to be drafted, and Hope thought they could be depended on to remain at the school until he returned. He was therefore shocked to receive a letter from the temperamental Brawley in the middle of May announcing his resignation.[56]

Hope should not have been totally surprised. Brawley had threatened several weeks before to resign but had promised to remain one more year. Given how quickly Brawley resigned after Archer's appointment, Hope was convinced that it was that announcement that had prompted Brawley's resignation. Rattled by Brawley's decision, Hope seriously considered remaining in Atlanta. Finally, following "many embarrassing situations and conversations," Brawley agreed to stay one more year, and Hope went on making plans to leave.[57]

Hope divided his time that summer between Morehouse and New York, where he attended training sessions at Columbia University. Du Bois, apparently fully recovered from his surgery, was back at work publishing the *Crisis*, and Hope spent a great deal of his spare time in his friend's office, which he used frequently as his New York mailing address. In July 1917 Du Bois's famous "Close Ranks" editorial appeared in the *Crisis*, encouraging African Americans to subordinate their "special grievances" to the greater need to fight to "save the world for democracy." Many African American leaders did not respond favorably to it. Hope did not publicly reveal his thoughts about the editorial, although it probably caused him as much concern as it did other African American leaders.[58]

In Hope's view, African Americans could close ranks with their white fellow citizens *without* forgetting their special grievances. After the passage of the Espionage and Sedition Acts of 1917 and 1918, Hope remained silent about rumors of racial discrimination in the military, even while continuing to protest inequality and violence in the civilian sphere. He may have found it difficult to tell his old friend what he really thought in face-to-face conversation, but he got an opportunity to address the issue indirectly when Du Bois sought his advice about an opportunity that had come his way from Joel Spingarn.

In early June 1918 Spingarn had approached Du Bois about a commission in the Intelligence Bureau of the General Staff of the United States Army. Some historians now believe, in spite of what Du Bois later wrote, that "Close Ranks" was linked to his desire to have that military commission.[59] Du Bois informed John Hope of Spingarn's offer on 12 July. Hope, of course, did not know that Du Bois had already made a tentative decision to accept the commission. As far as he knew, Du Bois had just been approached about it, which probably explained why the *Crisis* editor appeared hesitant. Hope tried to provide some context for his friend to make a decision.

In typical John Hope fashion, he wrote a poignant letter in which he posed several critical points for Du Bois to consider before accepting the commission. First, Du Bois would have to admit that his greatest concern, or "thorn in the flesh," as Hope put it, was the criticism he knew would come from African American leaders who were already critical of his "Close Ranks" editorial. Second, Hope asked, "Do you *know* that you will be able to do constructive work or will you find yourself a secret service man pure and simple?" Then came the pivotal question. Hope assured Du Bois that the job was an honorable one, but he wanted Du Bois to answer honestly: "Is it your job?" In other words, was a job in military intelligence a position for W. E. B. Du Bois? Du Bois did not respond to Hope's letter in writing, but the two undoubtedly discussed it. In the end, Du Bois did not receive the commission, but it had more to do with the War Department's rejection of his application than a change of heart by Du Bois.[60]

Hope's departure for Europe was delayed several times, but finally, on 24 August 1918, he stood on the banks of the Hudson River with Lugenia, Edward, and John II. Soldiers had already begun to board the imposing ship, but Hope waited almost to the last minute. Except for young John II, the family members managed to keep their emotions in check. With Hope waving farewell, the ship disappeared into the early morning fog.[61]

That June, Hope had turned fifty. His hair was almost completely gray, the horn-rimmed glasses were now a permanent fixture on his face, and a slight bulge had appeared around his waist. Though small in stature, Hope nevertheless remained a commanding figure. Most photographs taken during this period picture him immaculately dressed in a tailored suit, standing very erect with both hands tucked deep into the pockets of his trousers, exposing his matching vest and the watch chain curving into one of his vest pockets (the other usually carried a pocket version of the New Testament). With his chiseled features and blue eyes, he could have easily been mistaken for a diplomat, statesman, or ambassador.

Hope had not been abroad since his first trip in 1912, and he had hoped that his second trip would include his wife and sons. Before long, the grim realities of his destination dawned on him. He was going to war, and in spite of his civilian status, death was a real possibility. The ship's careful maneuvers during the journey were solemn reminders. In vivid detail, Hope wrote to Lugenia about the "lifeboat drill, the unlighted decks . . . the careful lookout . . . [and] the guns mounted on deck ready to fire any second." Only a few days out to sea, Hope wrote, "it is war and we are all resigned. What strikes me most forcibly is the composure of everybody, and when I say everybody, I include myself."[62]

His early letters do not mention any other black YMCA secretaries or African American soldiers aboard his ship. The black Ninety-second Division had been ordered overseas in May, and most of them had already arrived in France by early July. American racism had not "missed the boat" either. Special Assistant Emmett Scott would later report that black soldiers were ordered off the battleship *Virginia* because "no colored troops had ever traveled on board a United States battle-ship." The soldiers were removed from the ship, put on a tugboat, and, according to Scott, "subjected to numerous hardships in being brought back to port." [63]

Hope's ship arrived in France in mid-September 1918 without incident. The green fields, vineyards, and old Gallic ruins of Bordeaux recalled his first trip there in 1912. As the ship pulled into port, however, there were sharp reminders that he was in a war zone. Almost as far as the eye could see, there were soldiers and laborers from practically every race and nationality, their different uniforms providing clues to their identities. In one direction there were African colonial troops; in another there were American troops, both black and white. In still another direction, camps of French soldiers and Chinese laborers dotted the landscape. Hope did not linger in Bordeaux but went on to Paris, where he met with Edward C. Carter, the head of all YMCA work. After that he settled in at the Grand Hotel du Louvre near YMCA headquarters at 12 Rue d'Aguesseau. In less than a week, he was in the field. [64]

In Paris, Hope learned that he would be responsible for all YMCA war work with African Americans in France, and directly accountable to Carter. His title, "Field Secretary for Work among Colored Troops," aptly describes his position, which amounted to the equivalent of Jesse Moorland's responsibilities in the United States. Moorland himself could not go to France. He had been denied a passport after someone in the Intelligence Bureau charged him with disloyalty, citing his "sympathy with people thought to be seditious, and . . . his appointment to war service of those of radical temper." [65] He was later cleared of the charges.

Obviously, John Hope was not on the "radicals" list. He was considered safe, perhaps even conservative, by government standards. Since he could not be there himself, Moorland entrusted Hope with the enormous responsibility of supervising the work of African American secretaries and looking out for the interests of black soldiers in the field. Hope soon learned these would not be easy tasks. In addition to elementary and high school education, the YMCA provided religious instruction, contracted with the U.S. Army to run canteens, and arranged athletic activities. Fewer than one hundred of the almost thirteen thousand secretaries in the segregated YMCA overseas workforce were African American. Yet they were responsible for administering to the needs of approximately 140,000 black troops living in makeshift tents, or "Y huts." Hope often had to take up the slack himself, serving as teacher, minister, recreation supervisor, and sometimes even storekeeper. An undated scratchpad from France shows the range of his duties:

> go to explain my work; select offices for working. Don't send illiterate back, if you do, they will never learn and you will lose great power in rural districts of society. Talk to Dr. Kingsburn about the ballot and about public schools as this relates to teaching civics to Negroes. See Kingsbury and Carter about Griffith's Movie [probably *Birth of a Nation*]. Movie propaganda against Negroes—e.g. the movies I saw in Paris.[66]

Hope was often dangerously close to the fighting. He learned early to use a gas mask and was instructed never to be without it. "About an hour and a half ago I told you good night and went to bed with part of my clothes on," he wrote to Lugenia from a small town only twenty miles from German territory in September. "But the long whistle of sirens woke me, and when I heard the report of guns it seemed time to 'beat it' so I moved downstairs to the abri [cellar]."[67] African American combat troops tended to move more frequently than other members of the American Expeditionary Forces (AEF), and that kept Hope on the move as well. In less than three months he visited all of the large ports of France—making stops in several camps in the interior—and went to at least three different sectors along the western front. In addition to the Ninety-second Division, Hope came into contact with just about every other black unit serving in France and spoke to hundreds of black and white enlisted men and officers. Practically every African American the YMCA sent overseas met Hope.

It was not long before complaints began to pour in from the black YMCA secretaries serving in France. "The tents are too small, the electric lights do not work, there are no Y furnishings and equipment. I am unable to get any consideration from the other [white] Y," wrote one disgruntled secretary. Hope was asked to "press the question of supplies for the educational work to the limit." He did what he could, but he was up against a YMCA policy that had never intended to provide equal services for African American troops. Hope knew the African American secretaries were understaffed, overworked, often discriminated against, and left out of the decision-making process in France. He did not reveal his frustrations, however, and admittedly was restrained in his complaints to YMCA and military authorities. Explaining his silence a year later to Moorland, Hope wrote that he understood he "was there to win the war and not to write criticisms."[68]

But another part of Hope's job, at least as he understood it, filled him with bitterness and caused him to question whether the War Department and the YMCA had ever intended to treat African Americans fairly. It involved his investigation of black soldiers' complaints of racist and discriminatory behavior. He received complaints in letters given directly to him, in private conversations with the men, and from black chaplains and YMCA secretaries. He had been briefed on arrival about the low morale of African American soldiers, which deteriorated further as the war dragged on. At first Hope believed that the AEF and the YMCA were genuinely interested in blacks' complaints of discrimination and were doing what they could to raise the morale of African American soldiers. He soon realized he was wrong. Officials of the AEF and the YMCA were unwilling to make any structural changes that would eliminate racist behavior or discrimination in either organization.[69]

Hope learned early from the men about "Special Order No. 40," which forbade African Americans to associate with French women. He was also aware of the infamous "secret information" on African American soldiers intended for French officers with black troops in their commands. The French were advised to keep in mind the position of African Americans in the United States and were told that blacks were a "menace of degeneracy," were given to the "loathsome vice of criminally assaulting women," and were regarded by whites as "inferior, lacking intelligence, discretion, civic and professional conscience." Black troops were well aware of the "secret" document's existence and were outraged by its content.[70]

Black soldiers at the front were not welcome in YMCA huts, and black troops in labor battalions correctly believed they were given the most unpleasant tasks of the war. Among other things, they were responsible for exhuming, transporting, and reburying the American dead during the hot summer months. Du Bois later reported in the *Crisis* that these soldiers were often under the command of southern white officers accustomed to "managing gangs of Negroes on plantations, turpentine farms or construction of public works." Their morale was extremely low. "That is the sort of thing that colored soldiers and colored secretaries were up against," Hope later wrote to Moorland. "That and worse."[71]

Although angered by the complaints of overt racist behavior and discrimination, Hope bottled his indignation and continued to remain relatively silent. He was perhaps torn between two painful choices. He could wage a vigorous protest against the AEF and the YMCA and risk being sent back to the United States as an "undesirable" or "radical." Or he could quietly work within the system to effect change and perhaps reap some benefits for African American soldiers when the war ended.

Hope decided to work within the system, to express his views with YMCA and AEF officials in ways that did not seriously challenge the war effort or the role set aside for African American troops in it. In return, Hope probably convinced himself that at least the educational programs, inadequate though they were, would continue; black officers would get valuable experience; more African American secretaries would be sent to France; and perhaps once the war was over, black support at home and abroad would yet result in the dismantling of racism and discrimination in America. In addition, Hope enjoyed his work with African American soldiers in France and did not want to risk being sent home as an "undesirable."

Hope's actions certainly imply that he followed that line of reasoning. The "Bordeaux situation" is an example. It involved a large region with thousands of African American soldiers and not a single African American secretary. Mrs. Helen Curtis, the first African American woman sent overseas as a YMCA secretary, and Matthew W. Bullock, a former Morehouse faculty member and also a secretary, had been sent to the region, but were made to feel unwelcome by military officers who wanted the area to remain exclusively white. A short time later, the two African American secretaries were removed by YMCA officials after a white secretary and a minister from a nearby camp reported that they were not "running their camp right." The commanding general of the district agreed that "so much instruction, and athletics and games was not good for a colored soldier," and therefore ordered their camp disbanded. Quietly, Hope lobbied successfully to have the two black secretaries sent elsewhere instead of back to the United States. He also pushed to increase the number of African American secretaries in France. However, unlike Curtis and Bullock, Hope did not expose, or even report, the YMCA officials and AEF officers responsible for ignoring the rights of the black soldiers and secretaries even in their segregated camps.[72]

The question of leave areas is another example of Hope's conservative quiet diplomacy. During the war, black and white soldiers had congregated at the leave area at Aix-les-Bains, although the number of African Americans there was small. After the armistice, however, a few southern white male and female YMCA secretaries objected to the presence of the African American soldiers, and Hope was summoned to discuss a plan to put African American soldiers in a separate leave area. Pressured by Carter and AEF officials to go along, Hope at first rejected the plan because there seemed to have been no significant problems at the integrated facility at Aix-les-Bains. He eventually acquiesced, allowing himself to be convinced that separate leave areas would reduce race friction. Blacks and whites could visit the other's leave areas during the day (they were a short distance apart) as long as they returned to their proper areas by midnight.[73]

Hope's position represented a compromise that had been acceptable to him on a few occasions in the past and would become a dominant component of his philosophy in the future. In spite of his ideological belief in a fully integrated society, he increasingly accepted legal separation as long as it provided for some formal and systematic contact between the races. His willingness to compromise had already begun to endear him to influential whites, including officials of the YMCA and the AEF. In this case, however, as in many others, his strategy did not work out as he had intended. Planned interracial meetings between African American soldiers and whites were extremely rare, and whites did not restrict themselves to their facilities even though the segregation policy was strictly enforced among blacks at Chambéry and Challes-les-Eaux.[74]

In spite of his heavy responsibilities, Hope always found time to write home. Because of the laws regarding censorship, he took special care not to reveal his activities in France, including his disgust with the sad state of race relations. At first Lugenia did not understand: "You tell us so little about your work. We want to know what our boys are doing and how they are treated." Lugenia was also John Hope's best friend, and he found it difficult to keep important things from her. Sometimes he seemed almost ready to take the chance: "Well, my dear," he wrote late in October, "I am so full of things to tell that I am almost ready to pop, but I can't tell them.[75]

Hope's letters reveal a brutal schedule that would have taxed a man half his age. He traveled up to two hundred miles a day, often over almost impassable roads in a Ford car or a motorcycle sidecar, to speak with African American troops and black secretaries. Scripture readings and prayer services were frequently conducted amid the "roar of thundering guns, some of them only two city blocks away." His letters often seem to drift, as though they were interrupted by brief intervals of light sleep. Outside Paris, he wrote to Lugenia that the "average hotel is a cold, fireless place." He often retired early, at times going to bed fully dressed, including his overcoat.[76]

Lugenia Hope was her husband's primary source of stateside information, and he, in turn, was the sounding board for her own mounting frustrations. She hated her temporary job as the Morehouse College bookkeeper: "I am not constituted for this particular kind of work—I want my mind free from figures," she wrote halfway through the first semester. She yearned for her work with the YWCA War Work Council and was letting Hope know that she would resume it as soon as she could get someone to take over the work at Morehouse.[77]

Lugenia also disliked the Student Army Training Corp (SATC) unit housed at Morehouse College. The program allowed students to remain in college while receiving basic army training on campus, but the students who participated acted more like soldiers than "Morehouse men." The War Department allowed smoking and chewing tobacco and sanctioned dancing and card playing. Lugenia wrote to Hope that the SATC boys were taking over the campus, "and they make me sick. They swear, quarrel and have taken on all the vices of seasoned *common* soldiers." In her view, "the values and principles of the college were being swept away with a wave of the hand." [78]

Hope's work with African American soldiers, especially the Ninety-second Division, in which he took great pride, made it easy for him to block out the problems of Morehouse College. He had not yet been "in country" for three months when Germany surrendered and the armistice was signed on 11 November 1918, but that did not affect his enthusiasm for the celebration that ensued. He joined in the marching, singing, pistol shots, and jubilation. "The war, the long, weary hellish war" was over. To Lugenia he wrote that it "sounds like an *old* time noisy southern Christmas. . . . *Fini, Fini!* That word is everything." Back home, word that the war was over aroused just as much jubilation among family and friends. Edward wrote to his father that "Mr. Brawley jumped four feet in the air, the boys cheered and the girls cried." Everybody, he wrote, waited with "breathless suspense" when a returning official of the YMCA told them that Hope had been offered a cigarette, "until he told how you took it and yet didn't smoke it." [79]

Hope's celebration of the war's end was short-lived. Phase II of the YMCA's program for demobilization began immediately, and Hope still had much to do. By now, word of the problems experienced by black soldiers had leaked back to the States. African Americans were shocked to learn that black officers of the Ninety-second Division were special targets of overt white discrimination, promotions of black officers were few, and white officers who refused to join antiblack campaigns were dismissed or demoted. There were also rumors of African American cowardice, poor performance in battle, raping of French women, and other crimes. [80]

The facts about the poorly trained and ill-equipped Ninety-second were still coming to light, but John Hope was already outraged. He was with the Ninety-second Division during the early days of the Battle of the Argonne Forest and personally witnessed many acts of bravery. He wrote to Secretary Moorland later, "[When] I think of the demeanor of those men during those days and then read the contemptible reports of cowardice that I have heard since, I am simply amazed at the successful propaganda that can be 'put over' with reference to those fine fellows." [81]

Hope learned from Lugenia that conditions for African Americans had not improved in America, and in some ways had gotten worse. "The people here in the South are organizing home guards—Klu Klux Clans . . . to keep the Negro in his place when he returns all wornout and maimed fighting for democracy. Ha! Ha! what a sham." There was an unfamiliar tone of pessimism in Lugenia Hope's letter. She was very worried about the future: "I wonder if our country will care for our [black] heroes or will they be treated as they always have been. . . . we have backed our country with every thing we have—

money, our boys and our lives—but we are not happy. None of *us*." The night before Lugenia Hope wrote that letter, she joined the NAACP. Edward, who expected to graduate from the Morehouse Academy in the spring, revealed his thoughts about the future in a letter written to his father the day before the armistice was signed: "The same paper which announced peace announced a lynching in Alabama. I wonder whether I should leave for the *real* land of the free—France—or stay here. I am taking military training voluntarily so that if I have to I can sell my life dearly."[82] Edward's grim words were perhaps close to the attitude of many black soldiers. It was clear that something had to be done.

Woodrow Wilson arrived in Paris in December 1918 to attend the peace conference and to press his case for the League of Nations. Also in December, several people, blacks and whites, arrived in France to investigate the conditions and rumors about black troops and to get some sense of what black soldiers expected once they returned home. Among them were Special Assistant Emmett Scott and Thomas Jesse Jones, the alleged "Negro expert" whose controversial report on education had appeared in 1917. Joel Spingarn also came, as did Robert Moton and W. E. B. Du Bois, with their contrasting personalities. Moton was an official representative of the Wilson administration, which was very concerned about the attitude of the returning black soldiers. Many black leaders believed—and black soldiers confirmed—that Moton's major objective was to pacify black troops and reduce their expectations. Du Bois was there to investigate black complaints, convene a Pan African Congress if possible, and gather data for a proposed history of African Americans' role in the war, which he hoped to get John Hope's help in writing.[83]

The arrival of Du Bois and Moton provided Hope with an opportunity to talk openly without fear of the censor. He was determined that Moton and Du Bois should learn firsthand what African American soldiers had been forced to endure. With Du Bois it was easy; they lodged at the same hotel and spent days discussing the situation. Hope knew it would be more difficult to see Moton. He had already written to his wife shortly before Moton arrived that "I will have to throw myself in his way, so that he may let me talk to him."[84]

Eventually, he did see Moton alone and provided him with the same information he had given Du Bois. Neither Hope nor Du Bois was pleased with Moton's work in France. Du Bois later wrote a blistering article criticizing Moton. In it, he mentioned that a "colored man of national reputation and unquestioned integrity who had been in France six months took him [Moton] aside and told him frankly" about "rampant American prejudice against black troops and officers." That "colored man" was John Hope.[85]

African American demobilization was a frequently discussed topic in the conferences with AEF and YMCA officials that Hope attended. After the armistice they were often joined by representatives from the United States government. The meetings were often tense, sometimes even hostile, pitting black against white and military against civilian. The discussions resonated with charges and countercharges, facts and rumors, rationalizations and justifications. Late in December, for example, Hope and a small group of southerners and northerners of both races were summoned to discuss "what should be the attitude on the Negro problem in America." Hope believed he upset many whites in attendance when he stated that "whatever might be done the attitude of colored people was such that from now on white people would have to 'come clean.'" The latter term was offensive to most whites in the group, and Hope was forced to explain just what he meant. By his own account, Hope's position was not a radical one; in fact, it was quite the contrary, he later wrote to Du Bois. As he explained many times later, "I simply meant . . . that they [whites] would have to be honest and straightforward in their dealings because colored people had got a new vision and would not stand for much that they had endured."[86]

From that point forward, Hope's responsibilities in France increased significantly. He not only advised Moton and Du Bois in their investigations, he also intensified his own inquiries for the YMCA. He also spoke at religious gatherings and counseled many soldiers individually about their plans after they returned home. Hope was convinced that the future was especially bleak for African American officers. "These young fellows," he wrote to Lugenia, "many not yet out of college—have had more than a year of this easy salary, this giving of commands. It is so abnormal and so new. Never among our people has such happened." Even if commanding troops in war was not exactly earning an "easy salary," Hope's concern for the limited opportunities available to black officers in America was valid. He tried to interest many of them in YMCA work associated with the Colored Men's Department, and he talked to a few about teaching.[87]

Edward Carter, the chief YMCA executive in France, pleaded with Hope to remain until every black soldier had returned home. With little hesitation, and without asking permission from the Morehouse trustees, Hope agreed to extend his stay for another six months and was made a "Field Staff" member of the AEF. Hope immediately put forth his own solutions for resolving what he believed were some of the most pressing problems. Late in January he wrote a long report to Carter in which he practically insisted that Carter agree to send for more African American secretaries from the States to help in the demobilization. He also strongly recommended a "gradual but not ruthless" withdrawal of the white secretaries who did not feel comfortable serving African American troops. The report was a measured proposal that was acceptable within the conservative policies of the YMCA and the AEF. He did not propose drastic changes in behavior, but rather a more or less quiet replacement of the "problem" (the uncomfortable white secretaries) with an equally quiet "solution" (eager black replacements).[88]

A letter Hope wrote to Carter one day after attending the Pan African Congress revealed his long-held desire to go to Africa. "No doubt some colored men may be valuable as workers, administrators, and advisers in the new efforts to develop the Africans in ways educational, industrial, economic, moral, and religious," he wrote. "Perhaps I could render some service." Obviously, Hope had been impressed by the deliberations of the congress and the likelihood of "new adjustments" in the German colonies—and perhaps other colonies as well. The Pan African Congress may also have rekindled the strong emotions he had felt when reading Du Bois's "African Roots of the War" in the May issue of the *Atlantic Monthly* a few years earlier. Hope continued to view Africa through a lens that was more or less Victorian and centered in the Western Christian tradition. Yet his desire to advance African interests as he understood them was sincere. Throughout his time in France he had consulted with officers commanding Belgian, English, and French troops to ascertain if there were problems in their integrated units. He also spent time with African troops from the various European colonies to determine their views on their military experiences, their aspirations, and the problems they anticipated when they returned home.[89]

Ironically, in the same letter in which he seemed to be creating a position for himself in Africa, Hope asked to return home to Atlanta. He wanted "to get the college work in shape" and then return as quickly as possible to France. Throughout that winter Hope found it increasingly difficult to concentrate exclusively on the problems of blacks in France or anywhere else. Sam Archer, the acting president at Morehouse, bombarded him with pleas to return. There were discipline problems with the SATC unit. Nine-year-old John II did not help matters with his first letter describing how exciting it was to witness a Morehouse student being locked up in the military guardhouse. There had been student rebellions in the dining and study halls, and there was a general disrespect for faculty authority on the campus. Lugenia Hope believed the situation had gone beyond Archer's and Brawley's ability to control it.[90]

Student discipline, however, was not Archer's most immediate concern. He believed there were significant financial changes in store for Morehouse and perhaps other black colleges in Atlanta as well. Rumors abounded; one of them linked the future of Morehouse with that of Atlanta University. For years, unsuccessful efforts had been made to get the two schools to cooperate. During their fall meeting in 1918, according to Archer, Atlanta University's trustees had voted to sell all the school's Atlanta property and invest the proceeds in Fisk University. In October, Archer wrote to Hope urging him to return. Hope responded with a letter that probably indicated his ambivalence about returning at all. Late in November 1918, Archer wrote again: "You spoke of having rounded out your career here. You have rounded out a career of sacrifice and privation. Now when the opportunity to see the fulfillment of your hopes is at hand, it is not quite fair to yourself and family and to the institution to quit to take less responsibility. I know what you suffered and endured. Give yourself to the larger things of the administration."[91]

That winter the General Education Board gave Morehouse an unexpected gift of $100,000 to upgrade salaries. There were even rumors that three major black universities were to be established in America: Howard, Fisk, and Morehouse College. Hope was still not moved. Archer, of course, did not know what was going on in France, although he did know what was being said at home about black soldiers. Although Hope tried without being specific to convince Archer that his work for the YMCA was important, Archer could not see how "passing 'smokes' to soldiers" could be more important than directing "the educational future of a race."[92] Hope was probably perturbed at Archer's disparagement of his YMCA work, but he also understood that Archer was unaware of the total picture. He chose to continue his work as a professional African American leader, even though it meant neglecting his responsibilities as a black college president.

Neither Hope nor Archer knew everything there was to know about the changes taking place within the ranks of northern foundation heads in 1918. For years, black leaders like Hope, Du Bois, and others had tried unsuccessfully to convince them of the need for trained African American leaders. But most of the philanthropic foundations—the General Education Board, for example—had been committed to vocational institutions like Hampton and Tuskegee and paid only scant attention to black liberal arts schools. In 1918 GEB officials decided it would be wise to upgrade the quality of selected black colleges while continuing to focus their support on vocational schools. Their decision was prompted at least in part by the deterioration of race relations in America, despite blacks' overwhelming support of the war effort. The GEB recognized the potentially explosive racial situation and believed the need for trained black leaders was perhaps more important than ever before in the history of American race relations.[93]

Morehouse College was targeted to receive special financial help from the GEB for several reasons. First, the college was run entirely by African Americans, "who in point of ability," noted one official, compared "favorably with white college teachers." In addition, Morehouse was well administrated, the teaching was excellent, and it was popular among blacks in the state of Georgia and elsewhere. Most significant, John Hope was its president. Not only was he

recognized as an educational statesman, he was also known as a calm and reserved race leader who "would tell the truth to white folks plainly without
insulting them."[94]

By increasing funding for Morehouse College the GEB expected to accomplish two objectives. On one level, the board assumed (incorrectly, as it
turned out) that Hope's sane (meaning restrained and compromising) leadership would influence Morehouse students to follow his direction, thereby ensuring another generation of conservative black leaders. For the GEB and its
supporters, "sane" black leadership was a vital part of a long-range solution to
the race problem in America. On another level, additional support for Morehouse and Hope would, they hoped, raise the morale of the black community
in general and perhaps help defuse a volatile racial situation. An exchange of
letters between Wallace Buttrick, then president of the GEB, and the board's
secretary, Abraham Flexner, expressed this view only days before the $100,000
was given to Morehouse. Flexner wrote to Buttrick that

> before long, Morehouse . . . would draw to itself a larger student body which
> would emerge in a few years, better trained for the responsibilities which, trained
> or untrained, the leaders of the race are going to bear. The possession of such an
> institution for higher education would, I believe, have weight in convincing the
> Negro that he is getting a fair deal; our aid would represent a fundamental con-
> tribution to the solution of a grave and pressing problem.[95]

There is no doubt that the GEB's decision to officially support Hope and
Morehouse College represented a watershed. It was also part of a gradual but
marked change in the thinking of northern white charitable organizations.
The organization's views about black and white separation and its interest in
avoiding friction between the races remained unchanged. Perhaps more than
ever before, the GEB did not envision African American integration into the
mainstream of American society. Segregation was expected to continue, with
African Americans operating in their own more or less enclosed world.[96]

Archer was correct that the turmoil created by the SATC, the student rebellions, and the more militant attitude at Morehouse made the GEB nervous.
The General Education Board had little faith in Archer's or Brawley's administrative abilities, or in their ability to give the students what Lugenia Hope
called the "right sort of teaching" to prevent racial friction.[97] Hope, of course,
was still unaware that the explosive racial situation in America had moved the
GEB in what appeared to be a new direction. Nor did he know that he was
expected to play a prominent role in the GEB's plans.

Eventually Lugenia wrote a letter to Hope that hit a nerve. There were
rumors among the Morehouse faculty and staff that the GEB had decided to

commit its support to Atlanta University (AU), and that the rest of the schools, including Morehouse, would become subordinate to AU. Archer, noted Lugenia, had stated in a faculty meeting that "there was no more Morehouse Spirit." On 19 January 1919, Archer made his final appeal to Hope: "We shall have either a larger college or a small academy. Your absence may mean an academy. *Are you Coming? Do not keep us in suspense.* If you are not then I must get busy on the assumption that it is up to us on campus to force ourselves and our plans on G.E. Board. You must be here by April 1st."[98]

Hope decided to return home for three weeks. Even then, he did not completely abandon his war work, for he planned to use the trip as an opportunity to recruit several black YMCA secretaries to send to France. When he arrived in New York in late March, he realized the rumor about Morehouse becoming a small academy subordinate to AU had been incorrect. Archer's suspicion about increased funding, however, was correct. The GEB planned to give Morehouse $165,000 for overall improvements and expansion, and increased its annual appropriation for operating expenses to $10,000. The executive secretary of the American Baptist Home Mission Society reported that the $165,000 was the largest gift ever received by an ABHMS mission school in the South. In addition to recruiting YMCA secretaries, Hope spent the next three weeks traveling between Atlanta and New York trying to work out the final details for implementing the "Greater Morehouse Plan." He also managed to find the time to discuss the problems of black soldiers in France and their expectations once they returned home with close friends and a number of influential northern whites such as Buttrick and Flexner of the GEB, George Peabody, and Julius Rosenwald.[99]

By early May he was on his way back to the war zone. In France, Hope went back to work with even more intensity than before, unaware that Archer had appealed directly to Wallace Buttrick in June to have him sent home permanently.[100] Archer's letter to Buttrick points up Hope's inseparable roles as a capable black college educator and an increasingly conservative African American leader. Archer wrote to Buttrick that in addition to overseeing the financial improvements at Morehouse, Hope was needed immediately to help with "race relations in the process of adjustment." He felt that the "radical" leaders were negative influences, and that "we should have the progressive conservatism of President Hope," who in "this section [the South] we look to for advice and counsel." Though Archer was probably more concerned with being able to relinquish his heavy responsibilities, he was nevertheless astute enough to recognize that during the summer of 1919 there was a core of northern whites interested in moderate change in the South that included John Hope as a key player.[101]

Hope returned to the United States permanently in July and went immediately to the GEB offices in New York City to iron out the particulars of the GEB grant. As usual, the $165,000 gift, earmarked exclusively for physical improvements, was based on the ability of African Americans to raise an additional $5,000. Hope therefore spent the remainder of the summer crisscrossing the country in an effort to raise the matching sum. For the first time in months, Hope seemed satisfied, excited, and even cheerful as he prepared for the opening of the fall semester in 1919. One GEB official wrote of Hope during that period: "He is as happy as 'a bug in a rug' and . . . anticipates no difficulty in raising the $5,000 which the colored people are to subscribe." [102]

Privately, however, Hope's cheerfulness was tempered by sadness. Racial violence was spreading like wildfire throughout America. His arrival coincided with race riots in Longview, Texas, Washington, D.C., and Chicago. In Chicago alone, thirty-eight people had been killed and more than five hundred injured. It was the most devastating riot ever in the United States—worse, even, than in East St. Louis two years earlier. Before what James Weldon Johnson called the "Red Summer" of 1919 ended, more than twenty-five riots took place in other cities such as Knoxville, Omaha, and Elaine, Arkansas. The violence was mainly rooted in urban black migration, labor problems, and economic competition, but much of it was also triggered by returning black veterans and other African Americans who were fed up with discrimination and determined to resist and defy demands that they "remain in their place." In some instances black soldiers still in uniform were beaten, others were lynched, and still others died defending their lives, families, and property. Hope's namesake, historian John Hope Franklin, wrote that the violence of 1919 "shocked even the most indifferent persons into a realization that interracial conflicts in the United States had reached a serious stage." [103]

John Hope had his own thoughts about that bloody summer of 1919. Like Du Bois and a number of other African American leaders, he had convinced himself that the war would bring significant positive change in the lives of African Americans. His private letters, particularly the ones written in August 1919, reveal his disappointment: "I wish people in authority beginning with the President of the United States and reaching down to mayors and sheriffs of the smallest counties and towns would at least guarantee to Negroes the protection of their life and property." In another letter he was less disturbed with the "lawless element" than he was with the "flabby, helpless, impotent attitude of people in authority." The war should have "stiffen[ed] their backbone." And to a white friend in Providence he lamented that there "has never been in our lifetime anything at all approximating the problem that is facing this country today." [104]

Finally, in September 1919, Hope wrote his report to Jesse Moorland revealing his activities in France and the terrible treatment of African American soldiers there. This three-thousand-word document epitomizes Hope's disillusionment with race relations in America, yet he also managed to say that, like "colored men in general," he was still a patriot who loved his country. Nevertheless, he and other African Americans "reserved the right to express our grievances and to endeavor to correct the attitude which is so unfavorable to colored people and so embarrassing to our peace and happiness."[105]

Unlike professional race leaders, Hope faced still another dilemma when he returned home. Should he move to the left, as his friend Du Bois had done, and return to his old uncompromising position, or should he return to the conservatism that he increasingly recognized was required of an African American college president in the South? Hope had just received a tangible commitment to upgrade Morehouse College, and he believed new opportunities for black higher education in general were just over the horizon. His vision of greater opportunities for blacks during the war had taken an unexpected turn. Initially, he was convinced that conditions would improve across the board, not just inside the segregated setting. In a way he was now forced to decide whether the glass was half empty or half full. Both ideological directions pulled him strongly. Should he insist that his people had earned the right to full racial equality as a result of their support for the war both at home and abroad, or should he accept the commitment to improvements within black America and soft-pedal other issues that seemed less attainable? It was impossible to do both. The philanthropic foundations that channeled money into black education would not accept a "Du Bois–type" leadership unwilling to compromise with whites in the South. If Hope chose that direction, Morehouse, and perhaps black higher education in general, would die a slow death.

When school began in September 1919, Hope gave no clues to his decision, or even indicated that he had given his choices much thought. As usual, he was able to maintain two contradictory images. African American leaders like Du Bois, Walter White, and even William Monroe Trotter in the traditionally radical camp still counted him as an ally. But Hope had also managed not to alienate more conservative leaders like Emmett Scott and Robert Moton, and leaders working directly within the African American community like Channing Tobias and Moorland. He also remained popular with community activists in Atlanta like Ben Davis, A. D. Williams, W. S. Cannon, and a number of others. Hope was so busy with school business that there was no hint of the direction he would take until 1920.

One thing, however, was clear. He had decided to remain at Morehouse College. Several factors contributed to that decision. First, there had always been competition between Atlanta University and Morehouse College. Morehouse's autonomy was important to Hope, and he did not want to see it subordinated to any institution in Atlanta. Second, quite simply, Hope loved Morehouse College. It had become as much a part of him as he had become a part of it. Throughout most of his life, only brief periods of disillusionment with his job had caused him to think about leaving it. For practically an entire year Hope had worked as a professional race leader and had enjoyed it immensely. He no doubt came closer then to giving up his work at Morehouse than ever before, but once he returned and recognized the new opportunities there, he realized it was where he wanted to be.

Mary Frances (Fanny) Butts, n.d., mother of John Hope. (Photograph courtesy of the Hope family.)

John Hope as a student at Worcester Academy in Worcester, Massachusetts, ca. 1890. (Photograph courtesy of Worcester Academy Archives photo collection.)

The *Brown Daily Herald* staff, 1893–94. Hope is standing at far left. (Photograph courtesy of John Hay Library Archives, Brown University.)

Graduation picture of John Hope, Brown University, 1894. (Photograph courtesy of John Hay Library Archives, Brown University.)

John Hope, ca. 1906, when he first became president of Atlanta Baptist College. (Photograph courtesy of the Hope family.)

Hope's first Niagara Movement meeting, 1906. He is standing, second row from front, fifth from left. W. E. B. Du Bois is on front row, seated, third from left. (Photograph from the black *Cleveland Gazette*, 1906.)

Hope's first major educational conference as president of Atlanta Baptist College, 1908. He is in the center of back row. George Sale, Hope's mentor and former president of Atlanta Baptist College, is on front row, third from right. (Photograph from W. N. Hartshorn, *An Era of Progress and Promise, 1863–1910* [1910].)

Professor William E. Holmes, 1908. The faculty member most responsible for Hope's employment at ABC, Holmes later left to start Central City College in Macon, Georgia, and encouraged ABC's students to follow him. (Photograph from W. N. Hartshorn, *An Era of Progress and Promise, 1863–1910* [1910].)

Henry L. Morehouse, influential leader of the American Baptist Home Mission Society, 1908. Atlanta Baptist College honored him by changing its name to Morehouse College in 1913. (Photograph from W. N. Hartshorn, *An Era of Progress and Promise, 1863–1910* [1910].)

First Amenia Conference, 1916. John Hope is standing on back row, center; W. E. B. Du Bois is on front row, kneeling, second from right; James Weldon Johnson is kneeling; Mary Church Terrell is standing, third from right. (Photograph courtesy of the Moorland-Spingarn Research Center, Howard University.)

First Amenia Conference, August 1916. John Hope is barely visible on the last row, sixth from left; W. E. B. Du Bois is standing, third row, third from left; Mary Church Terrell is seated in second row, third from left; Lucy Laney is second from right. (Photograph courtesy of the Moorland-Spingarn Research Center, Howard University.)

The John Hope family on the porch of the president's house, ca. 1916. From left, John Hope, John Hope II, Edward S. Hope, and Lugenia Burns Hope. (Photograph courtesy of the Hope family.)

Officers and Executive Committee of the Atlanta Branch of the NAACP, 5 April 1917. Standing, from left to right: Peyton A. Allen, George A. Towns, Benjamin J. Davis Sr., Rev. L. H. King, Dr. William F. Penn, President John Hope, David H. Sims. Seated, left to right: Harry H. Pace (of Standard Life Insurance Company), Dr. Charles H. Johnson, Dr. Louis T. Wright, and a young Walter F. White. (Photograph courtesy of the photo Collection of the Library of Congress.)

John Hope in uniform during World War I in service of the Colored Department of the YMCA as "Field Secretary for Work among Colored Soldiers." The photograph was taken shortly before he left for France in 1918. (Photograph courtesy of the Hope family.)

Group of African American YMCA workers in France. John Hope is standing, front row, far left. (Photograph from Emmett J. Scott, *Scott's Official History of the American Negro in the World War*, published 1919.)

Session of the Pan African Congress, 1919. John Hope is in the background near the center, about three rows back from W. E. B. Du Bois, who is in front, center. (Photograph courtesy of the Moorland-Spingarn Research Center, Howard University.)

John and Lugenia Hope early in 1927, a few months after their return from their one and only European trip together. (Photograph courtesy of the Hope family.)

John Hope, seated, signing the agreement of affiliation, April 1929. President Florence Read of Spelman College is standing to his left, and President Myron Adams of Atlanta University is to his right. (Photograph courtesy of Special Collections, Robert Woodruff Library, Clark Atlanta University.)

John Hope at the ground breaking of of A. U.'s Trevor Arnett Library, ca. 1930. Florence Read is slightly to his right in the background. (Photograph courtesy of Special Collections, Robert Woodruff Library, Clark Atlanta University.)

Graduation ceremonies at Atlanta University, early 1930s. Hope is second from left, Florence Read is in the center, A.U. Board of Trustees member James Weldon Johnson is on her right. (Photograph courtesy of the Special Collections, Robert Woodruff Library, Clark Atlanta University.)

President John Hope at a commencement ceremony at Atlanta University in the 1930s. (Photograph courtesy of the Hope family.)

From left to right, W. E. B. Du Bois; William Harrison, who played "De Lawd" in the popular *Green Pastures;* John Hope; and W. W. Alexander of the Commission on Interracial Cooperation, ca. 1934 or 1935. (Photograph courtesy of Special Collections, Robert Woodruff Library, Clark Atlanta University.)

President John Hope and W. W. Alexander, n.d. (Photograph courtesy of Special Collections, Robert Woodruff Library, Clark Atlanta University.)

John Hope and Howard Archer at dedication of Morehouse College tennis courts, n.d. (Photograph courtesy of Special Collections, Robert Woodruff Library, Clark Atlanta University.)

President John Hope, ca. 1935. (Photograph courtesy of the Hope family.)

President John Hope and Governor Marland of Oklahoma in Oklahoma City, February 1936. (Photograph courtesy of Special Collections, Robert Woodruff Library, Clark Atlanta University.)

Group of African American women at New York's Camp Upton Hostess House. Lugenia Burns Hope, who trained many of the workers, is standing at center; Hope's good friend, Mary E. Jackson, is fourth from the left. (Photograph from Emmett J. Scott, *Scott's Official History of the American Negro in the World War* [1919].)

Secretary of the Interior Harold Ickes, ca. 1934, at demolition of "Beaver Slide" housing, soon to be replaced by construction of University Homes. John Hope is to the immediate right of Ickes. (Photograph courtesy of Special Collections, Robert Woodruff Library, Clark Atlanta University.)

Figures written on blackboard by John Hope during Negro History Week at Oglethorpe School in Atlanta, February 1936, only four days before Hope's death. (Photograph courtesy of Special Collections, Robert Woodruff Library, Clark Atlanta University.)

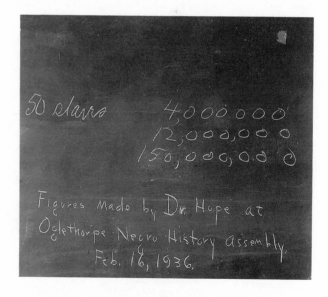

Funeral of President John Hope, February 1936. (Photograph courtesy of the Hope family.)

Annual
pilgrimage to
John Hope's
grave by
Morehouse
students at their
commencement
exercises. It is
unknown when
this observance
was discontinued.
(Photograph
courtesy of the
Hope family.)

10
The "New Negro" and John Hope in the 1920s

In 1924 John Hope wrote an insightful letter to W. E. B. Du Bois that included the following passage:

> An institution of learning is such a delicate organism, it is almost human. It is human. The slightest touch sometimes disturbs its healthy function. . . . Courage, the necessity of the enterprise, and a certain amount of pugnacity, along with a modicum of self-respect, make me continue rather ceaselessly in the fight, but I am bound to tell you, my dear friend, that blowing one's brains out is a great sight easier than some of the things we have to do and stand.

Hope's words illuminate the fragile position of African American higher education in the 1920s. Ironically, it was a precariousness that was at least partly the result of increasing support from the philanthropic foundations. The passage also reveals that John Hope continued to walk a tightrope in the 1920s, desperately trying to balance his role as a principled African American leader with his responsibilities as the president of an increasingly popular African American college in the South.[1]

The postwar backlash against African Americans continued into the 1920s. But so did black resistance. The postwar black militancy was one of two major components of the New Negro Movement, as its contemporaries called it. The cultural dimension of the movement, often called the Harlem or Negro Renaissance, was an urban, northern-based outpouring of African American artistic expression that was based on the collective experiences of America's black people. Among other things, especially under the influence of Jamaican-born ultranationalist Marcus Garvey, it included a celebration of black identity, black pride, increased racial solidarity, and an insistence on the value of a distinct African American way of life. African Americans in both lay and academic communities expressed an interest in courses on Negro and African history.

The political dimension of the New Negro Movement was no less dynamic. In addition to individual expressions of postwar resistance, organizations like the National Equal Rights League and the NAACP intensified black protests against lynching and discrimination in southern primaries. The NAACP also continued to chip away at racial discrimination through the courts. Black Socialists A. Philip Randolph and Chandler Owen often took a more uncompromising stance against segregation in their writings in the *Messenger* than the NAACP did. In addition to full racial equality, Randolph and Owen called for working-class solidarity and a "square deal" for African American workers.

In the South, the New Negro Movement included increased efforts to create equality within the legally segregated black world. Black southerners continued to petition and confront city councils and school boards for their own public libraries and better schools, housing, health care facilities, and city services. They also celebrated the continued development of black businesses and worked hard to see that these cherished enterprises survived. African American students on black college campuses, where rebellions erupted throughout the decade, were an important part of the "New Negro" militancy. Students demanded everything from a more democratic atmosphere on campus to more black control, including African American presidents. Thus, at the same time some proponents of the New Negro Movement were fighting to participate fully in American life, others were celebrating their racial distinctness and insisting that race-based factors should play a larger role in their daily lives. Hence the New Negro Movement tended to be both integrationist and separatist, and included both accommodation and confrontation. It thus looked both backward and forward.[2]

The changes that took place in America during the 1920s certainly posed problems for John Hope. The more militant attitude of African American leaders, especially in the North, challenged his own leadership style of quiet diplomacy. Northern leaders questioned Hope's support of conservative southern organizations like the Commission on Interracial Cooperation (CIC) and conservative leaders like Wallace Buttrick of the GEB and Thomas Jesse Jones of the Phelps-Stokes Fund. Like many other African American leaders of his generation, Hope found it difficult to adjust to the rapidly changing social milieu of the 1920s.

John Hope faced many challenges during his first semester back at Morehouse. Student enrollment was higher than ever before (550 students), and students were actually being turned away. Requests piled up on Hope's desk for teachers to fill vacancies in African American schools at every educational level. He wrote to a friend, "If you would see the requests on my desk for teachers in colleges, high schools and the grades you would think that we had not begun to furnish men and women for the teaching world." Hope also wanted to create a first-rate course in business and commerce at Morehouse and had already contacted the man he wanted to establish the program. He never expected Morehouse to become a university, but he did envision it becoming one of the best small colleges in the country.[3]

In addition to interacting with his own Morehouse students, Hope kept in touch with veterans from all across the country. He had become a surrogate father to scores of black men in France, and he felt bound to help them make the transition from soldiers to civilians. Some veterans enrolled at Morehouse, and he tried to find jobs for others. Still others wrote to him that they wanted to work for the YMCA, NAACP, and other black organizations. Hope was especially vigilant, however, over his own Morehouse graduates. He gave his former students very practical advice to help them get on in the world, assisted them in finding their first jobs, and was careful to investigate suspicious companies that sought to employ Morehouse graduates. Although most Morehouse men continued to become ministers or teachers, some went on to study in prestigious northern universities. A few went into business for themselves or found positions with black businesses. Still others worked at social service agencies like the YMCA and Urban League, and a few found positions with the NAACP.[4]

There were times when recent graduates tried to use the school's teachings and Hope's religious zeal to justify abandoning jobs they did not like, and their letters to Hope are sometimes amusing. A student required to work on Sundays wanted another position that would enable him to attend "Sunday School in the Name of the Lord." Hope told him to "stay put until you can get more experience in the work place." A graduate he placed at a black insurance company insisted on a pay raise after a very short period. "You always told us as Morehouse Men to ask for what we wanted," the student explained. Hope advised him to "learn the business, be quiet, and you shall get your raise in time."[5]

But it was not always that easy. When the issue involved race, Hope was usually much more cautious. It was often difficult to balance practical considerations with the high ideals that were part of the Morehouse tradition. In principle, students were taught that segregation was wrong and that Morehouse men were not expected to take part in any voluntary segregation. The students rarely questioned this ideal and believed it was practiced by most African Americans, especially in the North. When they set foot in the real world, however, the differences between the ideal and the practice became immediately apparent. One former student in 1923 was surprised and outraged when he saw northern black workers at a freight yard in Philadelphia "segregate themselves in one dining hall while whites occupied another."

When the student was offered a job there, he faced a difficult choice. He needed the job but was unwilling to compromise his ideals. At that point the student wrote to Hope for both an explanation and advice. Hope cautioned him to "keep your eyes open and not allow a desire for a dollar or for popularity to make you do things that you know are absolutely against our progress in the long run." He went on to criticize northern blacks who allowed "large wages and a relief from the more flagrant forms of injustice to blind them to the dangers of accepting segregation and discrimination," a practice Hope believed would "react against us in the North for fifty years to come." John Hope was no stranger to voluntary segregation, of course. He had done the same thing in his many jobs in restaurants and resorts while he was a student at Brown. More recently, he had recruited students to work in northern areas where de facto segregation was the rule. This student, however, was young, and since he was undecided and had asked Hope for advice, Hope felt compelled to emphasize the ideal. Perhaps Hope's decision shows that he had not completely lost his optimism—his belief that at some point in the future things would change for the better, "surely at least in the North," he told the student. If that did not occur, the student would eventually learn to make his peace with the system and do whatever was necessary to survive with some degree of sanity and self-respect.[6]

Not all of Hope's relationships with Morehouse students in the 1920s were positive. Student discipline had gotten completely out of hand while Hope was in France,[7] and he went after the student dissidents with a vengeance. His correspondence is full of his intolerance for anyone, regardless of age, who refused to accept the traditional Morehouse rules. He quickly reinforced and strengthened regulations against smoking, drinking, dancing, card playing, and fraternizing with female students without chaperons. He also instituted a highly regulated schedule that extended from the time students rose in the morning until they retired at night. Leaving the campus, for example, was strictly forbidden without permission from someone in authority. Students who dared to break the rules were subject to immediate expulsion without any opportunity to plead their case.[8]

Hope was often tested in those early years after the war. Many of the veterans believed he was bluffing and would not expel them for minor rule violations. They were mistaken. Hope carried through on his threats to expel both men and boys, in the college department as well as in the academy. His insistence on following the rules sometimes seems a bit extreme. One student remembered what happened at a football game after a student was knocked unconscious and carried off the field. When the dazed and obviously disoriented player began to come around, he uttered some words of profanity. Hope heard the student, rushed out of his seat, bent down on one knee, and shook his finger in the uncomprehending player's face, scolding him for his language.[9]

Hope's tyrannical and sometimes paternalistic rule extended to his faculty as well. Benjamin Mays joined the faculty in 1921 and eventually became Morehouse College's third African American president. Mays hated Hope's policy of charging faculty members with the responsibility of "spying on students for rule infractions" and then using that information to send students home. Without Hope's knowledge, Mays simply did not comply. Mays also remembered an incident that occurred during his first year when Hope denied him an opportunity to give his students a second final examination after the first one was stolen. Mays protested, invoking his "rights of academic freedom," but finally capitulated when it became clear that his job was on the line.

Another faculty member remembered that Hope was a "tyrant," and that his rule was "autocratic." He did not hesitate to counsel (and sometimes warn) his faculty about their marital relations, interactions with girlfriends, and off-campus social behavior. According to Ed Jones, a Morehouse graduate who later taught at the school, "not everyone appreciated . . . Dr. Hope's fatherly interest in his teachers." It was regarded as a "sort of administrative paternalism which merited for him the designation 'Father John' by those who resented the father-child relationship."[10]

Hope's leadership style became increasingly outdated as the 1920s proceeded. Yet he was deeply respected even by disgruntled faculty, who in most cases did not defy him. During those years the Morehouse faculty consisted mostly of young African American men who had no memory of Morehouse College without John Hope. Part of their respect came from loyalty to their alma mater (a significant number were Morehouse graduates). Others were simply committed to Morehouse as a prestigious race institution that had done well under its first African American president. Since denominational affiliation was no longer as relevant in hiring practices as it had been in the past (although it still remained a factor), Hope often used the faculty's pride in the school to help him keep track of outstanding black graduates elsewhere in the country.

Potential faculty members were flattered by Hope's personalized attention when he visited their institutions, often before they graduated with their A.B. degrees. Mays, for example, remembered that Hope first approached him during the summer of 1921 at the University of Chicago library and invited him to teach college math and high school algebra. By the late 1920s, Hope had personally recruited sociologists E. Franklin Frazier and Walter Chivers, Claude Dansby in mathematics, Samuel Nabrit in biology, and Brailsford R. Brazeal in economics. He also recruited theologian Howard Thurman to teach at Spelman College in 1928. Like most of the others, Thurman was a Morehouse graduate, which made Hope's recruiting job less difficult than it might have been. Regardless of what school they had attended, most of these men were also attracted to Morehouse by Hope's standing as an African American leader. They believed he was generally fair in spite of his tyrannical rule, and he did not hesitate to give them outstanding recommendations even when they decided to leave Morehouse to take other jobs.[11]

Although occupied with problems related to Morehouse, Hope did not abandon his concern with issues beyond the academy. He was disillusioned, skeptical, and bitter at the government's inaction in the face of deteriorating conditions in the early 1920s. He had believed briefly before the war that a new group of southern white progressives were beginning to emerge who would in time support full equality. But the war shattered that optimism, and he no longer believed any such group existed. He retreated once again to trusting only transplanted white northerners associated with Atlanta's African American institutions and his white allies in the North.

The winds of change, however, were already beginning to stir. As early as 1918, a small cadre of northern and southern whites began discussions about the kind of America African Americans would face once the war ended. These discussions took place over breakfast at the Harvard Club in New York City, over lunch and dinner at Atlanta's Georgian Terrace, and at meetings at the Ansley Hotel and City Club in New York.[12] Over time, these men came to believe that an interracial commission made up of prominent southern blacks and whites could prevent the race war many saw looming on the horizon in the United States. Earlier attempts at interracial cooperation had by and large been unsuccessful. The South frowned on any organization interested in African American equality, and even during the 1920s it was not a widely accepted idea. Nevertheless, the volatile racial climate after the war demanded a radical solution. In the South, that radical solution became the Committee on Interracial Cooperation (CIC).

"Radical" is perhaps too strong an adjective. The CIC was radical only within a southern context. By no means, as Benjamin Mays stated, were "the organization's goals equal to those of the NAACP." The CIC's idea of interracial cooperation included meetings with selected African American leaders and occasional unpublicized meetings between black and white student groups. The CIC did advocate equal justice before the law and sought in its own quiet way to protect African Americans from lynching and mob violence. The commission also supported separate—but truly adequate—educational and recreational facilities and travel accommodations, and the abolition of peonage. It failed, however, to challenge disfranchisement or to advocate the overthrow of Jim Crow.[13]

The Commission on Interracial Cooperation was officially organized in

Atlanta in January 1919. Its first members were southern white men who, for one reason or another, shared an interest in improving race relations through-out the South, including industrialists interested in reversing the black exo-dus from the South, leaders of philanthropic foundations, members of church bodies, and official members of the War Work Council of the YMCA. Only two prominent white northerners served on the commission, and then only in an advisory capacity: GEB executive director Wallace Buttrick and the con-troversial director of the Phelps-Stokes Fund, Thomas Jesse Jones. Both were conservative to moderate when it came to the race question, and both favored decreasing racial friction and improving race relations within limits that did not threaten the southern social order.[14]

Most CIC members were native southerners, such as R. H. King and Wil-lis D. Weatherford of the YMCA, educator James Dillard, and Meredith Ash-by Jones, the minister of Atlanta's prominent Ponce De Leon Baptist Church. Jones joined the CIC in 1919 because he felt "a high and holy responsibility for the future of the weaker race." Plato Durham, a Methodist minister and the first dean of Emory University's Candler School of Theology, was also an early member. The guiding light of the CIC was its liberal executive di-rector, Will W. Alexander, a Methodist minister who had worked among Afri-can Americans during the war as an official of the YMCA. Alexander had been an acquaintance of Hope's since 1911 and would become one of his dearest friends.[15]

The CIC met secretly and deliberated long and hard over the issue of black membership. It was not until March 1920, well over a year after the CIC was founded, that the first African Americans were invited to join. Despite his friendship with Alexander, Hope was not the first African American invited to join the CIC Executive Committee. That honor went jointly to Robert Moton of Tuskegee and R. E. Jones, the only African American bishop of the Meth-odist Episcopal church. Both Moton and Jones were known for their conser-vatism, and both had already developed close relationships with a number of southern whites. But even Moton and Jones were suspicious of white men who professed a desire for cooperation. Past experiences with interracial commit-tees had taught them that white members made decisions in separate meetings and then told blacks meeting elsewhere what they expected them to do. Afri-can Americans were responsible only for implementing policy; they had no role in creating it.

Indeed, this "southern form" of interracial cooperation proved hard to abandon. At first, white CIC members treated the black members with the usual condescension. Whites set the agenda, defined the objectives, and di-rected black members how to act. "Leading Negroes such as the Negro mem-bers of this Commission ought to prepare a Hand Book for use among Negroes to show their approval of the Inter-Racial program of cooperation," said a white member at an early meeting with blacks present. The "Negro members," however, said no. No white group must tell the Negro what to say, a black member stated. "The Negro does not object to any mechanism set up provided he be given the liberty of free thought."[16] The white members of the organization tempered their remarks thereafter, but they did not intend to give African American radicalism a voice on the CIC. The few African Americans invited to join the Executive Committee had already demonstrated a willingness to work with leaders of the New South. Most significant, they also accepted the CIC's goals of black improvement only along the lines of separate development. It was a conservative agenda meant for a conservative membership.

When Hope attended his first meeting as a member of the CIC on 25 June 1920, Moton and Jones had already been members for three months. In addition to documenting his local activism, the story of Hope's membership in the CIC pinpoints a significant shift in his public philosophy and helps to illuminate the CIC's initially ambiguous attitude toward him. At first, not all the CIC members trusted Hope. They did not know whether he was a true conservative or a "hopeless" radical. Although highly respected as an educational statesman, Hope's ideological commitment to black equality (not to mention his close friendship with W. E. B. Du Bois) bordered on the type of radicalism the CIC wanted to avoid. As yet, CIC members had not seen any evidence of Hope's willingness to compromise. They also had no reason to think that Hope's insistence on full racial equality was meant to apply only in the North. Prominent CIC member M. Ashby Jones, for example, later said that the "hopeless John Hope was regarded at first as an obstacle."[17]

Two factors influenced John Hope's appointment to the Executive Committee of the Commission on Interracial Cooperation: what John Hope expected of the CIC and what the CIC expected of John Hope. Hope was most impressed with the CIC's role in helping black Atlantans secure funds for the city's first African American high school. Southern leaders in the past had done very little to help African Americans achieve even limited goals within the black world. Shortly after the creation of the CIC in 1919, the city floated a bond referendum to expand and upgrade its public schools. African Americans had grown weary of supporting referendums and then seeing improvements made in white schools while their own schools were neglected. They surprised city officials by using their limited municipal political power to block the referendum several times during the next year.[18]

Hope was the chief spokesman for the NAACP committee that had helped organize black Atlantans to defeat the referendum. Through Hope, the CIC learned that African Americans knew that a sizable percentage of the bond money was slated for public high schools in Atlanta—and African Americans had no public high schools. Blacks also disliked the discrepancy in black and white teacher salaries and wanted the money generated by the referendum to go to equal pay for teachers as well. In the spring of 1920, Hope and other African American leaders, with the support of the CIC, struck a deal with the school board that included promises of more black grammar schools and a black high school when the next bond referendum was floated. In return, black leaders promised that African Americans would not block future referendums. The CIC's role in helping to improve and expand African American public educational facilities convinced Hope that the commission was serious.

Yet it was not what the CIC helped to accomplish that eventually brought Hope to the organization's Executive Committee, but what it did not. Although the city agreed to expand black educational opportunities, it did not equalize black and white salaries. The CIC lobbied black leaders hard to accept the city's decision, but Hope refused to budge. The stalemate went on for approximately a month. Hope finally capitulated and advised other African American leaders to accept the city's offer excluding equal teacher salaries. When M. Ashby Jones talked about the "hopeless John Hope" who was "at first an obstacle," he may very well have been referring to the negotiations over equal pay for black and white teachers. Only after Hope showed his willingness to compromise was he invited to join the Executive Committee.[19]

That Hope was invited to join the CIC *after* the bond fight is significant. Certainly Hope had compromised before, but his previous compromises had been closely connected to his responsibilities as president of Morehouse College and usually involved northern whites and funding for black education. Even more significant than that, however, is the fact that in joining the CIC, for the first time John Hope made a conscious decision to join a southern-based, mostly white organization that boasted of working for limited black progress. In 1920, the CIC envisioned no future time when African Americans would enjoy full equality in the South or escape the humiliation of legal separation.

Membership in the CIC might have been expected of Booker T. Washington, but it hardly seemed characteristic of John Hope. In part, his membership reflected his postwar pessimism regarding race relations in the South, which led him to see the CIC as the most progressive organization the region had to offer. Whether that rationalization cleared his conscience is, of course, unknown. In the final analysis, he played the hand he had been dealt, even though he knew the deck was stacked. As an African American leader, he decided to accept the CIC as a new ally and to work hard to ensure that the measured improvements succeeded.

By the end of Hope's first academic year back at Morehouse, the accolades and honors had begun to pour in. Shortly before the beginning of the first semester, the Morehouse Alumni Association held an elaborate banquet in Atlanta to honor him. The guests included the Honorable Fred R. Moore; Dr. George Rice Hovey, secretary of the Baptist Education Society of the ABHMS; Hope's Worcester Academy headmaster, D. W. Abercrombie; Eva Bowles of the YWCA; and Hope's good friend W. E. B. Du Bois. James Weldon Johnson, W. T. B. Williams, Robert Moton, and several others who could not be present sent telegrams that voiced their appreciation of his work. According to one guest, Du Bois "received great applause" when he summarized Hope's record at Morehouse spanning more than twenty years. Bowles, too, was congratulatory in her remarks, but she also took the opportunity to remind the banquet attendees of the role black women had played in the war, especially the "great services of Mrs. John Hope." [20]

Hope's banquet address reveals what he saw as the challenges facing African Americans in the 1920s, which included the needs for a concerted emphasis on racial self-help and an intensified role for college-trained African American leaders in rural areas as well as in the cities. The well-trained leader needed a "broad preparation that will enable him to think out and feel the difficulties of the man who farms, and to work out plans whereby the country man will be as prosperous and contented . . . as the most prosperous and contented city man is in his environment." Although it never materialized, Hope called for a conference in Atlanta "with the end view of working out a program for the immediate and permanent improvement of Southern Negroes in the country." [21]

In addition to the banquet, there were other rewards and honors. The Morehouse Alumni Association also raised funds to purchase an automobile to be placed at the president's disposal. Hope received the Dodge late in December. He never learned to drive it—or any car—and therefore had to have a chauffeur. One of his first drivers was Benjamin Davis Jr., the son of the newspaper editor and later a prominent attorney who went on to become a Communist and northern politician. Howard University awarded Hope an honorary doctorate in 1920. Publicly, Hope was uncomfortable with his new title of "Doctor" and preferred to be called simply "John Hope." Privately, however, he wrote to his friend Jesse Moorland that he "was happy to get the degree and it came at just the right time." Also in 1920, the NAACP held its eleventh annual meeting, for the first time in Atlanta. Between 1,500 and 3,500 (reports of numbers varied) delegates meeting at the Bethel AME Church paused to honor Hope for his work at Morehouse and in France. [22]

The impressive honors and rewards Hope received on behalf of Morehouse further convinced him that the General Education Board was committed to developing African American higher education. Early in 1920, John D. Rockefeller Jr. gave the GEB an additional $50 million to aid American higher education. In addition to allocations to increase salaries and update physical plants, Morehouse, Fisk University, and ABHMS schools Virginia Union University and Shaw University were slated to receive endowments from this second major Rockefeller gift. The $1.5 million the GEB allocated for African American schools was, of course, barely a fraction of the $20 million that was donated to white schools; however, presidents of African American institutions were grateful for any contributions to their endowments. In late July news reached the public that the GEB planned to contribute $200,000 dollars toward an endowment for Morehouse and that the Baptist Home Mission Society would contribute another $100,000.[23]

Predictably, Hope was elated. An endowment for Morehouse College was almost too good to be true. But the offer also brought problems. The gift was contingent on Hope raising an additional $5,000–$10,000 from African Americans within three years. Wallace Buttrick, who had become an ardent supporter of John Hope over the years, had lobbied other members of the GEB to support Morehouse in part because the state boasted more than 250,000 black Baptists who were solidly behind the institution. The ABHMS was also convinced that Hope could raise the conditional amounts. By early February 1922, however, John Hope was behind in the goals he had set for himself. Not only had he not raised the necessary funds to cover endowment money he had already received, he was also behind in securing the necessary matching funds for the "Greater Morehouse" money, and even the matching funds the GEB required for the next year's operating expenses.[24]

Hope's financial woes had less to do with his fund-raising ability than with the southern economy in the 1920s and—ironically—the frequency of financial gifts from the GEB. The South, with its agriculture-based economy, consistently lagged behind the more industrialized Northeast. Many African Americans in the South (and many whites as well) simply had little expendable income to contribute. With its stocks rising steadily toward an all-time high, the business side of the Rockefeller empire could easily have afforded to give Morehouse College the money over a two-year period without any strings attached. But conditional awards were an essential part of the GEB philanthropic formula, and there was no way to get around the practice.

In February 1922 Hope shocked GEB officials by offering to give up the Morehouse presidency to a younger man while he concentrated on fund-raising as the school's public relations officer. He had already talked it over with Lugenia and had come up with the proposition after first thinking about moving into another area of education altogether to fill out the five or ten years that remained before he retired. The GEB flatly refused to consider his offer and interpreted it as a need for rest. Hope and his wife needed a vacation, and Wallace Buttrick promised to use all of his influence to see that they received one. Buttrick did not realize that Hope had legitimate problems as an administrator and fund-raiser at Morehouse until late in May.[25]

Hope never mentioned leaving Morehouse to Dr. George Hovey, the Mission Society secretary to whom he was directly responsible, although he did let him know in his own way that he needed some time away from the "business side" of the college. In addition to being behind in raising the funds to match the conditional gifts, Morehouse was about to end the fiscal year with a deficit. In May 1922 Hope wrote to Hovey that he planned to "take the field" the coming summer to raise the necessary funds. He recognized that in order to erase the deficit, he would have to raise a lot of money from white people—a task, he wrote to Hovey, that had never been his "first business and obligation to the college." Despite Hope's pleas, however, the ABHMS did not relieve him of any of his responsibilities at Morehouse until the end of the decade.[26]

Approximately two weeks after Hope wrote to Hovey, he penned practically the same letter to Buttrick at the GEB. Neither Hovey nor Buttrick wanted to lose Hope, and both realized he had a difficult task and was already overworked. They also knew he sometimes lacked confidence and often needed encouragement, reassurance, and an acknowledgment that he was doing his best. Buttrick sent Hope a warm letter on 31 May giving him that encouragement and appreciation. More important, he arranged for the GEB to erase the $3,000 deficit and promised to speak to Hovey about giving him more time to raise the funds necessary to meet the conditional gifts.[27]

In fact, John Hope had not been completely honest with Hovey and Buttrick. He had been contacted about taking the presidency at black Lincoln University in Missouri and was warmly interested, even though a good friend was also being considered for the job.[28] Further, Hope's lack of time to attend to his responsibilities at Morehouse, including the fund-raising, was in part a problem of his own making. The side of John Hope that wanted to be a professional race leader had resurfaced. In addition to easing cautiously into the work of the CIC, Hope continued to support the national NAACP and spent considerable time writing letters, especially to northern white friends and associates, eliciting support for anti-lynching legislation. Hope also continued to provide Du Bois with valuable information for the *Crisis*, and he worked closely with the local NAACP on school issues and tried to promote the work of the fledgling Atlanta chapter of the Urban League as a member of its board of directors. Early in 1920, along with Lugenia Hope and others, Hope helped organize what eventually (in 1922) became the Atlanta School of Social Work.

Initially located on the Morehouse campus, the school attracted many More-house students and faculty, including E. Franklin Frazier, its first director.[29] But that was not all. Hope also continued his participation in the National Association of Teachers in Colored Schools (NATCS). He attended practi-cally all the association's meetings and helped to draft resolutions and plans for improving public and private black education.[30]

At the same time Hope also expanded his work with the YMCA. In addition to his work with the Colored Men's Department, Hope was frequently called on to represent the National Council and World Committee of the YMCA. Although he thoroughly enjoyed the work, it required a lot of his time. His duties often took him to Europe during the summers, and occasionally during the academic year as well. In May 1922, for example, only weeks before he wrote to Buttrick and Hovey of his desperate need for more time to raise money, Hope spent a couple of weeks in Europe attending the World Evan-gelism Conference sponsored by the YMCA World Committee. The ABHMS and GEB usually encouraged his participation in these outside activities, and sometimes even paid his expenses; in many ways it served their interests. While Hope's work among African Americans contributed to his popularity and was expected to result in increased funding, his work with the National and World Councils of the YMCA increased his popularity among whites, especially in Europe, and the ABHMS and the GEB may have believed it would result in increased financial support from abroad. Although Hope took every opportunity to talk about Morehouse in Europe, he viewed his trips abroad as a pleasure, not a burden. He relaxed while crossing the Atlantic Ocean, enjoyed the opportunity to provide a rare African American voice on the YMCA World Committee, and supported the YMCA's goal of worldwide Christian fellowship.[31]

In the early 1920s there were other pleasures as well. Hope loved to read, and though he rarely admitted it, he loved to write, too. His family certainly rec-ognized his writing ability and often encouraged him to put his thoughts on paper. Instead of helping Du Bois write his history of the First World War, Hope should write his own, Lugenia told him. Hope just did not feel he had the time; besides he loved reading Du Bois. Late in 1920 Hope took the time to read Du Bois's *Darkwater: Voices from within the Veil*. He began reading the book early one evening and did not put it down until after midnight, then scurried to find stationery to write a letter to Du Bois while his ideas were still fresh. The writing appears hurried, as if he was drifting off to sleep as he wrote, yet Hope managed nevertheless to convey how deeply the book had impressed him: "You have accomplished what seemed impossible, you have given us a better book than Souls of Black Folk." *Darkwater* is more than "just literature . . . more than even exalted propaganda," Hope wrote. "It is the life and soul of Du Bois." [32]

Late in December 1922 the Hopes celebrated their twenty-fifth wedding anniversary. There had not been much of a celebration for their twentieth anniversary in 1917 because John and Lugenia were too busy with their war-time activities. That was not the case in 1922. Family members and several mutual friends were invited to the celebration. Hope was disappointed when an illness in the family kept the Du Boises from attending. Yet Du Bois's letter of congratulations (and "commiseration" Du Bois jokingly added) illuminates the two men's deep and abiding friendship. In closing, the *Crisis* editor wished Hope and his wife holiday greetings and "another twenty-five years if you think you could stand it." Hope and Lugenia probably had a good laugh over that. [33]

The Hopes, however, took their twenty-five-year marriage seriously. During the early years in Atlanta, when neither was as busy, they took long, leisurely strolls through the countryside. West Atlanta was still rural in those years, and one was as apt to meet a stray cow, goat, or chicken as another human being. It was quite a contrast, Hope later wrote, from the "rushing into and out of the automobile" that was so much a part of their lives in the 1920s. He also remembered that in those early days "we had time to *be* together." Later, their lives were so "*un*private" that they had to "leave home to see the family, to know it and find the beauty, the rest, and the inspiration of it." [34]

John and Lugenia Hope were not only husband and wife, but best friends as well. Each valued the other's counsel on race work, family matters, and their responsibilities to Morehouse and the Neighborhood Union. They nevertheless had distinct personalities. Hope was gentle, at times even timid and evasive. Lugenia was more aggressive, usually direct, and could be terribly blunt. On occasion, Lugenia pushed Hope in directions he hesitated to go; sometimes she restrained him when she sensed that a certain path was dangerous. He was the more intellectual of the two, and more comfortable on the campus of Morehouse; she seemed more worldly, less shocked by life outside the ivory towers of academia.

Nevertheless, their twenty-five years had not been without conflicts and disagreements. Not only did Lugenia have a "womanist consciousness," to use historian Elsa Barkley Brown's term, refusing to separate the race struggle from women's struggle, she also insisted on placing her outside role as a race woman on the same plane as her roles as homemaker, wife, and mother. While there is no doubt that she loved her family dearly, Lugenia Hope was just as committed to her people and to general societal reform as her husband was. John and Lugenia Hope struggled hard throughout their lives to balance commitment to family—love for each other and their sons—with their commitment to racial progress. It was never easy for either of them.[35]

By the 1920s John Hope's views of women, especially middle-class African American women, had gone through several stages. As an idealistic student at Worcester and Brown, Hope's idol was Ida Wells-Barnett, the fiery newspaper editor and African American leader who took every opportunity to protest lynching and disfranchisement and insisted on nothing less than full equality for black Americans. He often wrote to friends and family about his fondness for this "spirited" African American woman. In the 1890s Hope was a follower of what was then called the "Ida B. Wells Movement" and seemed not to be bothered by her sex or gender.[36]

By the time Hope had graduated from college, married Lugenia, and moved to Atlanta, however, his thinking about African American women had changed significantly. His speeches to several African American women's groups in the early 1900s show that, not unlike many black male leaders, Hope was intimidated by black women who moved beyond what he believed was their proper "sphere of influence." He was comfortable with women who worked to improve conditions for poor children and working girls and women. He also felt comfortable with those who worked quietly within the African American community to improve housing, living conditions, and public education. He was suspicious, however, of women who insisted on publicly protesting racial inequality and questioned male dominance in certain organizations and institutions, both religious and secular. Moreover, also like many other African American male leaders at the turn of the twentieth century, Hope questioned African American women who dared venture into occupations that were considered unsuitable for women or were believed to be the exclusive domain of men. The draft of a blistering speech Hope made to a group of African American women sometime in the early twentieth century illuminates these attitudes. Apparently he lectured the women about "staying in their place" and allowing African American men "to be men."[37]

Like most African American men at the turn of the century, Hope accepted the culture of male privilege, which was supported by a Victorian code of patriarchy. By the 1920s, however, Hope had grown to view women differently, to see again the relationship between race struggle and women's struggle. In addition, his increasing contacts with African American women who were running schools, complex organizations, and businesses expanded his view of women's abilities. Once his perspective widened, Hope used his position as a prominent male leader within the African American community to help increase opportunities for middle-class African American women.

His new attitude was evident in his unsuccessful support of Mary E. Jackson for the field organizer position in the NAACP (see chapter 9). Along with

Du Bois, he strongly advocated awarding the Spingarn Medal to Mary B. Talbert, a president of the National Association of Colored Women and an NAACP official, and he supported educator Maria L. Baldwin for the medal as well. He admired these women and respected their abilities, but his enlightenment also came about through his association with women such as Lucy Laney, Charlotte Hawkins-Brown, Addie Hunton, Nannie H. Burroughs, Maggie Lena Walker, Madam C. J. Walker, Eva Bowles, and Mary McCloud Bethune, and he used his influence to support the work of these women as well.[38]

Without doubt, however, the most important figure in Hope's enlightenment was his own wife, Lugenia. Although Lugenia Hope's contributions to the early development of Morehouse were clearly understood by her husband and sons, they were virtually unknown outside the family until Jacqueline Rouse's revealing biography of her was published in 1989. In addition, Lugenia's masterful administration of the Neighborhood Union, her nationally acclaimed efforts during the First World War, and even her refusal to allow her husband to drown her in a sea of guilt for neglecting her family shattered John Hope's narrow early twentieth-century image of African American women's abilities and capabilities. Hence, by the early 1920s Hope was as progressive in his ideas about African American women as any of his male contemporaries. John Hope had more to celebrate after twenty-five years of marriage to Lugenia Hope than he probably realized.[39]

In the early 1920s Hope became increasingly valuable as an adviser to the American Baptist Home Mission Society and to philanthropic foundations such as the Rosenwald Fund, the Phelps-Stokes Fund, and the GEB, all of which contributed various sums to Morehouse College through the agency of the ABHMS. The GEB and ABHMS often requested Hope's advice before making personnel decisions at African American institutions and when considering financial requests from these schools. Hope also initiated requests for economic assistance to faculty members, staff, and other personnel for scholarships, loans, and jobs. He never served on the board of trustees of any college, nor did he ever come close to wielding the power Booker T. Washington had with philanthropists. Yet no contemporary African American college president surpassed his influence with the foundations and other organizations dominated by moderate to conservative whites.[40]

That influence did not come without a price. Directors of foundations often asked Hope confidential and sensitive questions. They were usually unapologetic and expected him to provide quick, truthful, and detailed answers. Wallace Buttrick of the GEB, for example, asked Hope to find out if rumors that certain black educators were "not Christians" were true, and if certain administrators were mismanaging funds. On another occasion the director of the ABHMS asked Hope for a "very frank and full statement" regarding a faculty member, promising that it would be "regarded as entirely confidential." The target of the specific inquiry was Benjamin Brawley, a former Morehouse faculty member who at one time was one of Hope's closest associates. "I want to know especially about his tact in getting along with people and his attitude on race matters," the official stated.[41]

There is evidence that Hope was privately uneasy with these requests, but he answered them promptly and honestly. Regarding Brawley, Hope's answer was not entirely favorable, but neither was it vindictive: "His last days at Morehouse should not overshadow so many happy years of association that had gone before." On racial matters, Hope wrote, he "feels things and talks about things . . . as most colored men of his quality and experience. It is true that he is . . . more temperamental than some of us, but I should say that his many years in Atlanta, and his . . . years at Howard ought to indicate that he knows how to be useful." Hope's candor only enhanced his prestige among influential whites.[42]

Hope's advice was not restricted to educational issues. The question about "race matters" shows that philanthropic organizations and the ABHMS also exploited Hope's role as a national black leader. The ABHMS, for example, consulted Hope on representatives for the National Baptist Convention, sought his advice before selecting speakers for specific functions, and asked what subjects the speakers should address. Either he kept files on a number of African American leaders, or he was simply able to get accurate and detailed information quickly. Less than three days after receiving a request from the ABHMS, Hope provided information on a minister that included the name of his Cleveland, Ohio, church, whether he had moved there before or after the great migration, the names of his wife and children, where they had been educated, his views on race relations, his familiarity with "southern work," and his church's support of the Northern Baptist Convention.[43]

As the years went by John Hope continued to operate in two worlds. Holding on to the support of prominent whites was difficult, but it was just as difficult to please moderate to conservative black supporters in the South while simultaneously appeasing less compromising constituencies in the North. In 1923, for example, Hope joined Robert Moton in his frustration with the "Tuskegee situation." The Harding administration had recently endorsed the construction of a hospital for black veterans in Tuskegee, Alabama, adjacent to the Tuskegee Institute campus; however, there was a potentially explosive controversy over whether the hospital would be managed and staffed by blacks or whites. Hope spent many hours with Robert Moton, W. T. B. Williams, and others at Tuskegee discussing the best way to resolve the problem. He sincerely believed that the hospital should be directed by an African American administrator assisted by a predominantly, if not completely, African American staff. He also agreed with Moton's strategy to remain quiet and allow the NAACP to lead the campaign against the groundswell of southern white opposition, especially in Tuskegee.[44]

Privately, Hope allegedly confided to an Atlanta University science teacher, presumably one ideologically to the left of Moton, that the Tuskegee situation provided new lessons for Moton. The teacher secretly reported to Du Bois that Hope believed that "Tuskegee is learning what we have always told her that the southern white man cannot be trusted." Hope also reportedly said that the Alabama controversy provided a much-needed "psychological moment for the two factions presented by the N.A.A.C.P. and Tuskegee to come together."[45]

A number of African Americans found the NAACP's support of the segregated facility unacceptable. Young black Socialists Chandler Owen and A. Philip Randolph, who had loudly protested the segregated officer training camp during the First World War, used the *Messenger* to warn African Americans against accepting any government-sanctioned segregation at all: "For the Negroes it is a dangerous precedent. . . . The hospital should be mixed with white and black porters, black and white physicians, nurses and maids. We are not impressed by the arguments that it can't be done." Hope understood their position but paid little attention to them at the time.[46]

Hope endorsed other issues that met with no opposition from African Americans. He was a part of the massive NAACP-sponsored campaign to pass the Dyer Anti-Lynching Bill, and was disappointed at its defeat by filibuster in the Senate. In 1923 Du Bois asked fifty African Americans leaders, including Hope, to publicly comment on the future of the bill. Hope's response was characterized by optimism, though his disappointment was clear: "Too soon to say what is the next political step," he wrote, "but Negroes are meditating" and "America has been compelled to look Lynching in the face." He also believed the NAACP was correct in trusting "the promises of gentlemen" who said they would support the bill, but added that "politically Negroes will have to pay due regard to the disloyalty of parties and friends." Privately, Hope did not think the legislation would ever pass the Senate. Earlier in December he had written to his old Niagara friend (and family dentist) Charles Bentley of Chicago that "the Dyer Bill is dead."[47]

Hope increasingly believed that the predominantly white Commission on Interracial Cooperation would supplant the NAACP in the South as the most effective civil rights organization. The Atlanta branch of the NAACP was reorganized in the mid-1920s but was relatively inactive for the rest of the decade. Hope tried desperately to persuade the national and local NAACP organizations to embrace the conservative CIC, but met with limited success. "There is one thing that is inspiring to all classes of colored people in Atlanta," he wrote to Walter White in 1924. "There is an increasingly large group of white people who are seeing that colored people ought to have a square deal." The NAACP remained suspicious of the organization, and Du Bois was generally hostile to it.[48]

The NAACP did acknowledge the CIC's good works, but, except for Hope, was critical of its conservative black membership and its refusal to work for full black equality. Du Bois could be particularly harsh in his *Crisis* editorials. On one occasion he advised the CIC not to "fill your committees with pussy footers like Robert Moton or white-folks Niggers like Isaac Fisher." Another time he urged the organization to "face the fundamental problems—the Vote, the Jim Crow car, Peonage and Mob-law." Although Du Bois eventually developed some respect for the commission, he continued to insist that "any honest inter-racial commission working in the South" must have a program that included social and political equality.[49]

Despite his good friend's views, Hope continued to defend the CIC and its leaders, both publicly and privately. In 1926 the black *Amsterdam News* of New York published an article by Hope in which he said that the CIC's record was already impressive. By the mid-1920s, he wrote, its accomplishments included improved protection of blacks by the courts and police, better school facilities, and "an increasingly large number of instances all over the South of the two races having better opportunities to come together . . . for the common good." In spite of its shortcomings, the CIC "represented the most inspiring and significant movement in racial matters in the South today."[50]

In truth, Hope's apparent optimism did not match the reality of the 1920s. Most African Americans in the South did not enjoy police protection. And although lynching was generally on the decline, the lynchings that occurred were as brutal as ever. In addition, the gap between black and white school expenditures was growing progressively wider. Hope's optimistic view embodied a conservative African American leadership posture that was more and more perceived as typically "southern" and out of step with the more militant and ever more popular northern-based New Negro ideology, which was unwilling to embrace any organization that did not include fundamental changes in the South. Not unaware that this new mood was also appearing among some African American leaders, Hope usually defended the CIC most vigorously in private.

In 1926 Hope wrote a detailed letter to Du Bois in support of the CIC's executive director, Will Alexander. Commission members throughout the

South had criticized Alexander for delivering a speech in Birmingham that mildly supported social equality and the end of segregation. It was widely rumored that Alexander in another speech had then retracted his most controversial statements, which upset the African American community.[51] Hope had been present at the second speech, and he wrote to Du Bois that Alexander had not retracted his views on social equality. Hope feared there was a "conspiracy to discredit white friends of the race." Further, "it would be a clever thing on the part of reactionaries in his [Alexander's] own race," Hope wrote, "if they could have him discredited by the colored people, in whose interest he has worked and is working."[52] Increasingly aware of his image among the younger, more militant wing of the New Negro leadership—perhaps even including Du Bois—Hope did not want his defense of Alexander and his views on social equality published in the *Crisis*. Rumors that he was naive, too gentle and trusting of conservative whites, were already beginning to surface. He hinted at these rumors in his letter to Du Bois: "I know you fear the Greeks though bearing gifts. I myself am not so guileless as some think, but I do know of the pressure to which a few Southern white men are now being subjected, and I know somewhat of the cruel influence brought to bear by their people to crush them while they are working for better things for Colored people." Hope's defense of Alexander indicates that there were exceptions to his distrust of the "southern white man."[53]

Hope's "private" defense of Alexander's views on social equality probably stemmed as much from his role as president of Morehouse College as from his sensitivity to his growing image as a respected but conservative African American leader. No one understood better than Hope the need to balance his concerns as a leader with his role as a black college president dependent on northern philanthropists for financial support. Hope knew the issue of social equality made philanthropists uneasy, and he preferred to do nothing that might upset their faith in him as "a sane and conservative spokesman for his people." In fact, many philanthropists viewed Du Bois as just the opposite—as radical and irrational, the quintessential black advocate of social equality, a propagandist and opportunist. George Foster Peabody believed Du Bois's leadership and influence made things hard for his people and would "greatly delay the right outcome." The more virulently racist executive secretary of the Mississippi Welfare League described Du Bois's influence as "vicious and dangerous, and his connection with anything is sufficient to damn it forthwith." Hope, of course, did not agree with these accusations, but he knew the philanthropists were very concerned about image, perceptions, and associations. Thus, though he loved Du Bois, he would not share a spotlight with him in the pages of the *Crisis* defending the always explosive subject of social equality.[54]

Hope consistently faced problems in the 1920s that inextricably linked his roles as an educational statesman and a national African American leader, and it became more and more difficult for him to strike a middle-of-the-road balance between the two. He was faced with two such challenges in 1924 that eventually contributed to minor surgery and a short stay in the hospital.

The Standard Life Insurance Company was one of the older black businesses in Atlanta, a shining example of black self-help and solidarity, and a source of pride in the southern New Negro African American community. Early in 1924 the company's assets started to deteriorate. There were cash flow problems, and the company began a journey that would end in financial failure.[55]

Hope expended considerable energy and time (as well as money) to help reverse the company's situation. Like other African Americans in Atlanta and across the nation, he had stock in Standard Life and did not want to lose his money. However, his concern went beyond the economic incentive. Standard Life was a treasured African American enterprise, and no one wanted to see it fail. Hope spent long hours with Robert Moton and other leaders trying to come up with a successful strategy to save the company. An appeal for money was made to the African American community. There was a positive response, but it was not nearly enough. Hope appealed to southern white progressives within the CIC to supplement the black community's financial support. They were sympathetic but unwilling or unable to bail out the company.

By the end of the year Hope had just about given up. Yet there was one option left. He could appeal to the educational foundations for financial assistance. It was a difficult decision for him. Hope had rarely, if ever, approached the foundations for any purpose other than funds for education. Later in the decade he would ask the GEB for an appropriation for the CIC, but that was a different matter. Saving Standard Life would not help to reduce friction between the races; this was an economic problem with nationalist overtones rooted deep in the African American tradition. John Hope believed in the efficacy of black business development and the need for independent black institutions. It was an idea that transcended class and was shared by most African American leaders in the New Negro era.

The day after Christmas, Hope appealed to the Rosenwald Foundation in Chicago for $200,000 to keep Standard Life from being put into the hands of a white company that had given it a six-month loan. Earlier attempts to interest Rosenwald had failed because Standard Life's president was unwilling to give up managerial control. Drawing on his memories of his Augusta boyhood, Hope couched his request in a nationalist framework that perhaps exaggerated the impact the company's failure would have on "12,000,000 Negroes." Recalling the failure of the Freedmen's Bank many years earlier, Hope remembered the "terribly crushing influence upon Negro men and women who had recently emerged from slavery and were trying to develop thrift." He saw them "shed tears because of their losses," and they never again "got back the inspiration or the confidence to save." [56]

In his effort to elicit Rosenwald's support, Hope invoked his dual roles as African American leader committed to interracial cooperation and educational statesman: "There is a goodly number of southern white people who want the . . . insurance company saved to the control of Negroes, and feel the great loss of inspiration to the Negro group if it should fail or, even though not failing, should fall into the hands of white people who would be interested not so much in building up business among Negroes, as in making money out of Negroes." His final plea illuminated his role as an African American president: "As a teacher of Negro youth for now a little more than thirty years, I would make an appeal. As a father of two Negro sons, one already through college, I would make this appeal. It is not simply money that we are wanting, it is encouragement. A dozen white insurance companies might go by the board and hardly cause a ripple. Such is not the case with us." [57]

His effort was unsuccessful. Hope was so devastated by his failure to save the Standard Life Insurance Company that he resigned from the board of directors of the Citizens Trust Bank, another African American enterprise. It bothered Hope that Rosenwald and the other foundations did not believe they had an obligation to save the struggling black enterprise. Of course, Hope ignored the economic conditions that had facilitated the company's failure, and downplayed the reality of bad management. Instead, he chose to believe the company failed because there was too little contact between the races. [58]

Six months into his efforts to help save Standard Life, Hope found himself embroiled in another controversy that again publicly, and in his view negatively, linked his dual roles. There were rumblings on several African American college campuses that Hope and Moton, and others as well, believed threatened the financing of African American higher education. Black college presidents were usually careful guardians of an established tradition rooted in the New England culture of the missionaries who had established the institutions in the years following the Civil War. As the 1920s progressed, however, American colleges were changing; they were becoming more liberal and allowing students to express their individuality and influence campus policies.

Administrators at African American schools, especially the mission colleges, continued to exercise the same strict discipline and autocratic rule that had existed for decades, while their students, imbued with the New Negro ideology, resorted to strikes, boycotts, and rebellions to bring about the changes that were occurring on white campuses throughout the nation. In addition, the nationalist tendency of the New Negro Movement manifested itself in a push for black studies, or at least courses in African American history, and in some cases a desire for increased black control of institutions currently headed by whites. More often than not, the larger black community supported at least some of the students' demands.[59]

Like other college presidents, John Hope found himself caught in a difficult situation. On the one hand, he genuinely admired the students' spunk, their interest in expanding democracy on campus, and certainly their desire to see more of their own people in responsible positions at African American institutions. His support of the Standard Life Insurance Company and the Tuskegee veterans' hospital spoke to his own nationalist sentiment, and he understood the students' position.

Nevertheless, he recognized that African American higher education was still a precarious enterprise. So far, only Howard University was receiving significant state or federal support. Black higher education's most affluent supporters were the philanthropic foundations, which had not taken off their conservative coats since first donning them in the age of Booker T. Washington. The "uncontrolled behavior" on black college campuses frightened them. They labeled such behavior "radical" or "militant" and expected black college presidents to keep their students in check. Hope understood the political economy of the situation well, but his was not an easy task. African American higher education required financial support from both the black and the white worlds. He could afford to alienate neither the militant New Negro leadership, which often supported the students' demands, nor the conservative white financiers who were disturbed by them.

For Hope, the fuse was lit in Nashville during the Fisk University commencement exercises in June 1924. The previous March, Du Bois, Fisk's most distinguished graduate, had written an article for the *Amsterdam News* about the Fisk president's strict policies and rules and other student concerns. In June he delivered the alumni speech in conjunction with Fisk's commencement exercises and publicly lambasted the university's president and trustees over the alumni's "bitter disgust" with the school's problems.[60]

Du Bois's speech sent shock waves throughout middle-class black America, especially among students and administrators at other African American colleges. Almost ten years earlier, organized philanthropy had acknowledged the Nashville school as the most "promising Negro college" and decided to develop it as a model for African American higher education. Fisk, led by its young white president, Fayette Avery McKenzie, and a mainly white faculty and staff, was given $500,000 toward an endowment by the General Education Board. It was the largest sum pledged from the Rockefeller education gift of 1920 to any school for African Americans. When the GEB sum and other philanthropic gifts were added to $50,000 contributed from the Nashville community, Fisk University's endowment totaled $1 million, a sum unprecedented in any African American school.

However, in order to please the philanthropists (and many white southerners who also supported Fisk), McKenzie and the Fisk trustees marketed Fisk University as the college version of conservative Tuskegee and Hampton Institutes. Among other things, the Fisk administration was criticized for arranging separate accommodations for white guests, disbanding the student government association, and suspending publication of the *Fisk Herald*, the popular and long-standing student publication. Students were also subjected to strict codes of conduct and harsh discipline. Requests to establish an NAACP chapter on campus were refused, and librarians performed routine inspections to ensure that no "radical" NAACP literature reached the students. In the words of Raymond Wolters, the students were treated as if they were "freedmen" instead of men "who were born free."[61]

Du Bois helped to engineer and orchestrate a protest against Fisk's autocratic rule that eventually attracted the attention of black America. For some (although not for Du Bois and most Fisk students), the protest expanded to include demands for an African American president and more black control. The issue was finally resolved in 1925 when McKenzie resigned and was replaced by another white president, Thomas Elsa Jones. In time, Jones established an environment more in line with the enlightened policies that existed on white college campuses.

The situation at Fisk greatly disturbed John Hope, and also created a dilemma for him. He was as committed to strong discipline and strict rules of order as President McKenzie,[62] yet he disagreed with McKenzie's endorsement of campus policies that completely surrendered to what McKenzie thought were the expectations of southern whites and northern philanthropists. Hope believed that an African American institution of higher learning — even one operating in a city as segregated as Atlanta — had a duty to be a beacon of light and an oasis of freedom and complete equality. For that reason, there was no separation at Morehouse of black students from white faculty or from any of the white guests who visited the campus. Early in his career, Hope had been committed to encouraging students to embrace the NAACP and other organizations that addressed African American interests. Against a backdrop that included a repudiation of McKenzie and his policies at Fisk, Du Bois sang Hope's praises as a "colored man building one of the finest institutions in the South." Compared with Fisk under McKenzie in the middle 1920s, Morehouse was a model the African American community could embrace.[63]

Hope appreciated and was flattered by Du Bois's references to his work at Morehouse College. But what Du Bois failed to mention in his October *American Mercury* article, although he did refer to increased "church" funding at Morehouse, was that Hope had received considerable support from the same or similar philanthropists. Why did McKenzie feel compelled to move Fisk so far to the right when Hope, who depended on the same sources for funds, did not? On one level, McKenzie was simply stubborn. He might have avoided some of his problems if he had possessed better interpersonal skills that would have allowed him to deal more effectively with those who opposed his policies. In addition, McKenzie may simply have overestimated what he needed to do to keep the support of northern (but not southern!) philanthropists, especially the GEB.[64]

Although Hope had embraced the conservative CIC, there were still certain principles—which included insisting on integrated campus facilities—that he refused to violate. Hope's adherence to those principles may explain why Morehouse's contributors included practically no southern whites. It is also significant that Hope was the president of an African American institution with a mostly black faculty, staff, and board of trustees that was still closely connected to the American Baptist Home Mission Society and more than 250,000 black Baptists. Although Fisk had virtually cut its connection with the American Missionary Association, black Baptists were strong supporters of Morehouse, and the ABHMS and the GEB were acutely aware of that. This understanding gave Hope some leverage at Morehouse that did not exist at Fisk University.

In spite of all these considerations, Hope could not bring himself either to support the students at Fisk or to publicly denounce McKenzie. No matter how genuine the students' complaints, nothing was worse than adverse publicity about African American higher education just at the time when things were beginning to improve. He wrote to Du Bois that differences within black colleges were best resolved with the "opposing parties getting together quietly and trying to iron things out without a big fuss." He wanted the best for Fisk but believed it should come to pass "with the least commotion possible and with as little embarrassment as possible."[65]

Hope's refusal to support the Fisk student revolt involved more than tactics or strategy. He simply did not believe the rules were too strict or the discipline too strong. And in spite of his own nationalist tendencies, he did not support the widely held view among African Americans in the New Negro era of the 1920s that all African American colleges should have black presidents. He certainly did not believe the time was ripe for Fisk to have one. "Even if we have doubts about whether a faculty should consist of all one race or of two races," he later said in a conference, "we ought to settle that as far as possible without its worrying us or without making the thing a universal question. Settle it in whatever institution it might arise."[66]

Basically, Hope tried to do just that. Even before Du Bois's controversial alumni address at Fisk, Hope and Moton had already begun to talk about the situation. Hope also talked with Du Bois. In late June, after the speech, Hope visited his friend at the *Crisis* and advised him to have a personal conference with L. Hollingsworth Wood, an attorney and prominent Quaker, president of the Urban League, and a good friend of Hope's. More important, Wood was a vice chairman of the Fisk University Board of Trustees. Along with his fellow trustee William Baldwin, Wood already had reservations about McKenzie's policies. The initial meetings between Baldwin and Wood, Du Bois, and the New Fisk Alumni Chapter were tumultuous, and very little was accomplished. Wood nevertheless went on to play a major role in helping to resolve the conflict at Fisk University and secure McKenzie's resignation. He also helped his friend and fellow Quaker Thomas Elsa Jones to ease into his new position as president of Fisk in 1926.[67]

Early in 1925, Hope felt especially fatigued. He was concerned because he remained behind schedule in his Morehouse fund-raising. The problems at Standard Life and Fisk University generated stress that further deteriorated his physical and emotional well-being. But that was not all. Hope was very concerned about his oldest son.

Edward was in graduate school at the Massachusetts Institute of Technology (MIT). Like his father, Edward Hope was quiet, independent, and tended to worry about everything. At MIT, he worried about the high cost of tuition, his inability to relax in examinations, and his fear of not graduating on time. Hope advised him to relax, get plenty of exercise, and take frequent trips for mental stimulation. About graduating, Hope told him, "You do not *have* to get through Tech on schedule time . . . the main thing is to get through in fine shape physically and educationally at *some* time."[68]

At virtually all-white MIT, Edward was in a new and strange place far removed from the black world of Morehouse College. Practically none of the white graduate students he knew had college presidents as fathers, yet they seemed far less concerned than he about paying their bills. Hope usually talked very little about his finances, but he realized that Edward needed an explanation even though he had not asked for one. He first tried to reassure his son that the tuition would be paid, and in the future it would be paid on time. Then he addressed Edward's confusion about class and affluence in the black and white worlds, explaining that "social standing and wealth among Negroes is very different from social standing and wealth among whites."[69]

Despite what he told Edward, financial problems ranked high on John Hope's own list of worries. His entire adult life had been characterized by financial struggle. The ABHMS and other mission societies operating black schools had very little money, and faculty and administrators were paid ridiculously low salaries. Even with a supplement from the GEB, the Morehouse budget for faculty salaries in the early 1920s was only about $11,000 (it was $8,500 when Hope assumed the presidency). Hope's salary when he took office in 1906 was $1,500. It did not change until he returned from France in 1919, more than ten years later. Even then, it was raised to $2,250 only because the General Education Board added the additional $750. Shortly after his arrival in Atlanta in 1898, and several times thereafter, Hope borrowed against insurance policies in order to get extra money. He also received loans from black and white friends he had known since college, especially men like Ted Owens and W. T. B. Williams. The situation improved somewhat in the 1920s, but money continued to be a problem.[70]

Nevertheless, Hope was a college president, and hence not a poor man within the African American world. There were even a few additional sources of income. After his mother's death in 1903 he inherited property in Augusta that had belonged to his father. He also tried to make profitable investments. He owned a few shares of stock in a number of different enterprises, including the ill-fated Standard Life Insurance Company, and he continued to look for good investment opportunities. Hope also owned a house on Beckwith Street near Morehouse that he occasionally rented out. In 1912 he purchased a ninety-three-acre farm about thirty miles north of Atlanta in Powder Springs, Georgia, and planted cotton and other cash crops.[71]

Despite his efforts, John Hope's business dealings were often less than successful. The farm in Powder Springs caused him one headache after another. In addition to producing extra income, Hope had expected the farm to serve as a "summer place" where he and his family could relax away from the hustle and bustle of the city. Hope hired a caretaker, Mr. Hugh Favors, a semi-sharecropper who was paid a small wage and was allowed to take a percentage of the crop. Except for a few vegetables that Hope took himself, the farm was not profitable. Furthermore, Favors often pleaded with Hope to send money (money he did not have) to take care of the property or to come up to the farm to settle other business connected with his "investment."

Hope's foray into the stock market was also short on success. The dividends on his stocks were mediocre even before the crash of 1929, and he lost money when the Standard Life Insurance Company failed. The Augusta lots did not increase significantly in value—and, of course, Hope was responsible for the taxes on them. During the First World War, squatters built makeshift dwellings on vacant lots throughout the city, including Hope's property. Eventually, Hope allowed his sister Anna to sell most of his property at a price below market value.[72]

Hope's constant need for money can also be attributed to his overzealous generosity. Perhaps it was his view of social responsibility that motivated his reluctance to seek compensation for the hundreds of addresses and speeches he made. He asked only that sponsors pay his expenses. Furthermore, he was so attached to some of his Morehouse students that he often loaned them money, knowing it would probably never be repaid. He also aided family members in need—his mother before her death, his brother Tom, his sister Jane, and Jane's children in Washington, D.C. He also "loaned" money to the caretaker of his farm and to friends across the country. Hope simply had difficulty saying no to personal requests for financial assistance.[73]

Once he became the president of Morehouse, John Hope contributed above his means to "causes," organizations and institutions working for African American uplift. His financial records show regular contributions to the local and national "colored branches" of the YMCA, the NAACP, the National Association for Teachers in Colored Schools, and the Atlanta (Colored) Anti-Tuberculosis Association. Nor could he say no to Mary McLeod Bethune's Cookman College in Florida, Nannie Burroughs's National Training Institute for Women and Girls in Washington, and, in Georgia, among others, Lucy Laney's Haines Institute and Walker Academy in Augusta.[74]

Though meticulous in his accounting at Morehouse, Hope was often careless in managing his own personal finances. Bills were not always paid on time, and important financial deadlines were often missed. In 1924 William Lewis, the business manager of William Monroe Trotter's newspaper, the *Guardian*, wrote to tell Hope that he was behind in his subscription. Hope wrote jokingly back about his old friend and fellow former Niagarite that "the fact is I do not know how much I owe Trotter . . . and Trotter does not know. Now I am going to send a check for $5.00 with the understanding that you and Trotter call that square."[75] More serious was Hope's lack of attention to deadlines, especially with insurance companies, which often cost him extra money. In 1927 Hope wrote the black National Benefit Life Insurance Company (a Washington-based company that had reinsured many of Standard Life's old clients) that he did not understand why he would have to "start all over with a new policy"; no one had called him and told him his payments were past due. Two years later he wrote another insurance agent about the National Benefit Company policy, which was again about to expire: "It looks unbusinesslike for me to ask people to remind me of my own policy, but fortunately or unfortunately—I know not which—I have not been able to run Morehouse College and my own business well, so I chose to run Morehouse." The quip was obviously an exaggeration, perhaps even a bit of his dry sarcasm. Nevertheless, Hope continued to neglect his personal finances in ways that strained his already limited resources and increased his concerns about money.[76]

In early February 1925 John and Lugenia Hope attended a series of Quaker meetings in Pennsylvania at which Hope delivered speeches and tried to raise funds for Morehouse. While there, Hope learned that his half-brother, Madison J. Newton, had died in his sleep of a heart attack only weeks before his sixty-eighth birthday. Hope was devastated and immediately returned to Georgia.

There were other deaths in the 1920s. A year earlier, in 1924, he had attended the funeral in Augusta of Judson W. Lyons, his brother-in-law and a former register of the Treasury. A year later, in 1926, Wallace Buttrick, his dear friend at the General Education Board, died. That same year he lost his sister Grace. He felt these deaths deeply, but none engendered the grief he felt when Newton died in 1925.[77]

It is difficult to characterize Hope's relationship with the brother he affectionately called "Buddie." Newton was a father figure—a valued friend, counselor, and benefactor. He had assisted Hope financially in prep school and college, and had encouraged him to leave Nashville for Atlanta and to accept the Morehouse presidency in 1906. Newton was the Hope family's Rock of Gibraltar, a meticulous historian and a consummate guardian of the family's heritage and secrets. Hope had turned to him during the spring of 1918 for records of his father's citizenship. If Newton had not delivered, Hope might not have obtained a passport enabling him to go to France. With more ease, perhaps, than he felt with others, Hope could talk to Newton about issues that faced African Americans who bore no visible traces of their African blood. It was to the once golden-haired Madison that Hope revealed his belief that a fair complexion could have disadvantages as well as advantages in both the black and white worlds. Referring to an opening for an Urban League job previously held by a "much darker man," Hope wrote to his brother in 1918: "I have had many experiences in my work when I have found it [a very light complexion] a handicap."[78]

Yet, to Hope's dismay, the two men were never close. Age was probably a factor; Newton was eleven years Hope's senior. Hope's feelings about his own accomplishments may have been another. He tended to believe that his successes should have rightly gone to Newton. Like Hope, Newton too had once looked forward to attending school in the North, marrying the woman he loved, and successfully operating his own business. Instead, he was forced to leave Atlanta University shortly before he finished the academy; the woman he loved married another man; and though he had a good job as one of the first African American postmen in Augusta, most of his business ventures failed.

In 1917 Hope wrote his brother the most revealing letter about their personal relationship that has survived. The seven-page letter delicately imposed

Hope's own needs on his brother. On the one hand, he wanted an affirmation that his accomplishments met with Newton's approval: "I have been very ambitious all my life to live so as to satisfy your hopes and expectations. I wonder whether in the essentials I have quite come up to the man you hoped to make out of me when you sacrificed so much for me in your young manhood." He also wanted his brother's affection and reassurance that there were no unbridgeable gulfs between them. "I wonder how happy you are," he wrote, "and wish that you might let me more and more into your life." Hope dared to delve deeper into his brother's private world, perhaps cleansing his own soul in the process: "In fact, you have had all your days such an aloofness and self-sufficiency that men have hardly dared to intrude upon your holy of holies to find out what were the needs and the merits of the real, inside Madison Newton." In his own formal and reserved way, Hope asked his brother to "think of me occasionally and know always how much I love you." At the funeral in Augusta, Hope was probably glad he had poured his heart out to Newton eight years earlier in that passionate letter. Given Hope's personality, it is doubtful he could have done so in person.[79]

True to the tradition in African American families, Madison's funeral was in some ways a joyful family reunion. They had not all been together since the death of his mother in 1903. Present at Madison's funeral, but conspicuous for her absence at her mother's twenty-three years earlier, was Sissie (Georgia Frances Ladeveze), the sister who had moved to California and passed for white. Jane Hope Lyons reported years later that John Hope was not in a festive mood for the family reunion. He knew Georgia Frances and Madison Newton had unresolved differences (what they were Jane Hope Lyons refused to disclose). In addition, John still had not forgiven his oldest sister for failing to return for their mother's funeral, and he also resented her decision not to keep in touch with the family. "Sissie passed through Atlanta last night," Hope wrote before attending his brother's funeral. "It was the first time we had seen each other for about twenty-eight years, and really neither one of us quite knew the other. It was more pathetic than I had expected."[80]

Other family members had also left Georgia by then. Through the influence of Lugenia Hope and Eva Bowles, Anna had gone into YWCA work during the war and now directed the association's "colored work" in Cincinnati, Ohio. Thomas Hope had worked in several different jobs (gained through John's influence) without remaining very long in any of them. He had caused John considerable worry, for creditors hounded him about Tom's loans. By 1925, Tom had married and settled down in New Jersey. Alethea Hope Ladeveze, the sister who was passing for white in Providence, also came to Madison's funeral. She did not attend John Hope's funeral eleven years later, in 1936, according to his son John Hope II. "If she did," added Hope's daughter-in-law, "no one knew who she was." By the early 1930s Alethea Hope Ladeveze had ceased to exist as a member of the John Hope family.[81]

Another family member also harbored a troubling secret. Letters show that the relationship between Jane Hope Lyons and her husband, Judson, had been strained for a very long time. Two daughters and a son had not altered that relationship, and the couple quietly separated sometime after 1915. With Hope's help, Jane eventually moved to Atlanta (where her son, Judson Lyons Jr., went to school) and secured employment at Morehouse as a matron. Eventually she became the dean of women at Spelman. It appears that the Lyonses never obtained a divorce, although they remained separated until Judson Lyons died in 1924. Their estrangement was kept a secret, although close friends and family must have known about it. The federal census of 1920 lists Jane Hope Lyons as a widow living on the Morehouse College campus in Atlanta. The same census shows that her husband, Judson Lyons, was still very much alive (and listed as married) and renting a house on Telfair Street in Augusta with two other men. Jane Hope Lyons remained in Atlanta until her own death many years later.[82]

Hope went back to work shortly after Madison's funeral, feeling more fatigued than usual. "Just now I am so awfully tired that I almost fear anybody can see it in my correspondence," he wrote to an old friend. "I have no aches or pains. I just feel as if I could knock off for the rest of my life, never striking another lick and not caring whether people called me lazy or not." At almost fifty-eight years old, Hope did not even consider working at a slower pace. He had trained himself to survive on five hours of sleep a night, but many nights even that much was a luxury. He thought his tiredness came from the stress of his work, but he was only partly correct. Early in May 1925 Hope underwent surgery for a hernia and was confined to MacVicar Infirmary on Spelman's campus for a little more than three weeks.[83]

Hope recognized his need for rest, and his friends and family tried to protect him from the problems of the outside world while he was recuperating. After he left the infirmary, Hope spent a few weeks at the Virginia vacation home of his friend Robert Moton. Hope and his family were frequently invited to Moton's isolated fortress "in paradise" but were usually too busy to accept. That summer there was no excuse. By the beginning of July, however, against his physicians' orders, Hope had resumed his activities. In his view he was simply too far behind in his work to stay away any longer. He needed to get back on schedule with his fund-raising, and there were final preparations to make for the 1925–26 academic year. In addition, requests from the CIC, the YMCA, and the NAACP were piling up on his desk.

Increasingly in the 1920s, Hope's work with the NAACP took the form of providing Du Bois with information for the *Crisis*. The 1925 article he penned himself on the Colored Department of the YMCA was a rare exception. More typical work involved answering Du Bois's requests for what was often very sensitive information. Early in the decade, for example, Du Bois asked Hope for details of any incidents in which Thomas Jesse Jones had tried to hamper his war work in France. Jones had upset many African American leaders with his disparaging remarks in South Africa about African American YMCA work and African Americans in general. Fearful of Marcus Garvey's influence in America, and already opposed to black missionary activity in Africa, Jones had reportedly convinced some European colonial officials not to allow African Americans to work in Africa at all.

It was no secret that many African American leaders, especially those of the New Negro era, distrusted Thomas Jesse Jones. The Phelps-Stokes Fund director's reluctance to endorse full equality for African Americans was well known, as was his negative view of African American higher education. American blacks, including Lugenia Hope, were very concerned that a man like Jones was considered a leading expert on African Americans in the United States.[84]

Though fully aware of the controversy, Hope was unable to provide Du Bois with any information to document his assumptions. In fact, he noted that Jones had been generally supportive of his work in France, and was not there long enough to adversely affect it anyway. And regardless of how African American leaders felt about him, Jones was a staunch supporter of John Hope. He used his influence with the Phelps-Stokes Fund to help Hope move Morehouse College forward and elevate Hope's popularity among prominent conservative whites. Certainly Hope's very cordial relationship with Jones owed much to his responsibilities as an African American college president dependent on white funds. But it seems their relationship extended into Hope's role as an African American leader as well, and Hope considered Jones an important ally if not a close personal friend.[85]

Before Hope went back to Morehouse for the beginning of the 1925–26 academic year, he and Lugenia went to Europe for the first time together on a trip that was part vacation and part work. He had been selected to be one of two African American delegates representing the World Council of the YMCA at the annual conference being held at Helsingfors, Finland. The Hopes also stopped in Le Zoute, Belgium, to attend a conference on African affairs. Perhaps with Thomas Jesse Jones in mind, Hope reportedly argued vigorously with officials of colonial governments to allow African Americans to work in Africa. Lugenia Hope later said that the conference reinforced John's desire to visit Africa, a dream deferred ever since his youth in Augusta.[86]

Since Lugenia was with him, Hope was careful to allow time to visit the places he had described to her back in 1912. He took her to England and introduced her to families he had met on that first trip. They also visited Scotland, where he again included the "stomping grounds" of Robert Burns (but not Langholm, the birthplace of his father) on the itinerary. The Hopes went to France and ran across Alain Locke in Paris, where they spent several days, Hope wrote to Edward, "slumming." The fastidious Locke, a Harvard graduate, philosophy professor, and the first African American Rhodes Scholar, had first met Hope in 1912, and the two had been good friends ever since. The Hopes returned to Atlanta early in September.[87]

As the fall term at Morehouse began, the students were still buzzing about the student strike that had occurred at Howard University the previous May. Howard students had always been more militant and less pious than students in the mission colleges. By the second half of the decade, their demands included the appointment of an African American president, more emphasis in classes on the "Negro experience," fewer religious services, and relaxation of the rigid rules and strict discipline.[88]

Hope did not support these demands, and he was especially concerned about the students' religious intolerance. He fervently believed in the efficacy of daily religious services, which helped to "develop community spirit, and gave a dignified and recreative effect to students in the work day." Given Hope's academic background both as student and as teacher, his views about Howard were predictable, and his own students were aware of his opposition.[89]

By the time Hope returned from Europe, President Durkee had resigned and Mordecai W. Johnson had been chosen as Howard's first African American president. Hope enthusiastically supported Johnson, a Morehouse man and former pupil. After a stellar student career at Morehouse, Johnson had gone on to get degrees from the University of Chicago and Harvard. The thirty-six-year-old Johnson had served on the Morehouse faculty, was a prominent Baptist minister, and like his former halfback and roommate at Morehouse, John W. Davis (who was president of black West Virginia Institute, later West Virginia State College), had served as a colored secretary for the YMCA. Johnson was much like Hope had been thirty years earlier. With his very fair complexion, Johnson could easily have passed for white. He was idealistic, energetic, deeply committed to his religious convictions, sharp, and articulate. He was also a race man and a part of the emergent New Negro leadership in the 1920s.[90]

The ouster of the presidents at Fisk and Howard epitomized the New Negro militancy on African American campuses. But there were other expressions of militancy as well. African American publications such as the *Messenger* and the very popular *Crisis* did not hesitate to openly criticize leaders like Robert Moton and Thomas Jesse Jones and conservative organizations like the

CIC. They also criticized the philanthropic foundations, which many thought had a choke hold on African American education. Philanthropists and other whites fearful of what they called "militant colored leadership" were nervous, and a call went out for a "frank discussion" of the "race problem" to be held at Yale University in December 1927.

The Rockefeller-sponsored gathering, called the Negro Problems Conference, took place on 19–21 December 1927 and was attended by an impressive group of black and white leaders in education and philanthropy, economics and business, race relations, and religion. Among others, the invitees included Howard's brilliant professor Ernest E. Just, Hope, Moton, and Mordecai Johnson in black education, and the new white president of Fisk, Thomas Elsa Jones. Also in attendance were black entrepreneur C. C. Spaulding of the North Carolina Mutual Life Insurance Company and Channing Tobias, who had replaced Jesse Moorland as director of the Colored Men's Department of the YMCA. The Brotherhood of Sleeping Car Porters' leader, A. Philip Randolph, represented organized labor, and Forrester Washington represented the Atlanta School of Social Work. Among the CIC members present were Will Alexander and Bishop Jones of the Methodist church. Charles S. Johnson and Eugene Knickle Jones represented the Urban League, and Arthur Spingarn and James Weldon Johnson represented the NAACP. Representing the philanthropists were Edwin Embree, Frank Stubbs, and Leonard Outhwaite of the Laura Spelman Rockefeller Memorial, and the controversial Thomas Jesse Jones of the Phelps-Stokes Fund. Unable to attend were Hampton Institute's James Gregg (who had his hands full with student unrest), Anson Phelps-Stokes, and Hollingsworth Wood. In all, twenty-two men (and no women) attended the conference.[91]

Some of the African American leaders were critical of the invited participants even before the conference began. James Weldon Johnson, for example, wrote to the conference organizer that "many felt most of the participants were members of the old guard . . . and were not in tune with the aspirations of the New Negro." Others complained because W. E. B. Du Bois, certainly the spiritual leader of the student protests and the man viewed by many as the quintessential black leader of the decade, was not invited.[92]

Though relatively quiet throughout the proceedings, Hope made several statements that were controversial for the 1920s, at least in the eyes of his New Negro colleagues. He reiterated his disgust with the Fisk University rebellion and was particularly critical of the students' disruptive behavior. In his opinion, the way to resolve grievances was through "patience and quiet diplomacy." He was opposed to student activism and believed that students' time was best spent concentrating on course work:

I feel that we run a risk of making our institutions not institutions of learning but institutions of propaganda. We ought to try to give to all of these colleges an atmosphere of learning and to bring students as little as possible into these discussions that are not going to help them at all but will withdraw them from their objective and their occupation which for the time being is improving their minds in order that they might take their place in life wherever it might be.[93]

Hope also continued his unequivocal support for the CIC. Beginning in 1922, the CIC received most of its funds from philanthropic organizations such as the relatively new Laura Spelman Rockefeller Memorial (another Rockefeller fund), the Phelps-Stokes Fund, the Carnegie Corporation, and the GEB. Those same foundations routinely denied requests from the financially strapped NAACP. Few of the conference participants knew that Hope had helped secure funding for the CIC and was a key figure in raising money to get the organization a $1 million endowment.[94]

Both Johnsons, Mordecai and James Weldon, with a barely veiled plea to the foundation representatives, tried to explain the NAACP's desperate need for funds to help prosecute its cases against segregation and discrimination. Hope, however, seemed to try to stifle their appeals: "I can see what the two Johnsons have in their minds," Hope said, "but in the South, you are going to find the Interracial Commission—we are talking quite among ourselves of the interracial movement." There was only silence from the two Johnsons. "In time," Hope went on, "there may be . . . no NAACP but the principles of it will survive." A voice was raised in opposition to Hope's vision of a future without the NAACP, but Hope interrupted and explained exactly what he meant: "Don't be weary. In due time you will reap. Sometimes it is a question of how to do it, or, as we say, a question of technique, and in the South you have got to almost find your technique for your individual community, but wherever negroes are thinking about their well-being through their rights and privileges, there the N.A.A.C.P. exists in spirit."[95]

Shortly after the conference Hope heard rumors that some of the African American leaders who had been there thought his comments were "uninspiring and outdated" and "far too conservative." He had even been labeled, he wrote to a white participant in the conference, an "obstacle to race progress." These remarks brought home to Hope his growing disfavor among the New Negro leadership. On the other hand, his popularity increased among whites, who viewed his remarks and role in the conference proceedings as further proof of his conservatism.[96]

Hope had no time to sit back and reflect on his comments at the conference, or to interpret blacks' and whites' reactions to them. Before the end of December he was in Cleveland addressing the annual meeting of his fraternity (which he had joined only a few years earlier), Alpha Phi Alpha. Shortly after that, there were last-minute preparations for what was perhaps his most celebrated trip abroad.

On 25 February 1928, John Hope boarded the SS *Adriatic* bound for Jerusalem as a delegate to the World Missionary Conference taking place from 18 March to 9 April. He was accompanied by Will Alexander, another of the more than 250 delegates to the conference. Hope was one of only two African Americans expected to address the international gathering. He was also scheduled to co-chair the session on race relations. Among other things, the race relations session was designed to examine the "spirit of racial unrest" that the conference organizers saw spreading through the world and come up with a "Christian solution" to the problem that would allow missionary activity to continue.[97]

Back in the States, African Americans anxiously awaited Hope's address to the representatives of the fifty nations that had sent delegates to the conference. On 31 March 1928, Hope presented an abbreviated version of a paper prepared for one of the many pamphlets made available to the conferees at the Jerusalem conference. The pamphlet was called *Christian Mission in the Light of Race Conflict*, and Hope's speech was entitled "The Relations between the Black and White Races in America."

Looking out over an international audience dressed in traditional clothing from Africa, the Philippines, Japan, Singapore, India, and Korea, as well as the United States and Europe, Hope began with a brief history of slavery in the United States. He was careful, however, to overlook the horrors of the institution, choosing instead to emphasize blacks' resilience. "Nowadays people spend far too much time in explaining how the Negro came to be where he is, whereas time might better be given to efforts to extricate the Negro from where he is and the white people from where they are." Throughout, Hope was careful to couch his address in the context of the American creed, a vision of what America could become instead of what it was. Yet he inextricably linked the country's future to its treatment of its black citizens. Being careful not to point an accusing finger, Hope predicted that continued discrimination would inevitably degenerate into class conflict and severely affect the moral character of the entire nation.

> I have interest in the race problem for the effect it will inevitably have on all people alike, on the victims and on those who do the victimizing. I am not blaming the people in America today for what has happened. Prejudice resulting in injustice may go on until it becomes a caste problem that may well-nigh become

insoluble. From now on injustice to Negroes may have a serious moral reaction on the white people even in their dealings with one another.[98]

Gone was the negative and pessimistic tone of the YMCA report Hope sent to Jesse Moorland after the First World War. The Jerusalem address was moderate, even conservative, when compared with the conference speeches that spotlighted racial problems in South Africa, the Philippines, and other countries. Hope said nothing, for example, about America's failure to pass anti-lynching legislation, the denial of political and social rights in the South, the lack of adequate educational facilities for African Americans, and the lack of opportunities for employment.

In the longer version of the speech that was published in the pamphlet, Hope credited the CIC with being the most viable solution to the race problem in the United States. Nowhere did he mention the work of the NAACP and its program to erase all forms of American racial discrimination. With that omission, the northern, urban-based New Negro militancy of the 1920s and the NAACP, its most active proponent of African American civil rights, lost a golden opportunity to have their goals recognized in an international arena. The participants of the Jerusalem conference left believing that the CIC was the only organization addressing the problems of America's blacks.[99]

The address may have been influenced by a letter Hope received from Thomas Jesse Jones in December 1927, before the Negro Problems Conference took place. It was a short and concise, "private and confidential" letter with very specific instructions about what Hope was expected to say at the Jerusalem conference: "You are to stress first the influence of Christianity in interracial developments in America, and, second, you shall direct your interpretation to show the importance of the Interracial Commission and all that has developed from it." Apparently, Hope, a black college president dependent on funds from conservative white philanthropists, did not deviate from his instructions.[100]

Privately, however, Hope's work behind the scenes showed his willingness to work quietly for many of the NAACP's objectives as long as it did not jeopardize his public image among whites as a conservative African American leader. As co-chair of the Race Relations Committee at the conference, he reportedly lobbied hard for universal suffrage throughout the world and an end to social and economic discrimination based on race. He also discouraged immigration quotas that were racially discriminatory and advocated "universal education free of prejudice and racial stereotypes." The chairman of the Missionary Council, John R. Mott, later pointed to Hope as one of the great "contributors that Spring in Jerusalem," and a London journalist wrote that Hope

was "one of the formative influences at the great Meeting in Jerusalem." Another journalist summed up the committee's general conclusion that Hope
"pleaded the Negro cause in terms of quiet yet irrefutable reasonableness
which could not be withstood."[101]

When he returned to the United States early in May, Hope was met by a
host of friends from the New York offices of the YMCA and the GEB, who
congratulated him on a job well done. When he examined the mail that had
accumulated over the two months of his absence, he found two letters that
would be of immediate importance. The first summoned him right away to
the offices of the General Education Board. He decided to postpone reading
the other, which was from his new and very competent administrative assistant, Constance Crocker.[102]

Only after his meeting with the GEB did Hope read the second letter. In it
was news from Morehouse so terrible that it caused him to forget, for the moment at least, how uplifted he had been by the Jerusalem conference and the
events surrounding it. A white proprietor had shot a young Morehouse student in the back and killed him instantly. The student's "crime"? He worked
part time as a newspaper delivery boy and had failed to remove his hat when
calling on the store owner to collect the monthly bill. Atlanta officials, and
many black leaders as well, had completely ignored the incident, and the mur-
derer was never even taken into custody.

For a moment—perhaps too brief a moment—the old John Hope returned.
He wrote to his secretary that "to think that while I was away holding up the
Atlanta Plan of Interracial Cooperation my own student should be killed without my community—my home—giving a tinker's damn about a nigger college
boy being killed, wantonly killed, because it does not matter if you kill a mere
nigger, for after all, white supremacy must be upheld."[103]

Shortly after arriving back in Atlanta, Hope was scheduled to address Morehouse students in the Tuesday chapel service. Deeply hurt by their classmate's
murder, they anxiously awaited their president's remarks. Hope later said that
he did not know, even as he rose to speak, if he would pass on his pain, disgust,
and contempt for Atlanta—the city that had already begun to boast of "being
too busy to hate." When at last he spoke, he chose not to mention the murder
at all. To the students' disappointment, the talk was simply a travelogue of
Hope's experiences in the Mediterranean that included platitudes about high
Christian ideals, the students' responsibilities as good citizens, and the need
to "follow the teachings of Jesus Christ." Florence Read, the president of
Spelman College, later said that it was Hope's Christian beliefs that caused
him throughout his life to use restraint when faced with racial injustice and
oppression. Yet, Read said, the murder of this student caused him to "die daily

renewing the necessity for making the great decision not to mention the incident to his students." [104]

But it was more than his religious views that caused Hope to remain silent about the murder. He had to think about the future of Morehouse College. Though the news would not become public for a few weeks, Hope had learned that Morehouse was about to receive another $300,000 for its endowment. With matching funds raised among African Americans, the money could raise the college's endowment to $1 million, providing the school with the security Hope felt it badly needed. Any political action, protest, or other disruptive activity on the part of Morehouse College students could have placed that gift in jeopardy—or even worse, resulted in a deadly racial conflict. Hope therefore kept his personal pain to himself and hoped the tensions would evaporate. [105]

Hope was soon swallowed up in the accolades earned by his leadership at the Jerusalem conference. Shortly after returning to Atlanta, the local Morehouse Club sponsored a banquet for Hope at which more than two hundred guests honored him as a national race leader and educational statesman. Smaller celebrations were sponsored by black YMCAs in New York, Chicago, and Cleveland. In July he was awarded an LL.D. degree from McMaster University in Toronto, Canada. Late in December 1928, the Atlanta chapter of the NAACP chose Hope to deliver the Emancipation Day address because of his "grasp upon world problems affecting the Negro race." [106]

The Atlanta NAACP's decision to honor Hope is especially significant because it shows that the South of the 1920s, where most African Americans continued to live, was in many ways different from the urban North. While the NAACP on the national level was endeavoring to eliminate all vestiges of segregation and discrimination, the southern branches were still fighting to bring about equality within the segregated system. Prominent local NAACP leaders such as A. T. Walden, G. A. Towns, and A. D. King were on the separate "colored" membership rolls of the local committee of the CIC along with practically every other prominent male and female leader in Georgia. The ever-present likelihood of explosive racial violence, coupled with blacks' lack of political power, created the need for a distinctively southern style of leadership based on the pragmatic needs of a population whose lives were dominated by the reality of a deeply entrenched and legally enforced segregation.

In the Deep South of the 1920s, African Americans understood that racial progress was often measured as much by improvements within the black world as by changes in the larger society. Progress had to include new, though segregated, organizations like the Community Chest as well as improved and expanded services in old organizations and institutions like the separate YMCA and African American colleges. It was not that there was no New Negro militancy in the South. There was. In addition to rebellions in African American colleges, some black students actually rejected and abandoned the Colored Department of the YMCA. Instead of talking about improving race relations separately or through a process of infrequent meetings, black students tried to merge their work with that of white students in an integrated national organization.[107]

The New Negro Movement, however, was a wide umbrella that covered a variety of activities. John Hope seemed to have his finger on the pulse of the African American South when, at the Negro Problems Conference, he kept alluding to the importance of the CIC. The few white southerners who addressed inequalities within the segregated system in the 1920s were celebrated as shining examples of racial progress. In Atlanta, for example, hardly a week went by without headlines in African American newspapers celebrating the "revolution in interracial relations." The usually secret CIC meetings were often held at the black Butler Street YMCA. Southern African American leaders publicly applauded southern white liberals' attempts to quietly reduce lynching and improve segregated facilities in public accommodations.

Though Du Bois was critical, Hope and other African American leaders in the South endorsed the "interracial press service" designed, according to the *Atlanta Independent*, "to interpret colored and white people to each other in the most favorable light consistent with the facts." Its objective was not to bring the races together, but to distribute articles that focused on "Negro achievement" and interracial cooperation in improving separate black conditions to more than two thousand white newspapers. African American leaders were often invited to local radio stations, like WSB in Atlanta, to talk about African American achievements and the things leaders like John Hope, Robert Moton, Mary McCloud Bethune, and Charles S. Johnson were doing to promote interracial goodwill and cooperation.

In general, African Americans in the South did not endorse the CIC's limited goals; nor did they offer much financial support to the CIC. Yet, given the distinct realities of southern black life, African Americans leaders could ill afford to reject any allies willing to address the immediate needs of African Americans in the region.[108]

At the end of the 1920s, John Hope was still recognized as an educational statesman and prominent leader in the South even though northern New Negro leaders such as James Weldon Johnson, Walter White, A. Philip Randolph, and George Schuyler of the *Pittsburgh Courier* had begun to have their doubts about his leadership. His friend Du Bois, however, seemed to understand. He, too, had lived in the South and recognized the terrible strain placed on southern leaders of both races. He had written to James Weldon Johnson earlier that "no southerner, white or black, can attack the South and stay there." Perhaps he alone recognized that John Hope had not abandoned his principles but rather had altered his tactics to fit the peculiar circumstances of a black college president operating in the South. Whether it was supplying information on controversial leaders like Thomas Jesse Jones, helping promote "causes" like the anti-lynching campaign, or securing a pension for the widow of war hero Colonel Charles Young, Du Bois knew he could always count on his Atlanta friend to promote the NAACP's objectives as well as the concerns of the larger African American community.[109]

Hope's dual roles were not easy for him in the 1920s. He appreciated the fact that philanthropic organizations like the GEB, the Phelps-Stokes Fund, the Rosenwald Fund, and the Carnegie Corporation had opened their financial coffers to support certain new areas of black development. Nevertheless, neither those foundations nor the new southern white liberals were ready to promote African American progress in a fully integrated and nondiscriminatory society. Hope's leadership and the continued development of Morehouse College were inextricably tied to a leadership paradigm that did not include some aspects of the New Negro militancy, which was often defiant, outspoken, proud, and uncompromising.

Yet, Hope's acceptance of a more conservative role in the 1920s to appease influential whites was only partly responsible for the stress he felt. Since philanthropic organizations required African Americans to contribute large matching sums in order to secure their financial gifts, Hope had to keep the good opinion of his own people as well. A man in his position could not stray far from the interests and concerns of African Americans in the South, whose lives were dictated largely by the exigencies of a separate black world. Although it kept him incredibly busy, Hope could not deny requests to be on the front lines of protests against unequal separate facilities. Within their enclosed world, African Americans in the South expected Hope, and other leaders, to try vigorously to save race institutions like the Standard Life Insurance Company, to be on the boards of the YMCA and other treasured organizations, and to support their separate lodges, fraternities, sororities, and other race enterprises, even if he was opposed to separation in principle. By the late 1920s, Hope had become a master of the balancing act.

At the 1927 Negro Problems Conference, Mordecai Johnson described how difficult it was for African American leaders, especially in the South, to remain an active part of the separate African American world while at the same time working hard to make that world someday fade away. For Johnson, black America operated as a separate nation within a nation that included both domestic relations and foreign relations. Domestic relations consisted of policies designed to improve the lives of the "black nation's" citizens; foreign relations had more to do with policies designed to improve relations with whites. "It would be perfectly foolish if we spent ninety percent of our time in foreign relations," Johnson said. "While we battle for liberty and equality we must develop these segregated institutions as if we expected them to last until the end of time." Johnson acknowledged that the two activities were inconsistent: "There will always be clashing in the soul, but both of them are absolutely necessary and must be carried on at the same time." As the 1920s ended, John Hope, an African American college president who was also a principled race leader, recognized that the clashing in his own soul would continue.[110]

11

"On Top of the Mountain"

On 1 April 1929, three presidents of African American colleges in Atlanta took turns signing an important document. Several historic photographs captured the session. One of them shows John Hope seated at a desk, appending his signature. To his left stands Florence Read of Spelman College, looking on with a smile of approval. On his right, also with his gaze fixed on the document, stands a more poker-faced Myron W. Adams, the outgoing president of Atlanta University. With the stroke of a pen, all three presidents had entered into an official affiliation that resembled nothing ever before seen in any Georgia college, black or white. A few months later, John Hope would become Atlanta University's first African American president and would begin his effort to lead the school in becoming a university in fact as well as in name.

Supporters of this revolutionary educational undertaking believed this affiliation was the beginning of the first and only "Negro university" in the Deep South. The blueprint for its future included schools of business, law, and medicine, and a community service component unmatched anywhere in black America. Snowy-haired John Hope, who in less than two months would celebrate his sixty-first birthday, was expected to bring this ambitious educational plan to fruition. At his insistence, he would do so while retaining the presidency of Morehouse College.

Hope's family and close friends were ambivalent about his new position. They knew there would be widespread criticism that would contribute to his already great stress. They also became disgusted with his refusal to curtail his responsibilities as a leader of the African American community, even after major surgery in 1929 and a near fatal heart attack in 1933. Ignoring Lugenia's misgivings, Hope would accept the presidency of the Commission on Interracial Cooperation (CIC), continue his work with the YMCA World Committee, and tackle new campaigns to benefit the black YMCA. The onset of the Great Depression would provide more opportunities for service outside academia. In 1933 Hope would head the "black side" of an advisory committee that brought the nation's first public housing project to Atlanta. These responsibilities, added to his duties as president of Atlanta University, would completely exhaust him.

Hope knew he was taking on too much. Yet all his adult life he had been unable to separate his roles as African American leader and college president. In 1929 he told Ludie Andrews, the director of Spelman's MacVicar Infirmary and a registered nurse: "I'm being asked to undertake this at an age when most men retire. I'm going to do it. But it's going to kill me." Perhaps Hope did not realize how close he was to the truth. He would live only another seven years. Before he died in 1936, like another southern African American leader who would follow thirty-two years later, Hope would reach the "top of the mountain and see the other side." He would not, however, be allowed to cross over.

According to the official version of events, the seed of the Atlanta University Affiliation was sown at the National Interracial Conference held in Washington, D.C., late in 1928. Approximately 150 delegates representing sixteen national organizations gathered to discuss contemporary black life and American race relations in the light of the most recent social science research. In fact, the official version is not quite correct.

John Hope attended that conference and delivered an unexpected speech at an evening session at the Howard University Medical School that attracted the attention of some influential delegates.[1] In his speech, entitled "Educational Achievements and Needs," Hope reminded the group of blacks' contributions to their own education before the Civil War, of an antebellum African American culture that included music, poetry, and an evangelical religion based on a belief in service that only deepened with the coming of the "Yankee schoolteachers." In Hope's view, that commitment to service had not diminished in 1928, yet public education facilities were still inadequate; African Americans needed medical training and opportunities for clinical practice. In closing, he challenged both races to go beyond their narrow focus on the "Negro problem" and think about the "best interests of both races." When he finished, the shouts of encouragement and standing ovation caught him by surprise.[2]

Hope left the next morning, on 17 December, to continue working on the Morehouse endowment campaign. That evening, the official version continues, Will Alexander of the CIC reportedly joined Jackson Davis of the GEB, Beardsley Ruml of the Laura Spelman Rockefeller Memorial, and Edwin Embree of the Rosenwald Fund at a dinner meeting at which Hope and the

Atlanta schools came up as a topic of conversation. "We're tired of giving out little dots of money first to one college, then to another, in Atlanta," Jackson said to Alexander. "There ought to be some way to bring them together." Ruml then turned to Alexander and said: "Damn it, you ought to do this." Alexander, who was a member of the Atlanta University Board of Trustees, took a morning walk the next day with twenty-six-year-old Clark Howell Foreman, a resolute interracial leader and the grandson of the publisher of the *Atlanta Constitution*. When asked what he thought about the Atlanta school situation, Foreman replied: "Why not elect John Hope as president of Atlanta University and then take the necessary steps to merge the institutions." These exchanges led to the widely circulated reports that the proposal to make John Hope Atlanta University's president and then merge the three schools emerged from the 1928 National Interracial Conference.[3]

Nothing could be further from the truth. The official version of the events leading to the affiliation and Hope's appointment as successor to President Adams appears to have been calculated to obscure the role of the philanthropists, especially the General Education Board, in the project. It had always been the official policy of the GEB to deny allegations that it encouraged educational institutions to move in *any* direction. The board preferred to make it look as though the initiative for change came from within. In fact, the GEB had been quietly suggesting different forms of cooperation among Atlanta schools for twenty years, especially among Morehouse, Spelman, and Atlanta University because of their close proximity. One early GEB proposal, vehemently rejected by Morehouse and Spelman, offered to develop Atlanta University into a college, with Morehouse and Spelman becoming high schools that would provide the majority of AU students. A few years later, in 1915, the Phelps-Stokes Fund quietly funded a joint course in Business Law and Ethics for Morehouse College and Atlanta University to engender closer affiliation. In spite of these efforts and others, there was very little meaningful cooperation between the institutions until the late 1920s.[4]

As early as 1904, while he was still a teacher at Atlanta Baptist College, Hope had envisioned an Atlanta university system that incorporated all the city's African American colleges. He had written in the premiere issue of the *Voice of the Negro* that someday all the schools would come together and "develop spheres of influence," with Atlanta University becoming a graduate school and "confining itself to the social sciences and *Belles Lettres*."[5] For most of his twenty-three years at the helm of Morehouse College, however, Hope had been lukewarm to consolidation. The black Atlanta schools had directed most of their energy and resources into becoming colleges in fact as well as in name, and each had deeply rooted traditions to guard. Hope believed there was too much denominational rivalry and competition in academics and athletics (especially between Morehouse and Atlanta University) to achieve meaningful cooperation, much less consolidation. Each school feared losing its unique identity. All were committed to meeting the educational needs of African Americans, but they wanted to meet that responsibility as separate collegiate enterprises with individual and distinct (and often denominational) historical identities.[6]

During the 1920s John Hope gradually modified his stance on close cooperation. It was probably not coincidental that the increase in philanthropic contributions to Morehouse after the First World War occurred at precisely the same time that Hope privately began to work with the American Baptist Home Mission Society and the GEB to engender more cooperation between Atlanta's African American colleges. Minutes of ABHMS board meetings show that as early as January 1920, George Rice Hovey, the ABHMS secretary, and John Hope were appointed as a "committee of two to confer with representatives of other Boards and schools with reference to the establishment of a university for Colored people in Atlanta, Georgia." In 1925 Thomas Jesse Jones of the Phelps-Stokes Fund got permission from the ABHMS to have Hope review and evaluate all the black schools in the South. What Hope thought about his expanded role with the philanthropists is impossible to discern. He still adamantly opposed consolidation at that time, but he was beginning to believe that closer cooperation posed no threat to Morehouse College. Pressure to move in that direction continued to mount.[7]

Cooperation among the black Atlanta institutions by the end of the 1920s or early 1930s was only the first step in a larger plan generated by the educational foundations. Their research and frequent trips south showed that college departments in most of the established black schools were increasing in size. Foundation officials interpreted that to mean that more graduate and professional opportunities were needed in the region to keep pace with the increasing number of black college graduates.

Members of the education boards remained conservative in their outlook on race relations. Though generally supportive of black progress in education, they continued to believe that progress would (and perhaps should) take place mainly along separate, race-specific lines. Since southern white universities were out of the question for African Americans and northern white universities could accept only a limited number, most of the blacks headed to graduate or professional schools would have to rely on opportunities within segregated black America. A few programs already existed at Howard University and Fisk; however, the five African American schools in Atlanta appeared to offer an excellent opportunity to continue the philanthropic policy of providing black opportunity along lines that did not challenge southern convention.[8]

Aware of the larger picture, the GEB quietly flexed its financial muscle.

Atlanta University, lacking the Rockefeller backing of Spelman or the Baptist support of Morehouse, had fallen on hard times. The school depended solely on its limited endowment, student fees, contributions from loyal alumni, and gifts from friends to meet its financial obligations. In spite of an annual grant of $12,000 from the GEB, Atlanta University had been plagued by large deficits for most of the twentieth century. By the mid-1920s the northern philanthropists had decided Atlanta University's undergraduate programs duplicated those already being vigorously supported at Spelman and Morehouse and began to withdraw their financial support. At the same time the philanthropists were being especially generous with endowment gifts to Morehouse and Spelman, they turned down requests from Atlanta University. A GEB official in 1925 responding to one of AU's many requests for financial help summed up the board's position: "The future of Atlanta University is tied up into closer cooperation with the other Negro colleges of the city. I shall be . . . delighted if some constructive plans for coordination and cooperation could be worked out."[9]

The General Education Board also took advantage of other opportunities to encourage cooperation. After thirty-seven years of service at Spelman College as a teacher and president, Lucy Hale Tapley announced plans to retire at the end of the 1926–27 academic year. The GEB moved quickly to replace her with Florence M. Read, a Phi Beta Kappa graduate of Mount Holyoke College who was already on the payroll of the New York–based Rockefeller Foundation as the executive secretary of the International Health Board. Read, forty-one years old, had served overseas in France during the First World War, but her only college administrative experience had been as secretary to the president of Reed College in Portland, Oregon. Nevertheless, the New York–born Read was a dynamo of boundless energy—just the person, the philanthropists believed, to develop Spelman into a top-notch liberal arts school for African American women and help move the other schools toward consolidation. A GEB memorandum from May 1927 indicates that several members of the education board met with John D. Rockefeller Jr. at the Princeton Inn in New Jersey and virtually decided to offer Read the presidency. She took office as Spelman College's fourth president on 1 July 1927.[10]

Hope had given his endorsement to Read's candidacy several months before that, but he also believed it was time to begin thinking about an African American woman as a future president for Spelman College. He had told John H. Dillard that "you could hardly have a colored woman at once, but . . . steps could begin in the direction of this." He did believe Spelman needed at least "half a dozen well educated young colored women as teachers" as soon as possible.[11]

When Read met Hope, she soon realized that he, too, although twenty years her senior, seemed blessed with unlimited energy. Hope and Lucy Tapley, Spelman's former president, had hardly interacted at all. Tapley had insisted on maintaining a code of southern etiquette that made it difficult for a real friendship to develop between a black man and a white woman. Florence Read, a newcomer to the South, brought a different code of behavior with her. She had worked closely with men in Oregon and New York, and she refused to honor Old South traditions when she arrived in Atlanta.

Years later, Read confided in an interview that shortly after her arrival at Spelman, Hope escorted Sir Gordon Guggisberg, then governor of the Gold Coast (now Ghana), to Read's residence at Reynolds Cottage after showing him the Morehouse campus. Read asked Hope to join the group for lunch, which also included Governor Guggisberg's official host, white southerner Clark Foreman. This may have been the first time an African American was asked to dine at the presidential cottage of Spelman College with a white southerner present. Caught off-guard, Hope declined the invitation, but less than a week later he wrote Read a strong letter of appreciation: "I think for one brief instant last week I saw you to the very innermost recesses of your soul. . . . When you asked me to dine, your very soul flung defiance at prejudice, snobbery, and a vicious outworn aristocracy." A new chapter had been written in the history of Spelman College, he proclaimed. Ever the classicist, he wrote to Read, "I think the god Thor smiled approval at his daughter. . . . The girls will feel her spirit though she may never say a word, and they will grow into the stature of their teacher." Thus began a close, and for some a controversial, friendship that would last until Hope's death.[12]

Read's developing friendship with Hope did not alter her responsibility as an agent of the GEB and the Rockefeller Foundation to help move the Atlanta schools toward cooperation. She had participated in several conversations with board members toward that end, and in September 1927 she was instructed to inform Hope that GEB president Wickliffe Rose needed to have a "long conversation" with him in New York. No notes were made of that conversation, but no doubt Rose revealed concrete plans for the affiliation in Atlanta and invited Hope to suggest other possibilities for black educational cooperation in the South.

After talking over the matter with GEB member Jackson Davis and Florence Read, Hope wrote a long letter to Rose voicing his approval. "To my mind," he wrote, "Atlanta is unquestionably well situated to become a great, if not the great, educational center for Negroes." He was particularly interested in developing a black medical center in Atlanta that would provide "Negro physicians and Negro nurses well trained in the field of public health." His vision then included Spelman, Morehouse, and Clark Colleges preparing undergraduates for the field of medicine, and Atlanta University becoming the medical school. Hope was shrewd enough to contextualize his comments about the medical center as a proposal that would "reach out into all the South as a project in interracial relations." Foreseeing a possible conflict with the training of white physicians at another local university, he wrote to Wickliffe that "Emory University could play a leading part in this movement without her students losing much of any advantage that they now have in the Negro ward of the Grady (city) Hospital."[13]

Elated with Hope's willingness to consider some form of cooperation, the GEB immediately intensified its efforts to move Atlanta University, Morehouse, and Spelman in that direction. On 22 December 1927, H. J. Thorkelson, then director of the college and university education division of the GEB, held individual conferences with Hope, Read, and Adams in Atlanta. It was then that Hope learned of the $300,000 addition to the Morehouse endowment. Thorkelson also casually mentioned the possibility of building a new library that would benefit Morehouse, AU, and Spelman, as well as the other Atlanta schools, if land could be found for it in the immediate vicinity. Two days later, President Adams of Atlanta University sent GEB officials a letter that discussed the possibility of expanding joint courses with Morehouse and Spelman with an ultimate goal of "some form of university organization with different constituent elements, some of them in due time graduate, and with some mutually agreed upon distribution of work between these different constituents."[14]

The GEB's maneuvering continued into the next year. In January 1928, the GEB rejected President Adams's suggestion that the board initiate a conference on cooperation because, Thorkelson said, "such a move should come from the colleges themselves." Nevertheless, Thorkelson wrote to T. B. Appleget, a Rockefeller representative, who with the approval of John D. Rockefeller Jr. began to secretly acquire land Hope had identified as a possible site for the library. A dummy Rockefeller company called the Seaboard Realty Company was created to serve that purpose, and by late fall the necessary land between Morehouse and Spelman had been acquired. Publicly, Hope remained lukewarm to cooperation, and that worried other education boards like the Slater Fund. He was unwilling to endorse any of the proposals then being floated in public until he could see a blueprint he could approve. No such plan had surfaced in the first part of 1928.[15]

By the time of the Morehouse commencement in May 1928, Hope was beginning to get a clearer picture of the possibilities. He observed a model of cooperation that summer when he received his honorary doctor of laws degree from McMaster University in Canada and spent some time at the University of Toronto. In the 1880s, Baptist-run McMaster University had declined an invitation to join the University of Toronto federation, which included an

Episcopalian, Methodist, Presbyterian, and even a Catholic college. Nevertheless, Hope was impressed with the federation's many professional schools and liberal arts colleges, each with the right to award its own theological degree. He later talked about the "Toronto merger" with Florence Read, Lugenia, and his administrative assistant, Constance Crocker Nabrit (Crocker had married Samuel Nabrit, a Morehouse faculty member, in 1927).

With the assistance of the GEB, Hope and Read conducted their first joint six-week summer school session in 1928. Since the joint project included a college course, Atlanta University reluctantly abandoned the eight-week program it had conducted for the last three years and joined Morehouse and Spelman to avoid duplication. Hope enthusiastically endorsed the GEB's decision to construct the joint library, and he encouraged Morris Brown College to move into the vicinity. Even by John Hope's exacting standards, the blueprint for effective cooperation was beginning to take shape by the summer of 1928.[16]

The events discussed above prove that the National Interracial Conference of 1928 was not the site of the first attempt to bring about cooperation among Atlanta's African American schools, nor was Clark Foreman the first person to mention Hope as a possible successor to President Adams. Further, GEB records of the important meeting that took place during the 1928 Washington conference in some respects contradict Will Alexander's recollections, which were recorded almost sixteen years later.

A meeting had actually been scheduled in the Biltmore Hotel room of the incoming GEB president, Trevor Arnett, specifically to discuss closer cooperation between the Atlanta schools. Alexander and the others identified earlier attended that meeting after their famous dinner conversation. In addition to Arnett, they were joined by W. D. Weatherford, Florence Read, and GEB member Leo Favrot. The NAACP's James Weldon Johnson, a graduate of AU and a member of the school's board of trustees, was also present, as was another AU graduate and board member, Willette R. Banks. Arnett opened the meeting by stating that the "time was propitious" for moving ahead on closer cooperation between Atlanta University, Morehouse, and Spelman because Adams would soon retire. According to a GEB memo from January 1929, Hope emerged as the group's first choice to replace Adams. Florence Read was directed to contact both Adams and Hope as soon as she returned to set up a meeting in January with Arnett, Favrot, and Ruml.[17]

By the middle of January 1929, the presidents of Morehouse, Atlanta University, and Spelman had secretly agreed to design a concrete plan of cooperation. John Hope also tentatively agreed to lead the effort, prompting Arnett to write in January that Hope was enthusiastic about the opportunity and "would be ready to undertake it with the whole-hearted cooperation of the friends of all three institutions." Privately, however, Hope still had reservations. While he was excited about the opportunity to make Atlanta a center for African American higher education, he knew there would be rough days ahead. Creating a cooperative spirit among the three schools, especially between Morehouse College and Atlanta University, would be exceedingly difficult.[18]

Some prominent whites involved in the secret deliberations were also concerned. They, too, understood that the affiliation was fraught with difficulties. Hope was the leading candidate because of his stature as an educational statesman and the respect he was accorded as an African American leader in the South. Despite such assets, however, Hope was not without liabilities. As late as the middle of January 1929, Will Alexander had serious doubts that the AU alumni would accept John Hope as president. A GEB member wrote that "already the alumni trustees are alert and suspicious, loyal to the old 'A.U.'" Jackson Davis of the GEB and W. D. Weatherford of the CIC and YMCA believed Hope's loyalty to Morehouse might ultimately prevent him from taking the position. Yet they were even more concerned that if anyone other than Hope was offered the presidency, the Morehouse alumni would reject the entire proposal. "My, my," wrote still another GEB board member, "it makes my heart sink when I foresee what a wrangle we may be in for."[19]

The three presidents worked hard in January, February, and March to hammer out a plan for closer cooperation. The final document that emerged was called the "Contract of Affiliation" and was officially signed by Hope, Read, and Adams in New York on the first of April 1929. They avoided the terms *consolidation* and *merger*, opting instead for *affiliation*. The contract provided for Morehouse and Spelman to limit their curricula to liberal arts undergraduate studies. Atlanta University would become the graduate school. Although each school maintained its individual board of trustees and management, a "university board" was created with an equal number of representatives selected from all three schools. The member schools would continue to raise funds individually, but not without consultation with and the mutual understanding of all three institutions. Although the other Atlanta colleges were in time expected to enter the affiliation, their admittance required the approval of the three original colleges, which could also withdraw with one year's notice.[20]

At the signing of the contract, the Atlanta University Board of Trustees unanimously invited John Hope to become president on 1 July 1929, the date President Adams would officially retire. Still Hope hesitated and asked for more time to think it over. There remained the question of his age; his wife was especially concerned about his physical condition; and negative reactions were sure to come from both Morehouse College and Atlanta University and their alumni. Moreover, there was also the Morehouse endowment campaign to consider.

Above all else, however, Hope knew that his refusal might be even more debilitating than his acceptance. If he declined, the affiliation would be still-born and might never come into existence. He had too much vision to allow that to happen. "If this affiliation did not occur," he later wrote, "it would be a definite and permanent backset to higher education for Negroes in one of the most important centers for Negroes in the United States." After more than thirty years as Atlanta University's "almost next-door neighbor," he knew the territory better than anyone else. Thus, in spite of the myriad problems sure to come, he reasoned later, anticipating criticism perhaps even after his death, "I was the man that could come nearer harmonizing things for all three schools than any other man that might have been appointed at that time."[21]

As an experienced college president well aware of the political economy of African American higher education, Hope knew that all three schools were tied to the purse strings of the GEB and other philanthropic foundations, which had played a major role in helping to bring the affiliation agreement to fruition. Low profiles and official policies notwithstanding, Hope knew that the GEB "wanted this thing to happen." There had been no assurances that the financial coffers of any of the three newly affiliated schools would swell, but the philanthropists were in a cooperative mode, and it was clear that the future of Morehouse was tied to the affiliation. Hope wrote later that "common sense and faith seemed to me to indicate that the affiliation would be a success, and that Morehouse's chances for actual life and development depended upon her coming in. It seemed to me it was the only thing to do. I therefore undertook the task."[22]

Hope's acceptance of the Atlanta University presidency included a deal unprecedented in the history of African American higher education. He did not feel comfortable turning over the Morehouse endowment campaign to Dean Samuel Archer, who admittedly was no more interested in fund-raising now than he had been during the First World War. In order to "put Morehouse on a sound basis," Hope thus accepted his new position without relinquishing the Morehouse presidency. He later wrote to his son Edward that "nothing but death could separate me from my interest in Morehouse." Understanding Hope's commitment to Morehouse College, the GEB accepted his proposition. In addition, GEB members correctly believed Hope's retention of the Morehouse presidency would reduce opposition to the affiliation from Morehouse. Hope remained president of both schools until 1931, when Archer was selected Morehouse College's fifth president.[23]

Hope could not totally immerse himself in the creation of the Atlanta University graduate school until he had completed the Morehouse endowment campaign. He would have to work harder—and much faster—to secure the college's financial future. For that reason he spent most of the early months of the affiliation on the road, crisscrossing the country on fund-raising trips. In April, after the affiliation agreement was signed, Hope spent eight days in Chicago, speaking both day and night in an attempt to secure funds for Morehouse. He planned to make as many trips as he could before the May commencement. It was a pace he surely could not maintain.[24]

Hope was aware that he was pushing his aging body dangerously close to its physical limits. Though he rarely discussed it, ever since his hernia surgery in 1925 he had lived with daily aches and pains—and a constant fatigue—that he associated with growing older. Particularly after the affiliation, Hope's deteriorating health became a sore point in his relationship with his wife, who for years had tried to convince him to take better care of himself. Lugenia Hope had always expected to leave Atlanta someday, but "I suppose that is not for us" she wrote to Edward in March 1929. After the affiliation, it seems that John and Lugenia, instead of talking with each other about the subject, increasingly vented their frustrations with other family members and close friends. In public, Lugenia Hope appeared enthusiastic about the new alliance. Privately, she had grave reservations about her husband taking on such an enormous responsibility. She confided to Edward on 1 May: "You know how head strong he is and he refuses to think of self at all. He can't stay fit if he works all night, goes all day and attends all the meetings—accepts all the possible invitations to speak everywhere in the U.S. and Europe—forgets self entirely. You know Edward the world wants you for your services [and] when you can't render service anymore it junks you."[25]

Lugenia Hope's disgust was no secret to her husband. Even as he avoided direct confrontations with her, he acknowledged her anger to friends like Robert Moton. "Genie is egregiously disgusted with me. I can tell it every time I come home and every time I depart from home. It isn't fair to her or the boys. But here I keep on working and deferring and postponing and procrastinating." Though he dared not mention it to Lugenia, Hope also told Moton that he was not feeling well. In his characteristic way, he tried to make light of it by enclosing the acknowledgment between a few lines of humor: "Of course Moton," he wrote, "there is a bare possibility that a man might have sense enough even to be president of a university, that he himself must build up, and yet be such a plumb fool that he does not look after his own physical condition. I am not saying that I have sense enough to build up a university, but I am saying that I am too big a fool to look after my personal interests."[26]

After a thirty-year friendship, Hope's veiled message did not go over Robert

Moton's head. He sensed that Hope felt worse than he actually indicated. For months Moton had been insisting that Hope visit the Mayo Clinic in Rochester, Minnesota, to get a thorough physical examination. Finally, knowing his friend so well, he bypassed Hope and wrote directly to the Mayo Clinic on Hope's behalf. Hope reluctantly went to Rochester early in May, submitted to a physical, and learned that he needed to have the hernia surgery of 1925 repeated. His tonsils were bad, and he also needed further tests on what appeared to be a malfunctioning prostate. Accompanied by Lugenia, who also needed a physical—and a tonsillectomy—Hope returned to the Mayo Clinic in June for what he expected to be a short stay. He had been assured that he would be back at work in three weeks. But Hope was slow to recover, and his physicians advised him to recuperate for the remainder of the summer.[27]

The month he spent at the Mayo Clinic provided ample time for deep introspection. In the last years of his life, Hope shared many of his deepest thoughts with Florence Read of Spelman and his administrative assistant, Constance Crocker Nabrit, the two people in Atlanta he needed most to help him bring his vision of a great "Negro University in the Deep South" to fruition. His letters to them show that he had begun to come to grips with his own mortality. He wrote to Read that he could "sometimes almost hear the Corybantes." He often had more questions than answers: "I wonder what it is all about—this coming into the world, struggling to stay, fighting fortune and disease, and finally yielding to the inevitable. Why not yield to the inevitable at the beginning rather than the end?" To Constance Nabrit he wrote more of the same.[28]

Hope also had time in Rochester to answer many of the congratulatory messages he had received on his appointment as president of Atlanta University. He was particularly pleased with Du Bois's editorial in the *Crisis*. "Little has been said and written of John Hope," Du Bois wrote, "because he is not the kind of man that wants or allows personal reference." Like Hope, Du Bois also recognized Atlanta's tremendous potential as a major educational center. The *Crisis* editor continued to soothe and comfort Hope with public pronouncements that showed he understood the constraints under which Hope operated. A letter Hope wrote to Du Bois on 2 June 1929, his sixty-first birthday, indicates that he expected his friend to play a role in developing the new Atlanta University. No other school—except, perhaps, Fisk—meant as much to Du Bois as Atlanta University, where he had spent thirteen very important years. In time, Du Bois did join Hope at the new graduate school.[29]

John Hope decided to put the development of Atlanta University on hold for the rest of the summer of 1929 and heed the advice of his physicians to take a much-needed vacation. Rather than being delighted, however, Lugenia was livid. She knew that Hope's "vacations" generally involved work in his alternate role as an African American leader. She was not incorrect. Hope had committed to attend the YMCA World Committee meeting in Geneva, Switzerland, early in 1929. That was, of course, before the announcement of the affiliation, before he had accepted the presidency of AU, and, most important, before his surgery at the Mayo Clinic. Hope's contributions to the World Committee meeting would include making speeches, drafting committee resolutions, and meeting with international diplomats from all over the world. He tried to placate Lugenia by insisting that it really was a vacation because he would take time to relax in several other European cities that were included on the expenses-paid trip. Lugenia was not convinced.

Nevertheless, Hope sailed for Europe on 25 July 1929. The voyage gave him more time to think about his remaining years. Once again he wondered if he would ever visit sub-Saharan Africa. He had earlier written to Edward: "The truth is this new arrangement has knocked your Dad's personal hopes and plans into a cocked hat, for I intended after raising the endowment to get away for at least six months and visit Africa. That has been my wish for the past five years." Hope was beginning to understand that his health and responsibilities at Atlanta University would prohibit him from ever realizing his African dream.[30]

As if by fate, the trip allowed Hope to channel his African interests in an unexpected direction. Disgusted with the "Second Cabin crowd," Hope ventured into third class in search of "our people" and discovered a group of teenagers and young adults who were headed to Moscow. "I began talking with the entire group so as not to seem to be singling out the colored boy," he wrote to Lugenia. Another young man of color soon entered the group, and Hope learned that he was Balamu Mukasa, a native of Uganda. The story from that point on is a Morehouse College legend.

At the Jerusalem conference in 1928, Hope had promised Sirwano W. Kulubya, a delegate from Uganda, that he would sponsor a Ugandan student at Morehouse College. Mukasa, a student of King's College in Uganda (actually a secondary school within the British system), overcame insurmountable odds to secure the scholarship and left his country to attend Morehouse. But he failed to notify Hope that he was coming. With no idea of the size of the United States, Mukasa arrived in New York looking for "Dr. John Hope." He eventually contacted Morehouse while Hope was in the Mayo Clinic and was informed by Dean Archer that "he knew of no arrangement for any student who could not meet the entrance requirements [Mukasa had not completed all of his high school work], pay the tuition fees, and meet his living expenses." Frustrated in his efforts and terrified by New York, Mukasa decided to return to Uganda. It was mere chance that he and Hope had traveled on the same ship.[31]

Hope made arrangements for Mukasa to return to the United States, where he remained for seven years, the first five of them in the Hope household. Hope became his benefactor and a surrogate father to whom Mukasa turned for advice on just about everything. After Mukasa completed his B.A. degree at Morehouse in 1935, Hope used his influence to secure the young Ugandan a graduate school scholarship to Yale University. After he received his master's degree in education, Mukasa returned to Uganda and taught for many years at Makerere University. One of his early students was Julius Nyerere, a leader in the African Independence Movement and Tanzania's first president after independence. By 1961, Mukasa had become Uganda's minister of education and agriculture.[32]

It is apparent from his letters home that Hope had not yet recovered from his ordeal at the Mayo Clinic. The handwritten words seem to vibrate across the page, as if they were written with an unsteady hand. In a rare instance, Hope shared his true feelings about his health to Lugenia. Their short walks in Rochester had fooled him into thinking, he wrote, that he was "his old self again." Now, in Europe, when he wanted to walk, his health demanded that he ride; when he wanted to stand, his health insisted that he sit—and on occasion lie down. "Nobody is telling me to do this," he wrote to Lugenia, "my body and my own sense tell me."[33]

Five days later, on 8 August 1929, Hope wrote a letter to his administrative assistant, Constance Crocker Nabrit. At ten o'clock that night he appended a revealing and emotional postscript. As one of four official representatives of the World Committee, Hope had just attended the funeral of the English economist Harold A. Grimshaw, who had championed the abolition of forced labor, especially in Africa. Hope was impressed with the ceremony's simplicity. The average funeral's "pomp and expense" seemed to him "flat and futile." He wrote to Nabrit, "If you are about when they are planning for me, do not let them do expensive things and lying things, but make it brief and honest; make it simple. Do not let the halting be too long." He then appended an eerie closing: "People should do their work and not spend too much time with the dead."[34]

Hope returned to Atlanta late in August 1929 and immediately plunged into the work of running two colleges. Mornings and early afternoons were spent at Morehouse College; the remainder of the afternoons and early evenings were spent at Atlanta University or at Spelman College with Florence Read, working on the plans for the new graduate school. Dean Archer addressed the day-to-day administrative functions at Morehouse, freeing Hope to set up appointments to solicit funds for the Morehouse endowment. The American

Baptist Home Mission Society had for years confined Morehouse and its other schools to certain northern locales when soliciting funds from white people. According to ABHMS board records, in 1929 those rules were abolished, allowing unrestricted solicitation. Hope also taught one class and allotted some time for meetings with Morehouse students, and he spent a good deal of time trying to convince suspicious Morehouse alumni that Atlanta University had not "absorbed their school." A contemporary student said in an interview years later that "there was a general belief that Hope had sold out to the big A.U. 'thing.'"[35]

The Morehouse alumni's suspicions barely made a ripple compared with the storm that exploded at Atlanta University when the affiliation was announced. The AU alumni looked at the affiliation as a dismantling of their institution, and in many ways they were correct. Most of the faculty members at Morehouse and other liberal arts schools for African Americans had only bachelor's degrees and were expected to be able to teach any subjects they had taken in college. New standards of accreditation in the late 1920s had shifted the academic tide in a new direction, even for undergraduate education, and specialization was certainly the rule for graduate schools. For that reason, most of the faculty at Atlanta University had to be replaced with specialists with earned M.A. degrees, and ultimately Ph.D.s.[36]

John Hope was saddled with the responsibility of replacing most of the AU faculty. It was a delicate issue, for Hope himself had earned only a bachelor's degree and could not have taught at the new graduate school. Rumors abounded, reaching practically everyone with any interest in the welfare of Atlanta University and its highly respected, but aging, faculty. The rumors even reached Du Bois at the *Crisis*, causing him to send a rare curt inquiry to John Hope asking for "the facts." Hurt by the tone of Du Bois's letter, Hope responded: "Among my many riches, friends stand at the head of the list. I have always had friends, and I have become so used to friendship that I doubt seriously what would become of me if my real friends failed me. Your recent letter is a message from a friend; and I thank you for it."[37]

Hope then proceeded to give Du Bois "the facts." Neither of the two people Du Bois mentioned specifically in his letter had been dismissed from Atlanta University without compensation. Along with ten others, including President Adams and Hope's good friend George A. Towns, they had received retirement allowances voted by the newly reorganized board of trustees "for teachers who had for many years devotedly given their services to Atlanta University." Hope had successfully encouraged the board to extend the allowances for at least another academic year. He was including a confidential list that included the names of all the retirees in a separately enclosed letter, Hope wrote to Du Bois, so "that you may see, not only the spirit of the Board of Trustees and of myself, but also the enactments that have already occurred in the interest of these workers." [38]

In spite of the many distractions, and some physical discomfort, Hope plowed forward in his new role as president of Atlanta University. Working closely with Constance Nabrit and Florence Read, he developed a series of five-, six-, and ten-year plans that included expanding existing academic programs, new facilities, and an updated physical plant. At the top of the list were a graduate school of liberal arts, a school of library science, a graduate school of social work closely affiliated with the Atlanta School of Social Work, and a graduate department of business administration. His vision for the future included new programs in teacher education and fine arts, and, with the cooperation of Atlanta's other black schools, an interdenominational theology program and schools of medicine, law, and dentistry.

With the backing of the foundations, Hope believed he was helping to create an African American university system in Atlanta that would someday include all the city's black colleges. The first step in that process had been the three-college affiliation. In addition to the specifics of developing new programs, however, Hope needed to create a more harmonious relationship between the affiliated schools and decide when the time was right to bring in the other Atlanta institutions. [39]

Had John Hope been able to concentrate solely on the development of the new Atlanta University, his last years might have been less strenuous. It was simply not to be. The stock market crash of October 1929 ushered in the worst depression in United States history. By 1930, Atlanta, like the rest of America, was feeling the full impact of the Great Depression. African Americans tended to lose their jobs first, creating unprecedented economic hardships. Contemporaries remembered people on the streets in Atlanta selling apples, children going through garbage cans, and abandoned houses being torn down for firewood. Hope later remarked that it was a "pitiful sight to see these impoverished human beings waiting in segregated soup lines, tin buckets in hand, to receive their daily rations of food." [40]

The Depression not only affected Hope's ability to raise money for the Morehouse endowment, it also escalated the demand for his services as an African American leader. Racial tensions increased throughout the South, and Hope responded by stepping up his participation in the CIC. The economic hardships affected both interracial and intraracial organizations all across the country, and Hope committed himself to raising funds to help the NAACP, the Urban League, the CIC, the YMCA, and numerous other organizations survive the Depression. With no hesitation, Hope divided his time between his commitment to develop the new Atlanta University and what he believed was expected of him by the black community.

It did not take long for an already volatile racial atmosphere in Atlanta to get worse. In June 1930 an organization called the American Facisti Order of the Black Shirts, patterned after fascist organizations in Germany, emerged in Georgia and a few other southern states. The Black Shirts believed no African Americans were entitled to jobs as long as white people were unemployed. With city permits, they conducted parades down Peachtree Street carrying signs that read "Niggers, Back to the Cotton Fields—City Jobs are for White Folks."

On 15 June 1930, eight months after the stock market crash, seven white men who were believed to be members of the Klan-like organization murdered a Morehouse sophomore. The semester had ended, and Hope was out of the city on a fund-raising campaign. The murdered student, Dennis Hubert, was a well-known member of a prominent African American family. According to his murderers, Hubert insulted the wife of one of the assailants as she emerged from some woods across from the playground of Crogman school, close to the Morehouse campus. An eyewitness reported that there was no insult, but that an unidentified black youth saw a man emerge from the woods with two intoxicated women and told him "you better take them women home." The man returned with six other men just as Hubert was passing by. Without warning, Hubert was shot in the back of the head and killed instantly. His father discovered his body on the playground as he returned from church.

The ordeal was not yet over. A group of whites who believed the assailants' story began a reign of terror a week later in the African American community. The home of the murdered student's father was burned to the ground; the family barely escaped with their lives. In the meantime, several white men were arrested, including the trigger man, T. L. Martin, and the city promised to bring them to trial. That decision set off another round of violence, attributed to the Black Shirts. Tear-gas bombs were tossed into black Wheat Street Baptist Church on Auburn Avenue during a rally to raise money to rebuild the Hubert home and help finance the prosecution. Another group tried to abduct Charles D. Hubert and his son, relatives of the murdered student, from their home, but the elder Hubert fought them off. To further intimidate African Americans before the trial, night riders hurled stones and shattered the lamps on the Spelman College campus.[41]

An outraged John Hope returned to Atlanta in July. His private papers include numerous clippings of news reports on the murder and trial. Unlike the Morehouse student killed two years earlier in 1928, Hope knew Hubert and his family well. Dennis Hubert had been Hope's driver on occasion, his father had attended Morehouse under Hope's tenure, and Charles D. Hubert was an esteemed professor of theology at Morehouse and later its president. "Must Morehouse students," Hope later wrote, "must all the colored youth of Atlanta, of Georgia, forever go about in terror of their lives?" Certainly Hope understood that the bad economic conditions produced by the Depression affected everyone, including poor whites, who increasingly took out their frustrations on African Americans. He also remembered the Atlanta race riot of 1906 and recognized that the situation in 1930 was potentially just as explosive. T. L. Martin's trial was set to begin on 22 July, and it was rumored that widespread rioting would result if he was found guilty.[42]

African Americans in Atlanta were tense and prepared. They could not legally purchase firearms in Atlanta, but guns had been quietly ordered and received by black retailers who supplied them to those who wanted them. On 28 July, an audience of blacks and whites that included John Hope filled the segregated courtroom when the jury found Martin guilty and imposed a sentence of twelve to fifteen years. Both races had been primed to remain quiet no matter what the outcome, which accounted for the eerie silence that followed the verdict and the sentence. That night, however, and for several nights thereafter, according to a former Morehouse faculty member, African Americans sat up all night protecting their families with .25 automatics (the professor still had his more than thirty-five years later). Fortunately, the city remained quiet.[43]

The Hubert case caused Hope to step up his activism. He worked closely with the CIC and African American activists to keep black and white Atlanta calm during the days following the Martin verdict. Along with A. T. Walden of the Atlanta NAACP, Hope assisted in gathering evidence on the Black Shirts that eventually resulted in a grand jury indictment. The number of lynchings had increased that year (Georgia again led the nation with five), and Hope allowed himself to become a member of a new organization— the CIC-inspired Southern Commission for the Study of Lynching. He recruited prominent Morehouse sociologist Walter Chivers to work with CIC researcher Arthur Raper as investigators for the new organization. Hope also continued to recommend other African Americans for membership in the CIC. Although he at first hesitated to accept the position, in 1932 Hope became the CIC's first African American president.[44]

The Depression also had an adverse effect on the work of the Colored Men's Department (CMD) of the YMCA, an institution Hope continued to believe was essential to black progress. With the retirement of Jesse Moorland in 1923, Channing Tobias, a fellow Augustan and good friend of Hope's, had become head of the CMD and was highly respected in that position. Local branches such as the Butler Street YMCA in Atlanta felt the Depression's effects early. Unemployed black men flocked to the Y for food and housing, and the organization expanded its outreach programs in 1930 to combat the increased adult and juvenile crime. The YMCA also provided employment counseling, educational and vocational training courses, and, as much as possible, distributed food, clothing, and other essentials to those in need.

Ironically, the Butler Street YMCA's workload increased at just the time the National Council of the YMCA was reducing staffs and cutting budgets because of declining revenues. Hope once again felt compelled to act. As a prominent member of Butler Street's powerful board of managers, Hope used his influence among philanthropists to secure a small appropriation from the Rosenwald Fund. He also helped to expand Butler Street's services westward, opening up Atlanta University and Morehouse for outreach programs. To offset the organization's dwindling finances, Hope backed loans for the Butler Street YMCA and donated substantial sums of his own money.[45]

As the Depression worsened, the National Council of the YMCA proposed eliminating African American student secretaries in the CMD by merging their work with the white Student Division created in 1927. For several years, the CMD had been at odds with the black student associations and the National Council over control of African American YMCA work. Fearing unequal treatment in the Student Division, the CMD rejected the National Council's merger proposal. Leading figures in the CMD such as Hope, Moton, and Tobias believed the merger would undermine the department's autonomy and decided to initiate a fund-raising campaign that would allow the CMD to maintain total control over all YMCA work associated with African Americans.[46]

John Hope accepted a key role in the national fund-raising campaign. The operation was largely conducted out of his AU office, with Constance Nabrit handling most of the administrative tasks. By 1932 Hope had successfully persuaded the CIC and John D. Rockefeller Jr. to donate money, and had contributed several hundred dollars of his own as well. When traveling the country soliciting funds for the Morehouse endowment campaign, Hope usually held separate meetings and made speeches to the same audience to elicit funds for the YMCA project. Only a thin line separated the two campaigns. Hope was aware that his role as an African American leader in this case came close to upstaging his responsibilities as an African American president—as were some GEB officials. Although he was once actually advised to save his fund-raising efforts for the Morehouse campaign, Hope rarely missed an opportunity to help the CMD.[47]

Despite his work in so many areas, Hope's leadership continued to evoke criticism. A memo circulated by the National Council of the YMCA, the

GEB, and the CIC in the early 1930s proudly compared John Hope's leadership with the "illustrious" and "conservative leadership" of Booker T. Washington and Samuel Armstrong. Most African American leaders of the time
did not look favorably on the leadership of either man. Many of the younger
leaders did not accept the CIC and GEB visions of black progress only within
the separate black world. Hope was occasionally condemned for his silence
on America's racial problems when he spoke in international forums. Other
leaders rejected his view that the solutions to Africa's problems existed in some
type of "missionary Christian idealism."[48]

African American students, especially those in the YMCA's black student
associations, were especially critical of Hope and Moton, who, they said, were
too closely tied to influential members of conservative white organizations
and put on a pedestal as models of African American leadership. This new
generation of African American students were convinced that Hope and
Moton controlled northern philanthropy. That many students held this view
was harshly revealed at an interracial conference in Atlanta sponsored by the
YMCA in 1932. It was widely rumored that an unknown student (or YMCA
secretary) on the planning committee had said that if "Dr. Hope, Dr. Moton
or Dr. Tobias should rise to speak in the Conference, then every Negro student would leave the auditorium." There were several variations on this story,
but all the versions included the names of Hope and Moton. It was clear,
a YMCA representative wrote, that Hope's and Moton's "positions in these
councils (religious, educational, social and otherwise) which so vitally direct
the course of Negro life in America give them a most unique opportunity to
influence public opinion and to direct public and private philanthropies." Like
Booker T. Washington before him, Hope did in fact channel philanthropy
in certain directions. Also like Washington, Hope made enemies as well as
friends by doing so.[49]

Hope's critics were not limited to those who disapproved of his leadership.
Criticism continued to mount at both Morehouse College and Atlanta University over his attempts to build a "Negro University" in Atlanta. Some
Atlanta University alumni, for example, refused to believe that their favorite
teachers had not been "tossed out without a penny," and continued to spread
those rumors throughout the country. John Hope was held responsible. In
1931 Hope conducted the last undergraduate commencement at Atlanta University. The AU alumni were especially vociferous on this occasion. They reportedly threatened to remove the stained glass from the chapel, the pictures
from the walls, and the clock from the tower. They also even threatened to
move the grave of Asa Ware, the school's first president, off campus.[50]

The response of Atlanta University's alumni was predictable, but Hope was surprised at the criticism that mounted among Morehouse faculty, administrators, and alumni who believed he had abandoned the college at a crucial point in its development. The onset of the Depression had wreaked havoc with Hope's plans to complete the endowment campaign before he gave up the presidency in 1931. In 1932, however, he had managed to get the GEB and other philanthropic foundations to extend the time allowed to meet their conditional gifts. With the help of the GEB, he was instrumental in persuading the ABHMS to cover the operational costs of the endowment campaign. In addition, in the name of his wife and mother, Hope and his sons contributed $2,000 to the campaign, calling it the Lugenia Frances Fund. Even after relinquishing the presidency Hope continued to closely monitor Morehouse's financial situation. Eventually he made a controversial proposal to combine the Morehouse and AU boards of trustees to help Morehouse survive the Depression.[51]

More and more, Hope discussed his problems with his son Edward, who had completed graduate school at MIT. In 1928, he had taken a job as a hydroelectric engineer in Brazil, but the job was terminated in 1931 as a result of the Depression. Edward went back to school at Columbia University, taught for a while at Howard University, and then became that school's superintendent of buildings and grounds. Thirty-year-old Edward provided the elder Hope with valuable advice and consistently encouraged him to rest and take care of himself. Like his father, Edward was apt to be solemn and serious minded, and Hope could count on his oldest son to tell him what he really thought about any subject, even if it was not what he wanted to hear.

John Hope was much less concerned about Edward in the 1930s than he was about his younger son, John Hope II. Young John entered Brown University's graduate program in economics in 1930, a few months shy of his twenty-first birthday. As he had with Edward, the elder Hope visited and wrote to young John often. He wanted to be sure the young man was eating properly, lived in decent housing, and had warm clothing. But beyond these physical needs, Hope wanted John II to use what he learned to benefit his "people, whether in Africa or America." Anticipating Edward's reaction, Hope assured him that his "feet were firmly planted on the ground," and that he was not "walking on the clouds." Yet Hope wanted his son John to balance his quest for economic security with some sense of social responsibility. He did not want John "to be so poverty stricken that he will not have the chance to think [or] . . . to have so much money to spend that he will not have time to think." Hope expected both of his sons to carry on the tradition of race leadership.[52]

But like many young graduate students, the youngest Hope was more interested in sharing his own new knowledge with his father—especially the economic theories in vogue during the Depression—than in taking his advice. Though impressed, the elder Hope was also disturbed. He eventually wrote young John an emotionally charged letter that reveals his deepest concerns:

> What is economics if it is not to help society to make such adjustments that the wheat which is almost bursting out of granaries but is being withheld from the mouths of men, women, and children shall have an equitable distribution? What is the matter when sheep and cotton are waiting to be made into clothes and naked people cannot get money to set the spindles going? What are we going to do about this situation? What are you going to do about the situation as it affects twelve millions of Negroes in city and country? I know you get tired of hearing me say this; I have been saying it for years. You have youth and education on your side. Work out a better future for people.[53]

It helped Hope to discuss his concerns about John II with Lugenia, but it was difficult to find the time; her schedule in the early 1930s was as busy as her husband's. Atlanta officials called on the Neighborhood Union to examine unemployment in the city's African American communities and to do what it could to ease the suffering caused by the Depression. Lugenia Hope also worked with the CIC in anti-lynching campaigns and was extremely valuable as chairperson of an NAACP drive in 1932 to educate and politicize African American voters. In 1933, at the twenty-fifth anniversary of the founding of the Neighborhood Union, Lugenia Hope was given a testimonial in honor of her more than thirty years of social service to Atlanta. Two years later, at sixty-four years of age, she retired from the organization, but she remained active as a race leader for many more years. Like Hope, Lugenia was ill in the 1930s and spent time at the Mayo Clinic. She often pushed herself beyond safe physical limits, but unlike her husband, she did not have the luxury of taking all-expenses-paid therapeutic vacations.[54]

John Hope continued to press forward in his dual roles. By 1933, Atlanta University was well on its way to becoming the "Negro university" he had long envisioned. Morris Brown College had moved into the historic buildings of the old Atlanta University on the west side of Atlanta. Discussions were under way between Hope and officials of Clark, Gammon Theological Seminary, and the Atlanta School of Social Work to bring those schools into closer cooperation with the affiliation. The new central library had been constructed, providing jobs for many of the city's unemployed. No African American was allowed in any of the city's white college libraries, so it was essential that the Trevor Arnett Library (named after the chair of AU's board of trustees) be well equipped.

Hope and Read, occasionally joined by members of the Atlanta University

Board of Trustees, often worked far into the night on the university plan. They had managed to secure significant sums from the GEB, the Carnegie Corporation, and the Rosenwald and Slater Funds for several university projects. Individual philanthropists such as John D. Rockefeller Jr. and Edward S. Harkness made substantial anonymous donations. In addition to furnishing the library, such contributions made Hope's plan for a graduate program in economics and business a reality in his lifetime, and also made possible a graduate department of sociology that would restore and strengthen the school's existing program, which had declined steadily since the departure of W. E. B. Du Bois more than twenty years earlier.[55]

Hope continued to try to interest Du Bois in joining him at Atlanta University. A decade-long dispute between Du Bois and the NAACP over control of the *Crisis* indirectly aided Hope's cause. Influenced by Marxism (as he understood it) and the despair created by the Depression, Du Bois advocated a not entirely new program of voluntary black cooperative economics that troubled NAACP leaders. To Walter White, other NAACP officers, and most NAACP board members, what Du Bois was promoting was the acceptance of segregation, pure and simple. Hope's vision of a Negro university in the South based on the cooperative efforts of several black colleges in Atlanta appeared increasingly attractive to Du Bois.[56]

At first Du Bois did what he could from New York to help move the project along, including introducing Hope to prominent educators such as the eminent John Dewey. He also passed along the names of promising African American graduate students matriculating at prestigious northern white universities. By late 1930, as tensions between Du Bois and the NAACP escalated, Du Bois began to show interest in an even closer affiliation with Hope and Atlanta University. Beginning in the spring of 1931, Du Bois conducted a series of annual lectures at AU on topics ranging from history, economics, and sociology to African American art and literature. He spent the entire spring semester of 1933 in Atlanta and was willing to consider a permanent return if he could spend half the year in New York working with the *Crisis*.[57]

The summer of 1933 began with Hope very busy as usual. In addition to conducting the Atlanta University commencement, he delivered addresses at Morris Brown and Tuskegee. Franklin D. Roosevelt, inaugurated earlier that year, had promised the American people a "New Deal," but programs were still in the process of being developed as the Depression continued to take its toll on the country. John Hope the African American leader took on even more responsibility. Concerned about the escalating juvenile delinquency, he called a meeting of African American leaders from throughout the state and led them in founding an organization designed to serve young African American males in rural areas where there was no YMCA. It was called the Georgia

State Council for Work among Negro Boys, and before he knew it Hope had become the organization's first president. The council eventually created a boy's camp in southwest Georgia that carried Hope's name.[58]

Also in 1933, Hope helped convince county and state officials to finance a summer program for children in an isolated outlying area not far from Atlanta. A Spelman teacher was slated to conduct the session in what Florence Read later described as a "dilapidated one-room building with a muddy yard on a rutted road." With no state money available for repairs, Hope arranged for students in the Atlanta University summer school to repair the building as part of a community service project. The AU students constructed steps, screened windows, and helped local parents and children plant flowers in the school yard. Accompanied by Read and Jane Hope Lyons, who was the dean of women at Spelman, Hope visited the renovated Red Oak School and was pleased with what he saw.[59]

Hope returned to Atlanta early in the evening on 15 June, not quite two weeks after his sixty-fifth birthday. The scorching Georgia sun had not yet begun to set. He went directly to Reynolds Cottage with Florence Read for a meeting with officials about the Red Oak School project. There he suddenly felt ill, and President Read immediately summoned Ludie Andrews, the resident nurse and director of MacVicar Infirmary. Hope insisted the two women take him home. That night, there were short, stinging pains in his chest. On 21 June he dictated a letter to Robert Moton that put the blame for his indisposition on the "hot weather, too much work, and a disgusted stomach." His self-diagnosis was wrong. The next day he was taken to MacVicar Infirmary, having suffered a major heart attack. For a while, the odds for his recovery seemed bleak.[60]

Hope remained at the Spelman facility for six weeks. There were good days and bad ones, but eventually he showed definite signs of improvement. The official diagnosis was angina pectoris, a condition that in itself was anathema to John Hope. Heart pains leading to another attack could occur with any exertion; only rest could ward it off. His physicians now demanded that he slow down, watch his diet, and get plenty of rest. According to his son John, he was sternly warned that, depending on how well he followed their advice, he had six months to five years or more left to live. Climbing stairs was simply too dangerous for him to attempt, and there were plans to install an elevator leading to Hope's office on the AU campus.[61]

Early in August, Hope improved enough to go to Clifton Springs Sanitarium, a New York rest home popular among prominent educators.[62] No comparable facility in the South would admit African Americans. His three months away from work provided ample time for another round of deep reflection. With doctors in New York echoing his Atlanta physicians' advice,

Hope's letters to family and friends show that he was completely aware of his fragile condition. Death had recently claimed many of his friends and relatives, including his sister Anna.[63]

Hope wrote to Lugenia from Clifton Springs that he "had been very near the edge" but was now calm. He insinuated that he had learned his lesson; he now wanted to "live and *work*." However, the haughty defensive posture he had learned to assume when questioned about his health was still there. Anticipating Lugenia's refrain, Hope wrote: "I want those nearest to me to help me to do it without even talking to me *about* my health. Never again, as long as I live shall I forget. But I shall not wish to talk about it or be further reminded of it." In words he hoped would soothe Lugenia's concerns, he tried to explain what his wife already knew: "I took two hard jobs, one in 1906, another in 1929, the latter when I was already as old as many men are when they retire from business. No regrets, my dear wife, *no* regrets; and absolutely *no* appeal or desire for pity."[64]

In July, John Hope II married Elise Oliver, a native of Louisville who had attended Spelman but finished her degree at the University of Cincinnati. John and his fiancée offered to postpone the wedding, but Hope would not hear of it. Also in July, Edward sent a telegram announcing his marriage to Marian Coniver, an attorney from Cleveland. Jane Hope Lyons had represented the family. "Please notify Mrs. Andrews, and break the news gently to Father if the doctors think it advisable," Edward wrote to Constance Nabrit. "Will tell Mother and John after latter's wedding."

John II had graduated from Brown and was teaching economics at Morehouse and Spelman, and Edward Hope was secure in his faculty position at Howard. John Hope still appeared troubled. He privately revealed to Andrews that although he was glad to see both young men happy, it reminded him that his own work remained unfinished. "I wonder whether my work is done," he said to her. "I'd like to live long enough to have my successor know what I was trying to do."[65]

Other family members were on John Hope's mind as well. Not all of them were doing as well during the Depression as Edward and John. Hope had taken on the responsibility for financing the education of his nephew Justin Hope (the son of his brother Tom) at Morehouse, and paid part of his medical school tuition as well. He also continued to help Thomas directly in New Jersey. When Tom was out of work, Hope used his influence to help him find jobs. When no jobs were available, Hope gave him money so his family would not suffer. During Hope's long recuperation, his thoughts of the present were often mixed with memories of the past. Those thoughts often centered on his early experiences in Augusta, the family homestead on Ellis Street, and the occupants as he remembered them through the eyes of a child.[66]

Seemingly for no other reason than to freeze the moment while it was still fresh in his mind, on 12 September Hope hurriedly copied down what he remembered of a vivid dream he had enjoyed the night before. He organized it into an essay, called it "A Dream of the Night of September 11, 1933," and used his narration to interpret what he believed was going on in his subconscious. The dream, as dreams tend to do, defied logic and showed no respect for historical order or chronology. In many ways it was an Augusta family reunion that included his mother and father as he remembered them from his childhood. Other deceased family members were in it, too—his brother Madison and several aunts and uncles. The mystical experience took place at the family homestead at 1108 Ellis Street in Augusta, a likely setting in that Hope had bought the house from Anna (who had inherited it as the last unmarried family member) in 1930 in order to help her pay her medical expenses.

Though Hope described practically every room in the house, the dream took place in the "old back room where life converged for my family." A young John and Edward occasionally darted in after a session of playing in the backyard. At other times he could hear them as adults talking with their wives in another room, which reminded him that he had missed their weddings. His Genie was at his side sewing. His conscious interpretation of that was that he continued to have mixed emotions about her work in the community. "Then her world was at home, not the great world outside into which I so much advised her to go. It is almost amusing to see her so perfectly innocent of the fact that she has been swallowed up." The dream switched back to the dead. He wanted to see his sister Anna: "I wish poor Anna . . . would come to see me. She would, if her coming could make me well." He had a morbid answer for the failure of some to appear: "Perhaps they cannot easily come," he wrote; "perhaps they know that I will soon be coming to them."

Overall, Hope gave the dream a positive meaning. Its setting in the Augusta household, which included his wife and their families, convinced him that "my home life must have been very beautiful." He wanted to believe that the parade of departed kinfolk was more than just a memory; perhaps it was even "a manifestation of immortality."[67]

Dabble though he might in the world of mysticism, the plight of his people in the real world was never far from his mind. Sometime during his stay in Clifton Springs, Hope jotted down the following note:

A man never lays down his gun until he does so in spirit. B[ooker] T. [Washington] got the N[egro] (the educated one) to lay down his gun. Most of us did. I did not lay mine down until I believed that Ashby Jones, Wilmer, Alexander, and Moton [members of the CIC] were really going to give us a gunless w[hite] man's civilization. The Indian never laid his down, and he is dead. And the w[hite] man, powerful as he is, will be dead if he does not lay down his g[un] in spirit, because he will be unable to trust anybody and nobody will trust him. Witness his situation now throughout the world.[68]

Hope arrived back in Atlanta late in September. Over his protests, his physicians insisted he spend his nights for the next two months at MacVicar Infirmary instead of at his home on Beckwith Street. He was given orders to avoid fatigue and to lie down in his office if he became tired. It was all very difficult for a man accustomed to working fourteen-hour days or longer. Jane Hope Lyons and Ludie Andrews remembered that it was not uncommon for Hope to lie down on a couch during long meetings in President Read's office or at her residence in Reynolds Cottage. Forewarned by his physicians of possible side effects, Hope revealed privately to W. T. B. Williams in October that pain in his hands and joints had already begun. And he was subject as well to a nervous irritability that caused him to become what he called "nettled" now and then. Though his family remained completely supportive, Hope was not always pleasant to be around after his heart attack.[69]

In spite of his physical limitations, life was work for John Hope, and he still found it difficult not to accept additional responsibilities. While he was recuperating at the Spelman infirmary, Hope had been approached by a prominent engineer and architect who needed his support for a new idea. A new National Industrial Recovery Act program had designated federal money for limited-dividend corporations interested in slum clearance and the development of low-cost housing. A plan was already in the works in Atlanta to clean up Techwood, a terrible nine-square-block slum area occupied by whites that was close to Georgia Tech University. However, the architect and engineer thought the proposal would be strengthened if a black area was added to the project, so the west Atlanta district known as "Beaver Slide," where conditions were even worse, had been included. Hope was enthusiastic and gave his endorsement to what eventually became the University Homes housing project.[70]

The housing project gradually came to dominate Hope's attention and time. He eventually contacted Charles F. Palmer, an Atlanta-based real estate developer who was organizing a delegation to present the proposal in Washington. When it was decided to create separate ad hoc advisory committees for each part of the project, Hope took on the responsibility of establishing and chairing the committee for University Homes. Still weak, he accompanied the other promoters to Washington, D.C., in October 1933 and remained there for five days to plead the cause for Atlanta's housing projects. By late December, after two more trips to Washington, Secretary of the Interior Harold L. Ickes had approved Atlanta's plans. By the spring of 1934 the federal government had scrapped the limited-dividend proposal, assumed full responsibility for building the housing, and transferred all projects to the Federal Emergency Housing Corporation. University Homes and Techwood Homes thus became the first housing projects approved for construction exclusively with federal funds.[71]

Opposition to the projects came from all sides, and fighting it drained Hope of practically all his energy. A hastily organized group of one hundred property owners came together under the sponsorship of the Atlanta Apartment House Owners Association and tried to block the development of the Techwood project in the Atlanta City Council and in Washington, D.C. There was too much housing in Atlanta already, they claimed. The federal housing projects would hurt their business and create unfair competition. In addition, according to one letter of opposition written from Atlanta to Washington, "none of the white residents in the Techwood area could pay the proposed rentals . . . else they would not now be living in cottages among negroes." Insurance companies were concerned that they would be forced to take over "distressed properties," and an Atlanta women's club thought the money would be better spent to build parks. John Hope II remembered that his father was so tired when he came home from housing meetings that he usually went straight to bed.[72]

Hope felt much better by the beginning of 1934. It was good that he did, because criticism of the federal housing projects in Atlanta soon zeroed in on the University Homes project. Leaders of the resistance first correctly noted (though it contradicted their earlier statements about a housing surplus) that there were African American areas more in need of slum clearance and housing than the community around the colleges in west Atlanta. Butler Street off Auburn Avenue was identified as an example, along with the slum district known as "Darktown" and the areas around the state capitol. Supporters of the project acknowledged that there were greater needs elsewhere; however, University Homes was an experiment, and the government hesitated to take on projects it considered too large. Both Techwood and University Homes were ideal, supporters contended, because they had the support of black Atlanta University and white Georgia Tech University.

The project's detractors (many of them owners of slum properties) then attacked the type of housing proposed. Assistant Director of Housing C. H. Pynchon was forced to respond to a rash of telegrams and letters criticizing apartments in particular. He in turn asked Senator Richard B. Russell Jr. of Georgia to talk to Clark Howell Sr., the publisher of the *Atlanta Constitution*, or Georgia Tech's president, M. L. Brittain, about the Techwood project, and further informed him that President John Hope of "Spelman University" could "enlighten him on the negro project." That was not good enough for P. C. McDuffie, the owner of numerous slum properties in the proposed University Homes area. As the chairman of an anti–federal housing organization called the Citizens Committee Representing the Civic and Public Welfare, McDuffie told Pynchon that apartments were unsuitable for African Americans: "I don't care what Dr. Hope or any other negro educator says," he wrote to Pynchon, "the small cottage type of house has proven for generations the very best type of habitation for these people. Ask any southern man in Washington if that isn't true."[73]

Hope fought back in his characteristic understated way. In addition to Florence Read, Will Alexander, Chairman of the Atlanta University Board of Trustees Dean Sage, and Kendall Weisinger, assistant to the president of Bell Telephone and Telegraph, Hope quietly added four black businessmen who were popular among African Americans to the University Homes advisory committee. His appointees included Lorimer D. Milton, chairman of AU's Department of Business and Economics, who with his partner, Clayton R. Yates, owned a string of black drugstores in Atlanta. In addition, Milton was vice president of the black-owned Citizens Trust Bank. There was also David T. Howard, a prominent funeral director; S. W. Walker, vice president of the Pilgrim Health and Life Insurance Company; and E. M. Martin, secretary of the Atlanta Life Insurance Company. When Du Bois arrived to deliver his lectures in the spring semester of 1934, Hope persuaded him to supervise a study of the University Homes area. The study, completed in May, showed a definite need for housing in west Atlanta, and also showed that the area's slum condition was due to poverty, not "vice or crime."[74]

Besides his involvement with the housing project in 1934, Hope continued to work on implementing his vision of a "Negro University" by looking at other cooperative models. In February he went to New Orleans to visit black Dillard University and its associated hospital, Flint Goodridge. His week in New Orleans with former Morehouse student (and later president of Dillard) Albert Dent, then superintendent of the hospital, provided Hope with more ideas. In March he went to California to visit the Claremont Affiliation, which had been his model for the Atlanta University Affiliation. The trips away from Atlanta were not all related to business. From California he wrote to Lugenia, "I was beginning to get on people's nerves [in Atlanta] because everybody urged me to leave town and get very far away."[75]

Hope was sixty-six years old when he took his last trip to Europe in July 1934. His family's pleas to remain at home fell on deaf ears, but he did yield to their insistence not to go alone. Lugenia was ill and could not go with him, so Hope first asked his new daughter-in-law Elise to accompany him. In an interview conducted sixty years later, John II and Elise recalled with sheepish smiles that young John II had declined the invitation for her. They had been married less than a year, and he was not willing to part with his wife for even a short time.[76]

Hope decided to take his administrative assistant, Constance Crocker Nabrit, who had never been to Europe. In many ways it was a good choice, for he expected to work on university business during the trip and also hoped to begin his memoirs. Unfortunately, Hope never completed more than seven pages of what he called his "autobiographical notes." They were started onboard the ship in a two-hour dictated session with Nabrit, but the last couple of pages were not written until a year later. Nabrit usually went sightseeing with a Morehouse faculty member in London while Hope was attending the conference in Oxford. She and Hope did a bit of sightseeing together as well, however, visiting some of the same sites John and Lugenia had seen on their one trip abroad together back in 1926.

Though writing was now painful for him, Hope's observations to Lugenia about what he saw and felt continued with the same poetic flare that had become his trademark in his letters to her: "My room looks out on the same blue lake. Across the lake are the same snowcapped peaks, and tonight the same moon stands high above everything and its white light streams across the lake. My thoughts are with you tonight as truly as they were that night when we stood in the wide window and looked across the lake." [77]

Lugenia Hope's biographer, Jacqueline Rouse, raised questions about John Hope's frequent trips without his wife: "Did she . . . understand and accept this constant absence of her husband, or did she remain behind because she wished to be alone?" Whatever her thoughts on the subject, the simple fact was that no one offered Lugenia Hope all-expenses-paid trips to Europe. And although John Hope's salary increased significantly when he became Atlanta University's president, for most of his life the money to pay his wife's travel expenses was simply not there. [78]

Sometime in the 1930s, perhaps even after his death, rumors began to circulate about John Hope's alleged infidelity. The woman most frequently mentioned was President Florence Read of Spelman College. Two facts are indisputable: John Hope and Florence Read were close, and Lugenia Hope and Florence Read disliked each other. Except for Constance Nabrit, Florence Read worked more closely with John Hope than anyone else in the last seven years of his life. In addition to her work as part of the AU Affiliation, Read played a major role in raising funds from philanthropists; she was a member of the CIC; she introduced Hope to influential international figures abroad; and she was deeply involved in the Atlanta federal housing project.

The two college presidents seemed to find in each other something that was missing in their separate lives. As Read continued to defy old South traditions by holding interracial gatherings in her home, Hope was convinced that she represented a major step forward in black-white relations. More important, Hope often remarked that Read "had youth on her side." She was in better physical and mental shape than both Hope and Archer. After Hope's surgery and heart attack in the 1930s, his envy of Read's youth and energy was even more obvious.[79]

It is Dr. Samuel Nabrit's view that Florence Read loved John Hope. Aside from Lugenia (and, perhaps, Constance Nabrit), Read knew details of Hope's life that he had not revealed to anyone else, including his sons. She was aware of his mixed-race family in Augusta, his experiences at Worcester and Brown, his family members scattered throughout the country, and his desires and wishes for his sons. Her private papers contain photographs of him at Brown, his sons, a grandson, and his sister Jane Hope Lyons. The Atlanta University collection of her papers once included a file box on subjects referring to John Hope, suggesting that Read at one time planned to write his biography.[80]

As Hope's health deteriorated during the last seven years of his life, Read became increasingly protective of him, at times even offering the family unwanted advice about how to ensure his comfort. On numerous occasions Read privately wrote to officials of the GEB and others that Hope needed to rest, that he was taking on too many responsibilities that imperiled his health. In the eyes of some family members, she stepped over the line and intruded on family responsibilities.[81]

There is some evidence that Read looked on John Hope as a father figure. Read never married, she was far away from her hometown in western New York, and her trips home were infrequent. According to her contemporaries, she had few friends among southern whites, and visits by relatives were rare. Read later wrote about Hope: "He was the most real Christian I have known. I would place my father in the same class, but my father did not have to conquer in his soul the hurts and scars of race discrimination."[82]

There is no doubt that Hope and Read cared deeply for each other. Hope may have filled a void in Read's personal life, and he certainly needed her energy. A man in his middle sixties, he was probably flattered by the attentions of a vibrant younger woman. Yet there is no evidence that their relationship was anything more than a deep and abiding friendship centered on mutual respect and professional ties. Even if he wished it otherwise, a contemporary correctly noted, the state of Hope's health in the 1930s would have been a major obstacle.[83]

Elise Oliver Hope offered a plausible explanation, based on her own experience, of how the unsavory rumors surrounding the Hope-Read relationship originated. Shortly after her husband, John Hope II, returned to Atlanta after finishing graduate school, he was summoned one evening by Read to go over some budgetary matters at Spelman College. He left his home at 9:00 P.M., and at 2:30 A.M. he still had not returned. Elise went to a neighbor's house (she and John did not have a phone) to call the campus and find out what was keeping her husband. Read answered the phone, either at her office in Rocke-feller Hall or at Reynolds College (both Hopes remember the incident, but they do not agree on where Hope II and Read were working), and said that she and John II were still working. Elise was furious. Though intellectually she understood that the two were working, emotionally she could only think, as she remembered in an interview years later, "that woman has my husband cornered over there at Reynolds Cottage." Her point was that her husband could have been the subject of rumors started by anyone who saw him leave Read's office (at either location on Spelman's campus) early in the morning.[84]

Elise Hope's recollections also explain, at least in part, why Lugenia Hope and Florence Read were not fond of each other. Although the two women were cordial when they first met in 1927, it soon became obvious to many that their personalities clashed. Both were strong, independent women fiercely committed to their beliefs. Both could be terribly blunt, and neither Lugenia Hope nor Florence Read allowed contemporary convention, as it applied to women, to define them.[85]

Nevertheless, Lugenia Hope and Florence Read operated from different centers: one was black and the other was white. Though both were centered in women's experience, Lugenia's identity as an African American woman separated her from the Spelman College president. Unlike her husband, Lugenia Hope was never quick to embrace interracial organizations, she was less impressed with personal acts of kindness and interracial goodwill, and she was certainly unwilling to entrust the welfare of any family member to an outsider. Read's stern personality and tendency to take control—as "if only she knew best," one of her contemporaries recalled—probably made matters worse. The animosity between the two women reached its peak after John Hope's death when Lugenia Hope was forced to get an attorney to help her collect several of her husband's personal possessions that Florence Read re-fused to return. As an African American woman, Lugenia Hope probably found it extremely difficult to accept a woman like Florence Read as an essen-tial part of her husband's life.[86]

There is no direct evidence that Hope was aware of his wife's feelings about Florence Read. He probably did know, but he was never one to confront controversy directly. His letters to Lugenia, however, do provide clues. The letters from the late 1920s frequently mention Nabrit and Read, describing how important they were to his work and how much he admired and needed both of them. By the early 1930s, Hope mentioned Read far less frequently, and when he did, he seemed to be timidly trying to coax Lugenia in Read's direction: "I do wish you would try and get to know Miss Read better for she could help you so much in your work." Though it may have been honestly motivated, Read's attention to the husband of a prominent African American woman was socially unacceptable within the African American world. Deep down, in spite of his sometimes apparent naiveté, that understanding was probably not lost on John Hope.[87]

There is nothing to suggest that John and Lugenia Hope did not love each other as they moved toward their thirty-seventh year of marriage in 1934. Sometime earlier the Hopes had purchased a beautiful tract of land about 125 miles from Atlanta in the north Georgia mountains. Located in Rabun County in Clayton, the property was situated high on a steep hill overlooking a picturesque valley. While Hope was in Europe in 1934, Lugenia supervised the building of a cabin there that they planned to use first as a hideaway during the summers, and later as a retirement home. John Hope II, accompanied by his wife and mother, took the elder Hope to see the house later that summer. It was his first and only visit to the cabin. John Hope was well pleased. The contractors had built a beautiful winding road embedded with huge stones leading up to the house, which featured a huge granite fireplace. The only neighbors were a black family, the Becklys, who lived across the road. Believed to be longtime residents of the area, they were reportedly well known in Atlanta and hosted many black visitors. Years later, the famous southern liberal and writer Lillian Smith would write *Strange Fruit* and other books in her cabin nearby. In Hope's time, however, Texas-born Maynard Jackson Sr. (father of Atlanta's first black mayor, Maynard Jackson Jr.) envisioned developing the entire area as a black resort and bought up several pieces of property toward that end. An early Morehouse graduate under Hope, Jackson was an astute businessman and minister, and he later served as the third pastor of the historic Friendship Baptist Church.[88]

The fall of 1934 brought a return to Atlanta and the beginning of a new academic year. On 29 September, Secretary of the Interior Harold Ickes arrived in Atlanta and detonated the dynamite charge that demolished a building on Greensferry Street and symbolized the beginning of the construction of the University Homes project. The next day, the *Atlanta Journal* reported that on an improvised platform close to Spelman College, Dr. "Frank Hope" of Atlanta University introduced Ickes, who made a short address. On 21 October, the *Journal* reported that "a gang of several hundred laborers had actually begun to demolish the shacks and shanties on the University project." Another gang was scheduled to begin work at the Techwood site in a few days. Though later it was widely assumed otherwise, University Homes, not Techwood, was the first federal housing project to undergo construction in the United States.[89]

Hope was aware that there were still problems with the project, problems that in part illuminated class differences within the African American community. The residents of Beaver Slide were not pleased that their homes were being destroyed. Most of them did not know where they were going to live, and no plans had been made to relocate them.[90] On the other hand, Atlanta's African American middle-class community viewed the Beaver Slide area as an eyesore. It had long been the object of jokes and ridicule that sometimes led to violent confrontations between its residents and other blacks and whites. Though he was a key player in the plan to destroy Beaver Slide, Hope nevertheless was sensitive to the residents' situation and applauded the pride many of them took in their community.

Charles F. Palmer, the man most responsible for the construction of University Homes, remembered Hope telling him that the conditions in Beaver Slide and similar areas were not the fault of the residents but the result of social, economic, and political conditions over which they had no control. One hot afternoon that fall in 1934, a frail John Hope climbed a slope of the Beaver Slide area with Palmer, who had to assist him up the hill. On reaching the top, Hope gazed down at the scene below with his clear blue eyes and said to Palmer: "I've dreamed about this place changing into something beautiful; not pretty, but straight and clean and full of light." In a speech later given in defense of the Beaver Slide residents, Hope told students that "Beaver Slide will never pass away until society all over the world learns how to do its duty by the underprivileged and underadvantaged. Beaver Slide is a condition of character, an economic condition, an educational and health condition. Beaver Slide is a state of mind."[91]

Hope's dual roles guided his actions with regard to the University Homes housing project and its residents. He continued to believe in the efficacy of the puritanical, evangelical, middle-class culture that had been a conscious part of his social makeup since his early educational experiences in New England. Though on the decline, that culture was still reflected in the curriculum and decorum of most African American colleges, and to some degree in the character of their graduates. For Hope, that culture still had a liberating influence that was worthy of emulation in the larger black society. In support of the housing project, Hope wrote in 1934 that "the families occupying the University Housing would be near social, educational, and cultural influences unsurpassed in any Negro neighborhood in the United States."[92] Yet, as an African American leader, Hope understood that culture alone could not satisfy concrete needs within any African American community, and he privately used his influence to see that African American laborers, skilled and unskilled, got jobs on the project. He also worked to ensure that a qualified black manager was selected to supervise University Homes once it was completed.[93]

Hope's plans for University Homes included the interests of both Atlanta University and the project's residents. His blueprint for the complex included a small library, playgrounds, and a nursery school and kindergarten for children of working mothers. He also envisioned central laundries and medical and dental care facilities. Atlanta University and its faculty would provide these services, and the housing project would in turn operate as a laboratory and training site for various university schools and departments. Hope also expected to bring the Atlanta School of Social Work within the "university organization" to provide services for the housing project. The federal government was interested in Hope's plan, and he made frequent trips to Washington to confer with housing officials, including Robert C. Weaver, then adviser to Secretary Ickes on the "economic status of the Negro." Because the plan was closely connected to Atlanta University, the GEB and the Spelman Memorial Rockefeller Fund were also interested, and their involvement continued after Hope's death.[94]

Hope was also beginning to put together an impressive faculty at Atlanta University. Du Bois's problems with the NAACP finally came to a head in 1934, and he joined the university that fall as a full-time professor of sociology. Despite Du Bois's reputation as a radical, there is no official record of any pressure to block his professorship, although John Hope II did believe (probably correctly) there was some opposition.[95]

There was definite opposition, however, when Ira De A. Reid, a Morehouse graduate with a master's degree from the University of Pittsburgh, joined the Department of Sociology in 1934. Hope had identified Reid's potential while he was still a student at Morehouse, and then tracked his development over the next several years. Before he came to Atlanta University, Reid had succeeded Charles S. Johnson as director of research for the National Urban League and was the editor of the league's magazine, *Opportunity*. He would go on to earn his Ph.D. at Columbia. Dean Sage, chairman of the Atlanta University Board of Trustees, wrote to Hope on 27 September concerning Reid's appointment to the faculty. Reportedly speaking for the board, Sage offered the opinion that "it would be a mistake to build up a faculty weighted with the radical element." Hope politely ignored Sage's advice and welcomed the brilliant Reid to the faculty in October.[96]

Dean Sage's concerns were not without merit. There was a radical element in AU's faculty. In addition to Du Bois and Reid, Hope had hired Rayford Logan in 1933 to chair the Department of History. Like the rest of Hope's graduate faculty, Logan, whom Hope first met in the Argonne Forest during World War I, came with impressive credentials and experience. He graduated Phi Beta Kappa from Williams College in Massachusetts, and in 1936 received his Ph.D. from Harvard. Once "respectfully" described by the *Chicago Defender* as a "bad Negro with a Ph.D.," Logan was a student of the renowned

Carter G. Woodson and had been active as a Pan Africanist, attending the congresses in 1921, 1927, and 1929.[97]

Logan had been fired from Virginia Union late in 1931 for politicizing students, demanding an African American president, and publicly criticizing the conservative black Virginia leader and sociology professor Gordon Blaine Hancock. Logan's radical reputation followed him to Atlanta when he arrived in 1933. His blistering critique of the occupation of Haiti by the United States earned him the disdain of Florence Read, who reportedly believed "students shouldn't be disturbed by global problems." As the highly publicized Angelo Herndon case of 1932 wound its way through the courts, Logan refused to remain quiet. His support of the Communist party made everyone nervous. Hope is said to have told Logan, "Say anything you like in the classroom but in Atlanta there are just some things that mustn't be said." While he obviously admired Logan, Hope also recognized that he was a ticking time bomb. A year later, Logan was scheduled to speak at a potentially explosive political interracial meeting in Atlanta. In a successful attempt to get Logan to decline the invitation, Hope reportedly said to him the day before: "Mr. Logan, we have a very small turn-over in Atlanta University. I wish you'd pull in your horns."[98]

Hope's interactions with Logan during the last years of his life are illuminating, for they show that his interests, his leadership style, and his humor remained intact. Hope could still be dictatorial in his relations with his faculty, insisting that they follow the same strict rules he had established for Morehouse years before (the one exception being Du Bois).

Logan remembered that when he ran into Hope at the annual Alpha Phi Alpha convention meeting in 1935, he asked his boss if he could spend a few extra days in Nashville, which meant missing his first day of classes for the spring semester. Hope felt strongly about professors attending their first classes of the semester and those immediately after a holiday, and he reiterated that point to Logan, then made him feel "two feet tall" by going back to Atlanta and holding his first day of classes for him. Hope also insisted that faculty make consistent progress on their dissertations. Logan was completing his doctorate on United States–Haitian relations and needed to go to Haiti to complete his primary research. Shortly before he left for the Caribbean in 1934, Hope told him: "I have nine members of my faculty who have *almost* got their doctor's degrees. I wish to God one of them would go ahead and get it."[99] Logan was in part responsible for Hope's interest in Haiti and other areas in the Caribbean, and he provided Hope with valuable contacts when Hope traveled there in 1935.

Hope took care to hire faculty who were both capable of assisting him in the development of Atlanta University and willing to play active roles as African American leaders. Reid and Du Bois took on the responsibility for a complete restructuring of the Department of Sociology, but they also played prominent roles in community work outside the academy. Du Bois's record spoke for itself, and he had already completed a study on the University Homes housing project earlier that year. In 1935 he proposed an elaborate seven-point scheme for AU and the affiliated schools in the future development of the University Homes housing project. Some of his points incorporated ideas proposed earlier by Hope to the GEB.[100] Reid conducted a special survey for the Federal Emergency Relief Administration during his first year on the faculty.

One of the first graduate faculty hired, history professor Clarence A. Bacote, joined Logan in restructuring the Department of History and was also prominent in Atlanta's African American Citizenship Schools, a brainchild of Lugenia Burns Hope. The Department of Economics and Business Administration's brilliant professors Lorimer D. Milton and Jesse B. Blayton were in constant demand for their expertise. Milton had been loaned to the Washington, D.C.–based National Benefit Life Insurance Company in 1932 in an unsuccessful effort to keep that company from going under during the Depression. Jesse B. Blayton graduated from black Langston University and later attended the Walton School of Business, and was reportedly the first African American CPA in Georgia. After first teaching at Morehouse, he joined the graduate faculty of AU in 1930. Like Milton, Blayton was an officer of Atlanta's black Citizens Trust Bank, and among numerous other community activities was the founder and president of the Atlanta Negro Chamber of Commerce.[101]

Hope did not relax during the fall of 1934, even though he was surrounded by an excellent faculty with strong commitments to community service. Retirement was certainly not on his mind, even though his friend Robert Moton retired that year and nudged the GEB about plans for Hope's retirement as well.[102] In February 1935 Hope canceled a speaking engagement at Emory University but felt obligated to accept another. In March, he and Lugenia were driven to Florida, where Hope spoke at the dedication of a new building at Bethune-Cookman College before the couple flew to Nassau for a brief vacation.

Before he left Atlanta for Florida, Hope dictated his wishes regarding his funeral arrangements to his assistant, who recorded them carefully: "He wished no elaborate ceremony—no sermon, no solos. As for the place of burial, if death occurred in a far place or country, he saw no need of going to the expense of bringing his body back here. Mr. Hope emphasized the fact that he wished a plain, very plain, casket, which might or might not be set inside a plain wooden box when lowered into the grave." Hope provided Constance Nabrit with precise directions for every phase of the burial in conjunction with the wishes of Lugenia Hope and Jane Hope Lyons. He even mentioned that he had once been promised a plot in Atlanta's Lincoln Cemetery, although he did not know if the offer still stood. He then dictated an important postscript: "These instructions were given by Mr. Hope so that they might be available whenever the need for them occurred; not because of any feeling of imminent disaster." It may have been his planned flight to Nassau that led Hope to record these explicit directions. Yet despite the explanatory postscript, it seems that he was also aware that his stepped-up activity might shorten his life. He may have even thought back to that summer in Europe when he had attended the simple but impressive funeral of Harold Grimshaw.[103]

Hope remained in the United States during the summer of 1935 to monitor the development of the University Homes housing project. He spent two days in Greensboro, North Carolina, where he was given mineral water to ease the pain in his joints, which had gotten worse. He wanted to spend at least a month at Clifton Springs Sanitarium but allowed himself only a week. Meanwhile, letters poured into his Atlanta office (some forwarded from Morehouse) from all sorts of people asking for all kinds of assistance. Inmates at a Pennsylvania penitentiary, for example, convinced their librarian to ask Hope to "furnish the prison library with studies on Negro life and culture." A Birmingham woman wrote to him for help in getting her nephew out of jail, and a former student wrote to him from Uganda asking Hope to assist in securing his release from a British prison. Hope made speeches and gave talks over the radio on Sunday evenings at 10:30 P.M. that were heard in most United States cities and even in parts of Africa and the Caribbean. It may have been these broadcasts that stimulated the flood of requests.[104]

Everything seemed to be going well in 1935. That fall, the American Baptist Home Mission Society relinquished its control of Morehouse College and placed the school in the hands of the Morehouse College Board of Trustees. With the encouragement of the GEB, the ABHMS also gave Morehouse a final $150,000 appropriation, thereby allowing the college to match most of the GEB's conditional funds. Hope was elated. Morehouse was well on its way to financial security. Nevertheless, he thought the frequently ill President Archer needed to become more involved in the school's finances. Archer, however, insisted on taking care of himself first and was already looking forward to retirement.[105]

Where Hope saw a college about to achieve financial security, however, the general Morehouse community saw a financially strapped college overshadowed by its affiliate, Atlanta University, which seemed to be on solid economic ground. Part of that apparent wealth had to do with long-standing commitments to AU's development as a university, and the other part was simply a matter of Hope's skills as a fund-raiser, a component sorely missing from Morehouse after he left. By the end of 1935, with Archer's approval, Hope had managed to merge the AU and Morehouse boards of trustees. The merger would allow him to keep watch over Morehouse's finances, as he had done from 1929 until his official resignation in 1931. Later, however, especially after Hope's death, there were some who thought the merger was simply another move to subordinate the interests of Morehouse to those of Atlanta University and erase the school's identity.[106]

Once Hope took office in 1929 and committed himself to the development of the new Atlanta University, he no longer envisioned AU as simply another college equal to Spelman, Morehouse, or any of the other black Atlanta colleges, including the old Atlanta University. His vision of AU as the centerpiece of an African American university system that would eventually include all the black colleges in Atlanta (though all would retain their distinct identities) influenced many of his decisions about Morehouse. With the encouragement of the GEB and the approval of the ABHMS, Hope endorsed plans that ceded land belonging to Morehouse College to Atlanta University. The GEB shared Hope's vision, and, according to reports in the African American press, many African Americans across the country believed the new Atlanta University represented the best hope for a black university in the Deep South. Understandably, it was a vision unappreciated by graduates of the old AU. It was also a vision increasingly disliked by the relatively impoverished Morehouse College community in the 1930s.[107]

By the beginning of the fall 1935 semester, only months before his death, the whispers that Hope had "sacrificed Morehouse" in order to build the new Atlanta University were out in the open. Few people outside his circle of family and friends realized how deeply the charge affected him. If there had been more time, he might have explained that he had done more than his share to move Morehouse forward. He might have also explained that Morehouse College's economic problems in the mid-1930s were another result of the Depression. The hard times had significantly reduced black Baptist support for mission schools, and that led to the ABHMS's decision to cut its ties with many of its mission schools, including Morehouse. Even though the parting gift of $150,000 from the ABHMS served an immediate need (by providing the money to secure the GEB's conditional gift), in the long run the loss of ABHMS support made Morehouse's road to recovery more difficult because the college was no longer linked to a strong and powerful northern missionary society. Just as AU and Fisk had suffered after losing American Missionary Association support many years earlier, the first years after termination would be difficult.

It would have been impossible for Hope to tell Morehouse partisans that their college needed a stronger administrator at the helm. Hope and Archer were extremely close, as were their families. Their sons sat virtually side by side in every classroom all through their school years. The issue remained a delicate subject for Hope's son fifty years later. John Hope II remembered that "Archer on the inside and Hope on the outside" were responsible for Morehouse College's development during his father's era. But both John Hope and Samuel Archer knew that the "outside" administrative work necessary to move Morehouse forward, especially during the Depression, was simply not in Archer's blood.[108]

Yet Hope kept his hurt to himself. His mildness and sensitivity had always caused him to shy away from controversy and kept him from placing himself in confrontational positions. At first, he thought that in time the rumor would run its course and die away. Perhaps he hoped that people would somehow realize that in order to promote the school he had at times been forced to compromise his principles, to remain silent when he wanted to speak out, and to speak out when he wanted to remain silent. It was the price one paid for being a black leader and college president in the segregated South. But it was a story John Hope himself would never tell.

Before the end of the year, Hope experienced two tragedies. In August, his chauffeur was shot and killed shortly before the beginning of the fall semester. Within four hours, a woman had informed Hope about the incident and asked him to hire her son as the dead driver's replacement. Shortly thereafter, the chauffeur's widow and her employer secured Hope's counsel in ensuring that her husband's killer was brought to justice. A few months later, in November, Hope wrote to an acquaintance that his nephew Judson Lyons, his sister Jane's only son, had died "as the result of an accident in Washington, D.C. He was either struck down by a street car or an automobile." Both of these deaths affected Hope deeply.[109]

He knew that his own time was running out. His nervous irritability had returned, and he could not ignore the occasional sharp, stinging pain in his left shoulder that vibrated down through the tips of his fingers. On 28 January 1936, Hope made out a will leaving everything to his wife. The next day he wrote to an insurance company in New York making "Genie the beneficiary of my policy, followed by my sons, equally, and then their heirs." He also wrote to the Dunbar National Bank in New York, where he had recently deposited $500, giving the same instructions.[110]

On 5 February 1936, Hope took a train to attend the annual meeting of the Oklahoma State Teachers Association in Oklahoma City. There he spent some time with black newspaper editor Roscoe Dunjee of the *Black Dispatch*. Dunjee was the son of John Dunjee, the minister at Augusta's Union Baptist Church who forty-five years earlier had helped Hope continue his education.

After the two-day conference in Oklahoma City, Hope traveled to several other cities, ending up in Tulsa. One of the last visits he made was in the home of Mollie and Buck Franklin. The Franklins had been his students at Roger Williams, and Buck had followed Hope to Atlanta Baptist College. They were also the parents of John Hope Franklin, the eminent historian who was named after John Hope. Dunjee later wrote to Lugenia Hope that her husband "apparently had some premonition of his own demise for the reason that he was obviously careful about what he did and how he exerted himself." [111] The Oklahoma winter was harsh and influenza was everywhere, yet Hope seemed to have escaped without problems.

He returned to Atlanta early on Lincoln's birthday in the midst of one of the coldest winters on record. After taking a hot bath, he went directly to his office to catch up on some work. Shortly thereafter, he complained of pain in his hands and feet. Lugenia Hope was already sick in bed with a severe cold, and had been there for two weeks. On 14 February, though he felt terrible, Hope spoke at Oglethorpe Elementary School at the Negro History Week assembly. Later that afternoon he went to see Florence Read. Feeling even worse, he decided to spend the night at MacVicar Infirmary.

The events that followed were rather bizarre. Hope asked the director of the infirmary, Ludie Andrews, to inform his wife of his plans to remain at the hospital. It was a routine call—he often stayed at the infirmary when he was not feeling well. A little later Hope phoned home in a rage to inquire why no one had called the hospital to ask about him and said that he was coming home immediately. Hope's flare-up, Ludie Andrews later said, was connected with his angina. John II, who was at the house along with his wife and mother, tried to reason with his father, but to no avail. When the elder Hope arrived home, he went straight to bed, coughing incessantly. The next morning the cough degenerated into short gasps for breath. With a temperature of 103 degrees and "pain over his entire body," Hope was immediately returned to the infirmary and his physician summoned.

Hope knew he was at the edge of death but continued to hold on. At one point he asked Andrews if he had pneumonia. The answer was soon apparent when he was placed inside an oxygen tent. His physician was worried about the possibility of another heart attack. At one point, briefly, Hope's fever seemed to have broken and Andrews wanted to inform Lugenia. Hope, however, told her, "You wait awhile. We don't know how this thing is going to pan out." His wife never saw him again after he was admitted to the hospital. Her own illness made it too dangerous. Lugenia later recalled that she pleaded with his physician to at least allow her to wave to him from the doorway of his

room, but even that was deemed too risky. "He might wave back," his physician warned, "and he must not even have that slight exertion." Hope was
visited, however, by Florence Read, his sister Jane Hope Lyons, and John
Hope II. To them all he repeated a familiar refrain: "If only I could tell my
successor what I was trying to do . . . there is so much work left to be done."

On 18 February he could hardly breathe or talk. Andrews recalled that the
next day, 19 February, completely aware of his situation, Hope simply refused
to die. "My wife's birthday is today," he told her. "I can't die today. I can't."
Somehow he managed to hold on for another day.

On 20 February 1936, Hope's temperature reached 104 degrees. At 2 : 15 p.m.
he quietly dropped off into an eternal sleep.[112] He was sixty-seven years old.
John Hope died believing that his work as an African American leader and
black college president was yet unfinished. Technically, he was correct; his
death was unexpected. But it would be up to others now, to a new generation
of African American leaders and black educators, to decide if the burden of
the dual roles was too heavy. It would be up to them to carry the torch forward. John Hope had made his contribution. He had packed the last seven
years of his life with perhaps fourteen years of living. Finally, perched high on
top of the mountain, his "clashing of the soul" would be no more.

Notes

Abbreviations

ABHMS	American Baptist Home Mission Society
ABHSA	American Baptist Historical Society Archives
AUC	Atlanta University Collection
BUA	Brown University Archives
DANB	*Dictionary of American Negro Biography*
GAH	Georgia Department of Archives and History
GEB	General Education Board
HMM	*Home Mission Monthly*
PUL	Princeton University Library
RAC	Rockefeller Archives Center
SCA	Spelman College Archives
SRM	Laura Spelman Rockefeller Memorial Archives
WAA	Worcester Academy Archives

Introduction

1. Gunnar Myrdal, *An American Dilemma: The Negro Problem and Modern Democracy*, 2 vols. (New York: McGraw-Hill, 1944).

2. W. E. B. Du Bois, *The Souls of Black Folk* (Chicago: A. C. McClurg, 1903; New York: Penguin Books, 1989), 5.

3. August Meier, *Negro Thought in America, 1880–1915: Racial Ideologies in the Age of Booker T. Washington* (Ann Arbor: University of Michigan Press, 1963).

4. The best study of Washington is still Louis R. Harlan's fascinating two-volume work, *Booker T. Washington: The Making of a Black Leader, 1856–1901* and *Booker T. Washington: The Wizard of Tuskegee, 1901–1915* (New York: Oxford University Press, 1972, 1983).

5. Willard B. Gatewood, *Aristocrats of Color: The Black Elite, 1880–1920* (Bloomington: Indiana University Press, 1990).

6. *Crisis* 55 (September 1948): 271; see also *Pittsburgh Courier*, 28 March 1936.

Chapter 1. "Oh Mary Don't You Weep"

1. For a history of Augusta's hinterlands, see J. William Harris, *Plain Folk and Gentry in a Slave Society: White Liberty and Black Slavery in Augusta's Hinterlands* (Middletown, Conn.: Wesleyan University Press, 1985).

2. The story of Mary's rape is from my interview with Dr. John Hope II, the younger son of John Hope. See also Ridgely Torrence's interview with Florence Read, former president of Spelman College and a close personal friend of John Hope's from the early 1920s until his death in 1936. This interview, like all those in the Torrence Papers, is undated, but all Torrence's interviews were conducted in the late 1930s and early 1940s. Torrence's papers are located in Special Collections of the Princeton University Library (hereafter PUL), Princeton, N.J.

3. On Lafayette's visit to Augusta and Hancock County, see *Augusta Chronicle*, 5 March 1925; see also Elizabeth Wiley Smith, *The History of Hancock County, Georgia: History, Heritage and Records*, 2 vols. (Washington, Ga.: Wilkes, 1974), 1:55.

4. Georgia Department of Archives and History (hereafter GAH), Estate Records of Hugh Taylor, Inferior Court, Ordinary Purpose Wills and Estate Records, Hancock County, book L, 1823–28, MFL 627, p. 442.

5. "Administration of Hugh Taylor Estate," Hancock County, book N, 1831–37, MFL 627–28, p. 13, GAH.

6. Ibid., 370–71.

7. A copy of Augusta's first map is in "Vertical File," Richmond County Historical Society, located in Augusta College Library, Augusta College, Augusta, Georgia.

8. See Edward J. Cashin, *The Story of Augusta* (Augusta: Richmond County Board of Education, 1980); see also U.S. Bureau of the Census, Population Schedules of the Eighth Census of the United States, 1860, drawer 332, reel 22, Georgia, vol. 12 (575–1038, Randolph and Richmond Counties); K. Woodward, *1841 Augusta Directory and City Advertiser* (Augusta: Brown and McCafferty, 1841); the *Augusta Chronicle* is also an excellent source on Augusta's cosmopolitanism and dynamic economy; see various issues from 1850 to 1870.

9. On Augusta's twin influences, see Cashin, *Story of Augusta*, 57.

10. See *Augusta Chronicle*, 21 April 1832; for other examples, see 26 November 1829, 12 June 1830, 23 June 1849, 4 September 1860.

11. For examples, see *Augusta Chronicle*, 16 December 1829, 20 June 1835, 1 July 1835, and 18 January 1860. For a general history of urban slavery, see Richard C. Wade, *Slavery in the Cities: The South 1820–1860* (New York: Oxford University Press, 1964).

12. See Whittington B. Johnson, "Free Blacks in Antebellum Augusta, Georgia: A Demographic and Economic Profile," *Richmond County History* 14 (Winter 1982): 10–22; also *Augusta Chronicle*, 1 July 1835, 18 June 1840, 4 July 1852. For a general history of free blacks, see Ira Berlin, *Slaves without Masters: The Free Negro in the Antebellum South* (New York: Random House, 1976); see also Michael P. Johnson and James L. Roark, *Black Masters: A Free Family of Color in the Old South* (New York: W. W. Norton, 1984).

13. *Augusta Chronicle*, 2 January 1852; see also *Acts of the General Assembly of the State of Georgia, 1851–1861*, 262.

14. Lethe's children first appear in the 1860 census. See Eighth U.S. Census, p. 861, GAH; Edward and Elizabeth [Taylor] Bustin also appear in this census, on p. 761, and in the Seventh U.S. Census, 1850, along with their slaves. The Bustins are also listed in the Augusta city directory for 1841. See Woodward, *1841 Augusta Directory*, 27; also Torrence interviews with Florence Read and Jane Hope Lyons, Torrence Papers, PUL; my interview with John Hope II.

15. See Ridgely Torrence, *The Story of John Hope* (New York: Macmillan, 1948), 5–6; also Alex Haley and David Stevens, *Alex Haley's "Queen": The Story of an American Family* (New York: William Morrow, 1993).

16. Torrence, *Story of John Hope*, 5–6.

17. Several studies document the treatment of enslaved African American women. Particularly useful in explaining enslaved female bonding and sexual encounters are Deborah Gray White, *Arn't I a Woman: Female Slaves in the Plantation South* (New York: W. W. Norton, 1985); Paul Giddings, *When and Where I Enter: The Impact of Black Women on Race and Sex in America* (New York: William Morrow, 1984); see also George Rawick, ed., *American Slave: A Composite Autobiography, Georgia Narratives, Parts 3 and 4*, 19 vols. (Westport, Conn.: Greenwood Press, 1972), 13:292–93.

18. See Ann F. Scott, *The Southern Lady: From Pedestal to Politics, 1830–1930* (Chicago: University of Chicago Press, 1970), especially pt. 1; Elizabeth Fox-Genovese, *Within the Plantation Household: Black and White Women of the Old South* (Chapel Hill: University of North Carolina Press, 1988).

19. On Mary Bustin's management of her slaves, see "Administration of Hugh Taylor Estate," Hancock County, book N, 1831–37, MFL 627–28, GAH; see also Eighth U.S. Census, reel 22, p. 861, GAH.

20. See Eighth U.S. Census, 1860, reel 22, p. 861, GAH; on the importance of slave names, see Herbert Gutman, *The Black Family in Slavery and Freedom, 1750–1925* (New York: Pantheon Books, 1976), especially chaps. 5, 6.

21. Eighth U.S. Census, 1860, reel 22, 861. Most likely Butt died sometime after 1854 in that Lethea's youngest daughter, Kate, is listed as seven years old in the 1860 census. A friend of the family later noted, "the Butts wouldn't have been listed as 'Free Persons of Color' because their father was a white man." The people required to register were those whose fathers were black. Though that conclusion is questionable, it nevertheless seems to coincide with the records and explains the children's absence from free black registers, tax digests, and other documents. See interviews with Miss Carrie Harper and Mrs. Price, "The Harper Family," Torrence Papers, PUL. Miss Carrie Harper, eighty-three years old when the interview was conducted, and her sister, Mrs. Price, then eighty-seven, were daughters of Robert Harper, a free black man in Augusta who knew the Hopes well.

22. Rawick, *American Slave*, 13:230.

23. See J. T. Trowbridge, *The South: A Tour of Its Battle-fields and Ruined Cities, a Journey through the Desolated States, and Talks with the People* (Hartford: L. Stebbins, 1866), 489.

24. Interview with Dart Family, Torrence Papers, PUL. John Dart was a minister and race leader who was responsible for Hope's conversion to Christianity and later influenced him to continue his education.

25. Ibid.; see also Johnson and Roark, *Black Masters*; also Michael P. Johnson and James L. Roark, *No Chariot Let Down: Charleston's Free People of Color on the Eve of the Civil War* (Chapel Hill: University of North Carolina Press, 1984); C. W. Birnie, "The Education of the Negro in Charleston, South Carolina, Prior to the Civil War," *Journal of Negro History* 12 (January 1927): 13–21; interview with Jane Hope Lyons, Torrence Papers, PUL.

26. Interviews with the Harper Family and Jane Hope Lyons, Torrence Papers, PUL; see also Eighth U.S. Census, 1860, reel 22, p. 861, GAH.

27. On Newton, see Kenneth Coleman and Charles Stephen Gurr, eds., *Dictionary of Georgia Biography*, vol. 2 (Athens: University of Georgia Press, 1983), 741–42; DeSaussure Ford, *An Address Embracing Biographical Sketches of Hon. Thos. W. Miller, Artemas Gould, George M. Newton, M.D., and Isaac Tuttle, Donors and Benefactors of the Augusta Orphan Asylum* (Augusta: Phoenix Printing Office, 1886), 8–11, pamphlet in possession of Emily Boyles, director of Tuttle-Newton Home, Augusta, Georgia; see also Phinizy Spalding, *The History of the Medical College of Georgia* (Athens: University of Georgia Press, 1987); Woodward, *1841 Augusta Directory*, 29.

28. See O. B. Bunce, "The Savannah at Augusta," originally published in *Appletons' Journal of Literature, Science and Art* 6 (November 1871): 575–77; Torrence, *Story of John Hope*, 20.

29. Spalding, *History of the Medical College of Georgia*, 23; *Southern Medical and Surgical Journal*, n.s., 15 (February 1859): 142–44.

30. R. A. Watkins, *Directory for the City of Augusta and Business Advertiser for 1859* (Augusta: R. A. Watkins, 1859), 27. People interviewed years later speculated on Newton and Taylor's relationship. Most did not think the two ever married, although the Harpers did say that Newton may have married her secretly (see interviews with Harper Family and Jane Hope Lyons, Torrence Papers, PUL). There is no evidence in Georgia or South Carolina marriage records, or in Newton's will, that a marriage ever took place. In addition, no member of the Hope family, including John Hope, ever suggested that Newton or James Hope ever married their mother.

31. Interviews with Mrs. R. C. Williams (Josephine White Williams), daughter of William Jefferson White (an outspoken race leader in Augusta during Hope's youth), Josephine Thomas White (reportedly Mary Frances Butts's best friend), and Harper Family, Torrence Papers, PUL.

32. See George Newton's will, Richmond County, Georgia, Ordinary Estate Records, Wills, vol. C, 1853–67, drawer 48, reel 74, pp. 212–14, GAH, hereafter cited as Newton will, GAH. For an example of a contested will, see Kent Anderson Leslie's *Woman of Color, Daughter of Privilege: Amanda America Dickson, 1849–1893* (Athens: University of Georgia Press, 1995), especially chap. 3.

33. John Hope to Lugenia Hope, 23 August 1912, John Hope Papers, Atlanta University Collection, Atlanta University, Atlanta, Georgia, hereafter cited as Hope Pa-

pers, AUC. My research in the Hope Papers was completed before they were micro-filmed, and I cite sources as they existed when I used them.

34. Quoted in Torrence, *Story of John Hope*, 14–15.

35. See John Hope, "Autobiographical Sketch," 22 July 1934, Hope Papers, AUC.

36. Eighth U.S. Census, 1860, reel 22, p. 860, GAH. James Hope owned real estate valued at $3,500, and his personal estate was valued at $80,000. His age appears in-correctly in the 1860 census as fifty; he was actually fifty-five. See also K. Woodward, *1841 Augusta Directory*, 56; *Augusta Chronicle*, 31 December 1842, 15 December 1845, 12 May 1847.

37. See Hope, "Autobiographical Sketch," Hope Papers, AUC; "General Index to Deeds and Mortgages," vol. 3, 1842–54, vol. 4, 1854–63, drawer 139, reel 8, Superior Court, Richmond County, book NN, p. 628, book 2N, 1858–60, reel 26, p. 463, GAH.

38. Torrence interview with Mrs. R. C. Williams, Torrence Papers, PUL.

39. "General Index to Deeds and Mortgages," vol. 3, 1842–54, vol. 4, 1854–63, drawer 139, reel 8, Superior Court, Richmond County, book GG, LL, HH, NN, p. 628, book 2N, 1858–60, reel 26, p. 463, GAH.

40. Interview with Mrs. R. C. Williams, Harper Family, Torrence Papers, PUL; Newton will, GAH; "Land Records," book 2N 1858–60, reel 26, p. 463, GAH.

41. Hope, "Autobiographical Sketch," Hope Papers, AUC.

42. These policing organizations are described in Harris, *Plain Folk and Gentry*, 35; on Augusta's notification and reaction to Harper's Ferry, see *Augusta Chronicle*, 20 Oc-tober 1859, 7, 28 December 1859.

43. See *Augusta Chronicle*, 7, 18 January, 26 February, 23 March, 5 May 1860.

44. *Augusta Chronicle*, 18 December 1860, 13, 20, 25 January 1861.

45. "Compiled Service Records of Confederate Soldiers Who Served in Organiza-tions from the State of Georgia," First Local Troops, Infantry, Augusta, Ga., drawer 254, reel 74, p. 764, GAH.

46. *Augusta Chronicle*, 9 January 1863.

47. *Augusta Chronicle*, 3 November 1864. On Augusta during the Civil War, see Cashin, *Story of Augusta*, chap. 8; Florence Fleming Corley, *Confederate City: Augusta, Georgia 1860–1865* (Columbia: University of South Carolina Press, 1960); Berry Fleming, ed., *Autobiography of a City in Arms: Augusta, Georgia, 1861–1865* (Augusta: Richmond County Historical Society, 1976). On Augusta's free blacks, see *Augusta Chronicle*, 6 June, 21 August, 5 March 1863, 1, 9 October 1864, 31 January 1865.

48. Rawick, *American Slave*, 13:225, 230.

49. See Hope, "Autobiographical Sketch," Hope Papers, AUC; also Torrence inter-views with Jane Hope Lyons and Mrs. R. C. Williams, Torrence Papers, PUL.

50. See Torrence interview with Lugenia Hope, Torrence Papers, PUL; Hope, "Autobiographical Sketch," Hope Papers, AUC.

51. Hope, "Autobiographical Sketch," Hope Papers, AUC; also interview with Jane Hope Lyons, Torrence Papers, AUC. Several works treat the life of Frederick Doug-lass; the latest biography is William S. McFeely's *Frederick Douglass* (New York: Simon & Schuster, 1991).

52. Torrence interview with Jane Hope Lyons, Torrence Papers, PUL.

53. See the Ninth U.S. Census, 1870, 69, Georgia, GAH.

Chapter 2. Identity

1. Hope, "Autobiographical Sketch," Hope Papers, AUC.

2. Rayford Logan, "Carter G. Woodson: Mirror and Molder of His Time, 1875–1905," *Journal of Negro History* 58 (January 1973): 1.

3. *Augusta Chronicle*, 25 March 1868.

4. Cashin, *Story of Augusta*, chap. 8; see also Edmund L. Drago, *Black Politicians and Reconstruction in Georgia: A Splendid Failure* (Athens: University of Georgia Press, 1992), chap. 6; *Augusta Chronicle*, 25 March, 21 April, 4 November 1868.

5. See interview with Mrs. Ursula Simpkins White, Torrence Papers, PUL. Mrs. White grew up in Augusta and knew the young John Hope well; see also interviews with Mrs. Claudia White Harreld (a daughter of William J. White) and Mrs. R. C. Williams, Torrence Papers, PUL.

6. Ninth U.S. Census, 1870, vol. 23, 69, Georgia, GAH. There are many inaccuracies in the ages of members of the Butts family in this census. For example, Anna Butts was 27, not 24; and James Butts was 23, not 15.

7. "Memo from John Hope's Dream," 11–12 September 1933, Hope Papers, AUC.

8. Hope, "Autobiographical Sketch," Hope Papers, AUC.

9. Speech delivered to the alumni of Atlanta University Laboratory High School, 27 April 1934, Hope Papers, AUC; see also interview with Jane Hope Lyons, Torrence Papers, PUL.

10. John Hope, "Extracts from Dr. Hope's Chapel Talks," *Spelman Messenger* 49 (February 1933): 23; see also interview with Jane Hope Lyons, Torrence Papers, PUL.

11. See A. Ray Roland and Helen Callahan, *Yesterday's Augusta* (Miami: E. A. Seemann, 1976), 15; see also Federal Writers' Project in Georgia, Works Progress Administration, *Augusta* (Augusta: Tidwell Printing, 1938), 128.

12. Rawick, *American Slave*, 13:292–93.

13. Federal Writers' Project in Georgia, *Augusta*, 128.

14. See Corley, *Confederate City: Augusta*; Roland and Callahan, *Yesterday's Augusta*, 27.

15. Hope, "Extracts from Dr. Hope's Chapel Talks," 23; see also interview with Jane Hope Lyons, Torrence Papers, PUL; Eugene Edmund Murphey, "Always the River," poem in Federal Writers' Project in Georgia, *Augusta*, 1–4.

16. Regarding the value of education, see in particular James D. Anderson, *The Education of Blacks in the South, 1860–1935* (Chapel Hill: University of North Carolina Press, 1988), especially chap. 1, for examples of black Augusta's educational efforts before the Civil War.

17. The Augusta teacher may have been Jane Holloway, the daughter of Frances Pickney Bonneau Holloway, who possibly ran the school Mary Frances attended back in the 1850s. Several black Holloways are listed in Augusta city directories after the Civil War; see also interview with Jane Hope Lyons, Torrence Papers, PUL.

18. See *Augusta Chronicle*, 1 October 1876; see also Edward Cashin, *The Quest: A History of Public Education in Richmond County, Georgia* (Columbia: R. L. Bryan, 1985), chap. 1; Torrence interview with Georgia Swift King, Torrence Papers, PUL.

19. On Laney, see Coleman and Gurr, *Dictionary of Georgia Biography*, 2:599–600; see also Sadie Iola Daniel, *Women Builders* (Washington, D.C.: Associated Publishers, 1931).

20. Interview with Mrs. Georgia Swift King, Torrence Papers, PUL.

21. The best treatment of the missionary teachers in Georgia is Jacqueline Jones, *Soldiers of Light and Love: Northern Teachers and Georgia Blacks, 1865–1873* (Chapel Hill: University of North Carolina Press, 1980).

22. James Hope did not make out a will until 16 October 1876, a week before he died. See Richmond County, Georgia, Ordinary Estate Records, Wills, vol. I, drawer 48, reel 57, GAH; on deeds, see Richmond County, Georgia, Superior Court Deeds and Mortgages, book 3C, 1874–75, drawer 138, reel 38, p. 208, GAH; see also interviews with Jane Hope Lyons and Mrs. R. C. Williams, Torrence Papers, PUL.

23. Hope, "Autobiographical Sketch," Hope Papers, AUC; see also interviews with Harper Family, Torrence Papers, PUL.

24. Hope, "Autobiographical Sketch," Hope Papers, AUC.

25. Federal Writers' Project in Georgia, *Augusta*, 89–90.

26. See *Augusta Chronicle*, 12, 28 March 1871.

27. For accounts of the Hamburg riot, see Cashin, *Story of Augusta*, 163; Federal Writers' Project in Georgia, *Augusta*, 88–90; *Augusta Chronicle*, 9, 11 July 1876; see also Joel Williamson, *After Slavery: The Negro in South Carolina during Reconstruction, 1861–1877* (New York: W. W. Norton, 1975), 270–71.

28. On Augusta's first lynching, see *Augusta Chronicle*, 27 August 1876; also Hope, "Autobiographical Sketch," Hope Papers, AUC.

29. Ordinary Estate Records, "Wills," vol. I, drawer 48, reel 57, GAH.

30. See Richmond County, Georgia, Ordinary Estate Records, Wills, vol. D, 1868–81, drawer 48, reel 74, pp. 148, 471–73; Inventory's Account Sales Divisions Years Support Book L–M, 1873–79, books N–O, 1879–88, books L–P, 1873–98, drawer 48, reels 57–58; see also "Annual Returns," drawer 48, reel 44, all GAH; Hope, "Autobiographical Sketch," Hope Papers, AUC.

31. Conscientious, honest, and tenacious administrators were essential in ensuring that black families received major inheritances from prominent whites. It seems James Hope recognized that, and he should have been more selective in choosing his executors. Not far away in Hancock County, free women of color Amanda Dickson and Susan Hunt survived legal challenges to their inheritances mainly because of excellent executors chosen by their white benefactors; see Adele Logan Alexander, *Ambiguous Lives: Free Women of Color in Rural Georgia, 1789–1879* (Fayetteville: University of Arkansas Press, 1991), especially chap. 5; Leslie, *Woman of Color, Daughter of Privilege*.

32. For a fuller discussion of this black elite, see Gatewood, *Aristocrats of Color*, especially chap. 1; A. E. Sholes, *Sholes Directory of the City of Augusta for 1877* (Augusta: A. E. Sholes, 1877).

33. Hope, "Autobiographical Sketch," Hope Papers, AUC; see also John Hope, speech delivered at Tuskegee Institute, 25 May 1933, Hope Papers, AUC.

34. See Hope, "Autobiographical Sketch," also John Hope to Dr. D. D. Crawford, 28 October 1930, Hope Papers, AUC; see also interviews with Rev. T. Dwelle, former pastor of Springfield Church, who knew Hope in his adolescent years, and Jane Hope Lyons, Torrence Papers, PUL.

35. On slaves being whipped, see Rawick, *American Slave*, 13:233; Hope's description of the Terri is from Torrence, *Story of John Hope*, 42.

36. Several studies document the importance of the African American church in the black community, irrespective of class; see, e.g., C. Eric Lincoln and Lawrence H. Mamiya, *The Black Church in the African-American Experience* (Durham: Duke University Press, 1990). For descriptions of the Negro Territory, see Diane Harvey, "The Terri, Augusta's Black Enclave," *Richmond County History* 5 (Summer 1973): 67; Federal Writer's Project in Georgia, *Augusta*, 45–50; my interviews with J. Phillip Waring, Augusta, June 1992, 1993. Mr. Waring grew up in Augusta and is in his eighties at this writing.

37. On Silver Bluff's and Springfield's beginnings, see Carter G. Woodson, *The History of the Negro Church* (Washington, D.C.: Associated Publishers, 1921); also the pamphlet *Springfield Baptist Church, Church History, 1787–1987*, by Betty Anderson (Augusta: Phoenix-Commercial Printers, 1987), located in the Richmond County Historical Society Collection, Augusta College Library, Augusta, Georgia.

38. Betty Anderson, *Springfield Baptist Church*. For the Augusta Institute's beginnings, see Edward A. Jones, *A Candle in the Dark: A History of Morehouse College* (Valley Forge, Pa.: Judson Press, 1967), especially chap. 1. On social activities in the church, see Torrence interviews with R. C. Williams, Jane Hope Lyons, Claudia Harreld, and Ursula Simpkins White, Torrence Papers, PUL; *Augusta Chronicle*, 26 April 1866.

39. Torrence interviews with Claudia White Harreld (daughter of William Jefferson White) and R. C. Williams, Torrence Papers, PUL.

40. Torrence interview with Claudia White Harreld, Torrence Papers, PUL.

41. In her interview with Torrence, Claudia Harreld said that her mother was a slave and that in March 1886 there was a thirtieth anniversary celebration, which would put the date of their union in 1856. If *she* was a slave, marriage would have been impossible, although White could have taken up residence in her master's home. Torrence interviews with Claudia Harreld and R. C. Williams, Torrence Papers, PUL. White does not appear in tax digests before 1869. See also Coleman and Gurr, *Dictionary of Georgia Biography*, 2:1059–61.

42. See Cashin, *Story of Augusta*, chaps. 8, 9; also Lloyd P. Terrell and Marguerite S. C. Terrell, *Blacks in Augusta: A Chronology, 1741–1977* (Augusta: Preston Publications, 1977), 10–21; Meier, *Negro Thought in America*, 156, 176, 221–22.

43. On the importance of Sabbath schools, see James D. Anderson, *Education of Blacks in the South*, chap. 1; William J. Simmons, *Men of Mark: Eminent, Progressive and Rising*, reprint ed. (Chicago: Johnson, 1970), 791–92.

44. See Cashin, *The Quest*, especially chap. 2; also Torrence interviews with Clau-

dia White Harreld and Georgia Swift King, Torrence Papers, PUL; on Ware High School, see James D. Anderson and Vincent P. Franklin, eds., *New Perspectives on Black Educational History* (Boston: G. K. Hall, 1978); for examples of White in the *Augusta Chronicle*, see 28 April 1870, 3 January, 24 July 1874.

45. John Hope to D. D. Crawford, 28 October 1930, Hope Papers, AUC.

46. See I. Garland Penn, *The Afro-American Press and Its Editors*, reprint ed. (New York: Arno Press, 1969); Gurr and Coleman, *Dictionary of Georgia Biography*, 1059–61.

47. Hope to D. D. Crawford, 28 October 1930, Hope Papers, AUC.

48. On Augusta Institute's move to Atlanta, see Jones, *Candle in the Dark*, chap. 1. On Booker T. Washington, see Harlan, *Booker T. Washington: Making of a Black Leader*, chap. 6. On attendance at Ware High School, see Torrence interview with Richard R. Wright, Torrence Papers, PUL; also J. Morgan Kousser, "Separate but Not Equal: The Supreme Court's First Decision on Racial Discrimination in Schools," *Journal of Southern History* 46 (February 1980): 22. On Paine College, see George E. Clary Jr., *Paine College: Augusta, Georgia, an Account of Its Beginnings, 1882–1903* (Brunswick: Lemmond Letter Shop, 1975); Hope, "Autobiographical Sketch," Hope Papers, AUC.

49. For descriptions of Henson's establishment, see Augusta city directories for 1872, 1879, and 1882. Copies are located under the names of various publishers in the Georgia State Archives in Atlanta, and in the Richmond County Historical Society, Augusta College Library, Augusta; see also *Augusta Chronicle*, 5 June 1885.

50. See *Augusta Chronicle*, 9 March 1875.

51. Hope appears in city records for the first time in 1882 as a clerk at Henson's Restaurant. See A. E. Sholes, *Sholes Directory of the City of Augusta, 1882* (Augusta: Chronicle Book Room, 1882); see also Torrence interview with the Harper Family, Torrence Papers, PUL.

52. Hope, "Autobiographical Sketch," Hope Papers, AUC; also Torrence interview with Levi White, Torrence Papers, PUL. White, not related to the William J. White family, grew up in Augusta and was the husband of Ursula Simpkins White, also interviewed by Torrence, who taught in Augusta's schools for more than forty years.

53. Torrence interviews with Levi White and Ursula Simpkins White, Torrence Papers, PUL; also Federal Writers' Project in Georgia, *Augusta*, 171–75; Harris, *Plain Folk and Gentry*, 23.

54. Cashin, *Story of Augusta*, 139, 161–64.

55. Torrence interviews with Jane Hope Lyons, Claudia White Harreld, and Channing Tobias, Torrence Papers, PUL.

56. John Hope to Lugenia Hope, 6 May 1919; also Hope, "Autobiographical Sketch," Hope Papers, AUC; Torrence interviews with Claudia White Harreld, Jane Hope Lyons, and Lucian Hayden White, Torrence Papers, PUL.

57. On southern education during this period, see Dorothy Orr, *A History of Education in Georgia* (Chapel Hill: University of North Carolina Press, 1950); David N. Plank and Rick Ginsberg, eds., *Southern Cities, Southern Schools: Public Education in the Urban South* (Westport, Conn.: Greenwood Press, 1990), especially chap. 4.

58. On activities of working-class black Augustans, see Howard N. Rabinowitz, *Race*

Relations in the Urban South: 1865–1890 (New York: Oxford University Press, 1978), especially chap. 10 on African Americans attending court sessions as entertainment; also my interview with J. Phillip Waring.

59. Torrence interviews with the Harper Family, Lucian Hayden White, R. C. Williams, and Claudia White Harreld, Torrence Papers, PUL. Newton appears in Augusta city directories as a postman from the late 1870s until his death in 1925.

60. See Augusta city directories for 1881–85; also Terrell and Terrell, *Blacks in Augusta*.

61. On these black Augusta leaders, see Coleman and Gurr, *Dictionary of Georgia Biography*, 2:646–47, 1:346–47, 2:1098–1100; see also Cashin, *Story of Augusta*, 113, 184; Torrence, *Story of John Hope*, 57–58; *Augusta Chronicle*, 3 January 1874, 21 March 1876, 21 February 1886; Terrell and Terrell, *Blacks in Augusta*, 6, 17–18, 21–23; Torrence interviews with Jane Hope Lyons and Lucian Hayden White, Torrence Papers, PUL; John Hope, "Emancipation Day Speech," undated (ca. 1904), Hope Papers, AUC.

62. Torrence interview with Harper Family, Torrence Papers, PUL; Horace Calvin Wingo, "Race Relations in Georgia, 1872–1908" (Ph.D. diss., University of Georgia, 1969); see also Free Negro Docket, Inferior Court Records, Office of Ordinary, Richmond County, 1848–63, GAH; Cashin, *Story of Augusta*, 184; *Augusta Chronicle*, 21 March 1876.

63. Cashin, *Story of Augusta*, 132; Cashin, *The Quest*, chap. 2; also *Augusta Chronicle*, 28 April 1870, 1 July 1866, 3 January 1874.

64. On the conservatism of Wright and Walker during the "age of Booker T. Washington," see Meier, *Negro Thought in America*, 156; see also *Augusta Chronicle*, 24, 25 April 1884, 10 October 1882, 14 December 1883, 5 June 1885; Torrence interview with Richard R. Wright Jr., Torrence Papers, PUL; Cashin, *Story of Augusta*, 163.

65. Torrence interviews with Jane Hope Lyons and Lucian Hayden White, Torrence Papers, PUL.

66. John Hope, "Talk to Students," undated but probably ca. 1904, Atlanta Baptist College, John Hope, "Sunday Afternoon Talk at Spelman Seminary," also undated, ca. 1900, both in Hope Papers, AUC.

67. The Union Baptist Church records are located in box 3, folder 4, notebook 8, Torrence Papers, PUL; on the question of color in Springfield Baptist Church, see Torrence interview with Richard R. Wright, Torrence Papers, PUL; my interview with J. Phillip Waring.

68. Torrence interviews with Dart Family, Jane Hope Lyons, and Mrs. R. C. Williams, Torrence Papers, PUL.

69. Hope, "Talk to Students," ca. 1904, also "Autobiographical Sketch," Hope Papers, AUC; Union Baptist Church Records; Torrence interviews with Claudia White Harreld and R. C. Williams, Torrence Papers, PUL.

70. Torrence interview with Dart Family, Torrence Papers, PUL; see also John Hope, "Speech at Gammon Theological Seminary," 14 May 1935, Hope Papers, AUC.

71. John Hope to Joseph B. Cumming, 13 August 1915, Hope Papers, AUC; also Torrence interview with Jane Hope Lyons, Torrence Papers, PUL; Hope, "Autobiographical Sketch," Hope Papers, AUC.

72. John Hope to Mr. R. R. Taylor, 24 August 1925, Hope Papers, AUC.

73. Torrence interview with Dart Family, Torrence Papers, PUL.

74. Channing H. Tobias, "Interracial Commission Honors Dr. Hope: Drs. Ashby Jones and Channing Tobias Pay Tribute to His Work for Better Relations," *Atlanta University Bulletin* 3 (July 1936): 17.

Chapter 3. Worcester and Brown

1. For descriptions of Worcester and its early history, see Mildred McClary Tymeson, *Worcester Centennial 1848–1948: Historical Sketches of the Settlement the Town and the City* (Worcester, Mass.: Worcester Centennial, 1948), 1–15; see also Edward A. Lewis, *The Blackstone Valley Line: The Story of the Blackstone Canal Company and the Providence & Worcester Railroad* (Seekonk, Mass.: Baggage Car, 1973), especially chap. 3.

2. For Hope's impressions after arriving in the North, see Hope, "Talk to Students," ca. 1904, Hope Papers, AUC; also Torrence interviews with Lucian Hayden White and Jane Hope Lyons, Torrence Papers, PUL.

3. On Worcester's history, see Tymeson, *Worcester Centennial*, 25–41.

4. On Worcester's African American population between 1860 and 1900, see Population Schedules of the Eighth, Ninth, Tenth, and Twelfth Censuses of the United States, Massachusetts, Worcester County, National Archives and Records Service, Washington, D.C.

5. Torrence interviews with John Swain, Erastus Starr, and Robert Drawbridge, Torrence Papers, PUL; all three men were Hope's classmates at Worcester Academy. On Worcester's rigid character, see Tymeson, *Worcester Centennial*, 4–8.

6. Cloyd E. Small, *Achieving the Honorable: Worcester Academy, 1834–1978* (Worcester, Mass.: Davis Press, 1979), 49; see also *Annual Catalogue of Worcester Academy* (Worcester: Goddard Publishers, 1887), 33–34, located in Worcester Academy Archives, Worcester, Mass., hereafter cited as Worcester Academy catalogue, year, WAA; see also *Academy* (February 1890), in Hope Papers, AUC.

7. Small, *Achieving the Honorable*, 51; interview with John Swain, Torrence Papers, PUL.

8. Small, *Achieving the Honorable*, 58–61; *Worcester Academy Bulletin*, December 1913, 16–19.

9. Small, *Achieving the Honorable*, 76–79; Worcester Academy catalogue, 1887, p. 28, WAA.

10. On Abercrombie, see Small, *Achieving the Honorable*, 103; also interview with Mrs. Edith Snow, Torrence Papers, PUL. Edith Snow was the daughter of D. W. Abercrombie. She was ten years old when Hope arrived at Worcester.

11. John Hope to D. W. Abercrombie, 5 November 1927, Hope Papers, AUC.

12. Ibid.; also Dr. Abercrombie to John Hope, 27 October 1925, Hope Papers, AUC; and Worcester Academy catalogue, 1887, pp. 1–3, WAA.

13. See D. W. Abercrombie to John Hope, 27 October 1925, Hope to Abercrombie,

5 November 1927, Hope Papers, AUC; see also Torrence interview with Edith Snow, Torrence Papers, PUL.

14. Small, *Achieving the Honorable*, 107; Worcester Academy catalogues, 1886–90, WAA; Worcester Academy scrapbook, 1886–90, WAA; Torrence interview with Edith Snow, Torrence Papers, PUL.

15. Interviews with Albert Bailey (another of Hope's classmates at Worcester), Erastus Starr, and John Swain, Torrence Papers, PUL; see also Worcester Academy catalogues, 1887, 1888, WAA.

16. Interviews with John Swain and Erastus Starr, Torrence Papers, PUL. See also interview with Edith Snow and Robert Drawbridge; *Worcester Academy Bulletin*, Spring 1964, 7–9; Worcester Academy catalogues, 1887, 1888, WAA; and D. W. Abercrombie to John Hope, 27 October 1925, Hope Papers, AUC.

17. Interview with Albert Bailey, Torrence Papers, PUL.

18. The Swain articles are in *Voice of the Negro*, December 1905, June 1906.

19. For examples of Hope's mischief, see "1890 Class History"; see also John Hope to Robert Drawbridge, 18 March 1912, Hope Papers, AUC; Torrence interviews with Erastus Starr, John Swain, and Robert Drawbridge, Torrence Papers, PUL. For biographical information on Hope's classmates, see Register of Alumni for class of 1890, WAA.

20. Torrence interviews with Erastus Starr and Albert Bailey, Torrence Papers, PUL; see also John Hope to Herbert Foster, 18 April 1924, Hope Papers, AUC.

21. Torrence interviews with Erastus Starr, John Swain, and Jane Hope Lyons, Torrence Papers, PUL.

22. Torrence interview with Dunbar Walton, Torrence Papers, PUL. Walton was one of Hope's co-workers at Henson's restaurant, where he worked for twenty years. He remembered Hope's return in 1887.

23. Torrence interviews with Jane Hope Lyons and Roscoe Dunjee, Torrence Papers, PUL. Dungee was the son of the man who was the minister at Union Baptist Church the summer of 1887.

24. Torrence interviews with Mrs. R. C. Williams and Jane Hope Lyons, Torrance Papers, PUL; see also Union Baptist Church records; selected material is also located in Torrence Papers, PUL.

25. Still's book, a large volume of 780 pages, chronicled the stories he heard from runaways while he was chairman of the Acting Vigilance Committee of Philadelphia. See William Still, *Underground Railroad Records* (Hartford, Conn.: 1886).

26. Torrence interviews with Lugenia Burns Hope, Jane Hope Lyons, and Roscoe Dungee, Torrence Papers, PUL; John Hope to Edward Burr Solomon, 10 October 1893, Hope Papers, AUC.

27. Torrence interviews with Albert Bailey, Erastus Starr, and John Swain, Torrence Papers, PUL.

28. Torrence interview with John Swain, Torrence Papers, PUL; Worcester Academy catalogues, 1887–90, WAA.

29. John Hope, "My First Trip to Boston," undated essay, Hope Papers, AUC.

30. Torrence interview with John Dart Family, Torrence Papers, PUL.

31. Torrence interview with Edith Snow, Torrence Papers, PUL; John Hope to D. W. Abercrombie, 18 February 1905, Hope to Robert Drawbridge, 18 March 1912, Hope Papers, AUC.

32. Du Bois reference quoted in David L. Lewis, *W. E. B. Du Bois: Biography of a Race, 1868–1919* (New York: Henry Holt, 1993), 145; the quote originally appeared in Du Bois's *Autobiography: A Soliloquy on Viewing My Life from the Last Decade of Its First Century* (New York: International Publishers, 1968), 145.

33. Commencement speech delivered at Gammon Theological Seminary, 14 May 1935, Hope Papers, AUC.

34. Ibid.

35. See Walter C. Bronson, *The History of Brown University, 1764–1914* (Providence: Brown University, 1914), chaps. 1, 2.

36. See *New York Examiner*, 25 September 1890, in "Brown University Scrapbook for Class of 1890," 109, in Brown University Archives (hereafter BUA), John Hay Library, hereafter cited as Brown University Scrapbook and page number, if applicable.

37. Ibid., 459. For descriptions of University Hall and other buildings at Brown University, see Federal Writers' Project of the Works Progress Administration for the State of Rhode Island, *Rhode Island: A Guide to the Smallest State* (Boston: Houghton Mifflin, 1937), 273–75; on student dormitories, see *Catalogue of the Officers and Students of Brown University 1890–91* (Providence: Snow & Farnham, 1890), 107–8, BUA; on Hope's room, see "Student File of John Hope," BUA.

38. On the struggle of women at Brown, see Bronson, *History of Brown*, 453–58; descriptions of the opening day ceremony are in the *Christian Inquirer*, in Brown University Scrapbook, 106.

39. The president's speech was published in the Brown University Scrapbook, 107; the name of Hope's roommate is in "Student File of John Hope."

40. Unable to shake his controversial views on the silver question, Andrews resigned from Brown University in 1898; see Bronson, *History of Brown*, 461–68.

41. John Hope to Dr. E. Benjamin Andrews, 9 November 1906, Hope Papers, AUC.

42. See transcripts of John Hope's grades at Brown University, 1890–94, BUA; see also Brown University catalogues, 1890–94, for names of courses, departments, and requirements; Bronson, *History of Brown*, 428–30.

43. John Hope to Mr. Justin M. Hope, 12 November 1932, Hope Papers, AUC.

44. Torrence interviews with Jane Hope Lyons, Lugenia Burns Hope, Florence M. Read, and Carrie Harper, Torrence Papers, PUL.

45. See *New York Times*, 21 March, 8 April 1890.

46. Ibid.; see also *New York Times*, 24 June 1890; John Hope to Lugenia Hope, 23 August 1912, Hope Papers, AUC; Torrence interview with Jane Hope Lyons, Torrence Papers, AUC.

47. John Hope to John Hope II, 2 November 1930, Hope Papers, AUC.

48. On Trimble, see Brown University Scrapbook, "Student File of John Hope," and "Registrar's Records of Brown University," BUA; see also James C. Collins to

Ridgely Torrence, 10 March 1944, Torrence Papers, PUL (Collins was a student at Brown while Hope and Trimble were there; he graduated in 1892); John Hope to John Hope II, 2 November 1930, Hope Papers, AUC; also my interview with John Hope II.

49. Collins to Torrence, 10 March 1944, Torrence Papers, PUL.

50. John Hope to John Hope II, 2 November 1930, Hope Papers, AUC; my interview with John Hope II.

51. On Hope as a Brown correspondent for several newspapers, see John Hope to William H. Edwards, 25 July 1916, Hope Papers, AUC. William was the son of Seebert Edwards, whom Hope credited with getting him into journalism. John indicated that he did some work for the *Providence Journal* and the *Chicago Tribune*, but I have been unable to find any identifiable bylines by Hope in those papers (bylines were usually not signed). On Hope's activities, see the *Liber Brunensis* (New Haven: E. B. Sheldon, 1894), the official Brown yearbook for 1894, BUA; on his boxing, see John Hope to George B. Hazard, 6 July 1916, Hope Papers, AUC.

52. Torrence, *Story of John Hope*, 96.

53. On the increase in popularity of Greek letter fraternities at Brown, see Bronson, *History of Brown*, 458.

54. Torrence interviews with Howard E. Sumner, Ted Owens, and Harold Hazeltine, Torrence Papers, PUL.

55. Torrence interview with Ted Owens, Torrence Papers, PUL.

56. John Hope, "The Relations between the Black and White Races in America," speech delivered at Geneva, Switzerland, 31 March 1928, Hope Papers, AUC.

57. See William J. Brown, *The Life of William J. Brown, of Providence, R.I. with Personal Recollections of Incidents in Rhode Island* (1883; reprint, Freeport, N.Y.: Books for Libraries Press, 1971), 47.

58. Irving H. Bartlett, *From Slave to Citizen: The Story of the Negro in Rhode Island* (Providence: Urban League of Greater Providence, 1954), 37.

59. Robert J. Cottrol, *The Afro-Yankees: Providence's Black Community in the Antebellum Era* (Westport, Conn.: Greenwood Press, 1982). Cottrol used the term *Afro-Yankees* to describe his belief that blacks in Providence had turned their backs on their African heritage; see pp. 46–47. For the black "sacred cosmos," see Lincoln and Mamiya, *The Black Church*, chap. 1; also Peter L. Berger, *The Sacred Canopy* (New York: Doubleday, 1967); Mechal Sobel, *Trabelin' On: The Slave Journey to an Afro-Baptist Faith* (Westport, Conn.: Greenwood Press, 1979); William H. Robinson, ed., *The Proceedings of the Free African Union Society and the African Benevolent Society: Newport, Rhode Island, 1780–1824* (Providence: Urban League of Rhode Island, 1976); Rhode Island Black Heritage Society, *Creative Survival: The Providence Black Community in the 19th Century* (Providence: Rhode Island Black Heritage Society, 1984).

60. See Lincoln and Mamiya, *The Black Church*, 8; also Cottrol, *Afro-Yankees*, especially chap. 3; Rhode Island Black Heritage Society, *Creative Survival*, 55–56; Bartlett, *From Slave to Citizen*, chap. 5. On Alexander Crummell, see Wilson Jeremiah Moses, *Alexander Crummell: A Study of Civilization and Discontent* (Amherst: University of Massachusetts Press, 1992), especially 34–37.

61. On Langston, see John Mercer Langston, *From the Virginia Plantation to the National Capitol, or the First and Only Negro Representative in Congress from the Old Dominion* (Hartford, Conn.: American Publishing Company, 1894), chap. 29 for election to Congress in 1888; see also William Cheek and Aimee Lee Cheek, *John Mercer Langston and the Fight for Black Freedom, 1829–65* (Urbana: University of Illinois Press, 1989), for an earlier period; also instructive is William J. Simmons, *Men of Mark: Eminent, Progressive and Rising* (New York: G. M. Rewell, 1887; reprint, Chicago: Johnson, 1970), 345–52.

62. Hope, "Talk to Students," ca. 1904, Hope Papers, AUC. Torrence identified the speech as being delivered in Nashville; however, notes written across it suggest it was given at Atlanta Baptist College sometime in 1904; see Torrence, *Story of John Hope*, 92.

63. See Meier, *Negro Thought in America*, 78; on Hope's reminiscences, see Hope, "Talk to Students," ca. 1904, Hope Papers, AUC. Frances Wayland and Ezekiel Robinson were much revered early presidents of Brown University. John Larkin Lincoln was a professor of Latin language and literature. Hope took his class before Lincoln died in 1891 and paid tribute to him in his class oration in 1894. See Bronson, *History of Brown*, on all three men.

64. Torrence interviews with Roberta Dunbar, Emily Tolliver, and Will Freeman, Torrence Papers, PUL.

65. See undated sheets of paper, Hope Papers, AUC.

66. On problems in Providence in the 1890s, see Bartlett, *From Slave to Citizen*, especially chap. 8; Rhode Island Black Heritage Society, *Creative Survival*.

67. On the importance of voluntary associations among upper-class African Americans, especially literary clubs, see Gatewood, *Aristocrats of Color*, especially chap. 8.

68. Torrence interviews with Florence M. Read and Lugenia Burns Hope, Torrence Papers, PUL.

69. Torrence interview with Florence Read, Torrence Papers, PUL.

70. On the working-class makeup of Providence's African American community, see Cottrol, *Afro-Yankees*, chap. 4; Bartlett, *From Slave to Citizen*, chap. 8. On what constituted a black upper-class elite in this period, see Gatewood, *Aristocrats of Color*.

71. Mary Frances Hope to John Hope, 13 October 1892, Hope Papers, AUC. University rules stated that all debts to the college must be paid before registering for the semester. On this and Aid Fund for "worthy students," see Brown University catalogues for 1890–94, BUA.

72. Hope, speech to alumni of Atlanta University Laboratory High School, 27 April 1934, Hope Papers, AUC; Torrence interviews with Florence M. Read and Lugenia Burns Hope, Torrence Papers, PUL; my interview with John Hope II.

73. Hope, speech to alumni of Atlanta University Laboratory High School, 27 April 1934, Hope Papers, AUC.

74. John relayed this story to Florence Read on 2 July 1933. She told it in detail to Torrence in an oral interview; see Torrence interview with Florence M. Read, Torrence Papers, PUL.

75. Jacqueline Anne Rouse, *Lugenia Burns Hope: Black Southern Reformer* (Athens: University of Georgia Press, 1989), 18–19; Torrence interview with Lugenia Burns Hope, Torrence Papers, PUL; my interview with John Hope II.

76. The events that unfolded at the World's Fair on Colored People's Day are described in William S. McFeeley, *Frederick Douglass* (New York: Simon & Schuster, 1991), 366–71; see also Alfreda M. Duster, ed., *Crusade for Justice: The Autobiography of Ida B. Wells* (Chicago: University of Chicago Press, 1972), 115–19.

77. See Rouse, *Lugenia Burns Hope*, chap. 1; my interview with John Hope II; Torrence interview with Lugenia Hope, Torrence Papers, PUL.

78. John Hope, Speech to alumni of the Atlanta University Laboratory High School, 27 April 1934, Hope Papers, AUC.

79. Torrence interview with Ted Owens, Torrence Papers, PUL. After Owens graduated from Brown University in 1897, he taught at a number of schools, eventually winding up at Tuskegee in 1903, where he remained until he retired in 1935. Owens and Hope remained close friends for the rest of their lives.

80. On both Page and Milford, see class albums and biographical files of Brown University, BUA; also on Page, see Simmons, *Men of Mark*, 315–20.

81. John's oration appeared in the Brown University Scrapbook, vol. 4, 1888–95, 233, BUA.

82. Du Bois's commencement oration is covered in David Lewis, *W. E. B. Du Bois*, 100–101.

83. Torrence interview with Ted Owens, Torrence Papers, PUL.

84. Brown University Scrapbook, vol. 4, 1888–95, 234–36, BUA.

85. John Hope to Benjamin Andrews, 9 November 1916, Hope Papers, AUC.

86. Hope, "Talk to Students," undated, AUC.

87. Torrence interview with Ted Owens, Torrence Papers, PUL; photographs of Appleton are in the Brown University Archives.

88. Ibid.

89. Brown University Scrapbook, vol. 4, 1888–95, 243; the scrapbook printed Hazeltine's and the other orations presented at the commencement exercises.

Chapter 4. The Return South: Nashville

1. On Williams, see Rayford W. Logan and Michael R. Winston, eds., *Dictionary of American Negro Biography* (New York: W. W. Norton, 1982), 661–62, hereafter cited as *DANB*.

2. See W. T. B. Williams to John Hope, 21 October 1894, Hope Papers, AUC.

3. On Hope's salary, see "Minutes of the American Baptist Home Mission Society," Board Book 13, p. 163, Records of the American Baptist Home Mission society (hereafter ABHMS), American Baptist Historical Society Archives (hereafter ABHSA), Valley Forge, Pa. The 1894 academic year was the last year faculty contracts required mandatory fund-raising. Also on Hope's salary, see Roger Williams University Teacher's Certificate no. 17714, undated, folder "Roger Williams University," ABHSA; a

copy of Hope's teaching certificate is also in the General Education Board File, folder R, Rockefeller Archives Center, Tarrytown, N.Y., hereafter cited as GEB File, RAC.

4. See J. Morgan Kousser, *The Shaping of Southern Politics, Suffrage Restrictions and the Establishment of the One-Party South, 1880–1910* (New Haven: Yale University Press, 1974), 71–76, 107; Rayford W. Logan, *The Betrayal of the Negro: From Rutherford B. Hayes to Woodrow Wilson* (New York: Collier Books, 1965), 48.

5. See Logan, *Betrayal of the Negro*, chap. 3.

6. Aunt Nannie to John Hope, 30 April 1893, Hope Papers, AUC. Hope's boyhood memories are in John Hope, "The Negro Vote in the States Whose Constitutions Have Not Been Specifically Revised," in Archibald H. Grimké et al., *The Negro and the Elective Franchise*, American Negro Academy Occasional Papers 11 (Washington, D.C.: American Negro Academy, 1905; reprint, New York: Arno Press and the New York Times, 1969), 56; for an example of Hope's brother-in-law and other African Americans protesting racist reporting, see *Augusta Chronicle*, 1 September 1881, 21 February 1886; *Georgia Baptist* criticism of the *Chronicle*'s racism is the 28 July 1898 issue. On scientific racism, see George Frederickson, *Black Images in the White Mind: The Debate on Afro-American Character and Destiny, 1817–1914* (New York: Harper & Row, 1971), especially chaps. 8, 9. On lynching in Georgia specifically, see W. Fitzhugh Brundage, *Lynching in the New South: Georgia and Virginia, 1880–1930* (Urbana: University of Illinois Press, 1993). On segregation, see C. V. Woodward, *The Strange Career of Jim Crow* (New York: Oxford University Press, 1974); in Georgia, see John Hammond Moore, "Jim Crow in Georgia," *South Atlantic Quarterly* 66 (Fall 1967): 554–65.

7. "Historical Sketch of Roger Williams University," folder "Roger Williams University," ABHSA; see also Eugene TeSelle, "The Nashville Institute and Roger Williams University: Benevolence, Paternalism, and Black Consciousness, 1867–1910," *Tennessee Historical Quarterly* 41 (Winter 1982): 360–79; Ruth Marie Powell, "The History of Negro Educational Institutions Sponsored by the Baptists of Tennessee from 1864 to 1934" (master's thesis, Tennessee State University, 1953), 5–30; Faye Wellborn Robbins, "A World-within-a-World: Black Nashville, 1880–1915" (Ph.D. diss., University of Arkansas, 1980), chap. 1.

8. See TeSelle, "Nashville Institute," 360–61; also Rabinowitz, *Race Relations in the Urban South*, 164–67. On missionary societies, including the ABHMS, see James M. McPherson, *The Abolitionist Legacy, from Reconstruction to the NAACP* (Princeton: Princeton University Press, 1975), especially chap. 9; see also "Historical Sketch of Roger Williams," ABHSA. On Fisk University, see Joe M. Richardson, *A History of Fisk University, 1865–1946* (University: University of Alabama Press, 1980), especially chaps. 2, 3.

9. "Historical Sketch of Roger Williams," ABHSA.

10. "Roger Williams University," undated newspaper clipping, December 1886, *Tennessee Star*, located in H. L. Morehouse File, folder "Roger Williams University Controversy, 1887," ABHSA; see also TeSelle, "Nashville Institute," 368–74; also important are James M. McPherson, "White Liberals and Black Power in Negro Education, 1865–1915," *American Historical Review* 75 (June 1970): 1371–72; and McPherson, *Abolitionist Legacy*, 287–88.

11. TeSelle, "Nashville Institute," 371–74; "Roger Williams University Controversy," H. L. Morehouse File, ABHSA; McPherson, "White Liberals and Black Power," 1370–71. McPherson viewed the scandal within the context of African Americans wanting to control missionary institutions where they constituted a majority. Perhaps that was a factor, but almost as many whites supported the students during the scandal as did not. Thus it seems that community control was just as important. See also McPherson, *Abolitionist Legacy*, 287.

12. Johnson defended his actions publicly after student accusations against him appeared in a local newspaper. See undated newspaper clipping, *Nashville Union*, in "Roger Williams University Controversy, 1887," H. L. Morehouse File, ABHSA.

13. Robbins, "World-within-a-World," 9; Torrence interview with J. W. Johnson, Torrence Papers, PUL.

14. Robbins, "World-within-a-World," 45–46; Powell, "History of Negro Educational Institutions," 17–18.

15. See Torrence interview with A. M. Townsend, Torrence Papers, PUL. On the curriculum and number of faculty and students at Roger Williams, see Powell, "History of Negro Educational Institutions," 15–16; TeSelle, "Nashville Institute," 364–67, "Historical Sketch of Roger Williams," ABHSA. On the science lab, see John Hope to Lugenia Burns, 22 March 1895, Hope Papers, AUC.

16. On courses Hope taught, see Torrence interviews with J. W. Johnson, A. M. Townsend, and W. A. Reed, Torrence Papers, PUL; also John Hope to Lugenia Burns, 23 October 1896, Hope Papers, AUC. On teaching loads at ABHMS schools, see "Historical Sketch of Roger Williams," ABHSA.

17. John Hope to Lugenia Burns, 10 June, 16 December 1896, 24 March 1897, Hope Papers, AUC.

18. On women at Roger Williams and rules governing their behavior, see Robbins, "World-within-a-World," 44–45; Powell, "History of Negro Educational Institutions," 18–19.

19. On students expelled, see John Hope to Lugenia Burns, undated, Hope Papers, AUC; Torrence interview with J. W. Johnson, Torrence Papers, PUL; see also McPherson, *Abolitionist Legacy*, 192.

20. John Hope to Lugenia Burns, 17 October 1896, Hope Papers, AUC.

21. On conditions in Nashville, see Don H. Doyle, *Nashville in the New South: 1880–1930* (Knoxville: University of Tennessee Press, 1985), especially chaps. 5, 6; see also his *New Men, New Cities, New South: Atlanta, Nashville, Charleston, Mobile, 1860–1910* (Chapel Hill: University of North Carolina Press, 1990), chap. 10; Joseph H. Cartwright, *The Triumph of Jim Crow: Tennessee Race Relations in the 1880's* (Knoxville: University of Tennessee Press, 1976), 168–77; Rabinowitz, *Race Relations in the Urban South*, 305–15.

22. Robbins, "World-within-a-World," 207–8; Doyle, *Nashville in the New South*, 142; Rabinowitz, *Race Relations in the Urban South*, 56.

23. Black aristocrats in this period are best described in Gatewood, *Aristocrats of Color*, chap. 1.

24. On Napier, see *DANB*, 470–71; on Nashville's black elite during this period,

see *Indianapolis Freeman*, 20 June 1896, 1 January 1898; Robbins, "World-within-a-World"; Doyle, *Nashville in the New South*, 109–10; Rabinowitz, *Race Relations in the Urban South*, 239–42, 246–49.

25. John Hope to Lugenia Burns, 10 June, 3 July 1896, and undated letter, Hope Papers, AUC.

26. On Nettie Napier, see *Black Women in America: An Historical Encyclopedia*, vol. 2, ed. Darlene Clark Hine (New York: Carlson, 1993), 833–34; Robbins, "World-within-a-World," 246.

27. Robbins, "World-within-a-World," 245.

28. Ibid., 245–47; Grigg's passage is quoted in Gatewood, *Aristocrats of Color*, 152; see also Rabinowitz, *Race Relations in the Urban South*, 239–43, 246–49.

29. Quoted in Gatewood, *Aristocrats of Color*, 51–52; see also his chapter 2 for an excellent description and analysis of Washington's upper-class elite; and *Indianapolis Freeman*, 13 May 1893.

30. John Hope to Lugenia Burns, 3 July 1896, Hope Papers, AUC.

31. Ibid.

32. John Hope to Lugenia Burns, 17 October 1896, Hope Papers, AUC.

33. John Hope to Jesse Moorland, 14 May 1929, Moorland Papers, Moorland-Spingarn Research Center, Howard University, Washington, D.C., hereafter cited as Moorland Papers, Howard University. See also John Hope to Lugenia Burns, 24 March 1897, Hope Papers, AUC.

34. On Booker T. Washington's rise from rags to riches, see his *Up from Slavery: An Autobiography* (New York: Doubleday, Page, 1902); also Harlan's two-volume *Booker T. Washington*, especially *The Making of a Black Leader*; on Judson Lyons, see Coleman and Gurr, *Dictionary of Georgia Biography*, 2:646–47; on Laney and Wright, see chapter 2 in this book.

35. See Doyle, *Nashville in the New South*, 110–13; Robbins, "World-within-a-World," 236–40; Alrutheus Taylor, "Fisk University and the Nashville Community, 1866–1900," *Journal of Negro History* 39 (April 1954): 120–26; Rabinowitz, *Race Relations in the Urban South*, 240–43; also helpful in this analysis is E. Franklin Frazier's classic work *Black Bourgeoisie: The Rise of a New Middle Class in the United States* (New York: Collier Books, 1962).

36. Robbins, "World-within-a-World," 244–45.

37. Torrence interviews with Ted Owens and Lugenia Burns Hope, Torrence Papers, PUL.

38. Anna Butts to John Hope, 12 March 1895, W. T. B. Williams to Hope, 2 January 1895, Hope Papers, AUC; see also Torrence interview with Ted Owens, Torrence Papers, PUL.

39. See Rouse, *Lugenia Burns Hope*, 20–23.

40. John Hope to Grace Hope, 21 November 1894, Hope Papers, AUC.

41. See John Hope to Lugenia Burns, undated, 16 December 1896, 22 April 1897, Mary Frances Butts to John Hope, ? August 1895, 12 April 1897, all in Hope Papers, AUC.

42. John Hope to Lugenia Burns, 10 June 1896, 10 June 1897, Mary Frances Butts

to John Hope, undated, 1892, 3 March 1900 or 1901, Madison J. Newton to John Hope, 14 December 1895, 20 June 1898, all in Hope Papers, AUC.

43. On Lyons, see Coleman and Gurr, *Dictionary of Georgia Biography*, 2:647.

44. Mary Frances Butts to John Hope, 12 April 1892, John Hope to Thomas Hope, 13 August 1893, Anna Butts to John Hope, date unreadable, 1895, Hope Papers, AUC; Torrence interviews with Jane Hope Lyons and Claudia White Harreld, Torrence Papers, PUL.

45. See *Indianapolis Freeman*, 28 September 1895, for the debate over the class of the lynching victims; see also *Indianapolis Freeman*, 19 October 1895; *Baltimore Afro-American*, 26 October 1895; *Atlanta Constitution*, 7 September 1895; also Doyle, *Nashville in the New South*, 140–42, on "lily whiteism" in Nashville. Hope revealed his discussions of this information in John Hope to Lugenia Burns, ? November 1895, Hope Papers, AUC.

46. John Hope to Lugenia Burns, November 1895, 9 December 1896, Hope Papers, AUC. Black interest in the liberation struggle in Cuba is scattered through black newspapers in 1895; e.g., *Indianapolis Freeman*, 19 October 1895.

47. See J. D. Anderson, *Education of Blacks in the South*, 66; see also McPherson, *Abolitionist Legacy*, 213–14.

48. See *Augusta Chronicle*, 18 September 1895; *Atlanta Constitution*, 15 September 1895; Doyle, *New Men, New Cities, New South*, 152–54. For the official history of the exposition, see Walter Gerald Cooper, *The Cotton States and International Exposition* (Atlanta: Illustrator Company, 1896).

49. See *Atlanta Constitution*, 8, 15 September 1895.

50. On descriptions, see *Atlanta Constitution, Atlanta Journal, Augusta Chronicle*, 18, 19, 20 September 1895; also Harlan, *Booker T. Washington: The Making of a Black Leader*, 214–15, Washington, *Up from Slavery*, 214.

51. Quoted in Harlan, *Booker T. Washington: The Making of a Black Leader*, 216; see also *Indianapolis Freeman*, 29 July 1899; *Atlanta Constitution* and *Atlanta Journal*, 19 September 1895.

52. See *Augusta Chronicle*, 21 September 1895; local analyses of the speech are in the *Atlanta Constitution, Atlanta Journal*, and *Augusta Chronicle*, 18, 19, 20 September 1895. All three papers printed the speech in its entirety and gave it a glowing commendation; see also *Washington Bee*, 2 November 1895.

53. John Hope to Lugenia Burns, November 1895; also W. T. B. Williams to John Hope, 9 November 1895, Hope Papers, AUC.

54. Hope's speech is quoted in Torrence, *Story of John Hope*, 114–15.

55. Quoted in Philip S. Foner, ed., "Is Booker T. Washington's Ideal Correct?" *Journal of Negro History* 55 (October 1970): 343–47; see also Daniel Walden, "The Contemporary Opposition to the Political Ideas of Booker T. Washington," *Journal of Negro History* 45 (April 1960): 88–103; Harlan, *Booker T. Washington: The Making of a Black Leader*, 226.

56. W. E. B. Du Bois to B. T. Washington, 24 September 1895, in *Booker T. Washington Papers, 1895–98*, ed. Louis R. Harlan (Chicago: University of Illinois Press, 1975), 4:26; W. E. B. Du Bois, *Dusk of Dawn* (New York: Harcourt, Brace, 1940), 55;

also quoted in Lewis, *W. E. B. Du Bois*, 174–75; see also Du Bois, *Souls of Black Folk*, especially chap. 3.

57. P. S. Foner, "Is Booker T. Washington's Ideal Correct?" 344–45; *Washington Bee*, 26 October 1895.

58. J. D. Anderson, *Education of Blacks in the South*, 41–42.

59. Ibid., 34. Anderson elaborates on these points convincingly throughout chapter 2 of this classic book.

60. Quoted in J. D. Anderson, *Education of Blacks in the South*, 68–69.

61. John Hope, "The Need of a Liberal Education for Us, and That, Too, in the South," speech delivered 12 April 1896, Hope Papers, AUC.

62. Ibid.

63. Officials of the ABHMS are mentioned in several letters Hope wrote or received earlier; see, e.g., William E. Holmes to John Hope, 17 December 1894, Madison J. Newton to John Hope, 14 December 1895, Hope Papers, AUC; also Torrence interview with Lugenia Burns Hope, Torrence Papers, PUL; and John Hope to Lugenia Burns, 10 January 1897, Hope Papers, AUC.

64. See John Hope to Lugenia Burns, 29 February 1896, 24 March 1897, Hope Papers, AUC.

65. John Hope to Lugenia Burns, 16 December 1896, undated (ca. early December 1897), Hope Papers, AUC; see also Rouse, *Lugenia Burns Hope*, 20–21.

66. John Hope to Lugenia Burns, 14 September 1896, 5, 12 October 1897, Hope Papers, AUC; also Torrence interview with Lugenia Burns Hope, Torrence Papers, PUL.

67. John Hope to Lugenia Burns, 12 March 1897, Hope Papers, AUC; also TeSelle, "Nashville Institute," 364–67; "Historical Sketch of Roger Williams," ABHSA.

68. Curiously, Ridgely Torrence's biography omits any mention of the event, even though it is prominent in Hope's correspondence.

69. On Lyons's appointment as postmaster and Ladeveze's leadership, see Cashin, *Story of Augusta*, 182–84.

70. John Hope to Lugenia Burns, 8, 12 October 1897, Hope Papers, AUC.

71. On the Tennessee Centennial Exposition, see Herman Justi, ed., *Official History of the Tennessee Centennial Exposition: Open May 1, and Closed October 30, 1897* (Nashville, 1898), 207–9; quotes also taken from Doyle, *Nashville in the New South*, 150–52.

72. Doyle, *New Men, New Cities, New South*, 268–69; Justi, *Official History*, 192–94, 196–98, 202; Doyle, *Nashville in the New South*, 149–50.

73. John Hope to Lugenia Burns, 10 June 1897, Hope Papers, AUC.

74. John Hope to Lugenia Burns, 20 June 1897, Hope Papers, AUC.

75. Ibid.

76. John Hope to Lugenia Burns, 25 August, 8 October 1897, Hope Papers, AUC.

77. See John Hope to Lugenia Burns, 8, 12 October 1897, Hope Papers, AUC.

78. My interview with John Hope II; John Hope to Lugenia Burns, 8, 12 October 1897, Hope Papers, AUC; see also Torrence interview with Claudia White Harreld, Torrence Papers, PUL. Harreld, one of William Jefferson White's daughters, said that "Georgia Newton married John Ladeveze and went to California. Dr. Hope didn't go

to see her—didn't want to embarrass her." Harreld is also the source on other relatives who may eventually have passed. The interview was probably conducted in the 1940s along with the others, but no reference appears anywhere in Torrence's book. On passing in general, see William M. Kephart, "The 'Passing' Question," *Phylon* 10 (1948): 336–40; Fannie Barrier Williams, "Perils of the White Negro," *Colored American* 13 (December 1907): 421–23; St. Clair Drake and Horace R. Cayton, *Black Metropolis: A Study of Negro Life in a Northern City*, vol. 1 (New York: Harcourt, Brace and World, 1945), 159–73.

79. John Hope to Lugenia Burns, 12 October 1897, Hope Papers, AUC.

80. John Hope to Lugenia Burns, 9 December 1896, 8, 12 October 1897, Hope Papers, AUC.

81. John Hope to Lugenia Burns, ? September 1897, 9, 16 December 1897, Hope Papers, AUC.

82. Hope to Lugenia, undated (ca. early December 1897), Hope Papers, AUC.

83. Lugenia Burns to John Hope, 23 December 1897, Hope Papers, AUC.

84. On Hope's wedding plans, see Hope to Lugenia Burns, undated (ca. early December 1897), Burns to Hope, 23 December 1987, Hope Papers, AUC; also Torrence interview with J. W. Johnson, Torrence Papers, PUL. On Grace Presbyterian Church and its founders, see Allan H. Spear, *Black Chicago: The Making of a Negro Ghetto, 1890–1920* (Chicago: University of Chicago Press, 1967), 94–95.

85. Torrence interviews with J. W. Johnson and Lugenia Burns Hope, Torrence Papers, PUL.

86. William Holmes to John Hope, 17 December 1894, George Sale to Hope, 15 March, 11 April 1898, Hope Papers, AUC.

87. John Hope to Lugenia Burns, 16 December 1896, Hope Papers, AUC.

88. See Madison J. Newton to John Hope, 20 April 1898, Hope Papers, AUC; Malcolm MacVicar to Hope, 15 May 1898, ABHMS Records, folder M, GEB File, RAC; Hope to MacVicar (penciled draft), undated; also George Sale to John Hope, 29 May 1898, Hope Papers, AUC.

89. John Hope to Owen James, 20 June 1898, ABHMS Records, GEB File, RAC.

Chapter 5. The Return South: Atlanta

1. For early descriptions of Atlanta Baptist College, see Benjamin Brawley, *History of Morehouse College* (Atlanta: Morehouse College, 1917), 35–36.

2. Ibid.; see also *Home Mission Monthly* 17 (March 1895): 89–94; also useful is Franklin M. Garrett, *Atlanta and Environs: A Chronicle of Its People and Events*, 2 vols. (Athens: University of Georgia Press, 1969), 1:954–55.

3. Torrence interview with James Nabrit, Torrence Papers, PUL. James Nabrit Sr. was a student at Morehouse College during Hope's early tenure who went on to become the minister of Atlanta's Mt. Olive Baptist Church. His son James Nabrit Jr. finished Morehouse in 1923 and became president of Howard University in the early 1960s. Another son, Samuel Nabrit, finished Morehouse in 1925 and went on to become president of Texas Southern University and in 1966 became the first African

American member of the Atomic Energy Commission; see also Brawley, *History of Morehouse*, chap. 5; and Jones, *Candle in the Dark*, 55–58, 283.

4. On the complex origins and relationship between the ABHMS and the National Theological Institute, see James Melvin Washington, *Frustrated Fellowship: The Black Baptist Quest for Social Power* (Macon, Ga.: Mercer University Press, 1986), 86–95; see also Harold Lyn McManus, "The American Baptist Home Mission Society and Freedmen Education in the South, with Special Reference to Georgia, 1862–1897" (Ph.D. diss., Yale University, 1953), especially chap. 3.

5. On these early struggles and examples of black self-help, see Brawley, *History of Morehouse College*, chap. 1; see also William Jefferson White, "The Founding of Atlanta Baptist College," speech to the Alumni Association, 13 May 1907, located in Alumni Office, Morehouse College. These events are also chronicled in Jones, *Candle in the Dark*, 23–29; also see McManus, "American Baptist Home Mission Society," 61–67; J. M. Washington, *Frustrated Fellowship*, 91.

6. Jones, *Candle in the Dark*, 28–29; see also "Charter of Atlanta Baptist College," ABHMS Records, GEB File, RAC.

7. On Morehouse becoming a college and its first graduates, see Brawley, *History of Morehouse*, chap. 6.

8. See chapter 2 of this volume for information on Walker and Lyons. On E. R. Carter, see his *The Black Side: A Partial History of the Business, Religious and Educational Side of the Negro in Atlanta, Georgia* (1894; reprint, Freeport, N.Y.: Books for Libraries Press, 1971), especially 263–80; also Coleman and Gurr, *Dictionary of Georgia Biography*, 75–76. On Love, see Clarence M. Wagner, *Profiles of Black Georgia Baptists: 206 Years of Georgia Baptist and 100 Years of National Baptist History* (Gainesville, Ga.: Bennett Brothers, 1980), 130–32; on his important role in the separatist movement, see J. M. Washington, *Frustrated Fellowship*, pt. 3; he is also mentioned in Simmons, *Men of Mark*, 321.

9. Torrence interview with Waldo Truesdale, Torrence Papers, PUL; Board Book 14, Executive Board Minutes, 13 June 1898, p. 342, ABHSA; see also Brawley, *History of Morehouse*, chap. 6.

10. Torrence interviews with James Nabrit and Lugenia Burns Hope, Torrence Papers, PUL; my interview with Samuel Nabrit.

11. Torrence interview with James Nabrit, Torrence Papers, PUL; also Wagner, *Profiles of Black Georgia Baptists*, 132. Wagner is also instructive in determining the opportunities open to African American ministers in the ABHMS organization. E. K. Love, for example, worked in an official capacity for the ABHMS for a time, as did William J. White, William Holmes, and numerous other ministers. On presidents and faculty at ABHMS schools and the importance of the ministry generally, see McManus, "American Baptist Home Mission Society," 313–50; J. M. Washington, *Frustrated Fellowship*, chaps. 6, 7; McPherson, *Abolitionist Legacy*, chap. 9. The ABHMS *Home Mission Monthly* occasionally highlighted administrators and faculty at other ABHMS schools who were also ministers or training for the ministry.

12. Torrence interviews with James Nabrit and Mordecai Johnson, Torrence Papers, PUL. Johnson was a student at ABC shortly before Hope became president and

was later a faculty member and worked in the YMCA; eventually he became the first African American president of Howard University. See also Jones, *Candle in the Dark*, 61–64; my interviews with John Hope II and Samuel Nabrit.

13. Torrence interview with James Nabrit, Torrence Papers, PUL; Jones, *Candle in the Dark*, 53–65; *Home Mission Monthly* 17 (March 1895): 89–94.

14. Torrence interview with James Nabrit, Torrence Papers, PUL; my interview with Sam Nabrit, the son of James Nabrit, who was in one of Hope's first classes.

15. On Holmes, see the ABC student publication *Athenaeum* 1 (May 1898): 8; *Georgia Baptist*, 5 October 1899; and Carter, *The Black Side*, 213–16.

16. Torrence interviews with James Nabrit and Charles Hubert, Torrence Papers, PUL. Hubert was another early Hope student.

17. Ibid.; also my interview with Sam Nabrit. On Morehouse and Roger Williams statistics, see W. E. B. Du Bois, ed., *The College-Bred Negro*, Atlanta University Publication 5 (Atlanta: Atlanta University, 1910), 8–9.

18. Interview with Charles Hubert, Torrence Papers, PUL.

19. Torrence interviews with John and Samuel Nabrit, John W. Johnson, and Charles Hubert, Torrence Papers, PUL; also quoted in Torrence, *Story of John Hope*, 138; see also Brawley, *History of Morehouse*, 91–95.

20. *Athenaeum* 1 (October 1898): 10; the students devoted an entire section of their magazine to their athletic activities. See also Brawley, *History of Morehouse*, 129–33; my interview with John Hope II; Torrence interview with James Nabrit, Torrence Papers, PUL.

21. See Hope, "Autobiographical Sketch," Hope Papers, AUC.

22. See Clarence A. Bacote, *The Story of Atlanta University: A Century of Service, 1865–1965* (Princeton: Princeton University Press, 1969), chap. 1; James Weldon Johnson, *Along This Way: The Autobiography of James Weldon Johnson* (New York: Viking Press, 1933), 64–77; Du Bois, *College-Bred Negro*, 8–9; Richardson, *History of Fisk*, chap. 1.

23. Torrence interview with George Towns, Torrence Papers, PUL; biographical sketch in George A. Towns Papers, AUC; little material on Towns is included in the George Alexander Towns Papers and Grace Towns Hamilton Collection located in the Atlanta History Center Library Special Collections; however, also see Coleman and Gurr, *Dictionary of Georgia Biography*, 95; J. W. Johnson, *Along This Way*, 103, 137; Bacote, *Story of Atlanta University*, 130.

24. Lewis, *W. E. B. Du Bois*, 253; see also Du Bois, *Autobiography*, 287; Du Bois, *Dusk of Dawn*, 315, 318.

25. Ibid., especially Lewis, *W. E. B. Du Bois*, chap. 3.

26. Du Bois explained the importance of culture in the quest for African American freedom in, among other things, his *Souls of Black Folk*. The theme is especially strong in the essays on Washington (III), Atlanta (V), and the training of African American men (VI). Hope's views on culture were usually more poignant in his speeches.

27. John Hope, undated speech to National Student Federation of United States of America, Hope Papers, AUC. On Hope's views on Christian character and the impor-

tance of religion, see Mordecai Johnson, "Report of Memorial Service in Honor of Dr. John Hope," speech delivered in Sister's Chapel, Spelman College, 2 December 1936, Hope Papers, AUC; also my interview with Samuel Nabrit.

28. On Du Bois's religious views, see Lewis, *W. E. B. Du Bois*, 153; Du Bois, *Autobiography*, 186–87.

29. On Pledger, see Meier, *Negro Thought in America*, 250–51; Coleman and Gurr, *Dictionary of Georgia Biography*, 2:802–4; *DANB*, 496–97. On Johnson, see Coleman and Gurr, *Dictionary of Georgia Biography*, 2:534; also Clarence A. Bacote, "The Negro in Atlanta Politics," *Phylon* 16 (1955): 333–43; see also Bacote, "The Negro in Georgia Politics, 1880–1908" (Ph.D. diss., University of Chicago, 1955).

30. On Clark College, see Alphonso A. McPheeters, "The Origin and Development of Clark University and Gammon Theological Seminary" (Ed.D. diss., University of Cincinnati, 1944).

31. On Crogman, see Coleman and Gurr, *Dictionary of Georgia Biography*, 235–36; *DANB*, 140–41; on African American boycotts against segregated streetcars in Atlanta and other Georgia cities, see August Meier and Elliott Rudwick, "The Boycott Movement against Jim Crow Streetcars in the South, 1900–1906," *Journal of American History* 55 (March 1969): 756–75.

32. Coleman and Gurr, *Dictionary of Georgia Biography*, 1:316–19, 2:816–17; see also Henry Hugh Proctor, *Between Black and White: Autobiographical Sketches* (Boston: Pilgrims Press, 1925).

33. John Hope to W. E. B. Du Bois, 19 October 1928, Hope Papers, AUC.

34. On lynching in Georgia, see Brundage, *Lynching in the New South*, chap. 7; Donald L. Grant, *The Way It Was in the South: The Black Experience in Georgia* (New York: Carol Publishing, 1993), 161; John Dittmer, *Black Georgia in the Progressive Era, 1900–1920* (Urbana: University of Illinois Press, 1977), 131.

35. See *Georgia Baptist*, 23 March 1899; Grant, *The Way It Was in the South*, 161–62.

36. *Georgia Baptist*, 23 March 1899.

37. On the Sam Hose (or Holt) lynching, see Brundage, *Lynching in the New South*, 82–85; *Atlanta Journal* and *Atlanta Constitution*, 15, 24, 25 April 1899, and issues of both for several weeks thereafter.

38. See Arthur F. Raper, *The Tragedy of Lynching* (Chapel Hill: University of North Carolina Press, 1933), 34; Grant, *The Way It Was in the South*, 163–64; for examples of newspaper reports on the need to prevent black men from raping white women, see *Atlanta Journal*, 12 August 1897; *Atlanta Constitution*, 2 November 1902.

39. Du Bois, *Autobiography*, 221–22; Lewis, *W. E. B. Du Bois*, 226.

40. Torrence interview with Lugenia Burns Hope, Torrence Papers, PUL.

41. See *Georgia Baptist*, 30 March 1899; *Atlanta Constitution*, 25 April 1899; *Atlanta Journal*, 24 April 1899; also Dittmer, *Black Georgia in the Progressive Era*, 132–35.

42. See *Atlanta Constitution*, 24 April 1899.

43. Although Holmes participated in the protest against the Palmetto murders, there is no evidence that President Sale or any other faculty member or administrator did so. In addition, it seems that even Holmes rarely involved himself in such activi-

ties. There is no evidence in either the *Georgia Baptist*, which frequently highlighted Holmes's ABHMS and ABC activities, or the local Atlanta papers that Holmes was an activist, although he may have been. The ABHMS policy on activism was rarely stated, but it is clear that it did exist.

44. Thomas J. Morgan to John Hope, 16 June 1899, Hope Papers, AUC; Torrence interview with Lugenia Burns Hope, Torrence Papers, PUL; W. E. B. Du Bois, "Two Negro Conventions," *Independent* 51 (September 1899): 2425–27.

45. W. E. B. Du Bois to John Hope, 10 May 1899, Hope Papers, AUC.

46. For a detailed and excellent analysis of the importance of the Atlanta University conferences, see Lewis, *W. E. B. Du Bois*, chap. 9; also W. E. B. Du Bois, ed., *The Negro in Business: Report of a Social Study Made under the Direction of Atlanta University; Together with the Proceedings of the Fourth Conference for the Study of the Negro Problems, Held at Atlanta University, May 30–31, 1899* (Atlanta: Atlanta University, 1899).

47. See Du Bois, *Negro in Business*, 51–55.

48. Ibid.

49. R. L. Wayland, a former president of the ABHMS, argued in favor of vocational education founded on the Hampton model in a conference that took place in Saratoga, N.Y., in 1896: "If schools like Atlanta and Fisk continued with dead languages, then the Baptists would simply withdraw funding from their students and give it to the support of Baptist young men at Hampton and Tuskegee" (quoted in Lewis, *W. E. B. Du Bois*, 266); see also J. D. Anderson, *Education of Blacks in the South*, 71–72.

50. On Lithia Springs, see Doris Lanier, "Henry W. Grady and the Piedmont Chautauqua," *Southern Studies* (Fall 1984): 216–42; also see T. J. Morgan to John Hope, 30 December 1898, Hope Papers, AUC.

51. John Hope to Lugenia Hope, 31 July 1899, Hope Papers, AUC.

52. John Hope to Lugenia Hope, 1 August 1899, Hope Papers, AUC.

53. John Hope to Lugenia Hope, 31 July, 2, 3 August 1899, Hope Papers, AUC.

54. Ibid.

55. John Hope to Lugenia Hope, 2 August 1899, Hope Papers, AUC.

56. Torrence interview with Lugenia Burns Hope, Torrence Papers, PUL.

57. The Beaver Slide on the west side of Atlanta should not be confused with the original Beaver Slide slum area in south Atlanta; see Charles F. Palmer, *Adventures of a Slum Fighter* (New York: Van Rees Press, 1955), 16; see also Louie D. Shivery, "The History of Organized Social Work among Negroes in Atlanta, 1890–1935" (master's thesis, Atlanta University, 1936); Garrett, *Atlanta and Environs*, 2:25–26, 910.

58. On the Neighborhood Union, see Rouse, *Lugenia Burns Hope*, chap. 4.

59. For examples, see John Hope to Lugenia Hope, 31 July, 2, 3, 12 August 1899, 3, 13 May 1903, Hope Papers, AUC; see also Torrence interview with Lugenia Burns Hope, Torrence Papers, PUL.

60. Quoted in Torrence, *Story of John Hope*, 141.

61. See Du Bois, *Souls of Black Folk*, chap. 11, "Of the Passing of the First Born," 152–56; see also Lewis, *W. E. B. Du Bois*, 226–29.

62. On Burghardt Du Bois's funeral, see ibid.

63. Torrence interviews with John Swain and Edward Burr Solomon Jr. (son of Ed-

ward Burr Solomon), Torrence Papers, PUL; Hope, "Autobiographical Sketch," Hope
Papers, AUC.

64. The Baptist Young People's Union, started in 1899, was designed to educate
African converts. A plan was initiated to bring them to America for education and return them to Africa as missionaries. See Wagner, *Profiles of Black Georgia Baptists*, 172.

65. See New York Life Insurance Company (Atlanta Branch Office) to John Hope,
18 December 1902; the dates on the other letters are illegible, but the years are 1898
and 1902, "Financial Records," Hope Papers, AUC.

66. Hope, "Autobiographical Sketch," Hope Papers, AUC.

67. Mary Frances (Butts) Hope to John Hope, 15 February 1900, Hope Papers,
AUC; see also Torrence interview with Claudia White Harreld, Torrence Papers,
PUL; Hope, "Autobiographical Sketch," Hope Papers, AUC.

68. See M. F. Hope to John Hope, 12 March, 30 April 1903, John Hope to M. F.
Hope, 9 April 1903; Lugenia Hope to John Hope, 12, 29 May, 5 August 1903, Hope
Papers, AUC; also Torrence interviews with Claudia White and the Harper Family,
Torrence Papers, PUL.

69. John Hope to Lugenia Hope, 5 August 1903, Hope Papers, AUC.

70. On Madison Newton, see Madison Newton to John Hope, 8 February, 5 March
1901, Hope to Newton, 11 May, 18 June, 25 July 1903, Hope Papers, AUC; see also
several letters from Judson Lyons to John Hope (some of text is illegible, but year is
1901) that show concern for Thomas Hope. Examples are 27 June, 4 November 1901,
also Jane Hope to John Hope, 10 February, 21 March 1903, all Hope Papers, AUC.

71. Sissie [Georgia Frances Ladeveze] to Aunt Nannie [Anna Butts], 7 August 1903,
Hope Papers, AUC.

72. See Gatewood, *Aristocrats of Color*, 174–76; also Sissie to Aunt Nannie, 7 August
1903, Hope Papers, AUC. Also instructive is Hope's letter written to an unknown
friend in 1925 when Newton died, quoted in Torrence, *Story of John Hope*, 251; see
also Torrence interview with Claudia White Harreld, Torrence Papers, PUL; Fourteenth U.S. Census, Schedule 1, California, vol. 31, Enumeration District 11, sheet 8,
line 74, National Archives, Southeast Regional Branch, Eastpoint, Ga.

Chapter 6. The Making of a "Militant"
African American President in a Southern City

1. J. M. Washington, *Frustrated Fellowship* (especially chap. 7), is a fine study of African American Baptist interests from around the Civil War to the beginning of the
twentieth century that convincingly shows that blacks' concern over racist tracts in
Baptist literature equaled their concern over white control of mission schools, and
eventually led to the creation of a separate black publishing company in Nashville; see
also McPherson, "White Liberals and Black Power," 1357–86; McPherson, *Abolitionist Legacy*, chap. 15.

2. J. M. Washington, *Frustrated Fellowship*; also on the black Baptist split in Georgia,
see Wagner, *Profiles of Black Georgia Baptists*, 79–82.

3. J. M. Washington, *Frustrated Fellowship*, 183–85.

4. On the creation of education societies in Georgia and other states, see Board Book 14, Executive Meetings of the ABHMS, 12 July 1897, 135, ABHSA; see also *Home Mission Monthly* (hereafter *HMM*) 19 (October 1897): 340–43; on amendment of the ABC charter to include more blacks on the board of trustees, see "Charter of Atlanta Baptist College," folder 512, GEB File, RAC.

5. *Georgia Baptist*, 7 September 1899.

6. *Georgia Baptist*, 5 October 1899; see also *HMM* 21 (November 1899): 431–34; *HMM* 22 (December 1899): 445–51.

7. See *Georgia Baptist*, 21 December, 14 December, 12 October 1899. In addition to those cited in the previous note, official views of the 1899 fiasco are scattered throughout the October, November, and December 1899 issues of the *HMM*.

8. "Holmes Gone to Macon," *Athenaeum* 2 (October 1899): 6.

9. On Holmes, see "William E. Holmes," *Athenaeum* 1 (May 1898): 8; E. R. Carter, *The Black Side*, 213; *Georgia Baptist*, 5 October 1899. It is possible Holmes had not been well. An opponent stated in the 5 October 1899 *Georgia Baptist* that perhaps Holmes had been duped into leaving ABC "given his recent nervous prostration." Perhaps the writer was being sarcastic, but it seems more likely that Holmes had been sick and perhaps had suffered a nervous breakdown.

10. William E. Holmes to H. L. Morehouse, 9 April 1887, ABHSA, quoted in Harold L. McManus, "The American Baptist Home Mission Society and Freedmen Education in the South, with Special Reference to Georgia: 1862–1897" (Ph.D. diss., Yale University, 1953), 448. Also useful are William E. Holmes to H. L. Morehouse, 8 March 1887, Morehouse to William J. White, 26 March 1887, ABHSA. According to the archivists, these letters have been lost in several moves of the Historical Society's holdings from New York City to Rochester, N.Y., to Valley Forge, Pa. However, there is no question of their authenticity. The letters are referenced and quoted extensively in McManus's dissertation (cited above, 443–51). On Holmes as corresponding secretary in 1883, see Wagner, *Profiles of Black Georgia Baptists*, 78.

11. William E. Holmes to H. L. Morehouse, 24 October 1891, ABHSA, quoted in McManus, "The American Baptist Home Mission Society," 450.

12. On the importance of a national black Baptist university and a centrally located Baptist college in Georgia, see Wagner, *Profiles of Black Georgia Baptists*, 65–67, 79–82; J. M. Washington, *Frustrated Fellowship*, 173–74.

13. On the Hardwick Bill, see Kenneth Coleman, Numan V. Bartley, et al., *A History of Georgia* (Athens: University of Georgia Press, 1991), 279–80; see also Grant, *The Way It Was in the South*, 201.

14. See W. E. B. Du Bois, "Suffrage Fight in Georgia," *Independent* 50 (November 1899): 3226–27; see also *Independent* 51 (December 1899): 3306–7; *Atlanta Constitution*, 10 November 1899. For a full explanation of the politics surrounding this early defeat of African American disfranchisement in Georgia, see Bacote, "The Negro in Atlanta Politics," 333–50; and also his massive dissertation, "The Negro in Georgia Politics, 1880–1908." On Proctor's involvement, see Proctor, *Between Black and White*,

102. Booker Washington's activity is covered in Harlan, *Booker T. Washington: The Making of a Black Leader*, 292.

15. Du Bois, "Suffrage Fight in Georgia," 3227; see also "Georgia Negroes on the Hardwick Bill, 1899," in Herbert Aptheker, *A Documentary History of the Negro People in the United States*, vol. 2: *From the Reconstruction Years to the Founding of the NAACP in 1910* (Secaucus, N.J.: Citadel Press, 1972), 784–86.

16. Hope, "The Negro Vote in the States," 55.

17. See Rabinowitz, *Race Relations in the Urban South*, 171–76; see also Jerry John Thornberry, "The Development of Black Atlanta, 1865–1885" (Ph.D. diss., University of Maryland, 1977), 94–111; Philip N. Racine, "Atlanta's Schools: a History of the Public School System, 1869–1955" (Ph.D. diss., Emory University, 1970), 35–41; *Atlanta Constitution*, 17, 26 July 1889.

18. On the conditions of Atlanta's schools during this period, see *The Negro Common School*, ed. W. E. B. Du Bois, Atlanta University Publication 6 (Atlanta: Atlanta University Press, 1901); see also W. E. B. Du Bois and A. G. Dill, eds., *The Common School and the Negro American*, Atlanta University Publication 16 (Atlanta: Atlanta University Press, 1911); Dorothy Orr, *A History of Education in Georgia* (Chapel Hill: University of North Carolina Press, 1950); also important are Philip N. Racine, "Public Education in the New South: A School System for Atlanta, 1868–1879," and Marcia E. Turner, "Black School Politics in Atlanta, Georgia, 1869–1943," both in *Southern Cities, Southern Schools: Public Education in the Urban South*, ed. David N. Plank and Rick Ginsberg (Westport, Conn.: Greenwood Press, 1990), 37–58, 177–98.

19. For an example of Hope's protest against education, see Dittmer, *Black Georgia in the Progressive Era*, 143; see also Du Bois, *Negro Common School*, 93–95. On segregation replacing exclusion, see Rabinowitz, *Race Relations in the Urban South*, preface, especially xv, xvi.

20. For example, Atlanta's African American leaders waged a major campaign against segregated streetcars in 1900; see Dittmer, *Black Georgia in the Progressive Era*, 16–17; also Meier and Rudwick, "The Boycott Movement against Jim Crow Streetcars," 267–89. It seems that what most perturbed these leaders were the filthy and undignified conditions set aside for African Americans, regardless of class, rather than the fact that they were separate.

21. On Morris Brown, see George A. Sewell and Cornelius V. Troup, *Morris Brown College: The First Hundred Years 1881–1981* (Atlanta: Morris Brown College, 1981); on Spelman College, see Florence M. Read, *The Story of Spelman College* (Princeton: Princeton University Press, 1961).

22. Quote from Clarence A. Bacote, "Negro Proscriptions, Protests, and Proposed Solutions in Georgia, 1880–1908," *Journal of Southern History* 25 (November 1959): 480.

23. On starting a colony along the coast of Georgia, see Torrence, *Story of John Hope*, 135; also Dittmer, *Black Georgia in the Progressive Era*, 179–80; see also Edwin S. Redkey, *Black Exodus: Black Nationalist and Back-to-Africa Movements, 1890–1910* (New Haven: Yale University Press, 1969), 142, 182–83 for Turner's activities during the

Chicago World's Fair; see also Stephen Ward Angell, *Bishop Henry McNeal Turner and African-American Religion in the South* (Knoxville: University of Tennessee Press, 1992), for a recent biographical treatment of Turner.

24. Hope, speech given at Morris Brown College, ca. 1900, Hope Papers, AUC. On African American attitudes toward Africa, see Walter L. Williams, "Black American Attitudes toward Africa, 1877–1900," *Pan-African Journal* 4 (Spring 1971): 173–94; also his "Black Journalism's Opinions about Africa during the Late Nineteenth Century," *Phylon* 34 (September 1973): 224–35; and "Ethnic Relations of African Students in the United States, with Black Americans, 1870–1900," *Journal of Negro History* (Summer 1980): 228–49.

25. Hope, speech at Morris Brown, Hope Papers, AUC.

26. Ibid.

27. My interview with Dr. Benjamin Mays, president of Morehouse College 1940–67. Hope first hired Mays in 1921, but he left three years later to continue his education, first at Virginia Union University, then at Bates College in Maine. See also T. J. Morgan to John Hope, 31 August, 6 November 1901, Hope Papers, AUC. Also on Virginia Union, see "A Century of Service to Education and Religion: Virginia Union University, 1865–1965," *Virginia Union Bulletin* (Centennial Issue) 65 (June 1965): 5–27.

28. See George Sale to T. J. Morgan, 29 November 1901, Hope Papers, AUC; also in ABHMS Records, folder M, GEB File, RAC.

29. Ibid.

30. Morgan to George Sale, 11 December 1901, ABHMS Records, folder M, GEB File, RAC.

31. Hope to Morgan, 21 December 1901, Hope Papers, AUC; Morgan to Hope, date illegible (ca. late December 1901), folder M, GEB File, RAC.

32. George Sale to T. J. Morgan, 29 November 1901, Hope Papers, AUC; see also Board Book 14, Minutes of Executive Board of ABHMS, 13 November 1899, p. 628, ABHSA; and *HMM* 20 (August 1898): 254, *HMM* 21 (July 1899): 264; also useful are McPherson, *Abolitionist Legacy*, 290; and McPherson, "White Liberals and Black Power," 1361. That Hope probably knew about the situation in Richmond is revealed in a letter from a family member who advised him to let the "Richmond situation take care of itself" (Grace Hope to John Hope, 21 November 1901, Hope Papers, AUC).

33. On these meetings, see McManus, "The American Baptist Home Mission Society," 435–72; Board Books 14 and 15, Minutes of Executive Board, September 1897, 1900, ABHSA; see also trips made in 1900 and 1901 in Lathan A. Crandall, *Henry Lyman Morehouse: A Biography* (Philadelphia: American Baptist Publication Society, 1919), 78–79.

34. For an example of black unity with the ABHMS on the issue of African American higher education, see *HMM* 22 (January 1900): 3, 4; *HMM* 23 (April 1900): 116–18.

35. See *69th Annual Report of the American Baptist Home Mission Society, Convened in Springfield, Massachusetts, May 23–24, 1901, Containing Minutes of the Meeting, Report of the Executive Board, Treasurer's Report, Report of Committees, and Missionary Tables* (New York: American Baptist Home Mission Society, 1901), 108, ABHSA. Subsequent

references to ABHMS annual reports will include only the number and year of the report and dates.

36. See John Hope, speech delivered at Clark College, December 1901, Hope Papers, AUC.

37. Ibid.

38. The minutes of the ABHMS for May 1902 include this statement: "Appoint Professor John Hope to visit churches and associations in Georgia in the interests of cooperation and education at a salary of $25 per month and necessary traveling expenses during actual time of service." Hope visited only black churches and associations in Georgia. A cursory check of the board minutes indicates Hope was the only faculty member performing this service that year, although the next academic year George A. Goodwin, another African American faculty member, would do the same. See Board Book 15, Minutes of the ABHMS Executive Board, 12 May 1902, p. 464, ABHSA.

39. See Sobel, *Trabelin' On*, 3; Patricia Collins, *Black Feminist Thought: Knowledge, Consciousness, and the Politics of Empowerment* (New York: Routledge, Chapman, Hall, 1991), 10.

40. For an excellent discussion of the factors that pushed some African American Baptists toward the separatist position, see James Melvin Washington, "The Origins and Emergence of Black Baptist Separatism, 1863–1897" (Ph.D. diss., Yale University, 1979), 107–8; see also his *Frustrated Fellowship*, 187–207.

41. Ibid.

42. Ibid.; see also Leroy Fitts, *A History of Black Baptists* (Nashville: Broadman Press, 1985), chap. 4; Hope, speech delivered at Clark College, December 1901, Hope Papers, AUC.

43. For examples of separatists who obviously disagreed with Hope and other co-operationists, see the debates carried out in the pages of the *Georgia Baptist* during 1898 and 1899; see also Wagner, *Profiles of Black Georgia Baptists*, chaps. 5, 6; Woodson, *History of the Negro Church*, 235–41; James D. Tyms, *The Rise of Religious Education among Negro Baptists* (New York: Exposition Press, 1965), 150–66. Reagon is quoted in Collins, *Black Feminist Thought*, 145.

44. See Garrett, *Atlanta and Environs*, 2:375–78; also W. E. B. Du Bois, "Opening of the Library," *Independent* 54 (April 1902): 809–10.

45. See *Atlanta Constitution*, 25 February, 7 March, 8 April, 28 July 1880, 2 June, 17 July, 26 October 1881, 18 July 1882; Thornberry, "Development of Black Atlanta," 308.

46. Garrett, *Atlanta and Environs*, 2:375–78; Du Bois, "Opening of Library," 810.

47. Ibid.; see also "Petition of Negroes to Use the Carnegie Library," reel 1, W. E. B. Du Bois Papers, University of Massachusetts, hereafter cited as Du Bois Papers, UMass; John Hope to W. E. B. Du Bois, 19 October 1928, Hope Papers, AUC; Annie L. McPheeters, *Library Service in Black and White: Some Personal Recollections, 1921–1980* (Metuchen, N.J.: Scarecrow Press, 1988), 18–20.

48. See A. L. McPheeters, *Library Service in Black and White*, 21–23.

49. See Louis Harlan, *Separate and Unequal: Public School Campaigns and Racism in*

the Southern Seaboard States, 1901–1958 (Chapel Hill: University of North Carolina Press, 1958), 84, 89; also quoted in J. D. Anderson, *Education of Blacks in the South*, 86. On the GEB's preference and support for industrial education in 1902, the first year the GEB operated, see "Appropriations," box 336, folder 3534, GEB file, RAC. An understanding of the philosophy of the GEB, which was not necessarily stated publicly on many of these issues (e.g., its preference for industrial education, its collaboration with southern state lawmakers and politicians on the course and type of black education, as well as the GEB's ideological assumptions), can be obtained from the report of an extremely interesting conference financed by the GEB and attended by its first executive director, Dr. Wallace Buttrick: "General Education Board, Secretary's Itinerary, Rock Hill, S.C., Athens and Atlanta, Ga., Concord, Tenn., Greensboro, N.C., September 6–17, 1902, and Report of Conference with Country School Commissioners, Athens, Ga., September 10–12, 1902," pp. 29–35, box 304, folder 3176, GEB File, RAC. For a general treatment of the GEB, see Raymond B. Fosdick, *Adventures in Giving: The Story of the General Education Board* (New York: Harper & Row, 1962).

50. On the characteristics of the Hampton model, see J. D. Anderson, *Education of Blacks in the South*, especially chap. 2.

51. John Hope, "A Plea for Higher Education," *Advance* 9 (January 1901): 2–3, Hope Papers, AUC; the actual publication has not been found, and the actual date of the speech is unknown, although it is probably late 1900.

52. Ibid.

53. "Articles and Notes on Negro Education and Business," ca. 1901–2, Hope Papers, AUC.

54. On Carnegie and Washington's relationship, especially Carnegie's gift for a Tuskegee endowment, see Harlan, *Booker T. Washington: The Wizard of Tuskegee*, 136–37.

55. Hope quoted this material from undated pages of the *Southern Workman* when he delivered a speech criticizing the article; see John Hope, Emancipation Day speech, ca. 1902, probably in Atlanta, Hope Papers, AUC.

56. In my interviews with them, Dr. Samuel Nabrit acknowledged that Emancipation Day activities were usually held at Wheat Street and Friendship Baptist Churches and were primarily all–African American affairs, and John Hope II confirmed Nabrit's recollections. See also Torrence interviews with Lugenia Burns Hope and Claudia White Harreld, Torrence Papers, PUL; also Hope, Emancipation Day speech, ca. 1902, Hope Papers, AUC.

57. On the origins of the academy, including Crogman's and Wright's connections and Hope's membership, see Alfred A. Moss Jr. *The American Negro Academy: Voice of the Talented Tenth* (Baton Rouge: Louisiana State University Press, 1981), 18, 73–74.

58. Ibid., 152, 157; see also John Hope, "The Negro Vote in the States," 51–60; on the organization's elitism, see Gatewood, *Aristocrats of Color*, 217–19.

59. Hope, "Negro Vote in the States," 51–60; see Dittmer, *Black Georgia in the Progressive Era*, 132–35; Grant, *The Way It Was in the South*, 165; *Voice of the Negro* 1 (September 1904): 375–76, 411–12; John Michael Matthews, "Race Relations in Georgia, 1890–1930" (Ph.D. diss., Duke University, 1970), 162; see also *Atlanta Constitution* and *Atlanta Journal*, 16, 17 August 1904.

60. John Hope to Lugenia Hope, 11 May 1903, Hope Papers, AUC. On Trotter, see Stephen R. Fox, *The Guardian of Boston: William Monroe Trotter* (New York: Atheneum Press, 1971), especially 50–51 on the Boston riot; another account of the disturbance is in Lewis, *W. E. B. Du Bois*, 299–301; also Du Bois, *Dusk of Dawn*, 87.

61. Several articles assessing African American views of Roosevelt appeared shortly before the election in *Voice of the Negro* 1 (September 1904); see also the January 1904 issue, p. 7; and Harlan, *Booker T. Washington: The Wizard of Tuskegee*, especially chap. 16.

62. Ironically, their objectives were not unlike those of the Afro-American League before it was reborn as the Afro-American Council under the disguised leadership of Booker T. Washington in the early 1890s. In 1905, however, Du Bois wrote that "the Afro-American Council, while still in existence, has done practically nothing for three years, and is today, so far as effective membership and work is concerned, little more than a name" ("The Niagara Movement," *Voice of the Negro* 2 [September 1905]: 619).

63. Ibid., 620–21.

64. August Meier was perhaps the first to place ideological positions of African American leaders from 1880 to 1915 in neat categories of accommodation and protest. See his very important and pioneering work, *Negro Thought in America*, especially the introduction and 178–82; also significant is Elliott Rudwick, *W. E. B. Du Bois: Propagandist of the Negro Protest* (New York: Atheneum Press, 1978), especially chap. 5; on Niagara Movement declarations, principles, and objectives, see Du Bois, *Dusk of Dawn*, 88–91; also memo, reel 2, Du Bois Papers, UMass; Lewis, *W. E. B. Du Bois*, chap. 12; Elliott Rudwick, "The Niagara Movement," *Journal of Negro History* 42 (July 1957): 177–200; J. Max Barber, "Niagara Movement," *Voice of the Negro* 2 (September 1905): 522, 619–22; Trotter, *Guardian of Boston*, 89–97; *Pamphlets and Leaflets by W. E. B. Du Bois*, ed. Herbert Aptheker (White Plains: Kraus-Thomson, 1986), 55–58.

65. *Voice of the Negro* 1 (January 1904): 9; see also W. E. B. Du Bois to John Hope, 31 July 1905, Hope Papers, AUC.

66. Ibid.; see also Rudwick, "Niagara Movement," 180–82; Lewis, *W. E. B. Du Bois*, 319–20; Dittmer, *Black Georgia in the Progressive Era*, 172–73. On Hope's position as state secretary in Georgia, see "Confidential Brochure," in folder "Secretaries and Committees of the Niagara Movement," 1 April 1907, box 95-6, folder 557, Joel Spingarn Papers, Moorland-Spingarn Research Center, Howard University, Washington, D.C., hereafter cited as Spingarn Papers, Howard University.

67. See *Voice of the Negro* 3 (March 1906): 163–64, 175–77; also *The Georgia Equal Rights Convention, Macon, Georgia, 13–14 February 1906*, pamphlet in Moorland-Spingarn Research Center, Howard University; see also John Hope to W. E. B. Du Bois, 19 October 1928, Hope Papers, AUC; *Atlanta Independent*, 24 February 1906.

68. *The Georgia Equal Rights Convention*, 13–18; also Dittmer, *Black Georgia in the Progressive Era*, 173; Bacote, "The Negro in Atlanta Politics," 435; *Atlanta Independent*, 6 May 1905, announcement that Holmes was to speak at the program on the "Reasons Negroes Should Help Themselves"; see also Meier, *Negro Thought in America*, 176, 221–22.

69. Du Bois became the undisputed leader of the anti-Washington group after the

publication of *Souls of Black Folk* in the spring of 1903. White was the editor of the *Georgia Baptist*, which did not deny its antiseparatist leanings. Both men delivered important addresses at the conference. Bishop Turner also addressed the audience, delivering his famous "the American flag is a dirty and contemptible rag" speech, but by this time emigrationist sentiment had waned significantly among even the few African American leaders who supported emigration. For White's and Du Bois's speeches, see *Georgia Equal Rights Convention*, 9–16; see also Lewis, *W. E. B. Du Bois*, 326–27; and *Voice of the Negro* 3 (March 1906): 175–77. For Turner's speech, see *Atlanta Independent*, 24 February 1906.

70. *Voice of the Negro* 3 (March 1906): 163–64; see also John Hope to W. E. B. DuBois, 19 October 1928, Hope Papers, AUC.

71. On African American resistance to the segregated streetcar, see *Voice of the Negro* 1 (June 1904): 216–17; for Davis's critiques of the Macon convention, Du Bois, and the Niagara Movement, see *Atlanta Independent*, 28 January, 5 August 1905, 24 February, 21 April 1906; on Benjamin J. Davis Sr., see *DANB*, 160–61; and the book by his son, Benjamin J. Davis Jr., *Communist Councilman from Harlem: Autobiographical Notes Written in a Federal Penitentiary* (New York: International Publishers, 1969), especially chap. 8, "Death of My Father."

72. Quoted in Gatewood, *Aristocrats of Color*, 158. For examples of Davis's attacks on the light-skinned elite, see *Atlanta Independent*, 9 January 1909, 30 May 1914, 23 October 1915.

73. See Brawley, *History of Morehouse*, 101–2; Jones, *Candle in the Dark*, 78–79; *HMM* 28 (May 1906): 178.

74. *Atlanta Independent*, 27 January 1906.

75. Mordecai Johnson, "Report of Memorial Service in Honor of Dr. John Hope," speech at Sister's Chapel, Spelman College, 2 December 1936, Hope Papers, AUC.

76. John Hope to H. L. Morehouse, 4 June 1906, GEB File, RAC.

77. See Board Book 17, Minutes of ABHMS Executive Board, 7 May 1906, p. 59, ABHSA.

78. See *HMM* 28 (August 1906): 312. Publicity on the permanent appointment in 1907 was highlighted in several white newspapers and received massive attention in the *HMM* and among important philanthropic agencies like the GEB.

79. ABHMS Executive Board minutes, annual reports, and the *Home Mission Monthly* throughout the late nineteenth century and into the twentieth show the organization pleaded for more financial support from African American Baptists generally, and specifically from Georgia. For the five-year period between 1899 and 1903, for example, annual contributions to ABC from black Georgia Baptists totaled less than $300; see ABHMS annual reports, 1899–1903. *HMM* 19 (July 1897): 260, and *HMM* 22 (December 1900): 336, are just two examples in the *Home Mission Monthly*. On the interest in the academies, see also McManus, "American Baptist Home Mission Society," 449.

80. Ibid.

81. Wagner, *Profiles of Black Georgia Baptists*, 79.

82. Torrence interviews with James Nabrit and Lugenia Burns Hope, Torrence Pa-

pers, PUL; my interviews with Dr. Benjamin Mays and Samuel Nabrit; see also Jones, *Candle in the Dark*, 79.

83. On continuing problems between Georgia's state conventions and their mutual support of ABC and Spelman, see Wagner, *Profiles of Black Georgia Baptists*, 79–83; on problems still remaining among black Baptists nationwide, see J. M. Washington, *Frustrated Fellowship*, chap. 7; McPherson, *Abolitionist Legacy*, 291–94.

84. Wagner, *Profiles of Black Baptists*, 73. On the comparison with Washington, see Frank W. Padel, *Christian Schools for Negroes* (New York: Board of Education of Northern Baptist Convention, ca. 1906), 12–13, in vertical file on various subjects related to Baptist African American history, ABHSA.

85. *Voice of the Negro* 3 (July 1906): 481.

Chapter 7. The Hope Presidency: The Crucial First Year

1. John Hope bragged about his participation in militant organizations as a black college president in John Hope to W. E. B. Du Bois, 17 January 1910, reprinted in *The Correspondence of W. E. B. Du Bois*, vol. 1, ed. Herbert Aptheker (Amherst: University of Massachusetts Press, 1973), 165–66; the letter is also in Hope Papers, AUC. Subsequent references to this letter use the Aptheker citation.

2. See Lewis, *W. E. B. Du Bois*, 328–29; Elliott Rudwick, "The Niagara Movement," 177–200; J. Max Barber, "The Niagara Movement at Harper's Ferry," *Voice of the Negro* 3 (October 1906): 403–11; see also Stephen R. Fox, *The Guardian of Boston: William Monroe Trotter* (New York: Atheneum Press, 1971), 101–3; *Washington Bee*, 25 August 1906.

3. Rudwick, "The Niagara Movement," 200; Barber, "The Niagara Movement at Harper's Ferry," 409; see also Rudwick, *W. E. B. Du Bois*, 103; Aptheker, *Leaflets and Pamphlets*, 63–65.

4. See John Hope to W. E. B. Du Bois, 17 January 1910, in Aptheker, *Correspondence of Du Bois*, 1:165–66. The photograph was widely circulated in African American publications throughout the country. See, e.g., *Washington Bee*, 25 August 1906; *Cleveland Gazette*, 25 August 1906; and *Voice of the Negro* 3 (October 1906): 403.

5. On the African American soldiers in Brownsville, Texas, see Bernard C. Nalty, *Strength for the Fight: A History of Black Americans in the Military* (New York: Free Press, 1986), 90–97; John D. Weaver, *The Brownsville Raid* (New York: W. W. Norton, 1970), 106–9; see also Emma Lou Thornbrough, "The Brownsville Episode and the Negro Vote," *Mississippi Valley Historical Review* 44 (December 1957): 469–93.

6. The best accounts of the Atlanta riot and its causes are still Charles Crowe's, "Social Reform: Origins of the Atlanta Riot of 1906," *Journal of Negro History* 53 (July 1968): 234–57; and "Racial Massacre in Atlanta, September 22, 1906," *Journal of Negro History* 54 (April 1969): 50–173; see also Dittmer, *Black Georgia in the Progressive Era*, 123–31. For examples of incendiary articles in the press, see various issues of *Atlanta Journal*, *Atlanta News*, and *Atlanta Constitution* from July, August, and September 1906; for the specific article from Columbus, Ohio, see *Atlanta Journal*, 14 September 1906.

7. See *Atlanta Constitution*, 30 August 1906; see also Louis R. Harlan and Raymond

W. Smock, *The Booker T. Washington Papers*, 14 vols. (Urbana: University of Illinois Press, 1981), 9:62–67.

8. *Atlanta Constitution*, 4 September 1906, and, on Proctor, 17 September 1906; also see Proctor, *Between Black and White*, 96–97.

9. See Crowe, "Social Reform," 150–73; also Coleman et al., *History of Georgia*, 304–5; Grant, *The Way It Was in the South*, 203–5.

10. Most of the activities designed to curb black crime are in the resolutions passed by Antioch AME Church and printed in the *Atlanta Constitution*, 4 September 1906.

11. See Walter White, *A Man Called White: The Autobiography of Walter White*, reprint ed. (Athens: University of Georgia Press, 1995), chap. 1, especially 8–9; also Torrence interviews with James Huth and Charles Wardlaw, Torrence Papers, PUL. Huth was then superintendent of buildings and grounds at Atlanta University. Wardlaw was a Morehouse graduate and faculty member who taught manual training; he later served as the superintendent of buildings and grounds. On Wardlaw, see also Jones, *Candle in the Dark*, 74; see also Torrence interview with Lugenia Burns Hope, Torrence Papers, PUL; and Rouse, *Lugenia Burns Hope*, 43–44.

12. See Crowe, "Racial Massacre in Atlanta," 150–73; *Atlanta Constitution* and *Atlanta Journal*, 23, 24 August 1906.

13. Crowe, "Racial Massacre," 158–61; W. White, *A Man Called White*, 9–10.

14. Torrence interviews with Charles Wardlaw and James Huth, Torrence Papers, PUL; see also Rouse, *Lugenia Burns Hope*, 43.

15. Torrence interviews with Charles Wardlaw and Lugenia Burns Hope, Torrence Papers, PUL; Crowe, "Racial Massacre," 166–67; *New York Times*, 24 September 1906; Rouse, *Lugenia Burns Hope*, 43.

16. The physical plant director at Atlanta University claimed he had furnished college residents with "Smith & Wessons" that were shipped in secretly from Springfield, Mass., when rumors of potential trouble first surfaced weeks earlier (Torrence interview with Huth, Torrence Papers, PUL); see also Rouse, *Lugenia Burns Hope*, 43. On guns shipped to Atlanta in a coffin, see Dittmer, *Black Georgia in the Progressive Era*, 126.

17. For accounts of the Brownsville episode, see *Atlanta Constitution* and *Atlanta Journal*, 25–27 September 1906, *Cleveland Gazette*, 13 October 1906; *New York Times*, 26 September 1906; Ray Stannard Baker, *Following the Color Line: American Negro Citizenship in the Progressive Era* (New York: Doubleday, Page, 1908), 5–9, 12–14; Dittmer, *Black Georgia in the Progressive Era*, 128–29.

18. *Atlanta Constitution* and *Atlanta Journal*, 25–27 September 1906; Baker, *Following the Color Line*, 5–9, 12–14; Dittmer, *Black Georgia in the Progressive Era*, 128–29.

19. Dittmer, *Black Georgia in the Progressive Era*, 129; Baker, *Following the Color Line*, 7–14; *New York Times*, 26 September 1906.

20. Told in the *Indianapolis Freeman*, 6 October 1906.

21. See "Why Mr. Barber Left Atlanta," *Voice of the Negro* 3 (November 1906): 470–72.

22. See *HMM* 28 (November 1906): 404–5; *Atlanta Independent*, 29 September,

6 October 1906; *Indianapolis Freeman*, 6 October 1906; *Augusta Chronicle*, 22, 26, 29 September 1906.

23. On Crogman, see Mary White Ovington, *The Walls Came Tumbling Down* (New York: Arno Press and the New York Times, 1969), 65. On views on leaving Atlanta because of the violence, see *Atlanta Independent*, 29 September, 6 October 1906.

24. On interracial meetings, see *Atlanta Independent*, ibid.; *Atlanta Journal*, 24 September 1906; Baker, *Following the Color Line*, 15–20; *Atlanta Constitution*, 26 September, 30 November 1906; also Proctor, *Between Black and White*, 96–102.

25. On the first and second wave of African American leaders contacted by whites to help resolve racial problems, see *Atlanta Constitution*, 25–28 September 1906, 2, 4, 13 October 1906. Black leadership in Atlanta was often confusing. All the men first approached by Atlanta's city leaders after the riot had been avid supporters of the Atlanta Exposition in 1895 and were enthusiastic supporters of Washington at the time. Herndon and Bowen had attended the first meeting of the Niagara Movement, although it seems that Bowen, at least, had become a Washington supporter by 1906, and possibly Herndon as well. Though the leaders mentioned here at times straddled the ideological fence, Hope, Du Bois, and Barber were certainly viewed as radicals in 1906. See Meier, *Negro Thought in America*, 211–12; Lewis, *W. E. B. Du Bois*, 320–21.

26. John Hope to W. T. B. Williams, 6 October 1906, W. T. B. Williams Papers, Special Collections, Tuskegee University, Tuskegee, Alabama, hereafter cited as W. T. B. Williams Papers, Tuskegee University.

27. Ibid.; also Torrence interviews with Lugenia Hope and Charles Wardlaw, Torrence Papers, PUL; *HMM* 28 (December 1906): 507–9. On parents' concern about students, see Richard Teasley to John Hope, 11 December 1906, Hope Papers, AUC.

28. John Hope to W. T. B. Williams, 6 October 1906, W. T. B. Williams Papers, Tuskegee University.

29. For Washington's influence on Crogman and Bowen, see Dittmer, *Black Georgia in the Progressive Era*; 167–68; Meier, *Negro Thought in America*, 211–12.

30. Hope wrote out these responsibilities in a letter to a friend a few years later. He was quick to point out that "the rules and regulations governing Morehouse were not in any booklet form"; see John Hope to J. E. Blanton, 4 January 1926, Hope Papers, AUC.

31. Jones, *Candle in the Dark*, 88; Brawley, *History of Morehouse*, 109–12.

32. Brawley, *History of Morehouse*, chap. 8; Jones, *Candle in the Dark*, 230–35; my interviews with John Hope II, Samuel Nabrit, and Dr. Hugh Glocester; Glocester, a former Morehouse president, was Hope's student at Atlanta University.

33. On Davis and Johnson, see *DANB*; also on Davis, see Patricia Angel Johnson, "A Study of the Life and Work of a Pioneer Black Educator: John W. Davis" (Ed.D. diss., University of Kentucky, 1981); on Mordecai Johnson, also see Walter Dyson, *Howard University: The Capstone of Negro Education, a History 1867–1940* (Washington, D.C.: Howard University, 1941), 398–401; Brawley, *History of Morehouse*, chap. 8. On sports at Morehouse and students, see monthly issues of the college magazine *Athenaeum*, 1907–12, Atlanta University Special Collections.

34. Torrence, *Story of John Hope*, 156.

35. Alonzo R. Raiford to John Hope, 23 June 1906, Lula Wanable to John Hope, 28 July 1906, Mrs. Janie Perkins to John Hope, 26 October 1906, R. Teasley to John Hope, 11 December 1906, Hope Papers, AUC.

36. Jeremiah Sherfield to John Hope, 18 November 1906, Alfred Lawton to John Hope, 26 November 1906, Hope Papers, AUC; Torrence interview with James Nabrit, Torrence Papers, PUL.

37. Mordecai Johnson to John Hope, 18 August 1907, 15 May 1909, Hope Papers, AUC.

38. Lawrence Green to John Hope, 5 January 1908, Hope Papers, AUC.

39. Mrs. C. T. Walker to John Hope, 23 December 1906, E. Augusta Deace to John Hope, 16 January 1907, Hope Papers, AUC; my interviews with William F. Crawl (former Morehouse student), 28 September 1983, and Samuel Archer Jr. (former student of Hope, graduate of Morehouse, and son of Samuel Archer, Hope's good friend and ABC's second black president), 15 December 1982, both in Atlanta.

40. H. L. Morehouse to John Hope, 9 May 1906, Hope to Morehouse, 4 June 1906, Hope Papers, AUC.

41. On Buttrick, see Fosdick, *Adventures in Giving*, 13–15; Harlan, *Separate and Unequal*, 92–94; on Buttrick's racial views, see J. D. Anderson, *Education of Blacks in the South*, 92; also "General Education Board, Secretary's Itinerary," 29–35, GEB File, RAC.

42. George Sale to Wallace Buttrick, 8 September 1904, 21 October 1905, GEB File, RAC.

43. W. T. B. Williams to Wallace Buttrick, 15 June 1904, George Sale to Buttrick, 8 September 1904, 21 October 1905, GEB File, RAC.

44. Both Hampton and Tuskegee received annual appropriations of $25,000; see General Education Board, *Annual Report 1902–1914* (New York: General Education Board, 1915), RAC.

45. See John Hope to Andrew Carnegie, 4 April 1907, GEB File, RAC; on Hope's correspondence with Washington about Carnegie, see Harlan and Smock, *Washington Papers*, 9:150, 164–65.

46. W. T. B. Williams to Wallace Buttrick, 22 May 1907, folder 1898, GEB File, RAC; also John Hope to Wallace Buttrick, 14 December 1907, Buttrick to Hope, 17 December 1907, Robert Moton to Buttrick, 19 October 1906, GEB File, RAC.

47. See Board Book 17, 12 March 1906–13 July 1908, ABHMS File, ABHSA.

48. See *HMM* 29 (December 1907): 443–44.

49. The material from the *Providence Journal* and *Boston Transcript* is quoted in ibid. On Sale's letter to Morehouse, see George Sale to H. L. Morehouse, 15 March 1907, GEB File, RAC.

50. See Rouse, *Lugenia Burns Hope*, 44–45, 57–65; Lester Rodney, "Henry Hugh Proctor: The Atlanta Years 1894–1920" (D.A. diss., Atlanta University, 1992); also Proctor, *Between Black and White*, 95–105; Dittmer, *Black Georgia in the Progressive Era*, 170–72; Dana F. White, "The Black Sides of Atlanta: A Geography of Expansion

and Containment, 1870–1970," *Atlanta Historical Journal* 26 (Summer–Fall 1982): 199–225.

51. Auburn Avenue was initially called Wheat Street. See D. F. White, "Black Sides of Atlanta," 220–23; Dana F. White and Timothy J. Crimmins, "Urban Structure, Atlanta," *Journal of Urban History* 2 (February 1976): 231–51; Alexa B. Henderson, "Alonzo F. Herndon and Black Insurance in Atlanta, 1904–1915," *Atlanta Historical Bulletin* 21 (Spring 1977): 34–35; Booker T. Washington, "The Golden Rule in Atlanta," *Outlook* 84 (December 1906): 913–16; Dwight Fennell, "A Demographic Study of Black Business, 1905–1908, with Respect to the Atlanta Race Riot of 1906" (master's thesis, Atlanta University, 1977), 30–33; also useful is Barbara Taggert's "The Atlanta Race Riot of 1906 and the Black Community" (master's thesis, Atlanta University, 1984), 65–71.

52. My use of the terms *culture* and *African American worldview* draws on the pioneering work of Lawrence Levine and others who see culture "not as a fixed condition but a process: the product of interaction between the past and present. . . . Its toughness and saliency are determined not by a culture's ability to withstand change . . . but by its ability to react creatively and responsively to the realities of a new situation" (Lawrence Levine, *Black Culture and Black Consciousness: Afro-American Folk Thought from Slavery to Freedom* [New York: Oxford University Press, 1977], 4–5). African Americans' interest in their own institutions is well documented, but on the period directly preceding the beginning of the twentieth century, see Rabinowitz, *Race Relations in the Urban South*, pt. 2.

53. I have in mind here the protest against the Carnegie Library, which clearly was not necessarily to impel the city to allow blacks to use it but to make the city establish a library for African Americans somewhere, and the protests against unequal expenditures in the financing of black and white schools, as well as the organized protests against many of the bond referenda that took place in Atlanta up through the 1920s. For the Carnegie Library protest, see chapter 6 in this volume; on public education protests, see chapter 9.

54. August Meier in his pioneering work, *Negro Thought in America*, separated African American leaders in the era of Booker T. Washington into those who accommodated to the system and those who protested against it; see especially chaps. 3, 5. Though his paradigm is still useful, it is perhaps incomplete because it ignores realities within black America that demanded bold and dangerous action from African American leaders. White city leaders and officials in Atlanta, for example, were often as hostile to individuals who protested inequalities within the segregated system as they were to those who publicly protested unequal political opportunities, segregation in general, and lynching. On Booker Washington, historians have begun to rethink the question of accommodationism. For a thought-provoking analysis of the Washington conservative paradigm, see Maceo Crenshaw Dailey Jr., "Neither 'Uncle Tom' Nor 'Accommodationist': Booker T. Washington, Emmet Jay Scott, and Constructionalism," *Atlanta History* 38 (Winter 1995): 20–33.

55. See *Atlanta Journal*, 25 January 1897; also *Savannah Tribune*, 5 August 1899; the physician was H. R. Butler, and the AU graduate and minister was L. B. Maxwell.

56. On the circular and the Home Mission Society's plans and expectations, see *HMM* 29 (February 1907): 41, 56; also "Publications" folder, ABHSA.

57. Georgia contributed $600 dollars to the campaign, second only to Alabama's sum of $650; see *HMM* 29 (April 1907):147–48.

Chapter 8. Continuity and Change after a Decade of Service

1. Aptheker, *Pamphlets and Leaflets*, 75–76; see also Rudwick, *W. E. B. Du Bois*, 108–10.

2. Lewis, *W. E. B. Du Bois*, 340; Rudwick, *W. E. B. Du Bois*, 110–12; Fox, *William Monroe Trotter*, 103–10.

3. On the origins of the African American YMCA, see Nina Mjagkij, *Light in the Darkness: African Americans and the YMCA, 1852–1946* (Lexington: University Press of Kentucky, 1994), especially chaps. 1, 3. Mjagkij correctly noted that the International Committee did not officially develop what it called a "Colored Department" until 1923. After Hunton and Jesse Moorland were hired as international secretaries in 1888 and 1898, most African Americans referred to their work as the Colored Department since almost all work associated with African Americans in the organization was handled by the two black secretaries. In fact, the stationery Hunton and Moorland used had "Colored Men's Department" as its letterhead. See, e.g., Jesse E. Moorland, "The Young Men's Christian Association among Negroes," *Journal of Negro History* 19 (April 1924): 127–38; William A. Hunton, "Colored Men's Department of the Young Men's Christian Association," *Voice of the Negro* 3 (June 1905): 388–94.

4. John Hope to Addie Hunton, 12 April 1916, Hope Papers, AUC; also Hunton, "Colored Men's Department," 388–94; Mjagkij, *Light in the Darkness*, 48–52;

5. Quotation from Mjagkij, *Light in the Darkness*, 18; see also Moorland, "Young Men's Christian Association," 127–38; W. A. Hunton, "Colored Men's Department," 388–96.

6. See *Athenaeum* 1 (November 1900): 5; W. A. Hunton, "Colored Men's Department," 396; Jesse Moorland to John Hope, 11 December 1902, Hope Papers, AUC.

7. On Weatherford, see Wilma Dykeman, *Prophet of Plenty: The First Ninety Years of W. D. Weatherford* (Knoxville: University of Tennessee Press, 1966), 68–70; Morton Sosna, *In Search of the Silent South* (New York: Columbia University Press, 1977), 16–17; on Hope's and Moorland's displeasure with Weatherford's first book, see Moorland, "The Young Men's Christian Association," 136; Mjagkij, *Light in the Darkness*, 103, 111.

8. See *Washington Bee*, 6 February 1909; W. E. B. Du Bois, "Y.M.C.A.," *Crisis* (December 1914): 77, 80. On the contradictory views of other African American leaders in black communities like Washington, Cleveland, Detroit, and Chicago, see Mjagkij, *Light in the Darkness*, 162, especially fn. 59.

9. John Hope to Clarence Mills, 12 April 1916, Hope to D. W. Abercrombie, 18 December 1916, Hope Papers, AUC; see also Rouse, *Lugenia Burns Hope*, 80–82; on the NATCS, see *Some Accomplishments of the National Association of Teachers in Colored Schools*,

undated leaflet in Hope Papers, AUC; also *Atlanta Independent*, 11 July 1908. That year Hope became the new president of the State Teacher's Association in Georgia.

10. Hope reminded Du Bois of his presence at the New York meeting in 1909 in an important letter written in January 1910, although neither Lewis nor Kellogg nor any other source mentions Hope as one of the participants. Yet there is no evidence that Du Bois ever disputed Hope's claim to be present at the meeting. See John Hope to W. E. B. Du Bois, 22 January 1910, Hope Papers, AUC. On the NAACP's beginnings, see Charles Flint Kellogg, *NAACP: A History of the National Association for the Advancement of Colored People*, vol. 1 (Baltimore: Johns Hopkins University Press, 1967), 19–20, 297–301; see also Lewis, *W. E. B. Du Bois*, 390–92.

11. On white liberals in the South and their reluctance to embrace full black equality, see Sosna, *In Search of the Silent South*, especially chap. 1; on northern liberals in the NAACP, see McPherson, *Abolitionist Legacy*, 368–93; Kellogg, *History of the NAACP*, 9–18, 297–308; B. Joyce Ross, *J. E. Spingarn and the Rise of the NAACP: 1911–1939* (New York: Atheneum Press, 1972); also Ovington, *The Walls Came Tumbling Down*, especially chap. 4. On Trotter's and Ida B. Wells-Barnett's doubts, see Fox, *The Guardian of Boston*, chap. 4; on Wells-Barnett, see Duster, *Crusade for Justice*, 321–33.

12. For example, George Sale to Wallace Buttrick, 8 September 1904, 21 October 1905, W. T. B. Williams to Buttrick, 22 May 1907, Hope to Buttrick, 14 December 1907, Buttrick to Hope, 17 December 1907, Robert Moton to Buttrick, 19 October 1906, GEB File, RAC. See also H. L. Morehouse to Hope, 9 October 1914, Hope to Morehouse, 12 October 1914, Hope Papers, AUC; Hope to Williams, 11 January 1908, W. T. B. Williams Papers, Tuskegee University.

13. John Hope to W. T. B. Williams, 11 January 1908, W. T. B. Williams Papers, Tuskegee University.

14. Ibid.

15. Harlan and Smock, *Washington Papers*, 10:96.

16. John Hope to W. E. B. Du Bois, 17 January 1910, in Aptheker, *Correspondence of W. E. B. Du Bois*, 1:165–66.

17. See Harlan and Smock, *Washington Papers*, 8:552–53.

18. See ibid., 9:50, 164–65; also "Conference of the General Education Board of the Rockefeller Foundation on Negro Education," 29 November 1915, GEB File, RAC, here cited as Negro Education Conference, GEB File, RAC. On the Tuskegee-Morehouse rivalry, see the *Athenaeum*, 1908–15. On Crogman and Bowen, see Meier, *Negro Thought in America*, 211–13; and Harlan and Smock, *Washington Papers*, 8:72–73, 571.

19. B. T. Washington to Andrew Carnegie, 13 November 1909, Washington to John Hope, 16 November 1909, in Harlan and Smock, *Washington Papers*, 10:96, 199.

20. Louis Harlan, *Booker T. Washington: The Wizard of Tuskegee*, 138.

21. On the amounts, circumstances, and conditions of the GEB and Carnegie money, see MS dated 1 February 1910, GEB File, RAC; Torrence, *Story of John Hope*, 159.

22. See W. T. B. Williams to Wallace Buttrick, 22 May 1907, W. T. B. Williams

Papers, Tuskegee University; the letter is also in folder 521, GEB File, RAC; see also George Sale to H. L. Morehouse, 15 March 1907, folder 520, GEB File, RAC.

23. On the GEB's continued reluctance to support black liberal arts education, see John Hope to Wallace Buttrick, 7 May 1912, Buttrick to Hope, 9 May 1912, GEB File, RAC; see also H. L. Morehouse to Hope, 9 October 1914, Hope to Morehouse, 12 October 1914, Hope Papers, AUC.

24. W. T. B. Williams to Wallace Buttrick, 22 May 1907, W. T. B. Williams Papers, Tuskegee University.

25. For Buttrick's impressions of Williams's letter, see ibid.; for the beginning of yearly appropriations to Morehouse College, see Wallace Buttrick to John Hope, 1 February 1910, GEB File, RAC.

26. John Hope to W. E. B. Du Bois, 17 January 1910, in Aptheker, *Correspondence of W. E. B. Du Bois*, 165–66.

27. Ibid.; see also John Hope to Lugenia Burns, 10, 20 June 1897, Hope Papers, AUC. Hope wrote to his future wife that he refused to attend any function where Washington was expected to be present because people would assume he approved of Washington's policies.

28. W. E. B. Du Bois to John Hope, 22 January 1910, Hope to Du Bois, 17 January 1910, Hope Papers, AUC.

29. For Washington's relationship with the NAACP, see August Meier and Elliott Rudwick, "Booker T. Washington and the Rise of the NAACP," in *Along the Color Line: Explorations in the Black Experience* (Urbana: University of Illinois Press, 1976), 75–93; also useful is Harlan, *Booker T. Washington: The Wizard of Tuskegee*, 367–68.

30. Hope to Moton, 21 November 1910, in Harlan and Smock, *Washington Papers*, 10:481–82.

31. Robert Moton to B. T. Washington, 2 December 1910, Washington to Emmett Scott, 8 December 1910, in Harlan and Smock, *Washington Papers*, 10:498, 501–2.

32. See John Hope to W. E. B. Du Bois, 29 June 1916, Hope Papers, AUC; also Hope to Roy Nash, 26 December 1916, Nash to Hope, 21 December 1916, Hope Papers, AUC.

33. See "Fifth Annual Conference Program," 23–25 April 1913, box B-1, 1913, NAACP Papers, Library of Congress, Manuscript Division, Washington, D.C., hereafter cited as NAACP Papers.

34. On Hope's association with Spingarn, see John Hope to J. E. Spingarn, 24 September 1913, Spingarn Papers, Howard University; also see Joyce Ross, *J. E. Spingarn and the Rise of the NAACP, 1911–1939* (New York: Atheneum Press, 1972); Oswald Garrison Villard to John Hope, 18 February 1911, Hope to Mary Childs Nerney, 16 August 1915, 4 September 1915, Hope Papers, AUC.

35. John Hope to William Freeman, 1 December 1915, Hope to Mary Jackson, 13 December 1915, Hope Papers, AUC; see also Bartlett, *From Slave to Citizen*, 64–66.

36. John Hope to Mary Childs Nerney, 27 January 1915, Nerney to J. P. Barbour, 30 January 1915, Barbour to Nerney, 24 February 1915, Walter White to James W.

Johnson, 16 January 1916, Roy Nash to Hope, 6 October 1916, NAACP Branch Files, box G-45 (1913–17), NAACP Papers.

37. Jones, *Candle in the Dark*, 91.

38. Hope's apparent unhappiness became even more apparent when the First World War began; his dissatisfaction comes through in his letters to people like Freeman and Jackson in Rhode Island, and Spingarn, Nerney, and others in New York; for his expression to Abercrombie, see John Hope to D. W. Abercrombie, 30 August 1915, Hope Papers, AUC.

39. Quotation from John Hope to W. T. B. Williams, 13 July 1910, W. T. B. Williams Papers, Tuskegee University. Actually, one (white) man became president of both institutions. On the dismissal of Crogman and Bowen, also see A. A. McPheeters, "Origin and Development of Clark University and Gammon Theological Seminary," 213–16.

40. Quotation from Jones, *Candle in the Dark*, 4; see also Addie Louise Joyner Butler, *The Distinctive Black College: Talladega, Tuskegee and Morehouse* (Metuchen, N.J.: Scarecrow Press, 1977), 100–109.

41. My interviews with Hugh Gloster, Sam Nabrit, and Samuel Archer Jr.; see also Brawley, *History of Morehouse*, 105–12.

42. John Hope to Professor Gilbert T. Stocks, 8 October 1911, Hope Papers, AUC.

43. My interviews with Samuel Nabrit, Benjamin Mays, John Hope II, and William F. Crawl. On faculty Hope hired during his first decade as president, see Jones, *Candle in the Dark*, 93–94, 96–97; also *Athenaeum* 10 (April 1908): 5; 13 (March 1911): 9; 16 (February–April 1914): 13, 18.

44. Rouse, *Lugenia Burns Hope*, 88, see especially chap. 4.

45. My interview with John Hope II, telephone interview with Edward Swain Hope, 12 May 1983; also Torrence interviews with Edward Swain Hope and Lugenia Burns Hope, Torrence Papers, PUL; for Hope's quote about the Atlanta public school system, see "Negro Education Conference," GEB File, RAC; for Hope's letter to Williams, see Hope to Williams, 13 July 1910, W. T. B. Williams Papers, Tuskegee University; see also Rouse, *Lugenia Burns Hope*, 32–34.

46. For examples of racial discrimination at Worcester Academy, see John Hope to P. E. Sabine, 12 April 1912, Hope to Robert Drawbridge, 18 March 1912, Hope Papers, AUC; on Abercrombie's pleas for Hope to send Edward to Worcester and Hope's response hinting it would not be appropriate, see D. W. Abercrombie to John Hope, 31 July 1916, Hope to Abercrombie, 8 August 1916, AUC.

47. My interviews with Edward Swain Hope and John Hope II; Torrence interview with Lugenia Burns Hope, Torrence Papers, PUL; see also Rouse, *Lugenia Burns Hope*, 31–32,

48. Lugenia Hope to John Hope, 17 August 1916, J. Hope to L. Hope, 27 August 1912, Hope to E. C. Amy, 15 August 1915, Hope to Anna Butts, 14 August 1915, Hope to Edward S. Hope, 6 September 1915, Hope Papers, AUC; see also Rouse, *Lugenia Burns Hope*, 31–32.

49. Samuel Priestley Smith to John Hope, 9 March 1912, Hope Papers, AUC.

50. See John Hope to Lugenia Hope, 20 June, 6 July, 8 July 1912, Hope Papers, AUC.

51. John Hope to Lugenia Hope, 29 May, 30 May 1912, Hope to Edward Hope, 30 May 1912, Hope Papers, AUC.

52. John Hope to Lugenia Hope, 30 May 1912, Hope Papers, AUC.

53. Rev. L. G. Jordan to John Hope, 13 January 1900, Hope Papers, AUC; also Wagner, *Profiles of Black Georgia Baptists,* 164; on Chilembwe, see George Shepperson, *Independent African: John Chilembwe and the Origins, Setting and Significance of the Nyasaland Native Rising of 1915* (Edinburgh: Edinburgh University Press, 1969).

54. John Hope to Edward Hope, 31 May 1912, Hope Papers, AUC.

55. Ibid.; see also Hope to Lugenia Hope, 5 July, 8 July, 18 July 1912, Hope to Edward Hope, 7 July 1912, Hope Papers, AUC.

56. John Hope to Lugenia Hope, 12, 18, 24 July 1912, Hope to Edward Hope 8, 12 August 1912, Hope Papers, AUC.

57. See John Hope to Lugenia Hope, 18 July, 23 August 1912, Hope Papers, AUC; also Torrence, *Story of John Hope,* 177.

58. Hope to Lugenia Hope, 23, 27 August 1912, Hope Papers, AUC.

59. On skin color prejudice and its complexity, see Gatewood, *Aristocrats of Color,* especially chap. 6, "The Color Factor"; Joel Williamson, *New People: Miscegenation and Mulattoes in the United States* (Baton Rouge: Louisiana State University Press, 1995), especially chap. 4; Frazier, *Black Bourgeoisie*; Dittmer, *Black Georgia in the Progressive Era,* 60–62; and, most important, St. Clair Drake and Horace R. Cayton, *Black Metropolis: A Study of Negro Life in a Northern City,* 2 vols. (New York: Harcourt, Brace and World, 1970), 2:495–505.

60. Atlanta newspaper columnist Ben Davis was known for his criticism of the city's light-skinned elite; see, e.g., *Atlanta Independent,* 9 January 1909, 30 May 1914, 23 October 1915.

61. John Hope to Lugenia Hope, 18 July 1912, Hope Papers, AUC.

62. See chapter 10 for a discussion of Hope's sister in Providence. It is unknown whether either of the boys realized that the Providence family was passing for white. Edward may have known, but John Hope II insists he did not.

63. Torrence, *Story of John Hope,* 183.

64. John Hope to J. E. Spingarn, 24 September 1913, Spingarn Papers, Howard University.

65. On John E. White, see Sosna, *In Search of the Silent South,* 15; also *Athenaeum* 8 (April 1906) and 10 (March 1908); on Weatherford, see Dykeman, *Prophet of Plenty.*

66. Sosna, *In Search of the Silent South,* 17; see also E. Charles Chatfield, "The Southern Sociological Congress: Organization of Uplift," *Tennessee Historical Quarterly* 19 (December 1960): 337–39, 346–47.

67. John Hope to J. E. Spingarn, 24 September 1913, Spingarn Papers, Howard University.

68. Ibid.

69. John Hope to W. T. B. Williams, 22 January 1917, W. T. B. Williams Papers, Tuskegee University.

70. On White's death, see *Athenaeum* 15 (May 1913): 1–2; on the death of George Sale, see W. T. B. Williams to John Hope, 30 January 1912, Hope Papers, AUC.

71. On Du Bois's illness, see Hope to D. W. Abercrombie, 15 January 1917, Hope Papers, AUC; on Lugenia Hope's mother's illness and death, see John Hope to Anna Hope, 16 February 1916, Hope to Lugenia Hope, 18 June 1916, Hope Papers, AUC.

72. See W. E. B. Du Bois, "Booker T. Washington," *Crisis* 11 (December 1915): 82, also in *Writings in Periodicals Edited by W. E. B. Du Bois: Selections from the "Crisis,"* vol. 1, ed. Herbert Aptheker (New York: Kraus-Thomson, 1983), 113.

73. John Hope telegram to John Warren Davis, 15 November 1915, Hope to Mrs. Booker T. [Margaret] Washington, 17 December 1915, Emmett Scott to Hope, 16 November 1915, Hope Papers, AUC; on Washington's death, see also Harlan, *Booker T. Washington: The Wizard of Tuskegee,* 455–57.

74. On the numerous black academies in Georgia still operating in 1915, see John Hope to W. T. B. Williams, 5 December 1914, W. T. B. Williams Papers, Tuskegee University. The dormitory Hope saw the need for in 1910 was extremely significant in the growth of Morehouse College (then still Atlanta Baptist College). Without it the school would probably have been unable to attract the students and faculty necessary to move it forward and increase its college department.

75. See John Hope to Margaret Washington, 17 December 1915, Hope Papers, AUC; also Meier, *Negro Thought in America,* 175–76 and chaps. 8, 10; Meier and Rudwick, *Along the Color Line,* 86.

76. "Negro Education Conference," 29 November 1915, GEB File, RAC.

77. A few years earlier Flexner had examined American medical schools. He concluded that there were too many of them and the weaker ones should be forced to discontinue. In 1911 the GEB employed him to provide guidance on medical schools' requests for aid and to look at duplication in African American schools. See Fosdick, *Adventures in Giving,* 151–55.

78. "Negro Education Conference," 29 November 1915, GEB File, RAC, 150; see also H. L. Morehouse to John Hope, 9 October 1914, Hope to Morehouse, 12 October 1914, Hope Papers, AUC.

79. See "Negro Education Conference," 29 November 1915, GEB File, RAC, 151–52; also, on earlier GEB interest in developing two or three "schools of higher learning for Negroes," including medical education, see John Hope to Wallace Buttrick, 7 May 1912, Buttrick to Hope, 9 May 1912, GEB File, RAC; also "confidential" report to members of the GEB, 27 October 1915, Jerome Green to Buttrick, 7, 10 January 1914; particularly useful are Oswald Garrison Villard to John D. Rockefeller Jr., 26 January 1914, John D. Rockefeller Jr. to Buttrick, 2 February 1914, Buttrick to Rockefeller, 5 February 1914, GEB File, RAC. In response to Villard's inquiries over lunch with Rockefeller and Jerome Green on paying more attention to African American higher education in the South, Rockefeller wrote to Buttrick on 2 February that he had for some time questioned whether the "Board was not performing its full duty to the negroes." Three days later, on 5 February, Buttrick wrote a response to Rockefeller that seemed to widen the interest of the GEB in African American higher education. It also

encompassed (pp. 4 and 5) views of W. T. B. Williams on black higher education, self-help, and duplication of resources communicated to Buttrick as early as 1907.

80. See "Report to the Board of Committees," 22 October 1914, GEB File, RAC; see also Fosdick, *Adventures in Giving*, 188–90; W. T. B. Williams to Wallace Buttrick, 22 May 1907, GEB File, RAC, also included in W. T. B. Williams Papers, Tuskegee University; J. D. Anderson, *Education of Blacks in the South*, 248. My reading of Williams's letter and report to the GEB is different from Anderson's. It seems to me that the letter and report of 1907 are about coming to grips with the reality of segregation and the development that would have to occur within that separate setting. The report was a plea to upgrade the institutions doing the best college work, not unlike Du Bois's position and Williams's belief that Morehouse deserved special attention as a "rising star" in the black higher education arena. Though I do believe the GEB by 1919 wanted to control African American higher education, including the kind of leaders black colleges produced, I do not think the board was necessarily committed to limiting black college opportunities any more than it wanted to limit or drastically reduce whites' opportunities for medical education when it advocated reducing the number of medical schools because of various structural weaknesses and needs for standardization and upgrading. As a financial enterprise that distributed funds, the GEB seemed genuinely concerned about duplication of resources as an economic issue, since practically all of the schools, black and white, asked the agency for funds. After John D. Rockefeller Sr. made a special gift to the GEB for medical education, the GEB put some financial resources into the development of black medical education as well. As early as 1916, some grants were made to Meharry Medical College. Students entering medical school needed college degrees. Thus, these developments seem consistent with the GEB's continuing recognition of the need for professionals, including doctors, for a separate yet relatively self-sufficient black world.

81. For examples of Hope's, Williams's, and Moton's complimentary remarks at the conference, see "Negro Education Conference," 29 November 1915, GEB File, RAC, 22–25.

82. John Hope to Mary E. Jackson, 1 December 1915, Hope to William P. Freeman, 9 December 1915, Hope Papers, AUC.

83. For accounts of the lynching, see *Atlanta Journal*, 15 January 1915; *Crisis* 9 (March 1915): 225–28; for Hope's involvement in the protest, see John Hope to John Swain, 27 August 1915, Hope Papers, AUC.

84. John Hope to May Childs Nerney, 21 January 1916, Hope Papers, AUC; W. E. B. Du Bois to Hope, 26 January 1916, reel 2, Du Bois Papers, UMass.

85. John Hope to W. E. B. Du Bois, 2 February 1916, reel 2, Du Bois Papers, UMass.

86. W. E. B. Du Bois, *The Amenia Conference: An Historic Gathering* (Amenia: privately printed at the Troutbeck Press, 1925), in the Moorland-Spingarn Research Center, Howard University.

87. See John Hope to W. E. B. Du Bois, 6 July 1916, Hope Papers, AUC; also *Crisis* 12 (July 1916): 36–37; Aptheker, *Selections from the "Crisis,"* 119; on the second letter to Moton, see Lewis, *W. E. B. Du Bois*, 519.

88. See J. E. Spingarn to John Hope, 16 August 1916, Hope Papers, AUC; Du Bois, *The Amenia Conference*; Hope to J. E. Spingarn, 21 October 1916, box 95-3, folder 221, "John Hope," Spingarn Papers, Howard University; see Lewis, *W. E. B. Du Bois*, 517–22, particularly on the Amenia Conference's aftermath, when many of the resolutions were violated by Du Bois and others.

89. John Hope to J. E. Spingarn, 21 October 1916, box 95-3, folder 221, "John Hope," Spingarn Papers, Howard University; see also Ross, *Spingarn and the Rise of the NAACP*, 79–80.

90. On Mary E. Jackson, see Hine, *Black Women in America*, 1:25–26, 558–59, 2:1288–89.

91. John Hope to Roy Nash, 26 December 1916, Mary W. Ovington to John Hope, 31 October 1916, Hope to Ovington, 24 October 1916, Hope Papers, AUC; see also Ross, *Spingarn and the Rise of the NAACP*, 80; August Meier and Elliott Rudwick, "The Rise of the Black Secretariat in the NAACP, 1909–1935," in their *Along the Color Line*, 94–127.

Chapter 9. The War Years: 1917–1919

1. See John Hope, "Negro Day Speech," n.d. except for year (1901), Hope Papers, AUC.

2. John Hope to Rev. George Hugard, 6 July 1916, Hope to Edmund Jenkins, 17 October 1916, Hope Papers, AUC.

3. John Hope to D. W. Abercrombie, 15 January 1917, Hope to Alice Coleman, 21 March 1917, Hope Papers, AUC.

4. John Hope to D. W. Abercrombie, 30 March 1917, Mrs. W. E. B. [Nina Gomer] Du Bois to Hope, 10 January 1917, Hope Papers, AUC.

5. On organizing the NAACP in Atlanta, see "Application for Charter," 31 January 1917, NAACP Branch Files, box G-45 (1913–17), NAACP Papers; see also W. White, *A Man Called White*, 29–32; on black Atlanta's attempts to get a new black YMCA building and problems with library facilities, see *Atlanta Independent*, 6, 20, 30 January 1917.

6. On the problems of Atlanta's segregated schools, see *Atlanta Independent*, 18 October 1913, 10, 17, 24 February 1917; Edgar A. Toppin, "Walter White and the Atlanta NAACP's Fight for Equal Schools, 1916–1917," *History of Education Quarterly* 7 (Spring 1967): 3–21; W. White, *A Man Called White*, 29–32; also useful is M. E. Turner, "Black School Politics in Atlanta," 177–97.

7. See Walter White to James Weldon Johnson, 22 February 1917, NAACP Branch Files, box G-45 (1913–17), NAACP Papers.

8. See *Atlanta Independent*, 24 February 1917; *Savannah Tribune*, 10 March 1917; Walter White to James Weldon Johnson, 22 February 1917; two letters were sent the same day: one describes general NAACP business and indicates that Hope's committee was to meet that afternoon at three o'clock, the second describes the positive outcome. See also White to Johnson, 19 April 1917, NAACP Branch Files, box G-45 (1913–17), NAACP Papers.

9. *Atlanta Independent*, 3 March 1917.

10. W. E. B. Du Bois to John Hope, n.d. (probably late January 1917), Hope Papers, AUC; see also Hope to Du Bois, 15 January 1917, reel 2, Du Bois Papers, UMass.

11. See *Atlanta Independent*, 10 March 1917, John Hope to H. L. Morehouse, 1 March 1917, Hope to Madison J. Newton, 15 March 1917, Hope Papers, AUC.

12. John Hope, "Fifty Years of Negro Education," speech delivered 25 February 1917, Hope Papers, AUC; see also *Atlanta Independent*, 10 March 1917; and *Athenaeum* 20 (March 1917): 5–8.

13. John Hope, "Fiftieth Anniversary Speech," Hope Papers, AUC; *Atlanta Independent*, 10 March 1917.

14. See John Hope to Clifton D. Gray, 17 March 1917, Hope to D. W. Abercrombie, March 1917, Hope Papers, AUC; see also ibid.

15. John Hope to E. A. Turner, 9 February 1917, Hope to Mrs. Michael Snyder, 27 March 1917, Hope Papers, AUC.

16. On the black migration in general, see James R. Grossman, *Land of Hope: Chicago, Black Southerners, and the Great Migration* (Chicago: University of Chicago Press, 1989); for Georgia and Atlanta, see Dittmer, *Black Georgia in the Progressive Era*, 186–91; see also my interview with Rev. William H. Borders, prominent minister in Atlanta and contemporary of the period, 12 September 1984; *Atlanta Independent* articles on the migration, 1916–17, e.g., 6, 13, 20 January 1917; Grant, *The Way It Was in the South*, 315–19.

17. John Hope to S. P. Smith, 1 September 1916, Hope Papers, AUC; Hope to W. T. B. Williams, 1 November 1919, W. T. B. Williams Papers, Tuskegee University; also useful is Grossman, *Land of Hope*, 63–64.

18. *Atlanta Independent*, 20 January 1917; see also John Hope to Benjamin Hubert, 15 August 1917, Hope Papers, AUC.

19. On southern reactions to the black migration, see Grossman, *Land of Hope*, chap. 2, also James R. Grossman, "Black Labor Is the Best Labor: Southern White Reactions to the Great Migration," in *Black Exodus: The Great Migration from the American South*, ed. Alferdteen Harrison (Jackson: University Press of Mississippi, 1991), 51–71; on Hope's views, see Hope to Benjamin Hubert, 15 August 1917, Hope Papers, AUC.

20. On Hope's role as an important contact for northern jobs, see John Hope to Jeremiah Smith, 27 January 1917, W. Willis to Hope, 18 April 1917, Hope to Philip Burner, 9 June 1917, Hope Papers, AUC; see also Hope to W. T. B. Williams, 13 September 1916, W. T. B. Williams Papers, Tuskegee University; *Atlanta Independent*, 16 September 1916. For Davis's criticism of black presidents (namely, Richard R. Wright of Savannah State College) sending their students north to work, see *Atlanta Independent*, 7, 14 July 1917.

21. See John Hope to E. N. Glover, Hope Papers, AUC. On rumors of black disloyalty and guarding of Washington, D.C., see *Atlanta Independent* 31 March, 7, 14 April 1917; Emmett J. Scott, *Scott's Official History of the American Negro in the World War* (Chicago: Homewood Press, 1919), 34–38.

22. John Hope to John Swain, 27 May 1917, Hope Papers, AUC. On early discrimi-

nation at recruitment centers and in the Selective Service Act, see Scott, *Official History*, 34–38; also Jack D. Foner, *Blacks and the Military in American History* (New York: Praeger, 1974), 117–22.

23. On the establishment of the separate black officer training facility, see Ross, *Spingarn and the Rise of the NAACP*, especially chap. 3; also "Sixth Annual Conference" (1913–17), box B-1, NAACP Papers; also useful is Scott, *Official History*, chap. 7.

24. On Hope's support of the proposal at the beginning of the year, see John Hope to J. E. Spingarn, 29 January 1917, Hope to George Cook, 5 April 1917, box 95-3, folder 221, "John Hope," Spingarn Papers, Howard University; on Du Bois and his reluctance to accept the separate camp, see Lewis, *W. E. B. Du Bois*, 528–32.

25. On the War Department's education programs, see Scott, *Official History*, 72, 77–79; Mjagkij, *Light in the Darkness*, especially chap. 6; also John Hope to Lugenia Hope, 2 April 1918; *Athenaeum* 20 (May 1918): 78.

26. Emphasis in original. See Scott, *Official History*, 96–98; Arthur E. Barbeau and Florette Henri, *The Unknown Soldiers: Black American Troops in World War I* (Philadelphia: Temple University Press, 1974), 86–88; Addie Hunton and Kathryn M. Johnson, *Two Colored Women with the American Expeditionary Forces* (New York: Brooklyn Eagle Press, 1920), 45–48; *Atlanta Independent*, 20 April 1918.

27. See John Hope to W. T. B. Williams, 5 August 1917, W. T. B. Williams Papers, Tuskegee University; Barbeau and Henri, *Unknown Soldiers*, 82–85; J. D. Foner, *Blacks and the Military*, 117–22; Dittmer, *Black Georgia in the Progressive Era*, 192–98; Grant, *The Way It Was in the South*, 302–3.

28. On Houston, see Robert V. Haynes, *A Night of Violence: The Houston Riot of 1917* (Baton Rouge: Louisiana State University Press, 1976); Barbeau and Henri, *Unknown Soldiers*, 26–32; John Hope Franklin, *From Slavery to Freedom: A History of Negro Americans*, 6th ed. (New York: Alfred A. Knopf, 1974), 406.

29. H. C. Terrell to John Hope, 5 July 1917, and undated newspaper clipping on Mississippi lynching, Hope Papers, AUC. The Chicago riot took place at Fifty-first and State Streets. On East St. Louis, see Elliott Rudwick, *Race Riot at East St. Louis: July 2, 1917* (Carbondale: Southern Illinois University Press, 1964); see also Barbeau and Henri, *Unknown Soldiers*, chap. 2; John Hope to W. E. B. Du Bois, 13 August 1917, reel 5, Du Bois Papers, UMass.

30. See John Hope to Grace Hope Birnie, 20 August 1917; John Hope to Anna Hope, 10 December 1917, Alethea Hope to John Hope, 12 August 1917, Hope Papers, AUC.

31. Twelfth Census of the United States, 1900, Georgia, Schedule 1, Enumeration District 41, sheet 4, lines 90–94. My thanks to Mr. Bill Carrigan for uncovering information for this footnote and the next one while assisting me as a graduate student at Emory University.

32. Fourteenth Census of the United States, 1920, Schedule 1, Rhode Island, Enumeration District 248, sheet 13, line 13. I was unable to find the Ladeveze family in the census of 1910, and for that reason cannot pinpoint when they arrived in Providence or began to pass for white.

33. John Hope to Alethea Hope, 7 August 1917, James Ladeveze to John Hope,

12 August 1917, John Hope to James Ladeveze, 15 August 1917, Hope Papers, AUC. On Hope's sister Georgia Frances in California, see chapter 4 of this volume.

34. One of the Tolliver sisters told Ridgely Torrence that she knew about the Providence sister and tried to get Hope to visit her when he visited the city; see Torrence interview with Tolliver Sisters, Torrence Papers, PUL. Although he probably knew about both sisters passing, Torrence chose not to treat that part of Hope's life in his 1948 biography.

35. John Hope to W. E. B. DuBois, 13 August 1917, reel 5, Du Bois Papers, UMass; Hope to C. L. Haynes, 27 August 1917, Hope to B. F. Hubert, 15 August 1917, Hope to Wallace Buttrick, 18 October 1918, Hope Papers, AUC.

36. John Hope to C. L. Haynes, 27 August 1917, Hope to B. F. Hubert, 15 August 1917, also Hope to John Swain, 14 October 1917, Hope Papers, AUC.

37. On the Food Administration's special appeal to black Americans, see R. L. Willis (representative of the Food Administration) to John Hope, 22 September 1917, Hope Papers, AUC; see also Franklin, *From Slavery to Freedom*, 471. On the Colored American Society, see Hope to Rev. G. Hugard, 6 July 1916, Hope to M. Johnson, 31 March 1917, Hope Papers, AUC.

38. See John Hope to Benjamin Hubert, 15 August 1917, Hope Papers, AUC; also Walter White to James Weldon Johnson, 27 September 1917, NAACP Branch Files, box G-45 (1913–17), NAACP Papers; Hope to M. Murphy, 15 October 1917, Hope Papers, AUC.

39. John Hope to J. E. Spingarn, 18 September 1917, box 95-3, folder 221, "John Hope," Spingarn Papers, Howard University; *Atlanta Independent*, 11 August, 1 September 1917; Hope to M. Johnson, 5 October 1917, Hope to D. W. Abercrombie, 28 December 1917, Hope to Louis T. Wright, n.d. (January 1917), Hope Papers, AUC.

40. John Hope to D. W. Abercrombie, 28 December 1917, Hope to Louis T. Wright, January 1917, Hope to M. Johnson, 5 October 1917; see also Scott, *Official History*, 77, 105–8; J. D. Foner, *Blacks and the Military*, 123–24; undated notes on discrimination in the military, February 1918, box 126-72, folder 1376, Moorland Papers, Howard University; see also John Hope to Lugenia Hope, 22 February 1918, Hope Papers, AUC.

41. On the question of black loyalty, see Atlanta NAACP resolutions endorsing the war, encouraging African Americans to join the military, and dismissing concerns about black disloyalty printed in *Atlanta Independent*, 7 April 1918.

42. John Hope to L. Hollingsworth, 15 February 1918, A. L. Jackson to Hope, 20 May 1918, Hope to Jackson, 4 June 1918, Hope Papers, AUC.

43. John Hope to Madison Newton, 26 December 1917, Hope to Lugenia Hope, 18 January, 12, 22 February 1918, Hope Papers, AUC.

44. On Lugenia Hope's work during the war years, see Rouse, *Lugenia Burns Hope*, 94–96; also John Hope to Nellie Williams, 1 June 1917, Hope to Ophelia [Burns Bryant, Lugenia's sister], 26 March 1918, Hope Papers, AUC.

45. John Hope to Lugenia Hope, 22 February 1918, Hope to M. W. Reddick, 26 March 1918, Hope Papers, AUC.

46. Jesse E. Moorland to John Hope, 31 January 1912, Hope to Moorland, 5 February 1912, Hope to H. L. Morehouse, 8 April 1915, Morehouse to Hope, 10 April 1915, J. E. Moorland to Hope, 21 July 1916, Hope Papers, AUC; see also Mjagkij, *Light in the Darkness*, chap. 4.

47. John Hope to Wallace Buttrick, 23 January 1918, GEB File, RAC; see also Hope to John Swain, 22 January 1918, Jesse Moorland to Hope, 28 October 1917, Hope to Moorland, 6 November 1917, Hope Papers, AUC.

48. John Hope to Lugenia Hope, 5 March 1918, Hope Papers, AUC.

49. "Copy of Appeal to Hon. Wm. B. Baker," 5 March 1918, Hope Papers, AUC.

50. John Hope to Lugenia Hope, 4, 21 March 1918, Hope Papers, AUC; see also Board Book 21, 11 February 1918–23 September 1920, pp. 165–66, ABHSA.

51. Telegrams, J. E. Moorland to John Hope, 27, 30 April 1918, also John Hope to Lugenia Hope, 12 February 1918, Hope Papers, AUC; see also *Athenaeum* 20 (May 1918): 78.

52. See *Crisis* 17 (October 1918): 268; also Mjagkij, *Light in the Darkness*, 91–93.

53. See J. E. Moorland to John Hope, 18 June 1918, Hope Papers, AUC; on Hope's salary, see Board Book 21, 11 February 1918–23 September 1920, ABHSA.

54. John Hope to Lugenia Hope, 6, 10 May 1918, Hope Papers, AUC.

55. John Hope to F. T. Lane, 6 May, 4, 21 June 1918, Lane to Hope, 10 May, 8 June 1918, Edward Hope to John Hope, 12 June 1918, Hope Papers, AUC.

56. John Hope to Lugenia Hope, 15 May 1918, Hope Papers, AUC.

57. Ibid.; also George R. Hovey to John Hope, 9 August 1922, Hope to Hovey, 23 August 1922, Hope Papers, AUC.

58. On "Closed Ranks," see *Crisis* 16 (July 1918): 11; Lewis, *W. E. B. Du Bois*, 555–57.

59. In his biography of Du Bois, David Lewis wrote that the editorial was part of a deal struck to help influence the awarding of the commission. In an illuminating article in the *Journal of American History*, Mark Ellis claimed that Du Bois really wanted the captaincy, but as a militant African American leader, Ellis believed the *Crisis* editorial was a "colossal blunder." William Jordan, also in the *Journal of American History*, explained that on occasion Du Bois (along with Hope and a number of other African American leaders) often fluctuated between strategies involving accommodation or protest, depending on the specific situation. It seems to me that Jordan is correct without Lewis and Ellis necessarily being wrong. See Lewis, *W. E. B. Du Bois*, 555–56; Mark Ellis, "'Closing Ranks' and 'Seeking Honors': W. E. B. Du Bois in World War I," *Journal of American History* 79 (June 1992): 96–124; also his "W. E. B. Du Bois and the Formation of Black Opinion in World War I: A Commentary on 'The Damnable Dilemma,'" *Journal of American History* 81 (March 1995): 1584–90; William Jordan, "'The Damnable Dilemma': African-American Accommodation and Protest during World War I," *Journal of American History* 81 (March 1995): 562–83; see also Ross, *Spingarn and the Rise of the NAACP*, 98–101; Rudwick, *W. E. B. Du Bois*, 203–5.

60. John Hope to W. E. B. Du Bois, 22 July 1918, reel 6, Du Bois Papers, UMass; see also Lewis, *W. E. B. Du Bois*, 559–60.

61. John Hope to Lugenia Hope, 25 August 1918, Hope Papers, AUC.

62. Ibid.; see also John Hope to Lugenia Hope, 10 September 1918, Hope Papers, AUC.

63. Scott, *Official History*, 440.

64. John Hope to Lugenia Hope, 10 September 1918, Hope Papers, AUC; also see A. Hunton and Johnson, *Two Colored Women with the AEF*, 15–17.

65. On Moorland's problems in the United States, see Mjagkij, *Light in the Darkness*, 167.

66. Undated notes on scratchpad, Hope Papers, AUC; see Colored Men's Department MS entitled "History of Colored Men's Department, 1919," box 126-59, folder 1132, Moorland Papers, Howard University; see also Mjagkij, *Light in the Darkness*, 91–92.

67. John Hope to Lugenia Hope, 14 September 1918, Hope Papers, AUC.

68. See John Hope to Jesse Moorland, 24 September 1919, quoted in Torrence, *Story of John Hope*, 220–26, also see 209–10.

69. See John Hope to Jesse Moorland, 24 September 1918, quoted in Torrence, *Story of John Hope*, 220–26; Mjagkij, *Light in the Darkness*, 90–93; Barbeau and Henri, *Unknown Soldiers*, 40–42.

70. See Scott, *Official History*, 442–43.

71. John Hope to Jesse Moorland, 24 September 1919, quoted in Torrence, *Story of John Hope*, 225–26; *Crisis* 19 (November 1918): 230–26.

72. For an account of the "Bordeaux situation," see John Hope to Jesse Moorland, 24 September 1919, quoted in Torrence, *Story of John Hope*, 220–21; also "Miscellaneous File, World War I," clippings from *Boston Chronicle*, 15 March 1919, *St. Louis Argus*, 14 November 1919, and *Indianapolis Recorder*, 29 November 1919, Schomburg Collection, New York Public Library, New York.

73. John Hope to Jesse Moorland, 24 September 1919, quoted in Torrence, *Story of John Hope*, 221–22; also Hope to George Peabody, 2 April 1919, Hope Papers, AUC; Mjagkij, *Light in the Darkness*, 97.

74. John Hope to Jesse Moorland, 24 September 1919, quoted in Torrence, *Story of John Hope*, 221–22; also Hope to George Peabody, 2 April 1919, Hope Papers, AUC.

75. Lugenia Hope to John Hope, 15 October 1918, J. Hope to L. Hope, 29 October 1918, Hope Papers, AUC.

76. John Hope to Lugenia Hope, 25 October, 11 November 1918, Hope Papers, AUC.

77. Lugenia Hope to John Hope, 26 October 1918, Hope Papers, AUC.

78. Ibid.; see also Lugenia Hope to John Hope, 12 December, 1918, 7 July 1919, Hope Papers, AUC.

79. Edward Hope to John Hope, 11 November 1918, Hope Papers, AUC; see also ibid.

80. *Crisis* 17 (November 1918): 8–9; *Crisis* 18 (July 1919): 127–28; Barbeau and Henri, *Unknown Soldiers*, chaps. 7, 8.

81. Hope to Moorland, 24 September 1919, quoted in Torrence, *Story of John Hope*, 224.

82. Edward Hope to John Hope, 10 November 1918, Lugenia Hope to John Hope, 12 December 1918, Hope Papers, AUC.

83. John Hope to Lugenia Hope, 4, 11, 15 December 1918, Hope Papers, AUC; see also Robert Moton, *Finding a Way Out: An Autobiography* (New York: Doubleday, Page, 1920), 234–65; Scott, *Official History*, 114–16; *Crisis* 18 (May 1919): 9–10, in Aptheker, *Selections from the "Crisis,"* 1 : 189–90.

84. John Hope to Lugenia Hope, 11 December 1918, Hope Papers, AUC.

85. *Crisis* 18 (May 1919): 9–10, in Aptheker, *Selections from the "Crisis,"* 1 : 189; see also John Hope to Lugenia Hope, 15 December 1918, Hope Papers, AUC.

86. John Hope to W. E. B. Du Bois, 1 June 1921, reel 21, Du Bois Papers, UMass.

87. John Hope to Lugenia Hope, 16 January 1919, Hope Papers, AUC.

88. See John Hope to Jesse Moorland, 24 September 1919, quoted in Torrence, *Story of John Hope*, 225, see also 218; John Hope to Lugenia Hope, 15 December 1918, Hope Papers, AUC; Hope to W. E. B. Du Bois, 1 June 1921, Du Bois Papers, UMass.

89. The letter to Carter about Africa is quoted in Torrence, *Story of John Hope*, 218; see also W. E. B. Du Bois, "African Roots of War," *Atlantic Monthly* 115 (May 1915): 707–14; John Hope to W. E. B. Du Bois, 5 June 1915, reel 5, Du Bois Papers, UMass.

90. Lugenia Hope to John Hope, 26 October, 12 December 1918, 7 July 1919, John Hope II to John Hope, 10 October 1918, Hope Papers, AUC.

91. Samuel Archer to John Hope, 28 October 1918, 28 November, 15 December 1918, Hope Papers, AUC.

92. Samuel Archer to John Hope, n.d., Hope Papers, AUC.

93. Wallace Buttrick to W. T. B. Williams, 2 February, 4 March 1918; Abraham Flexner to Buttrick, 27 November 1918, Buttrick to Flexner, 3 December 1918, GEB File, RAC. Black schools targeted for increased support included Fisk in Nashville, AU and Spelman in Atlanta, Shaw University in Raleigh, N.C., and Virginia Union in Richmond; see Raymond B. Fosdick, *Adventures in Giving*, 196–97; Lugenia Hope to John Hope, 17 March 1919, Hope Papers, AUC.

94. Abraham Flexner to Wallace Buttrick, 27 November 1918, Buttrick to Flexner, 3 December 1918, GEB File, RAC; see also Samuel Archer to John Hope, 23 December 1918, Hope Papers, AUC; Fosdick, *Adventures in Giving*, 196–97.

95. See Abraham Flexner to Wallace Buttrick, 27 November 1918, Buttrick to Flexner, 3 December 1918, GEB File, RAC.

96. This view is also hinted at in two letters Wallace Buttrick wrote to Hope's good friend W. T. B. Williams; see Buttrick to Williams, 2 February, 4 March 1918, GEB File, RAC.

97. Ibid.; see also Lugenia Hope to John Hope, 17 March 1919, Hope Papers, AUC.

98. See Samuel Archer to John Hope, 19 January 1919, Lugenia Hope to John Hope, 31 December 1918, Hope Papers, AUC. Mail was extremely slow reaching Hope in France, and letters written bear no relation to the time they were actually received.

99. Charles L. White to Wallace Buttrick, 1 March 1919, also Samuel H. Archer to Buttrick, 3 June 1919, folder 521, GEB File, RAC; see also John Hope to Lugenia Hope, 14 February 1919, Hope Papers, AUC.

100. See John Hope to George Foster Peabody, 2 April 1919, Hope to Buttrick, 9 April 1919, Hope Papers, AUC.

101. Samuel Archer to Wallace Buttrick, 3 June 1919, GEB File, folder 521, RAC.

102. Abraham Flexner to Wallace Buttrick, 18 July 1919, also Charles L. White to Buttrick, 1 March 1919, GEB File, RAC.

103. Franklin, *From Slavery to Freedom*, 359. On the Chicago riot, see William M. Tuttle Jr., *Race Riot: Chicago in the Red Summer of 1919* (New York: Atheneum Press, 1970); see also Allan H. Spear, *Black Chicago: The Making of a Negro Ghetto 1890–1920* (Chicago: University of Chicago Press, 1967). On the violence of the summer of 1919 generally, see NAACP, *Thirty Years of Lynching in the United States, 1889–1918* (New York: NAACP, 1919); Arthur I. Waskow, *From Race Riot to Sit-In: 1919 and the 1960s* (Garden City, N.Y.: Anchor Books, 1966), especially chap. 2; Barbeau and Henri, *Unknown Soldiers*, 177–82; Grant, *The Way It Was in the South*, 307–27.

104. John Hope to Wallace Buttrick, 6 August 1919, GEB File, RAC; see also Hope to Daniel F. George, 6 August 1919, Hope to John Swain, 10 September 1919, Hope Papers, AUC.

105. John Hope to Jesse Moorland, 24 September 1919, quoted in Torrence, *Story of John Hope*, 226.

Chapter 10. The "New Negro" and John Hope in the 1920s

1. John Hope to W. E. B. Du Bois, 15 November 1924, Hope Papers, AUC.

2. Among the many sources on this period, James Weldon Johnson, *Along This Way*, xxix; Walter White, *A Man Called White*, especially chaps. 5–8; and Alain Locke, *The New Negro*, reprint ed. (New York: Atheneum Press, 1968), pages 3–16 are especially useful; also see Nathan Huggins, *Harlem Renaissance* (New York: Oxford University Press, 1971); David Lewis, *When Harlem Was in Vogue* (New York: Oxford University Press, 1989); Grant, *The Way It Was in the South*, and Dittmer, *Black Georgia in the Progressive Era*, 203–11.

3. See John Hope to B. H. Fletcher, 9 October 1920, Hope Papers, AUC.

4. For examples of Hope's interactions with veterans and other students, see P. J. Blackwell to John Hope, 13 December 1920, James Love to Hope, 20 March 1920, Hope to Clarence Burrell, 11 January 1923, B. H. Fletcher to Hope, 9 October 1920, Hope to Victor Daly, 7 February 1921, Hope to A. N. Marquis & Company, 14 March 1921, S. Hart to Hope, 16 April 1921, John Clark to Hope, 2 January 1923, Hope to Clark, 15 January 1923, Hope Papers, AUC.

5. D. Allen to John Hope, 15 May, 22 April 1926, Hope to J. Benson, 17 August 1926, Hope Papers, AUC.

6. John Hope to Mr. F. D. Gholston, 20 July 1923, Gholston to Hope, 12 July 1923, Hope Papers, AUC.

7. For a view of discipline problems at Morehouse during the First World War, see B. J. Davis Jr., *Communist Councilman from Harlem*, 31–39; Lugenia Hope to John Hope, 20, 27 November and especially 12 December 1918, Hope Papers, AUC.

8. My interviews with Samuel Archer Jr. (son of Hope's dean, Samuel Archer) and W. F. Crawl, both Morehouse students in the 1920s.

9. My interview with W. F. Crawl; see also John Hope to L. Broughton, 15 October 1919, Hope to P. Maxwell, 12 March 1920, Hope Papers, AUC; for other examples of Hope disciplining students and even expelling them in the early 1920s, see John Hope to George Hovey, 15 April 1920, GEB File, RAC; Hope to W. T. B. Williams, 26 September 1919, W. T. B. Williams Papers, Tuskegee University.

10. Jones, *Candle in the Dark*, 108–12; my interview with Dr. Benjamin Mays, September 1982, also Benjamin Mays, *Born to Rebel: An Autobiography*, reprint ed. (Athens: University of Georgia Press, 1987), 66, 92–93; see also Torrence interview with Rayford Logan, Torrence Papers, PUL; *DANB*, "John Hope," 324.

11. Jones, *Candle in the Dark*, 108–12; my interview with Dr. Benjamin Mays, September 1982, also Benjamin Mays, *Born to Rebel: An Autobiography*, reprint ed. (Athens: University of Georgia Press, 1987), 66, 92–93; see also Torrence interview with Rayford Logan, Torrence Papers, PUL; also Howard Thurman to John Hope, 20 June 1921, Hope to Thurman, 26 June 1921, 29 September 1922, Hope to George W. Johnson, Hope Papers, AUC; my interview with Samuel Nabrit; Torrence interviews with Walter Chivers, Nathaniel P. Tillman, and Claude B. Dansby, Torrence Papers, PUL.

12. Manuscript, "Note copied from diary of Dr. M. Ashby Jones, copied by his wife," box 1, Archives of the Commission on Interracial Cooperation, Atlanta University Special Collections, hereafter cited as CIC Papers, AUC. The CIC Papers are now part of the microfilmed version of the John and Lugenia Hope Collection at the Woodruff Library at Clark Atlanta University. When I conducted my research, they had not yet been microfilmed and existed as a collection separate from the Hope Papers. My citations are from that original arrangement.

13. Manuscript, "Origin and Purpose—Exhibit A," box 1, CIC Papers, AUC; also on the origins of the CIC, see Edward F. Burrows, "The Commission on Interracial Cooperation" (Ph.D. diss., University of Wisconsin, 1954); see also Ann Wells Ellis, "The Commission on Interracial Cooperation, 1919–1944: Its Activities and Results" (Ph.D. diss., Georgia State University, 1975); Wilma Dykeman and James Stokely, *Seeds of Southern Change: The Life of Will Alexander* (Chicago: University of Chicago Press, 1962), 59–76; my interview with Benjamin Mays.

14. Manuscript, "Origin and Purpose—Exhibit A," box 1, CIC Papers, AUC; also on the origins of the CIC, see Edward F. Burrows, "The Commission on Interracial Cooperation" (Ph.D. diss., University of Wisconsin, 1954); see also Ann Wells Ellis, "The Commission on Interracial Cooperation, 1919–1944: Its Activities and Results" (Ph.D. diss., Georgia State University, 1975); Wilma Dykeman and James Stokely, *Seeds of Southern Change: The Life of Will Alexander* (Chicago: University of Chicago Press, 1962), 59–76.

15. See Dykeman and Stokely, *Life of Will Alexander*; also Torrence interview with Will Alexander, Torrence Papers, PUL. Important for an understanding of the CIC is Sosna, *In Search of the Silent South*, chap. 2; M. Ashby Jones's reasons for joining the CIC are quoted on pp. 28–29. Also see Dykeman, *Prophet of Plenty*, 138–44.

16. The black member who objected to whites controlling black thought was Fisk University's Isaac Fisher; see Minutes of CIC, 25 June 1920, box 1, AUC. Most African American leaders did not realize that the CIC was operating and included black members until May 1920. Though he would soon change, the editor of the *Atlanta Independent* was at first suspicious of the "self-appointed" committee operating "somewhere in our community"; see *Atlanta Independent*, 22 May 1920.

17. Torrence interview with Will Alexander, Torrence Papers, PUL; also Dykeman and Stokely, *Life of Will Alexander*, 74–75; Torrence, *Story of John Hope*, 229–30.

18. On the Atlanta bond issue, see Toppin, "Walter White and the Atlanta NAACP," 15–18; Torrence, *Story of John Hope*, 230; Dykeman and Stokely, *Life of Will Alexander*, 75.

19. For an account of these activities, see *Atlanta Constitution*, 6, 24 March, 29 November 1919, 29, 31 January 1920, also 1, 6 March 1921; *Atlanta Independent*, 16 December 1920, 24 February 1921; Torrence, *Story of John Hope*, 230; Racine, "Atlanta's Schools," 185–87; Toppin, "Walter White and the Atlanta NAACP," 16–17; also Dykeman and Stokely, *Life of Will Alexander*, 74–75.

20. For an account of the proceedings at the banquet, see *Atlanta Independent*, 23 August 1919.

21. The meeting never took place, it seems, because officials at Tuskegee believed (1) that it would tread too closely on their own agenda by duplicating the work of the Tuskegee Farmer Conferences, and (2) that such a meeting should take place in a rural area instead of in urban Atlanta. See John Hope to W. T. B. Williams, 1 November 1919, Williams to Hope, 8 November 1919, W. T. B. Williams Papers, Tuskegee University.

22. On the NAACP meeting, see *Atlanta Independent*, 1 May, 5 June 1920. On Hope receiving a car from the Alumni Association, see Alumni Association form letter sent to "Friends" of the college, 7 August 1919, and W. T. B. Williams to S. H. Archer, 1 December 1919, W. T. B. Williams Papers, Tuskegee University. On Benjamin Davis Jr., see Torrence, *Story of John Hope*, 238–39; see also John Hope to Jesse Moorland, 14 May 1929, Hope Papers, AUC.

23. On Morehouse's endowment, see John Hope to Wallace Buttrick, 27 July 1920, Buttrick to Hope, 30 July 1920, GEB File, RAC. On appropriations to Fisk and other ABHMS schools, see "Total Subscriptions by the General Education Board from Mr. Rockefeller's Gift of December 18, 1919, up to and Including December 2, 1920," 12–13, GEB File, RAC.

24. See John Hope to George Rice Hovey, 20 May 1922, Wallace Buttrick to Raymond Fosdick, 10 February 1923, Hope to Buttrick, 27 February 1922, GEB File, RAC.

25. John Hope to Wallace Buttrick, 27 February 1922, Buttrick to Hope, 1 March 1922, GEB File, RAC.

26. John Hope to Dr. George Rice Hovey, 20 May 1922, GEB File, RAC.

27. Wallace Buttrick to John Hope, 31 May 1922, GEB File, RAC.

28. Hope was never formerly offered the job, although a Lincoln board member contacted him to determine his interest. Hope made it clear that he would be interested only if the school's future included its development as a bona fide college. Hope's

friend Nathan B. Young became Lincoln's next president and by the end of the decade was embroiled in a major feud over the school's direction. See John Hope to William Parish Curtis, 10 February 1922, Hope Papers, AUC. On the problems at Lincoln, see Raymond Wolters, *The New Negro on Campus: Black College Rebellions of the 1920's* (Princeton: Princeton University Press, 1975), chap. 5.

29. On the Atlanta School of Social Work (first called Atlanta School of Social Services) and the Urban League, see Nancy J. Weiss, *The National Urban League, 1910– 1940* (New York: Oxford University Press, 1974), 75–79; Rouse, *Lugenia Burns Hope,* 83–85; Shivery, "History of Organized Social Work among Negroes in Atlanta," 290–96, 497–506; John Hope to William A. Avery, 15 June 1922, Helen Pendleton to Hope, 2 January, 2 April 1926, Hope Papers, AUC. On interactions with the NAACP, see John Hope to W. E. B. Du Bois, 1 June 1921, reel 9, 20 May 1922, reel 10, 12 January 1927, reel 23, Du Bois Papers, UMass.

30. For an example of Hope's involvement and work with the NATCS, see the six-page penciled draft of resolutions Hope helped construct when he attended its annual meeting in 1922, MS, "National Association of Teachers in Colored Schools, July 28, 1922," W. T. B. Williams Papers, Tuskegee University.

31. On the World Evangelism Conference, see the first page of a two-page letter (second page is missing) Hope wrote to Du Bois about it. John Hope to W. E. B. Du Bois, 20 May 1922, reel 10, Du Bois Papers, UMass.

32. John Hope to W. E. B. DuBois, n.d. (the date 21 October 1920 appears on p. 2), reel 9, Du Bois Papers, UMass. On Lugenia advising Hope to write his own history of the war, see Lugenia Hope to John Hope, 12 December 1918, Hope Papers, AUC.

33. John Hope to John Swain, 12 May 1923, Hope Papers, AUC; also Torrence interviews with Jane Hope Lyons, Ted Owens, and Hope's Nashville friend J. W. Johnson, Torrence Papers, PUL; W. E. B. Du Bois to John Hope, 19 December 1922, reel 10, Du Bois Papers, UMass.

34. See John Hope to Lugenia Hope, 8 January 1930, Hope Papers, AUC.

35. On Elsa Brown's concept of "womanism," see her "Womanist Consciousness: Maggie Lena Walker and the Independent Order of Saint Luke," in *Unequal Sisters: A Multicultural Reader in U.S. Women's History,* ed. Vicki L. Ruiz and Ellen Carol Du Bois (New York: Routledge, 1994), 268–83; see also Rouse, *Lugenia Burns Hope,* 8–10.

36. For an example of John Hope's respect for Ida Wells-Barnett, see his ten-page letter, John Hope to Tolliver Sisters and Mary E. Jackson, 14 September 1894, also Hope to Grace Hope, 15 October 1896, Hope Papers, AUC.

37. See undated speech (ca. 1900) to "Women's Club in Atlanta," see also Lucille Gibson to John Hope, 18 (28?) October 1899 Hope Papers, AUC.

38. For other examples of Hope's support for African American women, see John Hope to Oswald Garrison Villard, 5 February 1918, Minnie L. Bradley to Hope, 19 April 1922, Hope to Eva D. Bowles, 28 January 1920, Bowles to Hope, 2 February 1920, Charles Bentley to Hope, 29 June 1921, Mrs. John D. Rockefeller Jr. to Hope, 16 November 1920, Nannie H. Burroughs to Hope, 5 December 1921, Hope Papers, AUC.

39. See Rouse, *Lugenia Burns Hope,* especially chap. 3. I chronicle Lugenia's influ-

ence at Morehouse, their relationship with their children, and her work outside the home in earlier chapters in this volume.

40. For examples of Hope's role as adviser to foundations and societies, see John Hope to Wallace Buttrick, 16 July 1920, 9 March 1921, S. Hart to Hope, 16 April 1921, GEB File RAC; George Hovey to Hope, 20 March 1922, Hope to Hovey, 23 March 1922, Hope Papers, AUC.

41. George Hovey to John Hope, 9 August 1922, Hope Papers, AUC.

42. John Hope to Lugenia Hope, 17 December 1922, Hope to George Hovey, 23 August 1922, Hope Papers, AUC; see also Hope to W. T. B. Williams, 21 December 1922, W. T. B. Williams Papers, Tuskegee University.

43. George Hovey to John Hope, 20 March 1922, Hope to Hovey, 23 March 1922, Hope Papers, AUC.

44. On the 1920 Tuskegee situation, see Wolters, *New Negro on Campus,* chap. 4; also John Hope to W. T. B. Williams, 19 May 1923, W. T. B. Williams Papers, Tuskegee University.

45. Edward H. Webster to W. E. B. Du Bois, 22 July 1923, reel 12, Du Bois Papers, UMass.

46. See *Messenger* 5 (August 1923): 783, and (September 1923): 807–8.

47. John Hope to Charles E. Bentley, 13 December 1922, AUC; *Crisis* 24 (February 1923): 56.

48. John Hope to Walter White, 17 January 1924, White to Hope, 21 January 1924, box G-43, NAACP Papers.

49. See *Crisis* 22 (May 1921): 7–9; also 37 (July 1930): 245.

50. "John Hope Sees Improved Race Relations," *Amsterdam News,* 7 July 1926, newspaper clipping in Schomburg Library, New York, filed under "John Hope" in "Clipping File."

51. During an address to white Methodists in Birmingham, Alexander was asked specifically if he supported segregation. Alexander answered that he could not "defend the Jim Crow Law," yet added, "its repeal under all of the circumstances, however, is another matter on which your judgement is as good as mine." The latter is what appeared to be a retraction of his position on social equality as stated in an earlier speech. See John Hope to W. E. B. Du Bois, 25 May 1926, reel 18, Du Bois Papers, UMass; Dykeman and Stokely, *Life of Will Alexander,* 33.

52. Hope to Du Bois, 25 May 1926, reel 18, Du Bois Papers, UMass.

53. Ibid.

54. Du Bois published reviews critical of his own leadership in *Crisis* 22 (April 1921): 246–47; see also George F. Peabody to W. E. B. Du Bois, 12 July 1921, reel 10, Du Bois Papers, UMass.

55. For the story of Standard Life Insurance Company and its failure during the Depression, see Alexa B. Henderson's outstanding book, *Atlanta Life Insurance Company: Guardian of Black Economic Dignity* (Tuscaloosa: University of Alabama Press, 1990), especially 100–104; see also *Atlanta Independent,* 31 January, 7, 14 February 1920; E. Franklin Frazier to W. E. B. Du Bois, 21 January 1925, reel 17, Du Bois Papers, UMass.

56. John Hope to Mr. William C. Graves, c/o Mr. Julius Rosenwald, 26 December 1924, Hope Papers, AUC.

57. Ibid.

58. Hope, "The Relations between the Black and White Races in America," speech delivered at Geneva, Switzerland, 31 March 1928, Hope Papers, AUC.

59. See Wolters, *New Negro on Campus*, 3–28.

60. My discussion of the student rebellion comes mainly from Wolters, *New Negro on Campus*, chap. 2; and Richardson, *History of Fisk*, chap. 7.

61. Wolters, *New Negro on Campus*, 33–36; Richardson, *History of Fisk*.

62. Many of the strict rules at Fisk, which included faculty spying, strict rules on interacting with women, and prohibitions against smoking, gambling, etc., were no different from the rules at Morehouse College and, as Joe Richardson has pointed out, most black mission colleges; see Richardson, *A History of Fisk*, 85–90.

63. See W. E. B. Du Bois, "The Dilemma of the Negro," in *Writings in Periodical Literature, 1910–1934*, ed. Herbert Aptheker, vol. 2 (New York: Kraus-Thomson, 1982), 222–29, especially 228; it originally appeared in *American Mercury* 3 (October 1924): 79–185.

64. On McKenzie's stubbornness, see Richardson, *History of Fisk*, 89–90; Wolters, *New Negro on Campus*, 46–48. Unlike Morehouse, Fisk received considerable funding from other philanthropic agencies in addition to the GEB. The Carnegie Corporation contributed $250,000 to Fisk's endowment campaign, while Morehouse seems to have received no money at all from this agency. This may have been because Hope did not take Morehouse as far to the right as McKenzie took Fisk.

65. See John Hope to W. E. B. Du Bois, 15 November 1924, reel 13, Du Bois Papers, UMass.

66. Ibid. See also John Hope to Robert Moton, 12 February 1925, Hope Papers, AUC; also see "Negro Problems Conference, 1927–28," box 98, folders 999–1001, box 101, folder 1001, pp. 64–65, Laura Spelman Rockefeller Memorial Archives, Rockefeller Archives Center, Tarrytown, N.Y., hereafter cited as SRM, RAC.

67. See W. E. B. Du Bois to L. Hollingsworth Wood, 23 June 1924, Wood to Du Bois, 9 July 1924, reel 13, Du Bois Papers, UMass; see also Richardson, *History of Fisk*, 93–110; Wolters, *New Negro on Campus*, 44, 60–61.

68. John Hope to Edward Hope, 10 December 1924, Hope Papers, AUC.

69. Ibid.

70. On Hope's salary, see Board Book 17, 2 March 1906–13 July 1908, pp. 59, 114–15, and Board Book 21, 11 February 1918–23 September 1920, pp. 386–87, ABHSA.

71. On Hope's Cobb County farm, see Hugh Favor to John Hope, 13 March 1912, 15 July 1913, Hope to Favor, 23 October 1915, Favor to Hope, 30 August 1916. On Hope's properties in Augusta, see Hope to Thomas McNutt, 15 April 1916, 12 August 1917; see also New-York Life Insurance Company (Atlanta Branch) to John Hope, 26 October 1916, Hope Papers, AUC.

72. For examples, see Anna Hope to John Hope, 11 April, 19 October 1917, Thomas McNutt to Hope, 25 September 1917, Hope to McNutt, 29 September 1917; see also Heman E. Perry (Standard Life Insurance Company) to "Stockholder" [John

Hope], 5, 19 June 1917, Perry to Hope, 28 December 1916, Hope to Perry, 19 February 1918; see also Hope to Hugh E. Favor, 7 June 1916, 8 June 1917, Hope Papers, AUC.

73. See, especially, John Hope to Collector of Internal Revenue, 9 March 1934, Hope Papers, AUC. In addition to other financial woes, including his unemployed brother, Tom, Hope talked about his "income from the farm amounting to about two bags of corn a year." He also wrote: "I not only supply help to the man working the farm by hiring mules and the necessary machinery, but I have been forced to give him some hundreds of dollars so that he, his wife and several small children will not suffer."

74. See MS "Individual Income Tax Return, Contributions list," 1928–34, also, e.g., Lucy Laney to John Hope, 11 January 1918, John Hope to M. W. Reddick, 17 May 1912, Hope Papers, AUC.

75. John Hope to William H. Lewis, 9 May 1924, Hope Papers, AUC.

76. See John Hope to Marcus A. Johnson, 30 November 1927, Hope to J. C. Arnold, 25 October 1929, Hope Papers, AUC.

77. On the death of Grace Hope Birnie, see John Hope to Dr. George Dwelle, 24 December 1926, Hope Papers, AUC. On Buttrick's death, see Torrence interview with Constance Crocker [Nabrit], Torrence Papers, PUL; also Torrence, Story of John Hope, 255. On Newton's death, see Hope to R. R. Taylor, 24 August 1925, Hope Papers, AUC; also Torrence interview with Jane Hope Lyons, Torrence Papers, PUL.

78. John Hope to Madison J. Newton, 5, 25 March, 27 June 1918, Hope Papers, AUC.

79. John Hope to Madison J. Newton, 26 December 1917, Hope Papers, AUC.

80. Quoted in Torrence, Story of John Hope, 251; see also Torrence interview with Jane Hope Lyons, Torrence Papers, PUL.

81. My interviews with John Hope II and Elise Oliver Hope, his wife. Though Dr. Hope faintly remembered the name, he did not recall meeting Alethea directly, and never saw her or heard her name when he attended graduate school at Brown in the early 1920s. She did not reveal herself to him or any member of the John Hope family at his father's funeral in 1936.

82. Information on Jane Hope Lyons and Judson Lyons was found in the Fourteenth Census of the United States, Georgia, vol. 88, Enumeration District 77, sheet 12, line 34, also vol. 35, Enumeration District 50, sheet 12, line 34.

83. John Hope to D. W. Abercrombie, 3 May 1925, Edward Hope to John Hope, 12 May 1925, John Hope to R. R. Taylor, 24 August 1925, John Hope to Mary Seymour, 18 March 1925, Hope Papers, AUC.

84. See Lugenia Hope to John Hope, 17 March 1919, Hope Papers, AUC; W. E. B. Du Bois, "Thomas Jesse Jones," Crisis 22 (October 1921): 252–56, in Aptheker, Selections from the "Crisis," 1:311–16.

85. For an example of Thomas Jesse Jones's support for Hope, see Board Book 23, 19 February 1923–19 April 1926, p. 298, ABHSA; also John Hope to W. E. B. Du Bois, 1 June 1921, reel 9, Du Bois Papers, UMass.

86. On this trip, see Torrence, Story of John Hope, 256–57; Torrence interview

with Lugenia Burns Hope, Torrence Papers, PUL; see also *Atlanta Independent* 24 July, 25 September 1927.

87. See Alain Locke to John Hope, 1, 17 April 1912, Hope Papers, AUC; Torrence interviews with Alain Locke and Lugenia Burns Hope, Torrence Papers, PUL.

88. On the rebellion at Howard, see Wolters, *New Negro on Campus*, 70–136.

89. On Hope's views, see John Hope to National Student Federation of the United States of America (undated but sometime in the 1920s), Hope Papers, AUC.

90. John Hope to Mordecai Johnson, 13 August 1929, Hope Papers, AUC.

91. "Proceedings of the Inter-racial Conference, December 19–21, 1927," "Negro Problems Conference, List of Participants," box 98, folder 1001, SRM, RAC.

92. James Weldon Johnson to Leonard Outhwaite, 7 December 1927, box 101, SRM, RAC.

93. "Negro Problems Conference," 81, SRM, RAC.

94. On funding for the CIC, see Mjagkij, *Light in the Darkness*, 105–6; Aptheker, *Selections from the "Crisis,"* 2 : 590–92; CIC Executive Committee Meeting, February 1923, Records of the CIC, 1919–25; on Hope's role and involvement in raising money for the CIC, see Will Alexander to John Hope, 21 October 1927, 9 September 1927, telegram, R. H. King to Alexander, Hope Papers, AUC; also Thomas B. Appleget to Wickliffe Rose, 16 March 1928, GEB File, RAC.

95. "Negro Problems Conference," 255–56, SRM, RAC.

96. Leonard Outhwaite to John Hope, 8 January 1928, Hope to John Swain, 31 December 1927, Hope Papers, AUC; Hope to W. T. B. Williams, 19 February 1928, W. T. B. Williams Papers, Tuskegee University.

97. See *Atlanta Independent*, 1 March, 14 April 1928; Torrence interview with Will Alexander, Torrence Papers, PUL.

98. Hope, "The Relations between the Black and White Races in America," speech delivered at Jerusalem Conference, 31 March 1928, Hope Papers, AUC; see also John Hope, *The Christian Mission in the Light of Race Conflict*, pamphlet in Hope files.

99. Ibid.

100. Thomas Jesse Jones to John Hope, 13 December 1927, Hope Papers, AUC.

101. Quoted in Torrence, *Story of John Hope*, 276; *Atlanta Independent*, 14 April 1928.

102. Edward Hope introduced young Bostonian Constance C. Crocker to Hope in 1925, and a year later she became John Hope's able and trusted administrative assistant. A few years after that she married Dr. Samuel Nabrit, a Morehouse graduate and faculty member at both Morehouse and AU. She remained Hope's most trusted employee until he died. About the letters Hope received on returning from his Jerusalem trip, see my interview with Samuel Nabrit; also Torrence interviews with Constance Crocker Nabrit and Samuel Nabrit, Torrence Papers, AUC.

103. Ibid.; see also John Hope to Constance Crocker, 30 April 1928, Hope Papers, AUC; and Torrence, *Story of John Hope*, 286–87.

104. Torrence interview with Florence Read, Torrence Papers, PUL.

105. On Morehouse receiving another endowment, see *Atlanta Independent*, 7 June, 22 November 1928; see also Board Book 14, 17 May 1926–26 April 1929, p. 306, ABHSA.

106. *Atlanta Independent*, 5 July, 15 September, 28 December 1928.

107. See Mjagkij, *Light in the Darkness*, 112; for black leaders' membership in the CIC, see second page of letter, R. H. King to John Hope, 18 February 1928, Hope Papers, AUC. For example, Hope and most black leaders in Atlanta were very much involved in the functioning of the newly organized separate Community Chest; see *Atlanta Independent*, 8 November 1928.

108. For examples of southern black support of interracial cooperation, see *Atlanta Independent*, 22, 29 November, 6 December 1928. For Du Bois's criticism of the CIC, see R. B. Eleazer to W. E. B. Du Bois, 23 February 1928, reel 18, Du Bois Papers, UMass.

109. Despite his critical essays in the *Crisis*, privately, Du Bois was sensitive to the delicate position of Will Alexander and the CIC. See Will Alexander to W. E. B. Du Bois, 7 November 1925, reel 15, 7 October 1926, reel 18, Du Bois Papers, UMass. For examples of Hope's efforts to aid NAACP campaigns other than those already cited, see memo to Mr. [James Weldon] Johnson, 14 March 1924, reel 14, Du Bois Papers, UMass; Mrs. Ada Young to "friend," 20 January 1928; John Hope to Young, 26 January 1928, Young to Hope, February 1928, Hope to Honorable Charles Brand, 16 February 1928, Brand to Hope, 21 February 1928, Hope Papers, AUC; Hope to Du Bois, 12 January 1927, reel 23, 28 September, 9 November 1925, reel 15, Du Bois Papers, UMass.

110. "Negro Problems Conference," 153, SRM, RAC.

Chapter 11. "On Top of the Mountain"

1. Actually, Hope was not expected to deliver a speech at all but rather to summarize the earlier sessions on black health and education given at the Department of the Interior. On the 1928 National Interracial Conference, see Du Bois's description in *Crisis* 36 (February 1929): 47, 69–70, in Aptheker, *Selections from the "Crisis,"* 2:540–41.

2. From John Hope, "Educational Achievements and Needs," speech delivered at the National Interracial Conference, 16 December 1928, Hope Papers, AUC; see also Torrence interview with Will Alexander, Torrence Papers, PUL.

3. Ibid.; see also Dykeman and Stokely, *Life of Will Alexander*, 170–71. The same version was reported in the Atlanta University president's report in April 1936, two months after Hope's death; see "Report of the President," 25 April 1936, Hope Papers, AUC. It is also the version given in Torrence, *Story of John Hope*, 296–97.

4. For examples of these early attempts at encouraging cooperation and others, see "Negro Education Conference," especially pp. 163–65, GEB File, RAC; also Wallace Buttrick to George Sale, 6 November 1907, Edward Ware to Anson Phelps Stokes, 27 January 1915, Stokes to Buttrick, 1 February 1915, Buttrick to Stokes, 9 February 1915, GEB File, RAC; on the GEB's policy of obscuring its efforts to promote activities within the colleges, see Fosdick, *Adventures in Giving*, chap. 14, especially p. 199; see also Bacote, *Story of Atlanta University*, 257–58; Myron W. Adams, *The History of Atlanta University, 1865–1929* (Atlanta: Atlanta University Press, 1930), 67; Read, *Story of Spelman College*, 231.

5. John Hope, "Our Atlanta Schools," *Voice of the Negro* 1 (January 1904): 10–16.

6. For examples of Hope's negative views on cooperation and consolidation, see chapter 8 in this volume.

7. See Board Book 21, 19 January 1920, pp. 386–87, and Board Book 23, 19 January 1925, p. 298, ABHSA.

8. See John Hope, *Leadership: The Heart of the Race Problem* (Atlanta: Atlanta University, 1931). Hope used this ten-page pamphlet to explain the importance of the affiliation in providing additional graduate opportunities. See also recorded conversation, "Atlanta University Campaign—Mr. Dean Sage, Mr. Jackson Davis in New York City," 19 March 1931, Dean Sage to Trevor Arnett, memo, "Financing the University," 3 September 1931, Trevor Arnett to Jackson Davis, "Visit to Southern Colleges," Trevor Arnett Diary, undated, February 1934, all in GEB File, RAC.

9. For examples of the GEB's change in policy toward Atlanta University and its denial of AU's requests for money, see Anson Phelps-Stokes to Edward T. Ware, 12 July 1925, Stokes to Abraham Flexner, 12 July 1925, Flexner to Stokes, 14 July 1925, MSS, President "M. W. Adams, A.U.," 30 October 1925, folder 446, "Atlanta University 1923–1928," GEB File, RAC; see also Bacote, *Story of Atlanta University*, 259–60; and Read, *Story of Spelman College*, 229–31.

10. "Memorandum of Conference regarding Spelman College," Thursday, 26 May 1927, Princeton Inn, Princeton, N.J., GEB File, RAC. This memorandum also points out that Read would be key in helping to move the Atlanta schools toward cooperation and eventually consolidation. See also folder "Correspondence 1927–35," Trevor Arnett, President, Board of Trustees, Spelman College to Spelman Alumnae, Students, Faculty, 22 June 1927, Florence Read Papers, Spelman College Archives, Atlanta, hereafter cited as Read Papers, SCA; see also Read, *Story of Spelman College*.

11. John H. Dillard to ? (perhaps Florence Read), 20 (or 21) April 1927, box 1, folder "Correspondence 1927–1935," Read Papers, SCA.

12. Torrence interviews with Florence M. Read, Torrence Papers, PUL; see also John Hope to Read, 22 October 1927, Read Papers, 20-G, Atlanta University Archives, Atlanta, Ga. When I first began my research back in 1982–84, the unorganized and uncatalogued Florence Read Papers were in the Woodruff Library Special Collections at Clark Atlanta University as part of the Atlanta University Archives (then called the Atlanta University Collection, or AUC). These papers are different from the Spelman College Archives papers at Spelman College. Subsequent references to these Read Papers will cite Read Papers, AUC.

13. See Wickliffe Rose to Trevor Arnett, 11 October 1927, John Hope to Rose, 21 October 1927, GEB File, RAC.

14. See "Interview between John Hope and H. J. Thorkelson, regarding cooperation and Morehouse Endowment," 22 December 1927, also M. W. Adams to Jackson Davis and H. J. Thorkelson, 24 December 1927, GEB Files, RAC. Fortunately for the historian, in the late 1920s GEB officials began to record summaries and oftentimes direct quotes of conversations they had with people connected to their many activities.

15. For examples of this maneuvering, see "Interview between Thorkelson and M. W. Adams of Atlanta University," 23 January 1928; Thorkelson to T. B. Appleget,

24 January 1928, Appleget to John D. Rockefeller Jr., 2 February 1928, Rockefeller to Wickliffe Rose, 8 February 1928, all in GEB File, RAC; see also Fosdick, *Adventures in Giving*, 199–200. On John Hope's hesitation to speak out in public about cooperation, see W. T. B. Williams to Jackson Davis, 11 December 1927, Davis to Williams, 20 December 1927, GEB File, RAC; see also John Hope to Williams, 20 December 1927, W. T. B. Williams Papers, Tuskegee University.

16. See "Atlanta University's President's Report to the Trustees, 1928," GEB File, RAC; also Torrence interviews with Florence Read, Lugenia Burns Hope, and Constance Crocker Nabrit, Torrence Papers, PUL; my interview with Samuel Nabrit; Bacote, *Story of Atlanta University*, 168; and *Atlanta Independent*, 14 June 1928. The president of Morris Brown was interested in acquiring land closer to Morehouse and Atlanta University but was hampered by the school's affiliation with the African Methodist Episcopal church, which provided most of its financial support; see W. T. B. Williams to Jackson Davis, 11 December 1927, GEB File, RAC.

17. "Interview with Trevor Arnett regarding conversation with Will. W. Alexander, 15 January 1929," also memo, "RE: Atlanta University, Atlanta, Georgia, January 15–17, 1929," GEB File, RAC.

18. Ibid., memo regarding Atlanta University.

19. See Frank Shipman to H. J. Thorkelson, 7, 24 May 1928, "Interview with Trevor Arnett regarding conversation with Will. W. Alexander, 15 January 1929," memo "RE: Atlanta University, Atlanta, Georgia, January 15–17, 1929," W. E. Weatherford to Jackson Davis, 28 December 1928, all in GEB File, RAC.

20. "Contract of Affiliation," 1 April 1929, Hope Papers, AUC; a copy of the contract is in GEB File, RAC.

21. See memo, "John Hope to Constance Crocker Nabrit regarding Atlanta University Affiliation," dictated in 1934 as part of autobiographical notes put together for memoirs, Hope Papers, AUC; a copy of this is also in Torrence Papers, PUL.

22. Ibid.; see also John Hope to Edward Hope, 19 April 1931, Hope Papers, AUC.

23. John Hope to Edward Hope, 19 April 1931, Hope Papers, AUC; see also MSS, "Morehouse College," 14 December 1931, "Samuel Archer to General Education Board," GEB File, RAC.

24. John Hope to Edward Hope, 14 May 1929, Hope to Robert Moton, 27 April 1929, Lugenia Hope to Edward Hope, 1 May 1929, Hope Papers, AUC.

25. Lugenia Hope to Edward Hope, 1 May 1929, see also Lugenia Hope to Edward Hope, 27 March 1929, Hope Papers, AUC.

26. See Robert Moton to John Hope, 15 April 1929, Hope to Moton, 27 April 1929, Hope Papers, AUC.

27. Ibid.; see also Torrence interviews with Florence Read, Lugenia Burns Hope, and Alain Locke, Torrence Papers, PUL.

28. See John Hope to Florence Read, 28 May, 29 June, 4 July 1929, also Hope to Constance Crocker, 15 July 1929, all in Torrence Papers, PUL; see also Torrence, *Story of John Hope*, 305–7.

29. John Hope to W. E. B. Du Bois, 2 June 1929, reel 30, Du Bois Papers, UMass;

also *Crisis* 36 (June 1920): 203–4, also in Aptheker, *Selections from the "Crisis,"* 2: 552–54.

30. John Hope to Edward Hope, 14 May 1929, Lugenia Hope to Edward Hope, 11 October 1929, Hope Papers, AUC. Hope was offered a position later that year to work in Africa for six months. He really wanted to go, but an official of the GEB and the chairman of the AU Board of Trustees advised against it, as did Hope's physicians. Hope never again seriously considered the trip. See also "Interview: President John Hope of Atlanta University, with Trevor Arnett: *November 9, 1929*," [underlined in source], GEB File, RAC.

31. John Hope to Lugenia Hope, 25 July 1929, Balamu Mukasa to Hope, 20 January, 22 October 1934, Hope to Mukasa, 18 September 1934, Hope Papers, AUC.

32. Ibid.; see also John Hope to W. Edward Ricks, 12 July 1934, Ricks to Hope, 18 July 1934, Hope Papers, AUC; the story of Balamu Mukasa is also in Jones, *Candle in the Dark*, 277–80.

33. John Hope to Lugenia Hope, 3 August 1929, Hope Papers, AUC.

34. John Hope to Constance Crocker, 8 August 1929, Hope Papers, AUC.

35. My interview with B. A. Traylor; Torrence interview with Nathan Tillman, Torrence Papers, PUL.

36. My interview with Samuel Nabrit.

37. See John Hope to W. E. B. Du Bois, 27 October 1929, Du Bois to Hope, 23 October 1929, reel 27, Du Bois Papers, UMass.

38. Two separate letters, Hope to Du Bois, 27 October 1929, reel 27, Du Bois Papers, UMass. One of the retirees, E. H. Webster, may have had something to do with the rumor. He certainly appeared to be Du Bois's eyes and ears at AU, and had in the past secretly passed along information to Du Bois about other developments in the South. He had recently sent Du Bois a long letter on what he believed was the problem at AU and the reason Adams retired. On the retirement allowances, Du Bois also wrote to George A. Towns, who more or less confirmed Hope's reply. See E. H. Webster to W. E. B. Du Bois, 16 June 1929, reel 30, George A. Towns to Du Bois, 31 October 1929, reel 29, Du Bois Papers, UMass.

39. See Bacote, *Story of Atlanta University*, 277–81; also Jackson Davis to Trevor Arnett, 21 January, 23 July 1930, John D. Rockefeller Jr. to Trevor Arnett, 4 February 1931, and recorded interview: "President John Hope of Atlanta University and Morehouse College, President Florence M. Read of Spelman College, Mssrs. Trevor Arnett and W. S. Richardson, New York City," 25 October 1930, all in GEB File, RAC.

40. John Hope to W. T. B. Williams, 18 September 1932, W. T. B. Williams Papers, Tuskegee University; see also "Depression Years," series of interviews with Depression-era black residents of Atlanta, on tapes called *Living Atlanta*, recorded January–June 1979.

41. For coverage of the Hubert killing, see the *Atlanta Constitution*, 11, 22 July 1930; *Atlanta Independent*, 15, 22 June 1930; the *Georgian*, 22 July 1930, all in "Atlanta University Scrapbook clippings," some undated, Hope Papers, AUC; also the *Atlanta Jour-*

nal, 23 July 1930; my interview with Samuel Nabrit; Grant, *The Way It Was in the South*, 327–29.

42. Ibid.; see also "Commission on Interracial Cooperation, Inc. The Black Shirts Meet Defeat," (1930), memorandum in Hope Papers, AUC; John Hope to Edward S. Hope, 7 August 1930, Hope Papers, AUC.

43. My interview with Samuel Nabrit.

44. For Hope's responsibilities and service as the CIC's first black president, see "Commission on Interracial Cooperation, Miscellaneous 1932," 1033, box 17-B-1, and "Meeting of Executive Committee," July 1932, CIC Papers, AUC, also included in Hope Papers, AUC; see also *Atlanta Constitution*, 22 July 1931; Grant, *The Way It Was in the South*, 329.

45. See memo, "Butler Street YMCA Prepared for Rosenwald Fund," 1930, J. M. Choles to John Hope, 24 February 1930, Hope Papers, AUC.

46. Ibid., see also Mjagkij, *Light in the Darkness*, 110–17.

47. For Hope's involvement in this campaign, see ibid.; R. H. King to John Mott, 4 May 1932, also "Minutes of the Call Meeting of the Colored Work Department Committee, Hotel Shelton, New York City, April 27, 1931," all in Hope Papers, AUC.

48. See "Secretarial News Letter, Colored Work Department," July 1934, Hope Papers, AUC. For critics of his views on Africa, see John Hope to W. T. B. Williams, 17, 27 May 1934, Williams to Hope, 30 May 1935, W. T. B. Williams Papers, Tuskegee University.

49. R. H. King to Frank T. Wilson, 13 January 1933, King to Wilson, 5 January 1932, Tracy Strong to John Hope, 17 August 1934, Hope Papers, AUC; also "Annual Meeting of Board of Trustees," 29 April 1933, Read Papers, AUC; W. E. B. Du Bois to Hope, 4 February 1930, Hope to Du Bois, 17 February 1930, reel 30, Du Bois Papers, UMass.

50. See E. M. Martin, "Open Letter to Trustees, Graduates and Friends of Liberal Education in America," n.d. (ca. 1931), Hope Papers, AUC. Martin was a graduate of Atlanta University and president of the AU Alumni Association. He was also a businessman whom Hope later recruited to help in the University Homes project; on AU criticism, see also Torrence interview with Florence Read, Torrence Papers, PUL.

51. See John Hope to Edward Hope, 3 August 1930, John Hope to Justin Hope, 14 November 1933, Hope Papers, AUC; also Board Book 25, 20 May–20 June 1932, pp. 96–101, 340–41, ABHSA.

52. John Hope to Edward Hope, 7 August 1930, Hope Papers, AUC.

53. John Hope to John Hope II, 18, 23 January 1931, Hope Papers, AUC.

54. On Lugenia Hope's activities in the 1930s, see Rouse, *Lugenia Burns Hope*, 86–88, 115–21; *Atlanta Daily World*, 27 January 1932.

55. Jackson Davis to Trevor Arnett, 21 January, 11 July, 23 July 1930, also John D. Rockefeller Jr. to Arnett, 4 February 1931, GEB File, RAC; see also "Minutes of Annual Meeting of Board of Trustees," 29 April 1933, Read Papers, AUC.

56. On Du Bois's problems with the NAACP, see Arnold Rampersad, *The Art and Imagination of W. E. B. Du Bois* (New York: Schocken Books, 1990), 163–69; Ross, *Spingarn and the Rise of the NAACP*, 187–216; Rudwick, *W. E. B. Du Bois*, 266–85.

57. See W. E. B. Du Bois to John Hope, Du Bois to John Dewey, both 2 April 1930, Du Bois to Hope, 5 January, 19 December 1930, Hope to Du Bois, 30 December 1930, reel 30, also Du Bois to Hope, 15, 27 January, 9 February 1931, Hope to Du Bois, 26 March 1931, reel 34, Du Bois to Hope, 9, 11 January, 10 October, 28 November 1932, Hope to Du Bois, 14 January, 24 April, 28 December 1932, reel 36, Constance Crocker to Du Bois, 14 July 1932, reel 38, all in Du Bois Papers, UMass.

58. On Hope's work in this organization, see John Hope to Homer P. Rainey, 21 October 1935, Hope Papers, AUC.

59. Torrence interviews with Florence Read and Jane Hope Lyons, Torrence Papers, PUL.

60. See John Hope to Robert Moton, 21 June 1933, Robert Moton Papers, Tuskegee University Library, Tuskegee, Ala.; see also Torrence interviews with Read, Jane Hope Lyons, and Ludie Andrews, Torrence Papers, PUL.

61. See John Hope to Lugenia Hope, 14 August 1933, Hope Papers, AUC; also my interview with John Hope II.

62. Clifton Springs Sanitarium and Clinic in Clifton Springs, N.Y., was a rest home that had been suggested to Hope years ago by Harriet Giles, a founder of Spelman College.

63. John Hope to Lugenia Hope, 14 August 1933, John Hope to Jane Hope Lyons, 30 May 1930, telegram from Jane Hope Lyons to John Hope, 4 June 1930, Hope Papers, AUC.

64. Hope to Lugenia Hope, 14 August 1933, Hope Papers, AUC.

65. Torrence interviews with Jane Hope Lyons and Ludie Andrews, Torrence Papers, PUL; my interview with John Hope II and Mrs. Elise Oliver Hope; Edward Hope telegram to Constance C. Crocker, 17 July 1933, Hope Papers, AUC.

66. See Florence Hope [Thomas Hope's wife] to John Hope, 4, 9 March 1933, 2 July 1934, 25 April 1935, Hope Papers, AUC.

67. Memorandum, John Hope, "A Dream of the Night of September 11, 1933," Hope Papers, AUC.

68. A copy of this note written on Clifton Springs Sanitarium stationery is in Torrence Papers, PUL, and is cited in Torrence, *Story of John Hope*, 350.

69. See John Hope to W. T. B. Williams, 18 October 1933, W. T. B. Williams Papers, Tuskegee University; also on the side effects of Hope's angina, see interview with Ludie Andrews, Torrence Papers, PUL. See same interview for his need for complete rest; also Torrence interviews with Jane Hope Lyons and John Hope II; and my interviews with John Hope II and Elise Oliver Hope.

70. On the initial development of the Atlanta housing project, see Palmer, *Adventures of a Slum Fighter*, 7–21; also O. I. Freeman to Charles F. Palmer, 20 May 1934, Palmer to John Hope, 14 October 1933, Charles F. Palmer Papers, Emory University Library Special Collections, Atlanta, Ga.

71. "Interviews: President Hope of Atlanta University, with Mr. Trevor Arnett, October 17 and 18, 1933," Trevor Arnett Diary, also "Interviews: President John Hope of Atlanta University with Ruth D. Evans, December 14, 1933," both in GEB File, RAC; see also Record Group (hereafter RG) 196, Public Housing Administration

Records, Atlanta Housing, box 23, "Memorandum, Agreement between Public Works Emergency Housing Corporation, and Dean Sage, Dr. John Hope, et al.," January 1934, Records H-1100, National Archives, College Park, Md., hereafter cited as Public Housing Records, NA.

72. My interview with John Hope II; see also C. H. Pynchon [assistant director of housing] to Hon. Richard B. Russell Jr., n.d., also memorandum, Pynchon to M. D. Carrel, Public Housing Records. The latter document is actually a copy of the Atlanta City Planning Commission report, box 23, Public Housing Records, NA.

73. Ibid. See also P. C. McDuffie to Colonel Horatio B. Hackett, 15 March 1934, Pynchon to McDuffie, 5 March 1934, box 23, Public Housing Records, NA.

74. See W. E. B. Du Bois et al., "A Study of the Atlanta University Federal Housing Area, May, 1934." A copy of the report is in "Housing Project File," Hope Papers, AUC. For members of the black advisory housing committee, see "Atlanta University Report of the President," 22 April 1934, Hope Papers, AUC; a copy of the list of advisory members for both projects is in box 23, Public Housing Records, NA.

75. See John Hope to Lugenia Hope, 18, 22 March 1934, 9 February 1934, Hope Papers, AUC; also Torrence interviews with Constance Nabrit and Albert Dent, Torrence Papers, PUL.

76. My interview with John Hope II and Elise Oliver Hope.

77. John Hope to Lugenia Hope, 16 August 1934, 26 July 1934, Hope Papers, AUC.

78. On rumors of Hope's infidelity and Rouse's treatment of this sensitive issue, see Rouse, *Lugenia Burns Hope*, 50–54.

79. My interviews with Dr. Milicent Jordan [a student and later faculty member at Spelman College], Benjamin Mays, Samuel Nabrit, and John Hope II and Elise Oliver Hope; also Torrence interviews with Mrs. Ludie Andrews and Mrs. Jane Hope Lyons, Torrence Papers, PUL.

80. It was Read who recruited Torrence to write Hope's story and provided valuable information and leads for his research. On Read's vast knowledge of John Hope and his family and background, see Torrence interview with Florence M. Read; also important are Torrence interview with Constance Crocker Nabrit, Torrence Papers, PUL; and my interview with Samuel Nabrit. Photographs of several Hope family members are in Read Papers, SCA. Material obviously meant for a Hope biography is in Read Papers, AUC.

81. Florence Read to Rayford Logan, 4 July 1955, box 1, Read Papers, SCA; also my interview with Elise Oliver Hope.

82. Ibid.

83. My interview with Elise Oliver Hope.

84. My interview with Elise Oliver Hope and John Hope II.

85. Information on this point in Read's personality is from my interviews with Dr. Milicent Jordan, Ben Mays, and Samuel Nabrit.

86. On Lugenia Hope's attempts to get her husband's personal belongings, see Attorney Thomas J. Henry Jr. to Mrs. Hope, 1 April 1937, Lugenia Hope to Henry, 5 April 1937, Hope Papers, AUC.

87. For examples of these letters, see John Hope to Lugenia Hope, 17 June 1927, 16 December 1928, 30 August, 11 October 1930, 20, 22 March 1934, 9 October 1935, Hope Papers, AUC. It could be purely coincidental that Hope failed to mention Read while continuing to mention Nabrit, but I am convinced Hope did this purposely because he knew how Lugenia felt about her. Lugenia Hope was not one to keep her feelings to herself, although she understood Hope's need to keep Read in his life.

88. My interviews with John Hope II and Mrs. Elise Oliver Hope, and John Hope's grandson, Dr. Richard Hope.

89. See *Atlanta Journal*, 30 September 1934, "Magazine Section," 21 October 1934; a copy of this article and other information on Ickes in Atlanta is in RG 196, box 23, Public Housing Records, NA.

90. Du Bois et al., "Study of Atlanta University Federal Housing Area," 3, 4, 23.

91. See John Hope, "Speech to All-University Assemblies," 18 November 1935, Hope Papers, AUC. Beaver Slide got its name after an Atlanta police chief lost his balance on a cold winter day and slid all the way down the steep hill that overlooked the community; see Palmer, *Adventures of a Slum Fighter*, 16–17.

92. See John Hope to C. H. Pynchon, Assistant Director of Housing, Federal Emergency Administration of Public Works, 6 February 1934, Read Papers, AUC; a copy of this letter is also in RG 196, box 23, Public Housing Records, NA.

93. See "Atlanta University Report of the President," 25 April 1936 (delivered by Florence Read), Hope Papers, AUC; see also Alonzo G. Moron to John Hope, 16 July 1935, Hope to Moron, 5 August 1935, Hope Papers, AUC. Moron was then associated with or was the commissioner of public welfare for the Virgin Islands, but he later became the first housing manager for the University Homes project. See also Florence Read to Dean Sage, 8 October 1935, GEB File, RAC.

94. On Hope's plans for the housing project and the role of Atlanta University, see "Interviews, President Hope of Atlanta University with Lawrence K. Frank, May 8, 1934," also "Housing Project, Atlanta University Community Service Program," undated MS, both in GEB File, RAC; for the role of the GEB in supporting this project within the context of other community program proposals during the Depression, see Fosdick, *Adventures in Giving*, 259–65.

95. My interview with John Hope II. Read mentioned to Torrence later that a member of AU's board of trustees was skeptical about Du Bois and had voiced his concern at a dinner at Read's residence in 1934 when Hope was present, but I have not found anything else on this in any of the records; see Torrence interview with Florence Read, Torrence Papers, PUL.

96. See Dean Sage to John Hope, 27 September 1934, Hope Papers, AUC; also on Reid, see *DANB*, 520–21; on Reid and other outstanding AU faculty, see Bacote, *Story of Atlanta University*, 284–91.

97. See Kenneth Robert Janken, *Rayford W. Logan and the Dilemma of the African-American Intellectual* (Amherst: University of Massachusetts Press, 1993).

98. Torrence interview with Rayford Logan, Torrence Papers, PUL; see Janken, *Rayford W. Logan*, especially 107–11, for a variation on this story. On Herndon, see

Sasha Small, *Hell in Georgia: What Angelo Herndon Faces* (New York: International Labor Defense, 1935); also Charles H. Martin, *The Angelo Herndon Case and Southern Justice* (Baton Rouge: Louisiana State University Press, 1976).

99. Torrence interview with Rayford Logan, Torrence Papers, PUL.

100. "Memorandum to President Hope on Possible Activities at Atlanta University and Affiliated Institutions in the Federal Housing Project," March 1935, reel 43, Du Bois Papers, UMass.

101. See Bacote, *Story of Atlanta University*, 285–86. Hope had money in both Citizens Trust and the National Benefit Life Insurance Company.

102. "Conversation between Jackson Davis and Robert Moton," 1 June 1934, GEB File, RAC; see also John Hope to Robert Moton, 5 June 1932, Moton Papers, Tuskegee University.

103. Hope memorandum dictated to Constant Crocker Nabrit, 4 March 1935, Hope Papers, AUC.

104. On the radio speeches, see Lugenia Hope to John Hope, 3 December 1933, John Hope to Virginia Anderson, 6 January 1936; for examples of Hope's help, see Annie B. Hooks to John Hope, 10 March 1935, Hope to Hooks, 12 March 1935, Hope to John Terentine, 12 March 1935, Hope to Baluma Mukassa, 15 December 1935, Mukassa to Hope, 21 December 1935, all in Hope Papers, AUC.

105. See Board Book 26, 19 September 1932–27 April 1936, especially 20 May 1935, 336–38, ABHSA; on Archer, who returned in 1937, see Jones, *Candle in the Dark*, 128–29, 148; on Archer's role at Morehouse and shying away from administrative duties, see chap. 9; also important are Torrence interview with Morehouse faculty member Nathaniel Tillman, Torrence Papers, PUL; and my interview with John Hope II.

106. On combining the AU and Morehouse boards of trustees, see Board Book 26, 338, ABHSA; see also in ABHSA folder "Negro Schools, General Information," undated paper titled "Change in Administration." See also Samuel Archer to John Hope, 30 December 1933, Hope to Archer, 2 January 1934, Hope Papers, AUC. These letters as well as other references to these transactions are in Jones, *Candle in the Dark*, 339–43.

107. On Morehouse land ceded to AU, see Board Book 25, especially 20 June 1931, 342–43, 348; see also Jones, *Candle in the Dark*, 328–58. In addition to previously cited references in the *Crisis* and others in support of the affiliation across the country, see *Atlanta Daily World*, 27 January 1932; *Atlanta Constitution*, 5 June 1930; *Pittsburgh Courier*, 7 October 1931.

108. My interviews with John Hope II and Elise Oliver Hope; Torrence interviews with Jane Hope Lyons, Florence Read, and Nathaniel Tillman, Torrence Papers, PUL.

109. See John Hope to Channing Tobias, 11 November 1935, Hope Papers, AUC; Florence Read to Dean Sage, 8 October 1935, GEB File, RAC.

110. See John Hope to James Harris [of the Beneficial Insurance Company], 28 January 1936, Hope to Malcolm Clayton [of the Dunbar National Bank], 7 February 1936, Hope Papers, AUC; see also "Hope Itineraries for 1935 and 1936," Read Papers, AUC; a copy of these itineraries is in the Torrence Papers, PUL.

111. Roscoe Dunjee to Mrs. John Hope, 22 February 1936, Hope Papers, AUC.

112. For accounts of Hope's death, see Constance Crocker Nabrit to Thomas Hope, 19 February 1936, Hope Papers, AUC; see also copies of Hope medical charts from MacVicar Infirmary in Torrence Papers, PUL; Torrence interviews with Florence Read, Jane Hope Lyons, Lugenia Burns Hope, John Hope II and Elise Oliver Hope, Constance Crocker Nabrit, and Roscoe Dunjee Jr., all Torrence Papers, PUL; also my interviews with Samuel Nabrit, John Hope II, and Elise Oliver Hope.

Selected Bibliography

Manuscript Collections

American Baptist Historical Society Archives, Valley Forge, Pennsylvania
    Minutes of the American Baptist Home Mission Society
    Records of the American Baptist Historical Society
Atlanta Historical Society, Atlanta, Georgia
    Atlanta Municipal Records
Augusta College, Augusta, Georgia
    Richmond County Historical Society Records
Brown University, John Hay Library, Special Collections, Providence, Rhode Island
    J. B. Watson Papers
Clark Atlanta University, Special Collections, Atlanta, Georgia
    John and Lugenia Hope Papers
    Commission on Interracial Cooperation Papers
    Athenaeum (Morehouse student publication)
    Spelman Messenger (Spelman College student publication)
    Atlanta University Bulletin (Atlanta University publication)
Georgia Department of Archives and History, Atlanta, Georgia
Howard University, Moorland-Spingarn Research Center, Washington, D.C.
    Jesse Moorland Papers
    Joel Spingarn Papers
Library of Congress, Manuscript Division, Washington, D.C.
    Booker T. Washington Papers
    NAACP Papers
Princeton University Library, Special Collections, Princeton, New Jersey
    Ridgley Torrence Papers
Rockefeller Archive Center, Tarrytown, New York
    General Education Board Papers
    Laura Spelman Rockefeller Memorial Fund Papers
Tuskegee University, Tuskegee, Alabama

R. R. Moton Papers
W. T. B. Williams Papers
University of Massachusetts, Amherst, Massachusetts
   W. E. B. Du Bois Papers (microfilm edition)
Worcester Academy Archives, Worcester, Massachusetts

Newspapers

Amsterdam News
Atlanta Constitution
Atlanta Daily World
Atlanta Independent
Atlanta Journal
Augusta Chronicle
Boston Chronicle
Indianapolis Freeman
Indianapolis Recorder
New York Examiner
New York Times
Providence Journal
Savannah Tribune
St. Louis Argus

Interviews

Archer, Mr. Samuel A. Jr., September 1983, Atlanta, Ga.
Borders, Rev. William H., January 1982, Atlanta, Ga.
Calloway, Mr. W. L., October 1989, Atlanta, Ga.
Crawl, Mr. William F., September 1983, Atlanta, Ga.
Franklin, Dr. John Hope, 1996, Atlanta, Ga., and San Francisco, Calif.
Gloster, Dr. Hugh, August 1995
Hope, Dr. Edward Swain, telephone interview, 12 May 1983, Cleveland, Ohio
Hope, Mrs. Elise Oliver, summers, 1993–96, Washington, D.C.
Hope, Dr. John, II, summers, 1993–96, Washington, D.C.
Hope, Dr. Richard, summer 1993, Princeton, N.J.
Jordan, Dr. Milicent, October 1982, Atlanta, Ga.
Mays, Dr. Benjamin, October 1982, Atlanta, Ga.
Nabrit, Dr. Samuel, February, March, and April 1995, Atlanta, Ga.
Terrell, Rev. James, November 1982, 1985–86, Atlanta, Ga.
Traylor, Mr. A. Z., September 1983

Published Works

Adams, Myron W. *A History of Atlanta University*. Atlanta: Atlanta University Press,
   1930.

Alexander, Adele L. *Ambiguous Lives: Free Women of Color in Rural Georgia, 1789–1879*. Fayetteville: University of Arkansas Press, 1991.

Allen, Ivan. *Atlanta from the Ashes*. Atlanta: Ruralist Press, 1929.

Anderson, Betty. *Springfield Baptist Church, Church History, 1787–1987*. Augusta: Phoenix-Commercial Printers, 1987.

Anderson, James D. "Education for Servitude: The Social Purposes of Schooling in the Black South, 1870–1930." Ph.D. diss., University of Illinois at Urbana, 1973.

———. *The Education of Blacks in the South, 1860–1935*. Chapel Hill: University of North Carolina Press, 1988.

Anderson, James D., and Vincent P. Franklin, eds. *New Perspectives on Black Educational History*. Boston: G. K. Hall, 1978.

Angell, Stephen W. *Bishop Henry McNeal Turner and African-American Religion in the South*. Knoxville: University of Tennessee Press, 1992.

Aptheker, Herbert, ed. *The Correspondence of W. E. B. Du Bois*. 3 vols. Amherst: University of Massachusetts Press, 1973.

———. *A Documentary History of the Negro People in the United States: From the Reconstruction Years to the Founding of the NAACP in 1910*. Secaucus, N.J.: Citadel Press, 1972.

———. *Pamphlets and Leaflets by W. E. B. Du Bois*. White Plains, N.Y.: Kraus-Thomson Organization, 1986.

———. *Writings by W. E. B. Du Bois in Non-Periodical Literature Edited by Others*. 2 vols. Millwood, N.Y.: Kraus-Thomson Organization, 1982.

———. *Writings in Periodicals Edited by W. E. B. Du Bois: Selections from the "Crisis."* 2 vols. Millwood, N.Y.: Kraus-Thomson Organization, 1983.

Bacote, Clarence A. "The Negro in Atlanta Politics." *Phylon* 16 (1955): 333–50.

———. "The Negro in Georgia Politics, 1880–1908." Ph.D. diss., University of Chicago, 1955.

———. "Negro Proscriptions, Protests, and Proposed Solutions in Georgia, 1880–1908." *Journal of Southern History* 25 (November 1959): 480.

———. *The Story of Atlanta University: A Century of Service, 1865–1965*. Princeton: Princeton University Press, 1969.

Baker, Ray S. *Following the Color Line: American Negro Citizenship in the Progressive Era*. New York: Doubleday, Page, 1908.

Baker, Robert A. "The American Baptist Home Mission Society and the South, 1832–1944." Ph.D. diss., Yale University, 1947.

Baker, Ross K., ed. *The Afro-American*. New York: Van Nostrand Reinhold, 1970.

Barbeau, Arthur E., and Florette Henri. *The Unknown Soldiers: Black American Troops in World War I*. Philadelphia: Temple University Press, 1974.

Bartlett, Irving H. *From Slave to Citizen: The Story of the Negro in Rhode Island*. Urban League of Rhode Island, 1954.

Berger, Peter L. *The Sacred Canopy*. New York: Doubleday, 1967.

Berlin, Ira. *Slaves without Masters: The Free Negro in the Antebellum South*. New York: Random House, 1976.

Bigham, J. A., ed. *Select Discussions of Race Problems.* Atlanta: Atlanta University Press, 1916.

Birnie, C. W. "Education of the Negro in Charleston, South Carolina, prior to the Civil War." *Journal of Negro History* 12 (January 1927): 13–21.

Bond, Horace M. *The Education of the Negro in the American Social Order.* New York: Prentice-Hall, 1934.

———. *Negro Education in Alabama: A Study in Cotton and Steel.* Washington, D.C.: Associated Publishers, 1939.

Brawley, Benjamin. *History of Morehouse College.* Atlanta: Morehouse College, 1917.

———. *Negro Builders and Heroes.* Chapel Hill: University of North Carolina Press, 1937.

Broderick, Francis L. *W. E. B. Dubois: Negro Leader in a Time of Crisis.* Stanford: Stanford University Press, 1959.

Bronson, Walter C. *The History of Brown University, 1764–1914.* Providence: Brown University, 1914.

Brown, William J. *The Life of William J. Brown, of Providence, R.I.* 1883. Reprint. Freeport, N.Y.: Books for Libraries Press, 1971.

Brown University. *Historical Catalogue of Brown University.* Providence: Brown University, 1951.

Brown University Alumni. *Student Life at Brown.* Providence: J. C. Hall, 1915.

Bruce, Dickson D., Jr. *Archibald Grimké: Portrait of a Black Independent.* Baton Rouge: Louisiana State University Press, 1993.

Brundage, W. Fitzhugh. *Lynching in the New South: Georgia and Virginia, 1880–1930.* Urbana: University of Illinois Press, 1993.

Bullock, H. A. *A History of Negro Education in the South from 1619 to the Present.* Cambridge: Harvard University Press, 1967.

Bullock, Ralph. *In Spite of Handicaps.* New York: Association Press, 1927.

Bunce, O. B. "The Savannah at Augusta." *Appletons' Journal of Literature, Science and Art* 6 (November 1871): 575–77.

Burke, Emily P. *Reminiscences of Georgia.* Oberlin, Ohio: J. M. Fitch, 1850.

Butler, Addie L. J. *The Distinctive Black College: Talladega, Tuskegee and Morehouse.* Metuchen, N.J.: Scarecrow Press, 1977.

Calloway, W. L. *The Sweet Auburn Avenue Business History 1900–1988.* Atlanta: Central Atlanta Progress, 1988.

Carter, E. R. *The Black Side: A Partial History of the Business, Religious and Educational Side of the Negro in Atlanta, Georgia.* 1894. Reprint. Freeport, N.Y.: Books for Libraries Press, 1971.

Cartwright, Joseph H. *The Triumph of Jim Crow: Tennessee Race Relations in the 1880's.* Knoxville: University of Tennessee Press, 1976.

Cashin, Edward J. *The Quest: A History of Public Education in Richmond County, Georgia.* Augusta: Richmond County Board of Education, 1985.

———. *The Story of Augusta.* Augusta: Richmond County Board of Education, 1980.

Cate, Margaret D. *Early Days of Coastal Georgia.* St. Simons Island, Ga.: Fort Frederica Association, 1955.

"Chapel Talks." *Spelman Messenger*, April 1932, pp. 13–15.

Chapman, Abraham. *Black Voices: An Anthology of Afro-American Literature.* New York: New American Library, 1968.

Chatfield, E. Charles. "The Southern Sociological Congress: Organization of Uplift." *Tennessee Historical Quarterly* 19 (December 1960): 337–39, 346–47.

Cheek, Aimee L. *John Mercer Langston and the Fight for Black Freedom, 1829–65.* Urbana: University of Illinois Press, 1989.

Clary, George E. Jr. *Paine College: Augusta, Georgia: An Account of Its Beginnings, 1882–1903.* Brunswick, Ga.: Lemmond Letter Shop, 1975.

"Close Ranks." *Crisis* 16 (July 1918): 21.

Coleman, Kenneth, and Charles S. Gurr, eds. *Dictionary of Georgia Biography.* 2 vols. Athens: University of Georgia Press, 1983.

Coleman, Kenneth, William F. Holmes, F. N. Boney, Phinizy Spalding, and Charles E. Wynes. *A History of Georgia.* 2d ed. Athens: University of Georgia Press, 1991.

Collins, Patricia. *Black Feminist Thought: Knowledge, Consciousness and the Politics of Empowerment.* New York: Routledge, Chapman, Hall, 1991.

Cooper, Arnold. *Between Struggle and Hope: Four Black Educators in the South, 1894–1915.* Ames: Iowa State University Press, 1989.

Cooper, Walter G. *The Cotton States and International Exposition.* Atlanta: Illustrator Company, 1896.

Corley, Florence F. *Confederate City: Augusta, Georgia, 1860–1865.* Columbia: University of South Carolina Press, 1960.

Cote, Armand H. *Know Rhode Island: Facts concerning the Land of Roger Williams.* Providence: State of Rhode Island and Providence Plantations, 1947.

Cottrol, Robert J. *The Afro-Yankees: Providence's Black Community in the Antebellum Era.* Westport, Conn.: Greenwood Press, 1982.

Crandall, Lathan A. *Henry Lyman Morehouse: A Biography.* Philadelphia: American Baptist Publication Society, 1919.

Crimmins, Timothy J. "The Crystal Stair: A Study of the Effects of Class, Race, and Ethnicity on Secondary Education in Atlanta, 1872–1925." Ph.D. diss., Emory University, 1972.

Crowe, Charles. "Racial Massacre in Atlanta: September 22, 1906." *Journal of Negro History* 54 (April 1969): 150–73.

———. "Social Reform: Origins of the Atlanta Riot of 1906." *Journal of Negro History* 53 (July 1968): 234–57.

Culp, D. W., ed. *Twentieth Century Negro Literature.* Miami: Mnemosyne, 1969.

Dailey, Maceo C. Jr. "Neither 'Uncle Tom' Nor 'Accommodationist': Booker T. Washington, Emmett Jay Scott, and Constructionalism." *Atlanta History* 38 (Winter 1995): 20–33.

Daniel, Sadie I. *Women Builders.* Washington, D.C.: Associated Publishers, 1931.

D'Avino, Gail A. "Atlanta Municipal Parks, 1882–1917: Urban Boosterism, Urban Reform in a New South City." Ph.D. diss., Emory University, 1984.

Davis, Benjamin J. *Communist Councilman from Harlem: Autobiographical Notes Written in a Federal Penitentiary.* New York: International Publishers, 1991.

Day, Caroline B. *A Study of Some Negro-White Families in the United States.* 1932. Reprint. Westport, Conn.: Negro Universities Press, 1970.

Dick, Robert C. *Black Protest: Issues and Tactics.* Westport, Conn.: Greenwood Press, 1974.

"Disfranchisement Defeated in Georgia." *Independent,* December 1899, pp. 3306–7.

Dittmer, John. *Black Georgia in the Progressive Era, 1900–1920.* Urbana: University of Illinois Press, 1977.

Doyle, Don H. *Nashville in the New South: 1880–1930.* Knoxville: University of Tennessee Press, 1985.

———. *New Men, New Cities, New South: Atlanta, Nashville, Charleston, Mobile, 1860–1910.* Chapel Hill: University of North Carolina Press, 1990.

Drago, Edmund L. *Black Politicians and Reconstruction in Georgia: A Splendid Failure.* Athens: University of Georgia Press, 1992.

Drake, St. Clair, and Horace R. Cayton. *Black Metropolis: A Study of Negro Life in a Northern City.* Vol. 1. New York: Harcourt, Brace and World, 1945.

Du Bois, W. E. B. "African Roots of War." *Atlantic Monthly* 115 (May 1915): 707–14.

———. *The Amenia Conference: An Historic Gathering.* Amenia, N.Y.: privately printed at the Troutbeck Press, 1925.

———. *The Autobiography of W. E. B. Du Bois: A Soliloquy on Viewing My Life from the Last Decade of Its First Century.* New York: International Publishers, 1968.

———. "Booker T. Washington." *Crisis* 11 (December 1915): 82.

———. *Darkwater: Voices from within the Veil.* New York: Harcourt, Brace and Howe, 1921.

———. *Dusk of Dawn: An Essay toward an Autobiography of a Race Concept.* New York: Harcourt, Brace and Company, 1940.

———. *The Education of Black People.* Amherst: University of Massachusetts Press, 1973.

———. *The Negro Common School.* Atlanta University Publication 6. Atlanta: Atlanta University Press, 1911.

———. "The Niagara Movement." *Voice of the Negro* 2 (September 1905): 619.

———. "Opening of the Library." *Independent,* April 1902, pp. 809–10.

———. *The Souls of Black Folk: Essays and Sketches.* Chicago: A. C. McClurg, 1903.

———. "The Tragedy of Atlanta." *World Today* 11 (December 1906): 1174.

Du Bois, W. E. B., and A. G. Dill. *The College-Bred Negro American.* Atlanta University Publication 15. Atlanta: Atlanta University Press, 1910.

Durett, Dan, and Dana F. White. *An-other Atlanta: The Black Heritage, a Bicentennial Tour.* Atlanta: History Group, 1975.

Duster, Alfreda M., ed. *Crusade for Justice: The Autobiography of Ida B. Wells.* Chicago: University of Chicago Press, 1972.

Dutcher, Salem, and Charles C. Jones. *Memorial History of Augusta, Georgia.* Syracuse: D. Mason, 1890.

Dykeman, Wilma. *Prophet of Plenty: The First Ninety Years of W. D. Weatherford.* Knoxville: University of Tennessee Press, 1966.

Dykeman, Wilma, and Stokely James. *Seeds of Southern Change: The Life of Will Alexander.* Chicago: University of Chicago Press, 1962.

Dyson, Walter. *Howard University, the Capstone of Negro Education: A History, 1867–1940.* Washington, D.C.: Howard University Graduate School, 1941.

Ellis, Ann W. "The Commission on Interracial Cooperation, 1919–1944: Its Activities and Results." Ph.D. diss., Georgia State University, 1975.

Ellis, Mark. "'Closing Ranks' and 'Seeking Honors': W. E. B. Du Bois in World War I." *Journal of American History* 79 (June 1992): 96–124.

———. "W. E. B. Du Bois and the Formation of Black Opinion in World War I: A Commentary on 'The Damnable Dilemma.'" *Journal of American History* 81 (March 1995): 1562–83.

"Extracts from Dr. Hope's Chapel Talks." *Spelman Messenger*, February 1933, p. 23.

Federal Writers' Project in Georgia. Works Progress Administration. *Augusta.* Augusta: Tidewell, 1938.

Federal Writers' Project of the Works Progress Administration for the State of Rhode Island. *Rhode Island: A Guide to the Smallest State.* Boston: Houghton Mifflin, 1937.

Fennell, Dwight. "A Demographic Study of Black Business, 1905–1908, with Respect to the Atlanta Race Riot of 1906." Master's thesis, Atlanta University, 1977.

Fitts, Leroy. *A History of Black Baptists.* Nashville: Broadman Press, 1985.

Fleming, Berry, ed. *Autobiography of a City in Arms: Augusta, Georgia, 1861–1865.* Augusta: Richmond County Historical Society, 1976.

Fletcher, Marvin. *The Black Soldier and Officer in the United States Army, 1891–1917.* Columbia: University of Missouri Press, 1974.

Foner, Jack D. *Blacks and the Military in American History.* New York: Praeger Press, 1974.

Foner, Philip S. "Is Booker T. Washington's Ideal Correct?" *Journal of Negro History* 55 (October 1970): 343–47.

Ford, DeSaussure. *An Address Embracing Biographical Sketches of Hon. Thos. W. Miller, Artemas Gould, George M. Newton, M.D., and Issac Tuttle, Donors and Benefactors of the Augusta Orphan Asylum.* Augusta: Phoenix Printing Office, 1886.

Fosdick, Raymond B. *Adventures in Giving: The Story of the General Education Board.* New York: Harper and Row, 1962.

Fox, Stephen R. *The Guardian of Boston: William Monroe Trotter.* New York: Atheneum Press, 1971.

Fox-Genovese, Elizabeth. *Within the Plantation Household: Black and White Women of the Old South.* Chapel Hill: University of North Carolina Press, 1988.

Franklin, John Hope. *From Slavery to Freedom: A History of Negro Americans.* 6th ed. New York: Alfred A. Knopf, 1974.

———. *George Washington Williams: A Biography.* Chicago: University of Chicago Press, 1985.

Franklin, John Hope, and August Meier, eds. *Black Leaders of the Twentieth Century.* Urbana: University of Illinois Press, 1982.

Frazier, E. Franklin. *Black Bourgeoisie: The Rise of a New Middle Class in the United States.* New York: Collier Books, 1962.

Frederickson, George. *Black Images in the White Mind: The Debate on Afro-American Character and Destiny, 1817–1914.* New York: Harper and Row, 1971.

Garofalo, Charles P. "Business Ideas in Atlanta, 1916–1935." Ph.D. diss., Emory University, 1972.

Garrett, Franklin M. *Atlanta and Environs: A Chronicle of Its People and Events.* Vol. 1. Athens: University of Georgia Press, 1969.

Gatewood, Willard. *Aristocrats of Color: The Black Elite, 1880–1920.* Bloomington: Indiana University Press, 1983.

Gavins, Raymond. *The Perils and Prospects of Southern Black Leadership: Gordon Blaine Hancock, 1884–1970.* Durham: Duke University Press, 1977.

Giddings, Paula. *When and Where I Enter: The Impact of Black Women on Race and Sex in America.* New York: William Morrow, 1874.

Grant, Donald L. *The Way It Was in the South.* New York: Carol Publishing Group, 1993.

Grimké, Archibald, et al. *The Negro and the Elective Franchise.* American Negro Academy Occasional Papers No. 11. Washington, D.C.: American Negro Academy, 1905. Reprint. New York: Arno Press and the New York Times, 1969.

Grossman, James R. *Land of Hope: Chicago, Black Southerners, and the Great Migration.* Chicago: University of Chicago Press, 1989.

Gruber, Carol S. *Mars and Minerva: World War I and the Uses of the Higher Learning in America.* Baton Rouge: Louisiana State University Press, 1975.

Gutman, Herbert. *The Black Family in Slavery and Freedom, 1750–1925.* New York: Pantheon Books, 1976.

Haley, Alex, and David Stevens. *Alex Haley's "Queen": The Story of an American Family.* New York: William Morrow, 1993.

Harlan, Louis R. *Booker T. Washington: The Making of a Black Leader, 1853–1901.* New York: Oxford University Press, 1972.

———. *Booker T. Washington: Wizard of Tuskegee, 1901–1915.* New York: Oxford University Press, 1983.

———. *Separate and Unequal: Public School Campaigns and Racism in the Southern Seaboard States, 1901–1958.* Chapel Hill: University of North Carolina Press, 1958.

Harlan, Louis R., and Raymond W. Smock. *The Booker T. Washington Papers.* Vol. 4, *1895–98.* Urbana: University of Illinois Press, 1975.

———. *The Booker T. Washington Papers.* Vol. 5, *1899–1900.* Urbana: University of Illinois Press, 1976.

———. *The Booker T. Washington Papers.* Vol. 8, *1904–6.* Urbana: University of Illinois Press, 1979.

———. *The Booker T. Washington Papers.* Vol. 9, *1906–8.* Urbana: University of Illinois Press, 1980.

———. *The Booker T. Washington Papers.* Vol. 10, *1909–11.* Urbana: University of Illinois Press, 1981.

Harris, J. William. *Plain Folk and Gentry in a Slave Society: White Liberty and Black Slavery in Augusta's Hinterlands.* Middletown, Conn.: Wesleyan University Press, 1985.

Harrison, Alferdteen, ed. *Black Exodus: The Great Migration from the American South.* Jackson: University Press of Mississippi, 1991.

Hartshorn, W. N., and George W. Penniman, eds. *An Era of Progress and Promise, 1863–1910: The Religious, Moral, and Educational Development of the American Negro since His Emancipation.* Boston: Priscilla Publishing, 1910.

Harvey, Diane. "The Terri, Augusta's Black Enclave." *Richmond County History* 5 (Summer 1973): 67.

Hastings, William T., ed. *A Century of Scholars: Rhode Island Alpha of Phi Beta Kappa, 1830–1930.* Providence: Phi Beta Kappa Society, 1932.

Haynes, Robert V. *A Night of Violence: The Houston Riot of 1917.* Baton Rouge: Louisiana State University Press, 1976.

Henderson, Alexa B. "Alonzo F. Herndon and Black Insurance in Atlanta, 1904–1915." *Atlanta Historical Bulletin* 21 (Spring 1977): 34–35.

———. *Atlanta Life Insurance Company: Guardian of Black Economic Dignity.* Tuscaloosa: University of Alabama Press, 1990.

Hine, Darlene C., ed. *Black Women in America: An Historical Encyclopedia.* 2 vols. New York: Carlson, 1993.

Hoffman, Frederick L. *The Race Traits and Tendencies of the American Negro.* New York: Macmillan, 1896.

Holmes, Dwight O. W. *The Evolution of the Negro College.* College Park, Md.: McGrath, 1934.

Holt, Glen E., ed. *An American in the Army and YMCA, 1917–1920: The Diary of David Lee Shillinglaw.* Chicago: University of Chicago Press, 1971.

Hope, John. *Leadership: The Heart of the Race Problem.* Atlanta: Atlanta University, 1931.

Hughes, William H., and Frederick D. Patterson, eds. *Robert Russa Moton of Hampton and Tuskegee.* Chapel Hill: University of North Carolina Press, 1956.

Huggins, Nathan. *Harlem Renaissance.* New York: Oxford University Press, 1971.

Hunton, Addie W., and Katherine M. Johnson. *Two Colored Women with the American Expeditionary Forces.* New York: Brooklyn Eagle Press, 1919.

Hunton, William A. "Colored Men's Department of the Young Men's Christian Association." *Voice of the Negro* 3 (June 1905): 388–96.

Janken, Kenneth R. *Rayford W. Logan and the Dilemma of the African-American Intellectual.* Amherst: University of Massachusetts Press, 1993.

"John Hope Sees Improved Race Relations." *Amsterdam News,* 7 July 1926.

Johnson, Charles S. *A Preface to Racial Understanding.* New York: Friendship Press, 1936.

Johnson, Michael P., and James L. Roark, eds. *Black Masters: A Free Family of Color in the Old South.* New York: W. W. Norton, 1984.

———. *No Chariot Let Down: Charleston's Free People of Color on the Eve of the Civil War.* Chapel Hill: University of North Carolina Press, 1984.

Johnson, Patricia A. "A Study of the Life and Work of a Pioneer Black Educator: John W. Davis." Ed.D. diss., University of Kentucky, 1981.

Johnson, Whittington B. "Free Blacks in Antebellum Augusta, Georgia: A Demographic and Economic Profile." *Richmond County History* 14 (Winter 1982): 10–22.

Jones, Edward A. *A Candle in the Dark: A History of Morehouse College*. Valley Forge, Pa.: Judson Press, 1967.

Jones, Jacqueline. *Soldiers of Light and Love: Northern Teachers and Georgia Blacks, 1865–1873*. Chapel Hill: University of North Carolina Press, 1980.

Jordan, Lewis G. *Negro Baptist History U.S.A., 1750–1930*. Nashville: Sunday School Publishing Board, 1930.

Jordan, William. "'The Damnable Dilemma': African-American Accommodation and Protest during World War I." *Journal of American History* 81 (March 1995): 1562–83.

Justi, Herman, ed. *Official History of the Tennessee Centennial Exposition: Open May 1, and Closed October 30, 1897*. Nashville, 1898.

Kellogg, Charles F. *NAACP: A History of the National Association for the Advancement of Colored People*. Vol. 1, *1909–1920*. Baltimore: Johns Hopkins University Press, 1967.

Kephart, William M. "The 'Passing' Question." *Phylon* 10 (1948): 336–40.

King, Martin Luther Sr., with Clayton Riley. *Daddy King: An Autobiography*. New York: William Morrow, 1980.

Kousser, J. Morgan. "Separate but *Not* Equal: The Supreme Court's First Decision on Racial Discrimination in Schools." *Journal of Southern History* 46 (February 1980): 17–44.

Lamon, Lester C. *Black Tennesseeans, 1900–1930*. Knoxville: University of Tennessee Press, 1977.

Langston, John M. *From Virginia Plantation to the National Capitol, or the First and Only Negro Representative in Congress from Old Dominion*. Hartford: American Publishing, 1894.

Lanier, Doris. "Henry W. Grady and the Piedmont Chautauqua." *Southern Studies* 23 (Fall 1984): 216–42.

Leslie, Kent A. "Woman of Color, Daughter of Privilege: Amanda America Dickson, 1859–1893." Ph.D. diss., Emory University, 1990.

Levine, Lawrence. *Black Culture and Black Consciousness: Afro-American Folk Thought from Slavery to Freedom*. New York: Oxford University Press, 1977.

Lewis, David L. *W. E. B. Du Bois: Biography of a Race, 1868–1919*. New York: Henry Holt, 1993.

———. *When Harlem Was in Vogue*. New York: Oxford University Press, 1989.

Lewis, Edward A. *The Blackstone Valley Line: The Story of the Blackstone Canal Company and the Providence & Worcester Railroad*. Seekonk, Mass.: Baggage Car, 1973.

Lincoln, C. Eric, and Lawrence H. Mamiya. *The Black Church in the African-American Experience*. Durham: Duke University Press, 1990.

Locke, Alain. *The New Negro*. 1925. Reprint. New York: Atheneum Press, 1971.

Logan, Rayford W. *The Betrayal of the Negro: From Rutherford B. Hayes to Woodrow Wilson*. New York: Collier Books, 1965.

————. "Carter G. Woodson: Mirror and Molder of His Time, 1875–1905." *Journal of Negro History* 58 (January 1973): 1.

Logan, Rayford W., and Michael R. Winston, eds. *Dictionary of American Negro Biography.* New York: W. W. Norton, 1982.

Martin, Tony. *Race First: The Ideological and Organization Struggles of Marcus Garvey and the Universal Negro Improvement Association.* Westport, Conn.: Greenwood Press, 1976.

Matthews, John M. . "Race Relations in Georgia, 1890–1930." Ph.D. diss., Duke University, 1970.

Mays, Benjamin. *Born to Rebel: An Autobiography.* 1971. Reprint. Athens: University of Georgia Press, 1987.

McFeeley, William S. *Frederick Douglass.* New York: Simon and Schuster, 1991.

McManus, Harold L. "The American Baptist Home Mission Society and Freedmen Education in the South, with Special Reference to Georgia: 1862–1897." Ph.D. diss., Yale University, 1953.

McPheeters, Alphonso A. "The Origin and Development of Clark University and Gammon Theological Seminary, 1869–1944." Ed.D. diss., University of Cincinnati, 1944.

McPheeters, Annie L. *Library Service in Black and White: Some Personal Recollections, 1921–1980.* Metuchen, N.J.: Scarecrow Press, 1988.

McPherson, James M. *The Abolitionist Legacy: From Reconstruction to NAACP.* Princeton: Princeton University Press, 1975.

————. "White Liberals and Black Power in Negro Education, 1865–1915." *American Historical Review* 75 (June 1970): 1357–79.

Meier, August. *Negro Thought in America 1880–1915: Racial Ideologies in the Age of Booker T. Washington.* Ann Arbor: University of Michigan Press, 1973.

Meier, August, and Elliott Rudwick. *Along the Color Line: Explorations in the Black Experience.* Urbana: University of Illinois Press, 1976.

————. "The Boycott Movement against Jim Crow Streetcars in the South, 1900–1906." *Journal of American History* 55 (March 1969): 756–75.

Mjagkij, Nina. "History of the Black YMCA in America, 1853–1946." Ph.D. diss., University of Cincinnati, 1990.

Moorland, Jesse E. "The Young Men's Christian Association among Negroes." *Journal of Negro History* 19 (April 1924): 127–38.

Moses, Wilson Jeremiah. *Alexander Crummell: A Study of Civilization and Discontent.* Amherst: University of Massachusetts Press, 1992.

Moss, Alfred A. Jr. *The American Negro Academy: Voice of the Talented Tenth.* Baton Rouge: Louisiana State University Press, 1981.

Moton, Robert Russa. *Finding a Way Out: An Autobiography.* New York: Doubleday, Page, 1920.

Myrdal, Gunnar. *An American Dilemma: The Negro Problem and Modern Democracy.* 2 vols. New York: McGraw-Hill, 1944.

Nalty, Bernard. *Strength for the Fight: A History of Black Americans in the Military.* New York: Free Press, 1986.

National Association for the Advancement of Colored People. *Thirty Years of Lynching in the United States, 1889–1918*. New York: NAACP, 1919.

Orr, Dorothy. *A History of Education in Georgia*. Chapel Hill: University of North Carolina Press, 1950.

Ovington, Mary White. *The Walls Came Tumbling Down*. New York: Arno Press and the New York Times, 1969.

Padel, Frank W. *Christian Schools for Negroes*. New York: Board of Education of Northern Baptist Convention, ca. 1906.

Palmer, Charles F. *Adventures of a Slum Fighter*. New York: Van Rees Press, 1955.

Penn, I. Garland. *The Afro-American Press and Its Editors*. New York: Arno Press and the New York Times, 1969.

Perry, Geraldine J. "The Negro as a Political Factor in Georgia, 1896 to 1912." Master's thesis, Atlanta University, 1947.

Piersen, William Dillon. *Black Yankees: The Development of an Afro-American Subculture in Eighteenth-Century England*. Amherst: University of Massachusetts Press, 1988.

Plank, David N., and Rick Ginsberg, eds. *Southern Cities, Southern Schools: Public Education in the Urban South*. Westport, Conn.: Greenwood Press, 1990.

Powell, Ruth Marie. "The History of Negro Educational Institutions Sponsored by the Baptists of Tennessee from 1864 to 1934." Master's thesis, Tennessee State University, 1953.

Proctor, Henry H. *Between Black and White*. Freeport, N.Y.: Books for Libraries Press, 1971.

Rabinowitz, Howard N. *Race Relations in the Urban South: 1865–1890*. New York: Oxford University Press, 1978.

———, ed. *Southern Black Leaders of the Reconstruction Era*. Urbana: University of Illinois Press, 1982.

Racine, Philip N. "Atlanta's Schools: A History of the Public School System, 1869–1955." Ph.D. diss., Emory University, 1969.

Rampersad, Arnold. *The Art and Imagination of W. E. B. Du Bois*. New York: Schocken Books, 1990.

Range, Willard F. *The Rise and Progress of Negro Colleges in Georgia, 1865–1949*. Athens: University of Georgia Press, 1951.

Raper, Arthur F. *The Tragedy of Lynching*. Chapel Hill: University of North Carolina Press, 1933.

Rawick, George P., ed. *Georgia Narratives*. Parts 1–4. Vols. 12 and 13 of *The American Slave: A Composite Autobiography*. Westport, Conn.: Greenwood Press, 1972.

Read, Florence M. *The Story of Spelman College*. Princeton: Princeton University Press, 1961.

Redkey, Edwin S. *Black Exodus: Black Nationalist and Back-to-Africa Movements, 1890–1910*. New Haven: Yale University Press, 1969.

Rhode Island Black Heritage Society. *Creative Survival: The Providence Black Community in the 19th Century*. Providence: Rhode Island Black Heritage Society, 1984.

Richardson, Joe M. *A History of Fisk University, 1865–1946*. University: University of Alabama Press, 1980.

Riley, B. F. *A History of the Baptists in the Southern States East of the Mississippi.* Philadelphia: American Baptist Publication Society, 1898.

Robbins, Faye Wellborn. "A World-within-a-World: Black Nashville, 1880–1915." Ph.D. diss., University of Arkansas, 1980.

Robinson, William H., ed. *The Proceedings of the Free African Union Society and the African Benevolent Society: Newport, Rhode Island, 1780–1824.* Providence: Urban League of Rhode Island, 1976.

Ross, Joyce. *J. E. Spingarn and the Rise of the NAACP, 1911–1939.* New York: Atheneum Press, 1972.

Rouse, Jacqueline. *Lugenia Burns Hope: Black Southern Reformer.* Athens: University of Georgia Press, 1989.

———. "Lugenia D. Burns-Hope: A Black Female Reformer of the South, 1871–1947." Ph.D. diss., Emory University, 1983.

Rowland, A. Ray, and Helen Callahan. *Yesterday's Augusta.* Seemann's Historic Cities Series No. 27. Miami: Seemann, 1976.

Rozier, John. *Black Boss: Political Revolution in a Georgia County.* Athens: University of Georgia Press, 1982.

Rudwick, Elliott. *Race Riot at East St. Louis: July 2, 1917.* Carbondale: Southern Illinois University Press, 1964.

———. *W. E. B. Du Bois: Propagandist of the Negro Protest.* New York: Atheneum Press, 1968.

Ruiz, Vicki L., and Ellen C. Du Bois, eds. *Unequal Sisters: A Multicultural Reader in U.S. Women's History.* New York: Routledge, 1994.

Schuyler, George S. *Black and Conservative: The Autobiography of George S. Schuyler.* New York: Arlington House, 1966.

Scott, Ann F. *The Southern Lady: From Pedestal to Politics, 1830–1930.* Chicago: University of Chicago Press, 1970.

Scott, Emmett J. *The American Negro in the World War.* Washington, D.C.: Homewood Press, 1919.

Sewell, George A., and Cornelius V. Troup. *Morris Brown College: The First Hundred Years, 1881–1981.* Atlanta: Morris Brown College, 1981.

Shivers, Forrest. *The Land Between: A History of Hancock County, Georgia to 1940.* Spartanburg, S.C.: Reprint Company Publishers, 1990.

Shivery, Louie D. "The History of Organized Social Work among Atlanta Negroes, 1890–1935." Master's thesis, Atlanta University, 1936.

Sholes, A. E. *Sholes Directory of the City of Augusta, 1882.* Augusta: Chronicle Book Room, 1882.

———. *Sholes Directory of the City of Augusta for 1877.* Augusta: A. E. Sholes, 1877.

Simmons, William J. *Men of Mark: Eminent, Progressive and Rising.* 1887. Reprint. Chicago: Johnson, 1970.

Small, Cloyd E. *Achieving the Honorable: Worcester Academy, 1834–1978.* Worcester, Mass.: Davis Press, 1979.

Smith, Elizabeth W. *The History of Hancock County, Georgia: History, Heritage and Records.* 2 vols. Washington, Ga.: Wilkes, 1974.

Smith, Gerald L. *A Black Educator in the Segregated South: Kentucky's Rufus B. Atwood.* Lexington: University Press of Kentucky, 1994.

Sobel, Mechal. *Trabelin' On: The Slave Journey to an Afro-Baptist Faith.* Westport, Conn.: Greenwood Press, 1979.

Sosna, Morton. *In Search of the Silent South: Southern Liberals and the Race Issue.* New York: Columbia University Press, 1977.

Spalding, Phinizy. *The History of the Medical College of Georgia.* Athens: University of Georgia Press, 1987.

Spear, Allan H. *Black Chicago: The Making of a Negro Ghetto 1890–1920.* Chicago: University of Chicago Press, 1967.

Stanton, William R. *The Leopard's Spots: Scientific Attitudes toward Race in America 1815–59.* Chicago: University of Chicago Press, 1960.

Steinberg, Sheila, and Cathleen McGuigan. *Rhode Island: An Historical Guide.* Providence: Rhode Island Bicentennial Foundation, 1976.

Still, William. *Underground Railroad Records.* Hartford, Conn., 1886.

Taggert, Barbara. "The Atlanta Race Riot of 1906 and the Black Community." Master's thesis, Atlanta University, 1977.

Taylor, Alrutheus. "Fisk University and the Nashville Community, 1866–1900." *Journal of Negro History* 39 (April 1954): 120–26.

Terrell, Marguerite S. C. *Blacks in Augusta: A Chronology, 1741–1977.* Augusta: Preston Publications, 1977.

TeSelle, Eugene. "The Nashville Institute and Roger Williams University: Benevolence, Paternalism and Black Consciousness, 1867–1910." *Tennessee Historical Quarterly* 41 (Winter 1982): 360–79.

Thompson, Daniel C. *The Negro Leadership Class.* Englewood Cliffs, N.J.: Prentice-Hall, 1963.

Thornberry, Jerry J. "The Development of Black Atlanta, 1865–1885." Ph.D. diss., University of Maryland, 1977.

Thornbrough, Emma L. "The Brownsville Episode and the Negro Vote." *Mississippi Valley Historical Review* 44 (December 1957): 469–93.

Thwing, Charles F. *The American Colleges and Universities in the Great War, 1914–1919.* New York: Macmillan, 1920.

Tobias, Channing H. "Interracial Commission Honors Dr. Hope: Drs. Ashby Jones and Channing Tobias Pay Tribute to His Work for Better Relations." *Atlanta University Bulletin* 3 (July 1936): 17.

Toppin, Edgar A. "Walter White and the Atlanta NAACP's Fight for Equal Schools, 1916–1917." *History of Education Quarterly* 7 (Spring 1967): 3–21.

Torrence, Ridgely. *The Story of John Hope.* New York: Macmillan, 1948.

Trowbridge, J. T. *The South: A Tour of Its Battle-fields and Ruined Cities, a Journey through the Desolated States, and Talks with the People.* Hartford, Conn.: L. Stebbins, 1866.

Tuttle, William M. Jr. *Race Riot: Chicago in the Red Summer of 1919.* New York: Atheneum Press, 1970.

Tymeson, Mildred M. *Worcester Centennial, 1848–1948: Historical Sketches of the Settlement, the Town and the City*. Worcester, Mass.: Worcester Centennial, 1948.

Tyms, James D. *The Rise of Religious Education among Negro Baptists*. New York: Exposition Press, 1965.

Urban, Wayne F. *Black Scholar: Horace Mann Bond, 1904–1972*. Athens: University of Georgia Press, 1992.

Wade, Richard. *Slavery in the Cities: The South, 1820–1860*. New York: Oxford University Press, 1964.

Wagner, Clarence M. *History of the National Baptist Convention, U.S.A., Inc*. Decatur, Ga.: Tru-Faith, 1993.

———. *Profiles of Black Georgia Baptists: 206 Years of Georgia Baptist and 100 Years of National Baptist History*. Gainesville, Ga.: Bennett Brothers, 1980.

Walden, Daniel. "The Contemporary Opposition to the Political Ideas of Booker T. Washington." *Journal of Negro History* 45 (April 1960): 88–103.

Walker, Eugene P. "Attitudes towards Negroes as Reflected in the *Atlanta Constitution*, 1908–1918." Master's thesis, Atlanta University, 1969.

Warren, Mildred. *Community Building: The History of Atlanta University Neighborhoods*. Atlanta: Department of Budget and Planning, 1978.

Washington, Booker T. "The Golden Rule in Atlanta." *Outlook* 84 (December 1906): 913–16.

———. *Up from Slavery: An Autobiography*. New York: Doubleday, 1902.

Washington, James Melvin. *Frustrated Fellowship: The Black Baptist Quest for Social Power*. Macon: Mercer University Press, 1986.

———. "The Origins and Emergence of Black Baptist Separatism, 1863–1897." Ph.D. diss., Yale University, 1979.

Waskow, Arthur I. *From Race Riot to Sit-In: 1919 and the 1960's*. Garden City, N.Y.: Anchor Books, 1966.

Watkins, R. A. *Directory for the City of Augusta and Business Advertiser for 1859*. Augusta: R. A. Watkins, 1859.

Watts, Eugene J. *The Social Bases of City Politics: Atlanta, 1865–1903*. Westport, Conn.: Greenwood Press, 1978.

Weaver, John D. *The Brownsville Raid*. New York: W. W. Norton, 1970.

Weiss, Nancy J. *The National Urban League, 1910–1940*. New York: Oxford University Press, 1974.

"Welfare of Negro Troops." *Crisis* 19 (November 1918): 23.

West, E. Bernard. "Black Atlanta: Struggle for Development, 1915–1925." Master's thesis, Atlanta University, 1976.

White, Dana F. "The Black Sides of Atlanta: A Geography of Expansion and Containment, 1870–1970." *Atlanta Historical Journal* 26 (Summer–Fall 1982): 199–225.

White, Dana F., and Timothy J. Crimmins. "Urban Structure, Atlanta." *Journal of Urban History* 2 (February 1976): 231–51.

White, Deborah G. *Arn't I a Woman: Female Slaves in the Plantation South*. New York: W. W. Norton, 1985.

White, John. *Black Leadership in America: From Booker T. Washington to Jesse Jackson*. New York: Longman, 1985.

White, Walter. *A Man Called White*. New York: Viking Press, 1948. "Why Mr. Barber Left Atlanta." *Voice of the Negro* 3 (November 1906): 470–72.

Williams, Charles H. *Sidelights on Negro Soldiers*. Boston: B. J. Brimmer, 1923.

Williams, Fannie B. "Perils of the White Negro." *Colored American* 13 (December 1907): 421–23.

Williams, Walter L. "Black American Attitudes toward Africa, 1877–1900." *Pan-African Journal* 4 (Spring 1971): 173–94.

———. "Black Journalism's Opinions about Africa during the Late Nineteenth Century." *Phylon* 34 (September 1973): 224–35.

———. "Ethnic Relations of African Students in the United States with Black Americans, 1870–1900." *Journal of Negro History* 45 (Summer 1980): 228–49.

Williamson, Joel. *A Rage for Order: Black-White Relations in the American South since Emancipation*. New York: Oxford University Press, 1986.

Wingo, Horace Calvin. "Race Relations in Georgia, 1872–1908." Ph.D. diss., University of Georgia, 1969.

Wolters, Raymond. *The New Negro on Campus: Black College Rebellions of the 1920's*. Princeton: Princeton University Press, 1975.

Woodson, Carter G. *The History of the Negro Church*. Washington, D.C.: Associated Publishers, 1921.

Woodward, C. Vann. *The Strange Career of Jim Crow*. New York: Oxford University Press, 1974.

Woodward, K. *1841 Augusta Directory and City Advertiser*. Augusta: Brown and McCafferty, 1841.

Wright, Richard R. *87 Years behind the Black Curtain: An Autobiography*. Philadelphia: Rare Book Company, 1965.

Index

Moorland, Jesse E., 78, 185, 225, 234, 236, 240

Morehouse, Henry L., 89, 90, 92, 122, 155, 177

Morehouse College. *See* Atlanta Baptist College (Morehouse College)

Morgan, Clement Garnett, 163, 185

Morgan, Thomas J., 92, 117, 122, 132, 141

Morgan College for Negroes (Morgan State University), 225

Morris Brown College, 138, 210, 304, 318, 402 n16

Moss, Alfred, 150

Moton, Robert, 173, 179, 209, 213, 223; as intermediary for Booker T. Washington, 194–95; and Morehouse College 50th anniversary, 220, 221; and Committee on the Welfare of Negro Troops, 233; investigation of African American troop conditions in France, 246; on Commission on Interracial Cooperation, 261; and controversy about Tuskegee veterans hospital, 271–72; efforts to save Standard Life Insurance Company, 275; at Negro Problems Conference, 288–89; insistence upon Hope's Mayo Clinic visit, 308

Mott, John R., 291

Mukasa, Balamu, 309–10

Murphey, Eugene, 20

Myrdal, Gunnar, xxiv

NAACP. *See* National Association for the Advancement of Colored People (NAACP)

Nabrit, Constance Crocker, 292, 304, 326, 399 n102

Nabrit, James, Jr., 360 n3

Nabrit, James, Sr., 106, 159, 360 n3

Nabrit, Samuel, 107, 259, 304, 360 n3

Napier, Ida, 76, 78

Napier, James Carroll, 75, 213

Napier, Nettie Langston, 75–76

Nash, Roy, 213

Nashville, Tennessee: racial segregation and violence, 74–75; African American community, 75–76

National Association for the Advancement of Colored People (NAACP), xxiii, 188, 293; John Hope's work with, 188–89, 196, 212, 213–14, 218; creation of new position of "field organizer," 213; gender bias in regard to African American women, 214; endorsement of training camp for African American officers, 225; intensified protest against lynchings and discrimination, 256; criticism of Commission on Interracial Cooperation, 273; Atlanta Chapter, 293; dispute with Du Bois over control of *Crisis*, 319

National Association of Teachers in Colored Schools, 188, 267

National Baptist Convention, 96, 137; formation, 130–31

National Baptist Young People's Union, 125, 365 n64

National Benefit Life Insurance Company, 282

National Council of Churches, xxiv

National Equal Rights League, 256

National Interracial Conference, 1928, 298

Nationalism, African American, 143

National Negro Committee, 188

National Theological Institute (National Theological Institute and University), 103

National Training Institute for Women and Girls, 282

National Urban League, xxiv, 213, 331

Negro Education Society, 131

Negro Life in the South (Weatherford), 187

Negro Problems Conference, 288

Neighborhood Union (Atlanta), 123, 199–200, 201, 218, 318

Nerney, May Childs, 211–12, 213

New Negro Movement, xxv, 273; defined, 255–56; on African American campuses, 276–77, 287; criticism of conservative leaders and organizations, 287–88, 289

New South ideology: efforts to improve image of South, 84–85; support for industrial education for African Americans, 89

Newton, George M., 8–9

Newton, Madison J. (half-brother), 9, 11, 18, 22, 25, 32, 81; financial assistance for John Hope's education, 36–37; financial support of household, 81, 82; visit to Hope at Nashville, 96; death, 283

New York Independent, 89

New York Silent Parade, 229

Niagara Movement, xxiii, 152–53, 371 n62; Harpers Ferry meeting, 162–63; Boston meeting, 184–85

Walling, William English, 188

Walters, Alexander, 150

Wardlaw, C. H., 168, 374*n*11

Washington, Booker T., xxv, xxvi, 30, 79, 178; speech at Atlanta Cotton States Exposition, 83–84, 86–87; spokesperson for African American industrial education, 84; criticism of, in African American community, 87, 88; threat to African American higher education, 94, 95, 119–20, 147; speech at Tennessee Centennial Exposition, 95–96; *Up from Slavery*, 120; opposition to Hardwick Bill, 135; control of African American newspapers, 152; concern about African American crime, 164–65; fund-raising assistance to African American college presidents, 190, 191; relationship with John Hope, 190–91, 195, 208–9; appeal to Hope to speak out against NAACP, 195; death and funeral, 207–8

Washington, Forrester, 288

Washington, James, 131

Washington, Melvin, 144

Watson, John B., 174

Weatherford, Willis D., 186–87, 205, 206, 261, 304, 305

Weisinger, Kendall, 325

Wells-Barnett, Ida, xxv, 83, 188, 269

West Virginia Institute (West Virginia State College), 287

White, John E., 205

White, Josephine, 28, 125

White, Levi, 31

White, Walter, xxv, xxvii, 166, 167, 219, 294, 319

White, William Jefferson, xxvii, 170; political activism, 28–29; commitment to black leadership, 29; as editor and proprietor of *Georgia Baptist*, 29, 114; as Father of Negro Education in Georgia, 29; disputes with

Charles Walker and Richard Wright, 34; criticism of racist practices in 1890s, 69; and Augusta Institute, 103, 104; and dispute between African American Baptist and ABHMS, 133; call for Georgia Equal Rights Convention, 154–55; death, 207

Wigginton, John Harvey, 44

Williams, A. D., 154, 219, 220

Williams, Robert Bradford, 33, 34„ 36

Williams, William Taylor Burwell, 67, 79, 172, 209; friendship with John Hope, 67, 80, 100, 101; appeals to GEB on behalf of ABC, 178, 179, 191–92, 210; at first Amenia Conference, 213; and Morehouse College 50th anniversary, 220

Willis, Martha, 18

Wilson, Woodrow, 197, 217, 246

Wolters, Raymond, 278

Wood, L. Hollingsworth, 280, 288

Woodson, Carter, 215, 332

Worcester, Massachusetts, 39–40

Worcester Academy, 36, 40–42, 47–48

Workingman's Loan and Building Association, 34

World's Columbian Exposition of 1893, 60

World War I: effect on African American community, 222–23; racial violence stemming from treatment of African American soldiers, 227

Wright, Richard R., 29, 30, 33, 34, 79, 96, 150

Yates, Clayton R., 325

Young, Charles, 225

Young Men's Christian Association (YMCA): Colored Men's Department, xxiv, 185–86, 234, 314–15, 378*n*3; National War Work Council, 234, 261; activities in France in support of African American troops, 240–41; World Committee, 267; African American student associations, 315, 316